ZAGAT
2013

America's Top Restaurants

EDITOR
Karen Hudes

Published and distributed by
Zagat Survey, LLC
76 Ninth Avenue
New York, NY 10011
T: 212.977.6000
E: americastop@zagat.com
plus.google.com/local

ACKNOWLEDGMENTS

We're grateful to our local editors, Claudia Alarcon, Alicia Arter, Rudy Avalos, Olga Boikess, Nikki Buchanan, Suzi Forbes Chase, Ann Christenson, Bill Citara, Tracy Cumbay, Jeanette Foster, Mary Ann Castronovo Fusco, Rona Gindin, Meesha Halm, Lynn Hazlewood, Edie Jarolim, Valerie Jarvie, Elizabeth Keyser, Michael Klein, Rochelle Koff, Naomi Kooker, Gretchen Kurz, Sharon Litwin, Lori Midson, David Nelson, Jan Norris, Katie O'Connor, Jonah Ogles, Virginia Rainey, Laura Reiley, Mike Riccetti, Heidi Knapp Rinella, Julia Rosenfeld, Shelley Skiles Sawyer, Helen Schwab, Merrill Shindler, Jane Slaughter, Kelly Stewart, Eryn Swanson, Pat Tanner, Martha Thomas, Anne Trubek, John Turiano, Alice Van Housen, Carla Waldemar and Kate Washington. We also sincerely thank the thousands of people who participated in this survey – this guide is really "theirs."

We also thank Julie Alvin, Anne Bauso, Erin Behan, Simon Butler, Kathryn Carroll, Katharine Critchlow, Kara Freewind, Danielle Harris, Katherine Hottinger, Rebecca Salois, Hilary Sims, Stefanie Tuder and Alice Urmey, as well as the following members of our staff: Aynsley Karps (editor), Caitlin Miehl (editor), Brian Albert, Sean Beachell, Maryanne Bertollo, Danielle Borovoy, Reni Chin, Larry Cohn, Bill Corsello, John Deiner, Nicole Diaz, Carol Diuguid, Kelly Dobkin, Jeff Freier, Alison Gainor, Curt Gathje, Michelle Golden, Randi Gollin, Matthew Hamm, Justin Hartung, Marc Henson, Anna Hyclak, Ryutaro Ishikane, Cynthia Kilian, Natalie Lebert, Mike Liao, Vivian Ma, James Mulcahy, Polina Paley, Josh Rogers, Emil Ross, Emily Rothschild, Amanda Spurlock, Chris Walsh, Jacqueline Wasilczyk, Yoji Yamaguchi, Sharon Yates, Anna Zappia and Kyle Zolner.

Our reviews are based on public opinion surveys. The ratings reflect the average scores given by the survey participants who voted on each establishment. The text is based on quotes from, or paraphrasings of, the surveyors' comments. Phone numbers, addresses and other factual data were correct to the best of our knowledge when published in this guide.

© 2012 Zagat Survey, LLC
ISBN-13: 978-1-60478-520-3
ISBN-10: 1-60478-520-9
Printed in the
United States of America

Contents

Ratings & Symbols

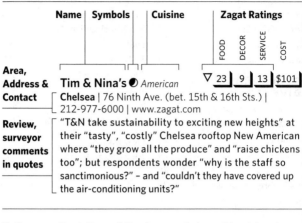

	Name	Symbols	Cuisine	Zagat Ratings			
				FOOD	DECOR	SERVICE	COST
Area, Address & Contact	**Tim & Nina's** ◑ *American*			▽ 23	9	13	$101

Chelsea | 76 Ninth Ave. (bet. 15th & 16th Sts.) | 212-977-6000 | www.zagat.com

Review, surveyor comments in quotes

"T&N take sustainability to exciting new heights" at their "tasty", "costly" Chelsea rooftop New American where "they grow all the produce" and "raise chickens too"; but respondents wonder "why is the staff so sanctimonious?" – and "couldn't they have covered up the air-conditioning units?"

Ratings   **Food, Decor** & **Service** are rated on a 30-point scale.

26 – 30	extraordinary to perfection
21 – 25	very good to excellent
16 – 20	good to very good
11 – 15	fair to good
0 – 10	poor to fair
▽	low response	less reliable

Cost   The price of dinner with a drink and tip; lunch is usually 25% to 30% less. For unrated **newcomers,** the price range is as follows:

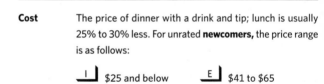

I	$25 and below	E	$41 to $65
M	$26 to $40	VE	$66 or above

Symbols
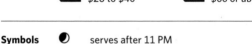

◑	serves after 11 PM
Ⓢ Ⓜ	closed on Sunday or Monday
⊘	no credit cards accepted

About This Survey

- 1,822 restaurants covered
- Over 225,000 surveyors
- Top Food Sampler: **Le Bernardin** (New York), **Urasawa** (Los Angeles), **Gary Danko** (San Francisco), **Alinea** (Chicago), **Bacchanalia** (Atlanta), **Fountain** (Philadelphia), **O Ya** (Boston), **Naoe** (Miami), **Joël Robuchon** (Las Vegas), **Cochon Butcher** (New Orleans), **Rover's** (Seattle), **Uchi** (Austin)

PEAK PICKS: Farm-to-plate menus run from **seasonal to daily changing** at hot spots like **Acme** (NYC), **Barbuzzo** (Philly), **Blackbird Kitchen & Bar** (Sacramento), **Boca Kitchen Bar Market, The Refinery** and **Indigenous** (Tampa/Sarasota), **Community Table** and **Oyster Club** (Connecticut), **Barley Swine** and **Foreign & Domestic** (Austin), **Skillet** (Columbus), **The Woodsman Tavern** (Portland), **State Bird Provisions** (San Francisco), **Braise** and **Odd Duck** (Milwaukee), **Late Harvest Kitchen, Bluebeard** and **Recess** (Indianapolis), **Oxheart** (Houston), **M.B. Post** (LA), **Local 127** (Cincinnati), **The Root** (Detroit), **Table & Main** (Atlanta) and **Linger** (Denver).

DINNER AND A SHOW: Nab a prime perch and **watch the kitchen action** at **The Crimson Sparrow** (Hudson Valley), **L'Atelier de Joël Robuchon** (Vegas), **Lukshon** (LA), **Max's Harvest** (Palm Beach), **Saison** (San Francisco), **Tavern Kitchen & Bar** (St. Louis), **Sbraga** and **Vernick Food & Drink** (Philly). Or join a **communal table** and feast with fellow eaters at **Travail Kitchen & Amusements** (Minneapolis), **A-Frame** (LA), **Black Market** (Indianapolis), **Communal** (Salt Lake City/Provo), **Corson Building** (Seattle) and **Sweet Cheeks Q** (Boston).

CASUAL GOES GOURMET: Pizza: **Settebello** (Vegas and Salt Lake City), **Supino Pizzeria** (Detroit), **Serious Pie** (Seattle) and **Dough** (San Antonio). Ice Cream: **Jeni's Ice Cream** (Columbus). Sandwiches: **Bäco Mercat** (LA), **Melt Bar & Grilled** (Cleveland) and **Barclay Prime** (Philadelphia). Burgers: **B Spot** (Cleveland) and **Flip Burger Boutique** (Atlanta). BBQ: **Union Woodshop, Slows Bar BQ** and **Zingerman's Roadhouse** (Detroit).

ABOUT ZAGAT: In 1979, we asked friends to rate and review restaurants purely for fun. The term "user-generated content" had yet to be coined. That hobby grew into Zagat Survey; 34 years later, we have loyal surveyors around the globe and our content now includes nightlife, shopping, tourist attractions, golf and more. Along the way, we evolved from being a print publisher to a digital content provider. We also produce marketing tools for a wide range of corporate clients, and you can find us on Google+ and just about any other social media network.

JOIN IN: To improve our guides, we solicit your comments – positive or negative; it's vital that we hear your opinions. Just contact us at **nina-tim@zagat.com.** We also invite you to share your opinions at plus.google.com/local.

New York, NY
November 1, 2012

Nina and Tim Zagat

Top Food Rankings by Area

ATLANTA
29 Bacchanalia
28 Antico Pizza
    Aria
    Bone's Restaurant
    Valenza

ATLANTIC CITY
27 Old Homestead
    Il Mulino
26 Chef Vola's
    White House
    Girasole

AUSTIN
29 Uchi
    Louie Mueller BBQ
28 Barley Swine
    Snow's BBQ
    Carillon
    Franklin Barbecue*

BALTIMORE/ANNAPOLIS
29 Charleston
28 Di Pasquale's
    Samos
    Vin 909
    Bartlett Pear Inn

BOSTON
29 O Ya
28 Oleana
    La Campania
    Neptune Oyster
    Lumière

CHARLOTTE
28 Barrington's
    McNinch House
27 Fiamma
    Fig Tree
26 Toscana

CHICAGO
29 Alinea
    Katsu
    Next
28 Riccardo Trattoria
    Les Nomades
    Takashi
    Avec
    Green Zebra
    MK
    Schwa

CINCINNATI
29 Jean-Robert's Table
28 Bakersfield
    Orchids at Palm Court
    Jeff Ruby's Steakhouse
    Nicola's

CLEVELAND
29 Chez François
    Giovanni's Ristorante
28 Lola
    Ty Fun
    Weia Teia

COLUMBUS
29 Pistacia Vera
28 L'Antibes
    G. Michael's Bistro & Bar
    Akai Hana
    Jeni's Ice Cream

CONNECTICUT
29 Le Petit Café
28 PolytechnicON20
    Thomas Henkelmann
    Mill at 2T
    Jean-Louis

DALLAS/FT. WORTH
29 Saint-Emilion
    Lucia
28 French Room
    Bijoux
    Pappas Bros. Steakhouse

DENVER AREA
29 Carlos' Bistro
    Junz
    Splendido at the Chateau
28 Penrose Room
    Fruition

DETROIT
29 Supino Pizzeria
28 Moro's Dining
    Lark
    Common Grill
    West End Grill

FT. LAUDERDALE
28 La Brochette
    Café Sharaku
27 Canyon
    Casa D'Angelo
    Eduardo de San Angel

---

* Indicates a tie with restaurant above

HONOLULU

29 La Mer
  Mitch's Fish Market
28 Alan Wong's
  Sushi Sasabune
27 Chef Mavro

HOUSTON

29 Da Marco
28 Chez Nous
  Mark's American Cuisine
  Pappas Bros. Steakhouse
27 Nino's

INDIANAPOLIS

29 Recess
28 Mo's a Place for Steaks
  Capital Grille
  Morton's
  Sakura

KANSAS CITY

29 Café Provence
28 Justus Drugstore
  Le Fou Frog
  Café Sebastienne
  Capital Grille

LAS VEGAS

29 Joël Robuchon
  Michael's
28 L'Atelier de Joël Robuchon
  Raku
  Picasso

LONG ISLAND

29 North Fork Table
28 Siam Lotus
  Mosaic
  Kitchen A Trattoria
  Maroni

LOS ANGELES

28 Urasawa
  Michael's/Naples
  Asanebo
  Sushi Zo
  Mélisse
  Piccolo
  Matsuhisa
  Echigo
  Providence
  Angelini Osteria

MIAMI

29 Naoe
28 Palme d'Or

Zuma
Palm
27 Il Gabbiano

MILWAUKEE

29 Sanford
28 Crazy Water
27 Eddie Martini's
  Ristorante Bartolotta
  Bacchus

MINNEAPOLIS/ST. PAUL

29 Travail
  Alma
  La Belle Vie
28 Lake Elmo Inn
  Lucia's

NAPLES

27 Côte d'Azur
  Bleu Provence
  USS Nemo
26 Truluck's
  Capital Grille

NEW JERSEY

29 Nicholas
28 Shumi
  Sapori
  Washington Inn
  Lorena's

NEW ORLEANS

28 Cochon Butcher
  Clancy's
  La Provence
  Brigtsen's
  GW Fins

NEW YORK CITY

29 Le Bernardin
  Per Se
28 Bouley
  Daniel
  Eleven Madison Park
  Jean Georges
  La Grenouille
  Mas (Farmhouse)
  Sushi Yasuda
  Sushi Seki

ORANGE COUNTY

29 Bluefin
  Marché Moderne
28 Basilic
  Blake's Place
  Gabbi's Mexican

ORLANDO

29 Cress
Victoria & Albert's
28 Nagoya Sushi
Chatham's Place
Norman's*

PALM BEACH

28 Marcello's La Sirena
Chez Jean-Pierre
27 11 Maple Street
Captain Charlie's
Café L'Europe

PHILADELPHIA

29 Fountain
Vetri
Birchrunville Store
Bibou
28 Sycamore

PHOENIX/SCOTTSDALE

28 Kai
Binkley's
Quiessence
Noca
27 Barrio Cafe

PORTLAND

29 Painted Lady
28 Le Pigeon
Genoa
Evoe
Cabezon

SACRAMENTO

29 Taste
Ambience
Mulvaney's
Kitchen
Sunflower Drive-In

SALT LAKE CITY

28 Foundry Grill
Mariposa
Takashi
Talisker on Main
Tiburon

SAN ANTONIO

28 Bistro Vatel
27 Sorrento
Bohanan's
Dough
Silo

SAN DIEGO

29 Sushi Ota
28 Tao

Market Restaurant
Tapenade
27 Pamplemousse

SAN FRANCISCO AREA

29 Gary Danko
French Laundry
28 Kiss Seafood
Seven Hills
Acquerello
Erna's Elderberry
Marinus
Kokkari Estiatorio
Sierra Mar
Evvia

SEATTLE

29 Rover's
Nishino
Staple & Fancy Mercantile*
Il Terrazzo Carmine
28 Herbfarm

ST. LOUIS

29 Bogarts Smokehouse
28 Citizen Kane's Steak
Pappy's Smokehouse
Sidney Street Cafe
Niche

TAMPA/SARASOTA

28 Beach Bistro
Pané Rustica
27 Bern's
Cafe Ponte
Maison Blanche

TUCSON

28 Fleming's Prime
27 Vivace
Dish
Le Rendez-Vous
Cafe Poca Cosa

WASHINGTON, DC, METRO

28 Rasika
L'Auberge Chez François
Komi
Marcel's
Prime Rib

WESTCHESTER/
HUDSON VALLEY

29 Sushi Nanase
28 Xaviars at Piermont
Il Cenàcolo
Freelance Cafe
Buffet de la Gare

Most Popular by Area

ATLANTA
1. Bacchanalia
2. Bone's Restaurant
3. Antico Pizza
4. Canoe
5. Atlanta Fish Market

ATLANTIC CITY
1. Ruth's Chris
2. P.F. Chang's
3. Morton's
4. McCormick & Schmick's
5. Chef Vola's

AUSTIN
1. Eddie V's
2. Uchi*
3. Salt Lick
4. Uchiko
5. Wink

BALTIMORE/ANNAPOLIS
1. Woodberry Kitchen
2. Double T Diner
3. Prime Rib
4. Charleston
5. G&M

BOSTON
1. Legal Sea Foods
2. Abe & Louie's
3. Craigie on Main
4. Blue Ginger
5. Oleana

CHARLOTTE
1. P.F. Chang's
2. Barrington's
3. Bad Daddy's
4. Capital Grille
5. Mac's Speed Shop

CHICAGO
1. Alinea
2. Frontera Grill
3. Girl & The Goat
4. Gibsons
5. Joe's Sea/Steak/Crab
6. Topolobampo
7. Lou Malnati's
8. Next
9. Blackbird
10. Tru

CINCINNATI
1. Jeff Ruby's Precinct
2. Montgomery Inn
3. Izzy's
4. Blue Ash Chili
5. Barleycorn's

CLEVELAND
1. Pier W
2. Melt Bar & Grilled
3. B Spot
4. Yours Truly
5. Great Lakes Brewing Co.

COLUMBUS
1. Cap City Fine Diner
2. Piada
3. Northstar Café
4. Schmidt's Restaurant
5. Thurman Cafe

CONNECTICUT
1. Frank Pepe
2. Barcelona
3. Union League
4. Coromandel
5. Thomas Henkelmann

DALLAS/FT. WORTH
1. Abacus
2. Fearing's
3. Al Biernat's
4. Stephan Pyles
5. Del Frisco's

DENVER AREA
1. Beau Jo's
2. Rio Grande
3. Elway's
4. 240 Union
5. Snooze

DETROIT
1. Andiamo
2. Buddy's Pizza
3. Fishbone's Rhythm
4. Kruse & Muer
5. Slows Bar BQ

FT. LAUDERDALE
1. Blue Moon
2. Casa D'Angelo
3. Greek Islands
4. Anthony's
5. Bonefish Grill*

HONOLULU
1. Alan Wong's
2. Assaggio
3. Big City Diner
4. Sansei
5. 3660 on the Rise

HOUSTON

1. Da Marco
2. Brennan's
3. Mark's American Cuisine
4. Carrabba's
5. Pappas Bros. Steakhouse

INDIANAPOLIS

1. Bazbeaux
2. El Rodeo
3. St. Elmo
4. Yats
5. Scotty's Brewhouse

KANSAS CITY

1. Fiorella's Jack Stack
2. Oklahoma Joe's
3. Arthur Bryant's
4. Hereford House
5. Gates BBQ

LAS VEGAS

1. Bouchon
2. Feast Buffet
3. Mon Ami Gabi
4. Joe's Sea/Steak/Crab
5. Aureole

LONG ISLAND

1. Peter Luger
2. Besito
3. Kotobuki
4. Bryant & Cooper
5. West End Café

LOS ANGELES

1. 101 Coffee Shop
2. Spago
3. 101 Noodle Express
4. Angelini Osteria
5. Brent's Deli
6. Bazaar/José Andrés
7. Cafe Bizou
8. Mélisse
9. Bouchon
10. Osteria Mozza

MIAMI

1. Joe's Stone Crab
2. Michael's Genuine
3. Prime One Twelve
4. Michy's
5. Il Gabbiano

MILWAUKEE

1. Sanford
2. Bartolotta's Lake Park
3. Eddie Martini's
4. Harbor House
5. Crazy Water

MINNEAPOLIS/ ST. PAUL

1. 5-8 Club
2. Big Bowl
3. Kincaid's
4. Axel's
5. Doolittle's

NAPLES

1. Campiello
2. P.F. Chang's
3. Bleu Provence
4. Cheesecake Factory
5. Truluck's

NEW JERSEY

1. Nicholas
2. Cheesecake Factory
3. River Palm
4. Cafe Panache
5. Highlawn Pavilion

NEW ORLEANS

1. Commander's Palace
2. Acme Oyster House
3. Café Du Monde
4. Galatoire's
5. August

NEW YORK CITY

1. Le Bernardin
2. Gramercy Tavern
3. Eleven Madison Park
4. Peter Luger
5. Daniel
6. Gotham Bar & Grill
7. Babbo
8. Union Square Cafe*
9. 21 Club
10. Jean Georges

ORANGE COUNTY

1. Marché Moderne
2. Anaheim White House
3. 21 Oceanfront
4. 3Thirty3 Waterfront
5. 230 Forest Avenue

ORLANDO

1. Bahama Breeze
2. 4 Rivers Smokehouse
3. Cheesecake Factory
4. Seasons 52
5. Charley's

PALM BEACH

1. Café Boulud
2. Abe & Louie's
3. Kee Grill
4. Seasons 52
5. Bonefish Grill

PHILADELPHIA

1. Buddakan
2. Amada
3. Iron Hill Brewery
4. Zahav
5. Vetri

PHOENIX/SCOTTSDALE

1. P.F. Chang's
2. Binkley's
3. T. Cook's
4. Lon's/Hermosa
5. Fleming's Prime

PORTLAND

1. Gustav's
2. Andina
3. Flying Pie
4. Higgins
5. Jake's Famous Crawfish

SACRAMENTO

1. Cheesecake Factory
2. Biba
3. Ella
4. Mulvaney's
5. Mikuni

SALT LAKE CITY AREA

1. Market Street Grill
2. Red Iguana
3. Rodizio Grill
4. Blue Iguana
5. Lion House Pantry

SAN ANTONIO

1. Biga on the Banks
2. Boudro's
3. Bohanan's
4. Dough
5. Rudy's Country Store

SAN DIEGO

1. Anthony's Fish
2. Brigantine Seafood
3. Phil's BBQ
4. George's Cal. Modern/Ocean
5. 94th Aero Squadron

SAN FRANCISCO AREA

1. Gary Danko
2. Boulevard
3. Slanted Door
4. Kokkari Estiatorio
5. French Laundry
6. Chez Panisse
7. House of Prime Rib
8. Absinthe
9. Zuni Café
10. A16

SEATTLE

1. 13 Coins
2. Dick's Drive-In
3. Canlis
4. Wild Ginger
5. Blue C Sushi

ST. LOUIS

1. Ted Drewes
2. Annie Gunn's
3. Blueberry Hill
4. Pappy's Smokehouse
5. Charlie Gitto's

TAMPA/SARASOTA

1. Bern's
2. Bonefish Grill
3. Columbia
4. Cevíche
5. Beach Bistro

TUCSON

1. Cafe Poca Cosa
2. Beyond Bread
3. Vivace
4. El Charro
5. P.F. Chang's

WASHINGTON, DC, METRO

1. Clyde's
2. 2 Amys
3. Zaytinya
4. Rasika
5. 1789

WESTCHESTER/ HUDSON VALLEY

1. X2O Xaviars
2. Blue Hill/Stone Barns
3. Tarry Lodge
4. Xaviars at Piermont
5. Harvest on Hudson

Latest openings, menus, photos and more on plus.google.com/local

RESTAURANT DIRECTORY

Atlanta

	FOOD	DECOR	SERVICE	COST

Abattoir *American*

| | 25 | 24 | 24 | $45 |

Westside | White Provision | 1170 Howell Mill Rd. (14th St.) |
404-892-3335 | www.starprovisions.com

"Whole-animal" dining is "shockingly delicious" but "still accessible"
at this "adventurous" Westside American, a meat-centric Bacchanalia
sibling that offers a "not-typical", "head-to-tail" menu in an "industrial", "butcher shop–chic" setting that hits the "perfect visual notes"
(along with some "loud" ones); its "foodie carnivore" following likes
the "relaxed service", "reclaimed wood and repurposed protein" on
offer, but it may be a challenge for those who "don't like organ meats."

Antico Pizza 🄼 *Pizza*

| | 28 | 17 | 19 | $19 |

Westside | 1093 Hemphill Ave. (Northside Dr.) | 404-724-2333 |
www.anticopizza.it

"Real-deal" ovens and "genuine Italian ingredients" make for "otherworldly" pizzas at this "family-run" Westside joint near Georgia
Tech, where "heavenly" Neapolitan pies with "perfect crusts" have
earned a "cult following"; "blaring" acoustics, "limited" communal
seating and "hectic" weekend scenes come with the territory, but in
return there's "opera on the speakers", "soccer on the telly" and a
money-saving BYO policy.

Aria 🄼 *American*

| | 28 | 26 | 26 | $60 |

Buckhead | 490 E. Paces Ferry Rd. NE (Maple Dr.) | 404-233-7673 |
www.aria-atl.com

Dubbed *the* place for "special occasions", this "longtime favorite" in
Buckhead via chef-owner Gerry Klaskala "continues to impress" with
"masterful" New American cuisine abetted by a "phenomenal wine
list" and "Kathryn King's fabulous desserts"; the "elegant", "contemporary art"–adorned digs work for both "business" and "romance",
service is "attentive" and the "expensive" tabs are "worth the money",
though nitpickers note that the waiters' "untucked shirts" seem out of
place at this otherwise "impeccable" experience; P.S. there's a tiny
"table in the wine cellar" that doubles as a "den of iniquity."

Atlanta Fish Market *Seafood*

| | 24 | 21 | 23 | $41 |

Buckhead | 265 Pharr Rd. NE (bet. Fulton Dr. & Peachtree Rd.) |
404-262-3165 | www.buckheadrestaurants.com

The "only thing missing is the ocean view" at this "steady" Buckhead
seafood "mecca" that offers "anything that swims" – "except Michael
Phelps" – and serves it, "still flapping", in a lofty setting with a "bustling", "big-city" feel; "loud" decibels, "long waits" and "crowded"
conditions are par for the course, but the pricing is "decent", the service "tight" and the specials "truly special."

Babette's Cafe 🄼 *European*

| | 26 | 22 | 25 | $39 |

Poncey-Highland | 573 N. Highland Ave. (Freedom Pkwy.) | 404-523-9121 |
www.babettescafe.com

Chef-owner Marla Adams "continues to please" at this "unassuming
bistro" in Poncey-Highland, where the "labor-of-love" European cooking shows "attention to detail" and is a match for the "quaint" setting;
a "dedicated local following" touts the "easygoing" mood, "charming
back porch" and "valet parking", while "reasonable pricing" makes it a
"best value" for "food of this caliber."

Bacchanalia ☒ *American* 29 | 26 | 28 | $111

Westside | Westside Mktpl. | 1198 Howell Mill Rd. NW (Huff Rd.) | 404-365-0410 | www.starprovisions.com

Holding fast as the "pinnacle of refined dining" (and again voted No. 1 for Food and Popularity in Atlanta), this near-"flawless" Westside New American "keeps it fresh year after year" with "absolutely outstanding" fare, served in a five-course, prix fixe–only menu that can be paired with an "impeccable" wine list for a "feast befitting its name"; the "well-trained" staff works with "panache", the setting is done up in "chic retro-industrial" style and there's a definite "sense of occasion" in the air, leaving the "extraordinary" prices as the only sticking point – though cheaper, à la carte dining is available at the bar.

BLT Steak *Steak* 26 | 23 | 23 | $62

Downtown | W Atlanta-Downtown | 45 Ivan Allen Jr. Blvd. NW (Spring St.) | 404-577-7601 | www.bltsteak.com

In a city with "a lot of great steakhouses", this "NYC transplant" in Downtown's W Hotel stands out for its "fantastic" chops and "to-die-for" popovers that are "worthy of a visit alone"; despite "noisy" acoustics and "not-cheap" tabs suited for the "expense-account" crowd, payoffs include "classy" quarters, a "trendy" mood and "on-top-of-everything" service – when it comes to "splurge" dining, this one's pretty "unforgettable."

Bone's Restaurant *Steak* 28 | 24 | 28 | $66

Buckhead | 3130 Piedmont Rd. NE (Peachtree Rd.) | 404-237-2663 | www.bonesrestaurant.com

"Hobnob" with the "who's who" of Buckhead at this "old-school" "cathedral of steak" renowned for "phenomenal" chops "cooked to perfection" and served by a team so "stellar" that it's been voted No. 1 for Service in Atlanta; "manly", "power-broker" decor, a "private-club" feel and an "epic wine list" ("presented on an iPad", no less) make the "platinum-card" prices easier to digest.

Buckhead Diner ☻ *American* 23 | 22 | 23 | $36

Buckhead | 3073 Piedmont Rd. NE (Paces Ferry Rd.) | 404-262-3336 | www.buckheadrestaurants.com

"Don't be fooled by the name" – this "high-end" Buckhead diner is "justifiably an Atlanta classic", offering "high-quality" American comfort chow (including "sinful" signature blue cheese potato chips) in an "aluminum"-lined "deco" setting; the no-reservations rule leads to "lines" at prime times, but "not-too-expensive" pricing and "happy-to-see-you" service make this 25-year-old a "tradition that never gets old."

Cakes & Ale ☒Ⓜ *American* 27 | 23 | 26 | $42

Decatur | Decatur Square | 155 Sycamore St. (Church St.) | 404-377-7994
Bakery at Cakes & Ale *Bakery*
Decatur | Decatur Square | 151 Sycamore St. (Church St.) | 404-377-7960
www.cakesandalerestaurant.com

Now relocated to "bigger", "more comfortable" quarters in a historic building on Decatur Square, this "assured" American "celebration" spot via "virtuoso" chef Billy Allin features "imaginatively prepared", "farm-fresh" dishes composed from "seasonal ingredients" and served by a staff versed in "attention to detail"; the arrival of a "fab" new adjacent bakery stocked with "tasty treats" has made the scene even more "happening" than before, so be prepared for "a little noise" along with a true "community feel."

Canoe *American*
27 | 27 | 27 | $50

Vinings | Vinings on the River | 4199 Paces Ferry Rd. SE (Woodland Brook Dr.) | 770-432-2663 | www.canoeatl.com
"Beautiful scenery" meets "exceptional" food at this Vinings "superstar", nestled in a "picturesque" setting overlooking the Chattahoochee River with "breathtaking gardens" that are a "gorgeous complement" to the "farm-to-table" New American cooking of "brilliant" chef Carvel Gould; "seamless" service and a "romantic" ambiance enhance the overall "sensational experience" that's so "well above the watermark", it's "easy to overlook" the "upscale" pricing.

Chops Lobster Bar *Seafood/Steak*
27 | 25 | 27 | $66

Buckhead | Buckhead Plaza | 70 W. Paces Ferry Rd. (Peachtree Rd.) | 404-262-2675 | www.buckheadrestaurants.com
"Still thriving after all these years", this "powerhouse" Buckhead Life Group surf 'n' turfer is "always packed" with "socialites", "businessmen" and "good ol' boys" with a hankering for "delectable" "man food" served by a "congenial", "old-school" team; upstairs, "dark wood and red leather" lend a "corporate-boardroom" feel, while downstairs, the tiled arched ceilings recall "Grand Central Station's Oyster Bar", but wherever you sit you can expect a "loud", "happening" scene and "wildly expensive" tabs.

Di Paolo Ⓜ *Italian*
27 | 21 | 25 | $42

Alpharetta | Rivermont Sq. | 8560 Holcomb Bridge Rd. (Nesbit Ferry Rd.) | 770-587-1051 | www.dipaolorestaurant.com
"Wow" is the word for this Alpharetta Northern Italian via chef Darin Hiebel, whose "excellent" cooking is so "superb" it's the kind of "food you'd expect to get in Buckhead" (the menu "changes with the season" and even includes "half portions for lighter eaters"); an "intimate" setting, "outstanding wine list" and "helpful", "first-name-basis" service offset the "high noise levels" and "depressing" strip-mall location.

Ecco *Continental*
26 | 25 | 25 | $42

Midtown | 40 Seventh St. NE (Cypress St.) | 404-347-9555 | www.ecco-atlanta.com
"Gorgeous patrons" frequent this "lively" Midtown Continental "crowd-pleaser" where the "modern", "ever-changing menu" includes "stunning small plates", "excellent" charcuterie and "higher-end entrees", all served in "beautiful", "fashionable" environs; granted, it's "not cheap" and some find it "more trendy than substantive", but the "good buzz" and staffers showing "pride in what they are doing" lead fans to say this one only "gets better with age."

Flip Burger Boutique *Burgers*
23 | 21 | 19 | $22

Westside | 1587 Howell Mill Rd. (Chattahoochee Ave. NW) | 404-352-3547
Buckhead | 3655 Roswell Rd. NE (Piedmont Ave.) | 404-549-3298
www.flipburgerboutique.com
Explore the "new burger frontier" at these "trendy" twins via *Top Chef* winner Richard Blais, who thinks "outside the bun" with "flippin' great", "nontraditional" patties washed down with "smoking milkshakes"

	FOOD	DECOR	SERVICE	COST

made with liquid nitrogen; devotees don't mind the "lines out the door" or "bumping elbows" at communal tables in the "witty", ultra-"modern" digs, but the "overly loud music" and "lackluster service" are another story.

Floataway Cafe ⊠Ⓜ *French/Italian* | 26 | 24 | 25 | $48 |

Emory | Floataway Bldg. | 1123 Zonolite Rd. NE (bet. Briarcliff & Johnson Rds.) | 404-892-1414 | www.starprovisions.com
"Seasonally" minded types seeking "creative" food paired with "superb wine" cite this "innovative" French-Italian near Emory, a Bacchanalia sibling with "all the flavor of the mother ship" – "without the cost or pretense"; a "knowledgeable staff" oversees the "newly renovated" digs (which lie somewhere between "soothing" and "stark", depending on who's talking), and though it's in a "funky", "industrial-wasteland" location, many say it's "worth finding" for those with "romance" in mind.

4th & Swift *American* | 26 | 24 | 25 | $47 |

Old Fourth Ward District | 621 North Ave. NE (Glen Iris Dr.) | 678-904-0160 | www.4thandswift.com
Quite the "foodie oasis" in the "up-and-coming" Old Fourth Ward District, this "progressive" New American via chef-owner Jay Swift offers a "seasonal", locally sourced menu paired with "awesome" cocktails that "meet at the corner of creative and delicious"; carved out of a "former dairy space", the "cavernous", "warehouse-chic" setting can be "louder than optimal" and a bit "hard to find", but appropriately "swift" service and "honest-value" pricing compensate; indeed, admirers say it's simply "perfect for every occasion."

Holeman & Finch ❶ *American* | 27 | 23 | 24 | $36 |

South Buckhead | 2277 Peachtree Rd. NE (Peachtree Memorial Dr.) | 404-948-1175 | www.holeman-finch.com
Ok, it looks like a "packed college bar", but this "cutting-edge" South Buckhead gastropub adjacent to sibling Restaurant Eugene puts forth a "smart", "meat-heavy" American menu built around the "whole animal concept" (it also offers a "pretty special" burger sold in "limited" quantities after 10 PM and all day Sunday); even though the dimensions are "tight" and the seating "cramped", the scene is "chic" and it "can be as expensive as you want."

Iberian Pig *Spanish* | 26 | 24 | 24 | $37 |

Decatur | 121 Sycamore St. (Church St.) | 404-371-8800 | www.iberianpigatl.com
An "homage to the wonderfulness of pork", this ultra-"popular" Decatur Spaniard serves "everything but the squeal" via "mouthwatering" tapas as well as a slate of "exquisite" non-porcine plates, all washed down with "crazy good" cocktails and a "terrific wine list"; the "dark", "modern industrial" setting has a "lively", "cool vibe", the price is "great" and the hospitality "exceptional", so it's no surprise that this one works for everything from a "romantic" date to a "night with friends."

JCT. Kitchen & Bar *Southern* | 25 | 23 | 23 | $35 |

Westside | Westside Mktpl. | 1198 Howell Mill Rd. (Huff Rd.) | 404-355-2252 | www.jctkitchen.com
"Down-home gourmet" cooking is "no contradiction" at chef Ford Fry's "trendy" Southerner on the "hip Westside", where the "updated" eats

include "heavenly shrimp and grits" and "delightful 'angry' mussels"; the interior exudes "Zen"-like charm, but when the "dining room volume" is comparable to the "Georgia Dome at kickoff", insiders escape to the "magical upstairs bar" and its view of the skyline; P.S. Sunday Supper, a meat-and-three for $24, is a "fabulous deal."

Kevin Rathbun Steak ⌧ *Steak*   27 | 26 | 26 | $59

Inman Park | 154 Krog St. NE (Lake Ave.) | 404-524-5600 | www.kevinrathbunsteak.com

"King of meat" Kevin Rathbun delivers "definitive" steaks and "modern twists on traditional sides" at this "contemporary" exercise in chophouse "perfection" in Inman Park; service is "unbeatable", the price tags "splurge"-worthy and the "dimly lit", "converted-warehouse" setting primarily illuminated by "cell-phone-lighting" apps, and overall most feel this one "really exceeds the hype"; P.S. those with "romance" in mind head for the "secluded tables downstairs."

Kyma *Greek/Seafood*   26 | 24 | 25 | $50

Buckhead | 3085 Piedmont Rd. NE (Paces Ferry Rd.) | 404-262-0702 | www.buckheadrestaurants.com

"Like a vacation escape", this "haute Greek" seafooder from the Buckhead Life Group offers "classically prepared" fish along with an "extensive selection" of Hellenic wine in a "sophisticated", "white palace"–like setting that's simply "transporting"; granted, the "exorbitant" pricing is "just slightly less than a round-trip ticket to Athens", but in return you get "impeccable" service and "quiet" acoustics – and Sunday's "magnificent meze" specials are an "exceptional value."

La Grotta ⌧ *Italian*   26 | 23 | 27 | $56

Buckhead | 2637 Peachtree Rd. NE (bet. Lindbergh Dr. & Wesley Rd.) | 404-231-1368

La Grotta Ravinia ⌧ *Italian*

Dunwoody | Crowne Plaza Ravinia Hotel | 4355 Ashford Dunwoody Rd. (Hammond Dr.) | 770-395-9925
www.lagrottaatlanta.com

"Sophisticated" and "elegant", this "old-money" Buckhead "tradition" is "still going strong", offering "beautifully prepared" Northern Italian cuisine and "wonderful" wines in a "mature", white-tablecloth setting that's got "special occasion" written all over it (there's also a "transporting" patio "straight out of *Rear Window*"); a "quiet", "relaxing" atmosphere and "read-your-mind" service make the "upscale" tabs easier to digest, while the equally "memorable" OTP Dunwoody satellite is a "welcome independent in a sea of chains."

La Pietra Cucina ⌧ *Italian*   27 | 21 | 25 | $48

Midtown | 1 Peachtree Pointe | 1545 NW Peachtree St. (Spring St.) | 404-888-8709 | www.lapietracucina.com

This "super" Midtown trattoria offers a contemporary Italian menu that includes "outstanding pasta" and "incredible" black spaghetti with rock shrimp; the "office-building" location on "busy" Peachtree Pointe can be "difficult to find", but payoffs include "polished" service and an "artistic setting" that's "perfect for pre-theater" or a "romantic" date; granted, the tabs are decidedly "high-end", but "worth every penny."

Local Three *American*   25 | 24 | 24 | $39

Buckhead | The Forum | 3290 Northside Pkwy. NW (Howell Mill Rd.) |
404-968-2700 | www.localthree.com

"Down-to-earth" despite its location in a luxury Buckhead complex,
this "something-different" enterprise via chef Chris Hall "lives up to
the hype", purveying an "honest" New American menu with "locavore" leanings paired with "unique cocktails" and a "great" wine list;
the "food fits the mood" of the "noisy", "energetic" space with a
"warm, witty" design, "handcrafted" wooden furniture and "laid-
back" "hipster waiters" – in sum, it's "upscale without uppityness"
and, best of all, comes at "un-Buckhead prices."

Miller Union ⊠ *American*   24 | 23 | 24 | $47

Westside | 999 Brady Ave. (10th St.) | 678-733-8550 | www.millerunion.com
"Hidden away" in an "off-the-beaten-track" Westside address, this
"hip" New American set in a "cool" space lures "farm-fresh" fans thanks
to the "brilliant" work of chef Steven Satterfield, whose "thoughtful",
Southern-accented cooking is highlighted by a "memorable" monthly
harvest dinner; "debonair" co-owner Neal McCarthy oversees the
"well-informed" staff, and even though critics cite a "smug" attitude
and "pricey" tabs, most affirm it's "as good as they say"; P.S. the ice
cream sandwiches enjoy a lot of "hype."

Nan Thai Fine Dining *Thai*   27 | 28 | 26 | $51

Midtown | 1350 Spring St. NW (17th St.) | 404-870-9933 |
www.nanfinedining.com

"Bring your camera" urge aesthetes "completely impressed" by this
"classy" Midtown Thai, voted No. 1 for Decor, with its "superb interior
design", "awesome bathrooms" and relaxing, "Zen-like ambiance";
the "beautifully presented", "top-drawer" cooking is on par with the
scenery and "gracious service" adds to the "winning formula", but
there are "no deals here", so be prepared for dining that's "quite expensive" for the genre.

New York Prime *Steak*   26 | 24 | 25 | $62

Buckhead | Monarch Tower | 3424 Peachtree Rd. NE (Lenox Rd.) |
404-846-0644 | www.newyorkprime.com

At this "upscale" Buckhead protein palace, "killer steaks" that you
can "hear across the room, sizzling with butter", are presented by an
"unmatched" team in a white-tablecloth, "dress up"–appropriate
setting; too bad about the "expensive" tabs, cigar "smoking at the
bar" and "loud, NYC-style" acoustics, but at least the scene is "active"
and the "people-watching" (think "young girls on the arms of old
businessmen") is choice.

No. 246 *Italian*   24 | 24 | 23 | $36

Decatur | 129 E. Ponce De Leon Ave. (Church St.) | 678-399-8246 |
www.no246.com

This "hot-spot" collaboration between chefs Ford Fry (JCT. Kitchen)
and Drew Belline (ex Floataway Cafe) "hits high notes" with "inspired"
Italian plates prepared in a wood-fired oven; the "hip" crowd, "feel-at-
home" ambiance and "place-to-be" outdoor patio lead some to label
it "Decatur's first destination restaurant"; P.S. it recently made "im-
provements" to the formerly "challenging noise levels."

	FOOD	DECOR	SERVICE	COST

Pricci *Italian* — 26 | 22 | 25 | $48

Buckhead | 500 Pharr Rd. NE (Maple Dr.) | 404-237-2941 |
www.buckheadrestaurants.com

"Beautiful", well-heeled Buckhead folk flock to this "classic old-world" Italian for "lovingly prepared" food served in an "elegant" setting by an "excellent" team; an "unapologetic '80s ambiance" and "loud" decibels from the "lively bar" come with the territory, and if a few feel it "needs to be updated", more say it's "improved over the years."

Quinones Room at — 28 | 27 | 29 | $163
Bacchanalia 🄢🄜 *American*

Westside | Courtyard of Bacchanalia | 1198 Howell Mill Rd. (Huff Rd.) | 404-365-0410 | www.starprovisions.com

"Fine dining at its best" is alive and well at this "super-duper fancy" Westside sibling of Bacchanalia, where "exquisite", "multicourse" New American meals backed up with "choreographed", "personalized" service add up to "memory-making experiences"; granted, this "three-hour event" doesn't come cheap (it's prix fixe only, starting at $125) and now is open Saturday nights only, but when it comes to "over-the-top" dining, this one's "in a league of its own."

Rathbun's 🄑 *American* — 27 | 24 | 25 | $51

Inman Park | Stove Works | 112 Krog St. NE (bet. Edgewood Ave. & Irwin St.) | 404-524-8280 | www.rathbunsrestaurant.com

Chef-owner Kevin Rathbun's flagship property, this "innovative" Inman Park American is "always spot-on" for "brilliant" dining, "whether you get a few large plates or a million small ones"; the "cool" warehouse setting and "outstanding" service lure a "lively" crowd of "celebrities" and "influential Atlanta natives", and if it gets too "loud", the patio is a "quieter" alternative; wherever you sit, however, the tabs are "quite pricey."

Restaurant Eugene *American* — 27 | 25 | 27 | $66

South Buckhead | The Aramore | 2277 Peachtree Rd. NE (Peachtree Memorial Dr.) | 404-355-0321 | www.restauranteugene.com

"Everything's just right" at this "spectacular" New American in South Buckhead, an "adult" exercise in "quiet sophistication" that's touted for chef Linton Hopkins' "rewarding" farm-to table menu and "superlative wine pairings"; granted, it's "costly" and what's "intimate" to some is too "staid" for others, but ultimately the "soft lights", "elegant" furnishings and "impeccable" service make for the "most consistent fine dining in Atlanta."

Seed *American* — - | - | - | M

Marietta | Merchant's Walk Shopping Ctr. | 1311 Johnson Ferry Rd. (Roswell Rd.) | 678-214-6888 | www.eatatseed.com

Boosters vie for a seat at this OTP newcomer from chef-owner Doug Turbush (ex Bluepointe) that brings affordable modern American eats with Asian and Latin accents to Marietta; the sleek, ai3-designed digs include a tucked-away patio and a bustling bar where carefully cultivated cocktails lure shoppers on breaks from Merchant's Walk; P.S. reserve ahead or you may be sprout of luck.

	FOOD	DECOR	SERVICE	COST

Sotto Sotto *Italian* — 27 | 22 | 25 | $46

Inman Park | 313 N. Highland Ave. NE (Elizabeth St.) | 404-523-6678 | www.sottosottorestaurant.com

A "heavenly" sibling of next-door Fritti, this "intimate" Northern Italian in Inman Park via chef-owner Riccardo Ullio "just gets better with age", dispatching "superb pasta" and "memorable risotto" paired with a "well-thought-out wine list"; "special-occasion" pricing and "tables packed on top of each other" to the contrary, this is the "kind of place you dream about" thanks to its "charming" mien and "precision" service "beyond compare."

Star Provisions ☒ *Deli* — 27 | 20 | 21 | $21

Westside | Westside Mktpl. | 1198 Howell Mill Rd. NW (Huff Rd.) | 404-365-0410 | www.starprovisions.com

Atlanta foodies "can find anything they want" at this Westside "gourmet-to-go" deli (basically sibling "Bacchanalia's grocery store") offering a "spectacular" variety of goodies – think meats, cheeses, baked goods – along with "brilliant lunch fare" that can be consumed on-site at tables scattered throughout; the "mega-rich" price tags "make Whole Foods look like Food Lion", but for such "top-notch" noshing, it's "worth it."

Table & Main ☒ *Southern* — – | – | – | M

Roswell | 1028 Canton St. (bet. Norcross & Woodstock Sts.) | 678-869-5178 | www.tableandmain.com

In a pristinely restored cottage, chef Ted Lahey lures Roswell residents with grown-up riffs on classic Southern comfort fare (think Velveeta bechamel mac 'n' cheese) washed down with small-batch bourbons; local art adorns the walls, and there's a relaxing patio overlooking the historic district's main drag.

Taka ☒ *Japanese* — 27 | 16 | 23 | $40

Buckhead | 385 Pharr Rd. NE (Grandview Ave.) | 404-869-2802 | www.takasushiatlanta.com

"Real sushi lovers" eschew "trendy" joints in favor of this "tiny" neighborhood Japanese in Buckhead where the eponymous chef's "artful presentation" and "huge flavors" keep things "honest and real", "without the glitz"; adherents ignore the "nondescript" decor and "small" dimensions, and "sit at the bar to get the whole experience."

Tomo ☒ *Japanese* — ▽ 28 | 20 | 23 | $49

Buckhead | 3630 Peachtree Rd. NE (Peachtree Dunwoody Rd.) | 404-835-2708 | www.tomorestaurant.com

"Sorry" Vinings surveyors regret that their beloved Japanese has relocated to "new quarters" in a "luxury" residential building in Buckhead, but the "seriously sensational sushi" from chef-owner Tomohiro Naito has made the trip intact, along with the "impeccable" service and "premium sake" list; followers say it's "like going to Nobu" but "without the NYC hassles", even if the "expensive" pricing made the move too.

Valenza *Italian* — 28 | 24 | 25 | $39

Brookhaven | 1441 Dresden Dr. (bet. Appalachee & Camille Drs.) | 404-969-3233 | www.valenzarestaurant.com

Brookhaven diners dig this "delightful" Northern Italian "neighborhood place" where chef Matt Swickerath offers "fine pastas" and other

	FOOD	DECOR	SERVICE	COST

"super-fresh" food in "large portions" paired with a "well-chosen" wine list; "prompt" service, "value" pricing and a "familial" setting with Venetian plastered walls add to the overall "pleasant" experience.

Woodfire Grill 🚭Ⓜ *American* | 27 | 22 | 26 | $58 |

Cheshire Bridge | 1782 Cheshire Bridge Rd. (Piedmont Rd.) | 404-347-9055 | www.woodfiregrill.com

Foodies swoon over this "stunning" Cheshire Bridge "splurge" where "sweetheart" Kevin Gillespie, a "*Top Chef* who actually works in the kitchen", produces "phenomenal" American "farm-to-table" fare on the "tantalizing" eponymous grill; servers make guests "feel beyond welcome" in the "unpretentious" setting, and though a few lament "micro portions" at "macro prices", overall this "not-to-be-missed" experience is "well worth it."

Atlantic City

TOP FOOD RANKING

	Restaurant	Cuisine
27	Old Homestead	Steak
	Il Mulino	Italian
26	Chef Vola's	Italian
	White House	Sandwiches
	Girasole	Italian
	Dock's	Seafood
	Mia	Italian
	SeaBlue	Seafood
	Buddakan	Asian
25	Little Saigon	Vietnamese

OTHER NOTEWORTHY PLACES

Amada	Spanish
American Cut	Steak
Bobby Flay	Steak
Capriccio	Italian
Luke Palladino	Italian
McCormick & Schmick's	Seafood
Morton's	Steak
Palm	Steak
P.F. Chang's	Chinese
Ruth's Chris	Steak

Amada 🚫Ⓜ *Spanish*
Atlantic City | Revel Resorts | 500 Boardwalk (Metropolitan Ave.) | 609-225-9900 | www.revelresorts.com
Luminary toque Jose Garces adds his Philly flagship to the star-studded firmament at AC's Revel Resorts, serving his signature upscale Spanish tapas and shareable plates in an airy room done up in brown, black and white, with ocean views on one side and the gaming floor on another; for more casual eats, Revelers can opt for Garces' Mexican cantina, Distrito, and American tavern, Village Whiskey.

American Cut 🚫Ⓜ *Steak*
Atlantic City | Revel Resorts | 500 Boardwalk (Metropolitan Ave.) | 609-225-9860 | www.americancutsteakhouse.com
Chef Marc Forgione modernizes the traditional American chophouse at this high-energy, high-decibel entry at AC's Revel Resorts, where surf 'n' turf morphs into chili lobster and tomahawk rib-eye for two, and old-school decor elements of brass, leather and dark wood become downright sexy; prices, alas, remain typically steakhouse stratospheric.

Bobby Flay Steak Ⓜ *Steak* 25 | 25 | 24 | $65
Atlantic City | Borgata Hotel, Casino & Spa | 1 Borgata Way (Huron Ave.) | 609-317-1000 | www.bobbyflaysteak.com
Bobby Flay, the "god of grilling", proves that he "sure knows how to grill a steak" at this "outstanding" chop shop set inside the Borgata

Hotel; a "superb" wine list and a "lavishly decorated" setting by David Rockwell embellish the overall "luscious" feel, but don't forget to bring all your credit cards – this one's priced for "high rollers."

Buddakan *Asian*
26 | 27 | 23 | $53

Atlantic City | Pier Shops at Caesars | 1 Atlantic Ocean (Arkansas Ave.) | 609-674-0100 | www.buddakanac.com

Stephen Starr's "phenomenal" Pan-Asian "scene" in the Pier at Caesars (a spin-off of the Philly and Manhattan branches) offers "beautifully realized" fusion specialties in an "over-the-top" setting complete with a "giant" gilded Buddha and "glorious" communal table; ok, it's fairly "pricey" and "noisy", but all agree that it's a "true experience" and "excellent for a special occasion."

Capriccio Ⓜ *Italian*
25 | 26 | 26 | $61

Atlantic City | Resorts Atlantic City Casino & Hotel | 1133 Boardwalk (North Carolina Ave.) | 609-340-6789 | www.resortsac.com

Diners "hit the jackpot" at this "outstanding" Italian in Resorts Casino, where the winnings include "skillfully prepared", "osso good" dishes served by a "wonderful" team in a "stunning", "Gilded Age" setting replete with "fantastic" ocean views; P.S. a post-Survey change in the hotel's ownership is not reflected in the ratings.

Chef Vola's Ⓜ⇗ *Italian*
26 | 12 | 23 | $53

Atlantic City | 111 S. Albion Pl. (Pacific Ave.) | 609-345-2022 | www.chefvolas.com

"Difficult reservations" is putting it mildly at this "hidden" Italian BYO on an AC side street, where the "just-like-mama's" cooking enjoys a fervid "cult following" despite a cash-only policy, "low-ceilinged basement" setting and "tables closer than Siamese twins"; it's "no longer a secret" – "everybody knows the unlisted number" – and first-timers are willing to "sell their first-born" for a table.

Dock's Oyster House *Seafood*
26 | 21 | 24 | $52

Atlantic City | 2405 Atlantic Ave. (Georgia Ave.) | 609-345-0092 | www.docksoysterhouse.com

A "throwback to the *Boardwalk Empire*" era of AC, this circa-1897 seafood "icon" still scores high for its "fabulous" fin fare served by an "outstanding" team in a "days-gone-by" setting; nightly piano music and a "good" wine list help distract from the "noise" and modern-day prices.

Girasole *Italian*
26 | 23 | 22 | $53

Atlantic City | Ocean Club Condos | 3108 Pacific Ave. (bet. Chelsea & Montpelier Aves.) | 609-345-5554 | www.girasoleac.com

Situated in a "nice spot" – a condo a block away from the boardwalk – this "superior" Italian boasts "refined", "old-fashioned" cooking served in a "cool", sunflower-themed setting festooned with "Versace decorations"; it feels as though it's "miles from the hustle and bustle of the casinos" and draws the "localin' crowd" unfazed by the "high prices" and service with "a little attitude."

Il Mulino New York *Italian*
27 | 23 | 24 | $71

Atlantic City | Trump Taj Mahal | 1000 Boardwalk (Virginia Ave.) | 609-449-6006 | www.ilmulino.com

For an "impeccable" Italian meal on a "big night out", it "doesn't get any better" than this Taj Mahal facsimile of the legendary NY original; expect "insanely good" classic cooking, "white-glove" service from a tuxedoed team and a "beautiful", traditionally appointed setting – but since it's a definite "splurge", "bring the credit card with no balance."

Little Saigon ⌿ *Vietnamese* | 25 | 10 | 20 | $26 |

Atlantic City | 2801 Arctic Ave. (Iowa Ave.) | 609-347-9119
"Authentic", "first-rate" Vietnamese cooking is the draw at this cash-only, off-the-boardwalk "find"; granted, this small BYO has "no atmosphere" and is parked on an "uncharming street", but service is "friendly" and the price tags "relatively meager."

Luke Palladino *Italian* | ▽ 26 | 18 | 23 | $49 |

Atlantic City | Harrah's | 777 Harrah's Blvd. (Brigantine Blvd.) | 609-441-5576 | www.harrahsresort.com
Modern Italian "dining bliss" lands at Harrah's via this new outpost from the eponymous chef, offering "beautifully prepared" seasonal dishes; frequently changing prix fixe dinners and tasting menus are available as well.

McCormick & Schmick's *Seafood* | 20 | 19 | 19 | $43 |

Atlantic City | Harrah's | 777 Harrah's Blvd. (Brigantine Blvd.) | 609-441-5579 | www.mccormickandschmicks.com
Popular for "business and pleasure", this "upscale" seafood chain link at Harrah's offers a "daily changing" menu of "freshly caught" fare in an "upbeat" atmosphere; though it feels too "stamped-out-of-a-mold" for some, its "professional" service is a plus and the "happy-hour bar menu" lures the after-work crowd.

Mia ⊠Ⓜ *Italian* | 26 | 25 | 24 | $57 |

Atlantic City | Caesars on the Boardwalk | 2100 Pacific Ave. (Arkansas Ave.) | 609-441-2345 | www.miaac.com
Diners encounter an "amazing", "Roman temple–style" space just off the lobby of Caesars at this "classy" Italian "getaway" via Georges Perrier and Chris Scarduzio; patrons "feel like Zeus himself" as they dine on the "stellar" specialties, and though it's "quite expensive", the prix fixe dinner specials are an "outstanding value."

Morton's The Steakhouse *Steak* | 25 | 23 | 25 | $67 |

Atlantic City | Caesars on the Boardwalk | 2100 Pacific Ave. (Arkansas Ave.) | 609-449-1044 | www.mortons.com
A steakhouse "standard-bearer", this "big-ticket" chain link at Caesars offers "excellently prepared" cuts of beef and "grand sides" "served professionally" amid an "ambiance of wealth and class"; some find it a bit "staid" and could do without the "high" wine pricing, but overall it's considered "one of the best."

Old Homestead ⊠ *Steak* | 27 | 25 | 26 | $72 |

Atlantic City | Borgata Hotel, Casino & Spa | 1 Borgata Way (Huron Ave.) | 609-317-1000 | www.theoldhomesteadsteakhouse.com
"Killer" steaks are "cooked to perfection" at this "cavernous" spin-off of the NYC original occupying a double-decker setting in the Borgata Hotel; "typical leather" decor and "prompt, unobtrusive" service come with the territory, and don't forget to bring "deep pockets" to settle the "outrageous" bill.

	FOOD	DECOR	SERVICE	COST

The Palm *Steak*
25 **21** **23** **$66**

Atlantic City | Quarter at the Tropicana | 2801 Pacific Ave. (Iowa Ave.) | 609-344-7256 | www.thepalm.com

"Perfect" lobster, "superb" steaks and "hefty" cocktails are the signatures of this "bustling", "special-occasion" chophouse chain link at the Quarter at the Tropicana with a "dark men's-club" look; "old-school" service seals the deal, so while it's "not cheap", most conclude it's "worth it."

P.F. Chang's China Bistro *Chinese*
20 **21** **19** **$34**

Atlantic City | Quarter at the Tropicana | 2801 Pacific Ave. (Iowa Ave.) | 609-348-4600 | www.pfchangs.com

"Light, delicious", "Americanized" Chinese food (and "standout" lettuce wraps) keeps fans "coming back" to this "upscale" chain link at the Quarter at the Tropicana; though some call it "ordinary" and "loud", the "consistent" service is a plus, ditto the "smart" menu "catering to people with allergies" and other needs.

Ruth's Chris Steak House *Steak*
25 **22** **24** **$63**

Atlantic City | The Walk | 2020 Atlantic Ave. (bet. Arkansas & Michigan Aves.) | 609-344-5833 | www.ruthschris.com

Loyalists love the "sizzling platters" of "oh-so-good buttery steaks" at the AC link of the "top-quality" chophouse chain that comes through with "winning" sides too; offering "old-style service" in a "traditional" setting, it's "expensive" but "utterly reliable", especially when you're "entertaining friends and clients."

SeaBlue *Seafood*
26 **25** **25** **$69**

Atlantic City | Borgata Hotel, Casino & Spa | 1 Borgata Way (Huron Ave.) | 609-317-8220 | www.theborgata.com

Celeb chef Michael Mina's "seafood experience" just off the Borgata casino floor is famed for its "decadent" signature lobster pot pie, served in a "picture-worthy" Adam Tihany–designed space; "stellar" service and a swanky mood make the "mortgage-payment" price tags "worth the splurge."

White House *Sandwiches*
26 **8** **16** **$14**

Atlantic City | Trump Taj Mahal | 1000 Boardwalk (Virginia Ave.) | 609-345-7827 | www.trumptaj.com
Atlantic City | 2301 Arctic Ave. (Mississippi Ave.) | 609-345-1564 ⊞

"Ridiculously large" submarine sandwiches arrive on "paper plates" at this cash-only AC "institution" that's "always crowded" but certainly "worth the wait in line", despite "tacky" decor and "major attitude" from the staff; P.S. the spin-off in the Trump Taj Mahal opened post-Survey.

Austin

TOP FOOD RANKING

	Restaurant	Cuisine
29	Uchi	Japanese
	Louie Mueller BBQ	BBQ
28	Barley Swine	American
	Snow's BBQ	BBQ
	Carillon	American
	Franklin Barbecue*	BBQ
	Congress	American
	Uchiko*	Japanese
27	Smitty's Market	BBQ
	Hudson's on the Bend	American

OTHER NOTEWORTHY PLACES

Restaurant	Cuisine
Eddie V's	Seafood/Steak
Fonda San Miguel	Mexican
Foreign & Domestic	American/European
La Condesa	Mexican
Olivia	French/Italian
Salt Lick	BBQ
Second Bar + Kitchen	American
Swift's Attic	American/Eclectic
Vespaio	Italian
Wink	American

Barley Swine ⏛ *American*　　28 | 19 | 25 | $47
South Lamar | 2024 S. Lamar Blvd. (Hether St.) | 512-394-8150 |
www.barleyswine.com
One of the "hottest" places in town, this "amazing" "locavore" American
in South Lamar from chef Bryce Gilmore (of the now-defunct Odd
Duck trailer) provides "truly memorable" small plates all made for
sharing and enjoying alongside an impressive list of beers; it's "foodie
central", but the space is "hopelessly small", so "arrive early or be prepared to wait for an eternity."

The Carillon *American*　　28 | 25 | 26 | $55
Campus | AT&T Executive Education & Conference Ctr. |
1900 University Ave. (Martin Luther King Blvd.) | 512-404-3655 |
www.thecarillonrestaurant.com
"Top-drawer for Austin", this "beautiful", "special-occasion" Campus-
area New American in the AT&T Executive Education and Conference
Center is where chef Josh Watkins "moves Texas-native materials
into haute cuisine territory", yielding "exceptional" dishes; considering such "superior" quality and service, many find the prices
quite "reasonable"; P.S. the lounge features a separate bar menu
with small plates.

---

* Indicates a tie with restaurant above

	FOOD	DECOR	SERVICE	COST

Congress 🖼️Ⓜ️ *American* — 28 | 28 | 27 | $90

Downtown | The Austonian | 200 Congress Ave. (2nd St.) |
512-827-2760 | www.congressaustin.com

"Hands-down" among the "best" in town proclaim fans of this "up-scale" Downtown restaurant spotlighting chef David Bull's "over-the-top", "no-holds-barred" New American creations served in prix fixe feasts "fit for a foodie"; "wonderful wines", "fantastic" service (ranked No. 1 in Austin) and a "sophisticated" setting make it "worth every penny for a special occasion" – go for the "full-monty chef's tasting" "if you can afford it"; P.S. the adjacent Bar Congress has its own menu of cocktails and small bites.

Eddie V's Prime Seafood *Seafood/Steak* — 26 | 26 | 25 | $55

Arboretum | 9400 Arboretum Blvd. (Capital of Texas Hwy.) |
512-342-2642
Downtown | 301 E. Fifth St. (San Jacinto Blvd.) | 512-472-1860
www.eddiev.com

This "vibrant" chophouse chainlet – tied for Most Popular in Austin – "stands out" with "super" steaks and "excellent" "seafood without gimmicks" ("oysters as fresh as if you'd gotten them off the boat"), plus "exemplary" service and "elegant", "well-appointed" surroundings attracting a "high-rolling" crowd of "wealthy lobby-ists and dealmakers"; "you pay dearly" for it all, so many seek out the half-price apps deals during happy hour; look for a "hopping" bar scene too.

Fonda San Miguel *Mexican* — 25 | 27 | 23 | $42

Highland Park | 2330 North Loop Blvd. W. (Hancock Dr.) | 512-459-4121 |
www.fondasanmiguel.com

"Colorful and full of beautiful pottery", this Highland Park hacienda has long been "a treat for the eyes as well as the taste buds" with "im-peccable" interior Mexican fare in a "casually elegant" setting tended by a "knowledgeable" crew; especially "memorable" is Sunday's boun-tiful buffet brunch – a long-standing "tradition" and quite the "event"; "don't eat all weekend" before you go.

Foreign & Domestic Ⓜ️ *American/European* — 23 | 17 | 21 | $40

Hyde Park | 306 E. 53rd St. (Ave. H) | 512-459-1010 |
www.foodanddrinkaustin.com

Riding both the farm-to-table and nose-to-tail waves is this "inven-tive" Hyde Park American-European offering an "adventurous" sea-sonal menu and a well-chosen array of wines and craft beers; reviews on the food are mixed ("tasty" vs. "disappointing"), although the "loud", "offbeat" setting in an old skate shop continues to draw diners in droves.

Franklin Barbecue Ⓜ️ *BBQ* — 28 | 11 | 19 | $17

East Austin | 900 E. 11th St. (Branch St.) | 512-653-1187 |
www.franklinbarbecue.com

Originally a trailer, this brick-and-mortar BBQ upstart in East Austin is "giving the big names a run for their money" with some of the "finest brisket in the entire state of Texas" plus pulled pork and other "excep-tional", "simple smoked meats"; the modest space opens at 11 AM and closes whenever the eats run out, which is usually early.

	FOOD	DECOR	SERVICE	COST

Hudson's on the Bend *American*

27 | 24 | 26 | $60

Lakeway | 3509 Ranch Rd. 620 N. (Hudson Bend Rd.) | 512-266-1369 | www.hudsonsonthebend.com

"Rattlesnake cakes, anyone?" – this "true Texas ranch house" in Lakeway spotlights Jeff Blank's "memorable" New American menu highlighting "elk, elk and more elk" and other "exotic" game served by a "savvy", "pleasant" staff in "romantic" digs; yes, it's "expensive", but it's truly a "unique experience" that makes any meal "feel like a special occasion"; P.S. reservations recommended.

La Condesa *Mexican*

23 | 26 | 22 | $38

Second Street District | 400 W. Second St. (Guadalupe St.) | 512-499-0300 | www.lacondesaaustin.com

"Fabulous, bold" takes on Mexican street food and "wonderful margaritas" await at this Second Street District destination set in "stunning", "sophisticated" digs with a patio; just know the "lively" atmosphere can be "a little too loud for conversation", and it's not exactly cheap, unless you "go at happy hour for deals on appetizers and drinks."

Louie Mueller BBQ 🅼 *BBQ*

29 | 16 | 21 | $21

Taylor | 206 W. Second St. (Talbot St.) | 512-352-6206 | www.louiemuellerbarbecue.com

The dining room itself is "charred with years of accumulating smoke" at this "real-deal" circa-1949 Taylor BBQer declared "one of the best in Texas" thanks to its "simply divine", "thickly crusted", "flavorful" brisket that "passes the doesn't-need-sauce test"; service is "cafeteria-style" and "neon beer signs" are the only decor, but it's "well worth the drive"; P.S. it "closes when they run out of food", so "get there early."

Olivia *French/Italian*

25 | 22 | 24 | $42

South Lamar | 2043 S. Lamar Blvd. (Oltorf St.) | 512-804-2700 | www.olivia-austin.com

A "lovely space with good buzz", this modern South Lamar spot "does fresh, seasonal, nice-night-out food" with an "innovative" French-Italian menu that will "change your mind about sweetbreads, lamb tongue and other oddities"; an "extremely attentive and knowledgeable" staff and wine list "filled with gems" help take the sting off somewhat pricey tabs.

Salt Lick *BBQ*

25 | 19 | 20 | $24

Round Rock | 3350 E. Palm Valley Blvd. (Harrell Pkwy.) | 512-386-1044
Southeast Austin | Austin-Bergstrom Int'l Airport | 3600 Presidential Blvd. (Bastrop Hwy.) | no phone 🍽
Driftwood | 18300 FM 1826 (FM 967) | 512-858-4959 🍽
www.saltlickbbq.com

"Bring your appetite" to these "true Texas" BBQers for a "first-class orgy of meat" via "piles" of pit-smoked "fork-tender brisket", "spicy sausage" and "fall-off-the-bone ribs" served "family-style" in a "rustic" atmosphere with "great" live music on weekends; it's cash only with "looong waits" at the Driftwood original, and although it's BYO beer, you can also pick up a bottle of wine from their new tasting room to open at the picnic tables; P.S. "buy a whole brisket at the airport to carry home and your friends will love you."

	FOOD	DECOR	SERVICE	COST

Second Bar + Kitchen ● *American* | 25 | 24 | 22 | $43 |

Downtown | The Austonian | 200 Congress Ave. (2nd St.) | 512-827-2750 | www.congressaustin.com

This more casual offshoot of chef David Bull's Congress specializes in "superb", "farm-to-table" New American fare served all day in small- and large-plates with "awesome" cocktails and wines; the "cool" modern-industrial Downtown space sports a wraparound bar for dining or drinks with maximum "people-watching", so the only downsides are the lack of happy hour and no-reservations policy.

Smitty's Market ⌐ *BBQ* | 27 | 14 | 15 | $18 |

Lockhart | 208 S. Commerce St. (bet. Market & Prairie Lea Sts.) | 512-398-9344 | www.smittysmarket.com

A "mecca" for "BBQ aficionados", this Lockhart butcher shop set in the original site of the Kreuz Market is cherished for its "superb" brisket, "thick pork chops" that "rock your socks" and links "to die for" (a good thing since "your arteries may never recover"); all comes served straight from the pit in an "old-time, fire-seared" setting abetted by a friendly staff and cold beer.

Snow's BBQ ▣Ⓜ *BBQ* | 28 | 15 | 22 | $18 |

Lexington | 516 Main St. (bet. 2nd & 3rd Sts.) | 979-773-4640 | www.snowsbbq.com

It's "only open on Saturday mornings" so diehards "show up at dawn and stand in line" for "melt-in-your-mouth" brisket and "tender" ribs at this Lexington smokehouse called "as close to heaven as meat eaters can get"; its "no-pretensions", "far-off-the-path" locale "down a back alley in a forgotten town" is definitely "part of the charm", and so is the "friendly" hospitality.

Swift's Attic *Eclectic* | - | - | - | M |

Downtown | 315 Congress Ave. (bet. 3rd & 4th Sts.) | www.swiftsattic.com

This highly anticipated Downtown New American features Eclectic small plates from a dream team of chefs – Mat Clouser, Zack Northcutt and Callie Speer – with experience at Uchi, Mulberry and Parkside between them; set in the historic Swift Building, the space is done in a modern style with a long bar.

Uchi *Japanese* | 29 | 25 | 27 | $56 |

Zilker | 801 S. Lamar Blvd. (Juliet St.) | 512-916-4808 | www.uchiaustin.com

"Heaven" for sushiphiles, this Zilker jewel box presents the "finest in forward-thinking Japanese" cuisine via chef Tyson Cole – from "delish" raw fare and the signature deep-fried shag roll to "incredible" fusion plates that "make you cry tears of joy" – earning it Austin's No. 1 for Food rating and tying it for Most Popular; a "sophisticated" vibe, "outstanding" service and a "great-looking clientele" mean it "surpasses expectations" for most, just "take another hit of sake before you look at the bill"; P.S. a Houston outpost is now open.

Uchiko *Japanese* | 28 | 26 | 27 | $59 |

Rosedale | 4200 N. Lamar Blvd. (42nd St.) | 512-916-4808 | www.uchikoaustin.com

"Simply brilliant", this "whimsical" Rosedale sib to Uchi features *Top Chef*'s Paul Qui's "wildly creative" Japanese fare in "beautiful" presentations capped by "dynamic" wines and "mind-blowing desserts"; service is "professional", the space is modern and while tabs are steep, that hasn't deterred the crowds.

Vespaio *Italian*

| 26 | 21 | 24 | $43 |

SoCo | 1610 S. Congress Ave. (Monroe St.) | 512-441-6100 | www.austinvespaio.com

"Long waits" are par for the course at this midpriced SoCo Italian, "hands-down one of the best in Austin" thanks to its "superb" cooking, "wonderful wines" and a warm setting that's "one of the best places to spot a movie star or politician"; an "eager" staff is "helpful" with suggestions, but it's "noisy, noisy, noisy" at prime times.

Wink ☒ *American*

| 27 | 21 | 25 | $64 |

Old West Austin | 1014 N. Lamar Blvd. (11th St.) | 512-482-8868 | www.winkrestaurant.com

On the scene for a decade and still utterly "original", this Old West Austin New American delivers "highly creative", "locavore"-driven fare with a tasting menu that will "blow you away"; service is "wonderful" too, so fans only "wish the space were a little hipper", and perhaps that the check were a bit lower; P.S. "happy hour in the wine bar is a steal."

Baltimore/Annapolis

TOP FOOD RANKING

	Restaurant	Cuisine
29	Charleston	American
28	Di Pasquale's	Italian
	Samos	Greek
	Vin 909	American
	Bartlett Pear Inn	American
	Prime Rib	Steak
	Tersiguel's	French
	Out of the Fire	American/Eclectic
	Sushi King	Japanese
	Milton Inn	American

OTHER NOTEWORTHY PLACES

Restaurant	Cuisine
B – A Bolton Hill Bistro	American
B&O American Brasserie	American
Cheesecake Factory	American
Double T Diner	Diner
Food Market	American
G&M	Seafood
Gertrude's	Chesapeake
Pabu	Japanese
Peter's Inn	American
Woodberry Kitchen	American

b – A Bolton Hill Bistro Ⓜ *American*   26 | 21 | 24 | $39

Bolton Hill | 1501 Bolton St. (Mosher St.) | Baltimore | 410-383-8600 |
www.b-bistro.com

"One of Bolton Hill's most valuable assets" is this "cute and quirky"
corner bistro with big picture windows, "a real neighborhood" spot
that nevertheless "outperforms trendier places" with its "creative"
American dishes made with "lovely locally sourced ingredients"
(though a recent chef change may outdate the Food rating); just be
prepared to sit "elbow-to-elbow" or grab a table "outside in summer."

B&O American Brasserie *American*   23 | 24 | 22 | $43

Downtown | Hotel Monaco | 2 N. Charles St. (Baltimore St.) | Baltimore |
443-692-6172 | www.bandorestaurant.com

At the Hotel Monaco's "historic" beaux arts digs Downtown, this "lively"
American turns out "innovative" charcuterie, small plates and seasonal
mains; the space is "very *Mad Men*", with a "chic" crowd downing "creative" drinks in the lounge and, overlooking the action from the mezzanine, a "swanky", almost "1950s boardroom"-esque dining room.

Bartlett Pear Inn Restaurant *American*   28 | 25 | 27 | $58

Easton | Bartlett Pear Inn | 28 S. Harrison St. (bet. E. Dover & South Sts.) |
410-770-3300 | www.bartlettpearinn.com

"Extraordinary doesn't begin to describe this culinary temple" rave
pear-amours of the "beautifully prepared" New American dishes pre-

sented by a "superb" staff at this "charming" and "gorgeous" Easton inn that dates to the late 18th century; prices place it "high on the romance and special-occasion scale", though the chef's tasting menu is a "relative bargain", and the bar offers a more casual approach.

Charleston ⑤ *American*   29 | 28 | 28 | $99

Harbor East | 1000 Lancaster St. (Exeter St.) | Baltimore | 410-332-7373 | www.charlestonrestaurant.com

Cindy Wolf remains "at the top of her game", applying "world-class technique" to "Low Country" cuisine to create "phenomenal" New American masterpieces at her Harbor East "destination", which ranks as "Baltimore's best restaurant" with its No. 1 scores for Food, Decor and Service; "no detail goes unnoticed" by the "superlative" staffers, who "spoil" guests with selections from an "epic" wine list in a "stunningly beautiful" space; just "be prepared" for the multicourse menu's "sticker shock" – for many, it's a "once-every-few-years kind of place."

Cheesecake Factory *American*   24 | 22 | 22 | $30

Inner Harbor | Harborplace Pratt Street Pavilion | 201 E. Pratt St. (South St.) | Baltimore | 410-234-3990
Columbia | Mall in Columbia | 10300 Little Patuxent Pkwy. (Wincopin Circle) | 410-997-9311
Towson | Towson Town Ctr. | 825 Dulaney Valley Rd. (Fairmount Ave.) | 410-337-7411
Annapolis | Annapolis Mall | 1872 Annapolis Mall Rd. (Jennifer Rd.) | 410-224-0565
www.thecheesecakefactory.com

"Folks need 15 minutes" just to "pore over" the "diverse", "book"-length menu at this "perennial favorite" (indeed, it's ranked the Most Popular chain in Baltimore) that has lots of fans thanks to "scrumptious", mid-priced American eats in "insanely large" portion sizes, including the "sinfully rich" signature cheesecakes ("wear your stretchy pants", or try the 'SkinnyLicious' options); service is "prompt and courteous", and the "loud", "brassy", glitzy setting makes for a "lively" meal, though tables are tightly packed, and "eternal" waits "require patience."

Di Pasquale's Marketplace ⑤ *Italian*   28 | 15 | 22 | $16

East Baltimore | 3700 Gough St. (Dean St.) | Baltimore | 410-276-6787 | www.dipasquales.com

"Bring your appetite" to this "old-fashioned" East Baltimore specialty store where Europhiles shop for "Italian staples" or sit in the cafe area for a quick meal of "homemade" soups and "big, fat" sandwiches heaped with "made-fresh-daily" mozzarella; staffers "make you feel at home", and though there is "no decor" to speak of, the "wonderful aromas" provide ambiance; P.S. closes at 6 PM.

Double T Diner *Diner*   20 | 16 | 21 | $18

White Marsh | 10741 Pulaski Hwy. (Ebenezer Rd.) | 410-344-1020 ◗
Catonsville | 6300 Baltimore National Pike (N. Rolling Rd.) | 410-744-4151 ◗
Ellicott City | 10055 Baltimore National Pike (Bethany Ln.) | 410-750-3300
Perry Hall | 4140 E. Joppa Rd. (Belair Rd.) | 410-248-0160 ◗
Pasadena | 1 Mountain Rd. (Ritchie Hwy.) | 410-766-9669 ◗
Annapolis | 12 Defense St. (Solomons Island Rd.) | 410-571-9070 ◗
www.doubletdiner.com

For "sinful" breakfasts or "a quick bite anytime", eaters of "all ages" flock to this "always busy", "subtly Greek", retro-looking Maryland diner chain; the menu is "novel"-length, and the "tasty" grub and "phenomenal" desserts – served "lickety-split" by "courteous" staff – are a "great value for the money"; P.S. the Annapolis location is open 24/7.

Food Market ● *American*

| − | − | − | M |

Hampden | 1017 W. 36th St. (Roland Ave.) | Baltimore | 410-366-0606 | www.thefoodmarketbaltimore.com

From the open kitchen of a former Hampden grocery store made famous in John Waters' film *Pecker,* Chad Gauss dishes up an inventive menu of traditional Americana loaded with twists; the sleek, modern interior with touches of rustic metal and wood, plus a bar pouring cool cocktails until late, have made it a fast favorite on the 'Avenue.'

G&M *Seafood*

| 24 | 16 | 20 | $29 |

Linthicum | 804 N. Hammonds Ferry Rd. (Nursery Rd.) | 410-636-1777 | www.gandmcrabcakes.com

"Bigger-than-your-head" crab cakes with "lots of lump meat" are the reason travelers "take cabs from BWI" during layovers to visit this "affordable" Linthicum "mecca", where the lengthy menu has Italian and Greek eats, but the crustacean creations are the "real star"; the simple, white-tablecloth setting is "pleasant" enough, and service is "old-school", but really, it's all about "one thing" here.

Gertrude's Ⓜ *Chesapeake*

| 22 | 25 | 23 | $37 |

Charles Village | Baltimore Museum of Art | 10 Art Museum Dr. (N. Charles St.) | Baltimore | 410-889-3399 | www.gertrudesbaltimore.com

"Manet and Cezanne would have stopped painting" to enjoy an alfresco meal "at the edge of the sculpture garden" or inside this "oasis" within the Baltimore Museum of Art say admirers of John Shields' "sassy, Southern", "Chesapeake Bay–oriented" menu presented by "knowledgeable" servers; prices are moderate, and $12 entrees on Tuesdays are "a great touch."

Milton Inn *American*

| 28 | 26 | 26 | $59 |

Sparks | 14833 York Rd. (Quaker Bottom Rd.) | 410-771-4366 | www.miltoninn.com

Dripping with "ambiance", this circa-1740 fieldstone inn is an "enduring treasure" in Sparks, with "cozy fireplaces, oil paintings and white tablecloths" spread over multiple rooms that provide suitably "elegant" backdrops for its "sophisticated" American cuisine; service is "impeccable", and while a typical experience is "pricey", the lounge menu offers "lesser-priced" options.

Out of the Fire 🅢Ⓜ *American/Eclectic*

| 28 | 24 | 26 | $42 |

Easton | 22 Goldsborough St. (Washington St.) | 410-770-4777 | www.outofthefire.com

"Sit at the bar and watch the action" in the kitchen at this "superb" Easton American-Eclectic where "amazing chefs" who really "get the magic of fresh, local ingredients" "artfully plate" "great things" cooked via the showpiece open hearth; it's not cheap for such an "informal" vibe, but service is "attentive" and the space is "inviting" with a "warm" "Tuscan" palette.

Pabu *Japanese*   - | - | - | E
Harbor East | Four Seasons Baltimore | 200 International Dr. (Aliceanna St.) | Baltimore | 410-223-1460 | www.michaelmina.net
Celebrity chef Michael Mina has made a foray into Japanese cuisine (with partner Ken Tominaga) with this high-end izakaya in Harbor East's Four Seasons (but accessed via a separate entrance on Aliceanna Street) that serves classic dishes from a robata grill and a sushi bar, washed down by a world-class sake selection; the rough-wood tables, bamboo ceiling and privacy panels keep things casual even though there's a sleek sheen to everything.

Peter's Inn 🗷Ⓜ *American*   27 | 17 | 22 | $35
Fells Point | 504 S. Ann St. (Eastern Ave.) | Baltimore | 410-675-7313 | www.petersinn.com
"What looks like (and once was) a dive bar is merely a front" for this Fells Point "foodie destination" with a "magic kitchen" plating up "farmer's market–inspired" New American "gourmet" "treats" served by a "friendly", "tattooed" staff; the "almost too hip" scene unfolds in "funky", "cramped quarters", so "go early" or "get in line", because they don't take reservations.

Prime Rib *Seafood/Steak*   28 | 26 | 28 | $71
Mt. Vernon | 1101 N. Calvert St. (Chase St.) | Baltimore | 410-539-1804 | www.theprimerib.com
Do as they do in *"Mad Men"* – "dress up, have a martini, take it easy and smile" – at this "classic" Mt. Vernon steakhouse that's still operating at the very "top of its game", delivering "fantastic" "slabs of meat" and "masterful seafood"; from the "sophisticated", "1940s supper-club vibe" to the "sublime" tuxedoed service, it's a "perfect evening out"; P.S. business-casual dress (with jackets required after 5 PM Saturday).

Samos 🗷⇪ *Greek*   28 | 16 | 24 | $21
Greektown | 600 Oldham St. (Fleet St.) | Baltimore | 410-675-5292 | www.samosrestaurant.com
"As close to the real thing as you can get" say ardent admirers of the "phenomenal" food "like *yia-yia* used to make", at this Greektown elder statesman where even the "salad dressing has a huge following"; the wait is often "long" since there are no reservations and only "limited seating" in the "underwhelming", mural-bedecked space, but it's "stupidly cheap" and "so very worth it"; P.S. it's cash only and BYO.

Sushi King 🗷 *Japanese*   28 | 20 | 24 | $32
Columbia | 6490 Dobbin Rd. (Rte. 175) | 410-997-1269 | www.sushikingmd.com
An "insiders' jewel", this "decently" priced Columbia Japanese "hidden" near the MVA "isn't flashy" but "completely rocks" for "consistently terrific" sushi "masterpieces" created by veritable "artists" and delivered by "courteous" servers in "traditional garb"; "seating is packed", so regulars suggest calling ahead, "even on weekdays."

Tersiguel's *French*   28 | 25 | 28 | $59
Ellicott City | 8293 Main St. (Old Columbia Pike) | 410-465-4004 | www.tersiguels.com
"Exquisite, delectable" French country "creations" comprised of "prime ingredients", including produce from the family farm, plus a "refined but

not stuffy" "white-napkin" ambiance and "attentive, unobtrusive" service have Ellicott City diners calling this "romantic" special-occasioner "a favorite for years"; it's "expensive", *oui,* but "a great treat when you want to play grown-up" (and prix fixe menus "help with the cost").

Vin 909 Ⓜ *American*   28 | 25 | 26 | $32

Annapolis | 909 Bay Ridge Ave. (Chesapeake Ave.) | 410-990-1846 | www.vin909.com

"Off the beaten path" in Annapolis, this "local walk-to" for Eastporters appeals to visitors as well with its "great-value" offering of "fabulous", "refined" New American fare and an "outstanding" wine selection; "exceptional" service and an "intimate", contemporary "cottage" setting create a "calming" backdrop "suitable for quiet conversation."

Woodberry Kitchen *American*   27 | 26 | 25 | $49

Clipper Mill | 2010 Clipper Park Rd. (Clipper Mill Rd.) | Baltimore | 410-464-8000 | www.woodberrykitchen.com

"A smash" since it opened and still "wildly popular" (in fact, it's Baltimore's Most Popular restaurant), this Clipper Mill New American in a "rebuilt old factory" hosts a "hip", "boisterous" crowd happily devouring the "complex" farm-to-table "amazingness" ferried by "friendly, smart" servers who "aim to please"; some find it "a bit pricey", but its huge fan base deems it "worth the trip many times over" – which is why it's "oh so hard to get into" ("reserve way in advance").

Boston

	Restaurant	Cuisine
29	O Ya	Japanese
28	Oleana	Mediterranean
	La Campania	Italian
	Neptune Oyster	Seafood
	Lumière	French
	Hamersley's Bistro	French
	Uni	Japanese
	T.W. Food	American/French
	Menton	French/Italian
	Mistral	French/Mediterranean
27	L'Espalier	French
	Sofra Bakery	Mideastern
	Duckworth's	American
	Oishii	Japanese
	Craigie on Main	French
	Clio	French
	No. 9 Park	French/Italian
	Bergamot	American
	Ithaki Med.	Greek/Mediterranean
	All Seasons Table	Asian

OTHER NOTEWORTHY PLACES

Restaurant	Cuisine
Abe & Louie's	Steak
Aka Bistro	French/Japanese
Bistro 5	Italian
Blue Ginger	Asian
Blue Inc.	American
Bondir	American
Catalyst	American
Ceia	European
Deuxave	American
80 Thoreau	American
51 Lincoln	American
Harvest	New England
Hungry Mother	Southern
Island Creek	Seafood
Legal Sea Foods	Seafood
Sorellina	Italian
Sweet Cheeks Q	BBQ
Ten Tables	American/European
Trade	Eclectic/Mediterranean
Troquet	American/French

	FOOD	DECOR	SERVICE	COST

Abe & Louie's *Steak*

26 | 24 | 26 | $64

Back Bay | 793 Boylston St. (bet. Exeter & Fairfield Sts.) | 617-536-6300 | www.abeandlouies.com

If you have an "über expense account", "you really can't go wrong" at this Back Bay "landmark" serving "sensational steaks" and "equally impressive everything else" in "huge portions", plus an "extensive wine list" that offers many "reasonable" selections; "impeccable" "professional service" and "dark" "gentleman's-club" decor impart a "classic feeling", but be prepared for "excessive decibel levels", particularly from the "hot scene at the bar."

Aka Bistro *French/Japanese*

25 | 21 | 23 | $55

Lincoln | 145 Lincoln Rd. (bet. Codman & Wells Rds.) | 781-259-9920 | www.akabistrolincoln.com

Nestled in the "leafy suburb of Lincoln", this "unique surprise" is a "great addition to the Metrowest dining scene", where worldly palates can "mix and match" from separate menus of "classic French bistro fare" and "imaginative sashimi" (the former "quite reasonably priced", the latter leaning toward "stratospheric" cost levels); the somewhat "sterile" yet "bustling" interior often gets "noisy", which is why most ask for the "lovely" patio in warm weather.

All Seasons Table *Asian*

27 | 25 | 23 | $32

Malden | 64 Pleasant St. (bet. Middlesex & Washington Sts.) | 781-397-8788 | www.astrestaurant.com

Malden locals are "excited" that they "don't need to go into Boston" for an "excellent variety" of "beautifully prepared", "inventive" Asian cuisine, including "melt-in-your-mouth sushi", thanks to this spot whose moderate prices seem like a "bargain" due to the "large" portion sizes; an "attentive" staff helps maintain a "relaxed atmosphere" in the "artfully decorated" space, which springs to life with live jazz Thursday–Saturday evenings.

Bergamot *American*

27 | 23 | 26 | $51

Somerville | 118 Beacon St. (Kirkland St.) | 617-576-7700 | www.bergamotrestaurant.com

"Nuanced, creative" and seasonal New American fare featuring "interesting juxtapositions of tastes and textures" is "backed by a sound wine list" and "well-trained, friendly" service at this "sophisticated but unpretentious" Somerville destination; all in all, "prices are not outrageous", although the "portions are on the smallish side" so big appetites recommend you "get three courses or you may leave hungry."

Bistro 5 Ⓢ Ⓜ *Italian*

27 | 23 | 26 | $48

West Medford | 5 Playstead Rd. (bet. High & Irving Sts.) | 781-395-7464 | www.bistro5.com

In a "surprising" (ok, "weird") location "near the commuter rail" in West Medford lies this "warm, elegant" Northern Italian "gem" where "passionate" chef-owner Vittorio Ettore's "high-concept", "fabulous" "seasonal menus highlight the freshest ingredients"; "knowledgeable, friendly" staffers can recommend "incredible pairings" of wine that, like the fare, is priced "extremely reasonably" "for the quality and presentation."

	FOOD	DECOR	SERVICE	COST

Blue Ginger *Asian*

| 27 | 23 | 25 | $58 |

Wellesley | 583 Washington St. (bet. Church St. & Weston Rd.) | 781-283-5790 | www.ming.com

"Taste-bud-tickling", "highly creative" Asian fusion fare comes from this Wellesley destination's open kitchen, where "justifiably famous" "wizard" chef Ming Tsai "actually cooks" when he's not "mingling with his guests"; "polished service" reigns, even though the "unpretentious" setting is often "packed" – indeed, you need to "make a reservation well in advance" or try for the bar and its "less expensive" but no less "intriguing menu"; P.S. "the foie gras shu-mai and the Alaskan butterfish may be the best appetizer–main course combination" ever.

Blue Inc. ☒ *American/Seafood*

| - | - | - | M |

Downtown Crossing | 131 Broad St. (John Fitzgerald Surface Rd.) | 617-261-5353 | www.blueincboston.com

From *Hell's Kitchen* runner-up Jason Santos, this New American addition in the Financial District showcases the chef's whimsical style; the intimate, funky, blue-and-white setting, adorned with mirrors and a print of model Twiggy, features a menu of homey, midpriced bites and specialty cocktails with names like the Anorexic Model.

Bondir *American*

| - | - | - | M |

Central Square | 279A Broadway (bet. Columbia & Elm Sts.) | Cambridge | 617-661-0009 | www.bondircambridge.com

Opened by chef-owner Jason Bond, this New American in Central Square offers a sustainable, daily changing menu that includes both small plates for sharing and pricey full entrees, accompanied by a petite but ambitious drink list with a focus on seasonal beers; the quaint cream-and-green dining room includes a portrait of a beloved pig painted by Bond's grandfather, and there's an alcove with tree stumps for tables and a fireplace.

Catalyst *American*

| - | - | - | E |

Kendall Square | 300 Technology Sq. (bet. Main St. & Broadway) | Cambridge | 617-576-3000 | www.catalystrestaurant.com

Chef-owner William Kovel (once of Aujourd'hui) offers fine dining in Kendall Square at this modern American where the local, seasonal menu includes housemade pastas and the drinks selection stars microbrew drafts at a perfect 34 degrees; the slick setting, done up with concrete floors and reclaimed barn wood, includes an exhibition kitchen, a patio, private dining and a lounge with a fireplace.

Ceia
Kitchen & Bar *European*

| - | - | - | M |

Newburyport | 25 State St. (bet. Essex & Middle Sts.) | 978-358-8112 | www.ceia-newburyport.com

This modern Mediterranean in Downtown Newburyport presents Portuguese specialties, housemade Italian pastas and other Euro coastline fare (with a complementary wine list); the chic, historic setting features exposed-brick walls, recessed mirrors and copper tables covered with butcher paper, plus a banquette overlooking bustling State Street and a bar offering a view of the open kitchen along with signature cocktails.

	FOOD	DECOR	SERVICE	COST

Clio ⊠ *French*
27 | 26 | 26 | $83

Back Bay | Eliot Hotel | 370A Commonwealth Ave. (Massachusetts Ave.) | 617-536-7200 | www.cliorestaurant.com

"As interesting as ever", this "subdued" yet "luxe" "special-occasion destination" in the Back Bay's Eliot Hotel "sets the standard for contemporary French" fare with chef Ken Oringer's "cutting-edge" "edible art" composed of "unexpected textures with surprising flavors" and paired with an "exceptional wine list"; service strikes most as "attentive" and "knowledgeable" (though a minority finds it "pretentious"), and although it's "hyper-expensive" for "relatively small" portions, it's "well worth it" if you want to "eat like royalty"; P.S. post-Survey, an expansion of the bar saw the advent of a new small-plates menu.

Craigie on Main Ⓜ *French*
27 | 23 | 26 | $65

Central Square | 853 Main St. (Bishop Allen Dr.) | Cambridge | 617-497-5511 | www.craigieonmain.com

"Formidable culinary presence" Tony Maws presents "unforgettable dining" at this "compelling" Central Square "destination" where "obsessive attention" to "local, sustainable" ingredients (not to mention a "worship of pig") is obvious in his "luscious" French fare with "mind-boggling flavors"; "with all of this perfection, one might expect snobbery", but the staff's "seasoned professionals" are "hospitable" as they navigate the "lively", "unpretentious" setting, which includes a "fantastic bar" boasting "outstanding drinks" and an "excellent menu with pared-down prices" – but even the normally "costly" tabs are "worth every penny."

Deuxave *American*
- | - | - | E

Back Bay | 371 Commonwealth Ave. (Mass. Ave.) | 617-517-5915 | www.deuxave.com

This sophisticated spot in the Back Bay offers a pricey menu of New American cuisine with nouvelle French influences; the fashionable setting features vaulted ceilings, dark wood and metallic accents, plus there's a gas fireplace, a semi-private dining room and a spacious, buzzing marble bar.

Duckworth's Bistrot Ⓜ *American*
27 | 20 | 25 | $46

Gloucester | 197 E. Main St. (Pirate Ln.) | 978-282-4426 | www.duckworthsbistrot.com

Disciples of this "crown jewel" of Gloucester "love that you can order" half portions of chef Ken Duckworth's "sublime" New American fare, "so you can try more stuff" and "save money", just as with half pours from the "terrific wine list"; the "cute", "casual" setting – which is patrolled by a "knowledgeable staff" – is "small" and "popular" to boot, so "make sure you make a reservation, or you'll be eating elsewhere."

80 Thoreau ⊠ *American*
- | - | - | E

Concord | The Concord Depot | 80 Thoreau St. (bet. Belknap St & Sudbury Rd.) | 978-318-0008 | www.80thoreau.com

Pedigreed hospitality veterans from Rialto and NYC's Per Se and Craft head this somewhat pricey white-tablecloth New American tucked inside a former train depot in historic Concord; the decor mixes Colonial accents (hand-forged iron chandeliers, wainscoting) with more modern design, while seating options include two dining rooms, four spots at a chef's counter overlooking the open kitchen and a soapstone bar.

51 Lincoln ⊠ Ⓜ *American*

24 | 20 | 23 | $48

Newton | 51 Lincoln St. (Columbus St.) | 617-965-3100 |
www.51lincolnnewton.com

Delivering "a Downtown experience" in Newton Highlands (and "for less money"), this "casual-upscale" spot shines with the "inspired", "terrific", seasonal New American fare of a chef whose artwork also adorns the walls, plus "superb cocktails" and "efficient, warm" service; the "cozy" main room gets "noisy" sometimes, so if that grates, ask for the "rustic, clandestine" downstairs wine room; P.S. the signature watermelon steak appetizer is "unbelievable."

Hamersley's Bistro *French*

28 | 25 | 26 | $61

South End | 553 Tremont St. (Clarendon St.) | 617-423-2700 |
www.hamersleysbistro.com

"Bravo, Gordon!" cheer champions of this South End classic's "terrific" celebrity chef-owner, who's "almost always visible in the open kitchen" prepping "extraordinary" seasonal French bistro fare that includes the "to-die-for" signature roast chicken ("famous for a reason"); its "country atmosphere" is "the epitome of grace", just like the "charming", "efficient" servers, and while the meal is "expensive", the "outstanding wine list" showcases many "reasonable" bottles.

Harvest *New England*

25 | 23 | 23 | $53

Harvard Square | 44 Brattle St. (Church St.) | Cambridge | 617-868-2255 |
www.harvestcambridge.com

"Timeless and fabulous", this "civilized" "haven in Harvard Square" "utilizes local suppliers" for its "tremendous" modern New England cuisine, which is enhanced by an "extensive wine list" and "personable" staff; a "plush", "elegant" interior and "lovely courtyard" foster the feeling that the "high prices" are "worth the splurge"; P.S. head to the "fantastic bar" for "lighter fare" and lighter tabs.

Hungry Mother Ⓜ *Southern*

26 | 21 | 25 | $45

Kendall Square | 233 Cardinal Medeiros Ave. (Binney St.) |
Cambridge | 617-499-0090 | www.hungrymothercambridge.com

"A splendid homage to fine Virginia kitchens", this "cozy, chic" Kendall Square spot spins "modern takes on traditional Southern cuisine", and while "the menu is limited", everything on it is "amazing" and "meticulously presented" by "people with demonstrable passion for their work" (they'll even "run across the street" to the theater and "purchase movie tickets for you at a discount"); fans forgive the slightly "high" prices because they're "reasonable for the quality", which is another reason they say it's "worth waiting" for a reservation.

Island Creek Oyster Bar ◑ *Seafood*

– | – | – | E

Kenmore Square | Hotel Commonwealth | 500 Commonwealth Ave. (Kenmore St.) | 617-532-5300 | www.islandcreekoysterbar.com

This chic seafood spot in the Hotel Commonwealth in Kenmore Square couldn't get closer to the source – owner Skip Bennett founded and operates Duxbury-based Island Creek Oysters, whose beds provide many area restaurants with plump, briny bivalves; the seaside-inspired setting is done up with oyster shells behind gabion cages and a photo of Duxbury Bay, plus there's a 25-seat bar offering raw fare and artisanal cocktails.

	FOOD	DECOR	SERVICE	COST

Ithaki Mediterranean

27 | 24 | 26 | $48

Cuisine Ⓜ *Greek/Mediterranean*
Ipswich | 25 Hammatt St. (Depot Sq.) | 978-356-0099 |
www.ithakicuisine.com

From the "classic Greek dishes" to the more "interesting", "fusion"-like
Mediterranean meals, everything made at this "real find in Ipswich" is
"extraordinary", and it comes via "wonderful service" to boot; the atmosphere has always been "relaxed but classy", but it benefits from
"lovely updated decor", so "run, don't walk to make a reservation –
you will not be disappointed."

La Campania Ⓢ *Italian*

28 | 24 | 25 | $59

Waltham | 504 Main St. (bet. Cross & Heard Sts.) | 781-894-4280 |
www.lacampania.com

"People come from far and wide" for this "transporting culinary experience" in Waltham, a "charming" "gem" providing both "inventive and
traditional" "Italian country" dishes, "all splendid" and priced for those
who "can afford luxury" (though the "staggering wine list" displays
many "affordable" options); the "professional" service is as "warm" as
the "beautiful", "rustic" "farmhouse"–like setting, but just "make sure
you have a reservation", "even for the bar."

Legal Sea Foods *Seafood*

22 | 18 | 21 | $41

Back Bay | Copley Pl. | 100 Huntington Ave. (Exeter St.) | 617-266-7775
Back Bay | Prudential Ctr. | 800 Boylston St. (Ring Rd.) | 617-266-6800
Park Square | 26 Park Plaza (Columbus Ave.) | 617-426-4444
Seaport District | Liberty Wharf | 270 Northern Ave. (D St.) | 617-477-2900
Waterfront | Long Wharf | 255 State St. (Atlantic Ave.) | 617-742-5300
Harvard Square | 20 University Rd. (Bennett St.) | Cambridge | 617-491-9400
Kendall Square | 5 Cambridge Ctr. (bet. Ames & Main Sts.) | Cambridge |
617-864-3400
Chestnut Hill | Chestnut Hill Shopping Ctr. | 43 Boylston St.
(Hammond Pond Pkwy.) | 617-277-7300
Peabody | Northshore Mall | 210 Andover St./Rte. 114 (Cross St.) |
978-532-4500
Burlington | Burlington Mall | 75 Middlesex Tpke. (Rte. 128) | 781-270-9700
www.legalseafoods.com
Additional locations throughout the Boston area

Again voted Boston's Most Popular restaurant, this "trustworthy" seafood chain "reigns supreme" thanks to a "huge variety" of "consistently
fresh" fish, not to mention the smarts to "adapt to changing times"
with "innovative touches" (e.g. what may be the "best" gluten-free
menu "in the world") while ensuring "solid value"; the decor of each
branch is "different" (ditto the service, though staffers generally "know
their stuff"), but when all is said and done, the "location doesn't
matter" – "they're everywhere" because "they know what they're doing"; P.S. the sprawling newish Seaport District destination offers a
casual ground floor, a more formal second story, a rooftop lounge and
an expanded menu featuring pizzas and pastas.

L'Espalier *French*

27 | 27 | 27 | $97

Back Bay | 774 Boylston St. (bet. Exeter & Fairfield Sts.) | 617-262-3023 |
www.lespalier.com

"If heaven were a restaurant", it would be this "regal experience" in
the Back Bay, where chef Frank McClelland's "exquisite", "inventive"

New French cuisine is "perfectly paired" with "outstanding wines"; modernists dig the "sleek" setting, while everyone appreciates staffers who "treat you like a king" – but then again, "they should since you're paying a king's ransom" (it's "so worth it").

Lumière   *French*   28 | 23 | 27 | $57

Newton | 1293 Washington St. (Waltham St.) | 617-244-9199 | www.lumiererestaurant.com

Exhibiting "panache" plus a "real devotion to all things local, sustainable and green", "genius" chef-owner Michael Leviton presents New French fare as "art" (and with "wonderful wine pairings") at his "classy" "West Newton gem"; "impeccable service" makes it a "good choice for that special occasion", and while it's a "little pricey", it costs "less" than if it were located Downtown.

Menton   *French/Italian*   28 | 27 | 29 | $145

Seaport District | 354 Congress St. (A St.) | 617-737-0099 | www.mentonboston.com

Barbara Lynch's "temple" of French-Italian gastronomy in the Seaport District earns the No. 1 scores for both Service and Decor thanks to its "unparalleled" staff and "elegant", "sophisticated" setting of earthy greens, grays and wood tones; the "phenomenal" prix fixe-only dinners, each course a "visual delight and a taste sensation" paired with "divine" wines, "set a new standard", as do tabs you may have to "mortgage your house" to pay – indeed, this ranks as Boston's "priciest restaurant."

Mistral   *French/Mediterranean*   28 | 25 | 26 | $70

South End | 223 Columbus Ave. (bet. Berkeley & Clarendon Sts.) | 617-867-9300 | www.mistralbistro.com

"Flashes of brilliance" illuminate this South End "legend" where dinner is an "event" thanks to chef Jamie Mammano's "imaginative", "sublime" French-Mediterranean cuisine paired with "glorious wines", "creative" cocktails and "terrific service"; an "elegant but not overly formal" aura permeates the "dramatic" high-ceilinged dining room and a "cool vibe" dominates the "chic bar" though it all comes at tabs that practically necessitate "a paycheck."

Neptune Oyster   *Seafood*   28 | 20 | 22 | $47

North End | 63 Salem St. (Cross St.) | 617-742-3474 | www.neptuneoyster.com

A "pearl" "floating among red-sauce" joints, this "classy", "divine" North End fishery specializes in "unreal lobster rolls", either "drenched with melted butter" or "New England–style with mayo", plus "superb rawbar" selections and "creative seafood concoctions", which the "knowledgeable staff" can help pair with "interesting wines"; however, be prepared for "expensive" checks, "sardine-can digs" and a "no-reservations" policy that leads to "frustrating waits" – all "well worth it."

No. 9 Park   *French/Italian*   27 | 25 | 27 | $77

Beacon Hill | 9 Park St. (bet. Beacon & Tremont Sts.) | 617-742-9991 | www.no9park.com

"Meticulously prepared" French-Italian plates deliver "tastes and textures beyond compare" at "genius" chef Barbara Lynch's "elegant" flagship on Beacon Hill, where the "revelatory" meals are enhanced by "brilliant wine pairings", "exceptional cocktails" and service that goes "the whole nine yards"; you probably "won't get stuffed on the portions" and you'll likely get a jolt of "sticker shock", but it's "well worth it" for such a "joyful experience."

Oishii ⓜ *Japanese* — 27 | 17 | 22 | $54
Chestnut Hill | 612 Hammond St. (Boylston St.) | 617-277-7888 | www.oishiiboston.com
Sudbury | Mill Vill. | 365 Boston Post Rd. (Concord Rd.) | 978-440-8300 | www.oishiitoo.com

Oishii Boston ⏺ⓜ *Japanese*
South End | 1166 Washington St. (E. Berkeley St.) | 617-482-8868 | www.oishiiboston.com

"True artistry" is on display in the "extravagant", "sublime" sushi crafted at this trio of "vibrant Japanese gems" where the service is mostly "kind" and "attentive"; while the scene is "chic yet serene" in the South End, you're "confined as tightly as the maki" at the Chestnut Hill original (where there's "usually a wait") and the setting is a "sparse", "tiny, dark cave" in Sudbury, but whichever you choose, you might "need to sell some stocks" first – and it's "worth every penny."

Oleana *Mediterranean* — 28 | 24 | 25 | $54
Inman Square | 134 Hampshire St. (bet. Elm & Norfolk Sts.) | Cambridge | 617-661-0505 | www.oleanarestaurant.com

"Exotic-spice" "guru" Ana Sortun makes "taste buds sing" at this Inman Square "diamond" where she weaves "layers of flavors" into "adventurous" Arabic-Mediterranean dishes that "emphasize locally grown" ingredients; the "enthusiastic servers" are "helpful with choosing a wine" from the "excellent" list, but just know that reservations are nearly "impossible to obtain" for the "cramped" but "warm" interior, while in summer, you have to "get there early" to score a table on the "lovely" patio, which doesn't accept bookings at all.

O Ya ⓩⓜ *Japanese* — 29 | 23 | 27 | $118
Leather District | 9 East St. (South St.) | 617-654-9900 | www.oyarestaurantboston.com

"Have you recently won a small fortune?" – then you have "the means" to enjoy this "cozy", unmarked izakaya in the Leather District, where "atomic" "bursts of texture and tastes" come from "every beautiful bite" of the "off-the-charts innovative" sushi, winner of Boston's No. 1 Food rating; suggestions from the "extensive sake list" by the "upbeat", "spot-on" staffers are just as "amazing" as the fare, but a caveat: even if you opt for the "luxurious" omakase, it's possible you will still "leave hungry", as everything "comes in amuse-bouche portions" – nonetheless, it's an "unforgettable" meal.

Sofra Bakery & Café *Mideastern* — 27 | 16 | 18 | $18
West Cambridge | 1 Belmont St. (Mt. Auburn St.) | Cambridge | 617-661-3161 | www.sofrabakery.com

"Anyplace that Ana Sortun touches is golden", and this "casual" West Cambridge Middle Eastern cafe is no exception, with its "huge variety" of "inspired", "delectable" light meals and pastries flaunting "exotic flavors" (at "half the price" of Oleana); it's "always busy", and the "cramped quarters" and "haphazard counter service" yield "long lines of rabid foodies fighting for a table", so it's best to "get it to go" or, in summer, "find a table outdoors."

Sorellina *Italian*

27 | 27 | 26 | $67

Back Bay | 1 Huntington Ave. (Dartmouth St.) | 617-412-4600 |
www.sorellinaboston.com

"Nothing but superlatives" rain down on Jamie Mammano's "chic",
"lively" Back Bay "temple" where "sumptuous", "elegant" Italian
dishes are conveyed by "detail-oriented" staffers in a "beautifully sophisticated", "spacious" black-and-white dining room filled with
"lovely light-paneled murals"; it's the sort of "decadently sublime experience" you save for "when you need to impress someone" – and
you should "save up" plenty of dough for it too.

Sweet Cheeks Q *BBQ*

- | - | - | M

Fenway | 1381 Boylston St. (bet. Kilmarnock St. & Park Dr.) | 617-266-1300 |
www.sweetcheeksq.com

Top Chef finalist Tiffani Faison brings wood-smoked Texas BBQ to the
heart of the Fenway with this moderately priced arrival serving brisket,
ribs, pork belly and the like accompanied by housemade sauce, biscuits
and sides; further enticements include communal high-top tables
made from church doors and bowling alley lanes, three patio areas
and all-American drinks, from single-batch bourbon to U.S. brews.

Ten Tables *American/European*

27 | 20 | 25 | $50

Jamaica Plain | 597 Centre St. (Pond St.) | 617-524-8810
Harvard Square | 5 Craigie Circle (Concord Ave.) | Cambridge | 617-576-5444
www.tentables.net

"True to its name", this Jamaica Plain "extravaganza" has just 10 tables,
and while the "tight" digs strike some as "romantic", others as "claustrophobic" (the attached bar "adds some space", but you should still
"make reservations" "a zillion years in advance"), most agree that the
"creative" European–New American dishes employing "locally grown
produce" are "absurdly delicious"; the "noisy" "basement location" of
the Harvard Square offshoot has more space, but similarly "beautifully
prepared" fare, "upbeat" service and "excellent value."

Trade *Eclectic/Mediterranean*

- | - | - | M

Waterfront | 540 Atlantic Ave. (Congress St.) | 617-451-1234 |
www.trade-boston.com

In a historic brick building on the Seaport District's Atlantic Wharf,
this second eatery from celeb chef Jody Adams presents a moderately
priced, small plates–focused Eclectic menu with heavy Mediterranean
influences and Southeast Asian flourishes; the sparsely decorated
digs feature vaulted ceilings, a bar/lounge with a brick pizza oven and
floor-to-ceiling windows framing views of the Greenway.

Troquet ⚼Ⓜ *American/French*

26 | 21 | 25 | $67

Theater District | 140 Boylston St. (bet. Charles & Tremont Sts.) |
617-695-9463 | www.troquetboston.com

A "wide variety" of "magnificent", "reasonably priced" wines by the
glass and half-glass makes this bi-level Theater District bistro an
oenophile's "Oz", while "exciting" pairings with the "progressive" New
American–French cuisine boasting "tantalizing flavors galore" help
justify the fare's "high cost"; "formal but not stuffy service" complements the "understated" setting, the highlight of which is a "beautiful
view" of the Common.

T.W. Food *American/French* | 28 | 22 | 27 | $58 |

Huron Village | 377 Walden St. (Concord Ave.) | Cambridge |
617-864-4745 | www.twfoodrestaurant.com

At this "extraordinary" Huron Village "hideaway", toque Tim
Wiechmann's "sublime", seasonal New American–New French fare is
"thoughtfully prepared" with local ingredients and "layers of complexity", then paired with wines from a "creative" list; the "casual", "minimalist" setting is "tight but charming" and conducive to "personal
attention" from the "impeccable" staff, another element that makes it
"worth the extra cost."

Uni *Japanese* | 28 | 23 | 25 | $70 |

Back Bay | Eliot Hotel | 370 Commonwealth Ave. (Mass. Ave.) |
617-536-7200 | www.unisashimibar.com

"Exotic", "excellent", "expensive" are just some descriptors for the
"impeccably fresh" sashimi prepared at this "cutting-edge" Ken
Oringer sibling to Clio in the Back Bay's Eliot Hotel; the "great attention to detail" in the "constantly changing" fare extends to the "huge
cocktail list" as well as "fabulous" staffers who are adept at "suggesting something to make your eyes twinkle"; P.S. post-Survey renovations
made the "intimate" setting a bit more casual, possibly outdating
the Decor score.

Charlotte

TOP FOOD RANKING

Restaurant	Cuisine
28 Barrington's	American
McNinch House	Continental
27 Fiamma	Italian
Fig Tree	Continental
26 Toscana	Italian
Good Food	American
Bonterra	American
Carpe Diem	American
Capital Grille	Steak
Soul Gastrolounge	Eclectic

OTHER NOTEWORTHY PLACES

Bad Daddy's	Burgers
BLT Steaks	Steak
Fern	Vegetarian
Halcyon	Eclectic
Harvest Moon Grille	American
Mac's Speed Shop	BBQ
Malabar	Spanish
Maverick Rock Taco	Mexican
P.F. Chang's	Chinese
Zebra	French

Bad Daddy's Burger Bar *Burgers*   25 | 19 | 22 | $17

Ballantyne | Ballantyne Commons | 15105 John J. Delaney Dr. (Johnston Rd.) | 704-919-2700
Dilworth | 1626 East Blvd. (Lombardy Cir.) | 704-714-4888
Huntersville | Birkdale Vlg. | 8625 Lindholm Dr. (Formby Rd.) | 704-237-4055
www.bigdaddysburgerbar.com
"Options, baby, options" are the draws at these "fairly priced", "super-upbeat" "joints" where the "huge burgers" (made from beef, poultry, pork, buffalo, tuna or black beans) are available with an "endless" array of "amazing" toppings, plus "wonderful" "build-your-own salads" and sides like "devilish tater tots"; "young hipsters" say "don't come before 7 PM unless you want to be surrounded by high chairs", but whenever you show up, prepare for it to be "crowded" and "noisier than a lawnmower."

Barrington's 🗷 *American*   28 | 23 | 27 | $53

SouthPark | Foxcroft Shopping Ctr. | 7822 Fairview Rd. (bet. Carmel & Colony Rds.) | 704-364-5755 | www.barringtonsrestaurant.com
Chef-owner Bruce Moffett's "sublime culinary imagination" yields "just plain wow" New American fare (starring gnocchi that's "better than sex") at this "one-of-a-kind" winner of Charlotte's No. 1 Food rating, in SouthPark; while "prices are high but worth it", wines are "limited but good" and digs are "charming" but "tiny" ("a

reservation is a must, even on a Tuesday"), the "experienced" staffers are unconditionally "impeccable."

BLT Steak *Steak*   25 | 24 | 25 | $62

Uptown | Ritz-Carlton | 110 N. College St. (5th St.) | 704-972-4380 | www.bltrestaurants.com

"The steaks are perfection" but "everyone's favorites" are the popovers at this "upscale" Uptown chophouse situated in the Ritz-Carlton, where the menu and decor "don't just cater to the 'men's club' crowd"; "exceptional service" and a "mod interior" get kudos, but it all comes with a "hefty price tag."

Bonterra Dining & Wine Room ⓩ *American*   26 | 27 | 26 | $52

Dilworth | 1829 Cleveland Ave. (E. Worthington Ave.) | 704-333-9463 | www.bonterradining.com

This "gorgeous restored church" in Dilworth is often "sedate" with foodies indulging in "shut-your-mouth-good" New American dishes, made with "thoughtfully sourced ingredients", and oenophiles studying the "amazing" selection of bottles and glasses, which comes from the "old altar that serves as a wine bar"; yes, it's "costly", but "sharp" service is part of the package; P.S. consider reserving the "choir loft for large groups" or the cellar for "intimate" gatherings.

The Capital Grille *Steak*   26 | 25 | 26 | $59

Uptown | IJL Financial Ctr. | 201 N. Tryon St. (5th St.) | 704-348-1400 | www.thecapitalgrille.com

With "professional" service, somewhat "formal", "dark-wood decor" and "expense-account" pricing, it's no surprise this "elegant" Uptown chain link caters to an "executive crowd", which comes for "power" lunches and "client dinners" of "cooked-to-perfection" steaks and "large", "delicious" sides; it's also "reliable" before a show at the nearby Blumenthal Performing Arts Center, and the bar is a "see-and-be-seen" scene for "cocktails after work."

Carpe Diem ⓩ *American*   26 | 25 | 26 | $43

Elizabeth | 1535 Elizabeth Ave. (Hawthorne Ln.) | 704-377-7976 | www.carpediemrestaurant.com

"The Old South meets the New World" at this "tastefully decorated", art nouveau–tinged, mahogany-and-marble Elizabeth "institution", which boasts a "reliable", "crazy-good" New American menu whose "nice vegetarian options" ensure diners can eat as "lightly or lavishly" as they choose; "sparkling service", "wonderful wines" and a "beautiful" bar that's a neighborhood "gathering place" mean you "can't go wrong with this one."

Fern ⓩⓜ *Vegetarian*   - | - | - | M

Plaza Midwood | 1323 Central Ave. (Clement Ave.) | 704-377-1825 | www.fernflavors.com

Vegetarian cuisine goes upscale in concept but not in price at this funky Plaza Midwood arrival from the owners of Halcyon, where the daily Laughing Buddha Bowl shuffles different combos of beans, rice, greens and veggies, the seitan is housemade and the chef's global influences put dashi ramen next to chiles rellenos made with quinoa; complementing the food are chakra-color-coordinated juices, kombucha cocktails (made from a local brew) and organic beers and wines, served in a soothing space with a fern-embedded wall and twinkly lights.

Fiamma *Italian*

27 | 19 | 25 | $35

Dilworth | Park Square Shopping Ctr. | 2418 Park Rd. (Ordermore Ave.) | 704-333-3062 | www.fiamma-restaurant.com

Don't let the "unassuming" strip-mall setting "fool you" – you're bound to be "blown away" by the *"bella e deliziosa"* Northern Italian cuisine, featuring "exquisite" homemade pastas, served in "generous portions" at this "homey", "welcoming" Dilworth "surprise"; tipplers toast the "fabulous wine list and limoncello", and everyone appreciates the price point: always "affordable", with lunch specials that are "incredible bargains."

Fig Tree *Continental*

27 | 26 | 27 | $52

Elizabeth | 1601 E. Seventh St. (Louise Ave.) | 704-332-3322 | www.charlottefigtree.com

"Romantic" and "elegant", this 1913 Craftsman bungalow in Elizabeth offers an array of "intimate", "lovely" rooms in which to serve its "inventive", "fantastic" Continental menu filled with "rare finds like elk and ostrich" and even "more obscure options", all "well worth the exorbitant prices"; "exceptional" staffers are "knowledgeable" about the fare as well as the "impressive" wine list, which stars in what oenophiles insist are the "best wine dinners in Charlotte."

Good Food on Montford ☒ *American*

26 | 22 | 23 | $37

SouthPark | 1701 Montford Dr. (Park Rd.) | 704-525-0881 | www.goodfoodonmontford.com

"Amazingly creative", "internationally inspired", "seasonally changing" small plates plus "cool", "rustic" digs make this "reasonably priced" SouthPark New American from Barrington's chef Bruce Moffett and his brother, Kerry, "a big hit" with both "sophisticated foodies" and a "trendy younger crowd"; helping to fuel the perennial "cacophony" is an "adventurous wine list", and overseeing it all is an "attentive but not intrusive" staff.

Halcyon *Eclectic*

23 | 27 | 22 | $38

Uptown | Mint Museum Uptown | 500 S. Tryon St. (College St.) | 704-910-0865 | www.halcyonflavors.com

Charlotte's "best views, indoors and out" are found at this "super-swanky" Eclectic in the Mint Museum Uptown, where the "gorgeous", "well-lit" contemporary dining room is bedecked with "tables crafted by local artists" and the patio is just as "wonderful"; "farm fresh is the key" to the "innovative", "fantastic" menu, which is loaded with "many small plates as well as entrees", not outrageously priced and offered alongside a "unique wine list."

Harvest Moon Grille *American*

23 | 18 | 21 | $32

Uptown | Dunhill Hotel | 235 N. Tryon St. (6th St.) | 704-342-1193 | www.harvestmoongrillecharlotte.com

"If it isn't in season, you don't eat it" at this "neat addition to the Uptown food scene" in the "historic Dunhill Hotel", where chef/co-proprietor Cassie Parsons' New American fare is not only seriously "farm-to-table" (she also co-owns a farm), but "inventive and delicious" to boot; "enthusiastic" service, an "excellent wine selection" and casual

digs also please fans who rave that they "would eat there every day" –
and with such moderate prices, they possibly could.

Mac's Speed Shop ● *BBQ*

25 | 20 | 21 | $19

Cornelius | 19601 Liverpool Pkwy. (Catawba Ave.) | 704-892-3554
Dilworth | 2511 South Blvd. (Remount Rd.) | 704-522-6227
Steele Creek | 2414 Sandy Porter Rd. (Camden Creek Ln.) | 704-504-8500
www.macspeedshop.com
"The hogs in front rival the hogs on the plate" at this "informal" trio
that draws everyone from "bikers" and "families" to "yuppies" and
"Junior Leaguers" for its "killer BBQ" and "to-die-for" sides, served in
"huge", "reasonably priced" portions alongside an "amazing" beer selection; though the "kitschy", "animated atmosphere" can get "too
loud" for some, most realize that's all part of the "fun", "down-home"
experience; P.S. try to "grab a picnic table" outside on a "pretty day."

Malabar ⧄Ⓜ *Spanish*

– | – | – | M

Uptown | Hearst Tower | 214 N. Tryon St. (bet. 5th & 6th Sts.) |
704-344-8878 | www.conterestaurantgroup.com
Uptown's Hearst Plaza gets a midpriced Spanish anchor with this tight,
bright tapas-and-more venture, where you can find a leg of Iberico
ham sliced to order at the bar, as well as paella for two, Spanish cheeses
and zarzuela (seafood stew); the spare, cosmopolitan setting includes
a small patio where people-watching is at a premium, given the
mid-arts-district milieu.

Maverick Rock Taco ⧄Ⓜ *Mexican*

– | – | – | M

SouthPark | 1513 Montford Dr. (Park Rd.) | 704-527-1400 |
www.xeniahospitality.com
Mexican fare wrapped in a rock 'n' roll atmosphere is the shtick at this
SouthPark newcomer, with tacos and burritos made with guajillo chile–
roasted pork, citrus-marinated poblano shrimp and the like, topped off
with a tequila-drenched bar menu; graffiti-style portraits of rock stars
and an enormous American flag made of reclaimed wood set a hipster
tone, but midrange prices and live music draw an eclectic crowd.

McNinch House ⧄Ⓜ *Continental*

28 | 27 | 29 | $103

Uptown | 511 N. Church St. (bet. 8th & 9th Sts.) | 704-332-6159 |
www.mcninchhouserestaurant.com
For an "extraordinary" "special occasion", book this "unique restaurant" in an "intimate", "lovingly renovated" "Victorian home in the historic Fourth Ward" near Uptown, where "exceptional" Continental
fare is "divinely presented" in prix fixes "tailored to your needs and
tastes" ("you order prior to going") by staffers exhibiting "out-of-this-
world charm and hospitality"; true, it's "extraordinarily expensive,
even for the high quality that you get", but it's "well worth every dollar"
for an "experience you will never forget."

P.F. Chang's China Bistro *Chinese*

23 | 23 | 22 | $28

SouthPark | Phillips Pl. | 6809 Phillips Place Ct. (Charlton Ln.) | 704-552-6644
Northlake | Northlake Mall | 10325 Perimeter Pkwy.
(bet. Perimeter Woods Dr. & Reames Rd.) | 704-598-1927
www.pfchangs.com
Charlotte surveyors deem the "Americanized Chinese" cuisine so
"fabulous" and the service so "responsive" at these Northlake and

SouthPark outposts of the national chain, they've voted them the area's Most Popular; indeed, with "something for everyone" on the "reasonably priced" menu, they're "always crowded", thus you should "expect a long wait at peak times" for a table in the "loud, chaotic" though "fun" setting.

Soul Gastrolounge ● *Eclectic*   26 | 23 | 21 | $27

Plaza Midwood | 1500 Central Ave. (Pecan Ave.) | 704-348-1848 | www.soulgastrolounge.com

"Yummy" Eclectic small plates in "clever combinations" (plus "tasty sushi" and "unique cupcakes") are as much of a draw as the "innovative" cocktails and "great grooves" from the "DJ spinning in the corner" at this "hip neighborhood hot spot" in Plaza Midwood, which also gets accolades for its "unreal value"; the "small" exposed-brick digs get "crowded" and "noisy" easily, so "get here early or late" or try for a "highly sought-after table" outside with "great views" of the skyline.

Toscana ▣ *Italian*   26 | 22 | 24 | $44

SouthPark | Specialty Shops on the Park | 6401 Morrison Blvd. (Roxborough Rd.) | 704-367-1808 | www.toscana-ristorante.net

"Pretend you're in the Tuscan countryside" at this "warm", "calmly festive" SouthPark eatery offering Northern Italian "dishes that never disappoint" alongside an "excellent and reasonable wine list"; if owner Augusto Conte is "on hand, you're doubly blessed", as he and his "appealing" staff "know how to make you feel welcome", and "they don't rush you" either; P.S. in nice weather, try for the "pleasant" patio "complete with charming fountain."

Zebra Restaurant & Wine Bar ▣ *French*   26 | 24 | 25 | $56

SouthPark | 4521 Sharon Rd. (bet. Fairview Rd. & Morrison Blvd.) | 704-442-9525 | www.zebrarestaurant.net

"Fantastic food", "fantastic wine list", "fantastic everything" fawn the "discriminating" fans of this SouthPark New French "special-event restaurant" that boasts "stunning" woodwork, "gorgeous" zebra art and "fabulous" service; sure, you need to "make sure you have a Brink's truck with you" to settle the check, but "you do get what you pay for": an "outstanding, romantic experience"; P.S. also offered are "wonderful breakfasts and lunches" on weekdays, plus wine tastings on Friday evenings, a "great deal."

Chicago

	Restaurant	Cuisine
29]	Alinea	American
	Katsu	Japanese
	Next	Eclectic
28]	Riccardo Trattoria	Italian
	Les Nomades	French
	Takashi	American/French
	Avec	Mediterranean
	Green Zebra	Vegetarian
	MK	American
	Schwa	American
	Topolobampo	Mexican
	Sprout	American
	Fontano's Subs	Sandwiches
	Tru	French
	Ruxbin	Eclectic
27]	Mixteco Grill	Mexican
	Arami	Japanese
	Longman & Eagle	American
	Girl & The Goat	American
	Frontera Grill	Mexican

OTHER NOTEWORTHY PLACES

Restaurant	Cuisine
Arun's	Thai
Balena	Italian
Blackbird	American
Everest	French
Gibsons	Steak
Goosefoot	American
Hot Doug's	Hot Dogs
Joe's Sea/Steak/Crab	Seafood/Steak
Lou Malnati's	Pizza
Mercat a la Planxa	Spanish
Morton's	Steak
Naha	American
Nellcôte	American
NoMI Kitchen	American
Publican	American
Pump Room	American
Purple Pig	Mediterranean
Shanghai Terrace	Asian
Spiaggia	Italian
Vie	American
Wildfire	Steak

	FOOD	DECOR	SERVICE	COST

Alinea ⓜ *American* 29 | 28 | 29 | $225

Lincoln Park | 1723 N. Halsted St. (bet. North Ave. & Willow St.) |
312-867-0110 | www.alinea-restaurant.com

Grant Achatz is "like a real-life Willy Wonka in his ability to imbue his
creations with magic" at this "ultimate" Lincoln Park New American
that earns No. 1 Food and Most Popular honors in Chicago thanks to a
"spectacularly innovative" multicourse "culinary art show" featuring
"playful", "awe-inspiring" "gastronomic delights" presented with "unparalleled attention to detail"; "impeccable" service ensures that
meals are "timed perfectly" in the "ultramodern" surroundings, so
while tabs are "sky-high", "if your wallet can take the hit" (and you
come with "an open mind and sense of adventure"), "serious foodies"
say it "ranks with seeing the wonders of the world."

Arami ⓜ *Japanese* 27 | 23 | 23 | $48

West Town | 1829 W. Chicago Ave. (bet. Wolcott Ave. & Wood St.) |
312-243-1535 | www.aramichicago.com

"Sushi lovers" are among the "converted" at this "hip, urban" West
Town storefront delivering "exceptionally fresh, amazingly creative"
rolls alongside other "delicious and serious Japanese" offerings from
a recently retooled menu (which may not be reflected in the Food
score); "helpful service" enhances the "relaxing" "spa"-like setting,
and if some dub it "Zen for a lot of yen", most counter "premium"
"quality is not cheap."

Arun's ⓜ *Thai* 27 | 23 | 27 | $94

Northwest Side | 4156 N. Kedzie Ave. (bet. Irving Park Rd. & Montrose Ave.) |
773-539-1909 | www.arunsthai.com

For a "Thai food experience that's unmatched in Chicago", fans rave
about this "legendary" Northwest Side "jewel" where chef-owner
Arun Sampanthavivat crafts "simply wonderful" prix fixe meals featuring dishes "so beautiful you feel guilty putting a fork in them"; while
the generally "pleasing" space falls a bit short of the cuisine, the "caring" staff ensures that guests feel "pampered" and "satisfied", even if
they need a "high-limit credit card" to cover it all.

Avec ● *Mediterranean* 28 | 23 | 24 | $48

West Loop | 615 W. Randolph St. (bet. Desplaines & Jefferson Sts.) |
312-377-2002 | www.avecrestaurant.com

Blackbird's "more playful", less expensive sibling, this adjacent
West Loop "small-plates delight" offers "inventive", "dream-worthy"
Mediterranean dishes ("don't miss the incredible chorizo-stuffed
dates") delivered by a "knowledgeable" staff in "hip", "cozy" environs
with a "lively buzz"; the "stranger-phobic" may be wary of "tight" seating at communal tables, but game guests don't mind, insisting the
"only drawback" is the no-reservations policy, which often results in
"long waits"; P.S. chef Koren Grieveson's recent departure may not be
reflected in the Food score.

Balena *Italian* - | - | - | M

Lincoln Park | 1633 N. Halsted St. (bet. North Ave. & Willow St.) |
312-867-3888 | www.balenachicago.com

Chef Chris Pandel helms this midpriced Lincoln Park Italian where
handmade pastas, wood-fired mains and pizzas, and ambitious des-

serts are accompanied by complex culinary cocktails and an endless wine list; the vaulted, earth-toned space includes a brown leather and steel bar, and private dining rooms upstairs provide an escape from the well-heeled throngs.

Blackbird Ⓢ *American* — 27 | 23 | 25 | $69

West Loop | 619 W. Randolph St. (bet. Desplaines & Jefferson Sts.) | 312-715-0708 | www.blackbirdrestaurant.com

"Inspired", "thoughtful" New American plates are "meticulously put together" by chef-owner Paul Kahan and his "passionate, talented" team at this "energetic" West Loop "winner" "fit for foodies"; with a "sleek" "pristine setting" and "sophisticated" service, it "nails the essentials of fine, hip dining", so though prices may attract "expense-account" types and "seating is crowded", fans say it's "not to be missed"; P.S. "don't forget" the "phenomenal" prix fixe lunch.

Everest ⓈⓂ *French* — 27 | 28 | 27 | $115

Loop | One Financial Pl. | 440 S. LaSalle St., 40th fl. (Congress Pkwy.) | 312-663-8920 | www.everestrestaurant.com

Perched on the 40th floor of the Chicago Stock Exchange, this Loop longtimer with a "knockout" view of the city is deemed "perfection in the clouds" thanks to its "exquisite" Alsatian-influenced French prix fixe menus by chef Jean Joho, plus a "grand" wine list, all delivered with "exceptional" service in an "elegant supper-club setting"; though "not for the light-walleted", it's a "pinnacle" of "fine dining" befitting "special occasions."

Fontano's Subs *Sandwiches* — 28 | 9 | 19 | $10

Loop | 20 E. Jackson Blvd. (bet. State St. & Wabash Ave.) | 312-663-3061 | www.fontanosonjackson.com Ⓢ
Hinsdale | 9 S. Lincoln St. (Chicago Ave.) | 630-789-0891 | www.fontanossubs.com
Naperville | 1767 W. Ogden Ave. (Aurora Ave.) | 630-717-7821 | www.antignana.com
Naperville | 2879 W. 95th St. (Cedar Glade Rd.) | 630-305-8010 | www.fontanossubs.com

"It's all in the bread" (and "finest deli meats") at this "native" Chicago chainlet cranking out "awesome" subs "the way they should be" ("no wimpy" offerings); "you know it's good because all the cops eat here", but plenty opt for takeout since "it's a slice of life, not a fine-dining atmosphere."

Frontera Grill ⓈⓂ *Mexican* — 27 | 22 | 24 | $44

River North | 445 N. Clark St. (bet. Hubbard & Illinois Sts.) | 312-661-1434 | www.fronterakitchens.com

"Celeb" chef-owner Rick Bayless' "deep passion" shows at his "legendary" River North flagship that "elevates Mexican cuisine to a higher order", offering "perfectly executed", "imaginative" dishes with the "right balance of flavor and spice" plus "heavenly margaritas", all set down by "consistently efficient", "well-informed" servers in "festive", "artwork-themed" digs; limited reservations mean it's "very difficult to get a table" and waits are "extremely long", but believers call it "the gold standard" for the genre (adjacent "Topolobampo is the platinum standard"), so "if it isn't worth the wait, what is?"

	FOOD	DECOR	SERVICE	COST

Gibsons Bar & Steakhouse *Steak* | 26 | 22 | 25 | $66 |

Gold Coast | 1028 N. Rush St. (Bellevue Pl.) | 312-266-8999 ◐
Rosemont | Doubletree O'Hare | 5464 N. River Rd. (bet. Balmoral & Bryn Mawr Aves.) | 847-928-9900 ◐
Oak Brook | 2105 S. Spring Rd. (22nd St.) | 630-954-0000
www.gibsonssteakhouse.com

A "first-class icon", this Gold Coast "beef palace" and its suburban sequels tempt "serious steak lovers" with "flavorful" meat and "all the trimmings", "towering" desserts, "stiff drinks" and a "wide wine selection"; the "cost, of course, goes with the quality" (it's more "reasonable for lunch"), and "the wait can be long, long, long – even with reservations" – but service "makes you feel like a regular whether it's your first time or 55th" and the "bustling" crowd of "heavy-hitters" is prime for "people-watching"; P.S. all locations feature live music.

Girl & The Goat *American* | 27 | 24 | 25 | $55 |

West Loop | 809 W. Randolph St. (bet Green & Halsted Sts.) | 312-492-6262 | www.girlandthegoat.com

"Energetic" chef Stephanie Izard "balances flavors like Monet did with his color palette", creating "top-notch nose-to-tail cuisine" ("duck tongues, lamb hearts" and "pig face, anyone"?), vegetables that "will blow your mind" and other "innovative" small plates that "grab the brass ring" at her "cozy", surprisingly "reasonable" West Loop New American where the "passionate" staff's suggestions will "never lead you astray"; "incredibly noisy" digs are easily overlooked by "foodies" who insist it's the "future of dining"; P.S. "good luck getting a reservation."

Goosefoot 🚫Ⓜ *American* | – | – | – | VE |

Lincoln Square | 2656 W. Lawrence Ave. (Washtenaw Ave.) | 773-942-7547 | www.goosefoot.net

Chris Nugent made a highly rated splash at old-school French bastion Les Nomades before opening this "impressive" fine-dining "BYO foodie haven" "off the beaten path" in Lincoln Square that offers a "gorgeous, creative" New American tasting menu; expect artisan ingredients, artful presentations, "stellar service" and the high prices that go with them, plus no corkage fee and menus printed on plantable seed paper.

Green Zebra *Vegetarian* | 28 | 23 | 25 | $49 |

Noble Square | 1460 W. Chicago Ave. (Greenview Ave.) | 312-243-7100 | www.greenzebrachicago.com

"Creativity reigns" at Shawn McClain's "sophisticated" Noble Square stop, "the best vegetarian in town" say surveyors touting the "high-quality", "beautifully presented" small plates with "flavors incredible enough to thrill carnivores"; extras like "impeccable service", a "sleek" setting and "great wine list" add allure, and if it's "a little expensive, you definitely get what you pay for", so acolytes advise "open your mind and go – immediately."

Hot Doug's 🚫⇄ *Hot Dogs* | 26 | 14 | 21 | $13 |

Avondale | 3324 N. California Ave. (Roscoe St.) | 773-279-9550 | www.hotdougs.com

"Genius" owner Doug Sohn often "greets everybody personally" and takes orders at the counter of his "iconic" Avondale "shrine to encased meats", bringing franks to "unbelievable heights" with "incredibly cre-

FOOD DECOR SERVICE COST

ative" gourmet concoctions like foie gras–topped Sauternes duck sausage and "scrumptious" Friday and Saturday–only duck fat fries, all for under $10; guests wait in "huge" lines to visit the "cramped", "tacky" ketchup-colored shop, but it is "well worth the wait" for these "pedigreed pups."

Joe's Seafood, Prime Steak & Stone Crab *Seafood/Steak*
27 | 23 | 26 | $66

River North | 60 E. Grand Ave. (Rush St.) | 312-379-5637 | www.joes.net
"Some of the sunshine from Miami Beach" shines at this River North surf 'n' turf "half sister" to the Florida flagship where "grilled-to-perfection" steaks, "tasty, tender stone crab claws as big as your hand" and other "lip-smackingly good" fare is ferried by "professional", "amiable" servers in dark wood–accented digs; it's "noisy and touristy" with "prime prices" but "who cares" when it "consistently delivers" say patrons whose "only problem is getting a reservation at a decent time."

Katsu Japanese Ⓜ *Japanese*
29 | 19 | 24 | $57

Northwest Side | 2651 W. Peterson Ave. (bet. Talman & Washtenaw Aves.) | 773-784-3383
"Utterly authentic" Japanese fare "spoils" diners at this Northwest Side longtimer, "one of the best traditional sushi bars in Chicago" where chef-owner Katsu Imamura transforms "quality ingredients" into "beautifully prepared" plates; "enthusiastic", "knowledgeable" staffers elevate the "serene", "minimalist" space, so though it's not cheap (or for "fans of crazy over-stuffed rolls"), it's "hands down" a place to "visit again and again."

Les Nomades ⒵Ⓜ *French*
28 | 27 | 28 | $123

Streeterville | 222 E. Ontario St. (bet. Fairbanks Ct. & St. Clair St.) | 312-649-9010 | www.lesnomades.net
"A refuge of civility", this Streeterville French evokes "a more elegant era" with its "superbly attentive, efficient" servers, "serene" "flower-filled townhouse" setting and "sublime" "haute cuisine" from recently returned "master" chef Roland Liccioni; a "remarkable" wine list further elevates it to "special-occasion" status, so though "pricey", fans say it's "worth every centime."

Longman & Eagle ❶ *American*
27 | 22 | 23 | $41

Logan Square | 2657 N. Kedzie Ave. (Schubert Ave.) | 773-276-7110 | www.longmanandeagle.com
"Off the charts for original fare" typifies praise for this Logan Square "hipster" "hot spot" where the "bordering-on-brilliant" New American menu "mixes game and offal with traditional comfort food" and the "pitch-perfect cocktails" from bartending "ar-teests" are "wonderful as well"; service is "knowledgeable" and "friendly" and the setting "relaxed", so though a no-reservations policy ("whatever happened to that civilized custom?") often results in a wait, most say it's "worth fighting the crowds"; P.S. it's also an inn, so if you overdo it, "they've got rooms upstairs."

Lou Malnati's Pizzeria *Pizza*
25 | 16 | 20 | $22

River North | 439 N. Wells St. (Hubbard St.) | 312-828-9800
Lincoln Park | 958 W. Wrightwood Ave. (Lincoln Ave.) | 773-832-4030
(continued)

(continued)

Lou Malnati's Pizzeria

Far South Side | 3859 W. Ogden Ave. (Cermak Rd.) | 773-762-0800
Printer's Row | 805 S. State St. (8th St.) | 312-786-1000
Evanston | 1850 Sherman Ave. (University Pl.) | 847-328-5400
Lincolnwood | 6649 N. Lincoln Ave. (Prairie Rd.) | 847-673-0800
Buffalo Grove | 85 S. Buffalo Grove Rd. (Lake Cook Rd.) | 847-215-7100
Elk Grove Village | 1050 E. Higgins Rd. (bet. Arlington Heights & Busse Rds.) |
847-439-2000
Schaumburg | 1 S. Roselle Rd. (Schaumburg Rd.) | 847-985-1525
Naperville | 131 W. Jefferson Ave. (bet. Main & Webster Sts.) | 630-717-0700
www.loumalnatis.com
Additional locations throughout the Chicago area

"Come with an appetite" to this "iconic" chain, "the place to go if you
want to experience Chicago-style deep-dish" say pie-zani "OMG"-ing
over the "thick", "incredible" butter crust, "ooey gooey, nicely stretchy
cheese" and sausage plenty "enough to feed an army", plus "respectable" thin-crust pies and "fantastic" salads too; the staff is "friendly" and
though the decor strikes some as "humble", most barely notice, wishing
only that "made-to-order" 'zas didn't result in "a bit of a wait."

Mercat a la Planxa *Spanish*   26 | 24 | 23 | $54

South Loop | Blackstone Hotel | 636 S. Michigan Ave. (Balbo Ave.) |
312-765-0524 | www.mercatchicago.com
Get an "introduction to the vitality of Spanish food" at this "swanky"
South Loop Catalan in the "beautifully restored" Blackstone Hotel where
"creativity abounds" in chef Jose Garces' "authentic", "amazing" tapas
offered alongside "inventive cocktails" and a "deep", "well-paired" wine
list; "attentive" but "not intrusive" service adds to the "wow"-worthy experience, and as for cost, it varies since "you can eat a few tapas for
very little money or spend quite a bit on the tasting menus."

Mixteco Grill Ⓜ *Mexican*   27 | 18 | 22 | $32

Lakeview | 1601 W. Montrose Ave. (Ashland Ave.) | 773-868-1601 |
www.mixtecogrill.com
"Uniformly superb" apps, "to-die-for" mole sauces and "out-of-this-
world" entrees make this Lakeview Mexican a "standout", especially
since BYO further tempers the "reasonably priced" tabs; service is
"friendly" and the art "eye-catching", so the "only negative is that it
can get quite noisy."

MK *American*   28 | 25 | 26 | $73

Near North | 868 N. Franklin St. (bet. Chestnut & Locust Sts.) |
312-482-9179 | www.mkchicago.com
"Among the finest in Chicago", this Near North New American from
Michael Kornick has "all the right ingredients", with "thoughtful, unique"
meals that "reflect the seasons", "show-stealing" desserts and a
"spectacular" wine list all offered by "accommodating" staffers; the
"swanky" loftlike area is "bustling", the mezzanine "more intimate"
and "everyone leaves happy – except the guy stuck with the tab."

Morton's The Steakhouse *Steak*   26 | 23 | 25 | $72

Loop | 65 E. Wacker Pl. (bet. Michigan & Wabash Aves.) | 312-201-0410
Gold Coast | Newberry Plaza | 1050 N. State St. (Maple St.) | 312-266-4820
Rosemont | 9525 Bryn Mawr Ave. (N. River Rd.) | 847-678-5155
Northbrook | 699 Skokie Blvd. (Dundee Rd.) | 847-205-5111

(continued)

Morton's The Steakhouse

Schaumburg | 1470 McConnor Pkwy. (bet. Golf & Meacham Rds.) | 847-413-8771
Naperville | 1751 Freedom Dr. (Diehl Rd.) | 630-577-1372
www.mortons.com

"Perfect for closing the big deal or celebrating a major milestone", this "original power brokers' steakhouse" (with locations area-wide, including the vintage-1978 State Street original) "sets the standard and maintains it" when it comes to "melt-in-your-mouth" chops and "super-fresh" seafood, all served via "truly professional" staffers in "hushed, formal" surroundings; "pricey" (some say "overpriced") tabs are tempered by "huge" portions and "bargain bar bites", so for many it's an all-around "favorite."

Naha ⊠ *American* `27` `24` `25` `$73`

River North | 500 N. Clark St. (Illinois St.) | 312-321-6242 | www.naha-chicago.com

"Imaginative" dishes featuring "complex combinations of ingredients" are chef-owner "Carrie Nahabedian's gift to all of us" effuse enthusiasts "astonished" by the "well-composed", "perfectly prepared" plates at this "top-notch" River North New American; "the staff is engaging in the best way" ("like that one brother-in-law you actually like") and the "contemporary" space "impresses" too (even when "noisy"), so most overlook "steep prices" and soak in the "Zen experience."

Nellcôte ● *American* `-` `-` `-` `M`

West Loop | 833 W. Randolph St. (Green St.) | 855-635-5268 | www.nellcoterestaurant.com

Old Town Social's Jared Van Camp unleashes his culinary imagination at this West Loop New American where the midpriced menu showcases handcrafted ingredients (even the flour is house-ground); the posh setting has soft chandelier lighting, an elevated mezzanine area and a marble staircase; P.S. it's named for the Riviera site where some Rolling Stones recording sessions took place.

Next M *Eclectic* `29` `26` `29` `$164`

West Loop | 953 W. Fulton Mkt. (bet. Morgan & Sangamon Sts.) | 312-226-0858 | www.nextrestaurant.com

"Genius" Grant Achatz "breaks the mold", completely redesigning the themed fixed-price menu every three months at his "dazzling" West Loop Eclectic, an "unparalleled culinary experience" where enjoying "life-changingly delicious food" offered in "thought-provoking presentations" is "more like being part of a story than simply eating"; "flawless" staffers (rated No. 1 for Service in Chicago) enhance the "cozy", modern confines, so despite "über-expensive" tabs and a "bizarre ticketing system" "requiring feats of psychological endurance" it's still "worth every penny and then some."

NoMI Kitchen *American* `26` `27` `25` `$72`

Gold Coast | Park Hyatt Chicago | 800 N. Michigan Ave., 7th fl. (bet. Michigan Ave. & Rush St.) | 312-239-4030 | www.parkchicago.hyatt.com

After a "remake", the "more relaxed" yet still "elegant" space "passes the test for excitement" say those revisiting this "top-drawer" New

American in the Gold Coast's Park Hyatt where the "inventive", "wide-ranging" menu also inspires high praise; "service remains excellent" too, and with "magnificent city views" and an "extensive" wine list most agree it's "special-occasion"-worthy, "especially if you have an expense account"; P.S. the outdoor roof garden remains, and is now visible from inside through a glass wall.

The Publican *American*   26 | 23 | 23 | $49

West Loop | 837 W. Fulton Mkt. (Green St.) | 312-445-8977 | www.thepublicanrestaurant.com

A "slam dunk" gush groupies of Paul Kahan's West Loop New American, a "temple to the pig" with its pork-centered, "finger-lican' good" eats plus a "wonderful selection" of "quality" oysters, one of the "best, smartest" beer lists in the city – and plenty of "deliciously prepared" veggies too; communal tables lend a "hip cafeteria" feel, service is "helpful" and while "prices aren't crazy", you can "spend a lot to get filled up", but as long as "you don't mind loud", you'll still "look forward to eating here again."

Pump Room *American*   21 | 27 | 24 | $59

Gold Coast | Public Hotel | 1301 N. State Pkwy. (bet. Banks & Goethe Sts.) | 312-229-6740 | www.pumproom.com

The "gorgeous" revamp of this Public Hotel–based landmark is "classy with a capital C" say habitués of Jean-Georges Vongerichten's "celebratory" Gold Coast arrival, where "upbeat" staffers relay "creative" New American dishes in a "glitzy" "see-and-be-seen" setting; you can still "plow through the throngs" to Sinatra's table, and while a few tut it "doesn't compare" to its "revered" predecessor, the masses "welcome" it back, adding "you never know who you'll run into" at the bar.

The Purple Pig ● *Mediterranean*   26 | 21 | 21 | $42

River North | 500 N. Michigan Ave. (Illinois St.) | 312-464-1744 | www.thepurplepigchicago.com

"Adventurous" foodies scarf "every part of the pig but the oink" at Jimmy Bannos Jr.'s midpriced River North Med where "thought-provoking", "richly flavored small plates eat large", making it a "favorite after two or three bites"; it's "very small and does not take reservations", but the "young and soon to be deaf" don't mind, as the wine list is "killer", the service "unpretentious yet attentive" and the overall "buzz justified"; P.S. don't miss "glorious outside seating by the Chicago River."

Riccardo Trattoria *Italian*   28 | 21 | 25 | $49

Lincoln Park | 2119 N. Clark St. (bet. Dickens & Webster Aves.) | 773-549-0038 | www.riccardotrattoria.com

"Best Italian in the city" honors go to this "small" and "casual" yet "urbane" Lincoln Park "gem", house of "homemade everything" offered in "breathtaking" "upscaled" "traditional dishes" that are further enhanced by a "varied" wine list; with "no airs", "attentive service" and "prices well below its competitors", it's unsurprisingly "tough to get a table."

Ruxbin Ⓜ *Eclectic*   28 | 23 | 24 | $45

Noble Square | 851 N. Ashland Ave. (Pearson St.) | 312-624-8509 | www.ruxbinchicago.com

Tasters are "transported into a culinary adventure" courtesy of chef-owner Edward Kim and his "delicious, innovative" Eclectic cooking at this "freakin' awesome" Noble Square BYO; the "small" space offers a "fascinating lesson in creative recycling" – "repurposed" decor includes "bench backs made of seat belts" – and service is "incredibly friendly", so grumps groaning "only the young can tolerate two-hour waits" (no reservations) are overruled by those who simply "love everything", including the "coolest bathroom", "hands down."

Schwa 🗷Ⓜ *American* | 28 | 16 | 24 | $107 |

Wicker Park | 1466 N. Ashland Ave. (Le Moyne St.) | 773-252-1466 | www.schwarestaurant.com

Willing "guinea pigs" devour the "mindbendingly creative" New American "experiments" of "punk rock cooking genius" Michael Carlson at his "cutting-edge" Wicker Park BYO where the "seriously amazing" prix fixe menu is served by the chefs; "there's no atmosphere" but those who consider it "fine dining without the stuffiness" roll with it, suggesting you "bring an open mind, some booze" (and some big bucks) and strap in for an "exhilarating" night out; P.S. "make reservations far in advance – and good luck with that."

Shanghai Terrace 🗷 *Chinese* | 27 | 28 | 25 | $71 |

River North | Peninsula Chicago | 108 E. Superior St., 4th fl. (bet. Michigan Ave. & Rush St.) | 312-573-6744 | www.chicago.peninsula.com

"Each dish is a masterpiece" at this "upscale" Chinese off the lobby of River North's Peninsula Hotel where the "exquisite" cuisine is matched by an "astounding" '30s-style dining room that earns it top Decor honors in Chicago; "polite" service and a "terrace perfect for summer days and nights" further ensure a "top experience", so "expensive" tabs come as no surprise.

Spiaggia *Italian* | 26 | 27 | 26 | $105 |

Gold Coast | One Magnificent Mile Bldg. | 980 N. Michigan Ave. (Oak St.) | 312-280-2750 | www.spiaggiarestaurant.com

An "ultimate special-occasion place", this Gold Coast "destination" "leaves nothing to be desired", from Tony Mantuano's "exquisite", "beautifully presented" "haute Italian" plates and the "deeply varied wine list" to the "warm, discreet" service known to treat guests "like royalty"; "spectacular views of the lake" feature in the "sterling setting", so though you need "a bag of gold to pay the bill", acolytes insist it's "worth the splurge"; P.S. jackets required.

Sprout Ⓜ *American* | 28 | 25 | 25 | $77 |

Lincoln Park | 1417 W. Fullerton Ave. (bet. Janssen & Southport Aves.) | 773-348-0706 | www.sproutrestaurant.com

Chef-"magician" Dale Levitski "excites taste buds" at his Lincoln Park New American, a "showplace for creative cuisine" with "innovative combinations", "clean flavors" and "outstanding tastes"; service is "warm and knowledgeable" and the stone-walled space "pleasant", which helps quiet those who find it "overpriced"; P.S. "brunch is a highlight."

Takashi Ⓜ *American/French* | 28 | 23 | 25 | $66 |

Bucktown | 1952 N. Damen Ave. (Armitage Ave.) | 773-772-6170 | www.takashichicago.com

"Meticulously crafted" New American–New French dishes revealing an "excellent melding" of "delicate", "complex" flavors highlight chef-owner Takashi Yagihashi's "magic" touch at this "exceptional" Bucktown "gem"; there's an "understated elegance" to the "cozy" space and servers "clearly take pride in their work", so it's "habit-forming" to those who can afford the pricey tabs.

Topolobampo ⊠Ⓜ *Mexican*   28 | 24 | 26 | $70

River North | 445 N. Clark St. (Illinois St.) | 312-661-1434 |
www.rickbayless.com

Celeb chef Rick Bayless "wrote the book on fine Mexican cuisine" (literally and figuratively) and he "keeps rewriting it" by "setting new standards" at his "upscale" River North "institution" where "inventive", "refined interpretations" result in "sublime", "mind-melting" moles and other "subtle" yet "complex" dishes served alongside "delicious" margaritas; "kind", "informative" servers are "as comforting as family" in the "elegant", art-enhanced dining room, so "if you win the fight to land a reservation, you will be a very happy camper"; P.S. for a "cheaper" experience try the adjoining Frontera Grill.

Tru ⊠ *French*   28 | 27 | 28 | $129

Streeterville | 676 N. St. Clair St. (bet. Erie & Huron Sts.) | 312-202-0001 |
www.trurestaurant.com

A "true pampering experience" awaits at this Streeterville "bastion of epicurean splendor" where Anthony Martin's "creative, sometimes daring" New French tasting menus are "beautifully presented" and offered alongside "excellent wine recommendations"; "world-class" servers manage to be "both ballerinas and ninjas at the same time" and the "minimalist yet elegant" "art-filled room" is "serene", so admirers attest it's "excellent in every respect" – just "plan to stay awhile and spend a lot"; P.S. jackets required.

Vie *American*   29 | 26 | 28 | $68

Western Springs | 4471 Lawn Ave. (Burlington Ave.) | 708-246-2082 |
www.vierestaurant.com

For a "gourmet experience miles from the Loop", foodies head to this "exceptional" Western Springs New American, a "culinary jewel" from Paul Virant (Perennial Virant) who "treats the freshest ingredients with great respect" while crafting "outstanding, inventive" plates highlighting "subtle spices and textures"; "thoughtful", "well-timed" service and a "beautiful" dining room featuring "mostly black and white decor" further make for an "incomparable" experience, especially since it's "reasonably priced" given its caliber.

Wildfire *Steak*   24 | 21 | 22 | $43

River North | 159 W. Erie St. (bet. LaSalle Blvd. & Wells St.) | 312-787-9000
Lincolnshire | 235 Parkway Dr. (Milwaukee Ave.) | 847-279-7900
Glenview | 1300 Patriot Blvd. (Lake Ave.) | 847-657-6363
Schaumburg | 1250 E. Higgins Rd. (National Pkwy.) | 847-995-0100
Oak Brook | Oakbrook Center Mall | 232 Oakbrook Ctr. (Rte. 83) |
630-586-9000
www.wildfirerestaurant.com

You'll get "a good meal every time" assure fans of this River North and suburban steakhouse "staple", where a "gracious" staff serves "insane" martinis and "outstanding" cuts of beef in a "vibrant" setting recalling a 1940s supper club; some call it "predictable", but those who find it an "excellent value" say there's a reason it's "always busy."

Cincinnati

TOP FOOD RANKING

Restaurant	Cuisine
29┃ Jean-Robert's Table	French
28┃ Bakersfield	Mexican
Orchids at Palm Court	American
Jeff Ruby's Steakhouse	Steak
Nicola's	Italian
Tony's	Seafood/Steak
Abigail Street	Mediterranean
Jeff Ruby's Precinct	Steak
Jag's Steak & Seafood	Seafood/Steak
Morton's	Steak

OTHER NOTEWORTHY PLACES

Barleycorn's	American
Blue Ash Chili	American
Boca	Italian
Bouquet	Eclectic
Dewey's Pizza	Pizza
Izzy's	Sandwiches
Local 127	American
Montgomery Inn	BBQ
Palace	American
Wildflower Café	American

Abigail Street ⊠Ⓜ *Mediterranean* 28 | 26 | 26 | $40

Over-the-Rhine | 1214 Vine St. (bet. 12th & 13th Sts.) | 513-421-4040 | www.abigailstreet.com

"Creative", "tempting" Med tapas are prepared with "local ingredients" and cooked with "soul" at this "vibrant" Over-the-Rhine "favorite" bolstered by "beyond-excellent" service and a "great wine bar" with vino on tap; though "a little pricey", the "portions are actually quite respectable" and the "bustling", "big-city feel" is a bonus; P.S. no reservations.

Bakersfield *Mexican* 28 | 25 | 26 | $24

Over-the-Rhine | 1213 Vine St. (bet. 12th & 13th Sts.) | www.bakersfieldotr.com

Regulars "crave" the "bold, perfectly balanced" tacos, "incredible" guac and other "excellent" eats at this Mexican joint – the "hippest newcomer" in Over-the-Rhine – that's also big on tequila, whiskey and the "best margaritas"; with reasonable prices and a staff that "takes care of you", no wonder it's "always crowded" with "lots of energy" from the "Vine Street" set.

Barleycorn's *American* 22 | 21 | 22 | $22

Florence | 8544 U.S. 42 (off Pleasant Valley Rd.) | 859-937-4100
Cold Spring | 1073 Industrial Rd. (bet. Alexandria Pike & Winters Ln.) | 859-442-3400

(continued)

(continued)

Barleycorn's

Crescent Springs | 2642 Dixie Hwy. (Hudson Ave.) | 859-331-6633
www.barleycorns.com

Fans "enjoy" the American eats on a "huge menu with something for
everyone" at this "sports-bar-extraordinaire" trio of "family-friendly"
chain links with "outgoing" service, "comfortable" surroundings and
"lots of screens" to watch the game; "happy-hour deals" keep it extra
popular, so all in all it's a "good time."

Blue Ash Chili 🅂 *American*

25 | 16 | 24 | $12

Blue Ash | 9565 Kenwood Rd. (Cooper Rd.) | 513-984-6107 |
www.blueashchili.com

This "diner"-like American dive in Blue Ash serves up "butt-kickin'"
"Cincinnati chili" and "huge, delicious" double-deckers "piled high with
meats and cheese" ("they do not skimp"); "don't expect it to be nice
inside", but do expect "perky caffeine-powered servers", a "crowded"
lunch scene and "a lotta food for the buck."

Boca 🅂Ⓜ *Italian*

27 | 25 | 26 | $53

Oakley | 3200 Madison Rd. (bet. Brazee St. & Ridge Rd.) | 513-542-2022 |
www.boca-restaurant.com

"Impassioned" eaters "swoon" over David Falk's "imaginative", "absolutely delicious" Italian dishes ("especially the Brussels sprouts")
matched by a "wine list that gets bigger and better all the time" at this
"buzzing" Oakley "gem", calling it a "must-go" "if you have the money";
servers "know their stuff", though a few note that it's currently in
transition and seems to be "focusing on its move Downtown", slated
for late 2012.

Bouquet 🅂Ⓜ *Eclectic*

27 | 23 | 24 | $52

Covington | 519 Main St. (bet. 5th & 6th Sts.) | 859-491-7777 |
www.bouquetrestaurant.com

Both a "small neighborhood bistro" and upscale "destination", this
"highly recommended" Eclectic in Covington pairs "phenomenal",
seasonal dishes by chef-owner Stephen Williams with "excellent
reasonable wines" in a "quaint" setting resembling a living room;
with "dependable" service too, it adds up to a "surprise find" across
the Ohio River.

Dewey's Pizza *Pizza*

26 | 20 | 24 | $19

Clifton | 265 Hosea Ave. (Clifton Ave.) | 513-221-0400
Oakley | Oakley Sq. | 3014 Madison Rd. (Markbreit Ave.) | 513-731-7755
Crestview Hills | Crestview Hills Town Ctr. | 2949 Dixie Hwy.
(Rosemont Dr.) | 859-341-2555
Newport | Newport on the Levee | 1 Levee Way (Monmouth St.) |
859-431-9700
Kenwood | 7767 Kenwood Rd. (Montgomery Rd.) | 513-791-1616
Symmes | Shops at Harper's Point | 11338 Montgomery Rd.
(bet. Harper Point Dr. & Kemper Rd.) | 513-247-9955
West Chester | 7663 Cox Ln. (University Dr.) | 513-759-6777
www.deweyspizza.com

The Most Popular chain in Cincinnati, this "upper-class" pie purveyor
bakes up "seriously outstanding" "designer" pizzas on "hand-tossed"
dough, sporting an "incredible" crust with red or white sauce and

"fresh", "creative" toppings, served in "efficient" style; throw in "amazing" salads, "specialty beers" and an "upbeat" atmosphere with a window to "watch the pizzas being made" ("enthralling" for kids), and it's easy to see why it's a "favorite."

Izzy's *Sandwiches*
25 | 17 | 24 | $14

Downtown | 610 Main St. (bet. 6th & 7th Sts.) | 513-241-6246 ☒
Downtown | 800 Elm St. (Garfield Pl.) | 513-721-4241 ☒
Covedale | 5098B Glencrossing Way (Glenway Ave.) |
513-347-9699 ☒
Forest Park | 1198 Smiley Ave. (off Winton Rd.) | 513-825-3888
Anderson Township | 7625 Beechmont Ave. (Forest Rd.) | 513-231-5550
West Chester | 8179 Princeton-Glendale Rd. (Smith Rd.) | 513-942-7800
www.izzys.com

"Longtime fans" "love" this "landmark Cincinnati deli" with locations throughout the city serving "hearty", "overstuffed" sandwiches (particularly the "terrific" Reubens) along with "famous pickles" and "second-to-none" potato pancakes; though the decor reminds some of a "grade-school lunchroom", it's inexpensive and the staff is "a hoot", so "how can you go wrong?"

Jag's Steak & Seafood ☒ *Seafood/Steak*
28 | 27 | 25 | $62

West Chester | 5980 West Chester Rd. (Mulhauser Rd.) | 513-860-5353 |
www.jags.com

"Unbelievable" steaks (the Kobe beef sets the "gold standard") and "top-of-the-line" seafood add up to "first-class" meals with "big presentations" at this West Chester chophouse boasting "grand" service and a "terrific" atmosphere with a "club feel"; dubbing it an "elite" locale to "meet with a client" or spend a "romantic" evening, diners say "you definitely get what you pay for here – and you will pay a lot."

Jean-Robert's Table ☒ *French*
29 | 25 | 27 | $44

Downtown | 713 Vine St. (bet. Garfield Pl. & 7th St.) | 513-621-4777 |
www.jrtable.com

"Berets off" to this Downtown "winner", voted No. 1 for Food in Cincinnati, where "sumptuous", "work-of-art" French fare by "outstanding" chef-owner Jean-Robert de Cavel meets "first-class" service in a "bustling", intimate room that's "not too formal or too casual" but "just right"; fortunately it's "not too expensive" either, and the 'lunch tray' special at the bar is a low-cost coup.

Jeff Ruby's Precinct *Steak*
28 | 26 | 28 | $57

Columbia Tusculum | 311 Delta Ave. (Columbia Pkwy.) | 513-321-5454 |
www.jeffruby.com

"Astoundingly good" cuts are "always tender with lots of flavor" (and the "mac 'n' cheese is a must") at this "Cincinnati tradition" voted the city's Most Popular restaurant – a "charming" "old police HQ" turned "warm", "lively" steakhouse (with "tight" tables) in Columbia Tusculum; fans say "fine service puts it over the top", though the "high prices" mean some save it for "special events"; P.S. jacket suggested.

Jeff Ruby's Steakhouse ☒ *Steak*
28 | 27 | 27 | $70

Downtown | 700 Walnut St. (7th St.) | 513-784-1200 |
www.jeffruby.com

"Incredible" dry-aged cuts are the standard at this "elite" Downtown meatery where "steaks and martinis rule" in a "glamorous" "art deco

	FOOD	DECOR	SERVICE	COST

room" boasting "exemplary" service and "live music" most nights; the "amazing" sides and desserts alone are big enough to "put you in a coma" – just "prepare to pay" the equally hefty bill.

Local 127 *American*

| 26 | 23 | 25 | $38 |

Downtown | 413 Vine St. (bet. 4th & 5th Sts.) | 513-721-1345 | www.mylocal127.com

Customers "could live off the cured-and-pickled menu alone" at this Downtown New American "find" delivering "adventurous", "succulent" dishes enhanced by chef Steven Geddes' "farm-to-table" approach and "supreme knowledge of wine and beer"; though it recently "moved around the corner", it still has a "stylishly casual" atmosphere, moderate prices and an engaged staff that serves with "pride."

Montgomery Inn *BBQ*

| 26 | 25 | 25 | $38 |

Downtown | 925 Riverside Dr. (Eggleston Ave.) | 513-721-7427
Ft. Mitchell | 400 Buttermilk Pike (I-75) | 859-344-5333
Montgomery | 9440 Montgomery Rd. (bet. Cooper & Remington Rds.) | 513-791-3482
www.montgomeryinn.com

"Legendary" ribs and other "finger-lickin'", "lip-smackin'" BBQ specialties (on the "sweet" side) "continue to please" at this slightly "pricey" trio of "local icons" well suited to "family, business or special occasions"; from the "festive", "memorabilia"-decked Montgomery original to the Downtown Boathouse branch with a "wonderful view of the river", it's staffed by a "prompt" crew that's "on top of everything", though don't expect to "linger at the tables" since folks are "waiting."

Morton's The Steakhouse *Steak*

| 28 | 26 | 27 | $65 |

Downtown | Carew Tower | 441 Vine St. (5th St.) | 513-621-3111 | www.mortons.com

"Expense-accounters" and others head to this "Chicago steakhouse" in Downtown Cincinnati for "incredible" steaks and sides in "portions that are huge with prices to match"; the "relaxing" setting on Fountain Square is "classy" though "not trendy", with "excellent" service.

Nicola's 🗷 *Italian*

| 28 | 26 | 27 | $51 |

Downtown | 1420 Sycamore St. (Liberty St.) | 513-721-6200 | www.nicolasrestaurant.com

"Transports you from Downtown Cincinnati to TriBeCa in the blink of an eye" boast admirers of this "chic", "top-performing" Tuscan serving "exquisite" pastas and other "innovative" dishes (not to mention the "best bread basket in the city") in a "lofty" space with exposed-brick walls; "personal" service and a "deep" wine list are further pluses, and while it is "expensive", most find it a "great value in upscale dining."

Orchids at Palm Court *American*

| 28 | 29 | 28 | $61 |

Downtown | Hilton Cincinnati Netherland Plaza | 35 W. Fifth St. (Race St.) | 513-421-9100 | www.orchidsatpalmcourt.com

"The ceiling alone is magical" at this Downtown art deco "stunner" in the historic Hilton Netherland Plaza hotel, voted No. 1 for Decor and Service in Cincinnati, where the "exquisite" setting is matched by chef Todd Kelly's "beautifully prepared", "highly satisfying" New American dishes, an "impeccable" wine list and "genuine hospitality" with "superior" "attention to detail"; it's certainly "pricey", but that's to be expected at such a "grande dame" of "civilized" dining.

The Palace *American*   27 | 26 | 27 | $65

Downtown | Cincinnatian Hotel | 601 Vine St. (6th St.) | 513-381-3000 | www.palacecincinnati.com

"Impressed" guests say "every plate" by "inventive" chef Jose Salazar is "like a work of art and tastes even better" at this "beautiful", "top-of-the-line" Downtown New American in the Cincinnatian Hotel, where the "distinguished" staff "attends to your every need"; it's "expensive" of course, but a "classy and classic" choice for "new-world cuisine served with old-world style"; P.S. breakfast-only on Sundays.

Tony's *Seafood/Steak*   28 | 24 | 25 | $67

Symmes | 12110 Montgomery Rd. (Fields Ertel Rd.) | 513-677-1993 | www.tonysofcincinnati.com

"Beyond-delicious" steaks ("fabulous filet mignon") and a "great raw bar" stand out at this "expensive" Symmes surf 'n' turfer offering "fine", "personalized" service ("Tony almost always makes a stop at your table") to go with the "wonderful food"; live music on the weekends enhances the "nice" ambiance, making it perfect for a "special night out."

Wildflower Café 🅂🅼 *American*   27 | 21 | 26 | $24

Mason | 207 E. Main St. (Dawson St.) | 513-492-7514 | www.wildflowercafeandcoffeehouse.com

Chef-owner Todd Hudson maintains an "innovative", reasonably priced menu of dishes made with local "fresh ingredients" (some of them "grown on-site") at this American "favorite" in Mason; the "small" setting in an "old house" is staffed by an "accommodating" team, but "don't even think about getting a table without a reservation"; P.S. the thoughtful beer selection is "wonderful" too.

Cleveland

TOP FOOD RANKING

Restaurant	Cuisine
29 Chez François	French
Giovanni's Ristorante	Italian
28 Lola	American
Ty Fun	Thai
Weia Teia	Eclectic
Red	Steak
Dante	American
Aldo's	Italian
L'Albatros	French
Parallax	Eclectic/Seafood

OTHER NOTEWORTHY PLACES

Bar Cento	Belgian/Italian
B Spot	American
Crop	American
Fire Food & Drink	American
Flying Fig	American/Eclectic
Great Lakes Brewing Co.	American
Lolita	American/Mediterranean
Melt Bar & Grilled	American
Pier W	Seafood
Yours Truly	Diner

Aldo's Ⓜ *Italian*   28 | 17 | 25 | $33

Brooklyn | 8459 Memphis Ave. (Roadoan Rd.) | 216-749-7060

"Loyal customers" love the "expertly made, genuine" Italian dishes and "blackboard specials" at this "family-owned gem", a "small", "intimate" locale "hidden" in a Brooklyn strip mall; while the ambiance is "decidedly not upscale" and "you may have to wait awhile for a table", the "moderate prices" and "charming" hospitality help keep it a "favorite."

Bar Cento ◗ *Belgian/Italian*   25 | 21 | 22 | $28

Ohio City | 1948 W. 25th St. (Lorain Ave.) | 216-274-1010 | www.barcento.com

"Hard rock plays while the chef rocks" at this "trendy", "late-night" Belgian-Roman bistro in Ohio City offering "smaller plates to full-on meals" ("try the Sunnyside pizza") that are always "fresh and well made with balanced flavors", and go well with the "rare brews" from the adjoining Bier Markt; "casual and energetic", it comes through with some of the "best bargains in town" and, many agree, "incredible" "garlic rosemary fries"; P.S. "go downstairs to Speakeasy" for an after-dinner cocktail.

B Spot *American*   25 | 23 | 23 | $21

Woodmere | 28699 Chagrin Blvd. (bet. Belmont Rd. & Roselawn Ave.) | 216-292-5567

(continued)

B Spot

Strongsville | 18066 Royalton Rd. (Pearl Rd.) | 440-572-9600
Westlake | 20 Main St. (bet. Detroit Rd. & Hillard Blvd.) | 440-471-8270
www.bspotburgers.com

"Outlandish combinations that are so wrong, they're right" hit the "b spot" at this "quirky" mini-chain by chef-owner Michael Symon proffering "burger bliss" with its "adventurous", "full-of-flavor" patties, "killer" milkshakes and "irresistible" fries (you'll also find "brats, bologna, beer" and a "pickle bar"); "cool" and "crowded", with "efficient" service, it can be "a tad pricey", but fans insist the "quality" lives up to the cost.

Chez François �M *French*   29 | 28 | 28 | $71

Vermilion | 555 Main St. (Liberty Ave.) | 440-967-0630 |
www.chezfrancois.com

The "crème de la crème" when it comes to "exceptional", "beautifully plated" French food and a "world-class" wine list, this lakeside destination in Vermilion again takes the title of No. 1 for Food in the Cleveland area; noting its "quaint", "romantic" interior, "nice outdoor patio on the canal" and "tight ship" of a staff that shows "careful attention to detail", reviewers agree it's the "ultimate" celebration place when you want to splurge – and the "specialty dinners throughout the year should not be missed."

Crop ☒ *American*   26 | 28 | 26 | $44

Ohio City | 2537 Lorain Ave. (25th St.) | 216-696-2767 | www.cropbistro.com

A "jaw-dropping" new location in a former bank provides a "soaring backdrop" for "original" cooking at this Ohio City New American by "mad scientist" chef-owner Steve Schimoler, known for "playfully" combining "local" ingredients into "extraordinary" dishes ("balsamic popcorn" is a "must-do"); service is "swift and accommodating" and the upscale prices "reasonable", plus "sitting at the chef's table is a blast"; P.S. try the monthly Sunday Supper for a real "deal."

Dante ☒ *American*   28 | 27 | 26 | $46

Tremont | 2247 Professor Ave. (Literary Rd.) | 216-274-1200 |
www.restaurantdante.us

"Preserving the grandeur" of its setting in an "old bank building" while adding "warmth", this savvy, upscale Tremont New American by chef-owner Dante Boccuzzi presents a "modern stage" for "robust", "imaginative" fare with a Mediterranean influence; the staff is "excellent" as well, so even if it's "too far out for the meat-and-potatoes crowd", "foodie" fans call it "wonderful" all around; P.S. "eat in the vault or kitchen for a special evening."

Fire Food & Drink �M *American*   27 | 25 | 25 | $43

Shaker Square | 13220 Shaker Sq. (Moreland Blvd.) | 216-921-3473 |
www.firefoodanddrink.com

"Committed to fresh, organic products", chef-owner Doug Katz "creates culinary bliss" in Shaker Square at this "remarkable" New American turning out "exciting" food in a "sophisticated" "upscale-brasserie" setting with an "open kitchen"; boasting a "knowledgeable" staff, "well-stocked" wine cellar and "high-energy" scene ("makes an aging gal feel hip again"), it's "worth the price" all around – plus brunch is an "extra-special treat" on the "wonderful" patio.

Flying Fig ⓜ *American/Eclectic* — 28 | 24 | 26 | $38

Ohio City | 2523 Market Ave. (25th St.) | 216-241-4243 | www.theflyingfig.com

You'll find an "innovative" menu of "splendid", "locally sourced" cuisine at this "intimate" New American–Eclectic "gem" "tucked in by the West Side Market", where "hands-on" chef-owner Karen Small "artfully prepares" small and large plates for "reasonable" prices; the "well-informed, engaging" staff and "must-do" happy hour make it a "neighborhood favorite", with a patio that's a "warm-weather magnet."

Giovanni's Ristorante ⓩ *Italian* — 29 | 26 | 29 | $60

Beachwood | 25550 Chagrin Blvd. (Richmond Rd.) | 216-831-8625 | www.giovanniscleveland.com

Voted No. 1 for Service in Cleveland, this Beachwood "classic" boasts a "black-tie" staff serving "exquisite" Tuscan food and wine with "unparalleled" care amid "serene", "handsome" surroundings; sure, "it'll cost you", but it's the "place to go to impress a date", "your parents" or a "power broker" in supremely "old-world" style; P.S. "wear a sport jacket or you'll feel underdressed."

Great Lakes Brewing Company ⓩ *American* — 22 | 23 | 22 | $25

Ohio City | 2516 Market Ave. (bet. 25th & 26th Sts.) | 216-771-4404 | www.greatlakesbrewing.com

"You feel a sense of neighborhood" at this Ohio City microbrewery in an "old building across from the historic West Side Market", where the "world-class" suds are matched by a "decently priced" American "pub-style menu with a little kick" (the "best beer cheese soup in town"); "hip" and "crowded", it's a "neat place to hang out" and "catch up with friends", whether in the "inviting" interior or the beer garden – a "warm-weather delight"; P.S. free brewery tours are offered Thursday–Saturday.

L'Albatros ⓩ *French* — 28 | 26 | 27 | $44

University Circle | 11401 Bellflower Rd. (bet. Ford Dr. & 115th St.) | 216-791-7880 | www.albatrosbrasserie.com

"Another winner" by chef/co-owner Zack Bruell, this "modern" French brasserie in University Circle rises to "stellar" heights with its "fabulous" dishes, "outstanding" cheese course and "well-selected" wines; the atmosphere is "gorgeous, lush" and "sophisticated" with a "beautiful patio" and "excellent" service, and the prices are "quite reasonable", making it one of the "best values of any fancy restaurant in Cleveland."

Lola ⓩ *American* — 28 | 27 | 28 | $51

Downtown | 2058 E. Fourth St. (Prospect Ave.) | 216-621-5652 | www.lolabistro.com

From start to finish, "everything is delicious, beautiful and inventive" at celebrity chef Michael Symon's "flagship" "in the heart of the bustling Fourth Street restaurant scene", where "masters of pork" do wonders with "updated rustic" (sometimes "daunting") New American dishes; it's "a little costly", but the service is "top-drawer" and the "attractive" surroundings "electric", rounding out a meal that "totally exceeds expectations."

	FOOD	DECOR	SERVICE	COST

Lolita Ⓜ *American/Mediterranean* | 28 | 25 | 26 | $43 |

Tremont | 900 Literary Rd. (Professor Ave.) | 216-771-5652 |
www.lolitarestaurant.com

"The flavors are bright and strong" and the "adventurous" dishes "exquisitely prepared" at "rock-star" chef Michael Symon's "casual, funky" New American–Med in Tremont ("easier to get into than Lola"), with a "cool", "simple" look and "professional" staff; in step with the "neighborhood-bar feel", it's a "top-notch" value too, especially when you dig into "happy-hour specials" or go with friends and "share a bunch of small plates."

Melt Bar & Grilled *American* | 26 | 23 | 22 | $19 |

Cleveland Heights | 13463 Cedar Rd. (Taylor Rd.) | 216-965-0988
Independence | Liberty Commons Shopping Center | 6700 Rockside Rd. (Brecksville Rd.) | 216-520-1415
Lakewood | 14718 Detroit Ave. (Warren Rd.) | 216-226-3699
www.meltbarandgrilled.com

With a "menu like the Kama Sutra of grilled cheese (they can do it in ways you didn't even think possible)", this "zany", "original" trio pleases with its "big", "inspired" creations that make customers "melt" at first bite; it's "shockingly low-priced" and "crawling with hipsters side-by-side with tourists", but the staff "keeps up with the crowd" – "if a restaurant could have swagger", this one "would have it"; P.S. the "enormous" beer list is a "welcome distraction" while you wait.

Parallax Ⓩ *Eclectic/Seafood* | 28 | 25 | 26 | $48 |

Tremont | 2179 W. 11th St. (Fairfield Ave.) | 216-583-9999 |
www.parallaxtremont.com

"Hip, creative", "simply prepared" Eclectic cuisine "focused on the freshest seafood" – particularly "any concoction" from the "amazing" sushi bar – "shines" at chef-owner Zack Bruell's "Tremont destination", where the wine list is "deep" and the service "personable" and "welcoming"; it is "expensive", but that doesn't keep the "chic", "understated" space from getting "tightly packed" at peak times.

Pier W *Seafood* | 27 | 28 | 26 | $49 |

Lakewood | Winton Place | 12700 Lake Ave. (bet. Cove & Nicholas Aves.) | 216-228-2250 | www.selectrestaurants.com

"Arguably the most beautiful location in which to dine" with an "awesome view of Lake Erie", this shipshape Lakewood destination – voted Most Popular in Cleveland – is favored for its "fine seafood" and "fantastic" Sunday brunch, provided with "polished, efficient" service; it's unsurprisingly "spendy" for a "romantic night out" (enlivened by a "piano bar on the weekends"), but popular for its "bargain" happy hour too.

Red, The Steakhouse *Steak* | 28 | 26 | 27 | $62 |

Beachwood | 3355 Richmond Rd. (Chagrin Blvd.) | 216-831-2252 |
www.redthesteakhouse.com

"Cooler" than the competition, this "hip" Beachwood "hideaway" offers "outstanding" steaks, "incredibly well-made" sides and a "strong" wine list in a "modern", "intimate" setting tended by a "top-of-the-line" staff; it's "definitely celebration central", and "tastes even better if someone else is paying the check."

Ty Fun *Thai*

28 | 23 | 26 | $29

Tremont | 815 Jefferson Ave. (Professor Ave.) | 216-664-1000 | www.tyfunthaibistro.com

"Small but charming", this "awesome" Thai in "historic" Tremont turns out "fresh", "beautiful" plates for moderate prices, including a "whole fish preparation" that's "simply the best"; there's also "excellent" service by a "caring staff and owner", so regulars who "love" it say they're "treated very well."

Weia Teia *Eclectic*

28 | 24 | 25 | $24

Oberlin | 9 S. Main St. (College St.) | 440-774-8880 | www.weiateia.com

"Absolutely incredible Asian fusion dishes with eye-popping presentations" make guests "grateful" for this Oberlin Eclectic ("what an odd place to find such wonderful food and service"); though tables are "a little tight for more than four people", the interior is "tasteful" and "lunch prices are silly low", so admirers assure it's "not to be missed."

Yours Truly *Diner*

23 | 20 | 23 | $17

Shaker Square | 13228 Shaker Sq. (Shaker Blvd.) | 216-751-8646
Chagrin Falls | 30 N. Main St. (Franklin St.) | 440-247-3232
Valley View | 8111 Rockside Rd. (Canal Rd.) | 216-524-8111
www.ytr.com

"Homey and cute", this local chain of "family-friendly diners" (a "Cleveland institution") gets a "big thumbs-up" for its "tasty" "comfort food", including "loaded fries", "thick" shakes and breakfasts "so good it's criminal"; with "pleasant" surroundings, "cheerful" service and "plenty for the money", it's as "comfortable" as "your favorite sweatshirt or those jeans that are broken in just right" (plus "kids love it" too).

Columbus

TOP FOOD RANKING

Restaurant	Cuisine
<u>29</u> Pistacia Vera	Bakery/French
<u>28</u> L'Antibes	French
G. Michael's Bistro & Bar	American
Akai Hana	Japanese
Jeni's Ice Cream	Ice Cream
Mazah	Mediterranean
Hyde Park Prime	Steak
Refectory	French
M	American
Hunan House	Chinese

OTHER NOTEWORTHY PLACES

Alana's Food & Wine	Eclectic
Cap City Fine Diner	Diner
Kihachi	Japanese
Max & Erma's	American
Northstar Café	American
Piada	Italian
Rigsby's Kitchen	Italian
Schmidt's Restaurant	German
Skillet	American
Thurman Cafe	Burgers

Akai Hana *Japanese*   28 | 23 | 25 | $26

Northwest | Kenny Ctr. | 1173 Old Henderson Rd. (Kenny Rd.) |
614-451-5411 | www.akaihanaohio.com

"Rewarding", "super-fresh" (and sometimes "unusual") sushi prepared by "chefs so skilled they could make the Creature from the Black
Lagoon taste good" earns kudos for this "remarkable", "fairly priced"
Northwest mainstay; "traditional" with "knowledgeable" service and
"simple but dignified" surroundings (that often get "packed"), it's "not
flashy" but "way better than any of the trendier" competitors in town.

Alana's Food & Wine 🅂 🅼 *Eclectic*   26 | 18 | 24 | $40

University | 2333 N. High St. (bet. Oakland & Patterson Aves.) |
614-294-6783 | www.alanas.com

"Local" long before local was cool, chef Alana Shock continues to "scour
Ohio" for the "freshest" ingredients, earning accolades as a "wizard in
the kitchen" for her "uncanny ability to mix flavors" and craft an "adventurous" range of meaty and "vegan" items on a "daily changing" Eclectic
menu matched by an "endless", "low-priced" wine list; staffed by a "personable" crew in a University-area "old house" with "wacky", "local art"
and a "lovely" patio, it's a "uniquely Columbus" establishment.

Cap City Fine Diner & Bar *Diner*   26 | 23 | 25 | $24

Gahanna | 1301 Stoneridge Dr. (Morse Rd.) | 614-478-9999

(continued)

(continued)
Cap City Fine Diner & Bar
Grandview Heights | 1299 Olentangy River Rd. (bet. 3rd & 5th Aves.) | 614-291-3663
www.capcityfinediner.com

These "upscale" riffs on '50s diners in Gahanna and Grandview Heights, voted Most Popular in Columbus, are "multitasking" favorites of "kids", "grown-ups" and "seniors" seeking "updated" "twists" on American classics (the meatloaf could make a "grandma jealous"); their "bright, airy" and kitschy "midcentury"-style digs are "almost always busy", but "courteous" service plus "amazing" chocolate cake sweetens the deal.

G. Michael's Bistro & Bar *American*   28 | 25 | 27 | $42
German Village | 595 S. Third St. (Willow St.) | 614-464-0575 | www.gmichaelsbistro.com

"Shrimp and grits are a must-try" at "passionate" chef/co-owner David Tetzloff's "bustling" upscale German Villager, where "quality" local ingredients plus "creative" "Low Country" cooking equals "incredible" "high-end" fare; with "terrific" service, a skylit interior and "fabulous" patio, it's a "special evening" all around – plus there's more "casual eating" at the bar, especially during one of the city's "best happy hours."

Hunan House *Chinese*   28 | 23 | 25 | $22
Northeast | 2350 E. Dublin-Granville Rd. (bet. Cleveland & Maple Canyon Aves.) | 614-895-3330 | www.hunancolumbus.com

Throngs of fans who have been orbiting this "original" star of "spicy", "upscale" Hunan-Sichuan "since it opened" on the Northeast side decades ago still hail it as an affordable "winner" with a "gourmet" touch; new and "wonderful" Thai dishes, "tasteful" decor and helpful service add to its appeal, even if a minority opines that the "shine is gone."

Hyde Park Prime Steakhouse *Steak*   28 | 26 | 27 | $52
Short North | 569 N. High St. (Goodale St.) | 614-224-2204
Dublin | 6360 Frantz Rd. (Rte. 161) | 614-717-2828 🖂
Upper Arlington | 1615 Old Henderson Rd. (Larwell Rd.) | 614-442-3310
Worthington | 55 Hutchinson Ave. (I-270) | 614-438-1000 🖂
www.hydeparkrestaurants.com

Boasting "high-quality" cuts and "exceptional" seafood accompanied by "excellent" martinis and "wonderful" wines, this quartet wins acclaim as one of the "best steakhouses in Columbus"; the "atmospheres differ" ("trendy" to "dated"), but they're largely "clubby" and "masculine", boosted by "primo" service to back up the "costly" tabs.

Jeni's Ice Cream *Ice Cream*   28 | 21 | 26 | $7
Arena District | 59 Spruce St. (Park St.) | 614-228-9960
Clintonville | 4247 N. High St. (Cooke Rd.) | 614-447-0500
German Village | 900 Mohawk St. (Whittier St.) | 614-445-6513
Short North | 714 N. High St. (Lincoln St.) | 614-294-5364
Bexley | 2156 E. Main St. (Parkview Ave.) | 614-231-5364
Dublin | 1 W. Bridge St. (High St.) | 614-792-5364
Grandview Heights | 1281 Grandview Heights Ave. (3rd Ave.) | 614-488-2680
Powell | 8 N. Liberty St. (Olentangy St.) | 614-846-1060
www.jenisicecreams.com

Vanilla visitors turn into "daredevils" sampling the "innovative", "taste bud–popping" flavors ("salty caramel", "goat cheese with red cherries") crafted from "local products" like Ohio cream and "seasonal" fruits at this "pricey" but "glorious" ice cream "empire" created by Jeni Britton Bauer; though there's a wait "even in the dead of winter", the "buzzing" line and generous "try-before-you-buy" policy lead the way to "heaven-in-a-cone" confections that "help you discover ice cream anew."

Kihachi ☒ *Japanese* | - | - | - | VE |

Dublin | 2667 Federated Blvd. (Sawmill Rd.) | 614-764-9040
Even "expats" deem this "hidden" Dublin "destination" "up to Tokyo izakaya standards" with its "seasonal" sushi and "fine, authentic" small plates highlighting "rare ingredients" (pro tip: "ask for a translation" of the Japanese specials on "Post-It Notes"); while the edible art doesn't come cheaply or quickly, most are content to savor the "experience" in the spare yet "beautiful" setting with tatami-matted "private rooms."

L'Antibes ☒M *French* | 28 | 23 | 28 | $55 |

Short North | 772 N. High St. (Warren St.) | 614-291-1666 | www.lantibes.com
Chef-owner Matthew Litzinger's twin passions – he studied cooking at CIA and music at Miami of Ohio – are evident in the harmonious, "flawless" dishes (enhanced by "subtle" sauces and "well-paired" wines) at this "intimate" French "gem" "hidden" in the rowdy Short North; though some feel the decor could use "more character", the "talented" staff lends "warmth" to the "expensive but incredible" dinner, a "two to three-hour" evening culminating with a "handwritten souvenir menu."

M ☒ *American* | 28 | 28 | 27 | $52 |

Downtown | 2 Miranova Pl. (Mound St.) | 614-629-0000 | www.matmiranova.com
It "should be called mmm" gush guests about Cameron Mitchell's "high-end" Dowtown "flagship" – a "sleek" and "chic" "eye-candy" palace (voted No. 1 for Decor in Columbus) with "pampering" service and a "fabulous" patio; "splendid" cocktails precede "stylish", "delicious" New American bistro fare tinged with "Asian fusion" accents, topped off with "new twists on old childhood-favorite" desserts; P.S. a post-Survey chef change is not reflected in the Food score.

Max & Erma's *American* | 23 | 22 | 22 | $21 |

Downtown | The Lofts Hotel | 55 E. Nationwide Blvd. (bet. High & 3rd Sts.) | 614-228-5555
Easton | Eastern Town Center | 178 Easton Town Ctr. (bet. Chagrin Dr. & Easton Loop) | 614-337-9090
German Village | 739 S. Third St. (Frankfort St.) | 614-444-0917
Polaris | 1515 Polaris Pkwy. (Lyra Dr.) | 614-840-9466
Dublin | 411 Metro Pl. N. (Frantz Rd.) | 614-889-8111
Dublin | 7480 Sawmill Rd. (Hard Rd.) | 614-760-8585
Gahanna | 1317 N. Hamilton Rd. (Morse Rd.) | 614-471-0009
Gahanna | Port Columbus International Airport | 4600 International Gateway (Stelzer Rd.) | 614-238-7398
Pickerington | 1281 Hill Rd. N. (Stonecreek Dr.) | 614-759-9989
Westerville | 790 N. State St. (Maxtown Rd.) | 614-891-9396
www.maxandermas.com
Additional locations throughout the Columbus area
Devotees of this "homegrown" "favorite", rated Most Popular chain in Columbus, appreciate its "reliable", "varied" all-American menu featuring famously "oversized" burgers, "out-of-this-world" tortilla soups

and "ooey-gooey" chocolate chip cookies for "moderate prices"; with "casual" decor ("plenty of things to look at") and "prompt, friendly" service, it's a "handy" choice that pleases the "whole family."

Mazah *Mediterranean*   28 | 19 | 27 | $17

Grandview Heights | 1439 Grandview Ave. (5th Ave.) | 614-488-3633 | www.mazah-eatery.com

The "exceptional" Mediterranean food is traditional (with some uncommon Lebanese items) and "just plain delicious" at this Grandview "jewel" whose owner hails from the family behind Sinbad's, a pioneering shawarma shop from decades past; accommodating with affordable entrees and meze, it's a "cute" "hole-in-the-wall" that many wish would "take over the whole block."

Northstar Café *American*   27 | 23 | 23 | $17

Clintonville | 4241 N. High St. (Deland Ave.) | 614-784-2233
Easton | Easton Mall | 4015 Townsfair Way (Chagrin Dr.) | 614-532-5444
Short North | 951 N. High St. (2nd Ave.) | 614-298-9999
www.thenorthstarcafe.com

"This place rocks!" effuse fans of this "hip" New American trio whose omnivorous, "organic"-leaning and "unique" (if "limited") American menu stars a veggie burger so "revelatory" that many "hard-core carnivores consistently choose it"; "generous" portions, "above-and-beyond" counter crews and "high-energy" interiors with "thoughtful touches" (like "well-stocked" magazine racks) ameliorate sometimes "annoying" lines and "above-average" prices; P.S. don't miss the "tasty" housemade sodas and "awesome" cookies.

Piada *Italian*   23 | 19 | 22 | $12

Easton | 4025 Easton Station St. (bet. Chagrin Dr. & Easton Square Pl.) | 614-532-6551
Bexley | 2585 E. Main St. (Remington Rd.) | 614-754-1834
Dublin | 6335 Perimeter Dr. (Avery-Muirfield Dr.) | 614-389-5394
Dublin | 6495 Sawmill Rd. (Banker Dr.) | 614-389-2069
Gahanna | 4697 Morse Rd. (Stoneridge Dr.) | 614-532-5073
Upper Arlington | 1315 W. Lane Ave. (North Star Rd.) | 614-754-1702
www.mypiada.com

Often called a "healthy" "Italian Chipotle", this "pick-and-choose" local chain has moved "refreshing" Boot-style "street food" into a sleek "industrial atmosphere" that stirs up a "busy" lunchtime scene; adherents applaud "huge" servings, numerous "veggie mix-ins" and "fast" assembly-line crews (even though "tons of combinations" mean you might "ruin your own dish").

Pistacia Vera *Bakery/French*   29 | 26 | 25 | $14

German Village | 541 S. Third St. (Hoster St.) | 614-220-9070 | www.pistaciavera.com

"Masterful desserts" like "true" French macarons and "amazing" tarts have "found a home" in German Village at this "spectacular", "tastefully modern" "boutique bakery", voted No. 1 for Food in Columbus, that easily rivals the "best" anywhere, "including Paris and Lyon"; "clean, bright" and "hip", it's not limited to sweets either, because "Provençal-baked eggs" and other specialties make it an "excellent" if "overlooked" brunch and lunch destination; P.S. closes at 7 PM.

	FOOD	DECOR	SERVICE	COST

Refectory ☒ *French*
`28` `26` `28` `$52`

Northwest | 1092 Bethel Rd. (Kenny Rd.) | 614-451-9774 |
www.refectory.com

Gleaming stained-glass windows and soaring rafter beams show this
"dreamlike", "romantic" Northwest "landmark" to be a 19th-century
"converted church", so it's not surprising that reverent diners of the
"inspired", "breathtaking" French cuisine by chef Richard Blondin
(who studied under Paul Bocuse) might offer up "prayers of thanks";
with a "superb" wine cellar and an "extraordinary" staff (earning it the
No. 1 score for Service in Columbus), it can be a "pricey" affair – unless you know about the "bistro menu" and "happy-hour" deals.

Rigsby's Kitchen ☒ *Italian*
`27` `26` `26` `$42`

Short North | 698 N. High St. (bet. Buttles Ave. & Lincoln St.) |
614-461-7888 | www.rigsbyskitchen.com

Synonymous with the resurgence of the Short North, this "cutting-
edge" Northern Italian stalwart – a "chic" hangout attracting a
"power crowd" – helped "change the Columbus food scene" over
two decades ago and remains "remarkable" for its "exciting" cuisine, smartly curated "Italo-centric" wine list and "snazzy" "SoHo"
vibe; with "professional" service completing the picture, many say it's
"still the king."

Schmidt's Restaurant und Sausage Haus *German*
`26` `24` `24` `$20`

German Village | 240 E. Kossuth St. (Purdy Alley) | 614-444-6808 |
www.schmidthaus.com

Since the 1960s, this "Columbus classic" has put the German in German
Village, and loyalists love its "famous", "rib-sticking" and "wurst"-heavy
Teutonic buffet (nicknamed "the autobahn") that offers "incredible
savings"; "tour buses of people" also show up for its "biergarten" atmosphere, live "sing-along" "oompah" music, a "happy" dirndl-
donning staff and "epic" cream puffs – despite occasional "long waits"
and "parking issues."

Skillet Ⓜ *American*
`26` `18` `20` `$21`

German Village | 410 E. Whittier St. (Beach St.) | 614-443-2266 |
www.skilletruf.com

The "masterful" (and often "pork"-centric) New American fare whipped
up at this "farm-to-table" German Villager has "taken the city by storm",
"blowing away other restaurants where you'd spend two or three
times" the money; while the staff "knows its stuff", a "no-rez" policy
means you'll "often have to wait" for a seat in the arty, "cramped"
quarters (the "lack of decor is the decor"), especially during weekend
brunch; P.S. closed Monday–Tuesday; no dinner Saturday–Sunday.

Thurman Cafe *Burgers*
`26` `20` `21` `$17`

German Village | 183 Thurman Ave. (Jaeger St.) | 614-443-1570 |
www.thethurmancafe.com

"If you love burgers" that are "wonderful, juicy, sloppy" and "ridiculously large" (with a "feast" of potential toppings), then "go hungry"
to this "must-hit" "rustic tavern" in German Village; but "if you're in a
hurry, go someplace else" because "two-hour waits" aren't uncommon, despite the efforts of the "busy" staff.

Connecticut

	Restaurant	Cuisine
29	Le Petit Café	French
28	PolytechnicON20	American
	Thomas Henkelmann	French
	Mill at 2T	American
	Jean-Louis	French
	Basso Café	Mediterranean
27	Isabelle et Vincent	Bakery/French
	Max Downtown	American/Steak
	Café Routier	French
	Bernard's	French
	Valencia Luncheria	Venezuelan
	Tawa	Indian
	Schoolhouse	American
	Woodward House*	American
	Union League	French
	Bricco	Italian
	Ibiza	Spanish
	Bonda	American/Eclectic
	Le Farm	American
	Da Pietro's	French/Italian

OTHER NOTEWORTHY PLACES

Restaurant	Cuisine
Bar Boucheé	French
Barcelona	Spanish
Boathouse	American
Columbus Park	Italian
Community Table	American
Coromandel	Indian
David Burke Prime	Steak
Frank Pepe	Pizza
Match	American
Max's Oyster Bar	Seafood
Mayflower Inn	American
Napa & Co.	American
Oyster Club	New England
Pip's at the Copper Beech	American
Rebeccas	American
Restaurant L&E	French
Still River	American
Thali	Indian
West Street Grill	American
Winvian	American

* Indicates a tie with restaurant above

FOOD | DECOR | SERVICE | COST

Bar Bouchée *French*

▽ 28 | 26 | 25 | $46

Madison | 8 Scotland Ave. (Rte. 1) | 203-318-8004

A "remarkable version of a classic small Paris bistro" can be found in Madison, courtesy of the folks behind New Haven's Union League Cafe, where "spectacular" Gallic dishes are served by a "welcoming" staff in a "charming", "Frenchy-chic" room; "good luck" securing a reservation say those suffering from "table envy" (seating in the bar is first come, first served).

Barcelona Restaurant & Wine Bar ◑ *Spanish*

24 | 21 | 21 | $42

Fairfield | Hi Ho Motel | 4180 Black Rock Tpke. (Rte. 15) | 203-255-0800
Greenwich | 18 W. Putnam Ave. (Greenwich Ave.) | 203-983-6400
New Haven | Omni Hotel | 155 Temple St. (Crown St.) | 203-848-3000
South Norwalk | 63 N. Main St. (bet. Marshall & West Sts.) | 203-899-0088
Stamford | 222 Summer St. (Broad St.) | 203-348-4800
West Hartford | 971 Farmington Ave. (bet. LaSalle Rd. & Main St.) | 860-218-2100
www.barcelonawinebar.com

"*Viva España!*" exclaim amigos over the "intense flavors" of the Spanish tapas that "take hold of your taste buds" at this "jumping" chainlet where the "young at heart in heat" share small plates, sangria and Iberian wines served by an "attentive" staff amid "eclectic, urbane" surroundings; frugal types grouse about "pricey" bites and "high markups", but give an "*olé*" to half-price vino on Sundays.

Basso Café Ⓜ *Mediterranean*

28 | 18 | 23 | $46

Norwalk | 124 New Canaan Ave. (Bartlett Ave.) | 203-354-6566 | www.bassobistrocafe.com

"Shhh" say fans of this "charming" cafe in an "unlikely" strip-mall location in Norwalk's Broad River, for it's still a "great secret" among those in the know with "discerning palates" who appreciate its "imaginative", "high-quality" Mediterranean fare with "interesting" South American accents; what's more, the "understated" space is "surprisingly comfortable" and "BYO keeps the price reasonable."

Bernard's Ⓜ *French*

27 | 26 | 27 | $68

Ridgefield | 20 West Ln. (Main St.) | 203-438-8282 | www.bernardsridgefield.com

Chef-owner Bernard Bouissou turns out "superbly crafted" "classic" French fare "with a twist" at this Ridgefield "favorite" situated in an "upscale", "comfortable country-inn" setting; a "warm" staff, "outstanding wine list" and live piano on weekends help make it "the place to go for a special occasion" and "worth every penny"; P.S. the "more casual" Sarah's Wine Bar serves a separate, less expensive bistro menu.

Boathouse at Saugatuck Ⓜ *American*

25 | 24 | 23 | $49

Westport | Saugatuck Rowing Club | 521 Riverside Ave. (Bridge St.) | 203-227-3399 | www.saugatuckrowing.com

"Hiding in the Saugatuck Rowing Club", this Westport New American is the showcase for John Holzwarth's "fabulous, fresh" "locavore" cuisine that comes in "beautiful presentations", served in a "tasteful", "nautical" setting with a "picturesque balcony" that commands a "gorgeous view" of the Saugatuck River; the staff is generally "friendly" and "attentive", and while the prices may be on the "high side" for some, fans insist the "quality is way up there" too.

Bonda ☒Ⓜ *American/Eclectic* | 27 | 22 | 25 | $55

Fairfield | 75 Hillside Rd. (Bronson Rd.) | 203-292-9555 | www.bondarestaurant.com

Jamie Cooper's globally influenced American-Eclectic cuisine remains "creative and consistently outstanding" and the "wonderful" staff "still makes you feel at home" at his establishment, which moved from Westport to Fairfield's tony Greenfield Hill section a couple years ago; many say the "inviting" space is "much improved" from the previous site and "really showcases his talents" – just "don't plan on a quiet intimate evening" some caution, since "it gets a bit noisy in the front."

Bricco *Italian* | 27 | 23 | 24 | $40

West Hartford | 78 Lasalle Rd. (Farmington Ave.) | 860-233-0220 | www.billygrant.com

Billy Grant's "clubby" "mainstay" in West Hartford is "always busy – for good reason": namely, "spectacular", "creative" Italian cuisine and a "wonderful wine list" that are both "reasonably priced"; a "caring, well-informed staff" oversees the "lively dining room filled with happy people" as well as the "busy bar scene", while the "outdoor space is especially inviting in warm weather"; and if "waits can be long" due to "no reservations for parties of five or less", Bricco's Trattoria in Glastonbury should help with the overflow.

Café Routier *French* | 27 | 22 | 25 | $48

Westbrook | 1353 Boston Post Rd. (bet. Burdick & Goodspeed Drs.) | 860-399-8700 | www.caferoutier.com

A "Shoreline star", this French bistro is an "oasis of quality" in Westbrook, serving "creative" seasonal menus featuring locally sourced ingredients, "eclectic" regional menus full of "surprises" from around the globe, "inventive" specials and its "regular winners", all complemented by a "superb" wine list and "impeccable" service; the dining room is "quiet" and "cozy", but some say the lounge (which offers a separate menu) can get "really noisy", and even though it's "tough to get into during the summer", many conclude it's "worth the wait."

Columbus Park Trattoria ☒ *Italian* | 25 | 20 | 23 | $47

Stamford | 205 Main St. (Washington Blvd.) | 203-967-9191 | www.columbusparktrattoria.com

"Authentic dishes not usually found outside Italy" (including "divine homemade pastas") have been "consistently palate-pleasing for decades" at this "always-friendly Downtown Stamford gem", where the "all-in-the-family operation" "bends over backward trying to please its guests"; some complain of "New York" prices and "cramped" quarters that get "noisy" when "crowded", but most insist its "tasty perfection" is "not to be missed."

Community Table *American* | ▽ 27 | 20 | 21 | $51

Washington | 223 Litchfield Tpke. (Wilbur Rd.) | 860-868-9354 | www.communitytablect.com

At this Washington New American, "inventive" chef Joel Viehland's "ever-changing menus" of "uniformly excellent" dishes emphasizing "fresh food from local farms" are "meant to entice knowing loca-

| | FOOD | DECOR | SERVICE | COST |

vores"; opinions are split on the spare room made with green building materials ("original and attractive" vs. "charmless" and "noisy"), but for most it's a "splendid addition to the Litchfield County dining scene", now taking reservations; P.S. closed Tuesdays and Wednesdays.

Coromandel *Indian*

25 | 18 | 22 | $34

Darien | Goodwives Shopping Ctr. | 25 Old Kings Hwy. N. (Sedgewick Ave.) | 203-662-1213
Orange | Hitchcock Plaza | 185 Boston Post Rd. (Diana St.) | 203-795-9055
South Norwalk | 86 Washington St. (bet. Main & Water Sts.) | 203-852-1213
Stamford | 68 Broad St. (Summer St.) | 203-964-1010
www.coromandelcuisine.com

Lovers of this "distinctive" Indian chain sing "Jai Ho!" over its "amazing", "aromatic" cuisine, including a "sensational lunch buffet" that's a "steal", as well as "courteous", "helpful" servers who are "always willing to educate" you about the "authentic" menu that "traverses all of India's regions"; while a few feel the decorator needs to "tone it down" a bit, others find the interiors "charming."

DaPietro's ⊠ *French/Italian*

27 | 20 | 25 | $64

Westport | 36 Riverside Ave. (Post Rd.) | 203-454-1213 | www.dapietros.com

Chef-owner "Pietro Scotti knocks 'em dead with his brilliant cuisine" at this French–Northern Italian "favorite for milestone celebrations" in Downtown Westport, whose large wine list, "impeccable" service and "high" tabs abet its reputation as a merchant of "everlasting memories"; just try to "make reservations far in advance", because the "jewellike" setting is "Lilliputian"; P.S. "don't miss" the "reasonably priced" weekday lunch prix fixe.

David Burke Prime *Steak*

26 | 24 | 25 | $70

Ledyard | Foxwoods Resort Casino | 350 Trolley Lane Blvd. (bet. Grand Pequot Ave. & Watson Rd.) | 860-312-8753 | www.davidburkeprime.com

Fans feel like they've "hit the jackpot" at this "nice-looking" ("if you like black-and-white cowhide") Foxwoods steakhouse where "terrific" dry-aged prime cuts come via "attentive" servers; of course, you might need a "platinum card" to pay for it, but go ahead, "treat yourself."

Frank Pepe Pizzeria Napoletana *Pizza*

24 | 11 | 17 | $21

Danbury | 59 Federal Rd. (White Turkey Rd.) | 203-790-7373
Fairfield | 238 Commerce Dr. (Berwick Ct.) | 203-333-7373
Manchester | 221 Buckland Hills Dr. (bet. Buckland & Deming Sts.) | 860-644-7333
New Haven | 157 Wooster St. (Brown St.) | 203-865-5762
Uncasville | Mohegan Sun Casino | 1 Mohegan Sun Blvd. (bet. Rtes. 2 & 32) | 860-862-8888 ◗

Frank Pepe's The Spot Ⓜ *Pizza*

New Haven | 163 Wooster St. (Brown St.) | 203-865-7602
www.pepespizzeria.com

"There's magic in that coal-fired brick oven" swear fans of the New Haven pizzeria "mecca" and its outposts, voted Connecticut's Most Popular for what many claim is "the most memorable pie you'll ever inhale", boasting thin, chewy crusts "with the right hint of smokiness" and toppings like "fresh shucked" clams, which is worth enduring "long waits" and "grumpy" service; while some find it "overrated" and accuse the branches of "living on New Haven's reputation", most aver that "all the fussing and the buzz is true."

Ibiza ⑤ *Spanish* 27 | 21 | 23 | $49

New Haven | 39 High St. (bet. Chapel & Crown Sts.) | 203-865-1933 | www.ibizanewhaven.com

Ibiza Tapas *Spanish*

Hamden | 1832 Dixwell Ave. (Robert St.) | 203-909-6512 | www.ibizatapaswinebar.com

At this "classy" New Haven Spaniard, the tapas (served at the bar) and tasting menus are "exotic and yet mainstream", complemented by an "ample" wine list and served by an "attentive" staff in a "contemporary" setting; meanwhile, its "non-tweedy" Hamden offspring is an "excellent addition" to an otherwise "run-down retail" district, offering the same "fabulous" flavors as the mother ship with a "more casual flair" and more affordable price points, though some caution it "does get loud" and no reservations can mean "long lines on weekends."

Isabelle et Vincent Ⓜ *Bakery/French* 27 | 22 | 22 | $19

Fairfield | 1903 Post Rd. (bet. Bungalow Ave. & Granville St.) | 203-292-8022 | www.isabelleetvincent.com

"Quiet your inner expat" at this "heavenly" patisserie that's a "virtual voyage to Paris" with its "immense selection" of "exquisite" breads and pastries and "world-class" chocolates; Strasbourg natives Isabelle and Vincent Koenig "greet you with a warm smile" in the "tiny" bakery, and while it's "not cheap", most agree "France's loss is Fairfield's gain."

Jean-Louis ⑤ *French* 28 | 24 | 25 | $75

Greenwich | 61 Lewis St. (bet. Greenwich Ave. & Mason St.) | 203-622-8450 | www.restaurantjeanlouis.com

"Food heaven" is what fans call chef-owner Jean-Louis Gerin's Greenwich French thanks to his "extraordinary" cuisine, "prepared with art, professionalism and love"; add an "excellent wine list", "impeccable" service and a "lovely" setting, and it's a "superb" package; those who can "only afford to go once a decade" will welcome the prix fixe lunch ($29), dinner ($59) and tasting ($69) menus, while a recent redo adds a chef's bar with a view of the kitchen and a $49 set-price dinner.

Le Farm ⑤Ⓜ *American* 27 | 20 | 23 | $61

Westport | 256 Post Rd. E. (bet. Compo Rd. & Imperial Ave.) | 203-557-3701 | www.lefarmwestport.com

At his high-end Westport New American, chef-owner Bill Taibe "wows you from start to finish" with his "fantastic", "fresh, seasonal" cuisine that demonstrates his "dedication to local producers"; the staff is "friendly and helpful", and the "cozy" space has a "farmhouse feel", so while it may be "oh-so-trendy", most agree this "winner" "walks the walk."

Le Petit Café Ⓜ *French* 29 | 24 | 28 | $68

Branford | 225 Montowese St. (Main St.) | 203-483-9791 | www.lepetitcafe.net

"As good as it gets" in Connecticut, Roy Ip's "charming" Branford bistro was voted the state's No. 1 for Food thanks to his "brilliant" cuisine that'll "leave you speechless" over a four-course prix fixe menu "with plenty of choices"; the "delightful" toque "greets you at the door", and he and his "gracious" staff make you "feel like a treasured guest" in the "attractive", "intimate" space, which is all the more reason many deem it one of the "best dining values in the U.S."; P.S. only two seatings per night.

Match *American* | 26 | 22 | 23 | $50 |
South Norwalk | 98 Washington St. (bet. Main & Water Sts.) | 203-852-1088 | www.matchsono.com
Chef/co-owner "Matt Storch's creativity is unmatched" and it shows in his "superb" "seasonal" New American cuisine boasting "inventive food combinations" at this "happening" SoNo favorite, while "friendly, knowledgeable" service enhances the experience; the scene is "hip but cozy", and there's "lots of good people-watching" in the "loud, crowded" bar and outdoor patio, so while it's "pricey", many reckon it's "worth every penny."

Max Downtown *American/Steak* | 27 | 25 | 27 | $57 |
Hartford | City Pl. | 185 Asylum St. (bet. Ann & Trumbull Sts.) | 860-522-2530 | www.maxrestaurantgroup.com
"Every meal is a celebration" at the "flagship" of the Max group in Downtown Hartford, a "big-time", "big-city" New American offering "delectable" steaks, "top-shelf seafood" and other "creative" dishes with a spotlight on "locally grown" ingredients; "superb" service helps you feel "comfortable" in the "steakhouse" setting with "tasteful modern decor", and contributes to the satisfying sense that "you're in the right place at the right time."

Max's Oyster Bar *Seafood* | 26 | 24 | 24 | $47 |
West Hartford | 964 Farmington Ave. (S. Main St.) | 860-236-6299 | www.maxrestaurantgroup.com
While the "raw bar rocks" with "fresh, exotic" oysters at this "bivalve blowout" in the West Hartford Center, fish "cooked to perfection" and "fabulous steaks" also impress, as do the "excellent wines by the glass" and "professional, helpful" service; the ambiance is "divine" in the upscale setting with a "big-city feel", though some say it's "not a place for a romantic dinner", with "too much going on" (read: "noisy"), and it's "expensive", so take care not to max out your plastic.

Mayflower Inn Restaurant *American* | 24 | 28 | 24 | $72 |
Washington | The Mayflower Inn & Spa | 118 Woodbury Rd. (Rte. 199) | 860-868-9466 | www.mayflowerinn.com
"Just setting foot in" this "elegant" Relais & Chateaux "country inn" and "destination restaurant" in Washington "will make you feel special" swoon surveyors smitten by the "heaven-on-earth" surroundings and "sophisticated" American cuisine "presented beautifully" by a "caring" staff; while it's "outstanding in all regards for the money-is-no-object set", it may be "overpriced for the cost-conscious", some of whom recommend dining in the Tap Room as a "nicer", more casual alternative to the main dining room.

Mill at 2T ⊠Ⓜ *American* | 28 | 28 | 26 | $57 |
Tariffville | 2 Tunxis Rd. (Rte. 189) | 860-658-7890 | www.themillat2T.com
Despite its bucolic location in the "woods by a river", Kelleanne and Ryan Jones' "elegant" 38-seat New American, housed in a "beautiful",

"inviting" converted mill in Tariffville, makes you "feel like you're in NYC" with Ryan's "consistently excellent, inventive" cuisine featuring "fresh, local" ingredients, which is backed by a "clever" wine list; husband and wife are "wonderful hosts" and their staff is "unfailingly pleasant and knowledgeable", so sure, it's "expensive", but most agree the experience is "worthy of the bill"; P.S. open for dinner Wednesday–Saturday, and a spot at the chef's counter can be reserved same day.

Napa & Co. 🗷 American — 24 | 23 | 22 | $56
Stamford | 75 Broad St. (bet. Bedford & Summer Sts.) | 203-353-3319 | www.napaandcompany.com

Oenophiles "know they're going to have a great night" once they "see the wall of wine" at this "trendy" Stamford New American where "creative", "locally sourced" farm-to-table fare and "excellent pairings" are served by a "professional" staff; while some critics find it "too noisy" and "overpriced", claiming it's trying too hard "to be NYC", others promise a "memorable meal", whether it's a "casual dinner or more formal night out."

Oyster Club New England — - | - | - | M
Mystic | 13 Water St. (Fort Rachel Pl.) | 860-415-9266 | www.oysterclubct.com

The menu changes daily at this farm-and-sea-to-table venture in historic Downtown Mystic serving reasonably priced New England coastal cuisine influenced by executive chef (and former River Tavern toque) James Wayman's travels in Thailand and Oaxaca, featuring classics such as lobster rolls and grass-fed hamburgers as well as creative bites (think chocolate chip–and-bacon cookies); there's a lively scene around the zinc-topped bar (with happy-hour raw bar specials) and in the rustic dining room under exposed beams.

Pip's at the Copper Beech American/French — - | - | - | E
(fka Brasserie Pip)
Ivoryton | Copper Beech Inn | 46 Main St. (Johnny Cake Ln.) | 860-767-0330 | www.copperbeechinn.com

The owners of the "gorgeous" Copper Beech Inn in Ivoryton have combined the erstwhile Copper Beech restaurant and Brasserie Pip under one *parapluie,* and the result is "a little more brasserie" than the former and "a bit more upscale" than the latter; a "less expensive" French–New American menu is served in a chic bistro and formal dining room.

PolytechnicON20 🗷 American — 28 | 28 | 29 | $64
Hartford | Hartford Steam Boiler Bldg. | 1 State St., 20th fl. (Columbus Blvd.) | 860-722-5161 | www.ontwenty.com

While the "open, airy" 20th-floor setting with "spectacular views" of the Connecticut River and "exemplary", "sophisticated" service earn this Hartford New American Connecticut's No. 1 Decor and Service honors, "masterful" chef Noel Jones' "divine" cuisine and "well-thought-out pairings" from an "extensive wine list" make it "truly something special"; it's "expensive", but most feel the prices are "fair", so the "only downside" seems to be "limited hours" (lunch only Monday–Friday, happy hour and dinner on Fridays).

	FOOD	DECOR	SERVICE	COST

Rebeccas 🛇 Ⓜ *American* | 26 | 21 | 23 | $80 |

Greenwich | 265 Glenville Rd. (bet. Pemberwick & Riversville Rds.) | 203-532-9270 | www.rebeccasgreenwich.com

The "tantalizing flavors" and "beautiful presentations" on chef/co-owner Reza Khorshidi's "imaginative menu" make this Greenwich New American a "culinary paradise", one that's "run like a well-oiled machine" by his "gracious" wife and partner, Rebecca, and their "professional" staff; "exquisite flowers" grace the "lovely environment", but some grouse that "regular customers" are favored, while wallet-watchers wince at the "*très* haute prices."

Restaurant L&E Ⓜ *French* ▽ 24 | - | 22 | $63 |

Chester | 59 Main St. (Maple St.) | 860-526-5301 | www.restaurantlande.com

This "real find" (the former Restaurant du Village) is "worth the drive" to Chester according to loyal followers, now buzzing about an expansion – an elegant, second-story salon, decorated with French country antiques, and roof deck – serving "superlative" seasonal New French fare from chef Everett Reid alongside a "superb" wine list; meanwhile, the more casual French 75 Bistro, with copper-topped tables and cozy banquettes, has taken over the street-level dining room; service remains "accommodating" both upstairs and down, with Madame Christine greeting all with a welcoming '*bonjour.*'

Schoolhouse at Cannondale Ⓜ *American* | 27 | 23 | 24 | $59 |

Wilton | 34 Cannon Rd. (Seeley Rd.) | 203-834-9816 | www.theschoolhouseatcannondale.com

Fans would stay "after school any day of the week" to savor chef-owner Tim LaBant's "fabulous" menu of "inspired" New American cuisine showcasing "locally grown produce" at his "pricey" Wilton restaurant, housed in a "charming former one-room schoolhouse" overlooking the Norwalk River; the toque "talks with every guest" while his staff provides "attentive" service, and though some surveyors say they could use a hall pass from the "cramped" quarters, most give it extra credit for a "delightful dining experience."

Still River Café Ⓜ *American* ▽ 28 | 26 | 27 | $67 |

Eastford | 134 Union Rd. (Centre Pike) | 860-974-9988 | www.stillrivercafe.com

A "destination in the beautiful Quiet Corner", this weekend-dinner-only (plus lunch on Sundays) Eastford New American set on a 27-acre farm is where Kara Brooks "turns up the volume of taste full blast" in her "fabulous" dishes prepared with "elegance, style" and "locally grown ingredients", including organic produce grown by husband Robert; "quietly competent" service and an "open, inviting" space in a refurbished barn also make it a "place to celebrate life"; P.S. closes end of October and reopens in spring, so call ahead.

Tawa *Indian* | 27 | 22 | 23 | $34 |

Stamford | 211 Summer St. (bet. Broad & Main Sts.) | 203-359-8977 | www.tawaonline.com

It's "worth the vertical trek" upstairs to the second-floor fine-dining area of this Indian in Downtown Stamford offering a "unique menu" of dishes filled with "gorgeous flavors", including a daily lunch buffet; a subtly bejeweled setting, "solicitous staff" and "incredibly low prices for the quality" are further draws, as is the small-plate Bread Bar on the ground floor.

Thali *Indian*
24 | 20 | 21 | $38

New Canaan | 87 Main St. (bet. East & Locust Aves.) | 203-972-8332
New Haven | 4 Orange St. (George St.) | 203-777-1177
Ridgefield | Ridgefield Motor Inn | 296 Ethan Allen Hwy. (Florida Hill Rd.) | 203-894-1080
www.thali.com

Thali Too *Indian*
New Haven | Yale University campus | 65 Broadway (Elm St.) | 203-776-1600 | www.thalitoo.com

"Sophisticated", "innovative" dishes and "generous" drinks are the specialties of these "decently priced" Indians; all branches boast "cool", "upscale" settings and generally "professional" service, but each offers its own distinct feature, among them an "aerial waterfall" in New Canaan, "well-prepared vegetarian" fare at Thali Too and a "no-tell motel setting" in Ridgefield ("don't be put off" by it).

Thomas Henkelmann ⊠Ⓜ *French*
28 | 28 | 28 | $90

Greenwich | Homestead Inn | 420 Field Point Rd. (bet. Bush Ave. & Merica Ln.) | 203-869-7500 | www.thomashenkelmann.com

"Everything is simply exquisite" at this "destination restaurant" in a "beautiful Victorian mansion" in Greenwich, from the eponymous chef's "fabulous", "memorable" New French cuisine served by a "seasoned staff" to the "luxurious", "tasteful" decor; "expensive" tabs match the "formal" (ok, "a bit stuffy"), jackets-required (at dinner) atmosphere, but "for that special occasion", it's "worth it."

Union League Cafe ⊠ *French*
27 | 27 | 26 | $60

New Haven | 1032 Chapel St. (bet. College & High Sts.) | 203-562-4299 | www.unionleaguecafe.com

A "destination for that special event or celebration", this "New Haven landmark" across from the Yale campus is the showcase for chef Jean-Pierre Vuillermet's "masterful", "precisely prepared" French cuisine, backed by a "superior" wine list and served in the "comfortable" environs of a "historic" building with a "wonderful old-school atmosphere"; the service is "impeccable" but "not snooty", and while many wince at the "bankers' prices", the $35 pre-theater prix fixe can give those who don't have "expense accounts" a taste of "what fine dining is meant to be."

Valencia Luncheria *Venezuelan*
27 | 10 | 17 | $22

Norwalk | 164 Main St. (bet. Center & Plymouth Aves.) | 203-846-8009 | www.valencialuncheria.com

"Let your taste buds become your primary sense" at this "inexpensive" Norwalk Venezuelan serving "heaping portions" of "innovative, perfectly prepared" food all day, including "incredible" arepas, "awesome" *pernil* (roast pork) and empanadas "thick with excellent fillings"; in a post-Survey move (that outdates the Decor score), it's taken over a larger space down the street, adding a bar and patio.

West Street Grill *American*
24 | 21 | 23 | $57

Litchfield | 43 West St. (North St.) | 860-567-3885 | www.weststreetgrill.com
Mixing "upscale dining with relaxed Connecticut countryside" "works very well" for this "iconic" Litchfield New American that offers "inven-

tive", "high-quality" fare and an "excellent" wine list in a "lovely" setting, garnering a "loyal following" that includes "locals and celebs"; while the service is "top-notch" and the owners "pay attention that all goes well", a few are put off by the "'in' crowd" vibe.

Winvian M *American* ∇ 27 | 28 | 26 | $87

Litchfield | Winvian Resort | 155 Alain White Rd. (bet. County & E. Shore Rds.) | 860-567-9600 | www.winvian.com

"Feel like landed gentry" in what seems like "your own private 18th-century dining room" on an "idyllic" country estate in the Litchfield Hills that specializes in seasonal, locally driven American cuisine; the "innovative" menu is a "delight to the senses" and the service is "sophisticated" (i.e. "attentive but not intrusive"), but "cash in your stocks before going" and consider trying to "stay the night in one of the very special cottages" on this Relais & Châteaux property, which many agree is also "out of this world."

Woodward House M *American* 27 | 27 | 26 | $63

Bethlehem | 4 The Green (West Rd.) | 203-266-6902 | www.thewoodwardhouse.com

Each of the four distinctly and "beautifully appointed" rooms in this restored Colonial-era saltbox in Bethlehem is an "intimate" and "memorable" setting for "exquisitely prepared" New American cuisine that most agree is "never less than wonderful"; though the departure of the original chef-owner is not reflected in the Food score, the remaining owner, Adele Reveron, is as "gracious" a host as ever, treating the whole enterprise like an "only child: lovingly and with great care"; P.S. the "special-occasion" tabs can be beat by a $28 three-course prix fixe (a "great buy").

Dallas/Ft. Worth

TOP FOOD RANKING

Restaurant	Cuisine
29	Saint-Emilion	French
	Lucia	Italian
28	French Room	American/French
	Bijoux	French
	Pappas Bros. Steakhouse	Steak
	Mercury	American
27	Abacus	Eclectic
	Bonnell's	Southwestern
	Stephan Pyles	Southwestern
	Cacharel	French
	Suze*	Mediterranean
	Nick & Sam's	Seafood/Steak
	Hattie's	American
	Cavalli Pizza	Pizza
	Sushi Sake	Japanese
	Al Biernat's	Steak
	Esperanza's	Mexican
	Fearing's	Southwestern
	Del Frisco's	Steak
	Lanny's Alta Cocina	Eclectic

OTHER NOTEWORTHY PLACES

Angelo's	BBQ
Bolsa	American
Charlie Palmer	American
Five Sixty	American
Grace	American
Joe T. Garcia's	Tex-Mex
Komali	Mexican
Lonesome Dove	Southwestern
Mansion	American
Mia's	Tex-Mex
Mi Cocina	Tex-Mex
Neighborhood Services	American
Nonna	Italian
Nosh	American
Oak Restaurant	Eclectic
Private Social	Eclectic
Salum	American
Tei An	Japanese
Village Marquee	American
Woodshed Smokehouse	Eclectic

* Indicates a tie with restaurant above

FOOD | DECOR | SERVICE | COST

Abacus ⊠ *Eclectic*
27 | 25 | 27 | $69

Knox-Henderson | 4511 McKinney Ave. (Armstrong Ave.) | Dallas |
214-559-3111 | www.kentrathbun.com
Once again voted Most Popular in Dallas/Ft. Worth, this Knox-
Henderson Eclectic is "still tops" thanks to "superstar" chef Kent
Rathbun's "sublime", "innovative" cuisine ("the lobster shooters are a
must") and "sophisticated" "see-and-be-seen" surroundings where
you feel equally "at home whether in jeans or dressed up"; service is
"smooth and polished" too, so despite a few gripes about "noise",
most are "blown away" – just "bring your sense of adventure" (and
your platinum card).

Al Biernat's *Steak*
27 | 24 | 27 | $65

Oak Lawn | 4217 Oak Lawn Ave. (bet. Herschel & Wycliff Aves.) |
Dallas | 214-219-2201 | www.albiernats.com
"A haven for star athletes and their fans who crave a good steak", this
"loud", lively Oak Lawn "classic" "stands out" with "top-notch" fare
and "supreme" service from Al himself that "makes you feel important"; all this comes at a "high price", though many find it worthwhile
given the "incredible ambiance for deal-making and celebrations."

Angelo's Barbecue ⊠ *BBQ*
25 | 15 | 17 | $16

Near West | 2533 White Settlement Rd. (bet. Henderson St. &
University Dr.) | Ft. Worth | 817-332-0357 | www.angelosbbq.com
"Eat here to understand what brisket is in Texas" proclaim fans of
this BBQ "standard" in Near West Ft. Worth where "exceptional"
meat is washed down with "frosty mugs of cold beer" in an atmosphere that's "a taxidermist's delight"; in sum, it's "a guaranteed good
time for little coin."

Bijoux ⊠ *French*
28 | 25 | 26 | $77

West Lovers Lane | Inwood Vill. | 5450 W. Lovers Ln. (Inwood Rd.) |
Dallas | 214-350-6100 | www.bijouxrestaurant.com
"Lovely for a special occasion", this "classy, quiet" West Lovers Lane
destination provides "superb" New French fare from chef Scott Gottlich
offered in five- and nine-course tastings with à la carte options available too; though it's expensive", many consider it among "Dallas' finest";
P.S. formality in the main dining area has been dialed back post-Survey
with a more relaxed, contemporary look.

Bolsa *American*
25 | 21 | 21 | $35

Oak Cliff | 614 W. Davis St. (Cedar Hill Ave.) | Dallas | 214-367-9367 |
www.bolsadallas.com
It can be a "mob scene" at this "foodie delight" in Oak Cliff cooking up
an "exciting", ever-"changing" New American menu backed by "awesome drinks" crafted by some of the "best mixologists in Dallas"; look
for an "energetic" vibe, "casual but attentive service" and a "fun" patio
packed with "hipsters"; P.S. Bolsa Mercado is a separate market vending local meats, charcuterie and cheeses.

Bonnell's ⊠Ⓜ *Southwestern*
27 | 24 | 27 | $53

Southwest | 4259 Bryant Irvin Rd. (Southwest Blvd.) | Ft. Worth |
817-738-5489 | www.bonnellstexas.com
"Where else can you get elk, ostrich, bison, antelope and boar?" but
at this Southwest Ft. Worth "treasure" specializing in Jon Bonnell's

own brand of "unique" "upscale" "cowboy cuisine" that's "always a treat"; it's not inexpensive, but add in "top-notch" service and "casually elegant" surroundings and it's a "pleasure on every level."

Cacharel ☒ *French* | 27 | 23 | 27 | $50 |

Arlington | Brookhollow Tower Two | 2221 E. Lamar Blvd., 9th fl. (Ballpark Way) | 817-640-9981 | www.cacharel.net
Set in an Arlington office tower "overlooking the Cowboys Stadium dome", this upscale entry delivers true "French fine dining" including "wonderful" Grand Marnier soufflés; it's "a little old-fashioned" and not inexpensive, but with "charming" service and a "spectacular view", it's "perfect" for a business lunch or "romantic dinner."

Cavalli Pizza Napoletana *Pizza* | 27 | 16 | 22 | $15 |

McKinney | 6851 Virginia Pkwy. (Stonebridge Dr.) | 972-540-1449
Irving | 3601 Regent Blvd. (Belt Line Rd.) | 972-915-0001
www.cavallipizza.com
Some of the "best pizza" "outside of Rome" with "chewy crusts" and "interesting" toppings turns up at this Neapolitan twosome in Irving (quick-bite) and McKinney (full service); "reasonable" prices and a BYO policy keep it "crowded" but "worth the wait."

Charlie Palmer Steak *American* | 25 | 26 | 25 | $68 |
(fka Charlie Palmer at the Joule)

Downtown Dallas | Joule Hotel | 1530 Main St. (bet. Akard & Ervay Sts.) | Dallas | 214-261-4600 | www.charliepalmer.com
A "jewel" in the "luxury" Joule Hotel Downtown, this glitzy showcase from celeb chef Charlie Palmer "pampers" guests with "excellent" New American fare, "impressive" wines and "gracious" service in an "elegant" room brimming with "business types"; "it's definitely a wow locale", even if a few find the fare "hit-or-miss" given the prices.

Del Frisco's Double Eagle | 27 | 24 | 26 | $67 |
Steak House *Steak*

North Dallas | 5251 Spring Valley Rd. (Dallas N. Tollway) | Dallas | 972-490-9000
Downtown Ft. Worth | 812 Main St. (8th St.) | Ft. Worth | 817-877-3999
www.delfriscos.com

Del Frisco's Grille *American*

Uptown | 3232 McKinney Ave. (Hall St.) | Dallas | 972-807-6152 | www.delfriscosgrille.com
You might just "need two stomachs" for the "outrageous", "buttery" steaks "cooked to perfection" at this high-end chophouse chain catering to an "expense-account" clientele with its "extensive wine list", "fine" service and setting akin to a "chic Western saloon"; it's especially "great for a special occasion" "if money is no object"; P.S. the Uptown Dallas Grille offers a lighter menu with a focus on cocktails, apps and burgers plus brunch in a more relaxed setting.

Esperanza's Mexican Bakery & | 27 | 17 | 23 | $16 |
Café *Mexican*

Hospital District | 1601 Park Place Ave. (8th Ave.) | Ft. Worth | 817-923-1992

FOOD DECOR SERVICE COST

(continued)

Esperanza's Mexican Bakery & Café
North Side | 2122 N. Main St. (21st St.) | Ft. Worth | 817-626-5770
www.joets.com

The "wow factor" is high at this Ft. Worth Mexican duo from descendents of the Joe T. Garcia–Lancarte family serving "superb" takes on the classics in "homey" surroundings; expect long lines, especially for the "unbeatable" Sunday brunch; P.S. the on-site bakeries vending pan dulce are "not to be missed on the way out."

Fearing's *Southwestern* 27 | 28 | 27 | $75
Uptown | Ritz-Carlton Hotel | 2121 McKinney Ave. (Pearl St.) | Dallas | 214-922-4848 | www.fearingsrestaurant.com

Smitten fans say it "doesn't get any better" than Dean Fearing's "fine-dining" venue in Uptown's Ritz-Carlton Hotel featuring his "spectacular", "sophisticated" Southwestern cooking that's "just plain awesome"; it follows through with "warm" service (Dean himself often "works the room") and a glitzy setting that's a total "scene", so even if some sniff "overrated", the "overall event" is "quite an experience."

Five Sixty Wolfgang Puck ⌷ *American* 24 | 26 | 24 | $69
Downtown Dallas | Reunion Tower | 300 E. Reunion Blvd. (Houston St.) | Dallas | 214-741-5560 | www.wolfgangpuck.com

A "perfect spot to take out-of-town guests", this New American from celeb chef Wolfgang Puck offers "spectacular" 360-degree vistas from a revolving room atop Downtown's Reunion Tower, "fabulous" Asian-accented cuisine and "top-notch" service; some prefer to "stick with drinks and appetizers", because "you pay for the view" dearly.

French Room ⌷Ⓜ *American/French* 28 | 29 | 29 | $90
Downtown Dallas | Hotel Adolphus | 1321 Commerce St. (Field St.) | Dallas | 214-742-8200 | www.hoteladolphus.com

"For a splurge night", fans tout this "top-flight" haute French inside the historic Hotel Adolphus, voted Dallas' No. 1 for Decor and Service thanks to its "breathtaking", "rococo" interior and "impeccable" hospitality; "creative", "perfectly executed" cuisine and "marvelous" wines round out a "superior dining experience" that's "memorable in every way"; P.S. jackets required.

Grace ⌷ *American* 25 | 26 | 25 | $60
Downtown Ft. Worth | 777 Main St. (7th St.) | Ft. Worth | 817-877-3388 | www.gracefortworth.com

"Contemporary, chic" surroundings, "perfectly prepared" steaks and "imaginative" New American dishes, along with a wine list that's "worth a night's reading" and "stellar" service, are the reasons this Downtown eatery is considered one of the "best places for a special evening in Ft. Worth"; though some wince at "expense-account" prices, most concur it's "well worth it."

Hattie's *American* 27 | 25 | 24 | $39
Oak Cliff | 418 N. Bishop Ave. (8th St.) | Dallas | 214-942-7400 | www.hatties.net

"Charleston comes to Dallas" via this American "gem" in a "buzzy area" of Oak Cliff turning out "contemporary", "fancified" takes on Low Country fare ("superb" shrimp and grits, chicken and waffles "to die for"), plus a standout Sunday brunch, in a "modern, civilized" setting; "impeccable" service, a "casual atmosphere" and moderate prices all "soothe the soul."

Joe T. Garcia's ⊉ *Tex-Mex*   20 | 23 | 21 | $24
North Side | 2201 N. Commerce St. (22nd St.) | Ft. Worth | 817-626-4356 | www.joets.com
Devotees dub this "iconic" Ft. Worth "institution" on the North Side the "Holy Grail of Tex-Mex", offering a "solidly good", "no-surprises" menu in the "huge" dining room or on the "massive", "beautiful" patio and poolside garden; some critics find the fare "routine" and contend its appeal is strictly the "scene that it offers" and the "fab" margaritas; P.S. cash only.

Komali *Mexican*   24 | 26 | 24 | $40
Uptown | 4152 Cole Ave. (Fitzhugh Ave.) | Dallas | 214-252-0200 | www.komalirestaurant.com
A "bright, cheery", "modern" space with a long bar and a mosaic fireplace is the backdrop for chef Abraham Salum's "exciting" "interior Mexican" cuisine at this Uptown sibling (and next-door neighbor) of Salum; "fabulous" margs and a "good selection of mezcals" help fuel a lively scene that "can redefine 'loud' on weekend nights."

Lanny's Alta Cocina   27 | 23 | 25 | $52
Mexicana 🆂🅼 *Eclectic*
Cultural District | 3405 W. Seventh St. (Boland St.) | Ft. Worth | 817-850-9996 | www.lannyskitchen.com
"A special-occasion place" that's "matured perfectly in sync with its chef", this upscale Eclectic in the Cultural District "shines" with an "excellent" "creative" menu of Mexican-inspired cuisine from chef-owner Lanny Lancarte (of the Joe T. Garcia's dynasty), backed by a "terrific selection of wines and beers"; the mood is "romantic" in the contemporary space, but some balk at the prices unless they can "dine on someone else's tab."

Lonesome Dove Western   27 | 24 | 26 | $55
Bistro 🆂 *Southwestern*
Stockyards | 2406 N. Main St. (24th St.) | Ft. Worth | 817-740-8810 | www.lonesomedovebistro.com
Celeb chef Tim Love's "signature cowboy cuisine" "shines" in a "Western-themed" setting "with a touch of elegance" at his flagship in the Ft. Worth Stockyards, where "innovative" takes on "game, pork and anything else you'd find on a ranch" are served by an "outstanding" staff amid a "cool", if "loud" scene; "extremely reasonable" lunch specials offset otherwise "high-end" prices.

Lucia 🆂🅼 *Italian*   29 | 21 | 25 | $58
Oak Cliff | 408 W. Eighth St. (Bishop Ave.) | Dallas | 214-948-4998 | www.luciadallas.com
"It takes weeks to get in" to chef David Uygur's tiny Oak Cliff Italian, but his "awesomely creative" cuisine that's "executed to perfection" is "worth the effort"; led by the chef's wife and co-owner, Jennifer, the front-of-house staff "treats you like beloved family" in the rustic 36-seat space, which is housed in a historic building dating back to the '20s.

	FOOD	DECOR	SERVICE	COST

The Mansion *American* | 26 | 28 | 27 | $89 |

Uptown | Rosewood Mansion on Turtle Creek | 2821 Turtle Creek Blvd. (Gillespie St.) | Dallas | 214-559-2100 | www.mansiononturtlecreek.com

"Divine as it's always been", this Uptown icon showcases chef Bruno Davaillon's "impeccable" French-influenced New American cuisine, served by a staff that "couldn't be kinder" in "elegant" environs in a historic boutique luxury hotel; while a few feel "it's not what it used to be", most "highly recommend" it when you want to "pamper yourself and a loved one", though all agree "it helps if the oil wells are still producing when the check arrives."

The Mercury ⊠ *American* | 28 | 24 | 25 | $62 |

Preston Forest | Preston Forest Vill. | 11909 Preston Rd. (Forest Ln.) | Dallas | 972-960-7774 | www.themercurydallas.com

Chef Chris Ward "blends tastes like a harmonious work of art" in his "exceptional" French- and Mediterranean-influenced New American cuisine, served "without attitude" by an "attentive" staff at this upscale sophisticate in Preston Forest; "don't be fooled by the strip-mall location", for it's "beautiful inside", with a "cool, New Yorkish" ambiance and "lively" lounge scene, making it a "must-visit" for many, including former President George W. Bush.

Mia's *Tex-Mex* | 23 | 13 | 19 | $22 |

Lemmon Avenue | 4322 Lemmon Ave. (Wycliff Ave.) | Dallas | 214-526-1020 | www.miastexmex.com

"Two words: brisket tacos" sum up much of the appeal of this Lemmon Avenue *cocina*, a "longtime favorite" for "wonderful", "no-fuss" Tex-Mex, as evidenced by the perpetual "lines" out front; no, there's "not much decor" or "elbow room" either, but bargain prices compensate.

Mi Cocina *Tex-Mex* | 21 | 19 | 20 | $25 |

Lake Highlands | 7201 Skillman St. (Walnut Hill Ln.) | Dallas | 214-503-6426
Park Cities | Highland Park Vill. | 77 Highland Park Vill. (Douglas Ave.) | Dallas | 214-521-6426
Preston Forest | Preston Forest Vill. | 11661 Preston Rd. (bet. Forest Ln. & Preston Haven Dr.) | Dallas | 214-265-7704
West Village | West Vill. | 3699 McKinney Ave. (bet. Blackburn St. & Lemmon Ave.) | Dallas | 469-533-5663
North Dallas | 18352 N. Dallas Pkwy. (Frankford Rd.) | Dallas | 972-250-6426
West Plano | Lakeside Mkt. | 4001 Preston Rd. (Lorimar Dr.) | Plano | 469-467-8655
West Plano | Shops at Legacy | 5760 Legacy Dr. (Bishop Rd.) | Plano | 972-473-8745
Southwest | Chapel Hill Shopping Ctr. | 4601 West Frwy. (Hulen St.) | Ft. Worth | 817-569-1444
Sundance Square | Sundance Sq. | 509 Main St. (bet. 4th & 5th Sts.) | Ft. Worth | 817-877-3600
www.mcrowd.com

It's "always a scene" at these "smartly designed" Tex-Mex cantinas favored by the "young and beautiful" for "well-prepared" "lighter alternatives" and "killer" Mambo Taxi 'ritas ("after two you'll want to mambo and need a taxi"); though a few critics find them "overrated" and "overpriced" for what they are with "spotty" service, defenders insist "these guys know how to run a restaurant."

Neighborhood Services 🗷 *American*   25 | 22 | 23 | $41
West Lovers Lane | 5027 W. Lovers Ln. (Inwood Rd.) | Dallas | 214-350-5027
Neighborhood Services Bar & Grill 🗷 *American*
Preston Royal | 10720 Preston Rd. (Royal Ln.) | Dallas | 214-368-1101
Neighborhood Services Tavern 🗷 *American*
Knox-Henderson | 2405 N. Henderson Ave. (Capital Ave.) | Dallas | 214-827-2405
www.neighborhoodservicesdallas.com

"Haute blue-plate specials" headline chef Nick Badovinus' "ingredient-driven" New American menu delivering "creative twists on homestyle food" at these "hip" "favorites"; the servers are "impressive", and while some critics cite "extremely long waits" (due to a no-reservations policy), others take the opportunity for a little "social networking" at the "trendy bar", or "call ahead and get your name on the list"; P.S. the Tavern on Henderson is a "scaled down, more casual" version of the original.

Nick & Sam's *Seafood/Steak*   27 | 25 | 25 | $75
Uptown | 3008 Maple Ave. (bet. Carlisle & Wolf Sts.) | Dallas | 214-871-7444 | www.nick-sams.com

Imagine, a "New York steakhouse in the middle of Texas" exclaim fans of this Uptown meatery, the "place to be seen" over "excellent" prime beef and seafood in "dark", "attractive" digs highlighted by a grand piano player in the kitchen; whether you're seated in the "gorgeous" dining room or "less formal, action-packed bar", you'll find "eye candy", "top-notch" service and "Texas-size" tabs.

Nonna 🗷 *Italian*   25 | 19 | 23 | $53
Lemmon Avenue | 4115 Lomo Alto Dr. (bet. Bowser & Lemmon Aves.) | Dallas | 214-521-1800 | www.nonnadallas.com

Chef Julian Barsotti's "sophisticated", "upscale" Northern Italian cuisine "reigns supreme" at this cozy "bit of heaven" off Lemmon Avenue; a wood-burning oven highlights the "small" contemporary space, and while some grouse about "terrible acoustics", many others insist "it's worth the wait", which may be unavoidable "even with reservations."

Nosh Euro Bistro 🗷 *American*   24 | 19 | 20 | $49
Oak Lawn | 4216 Oak Lawn Ave. (Wycliff Ave.) | Dallas | 214-528-9400 | www.nosheurobistro.com

Its roots may be in classic Gallic cuisine, but the attitude is anything but stuffy at prolific chef-restaurateur Avner Samuel's "lively" enclave in Oak Lawn; the crowd is chock-a-block with business types and luncheonistas tucking into "creative" French-influenced riffs on New American fare – including plenty of noshes from pâté to escargot fritters – that's served at a "brisk" pace and priced well for the times.

Oak Restaurant 🗷 *Eclectic*   - | - | - | E
Market Center | 1628 Oak Lawn Ave. (Hi Line Dr.) | Dallas | 214-712-9700 | www.oakdallas.com

Reservations are already a hot ticket at this Design District stunner in Market Center featuring a seasonal Eclectic menu from Jason Maddy (ex The Mansion) in posh neutral-toned digs and equally polished service; prices are high, but fair for dishes, like duo of Kobe beef and honey-glazed quail.

	FOOD	DECOR	SERVICE	COST

Pappas Bros. Steakhouse 🖪 *Steak* | 28 | 25 | 27 | $71 |

Love Field | 10477 Lombardy Ln. (Stemmons Frwy.) | Dallas |
214-366-2000 | www.pappasbros.com

The "melt-in-your-mouth" steaks "blow the competition away" at this
"classy" Love Field chophouse where the "excellent" cuts are matched
with an "unbelievable" wine list ("a sommelier's dream"); yes, it's
"pricey", but the "impeccable" service and "elegant, masculine" setting make it a "favorite for special occasions."

Private Social 🖪 *Eclectic* | - | - | - | M |

Uptown | 3232 McKinney Ave. (Hall St.) | Dallas | 214-754-4744 |
www.privatesocial.com

Two-time *Top Chef*-testant Tiffany Derry is at the helm of this Uptown
arrival proffering two moderately priced Eclectic menus: 'private',
comprising large plates for one, and 'social', filled with tapas meant
for grazing and sharing; the venue's already a hit with foodies and
scenesters who vie for prime placement in the pearl-colored booths.

Saint-Emilion 🖪 Ⓜ *French* | 29 | 26 | 28 | $57 |

Cultural District | 3617 W. Seventh St. (Montgomery St.) | Ft. Worth |
817-737-2781 | www.saint-emilionrestaurant.com

Bernard Tronche's "*fantastique*" "jewel" in the Cultural District is "always tops" proclaim fans who vote it No. 1 for Food in Dallas/Ft. Worth,
a tribute to the daily blackboard menu of "exquisite" fare from the
South of France complemented by a "fabulous" wine list; "impeccable" service and a "quaint old house" setting are more reasons why it's
a "favorite destination" of many.

Salum 🖪 *American* | 26 | 24 | 25 | $54 |

Uptown | 4152 Cole Ave. (Fitzhugh Ave.) | Dallas | 214-252-9604 |
www.salumrestaurant.com

Though it's hidden in an unassuming Uptown strip center, chef-owner
Abraham Salum's upscale "culinary haven" "takes its rightful place in the
upper echelon" of the Dallas dining scene thanks to his "superb", "eclectic" New American menu, which changes monthly and is served by a
"caring" staff; the "simple", "elegant" venue is adjacent to sibling Komali.

Stephan Pyles 🖪 *Southwestern* | 27 | 27 | 27 | $69 |

Arts District | 1807 Ross Ave. (St. Paul St.) | Dallas | 214-580-7000 |
www.stephanpyles.com

The "master of New Texas cuisine", Stephan Pyles "reigns" at his
"classy, modern" Arts District Southwestern where diners can watch
chefs create his "amazing", "constantly evolving" globally influenced
fare in the glass-enclosed display kitchen; with "outstanding" service
and a "cosmopolitan vibe", it's the "perfect place to take out-of-
towners" – "particularly if they're paying."

Sushi Sake 🖪 *Japanese* | 27 | 22 | 21 | $40 |

Richardson | 2150 N. Collins Blvd. (Campbell Rd.) | 972-470-0722 |
www.sushi-sake.com

You feel like "you're in Japan" at this discreet, "authentic" Richardson
hideaway serving "generous" portions of "amazing sushi" and plentiful sake choices; though critics say the "decor doesn't quite live up to
the phenomenal fish" and grouse over "indifferent" service, "excellent"
cuisine at "reasonable prices" makes up for most glitches.

Suze 🏠Ⓜ *Mediterranean*

27 | 20 | 25 | $53

Preston Hollow | Villages of Preston Hollow | 4345 W. Northwest Hwy. (Midway Rd.) | Dallas | 214-350-6135 | www.suzedallas.com

"Unpretentious and friendly", Gilbert Garza's "hidden gem" in Preston Hollow is a "high-end neighborhood place" offering "beautifully presented" Mediterranean fare, an "excellent wine list" and "perfect" service in an "intimate, quiet" setting; given its "reasonable prices", it's no surprise that it's "always booked."

Tei An Ⓜ *Japanese*

26 | 27 | 24 | $59

Arts District | One Arts Plaza | 1722 Routh St. (bet. Flora St. & Ross Ave.) | Dallas | 214-220-2828 | www.tei-an.com

Foodies "feel transported to Japan" by chef-owner Teiichi Sakurai's "brilliant" cuisine at this "cutting-edge" Japanese atelier in the Arts District showcasing "amazing" handmade soba, sushi and more "esoteric" specials, all "flawlessly served" in a "Zen-like" interior ("like a spa"); it's a splurge, yes, but the "price is right for the product"; P.S. there's also a rooftop cocktail bar.

Village Marquee Texas
Grill & Bar ❶ *American*

26 | 25 | 24 | $53

Highland Park Village | Highland Park Vill. | 33 Highland Park Vill. (Douglas Ave.) | Dallas | 214-522-6035 | www.marqueegrill.com

Top Chef alum Tre Wilcox stars in the kitchen and mixologist Jason Kosmas crafts cocktails in the lounge at this "hip, happening" "place to be seen", located adjacent to the Highland Park Village Theatre and presenting "excellent", "innovative" New Americana in a glam 1930s Hollywood setting; "attentive service" and "people-watching" galore, especially the "scene at the bar", add to the "delight."

Woodshed Smokehouse *Eclectic*

‒ | ‒ | ‒ | M

Cultural District | 3201 Riverfront Dr. (University Ave.) | Ft. Worth | 817-877-4545 | www.woodshedsmokehouse.com

Set on the banks of the Trinity River in the Cultural District, celeb chef Tim Love's Eclectic tribute to a smokin' backyard party showcases a mix of wood-enhanced dishes in a menu so esoteric it comes with a glossary; an enthusiastic staff provides a warm welcome in the casual garage-chic space spilling out onto picnic benches on the patio.

Denver & Mountain Resorts

TOP FOOD RANKING

Restaurant	Cuisine
29 Carlos' Bistro	American
Junz	Asian
Splendido at the Chateau	American
28 Penrose Room	French
Fruition	American
Keystone Ranch	American
Masalaa	Indian/Vegetarian
Amu	Japanese
Matsuhisa	Japanese
Sweet Basil	American
Zucca	Italian
Sushi Sasa	Japanese
Walter's Bistro	American
Palace Arms	American
Saigon Landing	Vietnamese
Hearthstone Restaurant	American
Twelve	American
Ski Tip Lodge	American
Zamparelli's	Italian
Sushi Den	Japanese

OTHER NOTEWORTHY PLACES

Barolo Grill	Italian
Beau Jo's	Pizza
Bistro Vendôme	French
CholLon	Asian
Elway's	Steak
Euclid Hall	Eclectic/Pub Food
Frasca	Italian
Kelly Liken	American
Linger	Eclectic
Luca d'Italia	Italian
Melting Pot	Fondue
Panzano	Italian
Restaurant Kevin Taylor	French
Rio Grande	Mexican
Rioja	Mediterranean
Snooze	American
Table 6	American
Tag	Eclectic
240 Union	American
Z Cuisine & A Cote	French

	FOOD	DECOR	SERVICE	COST

Amu *Japanese*   28 | 24 | 25 | $38

Boulder | 1221 Spruce St. (bet. Broadway & 13th St.) | 303-440-0807 | www.izakayaamu.com

"Just superb" say those who've gotten into this Boulder izakaya where a "highly professional chef and staff" "beautifully present" an "ever-changing" selection of "inspired" Japanese small plates alongside an "extensive sake list"; just come "willing to wait", as the "serene", "sparse" setting only has 10 bar seats and a couple of tatami tables – and "be prepared to take off your shoes."

Barolo Grill Ⓢ Ⓜ *Italian*   27 | 24 | 26 | $56

Cherry Creek | 3030 E. Sixth Ave. (bet. Milwaukee & St. Paul Sts.) | Denver | 303-393-1040 | www.barologrilldenver.com

"One of the standard bearers in Denver", this "flat-out wonderful" Cherry Creek venue presents "dreamy" Northern Italian creations for "premium prices" in a "beautiful" setting suited for "special occasions" and "romance"; what's more, the staff, which famously gets "flown to Italy every year for training", is as "scalpel sharp" as ever, while "the owner's passion for wine" shines on the "extensive", "impressive" list; just be sure to "make your reservations early", otherwise you might have to dine at the bar (though that's a "great experience" too).

Beau Jo's Pizza *Pizza*   25 | 20 | 22 | $21

Arvada | 7525 W. 53rd Ave. (Wadsworth Bypass) | 303-420-8376
Evergreen | 28186 Hwy. 74 (Co. Rd. 73) | 303-670-2744
Fort Collins | 100 N. College Ave. (Mountain Ave.) | 970-498-8898
Steamboat Springs | 704 Lincoln Ave. (7th St.) | 970-870-6401
South Denver | 2710 S. Colorado Blvd. (Yale Ave.) | Denver | 303-758-1519
Boulder | 2690 Baseline Rd. (27th Way) | 303-554-5312
www.beaujos.com

A "kitschy" "tradition", this "Colorado-themed" chain, voted Denver's Most Popular, slings "outrageous", "one-of-a-kind", "deep, deep-dish" pizzas with "plentiful toppings" and "honey for dipping" on the side, so essentially, the "amazing crust does double duty as dessert"; the cost can seem either "reasonable" or "pricey" depending on how many people you have to feed ("you order by the pound, not the size"), though the "decadent lunch buffet" is an undisputed "great deal", as is the "wonderful salad bar."

Bistro Vendôme *French*   26 | 25 | 24 | $47

Larimer Square | Sussex Bldg. | 1420 Larimer St. (15th St.) | Denver | 303-825-3232 | www.bistrovendome.com

"C'est si bon" purr the Gallophiles who frequent this "slice of the Left Bank" on Larimer Square (sib to Rioja and Euclid Hall) for its "pitch-perfect" decor and "dependable", "reasonably priced" French bistro fare, ferried by servers who "go the extra 1,600 meters"; lingering over "wonderful" wines and "clever cocktails" at the "lovely zinc bar" or in the "fetching" *jardin* fragrant with blooming foliage" is also "memorable."

Carlos' Bistro *Eclectic*   29 | 25 | 28 | $46

Colorado Springs | 1025 S. 21st St. (Cimarron St.) | 719-471-2905

"Phenomenal" "gastronomical pleasures" – voted tops for Food in Colorado – are "worth" the "fairly high prices" at this Colorado Springs

Eclectic with a "romantic" setting; "personalized service" comes from the "accommodating" staff and chef-owner Carlos Echeandia himself, a real "character" who's "always out on the floor meeting and greeting his customers."

CholLon Modern Asian Bistro ⊠ *Asian*

27 | 25 | 24 | $41

LoDo | 1555 Blake St. (16th St.) | Denver | 303-353-5223 | www.cholon.com

LoDo is "lucky to have" chef Lon Symensma, whose "talent is on display" in every "exquisite" Southeast Asian morsel (including "brilliant" sweet onion and Gruyère soup dumplings) that this "sleek" spot sends out of its open kitchen; fetched by "knowledgeable, efficient" servers and accompanied by "fantastic cocktails", the "artistic" small plates are "made to share" – and you may as well, since the "earsplitting noise level" promotes getting close.

Elway's *Steak*

25 | 24 | 24 | $59

Cherry Creek | 2500 E. First Ave. (University Blvd.) | Denver | 303-399-5353
Downtown Denver | Ritz-Carlton Denver | 1881 Curtis St. (19th St.) | Denver | 303-312-3107
Vail | 174 E. Gore Creek Dr. (Mill Creek Rd.) | 970-754-7818
www.elways.com

"Melt-in-your-mouth steaks" "score big" at the "posh" Cherry Creek flagship of the eponymous former pro quarterback's chophouse trio, but the real "highlight" may be its "meat-market" bar scene, comprised of "big-spending" "cougars", "sugar daddies" and other "beautiful" folk who can afford the "Super Bowl prices" (though there's "value" to be found on the "bold wine list"); similar offerings, including "smooth" service, are found in the "glitzy, ritzy" Downtown branch, sporting a "sushi bar that's the bomb", and the "bustling" new Vail offshoot.

Euclid Hall ● *Eclectic/Pub Food*

24 | 24 | 23 | $29

Larimer Square | 1317 14th St. (Larimer St.) | Denver | 303-595-4255 | www.euclidhall.com

The "gut-busting" "haute" Eclectic pub grub "won't break the bank" at this Larimer Square "necessity" (sibling of Rioja and Bistro Vendôme) with an "industrial"-"modern" "gastropub-chic" setting; though it's sometimes "loud", it remains an "awesome spot, especially late night", thanks to the "well-curated beer list" that boasts pours you might have "never heard of before" ("don't be afraid to ask questions" – the servers "always have an answer").

Frasca Food & Wine ⊠ *Italian*

28 | 25 | 28 | $80

Boulder | 1738 Pearl St. (18th St.) | 303-442-6966 | www.frascafoodandwine.com

"Sublime in every way", this Boulder "must" "lives up to the hype" thanks to Lachlan Mackinnon-Patterson's "exceptional" Northern Italian menu, which is "perfectly paired" with "informed, articulate sommelier" Bobby Stuckey's "spectacular" wines; a staff that has "hospitality down to a science" and "minimalist modern" decor only add to its appeal, and though "long lead times for reservations" and "exorbitant prices" are part of the deal, most deem it "well worth the wait" and expense for such a "transformative experience."

Fruition *American* | 28 | 23 | 26 | $56 |
Country Club | 1313 E. Sixth Ave. (bet. Lafayette & Marion Sts.) | Denver | 303-831-1962 | www.fruitionrestaurant.com

The menu at this Country Club "diamond" – ranked No. 1 for Food in Denver – reads "like a foodie romance novel", which its author, farmer-chef Alex Seidel, brings to life with his "seductive" approach to "garden-to-table" New American cuisine, by turns "rustic" and "ethereal", "nuanced" and "startling" (matched by a "well-thought-out wine list"); meanwhile, the "deft" manner of the "astute" staff makes the "close quarters" seem "charming", and everything comes for "fair prices."

Hearthstone Restaurant *American* | 28 | 26 | 27 | $45 |
Breckenridge | 130 S. Ridge St. (Washington Ave.) | 970-453-1148 | www.stormrestaurants.com

"Celebrate something" – anything – with an "outstanding" meal of "delicious" local American cuisine at this "magical" old home where everything from the "high-end Gold Rush–period decor" and "gorgeous mountain views" to the "friendly staff" oozes "warmth and charm"; though "one of the fanciest restaurants in Breckenridge", with "pricey" tabs to match, it "often offers special menus that are a bargain for the quality."

Junz *Asian* | 29 | 24 | 25 | $34 |
Parker | 11211 S. Dransfeldt Rd. (Twenty Mile Rd.) | 720-851-1005 | www.junzrestaurant.com

The "sushi is amazing", but the entire menu at this bright and cheerful Asian fusion "gem" in suburban Parker is "full of great (and sometimes unexpected) dishes", including "swell choices" for the raw-fish-phobic; what's more, affordable prices and solid service mean it's as "wonderful" for colleagues on their lunch break as it is "for families" at dinnertime.

Kelly Liken *American* | 26 | 25 | 25 | $81 |
Vail | Gateway Bldg. | 12 Vail Rd. (I-70 Frontage Rd.) | 970-479-0175 | www.kellyliken.com

Offering "exceptional" New American prix fixes and "always-changing" "gourmet cocktails" with service that "misses nothing" in an "elegant yet down-to-earth dining room", the eponymous chef-owner of this "total package" in Vail "would be a star anywhere"; however, critics crack that "you need a microscope to see the food" – "but not the huge bill" – so some recommend ordering fewer courses "for a reduced price."

Keystone Ranch ⑤Ⓜ *American* | 28 | 28 | 28 | $73 |
Keystone | Keystone Ranch Golf Course | 1437 Summit County Rd. 150 (Keystone Ranch Rd.) | 970-496-4161 | www.keystoneresort.com

"Year in and year out", the "perfectly prepared", "inventive" New American "mountain fare" at this "old working ranch house" in Keystone remains worthy of its setting, a "wonderful" "hunting lodge" suitable for "cowboy duds or uptown threads"; it's "not a place for the budget conscious", but with the added attraction of "professional, friendly" service (which extends through "dessert and after-dinner drinks by the fireplace"), it offers a level of "satisfaction few restaurants" achieve; P.S. reservations required.

Linger 🅂🅜 *Eclectic*

26 | 27 | 24 | $35

Highland | 2030 W. 30th Ave. (Tejon St.) | Denver | 303-993-3120 | www.lingerdenver.com

There's nothing "macabre" about this "old mortuary" turned "hip", "hopping" eatery in Highland, where "you'll definitely want to linger" either downstairs or on the "fantastic rooftop" lounge boasting "phenomenal city views" and a Lite-Brite bar; also "wonderful" are Justin Cucci's "outrageously delish" Eclectic small plates, "personable" service and a happy hour that's "lively" enough "to wake the dead."

Luca d'Italia 🅂🅜 *Italian*

28 | 23 | 27 | $54

Capitol Hill | 711 Grant St. (7th Ave.) | Denver | 303-832-6600 | www.lucadenver.com

Chef-owner Frank Bonanno "puts his heart and soul" into the "phenomenal" Italian "plates of beauty" at this Capitol Hill "foodie destination", where the wines are equally "fab" and service is "impeccable"; it may be true that the "unfinished-loft" decor "doesn't match" the "attention to culinary detail", but the prices sure do, though they are "lower" than "more upscale" sibling Mizuna.

Masalaa *Indian/Vegetarian*

28 | 17 | 21 | $16

Aurora | 3140 S. Parker Rd. (S. Peoria St.) | 303-755-6272 | www.masalaausa.com

"Excellent curries and dosas" as well as "lots of vegan and gluten-free options" "could make a vegetarian" out of the strictest carnivore at this unadorned Aurora eatery providing bargain rates and one of the "best Indian buffets in town"; "quick", "courteous" service adds to the altogether "satisfying" experience.

Matsuhisa *Japanese*

28 | 25 | 24 | $77

Aspen | 303 E. Main St. (Monarch St.) | 970-544-6628 | www.matsuhisaaspen.com
Vail | 141 E. Meadow Dr. (Village Centre Dr.) | 970-476-6628 | www.matsuhisavail.com

"The holy grail" of sushi is found at these Nobu siblings whose "world-class" "haute Japanese" "feasts for the senses" are as "jaw-dropping" as the "astronomical prices"; the Aspen branch is a "hip", "crowded" basement, the Vail venue boasts "dramatic" scenery and a "Zen vibe", while both feature a "savvy" staff and "raucous" bar scenes.

Melting Pot *Fondue*

26 | 26 | 26 | $58

Fort Collins | 334 E. Mountain Ave. (bet. Jefferson & Walnut Sts.) | 970-207-0100
Louisville | 732 Main St. (bet. Pine & Spruce Sts.) | 303-666-7777
Littleton | 2707 W. Main St. (bet. Curtice St.& Santa Fe Dr.) | 303-794-5666
Colorado Springs | 30 E. Pikes Peak Ave. (Cascade Ave.) | 719-385-0300
www.meltingpot.com

"An experience, not just a normal dinner" is what's offered at this "warm", "quaint" fondue chain whose "fabulous four-course meals" – served by a "skilled" staff – are "perfect for a date, special occasion" or "group event"; just "make sure you have plenty of time" and money, because meals "take about two to three hours" and are "pretty expensive" – though you will "leave stuffed."

FOOD | DECOR | SERVICE | COST

Palace Arms ⓧ *American* — 28 | 27 | 28 | $60

Downtown Denver | Brown Palace Hotel | 321 17th St. (Tremont Pl.) | Denver | 303-297-3111 | www.brownpalace.com

"A top choice for impressing out-of-towners" or for "a romantic anniversary dinner", this "impeccable" "grande dame" in Downtown's "elegant" Brown Palace Hotel presents "outstanding" New American creations both "classic" and "daring" in a "posh", "old-world" setting; "ouch, the price is high" warn wallet-watchers, but those wistful for "fine dining as it used to be" – complete with "superb" wines and "gracious service" – say it's "well worth the cost"; P.S. jackets and reservations suggested.

Panzano *Italian* — 26 | 24 | 25 | $44

Downtown Denver | 909 17th St. (Champa St.) | Denver | 303-296-3525 | www.panzano-denver.com

Chef Elise Wiggins "deserves all the praise heaped on her" fawn fans of the "scrumptious", "innovative" and "reasonably priced" Northern Italian fare (featuring "superb" freshly baked breads) she whips up at this "casually elegant" Downtown "jewel" in the "trendy Hotel Monaco"; a "polite" staff "puts the meal over the top", and "not-to-be-missed" happy hour "bargains" only add to the "pleasure."

Penrose Room ⓧ Ⓜ *French* — 28 | 29 | 29 | $98

Colorado Springs | Broadmoor Hotel | 1 Lake Ave. (Lake Cir.) | 719-634-7711 | www.broadmoor.com

After 50 years, the Broadmoor Hotel's signature "celebration" spot (maybe "the only place in Colorado Springs where you must wear a jacket") still offers one of "the most prestigious and posh dining experiences" around, with "heavenly" New French food, an "extensive wine list" and a "fabulous" staff – rated No. 1 for Service in Colorado – whose "attention to detail" makes for a "fairy-tale evening"; an "amazing" penthouse view of the lake and mountains is another reason the "unforgettable experience" is "well worth" the "expensive" tabs.

Restaurant Kevin Taylor ⓧ *French* — 27 | 25 | 27 | $69

Downtown Denver | Hotel Teatro | 1106 14th St. (Arapahoe St.) | Denver | 303-820-2600 | www.ktrg.net

"Astounding flavors" and "thoughtful presentations" continue to set the "benchmark of excellence" at chef Kevin Taylor's French flagship in Downtown's Hotel Teatro, where the "formal" "white-tablecloth" ambiance comes with commensurately "impeccable hospitality" and a "superior wine list"; a few find it "a bit too pricey", but it's "worth every penny" "if you lust for old-fashioned", "high-class" "magic."

Rio Grande Mexican Restaurant *Mexican* — 21 | 20 | 21 | $22

Fort Collins | 143 W. Mountain Ave. (College Ave.) | 970-224-5428
Lone Tree | 9535 Park Meadows Dr. (Yosemite St.) | 303-799-4999
Steamboat Springs | 628 Lincoln Ave. (7th St.) | 970-871-6277
LoDo | 1525 Blake St. (bet. 15th & 16th Sts.) | Denver | 303-623-5432
Boulder | 1101 Walnut St. (11th St.) | 303-444-3690
Greeley | 825 Ninth St. (9th Ave.) | 970-304-9292
www.riograndemexican.com

You go for the "superlative", "crazy-strong margaritas" at this "vibrant", "festive" local Mexican chain, but you "stay for the quesadillas" and "to-die-for chiles rellenos", all delivered by a "cheerful" staff; most of its "young, noisy clients" find the costs "reasonable", though a couple of "more refined palates" deem them "overpriced"; P.S. the Boulder location boasts an "incredible rooftop deck."

Rioja *Mediterranean*
28 | 24 | 26 | $49

Larimer Square | 1431 Larimer St. (bet. 14th & 15th Sts.) | Denver | 303-820-2282 | www.riojadenver.com

Jennifer Jasinki's "creative hand is evident" in every "meticulously thought-out" Mediterranean-inspired dish, each "presented like art-work" alongside an "extraordinary wine list" at this "cosmopolitan" "Larimer Square gem" (sib to Euclid Hall and Bistro Vendôme); the dining room with "Chihuly-esque blown-glass" fixtures gets "justifi-ably jam-packed", but "unobtrusive" service that "goes above and be-yond" helps mitigate the "raucous echoes"; P.S. it's "expensive", but the "killer brunch" is more "reasonably priced."

Saigon Landing *Vietnamese*
28 | 25 | 25 | $23

Evergreen | 28080 Douglas Park Rd. (Bear Creek Rd.) | 303-674-5421
Greenwood Village | 6585 Greenwood Plaza Blvd. (Arapahoe Rd.) | 303-779-0028 🏛
www.saigonlanding.com

"Not a typical Vietnamese menu", but "unique" (and "outstanding") dishes are what you'll find at this "cute", "spacious" Greenwood Village and Evergreen pair "par excellence"; with "friendly" staffers on hand, it remains many a local's "happy place."

Ski Tip Lodge 🏛Ⓜ *American*
28 | 27 | 29 | $90

Keystone | 764 Montezuma Rd. | 970-496-4202 | www.keystoneresort.com

Prepare to be "pampered" from the moment you "schuss" in from the mountain to "dessert in front of the fire" at this "rustic, romantic" for-mer stagecoach stop in Keystone; in between, you'll savor "black-diamond" New American fare (at "splurge"-worthy prices) from a "limited" but "sublime" prix fixe menu complete with "wonderful wine pairings" – a "relaxing way to end to a day on the slopes."

Snooze *American*
26 | 23 | 23 | $17

Ballpark | 2262 Larimer St. (Park Ave.) | Denver | 303-297-0700
Fort Collins | 144 W. Mountain Ave. (Mason St.) | 970-482-9253
Park Hill | 700 N. Colorado Blvd. (7th Ave.) | Denver | 303-736-6200
Boulder | 1617 Pearl St. (17th St.) | No phone
Centennial | 6781 S. York St. (Easter Ave.) | 303-734-9655
www.snoozeeatery.com

"Imaginative", "grown-up" "breakfasts of champions", "excellent coffee" and "spicy Bloody Marys" are shuttled by "happy" staffers amid "retro space-age kitsch" at this American mini-chain; however, if you don't "wake up before the roosters", you'll have to brave "outrageously long" lines (to pay prices some feel are "slightly high"), but "there's a reason for the wait"; P.S. a pared-down lunch menu is also offered (no dinner).

Splendido at the Chateau Ⓜ *American*
29 | 29 | 28 | $85

Beaver Creek | Beaver Creek Resort | 17 Chateau Ln. (Scott Hill Rd.) | 970-845-8808 | www.splendidobeavercreek.com

"Living up to the name", the "first-class kitchen" at this Beaver Creek "special-occasion" "experience" offers nothing less than "splendid" New American fare, which is complemented by an "exceptional wine list" pre-sented by an "impeccable" staff; "sure it's expensive", but "as you relax by the fire" in the "gorgeous setting" ("what views!") to the strains of "live piano from the bar", you can only conclude that "life is good."

Sushi Den *Japanese*   28 | 25 | 24 | $48

Platt Park | 1487 S. Pearl St. (Florida Ave.) | Denver | 303-777-0826 | www.sushiden.net

Be prepared to "wait for a table" at this "hot spot" in Platt Park, known for its "delightfully presented", "incredibly high quality" fish "flown in daily" from Tokyo, as well as lots of "people-watching" in the "packed" dining rooms ("ask to be seated" downstairs or at the sushi bar, because "the upstairs is a bit isolated"); though it can get a bit "spendy", most agree "it's always worth it."

Sushi Sasa *Japanese*   28 | 24 | 24 | $47

Highland | 2401 15th St. (Platte St.) | Denver | 303-433-7272 | www.sushisasadenver.com

The "exotic", "superb sushi" tastes so "fresh-off-the-boat", you'll think you're dining "by the ocean" and not in Highland at this "consistently outstanding" Japanese by "inventive" "rock star" chef-owner Wayne Conwell; "you'll certainly pay for the pleasure", but you're also getting an "artfully minimalist" environment and an "excellent" staff "at the top of their trade."

Sweet Basil *American*   28 | 25 | 26 | $65

Vail | 193 E. Gore Creek Dr. (Bridge St.) | 970-476-0125 | www.sweetbasil-vail.com

Still the "gold standard" in Vail, this "pioneer" of "forward-thinking" "luxury" presents "fab", "cutting-edge" New American cuisine and "pampering" service in an "energizing", "sexy" setting with "sparkling views" of Gore Creek through "picture windows"; "sky-high prices" are no issue for the "glitzy" "mountaineers" who frequent it – in fact, "the only downside is its popularity" (it's "achingly noisy").

Table 6 *American*   25 | 22 | 24 | $45

Capitol Hill | 609 Corona St. (bet. 6th & 7th Aves.) | Denver | 303-831-8800 | www.table6denver.com

Chef Scott Parker "perfectly executes" a "decadent" "high end–meets-low brow" "gourmet" New American chalkboard menu that's "heavy with meat" and complemented by a "well-advised" wine and beer selection at this Capitol Hill "locavore" destination; with "decent" prices and "attentive", "informal service" to match the "rustic" room, it's no wonder "all the cool kids are eating here."

TAG *Eclectic*   26 | 23 | 23 | $49

Larimer Square | 1441 Larimer St. (14th St.) | Denver | 303-996-9985 | www.tag-restaurant.com

While "it's difficult to peg" "magician" Troy Guard's "unexpected", "unreal" Eclectic eats (kampachi with Pop Rocks?) and "off-the-wall" drinks, this Larimer Square "hot spot" is proof his "star is on a Rocky Mountain high"; service is "super", and if a few bemoan that it's "kind of pricey" and the "brick interior with orange lights and upbeat pop music" is "noisier than a train station", well, that's the cost of "cool", so "dress hip" to fit in.

Twelve ⓈⓂ *American* | 28 | 23 | 27 | $51 |

Ballpark | 2233 Larimer St. (bet. Park Ave. & 22nd Ave.) | Denver | 303-293-0287 | www.twelverestaurant.com

The "menu changes every month", but "astounding gourmet" chef Jeff Osaka's New American fare is always "sublime and refined" at his "tiny" Ballpark eatery whose setting brims with "old-world charm"; "spot-on service", "great wines by the glass" and a "classic oak bar" are more reasons why fans "want to return often."

240 Union *American* | 26 | 23 | 25 | $40 |

Lakewood | 240 Union Blvd. (6th Ave.) | 303-989-3562 | www.240union.com

"Exceptional" New American fare, including "impressive" seafood and "to-die-for homemade bread", makes this "light, airy" "oasis of class" "off the beaten path" in a Lakewood strip center a "go-to" for locals and the "meet-and-greet business crowd"; some say that "the noise gets a little overbearing at times", but with "efficient", "unobtrusive" service" and "fair prices" to bolster the mood, most find the total package "reliably agreeable."

Walter's Bistro Ⓢ *American* | 28 | 25 | 27 | $46 |

Colorado Springs | 146 E. Cheyenne Mountain Blvd. (Vietnam Veterans Memorial Hwy.) | 719-630-0201 | www.waltersbistro.com

From the "famous lobster bisque" onward, the "splurges" to be had at this "classy" New American bistro in Colorado Springs are near "perfection"; the backdrop is fittingly "rich" yet "tasteful", and you're sure to "feel at home" thanks to the "gentlemanly" eponymous owner, who's "always there" to oversee his "knowledgeable" staff.

Zamparelli's Italian Bistro Ⓢ🍴 *Italian* | 28 | 21 | 26 | $28 |

Lafayette | 2770 Arapahoe Rd. (95th St.) | 303-664-1275 | www.zamparellis.com

For "amazing", "unusual wood-fired pizzas" with topping options like roasted poblanos and wine-poached pears, plus pastas, salads and gelato, this Italian bistro in Lafayette comes "strongly recommended"; add in some of the "friendliest service around", and locals say the simple dining room and bar area feel like their own *Cheers.*"

Z Cuisine & A Côté ⓈⓂ *French* | 27 | 24 | 24 | $44 |

Highland | 2239 W. 30th Ave. (Wyandot St.) | Denver | 303-477-1111 | www.zcuisineonline.com

"Magnificent" "French feasts" plus a "primo wine list" make for an "extraordinary culinary sojourn" at this "adorable", "postage stamp–sized" Highland bistro overseen by a "responsive" staff; "show up very early if you want any chance of finding a table" (reservations for large groups only) or "cool your heels next door" with a dram of absinthe at the "comfortable" A Côté bar.

Zucca Italian Ristorante *Italian* | 28 | 26 | 26 | $31 |

Louisville | 808 Main St. (Pine St.) | 303-666-6499 | www.zuccalouisville.com

"Some new ideas" in Italian cooking can be found on the "awesome" menu at this "heavenly" Louisville neighborhood spot whose fare is complemented by an "extensive wine list"; add in "terrific" service, a "snug", "warm" setting and "good prices", and it's no surprise that locals call it "a must-visit."

Detroit

TOP FOOD RANKING

Restaurant	Cuisine
29 Supino Pizzeria	Pizza
28 Moro's Dining	Italian
Lark	Continental
Common Grill	American
West End Grill	American
Union Woodshop	BBQ
Texas de Brazil	Steak
Roast	Steak
Assaggi Bistro	Mediterranean
Hill Seafood & Chop House	Seafood

OTHER NOTEWORTHY PLACES

Andiamo	Italian
Atlas Global Bistro	Eclectic
Beverly Hills Grill	American
Buddy's Pizza	Pizza
Fishbone's Rhythm	Cajun
Iridescence	American
Kruse & Muer	Seafood
Root	American
Slows Bar BQ	BBQ
Zingerman's Roadhouse	American

Andiamo *Italian*   25 | 24 | 25 | $46

Downtown | Renaissance Ctr. | 400 Renaissance Ctr. (Atwater St.) | 313-567-6700
Grosse Pointe Woods | 20930 Mack Ave. (Hampton Rd.) | 313-886-9933
Sterling Heights | 14425 Lakeside Circle (Eastbrook Dr.) | 586-532-8800
Royal Oak | 129 S. Main St. (2nd St.) | 248-582-9300
Livonia | 38703 Seven Mile Rd. (Haggerty Rd.) | 734-953-3200
Novi | 42705 Grand River Ave. (Novi Rd.) | 248-348-3838
Joe Vicari's
Andiamo Italian Steakhouse *Italian*
Bloomfield Hills | 6676 Telegraph Rd. (Maple Rd.) | 248-865-9300
Warren | 7096 E. 14 Mile Rd. (bet. Hollingsworth & Van Dyke Aves.) | 586-268-3200
Dearborn | 21400 Michigan Ave. (Brady St.) | 313-359-3300
www.andiamoitalia.com

Admirers say it's "always a pleasure" to eat at this "upscale local chain", voted Most Popular in Detroit, where an "impressive" staff delivers "flavorful" Italian in a "beautiful", "eclectic" setting that hosts an "animated" scene; it's slightly "expensive", but well suited to "business", "date night" or a "step-above-casual" outing; post-Survey, three of the locations have taken a new name and direction as steakhouses, retaining some of the same Boot-based menu.

DETROIT

	FOOD	DECOR	SERVICE	COST

Assaggi Bistro ⓜ *Mediterranean*   28 | 23 | 25 | $39

Ferndale | 330 W. Nine Mile Rd. (bet. Allen Rd. & Planavon St.) |
248-584-3499 | www.assaggibistro.com

A "bastion of civility" in Downtown Ferndale, this Mediterranean "jewel"
offers "outstanding", "refreshing" dishes (accented with ingredients
from the "lovely herb garden") along with "wonderful hospitality"
overseen by "warm", ever-present owners who lend a "homey" touch
to the "crowded" room; "reasonable" wines help keep the cost moderate, while the "cool cocktail bar" makes it a destination for drinks too.

Atlas Global Bistro *Eclectic*   25 | 22 | 23 | $37

Orchestra Hall Area | 3111 Woodward Ave. (Charlotte St.) |
313-831-2241 | www.atlasglobalbistro.com

"Elegant yet casual", this "stylish", moderately priced Eclectic bistro is
a "winner" for its "fantastic", seasonally "changing" menu, "intelligent" service and "inviting" ambiance, especially "if your evening en-
tails a little night music from Orchestra Hall"; with "huge windows
overlooking Woodward Avenue", it has an "open, airy" atmosphere
that makes it a "favorite" for the "well-executed" Sunday brunch;
P.S. reduced hours Sunday–Monday in the summer.

Beverly Hills Grill *American*   27 | 21 | 25 | $34

Beverly Hills | 31471 Southfield Rd. (bet. Beverly & 13 Mile Rds.) |
248-642-2355 | www.beverlyhillsgrill.com

"A hit for b, l and d", this "warm, inviting" New American in a "tough-to-
find" Beverly Hills locale delivers "phenomenal" "power breakfasts" and
brunches as well as "wonderful daily specials" to round out "terrific"
dinners, served by a staff that's "enthusiastic without being cloying";
it's "always jammed", with a frequent "line out the door" (no rezzies).

Buddy's Pizza *Pizza*   27 | 20 | 24 | $21

Grosse Pointe | Pointe Plaza | 19163 Mack Ave. (bet. Kingsville Ave. &
Moross Rd.) | 313-884-7400
Hamtramck | 17125 Conant St. (McNichols Rd.) | 313-892-9001
Auburn Hills | 2612 N. Squirrel Rd. (Walton Blvd.) | 248-276-9040
Bloomfield Hills | 3637 W. Maple Rd. (Lahser Rd.) | 248-645-0300
Farmington Hills | 31646 Northwestern Hwy. (Middlebelt Rd.) |
248-855-4600
Royal Oak | 32218 Woodward Ave. (Nakota Rd.) | 248-549-8000
Warren | 8100 Old Thirteen Mile Rd. (Van Dyke Ave.) | 586-574-9200
Dearborn | 22148 Michigan Ave. (bet. Howard & Mason Sts.) | 313-562-5900
Livonia | 33605 Plymouth Rd. (Farmington Rd.) | 734-261-3550
www.buddyspizza.com

"Everyone loves" this "legendary" local pizza chain producing
"phenomenal" square pies with "just the right sauce", "crunch"
and "lots of quality toppings", adding up to pure "deep-dish deliciousness"; despite some mixed opinions on its "vintage" looks,
most call it an "accommodating" place to "meet friends", "have a
party" or "take the little ones" for an "affordable", "satisfying" meal.

Common Grill ⓜ *American*   28 | 23 | 27 | $40

Chelsea | 112 S. Main St. (bet. Middle & South Sts.) | 734-475-0470 |
www.commongrill.com

"Amazing" cooking with a focus on "fresh seafood" "surpasses expectations" at this slightly "out-of-the-way" Chelsea New American offer-

ing a "fine-dining experience in a hometown setting"; while the "bistro atmosphere" does get "loud", most are taken with the "positive energy" and "top-notch" service, calling it an "ideal stop before the Purple Rose Theatre"; P.S. reservations for large groups only.

Fishbone's Rhythm Kitchen Café *Cajun* 25 | 24 | 23 | $37

Downtown | 400 Monroe St. (Brush St.) | 313-965-4600
Saint Clair Shores | 23722 Jefferson Ave. (Harbour Place Dr.) | 586-498-3000
Southfield | 29244 Northwestern Hwy. (Franklin Rd.) | 248-351-2925
www.fishbonesusa.com

Champions of this "unique" Cajun trio "crave" its "spicy", "out-of-the-ordinary" eats (including "awesome" alligator and even "fantastic" sushi) amped up by a "colorful", "hopping" atmosphere with frequent "cool music"; throw in "on-point" service and "generous" plates, and it's a natural for "group outings" that's well "worth" the "fair price."

Hill Seafood & Chop House Ⓢ *Seafood* 28 | 27 | 28 | $48

Grosse Pointe Farms | 123 Kercheval Ave. (Muir Rd.) | 313-886-8101 | www.thehillgrossepointe.com

It's "definitive Grosse Pointe: exclusive, high-quality and traditional" at this "superb" GPF steak and seafood place delivering "flawless" presentations of "comfortable food the area loves"; "pouring a generous drink" too, the "the bar is the place to see and be seen", making it your "club away from the club" where it's "kind of nice to dress up and wear a little Brooks Brothers."

Iridescence Ⓜ *American* 27 | 28 | 26 | $73

Downtown | Motor City Casino Hotel | 2901 Grand River Ave., 16th fl. (Brooklyn St.) | 313-237-6732 | www.motorcitycasino.com

Guests "love looking out over the city at night" at this Downtowner voted No. 1 for Decor in Detroit, boasting a "romantic" "bling-bling" setting on the 16th floor of the Motor City Casino Hotel; with "superior" New American food, an "incredible" wine list and "excellent" service too, it's a "go-to celebration place" that's "worth the high price tag."

Kruse & Muer *Seafood* 26 | 23 | 25 | $36

Lake Orion | 801 S. Lapeer Rd. (bet. Clarkston Rd. & Goldengate St.) | 248-814-9500
Rochester | 327 S. Main St. (bet. 3rd & 4th Sts.) | 248-652-9400
Rochester Hills | 134 N. Adams Rd. (Walton Blvd.) | 248-375-2503
Troy | 911 Wilshire Dr. (bet. Crooks Rd. & Troy Center Dr.) | 248-362-2700

Kruse's Deer Lake Inn *Seafood*

Clarkston | 7504 Dixie Hwy. (Deer Lake Rd.) | 248-795-2077
www.kruseandmuerrestaurants.com

A local chain specializing in "well-prepared", "reasonably priced" seafood, this northern 'burbs "classic" serves "house favorites that have been perfected to a science", but it's the "endless", "scrumptious" hot bread that "everyone comes back for"; some branches are a "tight fit" and the decor may be "a little outdated", but it "feels like a good neighbor, with a touch of class", and "every time you go it's packed."

The Lark Ⓢ Ⓜ *Continental* 28 | 28 | 28 | $116

West Bloomfield | 6430 Farmington Rd. (Maple Rd.) | 248-661-4466 | www.thelark.com

"Living up to its sterling reputation", this West Bloomfield Continental brings together "spectacular" prix fixe dinners (including "second

<table>
<tr><td>FOOD</td><td>DECOR</td><td>SERVICE</td><td>COST</td></tr>
</table>

helpings"), an "unbelievable" wine list and "outstanding", "old-world" service in a "Portuguese country-themed" setting with "charming" gardens; it requires some "deep pockets", and the "entertaining" owner's "hands-on" approach isn't for everyone, but many love that the Larks "make you feel like a guest in their home"; P.S. jacket required.

Moro's Dining *Italian*   28 | 21 | 28 | $40

Allen Park | 6535 Allen Rd. (Park Ave.) | 313-382-7152 | www.morosdining.com

"A hidden gem in Allen Park", this "exceptional" Italian (voted No. 1 for Service in Detroit) feels like "going back in time to 1962" where the "salads and flaming desserts made tableside" by the "pro" staff are "old-school fun"; even if the decor is "a bit outdated", it's "charming", "intimate" and sure to "impress your date"; P.S. reservations for big groups only.

Roast *Steak*   28 | 26 | 27 | $55

Downtown | Westin Book Cadillac Hotel | 1128 Washington Blvd. (Michigan Ave.) | 313-961-2500 | www.roastdetroit.com

"Meat lovers won't find a better place to gorge" on beef (or the daily "roast beast of the day") than Michael Symon's "top" Downtown steakhouse that "rewards your inner caveman/woman" with its "hearty", "incredibly flavorful" dishes served by a "superbly informed" staff; the atmosphere in the Westin Book Cadillac Hotel is "gorgeous" yet "casual", and while it's "expensive", the "happy-hour specials can't be beat."

The Root ☒ *American*   27 | 26 | 27 | $48

White Lake | 340 Town Center Blvd. (Highland Rd.) | 248-698-2400 | www.therootrestaurant.com

More than a "haunt for hipster locavores in an unlikely locale", this "modern" New American in way exurban White Lake serving "unique", "phenomenal" preparations of "locally harvested foods" and a "great wine selection" (with some Michigan bottles) "deserves a rave" from anyone who likes to eat; overseen by a "hard-to-beat" staff, the "lovely" interior is "peaceful" and casual, and a bit "spartan without being sparse"; P.S. the "reasonable" tasting menu is "terrific."

Slows Bar BQ *BBQ*   27 | 22 | 22 | $26

Corktown | 2138 Michigan Ave. (14th St.) | 313-962-9828 | www.slowsbarbq.com

"Killer" BBQ ("the yardbird sandwich, the ribs, the brisket") that "transports you to St. Louis, Texas and Kansas City all in one" – with "various styles" of sauces and "out-of-this-world" mac 'n' cheese – "draws lots of people" to this "hipster mecca" in a refurbished 1880s building "near old Tiger Stadium" in Corktown; while it's an "adventure getting there" and definitely "lives up to the name" given the "frustrating" waits (sometimes over an "hour or two"), service is "right on" once you're seated, and the "excellent" yet "reasonable" beer selection is a plus.

Supino Pizzeria ☒Ⓜ *Pizza*   29 | 18 | 22 | $18

Eastern Market | 2457 Russell St. (Napoleon St.) | 313-567-7879 | www.supinopizzeria.com

"The best pizza west of Brooklyn" earns this "bare-bones" Eastern Market pizzeria the Detroit Survey's No. 1 Food score, with kudos going to its "tissue-thin crust" and "unique", "especially fresh" toppings, from eggplant to a cracked egg; so "it doesn't matter that there's no decor" (just big tables to share) and a "long wait from order to eating", since you forget all that once you're "wolfing down" such "delicious" 'za.

Texas de Brazil *Steak*

28 | 27 | 28 | $60

Downtown | 1000 Woodward Ave. (Gratiot Ave.) | 313-964-4333 | www.texasdebrazil.com

Reviewers "relish" the "awesome" variety of meat – presented "straight from the grill" on swordlike skewers by an "attentive" crew – at this "elegant" Downtown Brazilian steakhouse, a "carnivore's paradise" where the salad bar is also "a meal in itself"; so "come hungry, leave stuffed" – it's "pricey" but "worth the money if you can tackle tons of food in one sitting."

Union Woodshop *BBQ*

28 | 25 | 25 | $31

Clarkston | 18 S. Main St. (Washington St.) | 248-625-5660 | www.unionwoodshop.com

"Everything is smoked in-house" and made from scratch at this "hip" BBQ joint, an "outstanding local success story" producing "pick-it-up-with-your-fingers food" of "fantastic deliciousness" to wash down with "Michigan beers on tap"; "rustic", "woodsy" and "family-friendly", it's "difficult to get into" unless you "go early" (there are no reservations) but "first-class" all the way, and a fine "value" too; P.S. whether it's a "plus or minus", there's "always the possibility of a Kid Rock sighting."

West End Grill 🚫Ⓜ *American*

28 | 25 | 27 | $47

Ann Arbor | 120 W. Liberty St. (bet. Ashley & Main Sts.) | 734-747-6260 | www.westendgrillannarbor.com

Offering "big-city dining in the small college town" of Ann Arbor, this "cozy, romantic" New American is a "tough reservation, so book early" if you want to hear the "full menu recited tableside" and scarf "scrumptious pre-dinner beignets" that "set the tone for a decadent, inventive meal"; the "chef puts interesting twists on standard dishes" and the staff provides "personal attention", so while "expensive", fans agree it's a "very special little" place.

Zingerman's Roadhouse *American*

25 | 23 | 25 | $29

Veterans Park | 2501 Jackson Rd. (Maple Rd.) | Ann Arbor | 734-663-3663 | www.zingermansroadhouse.com

"Comfort food taken to the nth degree" stands out at this "ultimate American restaurant" in Veterans Park, where "locally sourced" "premium" ingredients come together in "massive portions" of BBQ and "adult mac 'n' cheese" that are "homestyle but far from boring"; true, a "big wallet" may be needed, particularly for a "folksy, relaxed" place that's "somewhat rustic", but the staff "will get you anything you want."

Ft. Lauderdale

TOP FOOD RANKING

	Restaurant	Cuisine
28	La Brochette	Mediterranean
	Café Sharaku	Asian
27	Canyon	Southwestern
	Casa D'Angelo	Italian
	Eduardo de San Angel	Mexican
	Valentino's	Italian
	Kitchenetta	Italian
	Cafe Maxx	American/Eclectic
26	Thai Spice	Thai
	Sette Bello	Italian

OTHER NOTEWORTHY PLACES

Anthony's	Pizza
Blue Moon	Seafood
Bonefish Grill	Seafood
Capital Grille	Steak
Chima	Brazilian/Steak
Greek Islands	Greek
Grille 66	Seafood/Steak
Market 17	American/Eclectic
Steak 954	Steak
3030 Ocean	American/Seafood

Anthony's Coal Fired Pizza *Pizza*   22 | 16 | 20 | $23

Ft. Lauderdale | 2203 S. Federal Hwy. (SE 22nd St.) | 954-462-5555
Pompano Beach | 1203 S. Federal Hwy. (SE 12th St.) | 954-942-5550
Coral Springs | Magnolia Shops | 9521 Westview Dr. (University Dr.) | 954-340-2625
Pembroke Pines | Home Depot Shopping Ctr. | 11037 Pines Blvd. (Hiatus Rd.) | 954-443-6610
Weston | Weston Commons | 4527 Weston Rd. (Griffin Rd.) | 954-358-2625
Plantation | 512 N. Pine Island Rd. (bet. Broward & Cleary Blvds.) | 954-474-3311
www.anthonyscoalfiredpizza.com
"Deliciously scorched" thin-crust pizzas with "high-end toppings" – plus "killer" wings and "awesome" salads for two – have made this burgeoning Florida-based chain "a hit"; its self-described "well-done" pies strike a few as simply "burned" and the "nothing-fancy" settings can be "loud", but "prompt" service and "low costs" keep 'em "crowded."

Blue Moon Fish Co. *Seafood*   24 | 23 | 23 | $49

Lauderdale-by-the-Sea | 4405 W. Tradewinds Ave. (Commercial Blvd.) | 954-267-9888
Coral Springs | 10317 Royal Palm Blvd. (Coral Springs Dr.) | 954-755-0002 Ⓜ
www.bluemoonfishco.com
"Thoughtfully chosen and prepared" seafood and "gorgeous" views of the Intracoastal's "yacht parade" make this "upscale" Lauderdale-by-

FOOD | DECOR | SERVICE | COST

the-Sea fish house Broward's Most Popular eatery, whether "for a romantic dinner or just to show friends why you moved to South Florida"; there's "attentive" service plus "ambiance to spare" on the outdoor deck, though "steep" prices convince many to opt for the "doubly wonderful" two-for-one lunch "bargains"; P.S. Coral Springs is separately owned, sans view and cheaper.

Bonefish Grill *Seafood*
22 | 19 | 21 | $36

Ft. Lauderdale | 6282 N. Federal Hwy. (NE 62nd St.) | 954-492-3266
Coral Springs | 1455 N. University Dr. (Shadow Wood Blvd.) | 954-509-0405
Davie | Weston Commons | 4545 Weston Rd. (Griffin Rd.) | 954-389-9273
Plantation | 10197 W. Sunrise Blvd. (Nob Hill Rd.) | 954-472-3592
www.bonefishgrill.com

"Just-out-of-the-water fish in many forms" "draws droves" to these "delightful", "easygoing" seafooders ("hard to believe it's a chain"); "longish waits, even with a reservation" and "noise" are balanced by "prompt, courteous" service and "competitive prices"; P.S. the "Bang Bang Shrimp is bang-on."

Cafe Maxx *American/Eclectic*
27 | 19 | 24 | $57

Pompano Beach | 2601 E. Atlantic Blvd. (NE 26th Ave.) | 954-782-0606 | www.cafemaxx.com

Chef Oliver Saucy's "innovative" Eclectic–New American cuisine is "always prepared with a special touch" and complemented by co-owner Darrel Broek's "inspired" wine list and "pleasantly low-key" service at this "one-of-a-kind" "treasure" in Pompano Beach; it's "not cheap" and some gripe that the strip-mall setting "doesn't do [the experience] justice", but longtime loyalists plead "don't move – it's part of the charm."

Café Sharaku Ⓜ *Asian*
28 | 15 | 25 | $44

Ft. Lauderdale | 2736 N. Federal Hwy. (bet. E. Oakland Park Blvd. & NE 26th St.) | 954-563-2888 | www.cafesharaku.com

"Don't tell anyone!" say fans who worry they might "betray their own interests" by raving about the "sophisticated", "beautifully presented" Asian fusion cuisine at this "tiny" (18-seat) not-quite-so-"hidden gem" in Ft. Lauderdale; there's "not much" decor but it's "quiet", and chef-owner Iwao Kaita and his servers "work so well together to pace" meals that it's lovely to linger for a "romantic" repast.

Canyon *Southwestern*
27 | 22 | 23 | $52

Ft. Lauderdale | 1818 E. Sunrise Blvd. (N. Federal Hwy.) | 954-765-1950 | www.canyonfl.com

It's "quite a scene" at this "popular" Ft. Lauderdale bistro offering an "imaginative", "pricey" menu of Southwestern and American "fusion" fare; "enormous portions", prickly pear margaritas that "wow" and "helpful" service are the reward "once you are finally seated" after often long "waits", the result of a "small" space and a no-reserving policy that can be "a real drag."

The Capital Grille *Steak*
26 | 25 | 25 | $67

Ft. Lauderdale | 2430 E. Sunrise Blvd. (Bayview Dr.) | 954-446-2000 | www.thecapitalgrille.com

"Where the elite meet to eat meat" sums up this Ft. Lauderdale chophouse that admirers deem a "cut above other national steak chains" –

not just for its "perfect sear" but also for its "impeccable" service that ensures "everyone is treated like a VIP"; a "solid wine list", including many by the glass, and "clubby", "dark-wood" environs make for a "relaxing" time, so go ahead and "break the bank."

Casa D'Angelo Italian
27 | 22 | 24 | $61

Ft. Lauderdale | Sunrise Square Plaza | 1201 N. Federal Hwy. (bet. E. Sunrise Blvd. & NE 13th St.) | 954-564-1234 | www.casa-d-angelo.com

Chef-owner Angelo Elia's "outstanding" Northern Italian fare, including a "wide variety of homemade pasta", takes diners on a "delightful" "journey to Italy" without leaving Ft. Lauderdale; it's "expensive" (i.e. an excuse to "wear your Valentino") and tables are "a tad too cozy" in the "bustling" space, but "warm" service and a "wine room that has to be seen to be believed" help explain why it's "beloved" by many – reservations are highly recommended.

Chima Brazilian Steakhouse Brazilian/Steak
25 | 24 | 25 | $64

Ft. Lauderdale | 2400 E. Las Olas Blvd. (SE 25th Ave.) | 954-712-0580 | www.chimasteakhouse.com

"Come hungry" to this "upscale churrascaria" in Ft. Lauderdale where an "endless" variety of "meat, meat and more meat" is carved tableside by "cute" skewer handlers in gaucho-style "black pants" until "belts rip" (yours, not theirs) – and that's aside from the "expansive" salad bar (included in the *rodizio* fee); an outside bar/courtyard with an "old banyan" tree is the perfect place to enjoy an "authentic caipirinha."

Eduardo de San Angel 🗷 Mexican
27 | 22 | 26 | $59

Ft. Lauderdale | 2822 E. Commercial Blvd. (bet. Bayview Dr. & NE 28th Ave.) | 954-772-4731 | www.eduardodesanangel.com

This Ft. Lauderdale "favorite" is "not your typical" "neighborhood taco place" – rather, "under the artful eye" of chef-owner Eduardo Pria, it's a "scintillating" tribute to "refined" "haute Mexicano" that some find "even better than high-end Mexico City restaurants"; a "quiet" ambiance and staffers who "provide the fascinating history of each dish" make it "enjoyable" despite the slight "dent in your wallet."

Greek Islands Taverna Greek
25 | 15 | 21 | $37

Ft. Lauderdale | 3300 N. Ocean Blvd. (Oakland Park Blvd.) | 954-565-5505 | www.greekislandstaverna.com

"*Opa!*" exclaim fans of this "crowded", "convivial" Greek in Ft. Lauderdale offering "authentic" Hellenic fare, including "insanely good" lamb chops, at "unusually affordable prices"; "decor is not part of the deal" and there's no reserving, but "don't be discouraged" by "lines out the door" (or "down the street") because the operation "moves like clockwork" – which also means that service, though "courteous", can feel "rushed."

Grille 66 Seafood/Steak
24 | 24 | 24 | $66

Ft. Lauderdale | Hyatt Regency Pier 66 | 2301 SE 17th St. (23rd Ave.) | 954-728-3500 | www.grille66andbar.com

"Everything is right" at this "quality" surf 'n' turfer in Ft. Lauderdale's Hyatt Pier 66 complex – from the "professional" staffers to the "stylish" space and 800-bottle wine list; the "beautiful setting", with views of the Intracoastal and marina, makes the expense "worth it", and harbor rats suggest "wandering among the million-dollar yachts" "before or after dinner" to complete the experience.

Kitchenetta Trattoria
Tipica Italiana ⓜ *Italian*

| 27 | 18 | 22 | $41 |

Ft. Lauderdale | 2850 N. Federal Hwy. (bet. E. Oakland Park Blvd. & NE 26th St.) | 954-567-3333 | www.kitchenetta.com

"Monster portions" of "delicious" housemade Italian fare – including wood-fired brick-oven flatbreads that are "meals in themselves" – garner "raves" for this reasonably priced Ft. Lauderdale trattoria/enoteca; a "friendly" staff and open kitchen add to its "casual" appeal, but the "concrete" "industrial"-style space can be "deafening" on "busy nights", so conversationalists often "opt for an outdoor table."

La Brochette Bistro ⓜ *Mediterranean*

| 28 | 19 | 26 | $54 |

Cooper City | Embassy Lakes Plaza | 2635 N. Hiatus Rd. (Sheridan St.) | 954-435-9090 | www.labrochettebistro.com

"Who would expect to find" Broward County's top spot for Food and Service "tucked away" in a Cooper City strip mall "a couple doors down from Winn-Dixie"? ask fans who marvel at the "gastronomical delights" on chef-owner Aboud Kobaitri's moderately expensive, seafood-focused Med menu; the "intimate" "European" environs are conducive to "romantic" meals, and diners are "well cared for" by the "sweet, old-fashioned" staffers.

Market 17 *American/Eclectic*

| 26 | 25 | 25 | $58 |

Ft. Lauderdale | 1850 SE 17th St. (Eisenhower Blvd.) | 954-835-5507 | www.market17.net

"Innovative" New American–Eclectic fare made with a "deft" touch and "farm-fresh" ingredients earns kudos for this sophisticated spot in Ft. Lauderdale; "superlative" service, "elegant" environs and a "wonderful wine and cocktail list" also help justify the "expensive" tabs; P.S. a small private room hosts "memorable" "dining-in-the-dark" tasting meals "packed with sensory", if not visual, "delights."

Sette Bello *Italian*

| 26 | 21 | 25 | $52 |

Ft. Lauderdale | 6241 N. Federal Hwy. (NE 62nd St.) | 954-351-0505 | www.settebellofla.com

At this "authentic" "family-owned" Italian in Ft. Lauderdale, diners feel "welcomed" by a chef-owner who "oversees everything", both in the kitchen (preparing "tasty" pastas and other "reasonably priced" fare) and out ("appearing at tables" to "ask about the food"); the "attention to detail" extends to the "small" room's "pretty" decor and "nice" wine list, with staffers ready to "suggest good pairings."

Steak 954 *Steak*

| 24 | 26 | 23 | $76 |

Ft. Lauderdale | W Ft. Lauderdale | 401 N. Ft. Lauderdale Beach Blvd. (Bayshore Dr.) | 954-414-8333 | www.steak954.com

"A hot spot even for a W Hotel", this "chic" chophouse from Stephen Starr (Buddakan in Philly and NYC, etc.) dazzles the eyes with its "fascinating" 15-ft. jellyfish tank and "gorgeous" beach and ocean views, helping it grab the top Decor rating in Broward; taste buds are also treated to some "inventive twists on traditional steakhouse standards" delivered by an "attentive" crew making it "worth every one of the many dollars."

	FOOD	DECOR	SERVICE	COST

Thai Spice *Thai*   26 | 22 | 25 | $38

Ft. Lauderdale | 1514 E. Commercial Blvd. (bet. NE 13th Ave. & 15th Terr.) | 954-771-4535 | www.thaispicefla.com

With a "litany" of daily specials recited by a "smiling" staff plus an "extensive" printed menu, there's "way more than pad Thai" at this "excellent" Siamese in a Ft. Lauderdale strip mall; "fresh orchids" adorning "beautifully presented" plates and an "upscale" setting with "spectacular" "tropical fish tanks" set the scene for "romance", while "fair" prices seal the deal.

3030 Ocean *American/Seafood*   26 | 23 | 24 | $57

Ft. Lauderdale | Harbor Beach Marriott Resort & Spa | 3030 Holiday Dr. (Seabreeze Blvd.) | 954-765-3030 | www.3030ocean.com

"Ultrafresh" fish prepared with "imagination" by the "personable" Dean James Max is the lure at this "upscale" Ft. Lauderdale New American; it's in the "hectic" lobby of an "oceanfront" Marriott, so there could be "noisy conventioneers" or "a family in their bathing suits" nearby, but "get over it" and "ask for a window" with "beautiful" water views or a "quiet table at the rear" away from the "lively" bar.

Valentino's Cucina Italiana 🅂 Ⓜ *Italian*   27 | 16 | 25 | $71

Ft. Lauderdale | 620 S. Federal Hwy. (SE 6th St.) | 954-523-5767 | www.valentinoscucinaitaliana.com

The "innovative" fare at this "pricey" Ft. Lauderdale Italian is so "blow-you-away" good that some find themselves "creating excuses to call things 'special occasions'" just to go back again; service is "excellent", and those who found its former strip-mall locale "small" and "uninteresting" may be pleased by a recent move down the street to larger digs (not reflected in the Decor score); P.S. bonus: there's more parking space now too.

Honolulu

TOP FOOD RANKING

	Restaurant	Cuisine
29	La Mer	French
	Mitch's Fish Market	Japanese/Seafood
28	Alan Wong's	Hawaii Regional
	Sushi Sasabune	Japanese
27	Chef Mavro	French/Hawaii Regional
	Michel's	French
	Hiroshi Eurasion Tapas	Eurasian
	Le Bistro	French
	Orchids	Pacific Rim
	Hy's Steak House	Steak

OTHER NOTEWORTHY PLACES

Restaurant	Cuisine
Assaggio	Italian
Big City Diner	American
DK Steak House	Steak
Nobu Waikiki	Japanese/Peruvian
Pineapple Room	Hawaii Regional
Roy's	Hawaii Regional
Sansei	Japanese/Pacific Rim
3660 on the Rise	Pacific Rim
Town	American/Italian
Vino Italian Tapas	Italian

Alan Wong's *Hawaii Reg.* | 28 | 23 | 27 | $79 |

McCully | 1857 S. King St. (Pumehana St.) | 808-949-2526 | www.alanwongs.com

A "pioneer in Hawaiian regional cuisine", chef Alan Wong "continues to innovate", "plating up the best of local farms and island seas" at this McCully "nirvana", still rated a "perfect No. 1" as Oahu's Most Popular; the "exciting", "exceptionally prepared" food boasts "brilliant flavors" and the "wine list is top-notch", and it's all "expertly presented" by a "smart" staff versed in every "culinary nuance"; if a few quibble that it "lacks panache", most agree it's the "dining highlight" of the island.

Assaggio *Italian* | 25 | 23 | 24 | $39 |

Kailua | 354 Uluniu St. (Aarona pl.) | 808-261-2772
Kapolei | 777 Kamokila Blvd. (Alohike St.) | 808-674-8801
Mililani | Town Center Of Mililani | 95-1249 Meheula Pkwy. (Lanikuhana Ave.) | 808-623-5115
Ala Moana | Ala Moana Ctr. | 1450 Ala Moana Blvd. (bet. Atkinson Dr. & Piikoi St.) | 808-942-3446
Hawaii Kai | Koko Marina Ctr. | 7192 Kalanianaole Hwy. (Lunalilo Home Rd.) | 808-396-0756
Kahala | 4346 Waialae Ave. (Kallauea Ave.) | 808-732-1011
www.assaggiohi.com

"Never been disappointed" at this Italian chain declare diners who give "kudos" to the "savory, delicious" and "memorable" fare, "pleasant,

	FOOD	DECOR	SERVICE	COST

light" atmosphere and "courteous" service; portions are "plentiful" and "reasonably" priced and the Caesar salad made tableside is "heaven", especially for "garlicphiles" – little wonder this outfit is a "gathering spot for local folk" who live a "hop, skip and a jump" away; P.S. the view of the harbor at the Koko Marina branch is "very relaxing."

Big City Diner   *American*   21 | 17 | 22 | $22

Kailua | Foodland Mktpl. | 108 Hekili St. (Hamakua Dr.) | 808-263-8880
Waipahu | Waipio Shopping Ctr. | 94-800 Ukee St. (Oli Loop) | 808-678-8868
Aiea | Pearlridge Shopping Ctr. | 98-211 Pali Momi St. (Moanalua Rd.) | 808-487-8188
Kaimuki | 3565 Waialae Ave. (11th Ave.) | 808-738-8855
Ward | Ward Entertainment Ctr. | 1060 Auahi St. (Kamakee St.) | 808-591-8891
www.bigcitydinerhawaii.com

"Go in with an empty stomach and leave full" urge fans who frequent this "family-friendly" Oahu diner chain with "lively decor" specializing in "ono-licious local grinds" (or "excellent" American "comfort food" with an "authentic" Hawaiian "twist"); the "extensive menu" is packed with "simple pleasures", including an "out-of-this-world breakfast", "gigantic burgers" and "insane" kimchi fried rice, all dished out in "customary huge portions" and served "with a smile" at "affordable" prices.

Chef Mavro   Ⓜ *French/Hawaii Reg.*   27 | 25 | 28 | $103

Moiliili | 1969 S. King St (McCully St.) | 808-944-4714 | www.chefmavro.com
"Expert culinarian" George ('Mavro') Mavrothalassitis "delivers on all fronts", offering a "spectacular taste of the islands" at his Hawaii Regional–French "true gourmet experience" set in a "nondescript building" in Moiliili where his "wife greets you at the door"; "plan to take your time" – the chef "combines exquisite technique with his passion for local ingredients" ensuring that "every morsel" of the "pricey set menu" is a "series of unique surprises", while the sommelier does a "fantastic job" with wine pairings and service is "gracious."

DK Steak House   *Steak*   26 | 23 | 26 | $62

Waikiki | Waikiki Beach Marriott Resort & Spa | 2552 Kalakaua Ave. (bet. Ohua & Paoakalani Aves.) | 808-931-6280 | www.dkrestaurants.com
D.K. Kodama's "clubby" yet "elegant" Waikiki Beach Marriott steakhouse is "one of the best" places on the beach to "savor a real" hunk of dry-aged beef and enjoy the "spectacular sunset"; the meat is "earthy, juicy and well paired" with the "solid wine list" and a "dizzying array of delicious sides", all delivered by an "absolutely delightful" staff; if quibblers find the decor a "bit lacking" for that "special night out", for most the "awesome location" more than compensates.

Hiroshi Eurasion Tapas   *Eurasian*   27 | 24 | 26 | $56

Restaurant Row | 500 Ala Moana Blvd. (bet. Punchbowl & South Sts.) | 808-533-4476 | www.dkrestaurants.com
"Prepare to be seduced by the flavors" at this "modern" Eurasian tapas "favorite" on Restaurant Row, next to sister restaurant Vino; chef/co-owner Hiroshi Fukui is "constantly experimenting" with ingredients from "local farmers", dreaming up "well-conceived", "imaginative combinations to delight the palate" while his business partner (along with restaurateur D.K. Kodama) and "main attraction" master sommelier Chuck Furuya "happily guides you" and "never pushes expensive

wines"; service is "attentive but not smothering", and happy hour is "amazing", as are the occasional multicourse kaiseki dinners.

Hy's Steak House *Steak*
27 | 25 | 27 | $70

Waikiki | Waikiki Park Heights Hotel | 2440 Kuhio Ave. (bet. Kaiulani Ave. & Kapuni St.) | 808-922-5555 | www.hyshawaii.com

"No postage-stamp portions" here so "bring an appetite" to this "old-school" steakhouse in the Waikiki Park Heights Hotel, an "oasis in the bustle of Waikiki" with a "library feel" where you "expect to see the Rat Pack" in the "big leather booths"; the "exceptional" kiawe-grilled beef sets the "gold standard", the wine selection is "terrific", "service is supremely professional" and the live music "fits perfectly" with the "romantic" mood, making for a "memorable experience"; P.S. "save room for the cherries jubilee" prepared tableside.

La Mer *French*
29 | 29 | 29 | $143

Waikiki | Halekulani Hotel | 2199 Kalia Rd. (Lewers St.) | 808-923-2311 | www.halekulani.com

"By far the finest dining experience you will have on Oahu", this "elegant, intimate" French "keeper" in the "stunning" Halekulani Hotel "aspires to Parisian culinary decadence with prices to match", garnering No. 1 ratings in Hawaii for Food, Decor and Service; the "superbly prepared" prix fixe and tasting menus coupled with a "top-notch wine list", "supreme" setting overlooking Waikiki Beach and "utterly spectacular" sunset views give epicures the "best reasons to open the piggy bank and put on a jacket" or long-sleeve collar shirts (either one required).

Le Bistro *French*
27 | 22 | 25 | $60

Niu Valley | Niu Valley Shopping Ctr. | 5730 Kalanianaole Hwy. (Halemaumau St.) | 808-373-7990

"Leave the strip mall behind" as you enter this "true hidden gem" owned by "talented" Japanese chef Alan Takasaki and his wife, Debbie, serving "fantastic French" fare in an "unlikely" Niu Valley venue; the "service-oriented staff" is "committed" to delivering "beautifully prepared dishes" made with "lots of local ingredients" and an "outstanding" wine list while the "elegant" room retains a "cozy feel", making for a *magnifique* and "memorable" experience that's "well worth the price."

Michel's *French*
27 | 27 | 28 | $85

Waikiki | Colony Surf | 2895 Kalakaua Ave. (Poni Moi Rd.) | 808-923-6552 | www.michelshawaii.com

"Romantic, expensive, posh", yes, this "big date" Classic French "throwback" is "worth every penny" sigh sybarites who snag oceanfront seats at this "bastion of fine traditional cooking" in the Colony Surf Hotel at the foot of Diamond Head; "it's the view that captures your heart" – let the "sunset, ships and night lights of Honolulu woo you" as the "music of the surf caresses the shore" and you "feast on the sumptuous" prix fixe menu prepared tableside by "gracious" tuxedo-clad servers; in sum, "simply marvelous."

Mitch's Fish Market & Sushi Bar *Japanese/Seafood*
29 | 13 | 24 | $69

Airport | 524 Ohohia St. (Ualena St.) | 808-837-7774 | www.mitchsushi.com

"In-freakin'-credible!" cheer fin fans who dive into the "outstanding chirashi plates" and "large portions" of the "freshest" fish at this

| | FOOD | DECOR | SERVICE | COST |

Japanese seafooder, a reservations-only BYO set in a "nondescript" warehouse near the airport car-rentals; it's "not the prettiest" locale, and the "tiny 'dining' area" is reminiscent of "Ralph Kramden's *Honeymooners* apartment", but the master sushi chefs "ensure that every piece is a balanced work of edible art" that's "worth the high price."

Nobu Waikiki *Japanese/Peruvian*   26 | 25 | 24 | $84

Waikiki | Waikiki Parc Hotel | 2233 Helumoa Rd. (Lewers St.) | 808-237-6999 | www.noburestaurants.com

You can always expect an "ethereal meal at one of Nobu Matsuhisa's" namesake restaurants and the Waikiki Parc Hotel branch is "no exception" exult enthusiasts who suggest you "give yourself over" to your "super-attentive" servers who "delight you with a parade" of "original, brilliant" Japanese-Peruvian fusion "taste sensations"; the sushi is like "edible art" while the low-lit atmosphere is "mellow, yet classy" – "all in all a wonderful dining experience", though a few quip that it "takes a sophisticated palate to appreciate the cost."

Orchids *Pacific Rim*   27 | 28 | 28 | $75

Waikiki | Halekulani Hotel | 2199 Kalia Rd. (Lewers St.) | 808-923-2311 | www.halekulani.com

It's "less formal than La Mer upstairs", but "from the minute" you enter this "spectacular" Pacific Rim seafooder in the "famed" Halekulani Hotel you're "treated like an alii (royalty)" by the "stellar" staff; "with Diamond Head in the background" and a "gorgeous oceanside setting" plus "innovative global-class cuisine" (including the "justifiably famous" Sunday brunch) and the "quiet elegance" of the orchid-filled room, the stage is set for a "wonderful" "open-air experience."

Pineapple Room *Hawaii Reg.*   25 | 20 | 23 | $37

Ala Moana | Macy's, Ala Moana Ctr. | 1450 Ala Moana Blvd. (bet. Atkinson Dr. & Piikoi St.) | 808-945-6573 | www.alanwongs.com

"Affordable Alan Wong! what a concept!" – this is the place to try the famed chef's "scrumptious" Hawaii Regional "creations" "without the super-high price tag" gush fans who make fruitful expeditions to this "surprising find" on Macy's third floor in the Ala Moana Center; a meal is "both a bargain and a treat", the setting is "casual" and service "pragmatic" – it's a "wonderful combination", and while it can get "noisy", the "food makes up for all of it."

Roy's *Hawaii Reg.*   26 | 23 | 25 | $57

Kapolei | Ko Olina Resort & Marina | 92-1220 Aliinui Dr. (Kamoana Pl.) | 808-676-7697 | www.roysrestaurant.com
Hawaii Kai | 6600 Kalanianaole Hwy. (Keahole St.) | 808-396-7697 | www.roysrestaurant.com
Waikiki | Waikiki Beach Walk | 226 Lewers St. (Kalakaua Ave.) | 808-923-7697 | www.royshawaii.com

The "godfather" of Hawaii Regional cuisine "still shines" insist loyalists who patronize Roy Yamaguchi's "epicurean delight" (Honolulu's Most Popular chain), including the "original" Hawaii Kai "mother ship"; "pupus through dessert", "each morsel makes your mouth happy" (try the "terrific" signature blackened ahi and "sublime" chocolate lava cake) and it's all "complemented by a very sophisticated wine list", "cordial" service and "cosmopolitan" atmosphere; if a wistful few feel it was "more interesting once upon a time", for most it's "always a treat."

	FOOD	DECOR	SERVICE	COST

Sansei *Japanese/Pacific Rim*

| 26 | 20 | 23 | $47 |

Waikiki | Waikiki Beach Marriott Resort & Spa | 2552 Kalakaua Ave. (bet. Ohua & Paoakalani Aves.) | 808-931-6286
Kapalua | Kapalua Resort | 600 Office Rd. (Village Rd.) | 808-669-6286
Kihei | Kihei Town Ctr. | 1881 S. Kihei Rd. (Halelani Pl.) | 808-879-0004
Kohala Coast | Waikoloa Beach Resort | 69-201 Waikoloa Beach Dr. (Queen Kaahumanu Hwy.) | Kamuela | 808-886-6286
www.sanseihawaii.com

The "amazing array of exquisite" sushi coupled with "scrumptious" entrees and cocktails lure loyalists to this "fabulous", "clublike" Japanese–Pacific Rim chainlet; "sit at the sushi bar and leave it to the chefs to prepare fish so fresh, you'd think they just plucked it out of the sea", though prepare to wait "forever if you don't have a reservation"; P.S. "don't forget the early-bird specials" or weekend karaoke.

Sushi Sasabune 🅢 *Japanese*

| 28 | 18 | 21 | $106 |

Ala Moana | 1417 S. King St. (Keeaumoku St.) | 808-947-3800

"OMG . . . omakase!" – for "mindblowingly fresh sushi impeccably prepared", this "spartan" Japanese "favorite" in Makiki is a "must-visit for purists" who follow "perfectionist" Seiji Kumagawa's motto: "trust me"; yes, he can be "bossy" but his "bark may be worse than his bite – and his bites are worth" the steep costs, since "once you put a piece of signature negitoro in your mouth", it's "simply divine."

3660 on the Rise 🅜 *Pacific Rim*

| 26 | 22 | 26 | $57 |

Kaimuki | 3660 Waialae Ave. (Wilhelmina Rise) | 808-737-1177 | www.3660.com

"Away from the hustle and bustle", this Pacific Rim seafooder "surprisingly set in an office building" remains a "Kaimuki treasure" where chef Russell Siu dreams up "amazingly innovative" fare, including his signature "melt-in-your mouth" ahi katsu, "served with utmost courtesy" by the "welcoming staff"; if a few wonder "what's all the fuss about?", for most it's "well worth leaving the tourist throngs and joining the locals" at this "upscale, modern" place that "will never plateau."

Town 🅢 *American/Italian*

| 26 | 19 | 23 | $39 |

Kaimuki | 3435 Waialae Ave. (9th Ave.) | 808-735-5900 | www.townkaimuki.com

Diners leave Ed Kenney's "lively" and "totally non-fancy" New American–Italian "locavore heaven" in Kaimuki with "smiles across their faces", praising the "innovative use of local ingredients" ("not a single cliché could be found on my plate") and the industrial digs' "hip, young yet welcoming vibe"; while it can get "noisy" and "cramped", for most it "never fails to delight" with its "reasonably" priced "taste of urban chic."

Vino Italian Tapas & Wine Bar 🅢🅜 *Italian*

| 26 | 21 | 24 | $45 |

Restaurant Row | 500 Ala Moana Blvd. (bet. Punchbowl & South Sts.) | 808-524-8466 | www.dkrestaurants.com

"Wine, wine and more wine" lures oenophiles to D.K. Kodama's vino-centric Italian on Restaurant Row where master sommelier Chuck Furuya's "philosophy" of pairing "food-friendly" pours from Europe and California with chef Keith Endo's "perfectly prepared small plates" hits all of the "high" notes; for a "real adventure", come for an "informal" meal with a "small group of friends" and "sample the extensive variety" of tapas and "little-known varietals" – "what a combination."

Houston

	Restaurant	Cuisine
29	Da Marco	Italian
28	Chez Nous	French
	Mark's American Cuisine	American
	Pappas Bros. Steakhouse	Steak
27	Nino's	Italian
	Brasserie Max & Julie	French
	Brennan's	Creole
	Del Frisco's Double Eagle	Steak
	Kiran's	Indian
	Brenner's	Steak
	Tony Mandola's	Seafood
26	Uptown Sushi	Japanese
	Mockingbird Bistro Wine Bar	American
	Perry's Steakhouse & Grille	Steak
	Vic & Anthony's	Steak
	Dolce Vita Pizzeria Enoteca	Italian
	Irma's*	Mexican
	Morton's	Steak
	Backstreet Café	American
	Kanomwan	Thai

OTHER NOTEWORTHY PLACES

Restaurant	Cuisine
Américas	South American
Branch Water	American
Carrabba's	Italian
Coppa	Italian
Feast	British
Haven	American
Hugo's	Mexican
Indika	Indian
Kata Robata	Japanese
Le Mistral	French
Oxheart	American
Philippe	American/French
Reef	Seafood
RDG/Bar Annie	American/Southwestern
Ristorante Cavour	Italian
Tony's	American/French
Triniti	American
Uchi	Japanese
Underbelly	American
Valentino	Italian

* Indicates a tie with restaurant above

	FOOD	DECOR	SERVICE	COST

Américas *S American* | 24 | 25 | 23 | $47 |

River Oaks | 2040 W. Gray St. (bet. McDuffe St. & Shepherd Dr.) |
832-200-1492
The Woodlands | 21 Waterway Ave. (Lake Robbins Dr.) | 281-367-1492
www.cordua.com

"Sample the tastes of South America" at this upscale duo in River Oaks
and The Woodlands from the Cordúa family (Amazon Grill, Artista,
Churrascos) with "wonderful", "top-notch" cooking and "fanciful" decor; service receives mixed reviews, and beware of acoustics that "can
be painful at peak times"; P.S. the Galleria original has closed.

Backstreet Café *American* | 26 | 24 | 25 | $39 |

River Oaks | 1103 S. Shepherd Dr. (Clay St.) | 713-521-2239 |
www.backstreetcafe.net

There's "lots of character" at this "quaint old house" in River Oaks, a
perpetual "favorite" for "stellar" midpriced American fare "with something for everyone" backed by "great wines" selected by Sean Beck
(also "quite the mixologist"); "the backyard patio is lovely in pleasant
weather", and "Sunday brunch is a real treat" too.

Branch Water Tavern ●Ⓜ *American* | 25 | 20 | 24 | $36 |

Heights | 510 Shepherd Dr. (bet. Blossom & Gibson Sts.) | 713-863-7777 |
www.branchwatertavern.com

Smitten fans "can't say enough good things" about this Heights New
American putting out "fabulous" fare and small plates backed by "creative" cocktails and "amazing bourbons"; the pubby space is "loud",
but "pleasant" and "well-informed" service completes the picture.

Brasserie Max & Julie *French* | 27 | 24 | 25 | $44 |

Montrose | 4315 Montrose Blvd. (Richmond Ave.) | 713-524-0070 |
www.maxandjulie.net

The "quintessential" French brasserie, this "lovely" Montrose charmer
pairs "fantastic", "authentic" fare with "excellent" Gallic wines; the
"atmosphere will make you believe you're in Paris", and it's even more
of a kick "when someone else is treating."

Brennan's *Creole* | 27 | 28 | 27 | $56 |

Midtown | 3300 Smith St. (Stuart St.) | 713-522-9711 |
www.brennanshouston.com

A "landmark", this Midtown "grande dame" and sib of the famed
Commander's Palace in New Orleans is "the place to indulge" in "fabulous" Southwestern-Creole dishes like turtle soup and bananas Foster;
it's ranked No. 1 for Service and Decor in Houston thanks to "exceptional hospitality" that "makes you feel like royalty" plus an "absolutely gorgeous" interior cementing its status as a "go-to" for "birthdays
and special occasions" or the "amazing" jazz brunch on Sundays;
P.S. jackets suggested.

Brenner's *Steak* | 27 | 26 | 25 | $59 |

Memorial | 10911 Katy Frwy. (bet. Brittmoore Rd. & Wycliffe Dr.) |
713-465-2901
River Oaks | 1 Birdsall St. (Memorial Dr.) | 713-868-4444
www.brennerssteakhouse.com

A longtime "tradition" for beef, this steakhouse duo from the Landry's
chain boasts "impressive" cuts and a staff that "waits on you hand and

	FOOD	DECOR	SERVICE	COST

foot"; "you can't beat the" atmosphere either, with both the circa-1936 Memorial branch and its River Oaks offshoot featuring "dark", wood-trimmed quarters deemed "perfect for a special occasion."

Carrabba's Italian Grill *Italian*   23 | 20 | 22 | $29

Briargrove | 1399 S. Voss Rd. (bet. San Felipe St. & Woodway Dr.) | 713-468-0868
Champions | Champions Vill. | 5440 FM 1960 W. (Champion Forest Dr.) | 281-397-8255
Northwest Houston | 7540 Hwy. 6 N. (bet. Longenbaugh & Ridge Park Drs.) | 281-859-9700
Upper Kirby District | 3115 Kirby Dr. (Branard St.) | 713-522-3131
West Houston | 11339 Katy Frwy. (bet. Kirkwood Rd. & Wilcrest Dr.) | 713-464-6595
Webster | 502 W. Bay Area Blvd. (bet. Hwy. 3 & I-45) | 281-338-0574
Kingwood | 750 Kingwood Dr. (Chestnut Ridge Dr.) | 281-358-5580
Sugar Land | 2335 Hwy. 6 S. (bet. Lexington & Town Center Blvds.) | 281-980-4433
The Woodlands | 25665 I-45 N. Hwy. (bet. Briar Rock Rd. & Valley Wood Dr.) | 281-367-9423
www.carrabbas.com

"Mainstream" Italian cooking comes in "plentiful" portions at this "reasonably priced" franchise ranked a solid bet "for a casual night out" with the family; "long waits" prevail at most locales, although seasoned patrons proclaim "you're best off" with the "family-owned originals" in Briargrove and the Upper Kirby District in Houston.

Chez Nous 🔀 *French*   28 | 24 | 27 | $64

Humble | 217 S. Ave. G. (bet. Granberry & Staitti Sts.) | 281-446-6717 | www.cheznousfrenchrestaurant.com

In the "quiet city of Humble", this "expensive" foodie "mecca" is "worth the drive" thanks to its "outstanding" market-driven French cuisine, "excellent" wines and "superior service"; the setting in an old church is "romantic" enough that you may just see someone "pop the question"; P.S. jackets suggested.

Coppa *Italian*   ▽ 25 | 23 | 23 | $39

Heights | 5555 Washington Ave. (TC Jester Blvd.) | 713-426-4260 | www.copparistorante.com

A "pleasant surprise" in the Heights, this moderately priced Italian (and sibling of Brasserie 19 and Ibiza) has been hot since day one thanks to its "new takes on traditional dishes" like tuna crudo, goat ravioli and pizzas topped with ham and eggs; "knowledgeable" service and an "energetic" yet "comfortable" ambiance seal the deal.

Da Marco 🔀Ⓜ️ *Italian*   29 | 24 | 27 | $61

Montrose | 1520 Westheimer Rd. (bet. Ridgewood & Windsor Sts.) | 713-807-8857 | www.damarcohouston.com

"Tuscany" comes to Texas via this Montrose Italian – voted No. 1 for Food and Most Popular in Houston – whipping up "memorable" meals with "sublime", "homemade pastas" and "amazing things with truffles" in an "intimate" setting tended by a "knowledgeable" staff; yes, it's "crowded" and "you'll take a hit in the pocketbook, but you won't mind"; P.S. beer and wine only.

	FOOD	DECOR	SERVICE	COST

Del Frisco's Double Eagle
Steak House *Steak*

27 | 24 | 26 | $67

Galleria | 5061 Westheimer Rd. (bet. McCue Rd. & Post Oak Blvd.) |
713-355-2600 | www.delfriscos.com

You might just "need two stomachs" for the "outrageous", "buttery" steaks "cooked to perfection" at this high-end chophouse chain catering to an "expense-account" clientele with its "extensive wine list", "fine" service and setting akin to a "chic Western saloon"; it's especially "great for a special occasion" "if money is no object"; P.S. the Uptown Dallas Grille offers a lighter menu with a focus on cocktails, apps and burgers plus brunch in a more relaxed setting.

Dolce Vita Pizzeria Enoteca 🅼 *Italian*

26 | 17 | 21 | $32

Montrose | 500 Westheimer Rd. (Whitney St.) | 713-520-8222 |
www.dolcevitahouston.com

"Fabulous pizzas" with "beautiful blistered crusts" are the main attraction at this Montrose Italian from Marco Wiles (Da Marco), also putting out "innovative" antipasti and well-chosen wines; the room's bustling most nights with a "noisy" crowd, so "go early" or prepare to wait.

Feast *British*

24 | 18 | 23 | $43

Montrose | 219 Westheimer Rd. (Bagby St.) | 713-529-7788 |
www.feasthouston.com

"A must for any self-respecting foodie", this "homage to offal" in Montrose serves a "ballsy" British menu featuring "bold, adventurous and seriously delicious" "snout-to-tail" dishes; prices are "reasonable", while a "down-to-earth" staff and a "cute and cozy" Arts and Crafts setting complete the package.

Haven 🅇 *American*

25 | 24 | 24 | $43

Upper Kirby District | 2502 Algerian Way (Kirby Dr.) | 713-581-6101 |
www.havenhouston.com

Praised as a "pioneer in the eat-local movement", this "cool" Upper Kirby American from Randy Evans features "marvelous", midpriced small and large plates spotlighting artisanal and organic ingredients "in delicious new ways"; service is "attentive" and the setting has a "Texas-gone-green-and-sustainable vibe" with "sleek", "beautiful" decor designed from reclaimed materials.

Hugo's *Mexican*

26 | 23 | 23 | $41

Montrose | 1600 Westheimer Rd. (Mandell St.) | 713-524-7744 |
www.hugosrestaurant.net

This upscale Montrose Mexican is known for its "brilliantly executed", "modern" dishes "with a twist" and "kick-butt" margaritas "shaken at your table"; service is "excellent" and the attractive setting is always "humming with patrons", so "the only drawback is the noise level"; P.S. be sure to reserve ahead for Sunday's "fabulous brunch."

Indika 🅼 *Indian*

26 | 22 | 23 | $42

Montrose | 516 Westheimer Rd. (Whitney St.) | 713-524-2170 |
www.indikausa.com

"The flavors are fantastic" at this "modern" Montrose Indian attracting "adventurous" eaters with "fabulously inventive" cuisine that's "not your typical tandoori"; an "upscale" contemporary setting, "knowledgeable" service and an "inspired" cocktail list are clues that it's "not cheap", but certainly "worth it" for an "exciting" meal.

Irma's ⍒ *Mexican* | 26 | 20 | 23 | $23 |

Downtown | 22 N. Chenevert St. (Ruiz St.) | 713-222-0767 | www.irmashouston.com

"Menus? we don't need no stinkin' menus" is the m.o. at this funky Downtown Mexican where "Irma herself" "tells you what they've got each day" and customers choose from an array of "wonderfully authentic" dishes (don't miss the rightly famous lemonade); it's a "fun" place and a local "institution", though a few find fault with bills that feel a touch "overpriced"; P.S. dinner served Thursday–Saturday and often on game days.

Kanomwan ⍒ *Thai* | 26 | 6 | 13 | $21 |

Neartown | 736½ Telephone Rd. (Lockwood St.) | 713-923-4230
Gastronomes gush over this Neartown BYO Thai (aka 'Telephone Thai') whipping up "fabulous" food at "unbeatable" prices; the service and setting are no frills, but it remains an "institution" nonetheless.

Kata Robata *Japanese* | 25 | 21 | 22 | $41 |

Upper Kirby District | 3600 Kirby Dr. (Richmond Ave.) | 713-526-8858 | www.katarobata.com

"Fantastic sushi" with "modern twists" keeps crowds coming to this Upper Kirby Japanese also sending out "wonderful" small plates from the kitchen (like Kobe beef skewers) "for those who don't like the raw stuff"; though the "beautifully designed" space hosts a "chic" crowd, the bills "leave a surprisingly small dent in the wallet."

Kiran's *Indian* | 27 | 26 | 25 | $51 |

Galleria | 4100 Westheimer Rd. (Mid Ln.) | 713-960-8472 | www.kiranshouston.com

"The kitchen shows a lot of flair" at this Galleria-area venue specializing in "wonderful" Indian fusion cuisine like you might find at "Bombay's top restaurant"; "elegant" surroundings and an "attentive", "well-trained" staff help justify the "expensive" tabs and make it a "lovely place to dine."

Le Mistral *French* | 26 | 24 | 26 | $55 |

West Houston | 1400 Eldridge Pkwy. (bet. Brimhurst & Westerloch Drs.) | 832-379-8322 | www.lemistralhouston.com

"Paris meets Houston" at this "fantastic" upscale French in West Houston where the Denis brothers roll out "exceptional", "traditional" cuisine with especially "beautiful desserts" (the chocolate soufflé is a highlight); "attentive" service and a "warm, cozy" setting evoking "quiet luxury" make it "one of the best" in town.

Mark's American Cuisine *American* | 28 | 27 | 27 | $75 |

Montrose | 1658 Westheimer Rd. (bet. Dunlavy & Ralph Sts.) | 713-523-3800 | www.marks1658.com

"Magnificent" meals are had at this "delightful", "eccentric" converted church in Montrose where chef Mark Cox crafts "fabulous" New American dishes from "exceptional ingredients"; add in "impeccable" service, and it's "everything you could want in a restaurant", not counting the "expensive" bills.

Mockingbird Bistro Wine Bar *American*   26 | 24 | 25 | $50
River Oaks | 1985 Welch St. (McDuffie St.) | 713-533-0200 |
www.mockingbirdbistro.com
A "gem" "tucked away in a residential neighborhood" near River Oaks, this New American spotlights "wonderful, creative" seasonal cuisine from chef-owner John Sheely plus a wine menu that "shines"; it's a tad "expensive", but a "warm" staff and a "quaint" setting with an "old European feel" create an overall "inviting" mood.

Morton's The Steakhouse *Steak*   26 | 24 | 25 | $67
Downtown | 1001 McKinney St. (bet. Fannin & Main Sts.) | 713-659-3700
Galleria | Centre at Post Oak | 5000 Westheimer Rd. (Post Oak Blvd.) |
713-629-1946
www.mortons.com
"Corporate types" clamor for the "massive" steaks and "wonderful" sides and wines at these "manly" Downtown and Galleria outposts of the nationwide chophouse chain; they're "consistent", from the "top-notch" service to the "dark", "noisy" settings and premium prices, and if some find them "nothing special", they're "rarely disappointing" either.

Nino's ☒ *Italian*   27 | 22 | 25 | $39
Montrose | 2817 W. Dallas St. (La Rue St.) | 713-522-5120 |
www.ninos-vincents.com
Perhaps the menu's "not wildly creative", but this family-owned, mid-priced '70s-era Montrose mainstay is "always a pleasure" thanks to its "dependably *delizioso*" red-sauce dishes; there's a "real Italian feel" to the setting – an old house decorated with plants and pottery – and an ever-present owner who "greets guests warmly" adds to the charm; P.S. it shares a courtyard with sibs Grappino and Vincent's.

Oxheart *American*   - | - | - | VE
Downtown | 1302 Nance St. (Richey St.) | 832-830-8592 |
www.oxhearthouston.com
Set neatly in the Warehouse District Downtown, this ambitious, expensive New American – with a veggie-heavy menu and no à la carte – is an inaugural effort from married young chefs Justin Yu and Karen Man that has quickly stood out following its March 2012 opening; with an industrial yet comfortable feel – some bricks, light-colored walls and open kitchen – it's a cozy place (seating 31 at tables and the kitchen counter) that pairs well with the exacting contemporary fare.

Pappas Bros. Steakhouse ☒ *Steak*   28 | 25 | 27 | $71
Galleria | 5839 Westheimer Rd. (bet. Augusta & Bering Drs.) |
713-780-7352 | www.pappasbros.com
The "melt-in-your-mouth" steaks "blow the competition away" at this "classy" Galleria chophouse where the "excellent" cuts are matched with an "unbelievable" wine list ("a sommelier's dream"); yes, it's "pricey", but the "impeccable" service and "elegant, masculine" setting make it a "favorite for special occasions."

Perry's Steakhouse & Grille *Steak*   26 | 26 | 25 | $55
Champions | 9730 Cypresswood Dr. (Cutten Rd.) | 281-970-5999
Memorial | 9827 Katy Frwy. (bet. Bunker Hill & Gessner Rds.) | 832-358-9000
Clear Lake | 487 Bay Area Blvd. (bet. Sea Liner & Seawolf Drs.) |
281-286-8800

(continued)

Perry's Steakhouse & Grille

Katy | LaCenterra at Cinco Ranch | 23501 Cinco Ranch Blvd. (Grand Pkwy.) | 281-347-3600

The Woodlands | 6700 Woodlands Pkwy. (Kuykendahl Rd.) | 281-362-0569
www.perryssteakhouse.com

An "elegant place for business or special occasions", this chophouse chain is the place to "impress" with "wonderful" steaks, "outstanding" wines and a signature pork chop that's "not to be missed" ("everything pales next to the pork"); "top-notch" service and "attractive" settings are added perks, but it's "pretty damn expensive" "unless you're on an expense account"; P.S. live jazz and piano at most locales.

Philippe Restaurant + Lounge Ⓢ *American/French*

24 | 26 | 24 | $54

Galleria | 1800 Post Oak Blvd. (Ambassador Way) | 713-439-1000 | www.philippehouston.com

Very "chic", this Galleria-area entry from "tremendously talented" Philippe Schmit spotlights "top-line" French-American cooking with playful "Texas twists" (e.g. duck-confit tamales, burgundy beef cheeks); the "sexy" space features a first-floor zinc bar with its own menu plus a stylish industrial-contemporary upstairs dining room with near-"flawless" service and moderate-to-pricey bills.

RDG + Bar Annie *American/Southwestern*

24 | 25 | 22 | $59

Galleria | 1800 Post Oak Blvd. (Ambassador Way) | 713-840-1111 | www.rdgbarannie.com

"Old-guard Houston meets Robert Del Grande" at this "swanky" three-in-one concept in the Galleria with a cushy lounge, "noisy" bar and "excellent, creative" American-Southwestern menu presented in a "lavish" dining room; it's certainly a "place to be seen", although some are irked by "pricey" tabs and service "with an attitude."

Reef Ⓢ *Seafood*

25 | 21 | 22 | $47

Midtown | 2600 Travis St. (McGowen St.) | 713-526-8282 | www.reefhouston.com

"Hottie chef" Bryan Caswell "knows his seafood" gush fans of this midpriced Midtown "hot spot" known for its "fantastic", "creative" fare, "fabulous wines" and infamous deep-fried mac 'n' cheese ("don't miss it"); service can be "mixed" and the "modern" setting is plenty "noisy", but the "superb food makes it all bearable."

Ristorante Cavour *Italian*

▽ 24 | 26 | 25 | $62

Uptown | Hotel Granduca | 1080 Uptown Park Blvd. (Post Oak Blvd.) | 713-418-1004 | www.granducahouston.com

Hidden inside the ritzy Hotel Granduca Uptown, this dining room rolls out "excellent" (if "not the most creative") Italian cuisine in a "quiet", "elegant" setting; a few find the prices and the "white-glove service" "a bit precious", but it works for a "special occasion."

Tony Mandola's *Seafood*

27 | 23 | 25 | $39

River Oaks | 1212 Waugh Dr. (Clay St.) | 713-528-3474 | www.tonymandolas.com

A "home run" for the Mandola family, this River Oaks seafooder attracts "everyone in Houston" thanks to its "diverse" array of "fabulous" Gulf

FOOD | DECOR | SERVICE | COST

Coast–style dishes with Creole touches plus a handful of Italian favorites; it's a "bit fancy" with "professional" service and an attractive if "corporate" setting, though the consensus is it's "worth every dime."

Tony's ☒ Continental/Italian
26 | 26 | 26 | $74

Greenway Plaza Area | 3755 Richmond Ave. (Timmons Ln.) | 713-622-6778 | www.tonyshouston.com

"One of Houston's oldest and most elegant", this Greenway Plaza "legend" from Tony Vallone provides "true white-tablecloth" dining via "top-notch" Italian-Continental cuisine and "refined" service in a "date"-worthy setting adorned with world-class art; on the downside are "astronomical" prices and service that can be "a little stuffy" "unless they know you"; P.S. jackets suggested.

Triniti American
- | - | - | E

Lower Shepherd | 2815 S. Shepherd Dr. (Kipling St.) | 713-527-9090 | www.trinitirestaurant.com

Boasting plenty of local experience, chef Ryan Hildebrand and his team are behind this expensive New American in Lower Shepherd, which groups its artistically ambitious offerings into three categories: savory, sweet and spirits; modern chandeliers, artwork and other design touches are softened by warm woods for an ultimately inviting atmosphere, which includes an open kitchen with surrounding seats.

Uchi Japanese
- | - | - | E

Montrose | 904 Westheimer Rd. (Grant St.) | www.uchirestaurants.com

With inspired, exacting riffs on contemporary Japanese cooking and impeccably high-quality seafood, this Montrose newcomer – an offshoot of Austin's top spot – has lived up to the hype and been a tough reservation since its early 2012 launch; soft lighting, low ceilings and warm woods, including some arrayed Jenga-like, help provide an intimate feel to this coolly reconditioned space (for decades Tex-Mex pioneer Felix), which peers onto the bustling lower Westheimer scene.

Underbelly American
- | - | - | E

Montrose | 1100 Westheimer Rd. (Yoakum Blvd.) | 713-528-9800 | www.underbellyhouston.com

This much-anticipated first solo effort from Chris Shepherd, who wowed foodies at the now-closed Catalan, features an ambitious New American menu dedicated to all things porcine; the Montrose storefront is set in the middle of a newly bustling restaurant row and boasts an on-site butcher shop.

Uptown Sushi Japanese
26 | 22 | 22 | $45

Uptown | Uptown Park | 1131-14 Uptown Park Blvd. (Post Oak Blvd.) | 713-871-1200 | www.uptown-sushi.com

This "trendy" Uptown Japanese matches "outstanding" fusion rolls and sushi with creative cocktails; decor could be a little "less *Miami Vice*", and some find prices on the high side, but it's a "hot spot" nonetheless.

Valentino Italian
▽ 23 | 23 | 25 | $46

Galleria | Hotel Derek | 2525 W. Loop S. (Westheimer Rd.) | 713-850-9200 | www.valentinohouston.com

Los Angeles restaurateur Piero Selvaggio is behind this spin-off of his venerable Santa Monica–born Italian in the Galleria-area's sleek Hotel

Derek; extravagant multicourse meals are rolled out by a "terrific" staff in a "beautiful", cushy setting done up in dark tones and crimson, while the adjacent less-formal space is home to the Vin Bar spotlighting small plates, wines and some stellar people-watching.

Vic & Anthony's *Steak*   26 26 27 $64

Downtown | 1510 Texas Ave. (La Branch St.) | 713-228-1111 | www.vicandanthonys.com

This "classy" Downtown steakhouse near Minute Maid Park "gets it right" with "amazing" meats and "winning" wines deemed "damn expensive" but "worth" it; "top-notch" service and a dark, "romantic" setting with piano nightly cement its status as a "special-occasion" standby.

Indianapolis

TOP FOOD RANKING

	Restaurant	Cuisine
29	Recess	Eclectic
28	Mo's a Place for Steaks	Steak
	Capital Grille	Steak
	Morton's	Steak
	Sakura	Japanese
	Papa Roux	Cajun
	Santorini	Greek
	Tegry Bistro	Japanese
	Ruth's Chris	Steak
	City Café	American

OTHER NOTEWORTHY PLACES

Bazbeaux	Pizza
Black Market	Eclectic
Bluebeard	Italian/Eclectic
El Rodeo	Mexican
Late Harvest Kitchen	American
Libertine	Eclectic
Scotty's Brewhouse	American/Burgers
St. Elmo	Steak
Twenty Tap	Pub Food
Yats	Cajun

Bazbeaux *Pizza*
27 | 21 | 23 | $18

Broad Ripple | 811 E. Westfield Blvd. (College Ave.) | 317-255-5711
Carmel | 111 W. Main St. (bet. 1st & 3rd Aves.) | 317-848-4488
Mass Ave. | 333 Massachusetts Ave. (New York St.) |
317-636-7662
www.bazbeaux.com

"Gourmet-pizza lovers" say "nothing compares" to the "unique" combos on "incredible" crust at this "eclectic" pie trio, voted Most Popular in Indianapolis, serving "the stuff cravings are made of", including "huge", "delicious" salads (go for the "creamy basil dressing"); though priced slightly "higher" than your "run-of-the-mill joint", "timely" service and "family-friendly" settings with patio seating – especially at the Broad Ripple branch – are a perk.

Black Market ⊠ Ⓜ *Eclectic*
24 | 23 | 24 | $28

Mass Ave. | 922 Massachusetts Ave. (9th St.) | 317-822-6757 |
www.blackmarketindy.net

The "frequently changing menu always delights" at this "unique", modestly priced Mass Ave. Eclectic known for its "fresh ingredients" and "unusual" combinations ("who knew that peanut butter and pickles paired so well?"); "communal tables inside and out" mean you "get to meet people" in an "adults-only, modern atmosphere" where "knowledgeable" servers are happy to "guide you."

	FOOD	DECOR	SERVICE	COST

Bluebeard 🅢🅜 *Italian/Eclectic*

−	−	−	E

Fletcher Place | 653 Virginia Ave. (College Ave.) | 317-686-1580 | www.bluebeardindy.com

Named for a Kurt Vonnegut novel, this new Italian-Eclectic in Fletcher Place brings inventive, shareable dishes to a communal patio table and cozy (read: tight) interior suitably spiffed up with typewriters and books; expanding the horizons of its local, frequently updated menu is a shipped-from-Italy bread oven, producing crackly-crust pizzas and loaves that are also sold through Amelia's, the restaurant's bakery arm.

The Capital Grille *Steak*

28	27	29	$57

Downtown | 40 W. Washington St. (bet. Illinois & Meridian Sts.) | 317-423-8790 | www.thecapitalgrille.com

"Excellent and surprisingly so for a chain", this Downtown steak-house that some "hate to love" wins praise for its "exceptional" food and "massive" wine list served by an "awesome" staff that goes "above and beyond"; with "welcoming", "beautiful" surroundings too, most agree it's "worth the money" for a "special occasion" or "expense-account" outing.

City Café 🅢 *American*

28	20	23	$13

Downtown | 443 N. Pennsylvania St. (Michigan St.) | 317-833-2233 | www.indycitycafe.com

"Imaginative", "delicious and healthy" offerings prepared with "care-ful touches", including some of the "best sandwiches in town" and never-repeated daily specials, make this "delightful" Downtown American a "local favorite" for breakfast and lunch; the staff treats guests "like family", ensuring the "tiny" dining room "fills up fast"; P.S. closes at 2 PM weekdays, 1 PM Saturdays.

El Rodeo *Mexican*

23	20	23	$16

Avon | 8128 E. US Hwy. 36 | 317-272-0597 🅢🅜
Downtown | 250 S. Meridian St. (Georgia St.) | 317-638-5604
Fishers | 11452 N. Olio Rd. | 317-577-9520 🅢🅜
Geist | 11677 Fox Rd. (Oaklandon Rd.) | 317-823-5136
Greenwood | 3113 W. Smith Valley Rd. | 317-883-0379 🅢🅜
Northwest Side | 5501 W. 86th St. | 317-228-0863 🅢🅜
South Side | 7421 Heathrow Way | 317-856-9053 🅢🅜
West Side | 2606 N. High School Rd. (Embassy Row) | 317-328-7953

Delivering "flavorful" Mexican in portions "huge" enough "to feed two or three" (plus "jumbo" margaritas), this "festive, colorful" chain "tops the list" for many; the "personable" staff is "always spot-on" ("the chips keep coming") and the "price is right", so it works as "your basic, go-to" neighborhood place.

Late Harvest Kitchen 🅢 *American*

▽ 25	26	26	$44

Northeast Side | 8605 River Crossing (River Rd.) | 317-663-8063 | www.lateharvestkitchen.com

A "don't-miss newcomer" by chef-owner Ryan Nelson (ex The Oceanaire), this Northeast Side American offers "fresh, unusual" fare (aka "comfort food with a twist") that "changes" daily with the mar-ket; "upscale" yet "relaxing" with a "tastefully done", wood- and brick-accented interior and "quaint" patio, it's "perfect for a night out", and the care in the cooking and service makes simple meals feel like a "special event."

FOOD | DECOR | SERVICE | COST

The Libertine ⓈⓂ *Eclectic*   ▽ 27 | 26 | 25 | $36

Downtown | 38 E. Washington St. (Scioto St.) | 317-631-3333 |
www.libertineindy.com

"Indy's closest thing to a trendy Manhattan bistro", this "unique"
throwback Downtown joint offers "fab" "concoctions" ("sit at the
bar and watch the mixologists work") along with Eclectic small
plates that are "some of the best" in town; it'll cost a little "$$$",
but the "atmosphere couldn't be better if you want to feel like you're
hanging with Hemingway."

Morton's The Steakhouse *Steak*   28 | 25 | 26 | $60

Downtown | 41 E. Washington St. (Pennsylvania St.) | 317-229-4700 |
www.mortons.com

"Simply fabulous" say fans of this Downtown link in the "classic"
steakhouse chain, coming through with "outstanding" food and "old-
world" service in a mahogany-accented setting that's "cozy and ro-
mantic"; it's a "real treat for special occasions", even if sober sorts cite
"arm-and-a-leg" pricing; P.S. the selection of "bar bites" is easier
on the budget.

Mo's a Place for Steaks Ⓢ *Steak*   28 | 26 | 27 | $51

Downtown | 47 S. Pennsylvania St. (Maryland St.) | 317-624-0720 |
www.mosindy.net

"Top-notch" steaks and smart sides earn "lifetime customers" at this
Downtown chophouse that's "pricey but worth it for special occa-
sions"; the high-ceilinged dining room has an "awesome" atmosphere
enhanced by fine service, and it's a pleasure to "sit in the bar and enjoy
the piano" too.

Papa Roux Ⓢ *Cajun*   28 | 18 | 24 | $12

Downtown | 222 E. Market St. (Delaware St.) | 317-354-9525
East Side | 8950 E. 10th St. (Post Rd.) | 317-603-9861 Ⓜ
www.paparouxindy.com

"N'Awlins, Indy-style" impresses at this "bargain" East Side and
Downtown duo where the owner's "passion for food shows" in the
"genuine Cajun" specialties – "po' boys to die for" and "unlimited
sides" that draw "long lines for lunch"; "fantastic" service rounds out
the "down-home" feel of the place, where "you can write on the walls"
since "graffiti-izing is encouraged."

Recess ⓈⓂ *Eclectic*   29 | 21 | 28 | $60

SoBro | 4907 N. College Ave. (49th St.) | 317-925-7529 |
www.recessindy.com

Voted No. 1 for Food in Indianapolis, this "amazing" SoBro newcomer
boasts "inventive", "expertly prepared" Eclectic dinners by chef-owner
Greg Hardesty who turns his French techniques toward a daily four-
course prix fixe "based on the freshest of ingredients" and served by a
detail-oriented team; despite the stripped-down dining room and no-
choice menu, those who surrender call it the "perfect special-occasion"
place that's "worth it" all around; P.S. attached Room Four restaurant
offers a small menu of less expensive options.

Ruth's Chris Steak House *Steak*   28 | 26 | 28 | $70

Downtown | Circle Centre Mall | 45 S. Illinois St. (bet. Maryland &
Washington Sts.) | 317-633-1313

(continued)

Ruth's Chris Steak House

Near North | 9445 Threel Rd. (96th St.) | 317-844-1155
www.ruthschris.com

"The sizzle of the steak" haunts the dreams of diners who go for "searing hot and buttery" cuts at the Downtown and Near North branches of this "chain steakhouse with a personality", where the atmosphere is "warm and intimate" and the staff "meticulously takes care of your needs"; since prices are as hefty as the plates, it's ideal for "business" and "celebrations" (not to mention invitations from "someone richer than me").

Sakura *Japanese* | 28 | 18 | 21 | $25 |

North Side | 7201 N. Keystone Ave. (72nd St.) | 317-259-4171 |
www.indysakura.com

"Is there an ocean in Indy?" ask "sushi enthusiasts" who adore the "freshest" fish prepared by "amazing" chefs at this "consistent" North Side Japanese; with a "traditional setup", "gracious" service and affordable tabs, it does "get crowded", so be sure to make reservations.

Santorini ⊠ *Greek* | 28 | 23 | 26 | $25 |

Fountain Square | 1417 Prospect St. (Laurel St.) | 317-917-1117 |
www.santorini-greek-kitchen.com

Loyalists "love" the "real", "exciting" Greek food with a "bistro vibe" at this "classy", family-owned Fountain Square charmer where a "tremendous" staff "does an outstanding job with recommendations"; the modestly priced dishes are "huge" and "sharing is encouraged", so it's "fun with a group" or just for a "romantic dinner for two."

Scotty's Brewhouse *American* | 24 | 23 | 22 | $21 |

Downtown | 1 Virginia Ave. (Penn St.) | 317-571-0808
Northeast Side | 3905 E. 96th St. (Delegates Row) | 317-574-0101
www.scottysbrewhouse.com

Scotty's Lakehouse *Burgers*

Fishers | 10158 Brooks School Rd. (Fall Creek Rd.) | 317-577-2900 |
www.scottyslakehouse.com

"Two words: dill chips" declare regulars who dig into fried pickles, nachos and wings at these college and "post-college" pubs, including the "unique" burger-focused Lakehouse spot offering a "gourmet take on all-American food"; the "sports-bar" feel means you won't be out of sightline of a TV, though some find service "can be a little hit-or-miss."

St. Elmo *Steak* | 27 | 24 | 27 | $60 |

Downtown | 127 S. Illinois St. (Georgia St.) | 317-635-0636 |
www.stelmos.com

"Steak the way god intended" and a "famous", "fiery" shrimp cocktail pack plenty of "zing" at this Downtown "landmark" delivering "memorable" dinners in a "white-tablecloth" setting with "top-notch" service (and occasional "celeb sightings"); sure, you'll "pay handsomely", but most agree it "surpasses expectations" from "start to finish."

Tegry Bistro *Japanese* | 28 | 24 | 24 | $25 |

Brownsburg | 1521 N. Green St. (Garner Rd.) | 317-858-9505 |
www.tegrybistro.net

Customers "can't believe" they're "still in Brownsburg" at this "delightful" Japanese offering "luscious" sushi and "outstanding" grilled goods in a "great atmosphere" enhanced by a staff that "gets to know you"; while it "can get pricey depending on what you order", it's "reasonable" for the quality, so most are "always pleased" with the whole package.

Twenty Tap ☒ *Pub Food* 　　25 | 19 | 24 | $17

SoBro | 5408 N. College (54th St.) | 317-602-8840 | www.twentytap.com
Along with "killer cheese curds" and "fries to die for", even the "simple salad is delicious" (and a veggie banh mi isn't too far to venture) at this SoBro pub that "hasn't forgotten to focus on the food"; of course, it also taps "all the local beers" and other "awesome" brews ("actually 30-plus now"), so no wonder it's often a full, "noisy" house.

Yats *Cajun* 　　27 | 20 | 25 | $12

Broad Ripple | 5363 N. College Ave. (54th St.) | 317-253-8817 ⌀
Fishers | 8352 E. 96th St. (Kincaid Dr.) | 317-585-1792
Greenwood | 1280 US 31 (County Line Rd.) | 317-865-9971
Mass Ave. | 659 Mass Ave. (Park Ave.) | 317-686-6380
www.yatscajuncreole.com
"Go there now" for a "quick bite with flair" say devotees of these "deliciously different" Cajun joints offering "a slice of the Big Easy in the Midwest"; the "generous" plates of "tasty vittles" dished up in atmospheres ranging from "routine" to "funky" get added value from "solid", "enthusiastic" service steered by an "over-the-top outgoing" owner, so "why are you reading this?" when you could be chowing down for "cheap."

Kansas City

TOP FOOD RANKING

Restaurant	Cuisine
29 Café Provence	French
28 Justus Drugstore	American
Le Fou Frog	French
Café Sebastienne	American
Capital Grille	Steak
J. Gilbert's	Seafood/Steak
Osteria Il Centro	Italian
Bluestem	American
Bristol	Seafood
Oklahoma Joe's	BBQ

OTHER NOTEWORTHY PLACES

American Restaurant	American
Arthur Bryant's	BBQ
Fiorella's Jack Stack	BBQ
Gates BBQ	BBQ
Hereford House	Steak
Julian	American
Michael Smith	American
Room 39	American
Starker's	American
Webster House	Eclectic

The American Restaurant ⊠ *American*   26 | 24 | 25 | $68
Crown Center | 2511 Grand Blvd. (E. Pershing Rd.) | 816-545-8001 |
www.theamericankc.com
This is "what New American food is about" shout disciples of chef
Debbie Gold, who presides over this "jewel" in Kansas City's Crown
Center that's "stood the test of time" with its "fantastic" seasonal
menu and "excellent" service (even if the "quirky" decor may be "over-
due for a face-lift"); sure, the "elegant, urban dining experience" is
"heavy on the wallet", but, hey, the "million-dollar" skyline view alone
is worth a "splurge."

Arthur Bryant's *BBQ*   25 | 17 | 21 | $18
Kansas City, West | Legends at the Kansas Speedway |
1702 Village W. Pkwy. (Prairie Crossing) | 913-788-7500
18th & Vine | 1727 Brooklyn Ave. (18th St.) | 816-231-1123
Northland | Ameristar Casino Hotel Kansas City |
3200 North Ameristar Dr. (Birmingham Rd.) | 816-414-7474
www.arthurbryantsbbq.com
The "faint of heart need not apply" at this "hole-in-the-wall"
"Smithsonian of smoke" in Downtown's Historic Jazz District (with offshoots at the Kansas Speedway and Ameristar Casino) that attracts
"presidents, kings" and common folk for some of the city's "finest BBQ";
despite the "lunch-tray" self-serve line and "early greasy" decor, every-

one "bows to what comes out of the pit", and the accompanying "Wonder bread", "awesome" fries and "love-it-or-hate-it" "sauce with a kick" are all part of the "pilgrimage" ("do I hear an amen?").

Bluestem ⓂAmerican   28 | 23 | 26 | $60

Westport | 900 Westport Rd. (Roanoke Rd.) | 816-561-1101 | www.bluestemkc.com

"Complex" New American "culinary surprises await" at this "urbane", "occasionally magical" Westport "gem" from chef-owners Colby and Megan Garrelts, presenting multicourse tastings, "sensational" wines and "stellar" desserts; while the tables are close ("NY–style") and the "cost per bite" is high, the "polished" staff helps "earn it", plus the bar is "killer" for cocktails and a "can't-beat" happy hour.

Bristol Seafood Grill   Seafood   28 | 26 | 27 | $39

Downtown KCMO | Power & Light District | 51 E. 14th St. (Main St.) | 816-448-6007
Leawood | Town Center Plaza | 5400 W. 119th St. (Nall Ave.) | 913-663-5777
www.bristolseafoodgrill.com

KC landlubbers swear by the "superlative" seafood ("you won't find better in Chesapeake Bay") and "irresistible" biscuits at this "winning" pair in Downtown KCMO and Leawood; the atmosphere is "chic" and "hopping" with "professional" service (and "very few kiddies" in the crowd), so though a few balk at the bill, fans feel the "price is right", particularly for lunch and happy hour; P.S. Sunday brunch is "impressive."

Café Provence Ⓩ French   29 | 25 | 27 | $37

Prairie Village | Prairie Village Shopping Ctr. | 3936 W. 69th Terr. (bet. Mission & Tomahawk Rds.) | 913-384-5998 | www.cafeprovence.net

"Tucked away" in a Prairie Village shopping center, this "adorable", "family-owned" "neighborhood bistro", voted No. 1 for Food and Service in Kansas City, is a "hidden monument to flavor" and hospitality, providing "exquisite" French cooking in a "terrific" atmosphere with a crew that "makes you feel at home"; ideal for a "romantic" dinner or breezy lunch, it's "a little pricey" for the area, but the Tuesday night prix fixe is a "great value for the money."

Café Sebastienne Ⓜ American   28 | 28 | 26 | $29

Country Club Plaza | Kemper Museum of Contemporary Art | 4420 Warwick Blvd. (bet. 44th & 45th Sts.) | 816-561-7740 | www.kemperart.org

There's "art on the plate and on the walls" at this "hidden gem" inside the Kemper Museum of Contemporary Art, where the "superb", "eclectic and ever-changing" New American menu "won't bust your budget" (especially at lunchtime) and the courtyard atrium is a "beautiful refuge" that lets you "eat outside without being outside"; a "relaxed, knowledgeable" staff only adds to the "cool, understated" (if a bit "noisy") atmosphere; P.S. dinner Friday–Saturday only.

The Capital Grille   Steak   28 | 26 | 27 | $58

Country Club Plaza | Country Club Plaza | 4740 Jefferson St. (bet. 47th & 48th Sts.) | www.thecapitalgrille.com

"Even though it's a chain" chophouse competing in a "city known for steaks", this Country Club Plaza locale "executes on the highest level" with "mouthwatering, tender" cuts served by a "fantastic" staff that makes you "feel like a king"; the space is "elegant" with a "see-and-be-seen" bar attracting "power diners and wannabes", but you can also "dine in relative obscurity" for that "special occasion" – just be sure to "bring a thick wallet."

Fiorella's Jack Stack *BBQ*

| 28 | 25 | 26 | $24 |

Crossroads | Freight House | 101 W. 22nd St. (Wyandotte St.) | 816-472-7427
Country Club Plaza | 4747 Wyandotte St. (bet. 47th St. & Ward Pkwy.) | 816-531-7427
Overland Park | 9520 Metcalf Ave. (95th St.) | 913-385-7427
Martin City | 13441 Holmes Rd. (135th St.) | 816-942-9141
www.jackstackbbq.com

"Barbecue nuts" "cast their vote" for the "crazy good" "mix of tasty meats" with "perfect" "smoky" flavor, plus the "cheesy corn bake" and other "unrivaled sides" (the "subject of dreams") at these four branches of "burnt-end heaven", voted Most Popular in Kansas City; decked out with "clubby decor", it's "'cue with class" that commands you to "wait as long as necessary" and pay a relative "premium", but the "huge" portions ensure you'll be taking home a "doggy bag."

Gates Bar-B-Q *BBQ*

| 25 | 19 | 22 | $19 |

18th & Vine | 1221 Brooklyn Ave. (12th St.) | 816-483-3880 ◗
Midtown | 3205 Main St. (bet. Arbour Blvd & 36th St.) | 816-753-0828 ◗
Country Club Plaza | 1325 E. Emanuel Cleaver II Blvd. (Virginia Ave.) | 816-531-7522 ◗
Independence | 10440 E. 40 Hwy. (bet. Hardy Ave & Northern Blvd.) | 816-353-5880
Downtown KCKS | 1026 State Ave. (10th St.) | 913-621-1134
www.gatesbbq.com

"Newbies" may be "overwhelmed when they walk in", but the staff's "shouted" "hi, may I help you?" is as much a part of "the drill" at this "holy grail" of KC 'cue as "ribs that stick", sauces with a "spicier twist" and the "slight film of smoke residue covering the ceiling and walls"; even if some wallet-watchers feel the costs are "getting up there", it's pretty "affordable" nonetheless – and the "ritual" is "priceless."

Hereford House *Steak*

| 25 | 24 | 24 | $37 |

Leawood | 5001 Town Center Dr. (bet. Roe Ave. & 117th St.) | 913-327-0800
Shawnee | 17244 Midland Dr. (Elmridge St.) | 913-268-8000
Independence | 19721 E. Jackson Dr. (Little Blue Pkwy.) | 816-795-9200
Northland | Zona Rosa | 8661 N. Stoddard Ave. (bet. 87 Terr. & Prairie View Rd.) | 816-584-9000
www.herefordhouse.com

Guests of this suburban quartet make it their "go-to" for "cattleman-country" steaks that are "tender, juicy and seasoned just right"; it's "dark" and "intimate" with "courteous" service, and while some critics counter it's "hanging onto an old legacy", most are "pleased" with the results, recommending the "fantabulous" happy-hour and Sunday "deals."

J. Gilbert's *Seafood/Steak*

| 28 | 26 | 26 | $41 |

Overland Park | 8901 Metcalf Ave. (89th St.) | 913-642-8070 |
www.jgilberts.com

"Exceptional" steaks and "top-notch" seafood are the stars at this "high-end" Overland Park "favorite", complemented by a bar "mixing any drink you can imagine" to wet the whistles of "business" brokers and "romantics" alike; whether the interior's "classy" or "a little dated", "you don't care after you have eaten" and been treated to the "above-and-beyond" service by a "wonderful" staff.

Julian *American*

27 | 21 | 26 | $30

Brookside | Brookside Plaza | 6227 Brookside Plaza (62nd Terr.) | 816-214-8454 | www.juliankc.com

"Celeb" chef-owner Celina Tio crafts "top-notch" New American "comfort food with no cultural boundaries" at her "high-energy", moderately priced "scratch kitchen" in the "trendy Brookside neighborhood", where the staff makes customers "feel like locals each time they walk in"; the dining room's "a bit noisy", so when it's warm grab a spot on the "huge", "fab" patio for an "experience worth sharing"; P.S. no lunch Monday–Tuesday.

Justus Drugstore, A Restaurant Ⓜ *American*

28 | 23 | 26 | $61

Smithville | 106 W. Main St. (bet. Bridge & Mill Sts.) | 816-532-2300 | www.drugstorerestaurant.com

Chef/co-owner Jonathan Justus' "creations are unmatched" at this "local, fresh, imaginative" Smithville New American set in a "New Yorkish" "renovated drugstore" that's a real "destination north of the river" (and "would be worth it even if the drive were twice as far"); service has a "personal touch", so while it's "expensive" enough to blow a "monster bonus", you get "dinner and a show" thanks to the luxuriant pace – often "about three hours" – that you'll be "talking about for weeks."

Le Fou Frog Ⓜ *French*

28 | 23 | 26 | $47

River Market | 400 E. Fifth St. (Oak St.) | 816-474-6060 | www.lefoufrog.com

This "quirky" River Market French provides "marvelous" dishes in an atmosphere "so Parisian you expect Edith Piaf to jump onto a table and begin a chanson" – and the "serenading" chef who often "holds court in the bar" just might; despite "close quarters", it's a sought-out "celebration spot" drawing an occasionally "rowdy" "arts crowd" for "meals that measure up to the bill."

Michael Smith Ⓢ Ⓜ *American*

27 | 24 | 25 | $50

Crossroads | 1900 Main St. (19th St.) | 816-842-2202 | www.michaelsmithkc.com

"Not all interesting cuisine is east of the Mississippi or in California" declare converts of this Crossroads New American (sib to the adjacent Extra Virgin), a "metropolitan" standout by "star" chef-owner Michael Smith where the signature braised rabbit with potato gnocchi will "get you hopping", and "daring" yet "refined" dishes are de rigueur; a staff offering "spot-on" recommendations oversees the "minimalist, soothing" space ("more business than romantic"), and though some grumble about paying "double the price for half the food", many prize it for "special occasions."

Oklahoma Joe's Barbecue Ⓢ *BBQ*

28 | 18 | 23 | $15

Rosedale | 3002 W. 47th Ave. (Mission Rd.) | 913-722-3366
Leawood | 11723 Roe Ave. (W. 119th St.) | 913-338-5151 Ⓜ
Olathe | 11950 S. Strang Line Rd. (119th St.) | 913-782-6858
www.oklahomajoesbbq.com

"Who knew a gas station could crank out BBQ like this?" wonder "wowed" customers at this "bold" KCK original (with Olathe and

Leawood offshoots) whose "unbelievable" ribs ("perfect slabs of piggy goodness"), "amazing" pulled pork and "supreme" sides go for "terrific-value" prices; the lines do get "out of control", but "ecstatic loyal fans" insist it's "always worth the wait."

Osteria Il Centro 🖪 *Italian*   28 | 24 | 25 | $28

Country Club Plaza | 5101 Main St. (51st St.) | 816-561-2369 | www.osteria-ilcentro.com

Diners "adore" this *bellissimo* Italian "jewel" in the "pleasant" South Plaza neighborhood, a "popular date spot" serving "authentic" food that "takes you back to Verona"; since it's a "great value" and "crowded nearly every night", fans "wish they took reservations", but when faced with a "hardy wait" you can pass the time "people-watching" and chumming with the staffers ("who know pretty much everyone") over a glass from the "interesting" 1,000-bottle wine list.

Room 39   *American*   26 | 23 | 26 | $37

39th Street | 1719 W. 39th St. (bet. Bell & Genessee Sts.) | 816-753-3939 🖪
Leawood | Mission Farms | 10561 Mission Rd. (bet. I-435 & 103rd St.) | 913-648-7639
www.rm39.com

Customers commend the culinary "craftsmanship" at this "offbeat" pair of "fine-dining bistros" where the "imaginative" American menu driven by "local ingredients" "never feels contrived or forced", and there's "no rush to get out, so you get your money's worth"; "who cares about minimalist decor" at the "original" in Midtown (the Mission Farms outpost – where "Johnson County ladies lunch" – is a "dressed-up version"): you "gotta love the rotating local art on the walls", and the service is "perfectly attentive"; P.S. there's breakfast Monday–Saturday at 39th Street, and a "killer" weekend brunch at Mission Farms.

Starker's Restaurant 🖪 *American*   26 | 25 | 25 | $44

Country Club Plaza | 201 W. 47th St. (Wyandotte St.) | 816-753-3565 | www.starkersrestaurant.com

Views of the Country Club Plaza are "not the only thing that lights up" this "beautiful", "tucked-away" New American "treasure", where chef-owner John McClure's "inventive seasonal" dishes matched by an "endless list of fine wines" are served by a "wonderful" staff; admirers attest the experience "will leave you speechless" – just "go when someone else is paying."

Webster House 🖪 *Eclectic*   27 | 28 | 26 | $32

Crossroads | 1644 Wyandotte St. (17th St.) | 816-221-4713 | www.websterhousekc.com

On the second floor of an "elegantly restored" "old schoolhouse" (above a "wonderful antique store"), this "gorgeous" Eclectic "legacy spot" in the Crossroads, voted No. 1 for Decor in Kansas City, "gets it right" with "sublimely innovative" fare, "professional yet relaxed" service and "excellent views" of the Kauffman Center; ideal for pre-curtain eats, it also "goes well with a bright glass of wine and some girl talk" – especially during the "good-value" lunch and happy hour.

Las Vegas

	Restaurant	Cuisine
29	Joël Robuchon	French
	Michael's	Continental
28	L'Atelier de Joël Robuchon	French
	Raku	Japanese
	Picasso	French
	Guy Savoy	French
	Sen of Japan	Japanese
	Lotus of Siam	Thai
	Sage	American
	Steak House	Steak
27	Texas de Brazil	Brazilian/Steak
	SW Steakhouse	Steak
	StripSteak	Steak
	Prime Steakhouse	Steak
	Via Brasil	Brazilian/Steak
	Le Cirque	French
	I Love Sushi	Japanese
	Michael Mina	Seafood
	Nobu	Japanese
	Broadway Pizzeria	Pizza
	Kabuki	Japanese

OTHER NOTEWORTHY PLACES

Restaurant	Cuisine
Aureole	American
Bouchon	French
Cheesecake Factory	American
Feast Buffet	Eclectic
Fleur	Eclectic
Florida Café	Cuban
Hugo's Cellar	Continental
Jean Philippe Patisserie	Bakery
Joe's Sea/Steak/Crab	Seafood/Steak
Julian Serrano	Spanish
Marché Bacchus	French
Mon Ami Gabi	French
Monta Ramen	Japanese
Mundo	Mexican
P.J. Clarke's	American
Peppermill	Diner
Ping Pang Pong	Chinese
Pink's Hot Dogs	Hot Dogs
Settebello	Pizza
Todd English P.U.B.	American

Aureole *American* | 25 | 27 | 24 | $95 |

Strip | Mandalay Bay Resort | 3950 Las Vegas Blvd. S. (Hacienda Ave.) | 702-632-7401 | www.charliepalmer.com

Capped with a "spectacular" tower that slinkily clad "wine angels" scale "like mountain climbers" to obtain your vino, über-chef Charlie Palmer's "stunning" New American at Mandalay Bay (an outpost of the NYC original) has diners gawking at the "sophisticated", "one-of-a-kind" setting; the "stellar" fare's nearly as inspiring, and is bolstered by prix fixe options, a "grand" wine list and "extraordinary" service – just "don't worry about the cost", and you'll enjoy a "memorable evening."

Broadway Pizzeria *Pizza* | 27 | 17 | 23 | $13 |

Downtown | 840 S. Rancho Dr. (Palomino Ln.) | 702-259-9002 | www.broadwaypizzerialv.com

"Delicious" pizza "just like back east" whets patrons' appetites at this "reasonably priced" Downtown pie purveyor, where you can get 'za "by the slice" in true NYC fashion; while the digs are nothing special, the staff is up to speed whether you're dining in or taking out.

Bouchon *French* | 26 | 25 | 25 | $61 |

Strip | Venetian Hotel | 3355 Las Vegas Blvd. S., 10th fl. (bet. Flamingo Rd. & Sands Ave.) | 702-414-6200 | www.bouchonbistro.com

"Amazing from start to finish", Thomas Keller's "fab" French bistro in the Venetian (a spin-off of his Napa original) again wins the Most Popular title in Vegas with its "exquisitely prepared" dishes matched by "superb" wines in a "radiant", Adam Tihany–designed room; "outstanding" service is like icing on the gâteau, and though some say it's "hard to find" and "a little pricey", it remains a "best-seller."

Cheesecake Factory ● *American* | 25 | 23 | 23 | $30 |

Henderson | District at Green Valley Ranch | 160 S. Green Valley Pkwy. (Paseo Verde Pkwy.) | 702-207-6372
Strip | Forum Shops at Caesars Palace | 3500 Las Vegas Blvd. S. (Flamingo Rd.) | 702-792-6888
Summerlin | 750 S. Rampart Blvd. (Alta Dr.) | 702-951-3800
www.thecheesecakefactory.com

A famously "diverse" menu that "reads like a novel" is the gateway to "oversized" portions of "consistently good" American eats topped off with "phenomenal" cheesecakes at these "affordable" eateries, which rank as Vegas' Most Popular chain; sure, the "attractive" digs can get "loud" and "waits are looong", but "excellent" service helps compensate.

Feast Buffet *Eclectic* | 20 | 20 | 21 | $17 |

East Side | Boulder Station Hotel | 3770 Las Vegas Blvd. S. (Lamb Blvd.) | 702-432-7777
Henderson | Sunset Station Hotel | 1301 W. Sunset Rd. (Stephanie St.) | 702-547-7777
Henderson | Green Valley Ranch | 2300 Paseo Verde Pkwy. (Carnegie Dr.) | 702-617-6831
North Las Vegas | Texas Station Hotel | 2101 Texas Star Ln. (bet. Lake Mead Blvd. & Rancho Dr.) | 702-631-1000
North Las Vegas | Aliante Station Casino & Hotel | 7300 Aliante Pkwy. (Elkhorn Rd.) | 702-692-7777
Northwest | Red Rock Casino | 11011 W. Charleston Blvd. (I-215) | 702-797-7777

(continued)

(continued)

Feast Buffet

Northwest | Santa Fe Station Hotel | 4949 N. Rancho Dr.
(bet. Lone Mountain Rd. & Rainbow Blvd.) | 702-658-4900
West of Strip | Palace Station Hotel | 2411 W. Sahara Ave. (Rancho Dr.) |
702-367-2411
www.stationcasinos.com
Customers dig into "good food and plenty of it" at these Eclectic
buffet-o-ramas, known for providing a "vast" selection (extending out
to "another zip code") at Station Casinos sites across the valley; a "polite" staff further bolsters the "pleasant" settings, and while you may
have to endure "long lines", most say they're worth it for the "bargain."

Fleur *Eclectic*　　　　　　　　　　　25 | 23 | 22 | $70

Strip | Mandalay Bay Resort | 3950 Las Vegas Blvd. S. (Hacienda Ave.) |
702-632-9400 | www.mandalaybay.com
A "gastronomic symphony" awaits patrons of super-chef Hubert Keller's
"must-try" Eclectic at the Strip's Mandalay Bay, where "whimsical"
small plates offer culinary surprises; the "knowledgeable" staff works
well in "appealing" (and relatively "casual") surroundings, and though
it's not cheap, it remains a "favorite" for many – especially for lunch.

Florida Café *Cuban*　　　　　　　　22 | 17 | 18 | $22

North of Strip | Howard Johnson Hotel | 1401 Las Vegas Blvd. S.
(Park Paseo) | 702-385-3013 | www.floridacafecuban.com
For "savory" Cuban food that "sticks to your ribs at a price that doesn't
stick it to you", try this "friendly", north-of-the-Strip "oasis" by the Little
White Wedding Chapel; the eats come in "excellent portions", so it's
easy to go whole hog and ignore the "strange" location in a HoJo.

Guy Savoy Ⓜ *French*　　　　　　　28 | 27 | 28 | $199

Strip | Caesars Palace Hotel | 3570 Las Vegas Blvd. S. (Flamingo Rd.) |
877-346-4642 | www.caesarspalace.com
Deemed "very close to perfection", this "sublime" New French at
Caesars Palace – like its Paris sib – gives diners the chance to "luxuriate in the best of everything"; here, "food is art", with the canvas provided by the "exquisite" setting and "fantastic individualized" service,
and though you may have to "win a jackpot" to afford the bill, it's an
"absolute must" that "defines 'you get what you pay for.'"

Hugo's Cellar *Continental*　　　　　26 | 23 | 27 | $61

Downtown | Four Queens Hotel | 202 Fremont St. (4th St.) | 702-385-4011 |
www.fourqueens.com
An "Old Vegas standby", this "classic" Downtowner in the Four
Queens casino treats its guests "like royalty", with "roses for the ladies" heightening the ultra-"romantic" atmosphere; the "upscale",
wine-cellar–like space and "outstanding" Continental fare add to the
"throwback" feel, and though the "premium prices" are relatively
modern, diners are convinced there's "nothing like it."

I Love Sushi *Japanese*　　　　　　　27 | 23 | 25 | $31

Henderson | 11041 S. Eastern Ave. (Sunridge Heights Pkwy.) |
702-990-4055
"Locals" love this "affordable" Henderson Japanese offering "super-
fresh" sushi and an "amazing" selection of "inventive" rolls in an "exu-

	FOOD	DECOR	SERVICE	COST

berant" atmosphere; add in "skilled" chefs and "waitresses in kimonos" delivering "on-the-ball" service, and no wonder it's "often busy."

Jean Philippe Patisserie *Bakery*

	25	22	20	$22

Strip | Bellagio Hotel | 3600 Las Vegas Blvd. S. (Flamingo Rd.) | 702-693-8788
Strip | Aria Hotel | 3730 Las Vegas Blvd. S. (Harmon Ave.) | 702-590-8550 ◐
www.jpchocolates.com

"Skip breakfast, lunch and dinner and make a beeline straight for dessert" at this "chic" Strip-side French bakery/cafe pair, where "delicate" pastries and other "unique" treats delight with "incredible colors and flavors" (and the sidekick sandwiches are "tasty" too); the Bellagio location warrants a visit "just to see the chocolate fountain alone" (it also has sculptures made of the stuff, like its sister site in CityCenter's Aria), and though it may be "pricey" for the genre, it's a definite "wow."

Joël Robuchon *French*

	29	28	28	$227

Strip | MGM Grand Hotel | 3799 Las Vegas Blvd. S. (Tropicana Ave.) | 702-891-7925 | www.mgmgrand.com

"An experience from the moment you sit down", this "one-of-a-kind" dazzler at the MGM Grand – brought to you by chef extraordinaire Joël Robuchon – once again ranks No. 1 for Food in Vegas, with "stunning" New French cuisine that's "as close to heaven as you can get", plus "wonderful", purple-accented decor and "flawless" service; *bien sûr,* you may "faint when the bill arrives", but as to whether it's worth it – "yes, yes, yes!"

Joe's Seafood, Prime Steak & Stone Crab *Seafood/Steak*

	26	23	25	$66

Strip | Forum Shops at Caesars Palace | 3500 Las Vegas Blvd. S. (Flamingo Rd.) | 702-792-9222 | www.joes.net

Revelers say this Strip-side version of "Miami's classic" is the "real deal", boasting steaks and seafood (including those "wonderful" stone crabs) that "reign supreme" in a "large" "club-room" space at the Forum Shops at Caesars; the "terrific" staff delivers "tremendous" (even "over-the-top") service and the atmosphere's "amazing", so while tabs can get "hefty", it offers big-time "value for the money."

Julian Serrano *Spanish*

	26	23	23	$61

Strip | Aria Hotel | 3730 Las Vegas Blvd. S. (Harmon Ave.) | 702-590-8520 | www.arialasvegas.com

Less expensive than its northerly sib Picasso, this Spaniard by "master chef" Julian Serrano purveys "tapas as they should be", with a menu of "sublime" small plates (including "fantastic vegetarian" options) plus more substantial offerings like paellas in a "cool", "modern" space off the lobby of CityCenter's Aria; the "refreshing" drinks and "helpful" service also impress, and while it's "a little pricey", fans consider it a "keeper."

Kabuki *Japanese*

	27	25	25	$29

Summerlin | Tivoli Village | 400 S. Rampart Blvd. (Alta Dr.) | 702-685-7776
South of Strip | Town Sq. | 6605 Las Vegas Blvd. S. (Sunset Rd.) | 702-896-7440
www.kabukirestaurants.com

"Wondrous eats from the Land of the Rising Sun" delight diners at this Japanese chainster's south-of-the-Strip and Summerlin outposts, bastions of "very fresh" sushi and other savories – all laid out on a "huge" menu; with "friendly" service, "original" drinks and attractive settings, they recall an "elegant Tokyo meal", though without the high prices.

L'Atelier de Joël Robuchon *French*

28 | 26 | 27 | $132

Strip | MGM Grand Hotel | 3799 Las Vegas Blvd. S. (Tropicana Ave.) | 702-891-7358 | www.mgmgrand.com

"Although lower-key, it's still Joël Robuchon" say admirers of this New French "studio" in the MGM Grand, the more "affordable" (though still "wildly expensive") of the master's two outposts at the hotel, where you can sit at the counter for a "front-row seat" to the "chefs' show"; indeed, the "outstanding" small plates, accompanied by "finely tuned" service and "sensual" decor, may "redefine" dining for you, creating an "experience you'll recount for a long time."

Le Cirque Ⓜ *French*

27 | 27 | 27 | $117

Strip | Bellagio Hotel | 3600 Las Vegas Blvd. S. (Flamingo Rd.) | 702-693-7223 | www.bellagio.com

This Bellagio spin-off of the celebrated NYC original is a "first-class" destination in its own right, presenting "superb" New French cuisine and a "tremendous" wine list in a "whimsical", Adam Tihany–designed space that conjures up an "adult trip to the circus"; "attentive but not intrusive" service prevails, and while prices are as "grand" as the setting, it may well be the "dinner of your life."

Lotus of Siam *Thai*

28 | 15 | 23 | $33

East Side | Commercial Ctr. | 953 E. Sahara Ave. (bet. Maryland Pkwy. & State St.) | 702-735-3033 | www.lotusofsiamlv.com

It may be in an "unassuming" strip mall, but "don't let the outside fool you" – this longtime East Sider filled with "locals and foodies from across the country" is "off the hook" with "unusual, ultratasty" Northern Thai specialties elevated by a "clarity in the bright sauces and fresh ingredients", as well as a wine list that "could challenge the big dogs"; savants just suggest "disregarding the decor", an easy feat given the "gracious" staff ("ask for recommendations") and "embarrassingly modest" prices.

Marché Bacchus *French*

24 | 25 | 23 | $44

Summerlin | 2620 Regatta Dr. (Coral Shores Dr.) | 702-804-8008 | www.marchebacchus.com

"Transporting you out of the desert and onto the shores of a lake", this waterside Summerlin eatery is the "perfect date spot" – especially with an "excellent" on-site wine shop where "you can pick a bottle" to accompany your meal (with "just a $10 corkage fee"); the "lovely" French bistro fare, "discreet" service and "reasonable" rates more than satisfy, so locals feel "lucky" to have it.

Michael Mina *American*

27 | 25 | 26 | $104

Strip | Bellagio Hotel | 3600 Las Vegas Blvd. S. (Flamingo Rd.) | 702-693-7223 | www.michaelmina.net

"It's impossible to get a bad meal" at San Francisco chef Michael Mina's "exceptional" New American in the Bellagio, where diners dive into "magical seafood morsels" – including "must-have" lobster pot pie – in a "serene" room offering a "welcome oasis from the cacophony of the Strip"; "polished" service enchants too, and though you may have to "break open your cookie jar" for the privilege, it's a "special-occasion treat."

Michael's *Continental*
29 | 28 | 29 | $116

South of Strip | South Point Hotel | 9777 Las Vegas Blvd. S. (Silverado Ranch Blvd.) | 702-796-7111 | www.southpointcasino.com

"Old-school elegance" is alive and well at this "absolutely superb", "quite pricey" south-of-the-Strip Continental at the South Point hotel, where the "outstanding" black-tie service – rated No. 1 in Vegas – "makes you feel like you're a long-lost friend"; the "magnificent" dishes ("many prepared tableside") are matched by "upscale", "Victorian"-style surroundings, and though some say it's a little "hard to find", the "level of perfection is worth the hunt."

Mon Ami Gabi *French*
24 | 25 | 23 | $46

Strip | Paris Hotel | 3655 Las Vegas Blvd. S. (Flamingo Rd.) | 702-944-4224 | www.monamigabi.com

With a patio providing "incredible" views of the Bellagio fountains – plus "second-to-none" people-watching – this French bistro and steakhouse at the Strip's Paris Las Vegas promises a "lively" time; thankfully, "you don't feel like you have to mortgage the house" to enjoy the scenery, "delicious" food or "pleasant" service, and that suits the frequent "crowds" just fine.

Monta Ramen *Japanese*
25 | 16 | 21 | $13

West Side | 5030 Spring Mountain Rd. (bet. Decatur Blvd. & Hauck St.) | 702-367-4600 | www.montaramen.com

Even if you "swore you'd never eat ramen after college", you may happily do so again at this "shoebox-sized" West Side Japanese, where diners slurp down "stunningly good" noodles bathed in "savory, slow-simmered broths"; it's "always busy", but a "friendly" staff keeps things humming, and all in all there's "so much bang for your buck, it's ridiculous."

Mundo *Mexican*
23 | 25 | 22 | $37

Downtown | World Market Ctr. | 495 S. Grand Central Pkwy. (Bonneville Ave.) | 702-270-4400 | www.mundolasvegas.com

A striking space – mixing old-world Mexico and Vegas glam – sets the scene at this "upscale" Downtowner in the Las Vegas Design Center, which melds "traditional flavors" with "top-of-the-line ingredients" for a "different take on south-of-the-border cuisine"; moderate prices, "knowledgeable" service and "wowing" cocktails fit the bill too, plus it has an "awesome" location near the Smith Center.

Nobu *Japanese*
27 | 23 | 24 | $88

East of Strip | Hard Rock Hotel | 4455 Paradise Rd. (bet. Flamingo Rd. & Harmon Ave.) | 702-693-5090 | www.noburestaurants.com

Diners "dream" of the dinners at Nobu Matsuhisa's Japanese "hot spot" in the Hard Rock Hotel (one of his many venues), proffering "melt-in-your-mouth" sushi and "mind-blowing" cooked dishes like the "star"-quality miso black cod, plus omakase options; a "helpful" staff distributes everything in a "cool", "hopping" space ripe for "celeb sightings" – *hai*, it's "ultraexpensive", but "how could you not love it?"; P.S. watch for a new location slated for Caesars Palace.

Peppermill ● *Diner*
22 | 22 | 22 | $25

Strip | 2985 Las Vegas Blvd. S. (Convention Center Dr.) | 702-735-4177 |
www.peppermilllasvegas.com

A 24/7 bastion of "Old Vegas kitsch", this mainstay on the Strip rocks
"1970s-flashback" decor ("if you have any bell-bottoms or leisure
suits, wear them") while slinging "massive" portions of "sturdy" diner
victuals at "reasonable" prices; service that's "sassy with a smile"
heightens the groovy feel, while "glitz at its zenith" (along with "old-
school cocktails") can be found at the adjoining Fireside Lounge –
a Sin City "essential."

Picasso *French*
28 | 29 | 28 | $137

Strip | Bellagio Hotel | 3600 Las Vegas Blvd. S. (Flamingo Rd.) |
702-693-7223 | www.bellagio.com

"Who wouldn't want to eat surrounded by original Picassos?" wonder fans of chef Julian Serrano's "life-changing" New French at the
Bellagio, where the "unsurpassed" setting – once again rated tops
for Decor in Vegas – complements its "astonishing" art collection
with "spectacular views of the fountains"; meanwhile, a "top-
notch" staff serves prix fixe dinners as "opulent and rich" as the locale,
and if this "masterpiece" commands a "master price", it's earned for
delivering the "meal of your dreams."

Ping Pang
Pong ● *Chinese*
22 | 16 | 16 | $25

West Side | Gold Coast Hotel & Casino | 4000 W. Flamingo Rd. (Wynn Rd.) |
702-247-8136 | www.goldcoastcasino.com

"If this weren't in the Gold Coast, you'd think you were in Hong Kong" –
yet this West Side Chinese is Vegas all the way, with a big variety of
"delicious" dim sum and other "tasty" bites purveyed in "nicely decorated" Sino digs; prices that harken to the Sin City of yesteryear
complete the picture.

Pink's Hot Dogs ● *Hot Dogs*
20 | 13 | 17 | $14

Strip | Planet Hollywood Resort | 3667 Las Vegas Blvd. S.
(Harmon Ave.) | 702-405-4711 | www.planethollywoodresort.com

"In the tradition of Pink's in Los Angeles", this Planet Hollywood
outpost of the La Brea "legend" serves "sensational chili dogs" and
other "snappy" franks laden with "just about anything"; there's
only "outdoor seating on the Strip" ("great for people-watching"),
and if some think these wieners are "pricier than they should be",
late-night noshers say they're "just the thing after a long evening
at the tables."

P.J. Clarke's New York
Chophouse ● *American*
20 | 21 | 20 | $41

Strip | Forum Shops at Caesars Palace | 3500 Las Vegas Blvd. S.
(Flamingo Rd.) | 702-434-7900 | www.pjclarkes.com

It's "not the original", but this offshoot of the venerable NYC watering
hole – conveniently located in the Forum Shops at Caesars Palace –
apes its progenitor's look and feel, with "masculine" decor, capable
service and a "can't-go-wrong" American menu (big on burgers,
steaks and oysters); it's certainly choice for "casual" drinks, and the
sensible prices are the right chaser.

Prime Steakhouse *Steak*
27 | 27 | 27 | $103

Strip | Bellagio Hotel | 3600 Las Vegas Blvd. S. (Flamingo Rd.) | 702-693-7223 | www.bellagio.com

"What more can you say" about this "absolutely first-rate" steakhouse from Jean-Georges Vongerichten, where the filets are the "finest quality", the wine list "outstanding" and the "courteous" staff makes "everyone feel rich" – regardless of whether they win at the tables; let's not forget the "lovely" "chocolate-and-blue" setting or the views of the Bellagio's "dancing fountains", and though it's all quite "costly", "you're on vacation so enjoy"; P.S. no shorts, and no children under five allowed.

Raku ●Ⓩ *Japanese*
28 | 20 | 23 | $57

West Side | Seoul Plaza | 5030 Spring Mountain Rd. (Decatur Blvd.) | 702-367-3511 | www.raku-grill.com

Japanese food "like you've never had before" is the province of this "cozy" West Side robata grill, which instills its "exquisite", "high-end" small plates (no sushi) with "bold, complex flavors" and "elevates them to another level"; solid service and late hours are added benefits, so it's a "destination for foodies" as well as "chefs on their off-hours."

Sage Ⓩ *American*
28 | 27 | 25 | $82

Strip | Aria Hotel | 3730 Las Vegas Blvd. S. (Harmon Ave.) | 877-230-2742 | www.arialasvegas.com

"Intriguing flavor combinations" beguile at this "top-quality" New American in CityCenter's Aria, a showcase for Chicago chef Shawn McClain's "unique" fare and "farm-to-table philosophy"; "fantastic" drinks, "personal" service and "smashing" decor – tricked out with "sexy lighting" – enhance the experience, and with prices that may not reach the stratospheres attained by other upper-tier options, it leads fans to extend some "sage advice": try it.

Sen of Japan *Japanese*
28 | 19 | 26 | $53

West Side | 8480 W. Desert Inn Rd. (Durango Dr.) | 702-871-7781 | www.senofjapan.com

The "holy grail of Vegas sushi places", this West Side Japanese slices up "sensational", "highly nuanced" fin fare "without the Strip's hype or prices"; comfortable digs and "enthusiastic, prompt" service complete the package, and if you follow the experts and "ask for the omakase", you'll be fed "till your heart's content."

Settebello *Pizza*
26 | 18 | 21 | $22

Henderson | District at Green Valley Ranch | 140 S. Green Valley Pkwy. (Paseo Verde Pkwy.) | 702-222-3556 | www.settebello.net

It's "worth the trek to Henderson" for a taste of the "real Neapolitan pizza" baked up by this "authentic" spot, the flagship of a small chain (with Italian pizzaiolo certification), where a "wood-burning oven" creates "charred-crust" pies that "burst with fresh flavors"; the "relaxed" atmosphere gets a boost from "friendly" service, and though it may be "a bit pricey" for 'za, remember – this ain't your typical slice.

Steak House *Steak*
28 | 24 | 27 | $71

Strip | Circus Circus Hotel | 2880 Las Vegas Blvd. S. (bet. Desert Inn Rd. & Sahara Ave.) | 702-794-3767 | www.circuscircus.com

Maintaining a "standard that few have ever reached", this "hidden gem" of a steakhouse – surprisingly located in the "low-roller heaven" of Circus Circus – is a meat eater's mecca, dispensing "fantastically prepared cuts" in a "private-club" setting; with "top-rate" service, it offers "terrific value" for the quality, so "if you can get past the kiddies and the clowns, you're in for a great meal."

StripSteak *Steak*   27 | 24 | 25 | $90

Strip | Mandalay Bay Resort | 3950 Las Vegas Blvd. S. (Hacienda Ave.) | 702-632-7414 | www.michaelmina.net
"Serious meat eaters" have a field day with the "mouthwatering", buttery steaks proffered by this bastion of beef in the Strip's Mandalay Bay – another feather in the cap of San Fran celeb-chef Michael Mina; "personal" service and a "hip" vibe complement the "bright", modern setting, and despite "very expensive" tabs, it's a "must while you're in Vegas."

SW Steakhouse *Steak*   27 | 26 | 27 | $101

Strip | Wynn Hotel | 3131 Las Vegas Blvd. S. (bet. Desert Inn Rd. & Sands Ave.) | 702-248-3463 | www.wynnlasvegas.com
Aces for "grilled-to-perfection" steaks and a "not-to-be-missed" view of the show on the lake, this "wonderful" meatery at Wynn Las Vegas is "outstanding in every way" – making it a natural for "special celebrations"; overseeing the "elegant" setting is an "exceptional" crew, and though you may need to "bring your black card to support payment", most deem it a "spectacular place to dine."

Texas de Brazil *Brazilian/Steak*   27 | 25 | 25 | $55

South of Strip | Town Sq. | 6533 Las Vegas Blvd. S. (Sunset Rd.) | 702-614-0080 | www.texasdebrazil.com
"Only a T. rex wouldn't get enough meat" at this outpost of the Brazilian churrascaria chain in the Town Square mall, where servers "keep coming to your table" with "fantastic", rodizio-style steaks and other carnivoria; there's also a "luxe" salad bar and "superb" service bolstering the "classy-without-being-pretentious" atmosphere, so even if it's a little "expensive", diners "enjoy it every time."

Todd English P.U.B. *American*   21 | 21 | 20 | $37

Strip | Crystals at CityCenter | 3720 Las Vegas Blvd. S. (Harmon Ave.) | 702-489-8080 | www.toddenglishpub.com
With its "modern, pub-inspired" looks and a "convivial" atmosphere, Todd English's tavern in Crystals at CityCenter is a popular choice for "honest" American eats washed down with a "wicked" beer list; true, the "noise level" isn't for everyone, but "attentive" service, moderate prices and a patio option help appease.

Via Brasil *Brazilian/Steak*   27 | 26 | 26 | $58

Summerlin | 1225 S. Fort Apache Rd. (Charleston Blvd.) | 702-804-1400 | www.viabrasilsteakhouse.com
"Bring your appetite" to this Brazilian steakhouse in Summerlin, where "well-seasoned, delicious" meats are delivered to your table "hot off the skewer"; diners also dig the "awesome" staff and "relaxed" setting (yep, those are waterfalls), with relatively reasonable tabs for the feast – so "wear loose clothes" and come on down.

Long Island

TOP FOOD RANKING

	Restaurant	Cuisine
29	North Fork Table	American
28	Siam Lotus	Thai
	Mosaic	American
	Kitchen A Trattoria	Italian
	Maroni	Eclectic/Italian
	Nagahama	Japanese
	Lake House	American
27	Chachama	American
	La Piccola Liguria	Italian
	Kitchen A Bistro	French
	Kotobuki	Japanese
	Peter Luger	Steak
	La Plage	Eclectic
	Orient	Chinese
	Chez Noëlle	French
	Sempre Vivolo	Italian
	Aji 53	Japanese
	Dave's Grill	Continental/Seafood
	Il Mulino	Italian
	Piccolo	American/Italian

OTHER NOTEWORTHY PLACES

Restaurant	Cuisine
Barney's	American/French
Besito	Mexican
Bryant & Cooper	Steak
Dario's	Italian
Fifth Season	American
Harvest on Fort Pond	Italian/Mediterranean
Limani	Mediterranean/Seafood
Mirko's	Eclectic
Noah's	American
Plaza Café	Seafood
Rialto	Italian
San Marco	Italian
Snaps American Bistro	American
Starr Boggs	American/Seafood
Stone Creek	French/Mediterranean
Tellers Chophouse	Steak
Thai Gourmet	Thai
Tutto Il Giorno	Italian
Verace	Italian
West End Café	American

	FOOD	DECOR	SERVICE	COST

Aji 53 *Japanese*
27 | 24 | 23 | $43

Bay Shore | 53 E. Main St. (3rd Ave.) | 631-591-3107
Smithtown | Village Common | 1 Miller Pl. (E. Main St.) |
631-979-0697
www.aji53.com

An "all-around hit", this "chic", "modern" Japanese brings "NYC ambiance" to Bay Shore, with "stunning" decor, "incredible", "inventive"
sushi and "charming" (if at times "almost too eager") service; the
"cool vibe" and "martinis at the bar" make "waits worthwhile", while
dishes like "to-die-for black miso cod" are so "artful" you'll "forget
about the price tag" and the "noise" – just "don't even think of going
on a weekend without reservations"; P.S. the Smithtown branch
opened post-Survey.

Barney's Ⓜ *American/French*
26 | 23 | 24 | $63

Locust Valley | 315 Buckram Rd. (Bayville Rd.) | 516-671-6300 |
www.barneyslv.com

"Excellent from start to finish" declare diners about this "romantic"
"retreat" on a "hard-to-find" country byway in "tony Locust Valley",
offering "first-rate" American-French dishes delivered by a "cordial"
staff; the "chic, understated" setting "feels like a Vermont inn", especially in the "fireplace room" where a "log fire blazes and crackles" in
winter, so while it can be "expensive", many consider it a "must-go";
P.S. a prix fixe is offered Sunday–Thursday and an early-bird on Friday.

Besito *Mexican*
24 | 24 | 22 | $45

Roslyn | Harborview Shoppes | 1516 Old Northern Blvd. (bet. Northern Blvd. &
Remsen Ave.) | 516-484-3001
Huntington | 402 New York Ave. (bet. Carver & Fairview Sts.) |
631-549-0100
www.besitomex.com

Fans indulge in a "fiesta of the senses" at this "attractive" Mexican
twosome in Huntington and Roslyn where the "guac rocks", the "contemporary" *comida* is "different and delicious" and the "killer" margaritas lend extra zing to a "glowing" atmosphere that's "cool as the other
side of a pillow"; though it can all add up to a "pricey night", most
"shout 'arriba!'" and come back for more.

Bryant & Cooper Steakhouse *Steak*
26 | 21 | 23 | $69

Roslyn | 2 Middle Neck Rd. (Northern Blvd.) | 516-627-7270 |
www.bryantandcooper.com

Serving "phenomenal" cuts of meat "aged on-site" along with "ample
sides" and a "stellar wine list", this "carnivore's delight" in Roslyn "rivals Manhattan's finest" with some of the "most expertly prepared
steaks in the area" (you "can't go wrong" with the seafood either);
"well-trained" servers who "know their job" help justify the "pricey"
tabs, though some find the pace "rushed" and the whole package "too
much of a scene"; P.S. "lunch is a lot more affordable", and the adjoining butcher shop is "superb."

Chachama Grill *American*
27 | 21 | 27 | $52

East Patchogue | Swan Nursery Commons | 655 Montauk Hwy.
(S. Country Rd.) | 631-758-7640 | www.chachamagrill.com

"Star" chef Elmer Rubio crafts "marvelous" New American meals at
this "exciting", "Manhattan-type restaurant in a most unlikely loca-

tion" (an otherwise "dreary" strip mall) in East Patchogue; once inside, you'll "enter another world where one dish is better than the next" and they're all "beautifully served" by a "considerate" staff that "makes you feel every day is a celebration", so it's always a "winner"; P.S. the $26 prix fixe is one of the "biggest bargains on LI."

Chez Noëlle ⓜ French
27 | 19 | 25 | $55

Port Washington | 34 Willowdale Ave. (S. Bayles Ave.) | 516-883-3191 | www.cheznoellerestaurant.com

"Aging gracefully", this "old-fashioned French" in Port Washington is a "rare find" that "sticks to the basics and succeeds", attracting "well-dressed" guests who "appreciate" the "classic", "melt-in-your-mouth" cuisine, "gracious" greetings and the "owner's droll humor"; the "greatly improved", renovated setting boasts tables spaced out enough to "enjoy conversations", and though prices are "steep" (unless you go for the "bargain prix fixe"), it's worthy of a "special night."

Dario's ⓩ Italian
26 | 17 | 26 | $59

Rockville Centre | 13 N. Village Ave. (bet. Merrick Rd. & Sunrise Hwy.) | 516-255-0535

The "outstanding" Northern Italian food is "as good as it gets" at this Rockville Centre "old-schooler", leading guests to vow that if it's "served in heaven, I'll become a better person"; while it's "on the expensive side", and decor's a bit "stodgy", "gracious" "tuxedoed waiters" who "see to every request" offer an "elegant" diversion.

Dave's Grill Continental/Seafood
27 | 18 | 23 | $61

Montauk | 468 W. Lake Dr. (bet. Flamingo Ave. & Soundview Dr.) | 631-668-9190 | www.davesgrill.com

This "cozy", "pricey" Continental "right on the docks" in Montauk "rocks the East End" with its "extensive menu" of "impeccably prepared", "tremendous seafood"; while chef Dave's "gracious" wife, Julie, is the "best hostess anywhere", the "same-day reservation policy" is a "pain" for many who insist "the odds" of getting a seat "are about the same as winning the lottery"; P.S. closed in the off-season.

The Fifth Season American
26 | 23 | 23 | $48

Port Jefferson | 34 E. Broadway (bet. Main St. & Mariners Way) | 631-477-8500 | www.thefifth-season.com

"Top-notch all around", this Port Jefferson standout presents "artful", "locavore" New American cuisine served by a "caring" staff; the "warm" dining room has "beautiful" harbor views, so "sit by the windows" or "on the veranda" in summer, and offset the "high prices" with a BYO bottle – there's "no corkage fee" if it's from Long Island; P.S. closed Mondays in winter.

Harvest on Fort Pond ⓜ Italian/Mediterranean
26 | 22 | 22 | $53

Montauk | 11 S. Emery St. (Euclid Ave.) | 631-668-5574 | www.harvest2000.com

Remember that "one entree feeds two", so be ready to "share" at this "sensational" Tuscan-Med serving "simply wonderful" dishes that some call "the best on the South Fork"; it's ideal for "alfresco dining on a summer evening", with a "gorgeous garden" for watching the sunset over Fort Pond, but "long waits" for a table "even with reservations" make some yearn for the "off-season"; P.S. half-portions are now available.

Il Mulino New York   *Italian*

27 | 23 | 25 | $77

Roslyn Estates | 1042 Northern Blvd. (bet. Cedar Path & Searingtown Rd.) | 516-621-1870 | www.ilmulino.com

"Exceptional", "abundant" Northern Italian cuisine "delivered with panache" by a "superb" staff creates an "exquisite" (if "over-the-top") experience at this "romantic" Roslyn branch of the Manhattan classic, geared toward the "LI elite"; while some patrons pout about "dim" lighting and "too much of everything" for "shockingly expensive" tabs, most don't mind splurging on the "amazing" "feast"; P.S. the Sunday prix fixe is a more "reasonable" option.

Kitchen A Bistro   ⊭ *French*

27 | 19 | 23 | $51

St. James | 404 N. Country Rd. (Edgewood Ave.) | 631-862-0151 | www.kitchenabistro.com

Admirers adore this "super-relaxed" "rare find" in St. James, where "outstanding" chef-owner Eric Lomando crafts "awesome" French bistro dishes (including "unique" seafood specials) with "novel twists and turns"; it's a touch "less crowded" now that it's in "the old Mirabelle space", and the staff provides "helpful" service, plus it's a "bargain with BYO and no corkage charge"; P.S. cash-only and "reservations are a must", so "plan in advance."

Kitchen A Trattoria   🗷 🗹 ⊭ *Italian*

28 | 16 | 25 | $42

St. James | 532 N. Country Rd. (Lake Ave.) | 631-584-3518 | www.kitchenatrattoria.com

It's even "better than Kitchen A Bistro" marvel guests of this "exciting" St. James spin-off from chef-owner Eric Lomando, a "foodies' haven" proffering "inspired seasonal Italian dishes" you "dream about", served by a "terrific" staff; the "shockingly small" space is "still a bit rough" and it "takes a while to get a reservation" (required on weekends), but it's "worth adjusting your schedule to eat here"; P.S. the BYO policy and prix fixe specials "make it a steal."

Kotobuki   🗹 *Japanese*

27 | 18 | 20 | $41

Roslyn | Harborview Shoppes | 1530 Old Northern Blvd. (bet. Northern Blvd. & Skillman St.) | 516-621-5312
Babylon | 86 Deer Park Ave. (Main St.) | 631-321-8387
Hauppauge | 377 Nesconset Hwy. (bet. Brooksite Dr. & Hauppauge Rd.) | 631-360-3969
www.kotobukinewyork.com

"Best. sushi. ever." declare diners in awe of this "phenomenal" Japanese trio, "Long Island's answer to Nobu" serving fish so "sumptuous" it's worth getting in line and "waiting for the doors to open"; the "highly skilled chefs" create other "inventive" dishes as well, and the value's "amazing", but remember that variable service and "cramped" settings (apart from the Roslyn patio) are part of the deal; P.S. no reservations.

Lake House   🗹 *American*

28 | 24 | 26 | $60

Bay Shore | 240 W. Main St. (bet. Garner Ln. & Lawrence Ave.) | 631-666-0995 | www.thelakehouserest.com

"Spectacular meals" deliver "pure bliss in every aspect" at this Bay Shore "beauty" where co-owners Eileen and Matthew Connors (a "true artist" chef) provide "exquisite" New American dining accompanied by "gorgeous views" of the lake; the outdoor fire pit is "perfect for a romantic occasion" and the "exceptional" staff pulls it all together, so it's "well worth the cost" and the "drive" to experience "one of the best restaurants on Long Island."

La Piccola Liguria Ⓜ *Italian*   27 | 21 | 27 | $59

Port Washington | 47 Shore Rd. (bet. Mill Pond & Old Shore Rds.) | 516-767-6490

A "loyal cadre of regulars" "loves to hear" the "highly experienced" waiters recite a "mind-boggling" list of specials in "succulent detail" at this "outstanding" Port Washington Italian where the "brilliantly exe-cuted" dishes are among "the best on the Island"; the "minimally dec-orated", "sweet setting" fills up fast, so it's "hard to get a reservation" (and "not cheap"), but once inside you're treated "like royalty."

La Plage *Eclectic*   27 | 19 | 24 | $59

Wading River | 131 Creek Rd. (Sound Rd.) | 631-744-9200 | www.laplagerestaurant.net

Though it's an "unlikely location" for "truly inventive" cuisine, this "beachy" "oasis" in Wading River is a "special" "find" for "exuberant cooking" from chef-owner Wayne Wadington, whose "elegantly pre-pared", "beautifully presented" Eclectic dishes are matched with "knowledgeable" service; the "small" "cottage" setting may seem at odds with the "steep" tabs, but most maintain it's "totally charming" and "so worth the trip"; P.S. "reservations are a must" on weekends.

Limani *Mediterranean/Seafood*   26 | 27 | 24 | $71

Roslyn | 1043 Northern Blvd. (bet. Middle Neck Rd. & Port Washington Blvd.) | 516-869-8989 | www.limaniny.com

Bestowing a "beautiful atmosphere for beautiful people", this "gor-geous" Roslyn Mediterranean with teak floors, mosaic tiles and a "bar scene that's a bit of a show" also "wows" in the kitchen, providing "in-credible" fare ("fabulous" seafood "cooked to perfection") matched by a "formidable" wine list; "extremely accommodating" service is an-other plus, but just be ready for a "noise level that's off-the-charts" and tabs so "expensive" it might be "cheaper to go to Greece."

Maroni Cuisine Ⓩ Ⓜ ⇱ *Eclectic/Italian*   28 | 18 | 26 | $109

Northport | 18 Woodbine Ave. (bet. Main St. & Scudder Ave.) | 631-757-4500 | www.maronicuisine.com

"Inventive is an understatement" for chef-owner and "genial genius" Michael Maroni's "phenomenal" Eclectic-Italian tasting menu, which makes dining at his cash-only Northport standout an "exciting" "event" as "personable" servers convey course after course of "perfectly exe-cuted" "delicacies" (like those "famous" "tender" meatballs in "lush red sauce") till you "need help getting up"; it's "always worth" the "splurge" to be "wowed" by a "dream meal" "you'll never forget", but "reservations are a must" for a spot in the "shoebox" space; P.S. there's also a fair-weather courtyard and a party room.

Mirko's Ⓜ *Eclectic*   26 | 22 | 24 | $79

Water Mill | Water Mill Sq. | 670 Montauk Hwy. (bet. Cobb & Old Mill Rds.) | 631-726-4444 | www.mirkosrestaurant.com

"Absolutely exquisite" Eclectic fare via a chef who "really knows how to cook" and "clubby" service led by his co-owner/hostess wife lure a "loyal" clientele to this Water Mill class act set in a "lovely", country-style space with a fireplace and seasonal patio; even with "high prices" it's "often tough to get in", though a few opine "it helps to be known here"; P.S. open seasonally.

Mosaic ⊠Ⓜ *American* | 28 | 21 | 27 | $64 |

St. James | 418 N. Country Rd. (Edgewood Ave.) | 631-584-2058 | www.eatmosaic.com

The "spectacular" "ever-changing, five-course tasting menu" via "geniuses in the kitchen" Tate Morris and Jonathan Contes "never fails to please" at this diminutive St. James "gem", where "adventurous diners" are awestruck by the "flavors and textures" of "inspired" New American dishes "paired with exquisite wines"; add in "cheerful" servers who "never miss a beat" and a "cozy", "quiet" space, and it's an "unexpected treat for the palate" – "bravo!"

Nagahama *Japanese* | 28 | 15 | 22 | $37 |

Long Beach | 169 E. Park Ave. (bet. Long Beach & Riverside Blvds.) | 516-432-6446 | www.nagahamasushi.com

For "real quality", "you just can't beat" "inventive" chef-owner Hide Yamamoto's "pristine sushi" at this "reliable" Japanese, where the "incredibly fresh" fish and "warm" service have the natives feeling "lucky to live in Long Beach"; the renovated space is still "as small as a bento box" and "packed" to the gills, so dragon-roll disciples either get their "fix during the week" or "have them on speed-dial" for delivery.

Noah's *American* | 26 | 18 | 21 | $50 |

Greenport | 136 Front St. (bet. 1st & 3rd Sts.) | 631-477-6720 | www.chefnoahschwartz.com

"Adventuresome" chef/co-owner Noah Schwartz (formerly of Southold's now-defunct Seafood Barge) lends his "highly imaginative" flair to this "welcome addition to Greenport", where the New American menu showcases "inspired", seafood-centric small plates alongside full entrees and a raw bar; the "professional" staff is "helpful with choices", and despite a "stark", "too-noisy" setting that's "more SoHo than NoFo", the "fabulous" "grazing" ensures it's "always hoppin'."

North Fork Table & Inn *American* | 29 | 25 | 27 | $77 |

Southold | North Fork Table & Inn | 57225 Main Rd./Rte. 25 (bet. Boisseau & Laurel Aves.) | 631-765-0177 | www.northforktableandinn.com

Chef Gerry Hayden (ex Aureole) "has reached new heights" at this "stellar" Southold "destination", which secures the No. 1 rating for Food on Long Island with "a constantly evolving, brilliantly realized" New American menu crafted from "the freshest local ingredients" and matched with "gold-standard" desserts from Claudia Fleming (ex Gramercy Tavern); "impeccable, gracious" service that's also rated No. 1 on LI and a "civilized" "rural setting" round out an experience as "unforgettable" "as anything in NYC, period"; P.S. the Lunch Truck is planted out back, dispensing midday lobster rolls, artisan hot dogs and such at gentle prices.

The Orient *Chinese* | 27 | 9 | 19 | $27 |

Bethpage | 623 Hicksville Rd. (bet. Courtney & Fiddler Lns.) | 516-822-1010

As "authentic as going to Chinatown", this Bethpage Chinese is "the real thing" for "phenomenal", "richly flavored" Cantonese and "wonderful dim sum" that "can't be beat for quality and value"; "welcoming" owner Tommy Tan leads a team of "skilled waiters" who can "suggest terrific off-menu specials", and though it "gets completely packed" (on weekends particularly) "it's definitely worth the lines"; P.S. the Decor score doesn't reflect an extensive post-Survey renovation.

Peter Luger ⊄ *Steak*   27 | 17 | 21 | $71

Great Neck | 255 Northern Blvd. (bet. Jayson Ave. & Tain Dr.) | 516-487-8800 | www.peterluger.com

"Xanadu for steak", this Great Neck offshoot of the "iconic" Williamsburg meatery extends its run as Long Island's Most Popular restaurant by regaling "ravenous carnivores" in "traditional" style with "succulent" beef set down by "brusque" but "professional" "old-school waiters"; even loyalists concede the tabs are "gargantuan" and "cash will go out of existence before they accept credit cards", but it's still "the platinum standard": "calling them a steakhouse is like calling a Ferrari a car."

Piccolo *American/Italian*   27 | 20 | 25 | $56

Huntington | Southdown Shopping Ctr. | 215 Wall St. (bet. Mill Ln. & Southdown Rd.) | 631-424-5592 | www.piccolorestaurant.net

A "faithful crowd" stays true to this "upscale" New American–Italian in Huntington, which "deserves its reputation" for "superb cuisine" spanning "delicious pastas" to "phenomenal meat and fish"; the "top-notch" service and "intimate" setting with a pianist Sunday–Thursday will "make any occasion special", but "close quarters" lead to "long waits on weekends", so reserve ahead.

Plaza Café *Seafood*   26 | 22 | 24 | $70

Southampton | 61 Hill St. (bet. 1st Neck & Windmill Lns.) | 631-283-9323 | www.plazacafe.us

"They set the bar really high" at this "civilized" "Southampton gem", where chef/co-owner and "real pro" Douglas Gulija's "superb" seafood is prepared "with care" and "presented to perfection", paired with "unusual wines"; the "courteous staff" oversees a "cozy", "quiet" setting with "high ceilings and a fireplace", and while it's "a bit expensive", it's "worth seeking out" for "adult dining" "in a class by itself."

Rialto Ⓜ *Italian*   26 | 20 | 25 | $57

Carle Place | 588 Westbury Ave. (bet. Glen Cove Rd. & Post Ave.) | 516-997-5283 | www.rialtorestaurantli.com

"Top-notch" "each and every time", this "small" Carle Place Italian attracts adoring *amici* willing to go "out of the way" for "heavenly" "old-line" cuisine (including "wonderful whole fish") "served with style" by "warm hosts" who look after you like "their only customer"; it's "pretty pricey" and "worth every penny", but "they don't have room for a crowd", so "don't tell."

San Marco *Italian*   26 | 21 | 26 | $46

Hauppauge | 658 Motor Pkwy. (bet. Kennedy Dr. & Marcus Blvd.) | 631-273-0088 | www.sanmarcoristorante.com

"Everyone is treated like a VIP" by a "top-notch", "black tie"–clad staff wheeling "carts with appetizers and desserts" at this "tried-and-true" Hauppauge "special-occasion" "favorite" serving "some of the best" Northern Italian on the Island; although some suggest the decor "needs

FOOD | DECOR | SERVICE | COST

a bit of updating", "you can't go wrong" here, even "after all these years" – and it "won't break the bank" either.

Sempre Vivolo ☒ *Italian*   27 | 24 | 27 | $56
Hauppauge | 696 Vanderbilt Motor Pkwy. (Old Willets Path) | 631-435-1737 | www.semprevivolo.com
"Always a pleasure", this "refined" Hauppauge Italian is a "long-standing" source of "delectable" cuisine presented by "impeccable", "tuxedo-clad" pros; with "jackets required on Saturday night", it's a "fabulous" chance to "slow down" and "carry on a conversation" in a pleasant "old-world" atmosphere.

Siam Lotus Thai *Thai*   28 | 16 | 26 | $35
Bay Shore | 1664 Union Blvd. (bet. 4th & Park Aves.) | 631-968-8196 | www.siamlotus.us
A local "must" for a taste of "Bangkok at its best", this "exceptional" Bay Shore Thai brings you "all the classics" plus "delectable" daily specials, prepared "to a T" and "beautifully presented" courtesy of a kitchen that's "not afraid to use spice"; the "personal attention" is likewise "a cut above", so if the room's "nondescript", keep in mind "you don't go here for the decor."

Snaps American Bistro Ⓜ *American*   26 | 19 | 23 | $39
Wantagh | 2010 Wantagh Ave. (Sunrise Hwy.) | 516-221-0029 | www.snapsrestaurant.com
It's easy to "pass this diamond-in-the-rough" hidden in a Wantagh "strip of stores", but that would be a shame since "talented" chef/co-owner Scott Bradley creates an "ever-changing menu" of "extraordinary" New American dishes, including specials that "keep you coming back"; service is "excellent" and a recent "face-lift greatly improved" the "cool" space, plus the daily prix fixe and tasting menus make it such a "great value" you can't get in without "a reservation on weekends"; P.S. closed Monday–Tuesday.

Starr Boggs *American/Seafood*   26 | 23 | 22 | $62
Westhampton Beach | 6 Parlato Dr. (Library Ave.) | 631-288-3500 | www.starrboggsrestaurant.com
A perpetual Westhampton Beach "'in' spot", this "upbeat" New American shines bright with an "absolutely delicious" menu starring the eponymous chef-owner's "outstanding" seafood, served by a "terrific" team in "first-class" quarters flaunting original Warhols and a "gorgeous patio"; it provides "insanely sceney" "people-watching" on weekends, but if evading "pricey" tabs takes priority, there's a "wonderful" lobster bake deal on Mondays; P.S. open seasonally.

Stone Creek Inn *French/Mediterranean*   26 | 24 | 24 | $64
East Quogue | 405 Montauk Hwy. (bet. Carter Ln. & Wedgewood Rd.) | 631-653-6770 | www.stonecreekinn.com
There's "first-class" dining "nestled deep" in East Quogue at this "culinary tour de force", where the "adventurous" seasonal menu of "superior" French-Med cuisine shows off "fantastic variations and flavors" in discreetly "sophisticated" environs overseen by a "gracious" staff; the "noise level is certainly robust" and you may need to "negotiate a line of credit" to pay, but it's the stuff that "great memories" are made of; P.S. closed January–March.

	FOOD	DECOR	SERVICE	COST

Tellers American Chophouse *Steak*   26 | 27 | 25 | $70

Islip | 605 Main St. (bet. Locust & Nassau Aves.) | 631-277-7070 | www.tellerschophouse.com

Set in a "stately" "former bank building", this "high-class" Islip chophouse is "a cut above the rest" according to South Shore carnivores savoring "signature rib-eyes" (like "something out of *The Flintstones*") and other "superb" strips matched with wines from an "impressive" cellar in the former vault; you'll "drop a mortgage payment", but diners with "deep pockets" are happy to be "treated royally."

Thai Gourmet Ⓜ🚭 *Thai*   26 | 14 | 19 | $24

Port Jefferson Station | Common Plaza | 4747-24 Nesconset Hwy. (bet. Terryville Rd. & Woodhull Ave.) | 631-474-0663

Boosters feel "blessed" by the "best Thai food this side of Bangkok" at this strip-mall "treasure" in Port Jefferson Station, where the "tempting" dishes "burst with flavor" and "prices are dirt cheap"; just "hit the cash machine" first and "bring your own bottle and patience", since "you may have to wait for a seat" in the "kitschy" digs; P.S. there's a "substantial take-out business" as well.

Tutto Il Giorno *Italian*   25 | 19 | 20 | $62

Sag Harbor | 6 Bay St. (Rector St.) | 631-725-7009 Ⓜ
Southampton | 56 Nugent St. (bet. Main St. & Windmill Ln.) | 631-377-3611

"*Perfetto!*" cry partisans of the "absolutely amazing" cuisine and "warm service" that qualify this "creative" Italian as "a must-try" destination in Sag Harbor – and now in Southampton too, where a garden-equipped sibling arrived post-Survey; the "cozy quarters" and "wonderful" warm-weather terrace maintain an insidery vibe boosted by a "parade of celebrities" (Donna Karan's daughter Gabby is a partner in both branches), but be prepared for an "expensive" tab and a "queue to get in" (devotees "wish they would take reservations").

Verace *Italian*   26 | 26 | 25 | $47

Islip | 599 Main St. (bet. Locust & Willow Aves.) | 631-277-3800 | www.veracerestaurant.com

"Another winner" from the owners of next-door neighbor Tellers, this "sophisticated" Islip Italian takes an "inspired" approach to its fare, showcasing "mouthwatering" "small-plate servings" (plus full portions) presented by "professional" staffers tending the "stunning" interior and "cobblestone" patio; to sweeten the already "reasonable" cost, the "Monday wine dinner is a steal."

West End Cafe *American*   25 | 20 | 22 | $43

Carle Place | Clocktower Shopping Ctr. | 187 Glen Cove Rd. (bet. Old Country Rd. & Westbury Ave.) | 516-294-5608 | www.westendli.com

Despite its "oddball" location in the back of a strip mall, the "crowds" have "discovered" this "exceptional" Carle Place bistro whose "imaginative" New American creations deliver a "fantastic" "culinary experience"; a "mature, well-trained" staff and "NYC ambiance" complete the picture, but since the "tight" space is in demand, be sure to reserve "weeks in advance" – and if you nab a seat for the early-bird, "you've scored a home run."

Los Angeles

	FOOD	DECOR	SERVICE	COST

A-Frame *Eclectic*

23 | 18 | 21 | $34

Culver City | 12565 W. Washington Blvd. (Neosho Ave.) | 310-398-7700 | www.aframela.com

"Bold", "original" dishes by "genius" Roy Choi (of Kogi truck fame) deliver an "homage to LA's immigrant flavors" at this Culver City Eclectic set in a "stylish" "repurposed IHOP" done up à la "Dick Van Dyke's vacation lodge"; "spectacular" cocktails, "helpful" service and a firewarmed patio lend extra appeal, and while some could do without the "waits", "noise" and "awkward" seating at communal tables, others take the opportunity to "meet fellow foodies."

Angelini Osteria Ⓜ *Italian*

28 | 19 | 24 | $54

Beverly Boulevard | 7313 Beverly Blvd. (bet. N. Fuller Ave. & N. Poinsettia Pl.) | 323-297-0070 | www.angeliniosteria.com

"Every dish and nibble is a heavenly experience" at this "superb" Italian on Beverly Boulevard famed for chef-owner Gino Angelini's "incredible", "rustic" cooking including "pitch-perfect" pastas, "fabulous" roasted meats and "delectable" branzino; "budget-busting" tabs and a "constant din" in the "claustrophobic" room are drawbacks, and opinions are split on service, but most agree the "spectacular food wins out."

Asanebo Ⓜ *Japanese*

28 | 18 | 25 | $84

Studio City | 11941 Ventura Blvd. (bet. Carpenter & Radford Aves.) | 818-760-3348 | www.asanebo-restaurant.com

"Go with the omakase" and have a "sublime" time at Tetsuya Nakao's Studio City Japanese, a "shining star" where fish fanatics pay "flown-in-from-Japan" prices for "mind-boggling" results; forget "ridiculous novelty rolls", it's unadorned all around, from the "incredibly fresh" cuts to the "low-key" staff and "unassuming" digs, yet "always a total delight."

Bäco Mercat Ⓧ *Sandwiches*

26 | 20 | 21 | $33

Downtown | 408 S. Main St. (Winston St.) | 213-687-8808 | www.bacomercat.com

"Creative" chef-owner Josef Centeno (ex Lazy Ox Canteen) "must have made some sort of pact with the devil to create" the "ridiculously delicious" bäco, an "intense" "sandwich-taco fusion" that's the signature of this "dang original" Downtown newcomer; the "beautifully executed" Mex-Mideastern dishes and "hip but not off-putting" vibes draw a clientele that spans the spectrum from "suits and ties to tats and jeans."

Bashan Ⓜ *American*

28 | 21 | 26 | $57

Montrose | 3459 N. Verdugo Rd. (bet. Ocean View & Sunview Blvds.) | 818-541-1532 | www.bashanrestaurant.com

A "culinary highlight of the 818", chef/co-owner Nadav Bashan's "fabulous" "sleeper" in Montrose "hews to seasonal fare", offering "creative, exceptional" New American cuisine with "caring" service in a "small", "tasteful" setting decorated with grass wallpaper and Danish fixtures; though some would prefer more space, most agree the "expensive" tabs are "worth every bit."

Bazaar by José Andrés ❶ *Spanish*

27 | 28 | 25 | $83

Beverly Hills | SLS at Beverly Hills | 465 S. La Cienega Blvd. (Clifton Way) | 310-246-5555 | www.thebazaar.com

"Go with an open mind and be dazzled" by this "crazy gourmet circus" in the SLS Hotel from "mad genius" José Andrés that will leave you "giddy" thanks to "mind-blowingly delicious" Spanish-inspired small plates and cocktails "that look like they were made in chemistry class", all presented with "extra care"; just prepare for "sensory overload" when it comes to the "noisy", "luxe" Philippe Starck–designed space (including a "whimsical" patisserie), and "make sure your wallet can take it."

Bouchon *French*   25 | 25 | 25 | $63

Beverly Hills | 235 N. Cañon Dr. (bet. Dayton Way & Wilshire Blvd.) | 310-271-9910 | www.bouchonbistro.com

"*Vive* Bouchon!" gush *admirateurs* of Thomas Keller's "inviting", celeb-frequented Beverly Hills bistro – sib to the Yountville original – where "superbly trained" servers deliver "sublime", "meticulously prepared" French classics to industry "bigwigs" (and mere mortals) in a "bright" room that's like "Paris without the long flight"; while some "aren't dazzled", most feel for "special occasions", it's "money well spent", and you don't "have to drive to the wine country" to indulge.

Brent's Deli *Deli*   26 | 16 | 23 | $23

Northridge | 19565 Parthenia St. (bet. Corbin & Shirley Aves.) | 818-886-5679
Westlake Village | 2799 Townsgate Rd. (Westlake Blvd.) | 805-557-1882
www.brentsdeli.com

"The air is redolent with corned beef, stuffed cabbage" and other "NYC" eats at this "old-school" Northridge deli and "more luxurious" Westlake Village spin-off, where the "delish" "mile-high sandwiches" are "worth the schlep"; it's not inexpensive, but the "staff's a hoot" and "hefty portions" make for a "good value" – "bring an extra stomach."

Cafe Bizou *French*   23 | 19 | 22 | $33

Santa Monica | Water Gdn. | 2450 Colorado Ave. (26th St.) | 310-453-8500 Ⓢ
Pasadena | 91 N. Raymond Ave. (Holly St.) | 626-792-9923
Sherman Oaks | 14016 Ventura Blvd. (bet. Costello & Murieta Aves.) | 818-788-3536
www.cafebizou.com

It's "not expensive but feels like it" at this "upbeat" bistro threesome that's "always crazy busy" with "loyal customers" who "love" the "delightful" French food, "festive" atmosphere and "courteous" service; while a few surveyors find it too "ordinary", it remains a "safe choice" for "date night" and "celebrating something special", plus the "fantastic" $2 corkage makes it a BYO "bargain"; P.S. "make a reservation."

Cut Ⓢ *Steak*   27 | 25 | 26 | $102

Beverly Hills | Beverly Wilshire | 9500 Wilshire Blvd. (Rodeo Dr.) | 310-276-8500 | www.wolfgangpuck.com

"The apex of meatdom", Wolfgang Puck's "innovative, extravagant" take on the classic steakhouse in Beverly Hills "hits it out of the park" with "sublime cuts" and "divine" sides offered in a "sleek, modern", "star-studded" setting; it follows through with "exceptional" service, but you may "need to take out a loan" to foot the bill; P.S. a limited menu is available in the no-reservations Sidebar.

Echigo Ⓢ *Japanese*   28 | 10 | 21 | $58

West LA | 12217 Santa Monica Blvd. (Amherst Ave.) | 310-820-9787

"Purists" praise this "traditional" West LA Japanese specializing in simple, "ultrafresh", "tender" fish "harmoniously" paired with "warm, vinegary rice" at prices that are moderate for the genre; just overlook the strip-mall decor, grab a seat at the bar and "go for the omakase"; P.S. the lunch set is one of the "best deals in town."

Father's Office *American* | 24 | 17 | 15 | $24 |

Culver City | Helms Bldg. | 3229 Helms Ave. (bet. Venice & Washington Blvds.) | 310-736-2224
Santa Monica | 1018 Montana Ave. (bet. 10th & 11th Sts.) | 310-736-2224 ●
www.fathersoffice.com

The "out-of-this-world" blue-cheese burger is "perfection" and the "fantastic" beer list "will never let you down" at this "affordable", "order-at-the-bar" American gastropub duo in Santa Monica and Culver City that continues to outdo newcomers to the "gourmet burger trend"; no menu substitutions (or ketchup) are allowed and "it's a royal pain to find a place to sit", so "expect to wait awhile"; P.S. must be 21 to enter.

Hamasaku ⊠ *Japanese* | 28 | 19 | 24 | $67 |

West LA | 11043 Santa Monica Blvd. (Sepulveda Blvd.) | 310-479-7636 |
www.hamasakula.com

"Memorable enough to be your last meal", the "innovative" rolls named for celebs and "fresh" sushi (plus omakase) star at this "high-class" West LA Japanese in an unassuming strip mall; the "gracious" host treats everyone – from plebs to Hollywood luminaries – "like a VIP" in the upscale, homey space, but note that "the check will get your attention."

Kiwami *Japanese* | 28 | 19 | 24 | $52 |

Studio City | 11920 Ventura Blvd. (Carpenter Ave.) | 818-763-3910 |
www.katsu-yagroup.com

An "upscale version" of sibling Katsu-ya, this Studio City "jewel" impresses guests with "sublime" sushi, sashimi and "beautifully prepared" small plates; the vibe is "cool" without being "trendy", and though bills can be "painfully high" – especially for the hard-to-reserve private omakase with Katsuya himself – it's regarded as one of "the best" in town.

Lazy Ox Canteen ● *Eclectic* | 25 | 17 | 21 | $41 |

Little Tokyo | 241 S. San Pedro St. (bet. 2nd & 3rd Sts.) | 213-626-5299 |
www.lazyoxcanteen.com

Dubbed a "foodie paradise", this "exhilarating" little spot in Little Tokyo "wows" with an ever-"evolving" Eclectic menu featuring "amazing" "out-of-the-box" small plates based on "unique" seasonal ingredients and "all things pig", plus a "great burger"; prices are "moderate", servers are "informed" and the vibe is "cool", even if the "ear-splitting" music could "scare off anyone over 28."

Lucques *Californian/Mediterranean* | 27 | 25 | 26 | $66 |

West Hollywood | 8474 Melrose Ave. (La Cienega Blvd.) | 323-655-6277 |
www.lucques.com

"Take pride in being a local" at this "casually masterful" Cal-Med in WeHo where the "brilliant" Suzanne Goin (A.O.C.) "does wonders" crafting "thoughtful, seasonal" cuisine, complemented by a "smart wine list" and "gracious" service; set in an "old carriage house" with an

	FOOD	DECOR	SERVICE	COST

"ivy-lined courtyard", it's "pleasurable" all around and "well worth the cost" – plus the "value" prix fixe Sunday Supper is still a "big hit."

Lukshon ⊠ *Asian*   25 | 24 | 23 | $47

Culver City | Helms Bldg. | 3239 Helms Ave. (bet. Venice & Washington Blvds.) | 310-202-6808 | www.lukshon.com

Chef Sang Yoon (of Father's Office fame) earns kudos for his "highly original", "habit-forming" Southeast Asian small plates on a mid-priced menu "worth working your way through" at this "epicurean delight" inside Culver City's Helms Bakery; factor in "accommodating" service and a "gorgeous" "modern" setup with an open kitchen and patio, and it's "enjoyable" all around.

Matsuhisa *Japanese*   28 | 19 | 24 | $87

Beverly Hills | 129 N. La Cienega Blvd. (bet. Clifton Way & Wilshire Blvd.) | 310-659-9639 | www.nobumatsuhisa.com

"Impeccable in all respects", this Japanese "temple" from Nobu Matsuhisa – his first and some say "his best" – showcases his "stupendous sashimi with Peruvian flavors" employing "melt-in-your-mouth fresh" fish as well as other "tantalizing" creations; the "tranquil" setting is the most "low-key" in the Nobu empire, with a "professional" staff and a "comfortably modest" ambiance – just don't expect modest prices.

M.B. Post *American*   28 | 23 | 24 | $46

Manhattan Beach | 1142 Manhattan Ave. (Manhattan Beach Blvd.) | 310-545-5405 | www.eatmbpost.com

The "innovative small plates" come out "fast and furious" at this New American "hot spot" in Manhattan Beach where chef David LeFevre (ex Water Grill) creates a true "foodie experience" with his "amazing" locavore fare; it's housed in a former post office with exposed rafters and reclaimed wood lending a "cool vibe" – just remember to "bring earplugs", your premium plastic and start with the biscuits.

Mélisse ⊠Ⓜ *American/French*   28 | 26 | 27 | $120

Santa Monica | 1104 Wilshire Blvd. (11th St.) | 310-395-0881 | www.melisse.com

Admirers insist it "doesn't get any better" than this "stunning" Santa Monica French–New American from Josiah Citrin known for its "impeccable" prix fixe menus based on the seasons, "deep wine list" and "seamless service" that's "pampering without being obsequious"; it also features a "civilized" atmosphere "where your ears are not assaulted by the noise level", so even if some call it "just a bit outdated", the majority deems it "well worth the pennies."

Mezze *Mediterranean*   24 | 21 | 22 | $49

West Hollywood | 401 N. La Cienega Blvd. (bet. Beverly Blvd. & Rosewood Ave.) | 310-657-4103 | www.mezzela.com

"All I can say is 'yum'" sums up this "sensational" WeHo restaurant from Micah Wexler (ex Craft) whipping up "idiosyncratic, intelligent" "delicacies" "perfect for sharing" using "traditional ingredients from all over the Mediterranean in brilliant combinations"; the "beautiful" "sunwashed" tiled space feels like "a night out in Marrakesh", while "gracious" service makes the somewhat "dear prices" easier to handle.

LOS ANGELES

	FOOD	DECOR	SERVICE	COST

Michael's on Naples Ristorante *Italian* | 28 | 25 | 26 | $56 |

Long Beach | 5620 E. Second St. (bet. Ravenna & Tivoli Drs.) |
562-439-7080 | www.michaelsonnaples.com

Locals "can't come up with enough superlatives" for this "rare" Long Beach "treasure", an Italian "fine-dining" destination for "exquisite" market-driven dishes elevated by "wonderful wines" and "on-point" service; indeed, it's "pricey", but the "romantic" setting is "perfect for a special occasion" and "viewing the sunset from the rooftop bar" is a treat.

Michael's Pizzeria *Pizza* | 28 | 20 | 24 | $23 |

Long Beach | 5616 E. Second St. (N. Ravenna Dr.) | 562-987-4000 |
www.michaelspizzeria.com

An offshoot of the venerable Michael's on Naples, this "fabulous" Long Beach pizzeria loads up its "heavenly", "authentic" Neapolitan pies with "fresh", homemade mozz, plus more "creative" items like clams, egg and baby artichokes; with "excellent service" and "modest prices", the "simple", "noisy" setting is easily excused.

Mo-Chica ●☒ *Peruvian* | 24 | 8 | 16 | $26 |

Downtown | 514 W. Seventh St. (bet. Grand Ave. & Olive St.) |
213-622-3744 | www.mo-chica.com

What began as a stand in Downtown's Mercado La Paloma has grown to a full-service sit-down restaurant where Ricardo Zarate whips up "intriguing, but accessible", "delicious" Peruvian fare like "daily ceviches and other splendors" deemed a "revelation"; there's a full bar pouring pisco cocktails and a hip graffiti look, but best of all, the prices are still relatively "cheap."

Nobu Malibu *Japanese* | 27 | 21 | 25 | $86 |

Malibu | Malibu Country Mart | 22706 Pacific Coast Hwy. (Malibu Pier) |
310-317-9140 | www.noburestaurants.com

Though it's "much more low-key" than its West Hollywood sibling, Nobu Matsuhisa's Malibu Japanese still features "sublime", "novel" sushi and "delicious" Peruvian-inflected signatures that "have been copied at so many restaurants they almost sound pedestrian", delivered by a "stellar" staff; its locale right on the beach is "elegant" and "star-studded", just "take out a second mortgage before you go."

101 Coffee Shop ● *Diner* | 23 | 21 | 22 | $27 |

Hollywood | 6145 Franklin Ave. (Vista Del Mar Ave.) | 323-467-1175 |
www.the101coffeeshop.com

"Diner kitsch in its highest form" serves as a "hipster", "celebrity" and "tourist" magnet at this "late-night" Hollywood hang – voted LA's Most Popular restaurant – that dishes up plentiful portions of "spot-on" American coffee-shop eats, plus some "mean" java and "amazing" milkshakes at "fair prices"; an "enthusiastic" staff keeps it "vibrant", so it's "always hopping" whether curing "hangovers" in the morning or "getting them started" in the first place.

101 Noodle Express *Chinese* | 23 | 18 | 20 | $21 |

Culver City | Westfield Culver City | 6000 Sepulveda Blvd. (Slauson Ave.) |
310-397-2060

Arcadia | 1025 S. Baldwin Ave. (Arcadia Ave.) | 626-446-8855 ⇥

(continued)

(continued)

101 Noodle Express

Alhambra | 1408 E. Valley Blvd. (bet. New Ave. & Vega St.) | 626-300-8654 ◑⇄
www.101noodleexpress.com

Offering a "basic course in noodle-ology", this "no-muss, no-fuss" Sino trio dishes up "awesome" soups and dumplings as well as a "gotta-get-it" beef roll (picture a "Chinese burrito") served at a "prompt" pace; the settings vary, but most don't mind given the "generous" servings of "wonderfully cheap" eats.

Osteria Mozza *Italian*

27 | 23 | 24 | $68

Hollywood | 6602 Melrose Ave. (Highland Ave.) | 323-297-0100 | www.osteriamozza.com

"If you manage to score a reservation, you're in for a treat" at this "exquisite" Hollywood Italian from Nancy Silverton and Mario Batali that's "pure indulgence", from the "ethereal, unforgettable" pastas to the "luscious, milky-fresh" cheese at the mozzarella bar to the "sublime" desserts "even carb-phobe friends" enjoy; given the "fabulous" food, most don't mind if the "sophisticated", "star-studded" setting is "noisy" or the "knowledgeable" staff sometimes "snooty", but as for the bill – "start saving your paychecks."

Piccolo *Italian*

28 | 25 | 26 | $67

Venice | 5 Dudley Ave. (Spdwy.) | 310-314-3222 | www.piccolovenice.com

Surveyors say it "doesn't get much better" than this "quaint" Venice hideaway just "steps from the beach" serving "delectable", "refined" Venetian fare that "rivals the best in Italy"; prices are a "splurge", but with an exceedingly "knowledgeable" staff and "romantic" setting, "what's not to love?"

The Pikey ◐ *Pub Food*

- | - | - | M

Hollywood | 7617 W. Sunset Blvd. (Stanley Ave.) | 323-850-5400 | www.thepikeyla.com

Hearty pub food plus inventive cocktails crafted from an extensive list of spirits (absinthe, anyone?) make this well-priced Hollywood newcomer a happy-hour crowd-pleaser; tiled floors, dark wooden booths and cheery servers in suspenders add to the authentic English watering-hole feel.

Playa *Latin*

25 | 23 | 23 | $49

Beverly Boulevard | 7360 Beverly Blvd. (bet. Fairfax & La Brea Aves.) | 323-933-5300 | www.playarivera.com

"A winner" from "culinary rock star" John Sedlar, this Beverly Boulevard Pan-Latin serves "sensational", "clever" small plates and "terrific cocktails" in a "fun, flirty" setting that's an "informal, less expensive version of Rivera"; service is "knowledgeable" too, so the "insanely loud" acoustics are the only drawback; P.S. "the brunch is an undiscovered treasure."

Providence *American/Seafood*

28 | 26 | 28 | $104

Hollywood | 5955 Melrose Ave. (Cole Ave.) | 323-460-4170 | www.providencela.com

"Everything is exquisite" at this "world-class" fine-dining destination in Hollywood, where Michael Cimarusti turns out "amazing, innovative" seafood dishes like "delectable works of art" in a "luxurious" setting that's an "oasis of tranquility"; factor in "superb", "knowledgeable" service – fittingly rated tops in the LA Survey – plus a "fantastic" cheese platter wheeled tableside and it adds up to a "delightful gastronomic experience", albeit one that "doesn't come cheap"; P.S. the six-course dessert tasting menu will "blow your mind."

Rivera *Pan-Latin* · 26 | 24 | 23 | $60

Downtown | Met Lofts | 1050 S. Flower St. (11 St.) | 213-749-1460 | www.riverarestaurant.com
"A knockout every time", this Downtown Pan-Latin from "genius" chef John Sedlar presents "playful", "high-concept, beautifully executed" dishes that "look like art and taste like heaven" alongside "brilliant" cocktails in a "chic" dining room; service "always pleases" too, and although some complain the multiple menus are "confusing" and that it "needs to tone down the noise", most consider it a "privilege" "worth the high prices."

Spago *Californian* · 27 | 25 | 26 | $80

Beverly Hills | 176 N. Cañon Dr. (Wilshire Blvd.) | 310-385-0880 | www.wolfgangpuck.com
"What's left to say" about this "quintessential LA" hub in Beverly Hills – "the jewel in the crown" of the Wolfgang Puck empire – that's "going strong after all these years" turning out "knock-your-socks-off" Californian cuisine in a "glamorous", "glittering" setting sprinkled with "aging celebs", "power producers and socialites"; "everyone gets treated royally" and "with a little luck, you can get a handshake from the man himself" – in sum, there's "no finer place" to "impress", as long as you can handle the "sky-high" tabs; P.S. as we went to press Spago was closed for a remodel and menu revamp.

Sunny Spot *Eclectic* · ▽ 22 | 20 | 21 | $36

Marina del Rey | 822 Washington Blvd. (Abbot Kinney Blvd.) | 310-448-8884 | www.sunnyspotvenice.com
Kogi BBQ truck maven Roy Choi has transformed Marina del Rey's Beechwood into this "trendy" midpriced 'roadside cookshop' with a "tasty" Eclectic menu featuring "big, bold-flavored" dishes like jerk chicken wings, grilled shrimp and a standout burger; the "noisy" space is decked out with "bright and flowery" fabrics, island colors and a bar wrapped in burlap featuring a "top-notch cocktail menu."

Sushi Masu Ⓜ *Japanese* · 27 | 16 | 25 | $47

West LA | 1911 Westwood Blvd. (bet. La Grange & Missouri Aves.) | 310-446-4368
"Lots of loyal regulars" count on this West LA Japanese, a "quiet, neighborhood" "gem" for "fresh, delish", "expertly prepared" sushi at an "ideal cost/quality ratio"; though the simple space is "not fancy", chef Hiroshi Masuko is an "engaging host" who "makes you feel at home"; P.S. "sit at the bar" if you can.

Sushi Zo Ⓩ *Japanese* · 28 | 15 | 20 | $116

West LA | 9824 National Blvd. (Castle Heights Ave.) | 310-842-3977
"Beautiful little morsels" of "extraordinary, melt-in-your-mouth" sushi appeal to "purists" at this ultra-"expensive", omakase-only Japanese "indulgence" in West LA set in "spartan" digs; service can feel "rushed"

(and "too strict with requests"), but even that does "not detract from the exquisite experience."

Tar & Roses Ⓜ *Eclectic*　　　∇ 23 | 22 | 24 | $51

Santa Monica | 602 Santa Monica Blvd. (6th St.) | 310-587-0700 | www.tarandroses.com

Chef Andrew Kirschner (Joe's, Wilshire) is behind this "trendy" Santa Monica Eclectic pulling in a "beautiful" "LA" crowd with "interesting", "delicious" dishes built around his blazing wood-burning oven; service is "accommodating", but the rustic digs made from reclaimed and rough-hewn materials are frequently "packed", so prepare for "waits" and a "high noise level" "made more tolerable by the food."

Urasawa Ⓢ Ⓜ *Japanese*　　　28 | 25 | 27 | $488

Beverly Hills | 218 N. Rodeo Dr. (Wilshire Blvd.) | 310-247-8939

"Every dish is a work of art and a labor of love" at Hiro Urasawa's Beverly Hills Japanese – LA's No. 1 for Food – where the "sublime" omakase-only feasts are prepared by the "maestro" himself with the "utmost attention to detail" in a "tranquil" setting; service is "impeccable" too, so "put it on your bucket list", but "be ready to fork over your car payment" for the "once-in-a-lifetime treat."

Waterloo & City ◑ *British*　　　24 | 20 | 22 | $42

Culver City | 12517 W. Washington Blvd. (Mildred Ave.) | 310-391-4222 | www.waterlooandcity.com

"LA meets London gastropub" at this "hip" Culver City "favorite" from "innovative chef" Brendan Collins spotlighting a "sophisticated" Modern British menu "heavy on meat" with "lots of surprises", elevated by "awesome" beers and a "nicely curated" cocktail list; prices are "reasonable", the servers are "savvy" and the space has a pleasantly "ramshackle feel", although it's frequently "jam-packed", so "noise is an issue."

Miami

Restaurant	Cuisine
29] Naoe	Japanese
28] Palme d'Or	French
Zuma	Japanese
Palm	Steak
27] Il Gabbiano	Italian
OLA	Pan-Latin
Pascal's on Ponce	French
Michy's	American/French
Prime One Twelve	Seafood/Steak
Nobu Miami Beach	Japanese
Azul	European
Matsuri	Japanese
Michael's Genuine	American
Yakko-San	Japanese
Joe's Stone Crab	Seafood
Red	Steak
26] Oishi	Japanese/Thai
Frankie's	Pizza
La Dorada*	Seafood/Spanish
Francesco	Peruvian

OTHER NOTEWORTHY PLACES

AltaMare	Mediterranean/Seafood
Bazaar/José Andrés	Eclectic/Spanish
BLT	Steak
Bourbon	Steak
DB Bistro Moderne	French
Escopazzo	Italian
Estiatorio Milos	Greek
1500°	American
Forge	American
Hakkasan	Chinese
J&G Grill	American/Asian
Katsuya by Starck	Japanese
Makoto	Japanese
Pubbelly	Asian
Puerto Sagua	Cuban
Red Light	American
Scarpetta	Italian
Sugarcane	Eclectic
Timo	Italian/Mediterranean
Yardbird	Southern

* Indicates a tie with restaurant above

	FOOD	DECOR	SERVICE	COST

AltaMare *Mediterranean/Seafood* | 24 | 20 | 23 | $54 |

South Beach | 1233 Lincoln Rd. (bet. Alton Ct. & Alton Rd.) |
Miami Beach | 305-532-3061 | www.altamarerestaurant.com
Claudio the owner is always on hand, "ensuring all are satisfied" with
the "beautifully executed" Med-accented seafood, meats and "homemade" pasta emanating from the open kitchen of this SoBe spot; if it's
gotten more "pricey", it still pleases "locals" who "love" the "stylish"
space on a "mellow stretch" of Lincoln Road.

Azul 🅰 *European* | 27 | 27 | 26 | $76 |

Brickell Area | Mandarin Oriental Hotel | 500 Brickell Key Dr. (SE 8th St.) |
305-913-8358 | www.mandarinoriental.com
This "perennial favorite" in Brickell Key's Mandarin Oriental pleases its
well-heeled clientele with a Modern European menu that incorporates
American and Asian accents; cuisine aside, its "attentive but unobtrusive" service, "serious" wine list and "sleek" setting with "spectacular
bay views" help make it a "special-occasion" "delight" – "even if prices
are close to those for nearby condos."

Bazaar by José Andrés *Spanish/Eclectic* | - | - | - | VE |

South Beach | SLS Hotel South Beach | 1701 Collins Ave. (17th St.) |
Miami Beach | 305-674-1701 | www.thebazaar.com
DC-based superstar culinary magician José Andrés recently set up shop
in South Beach at the SLS Hotel with this Spanish-Eclectic in a sexy deco-
esque room (dominated by a huge seashell-encrusted chandelier), offering traditional tapas as well as more forward-thinking small plates with
Caribbean and Latin twists; either way, prices are high and reservations can be as difficult to obtain as snowshoes on Ocean Drive.

BLT Steak *Steak* | 25 | 23 | 23 | $71 |

South Beach | The Betsy Hotel | 1440 Ocean Dr. (bet. 14th & 15th Sts.) |
Miami Beach | 305-673-0044 | www.bltsteak.com
"A bit more hip" than old-school meat palaces, this Betsy Hotel outpost of a "quality brand" steakhouse chain excels with its "perfectly
charred" chops, "inventive" sides and "terrific" wine list – that's icing
on the cake for fans who admit "they had me at the popovers"; tabs are
"steep" and some "don't love the lobbyish atmosphere", but most
deem it a "refined" escape from the SoBe "riffraff."

Bourbon Steak *Steak* | 25 | 27 | 25 | $83 |

Aventura | Turnberry Isle Hotel & Resort | 19999 W. Country Club Dr.
(Aventura Blvd.) | 786-279-6600 | www.michaelmina.net
From its "gorgeous", "spacious" setup designed by Tony Chi to its
"decadent" chops, "delish" burgers and "addictive" fries, Michael
Mina's steakhouse in Aventura's Turnberry Isle Hotel strikes fans as
"ahead of the herd" in many respects; a "passionate" staff (a "rare find
in Miami") mixes "well-balanced drinks" and helps diners navigate an
"extensive" wine list that's loaded with "treasures" – and they'll gladly
accept your "gold card" at meal's end.

DB Bistro Moderne *French* | 26 | 25 | 25 | $76 |

Downtown | JW Marriott Marquis Miami | 255 Biscayne Blvd. Way
(bet. SE 2nd & 3rd Aves.) | 305-421-8800 | www.danielnyc.com
Proof positive that NYC's Daniel Boulud is a "genuine food god" is the
"perfectly prepared" French fare at this "chic" spot in Downtown

Miami's JW Marriott Marquis; service is "attentive" and the "airy" Yabu Pushelberg–designed trifecta of dining room, lounge and outdoor terrace is "beautiful", so if you "can handle the tab", "what's not to like?"; P.S. "burger fanatics" shouldn't miss the $34 sirloin, foie gras and truffle burger.

Escopazzo ●Ⓜ *Italian* | 25 | 19 | 24 | $62 |

South Beach | 1311 Washington Ave. (bet. 13th & 14th Sts.) | Miami Beach | 305-674-9450 | www.escopazzo.com

SoBe "insiders", "locavores" and "gourmets" know that this "nondescript storefront" on "busy" Washington Avenue houses a "hidden jewel", where chef-owner Giancarla Bodoni "does wonders" with the "fresh, organic ingredients" that go into "one-of-a-kind" Italian creations; her "love and creativity justify the high prices", so consider the "über-friendly" service, "quiet", "low-key" vibe and large wine selection pure gravy.

Estiatorio Milos *Greek* | – | – | – | VE |

South Beach | 730 First St. (Washington Ave.) | Miami Beach | 305-604-6800 | www.milos.ca

Fish flown in daily from the Mediterranean and displayed like jewels on a bed of ice compete with a spare-no-expense design that features white marble floors, raw exposed wood and ancient-looking pottery at this über-posh Greek chain outpost newly arrived in SoBe; the seafood is as breathtakingly expensive as it is impeccably fresh, with many species starting at $50 a pound and going up, with an epic wine list to match.

1500° *American/Steak* | 24 | 22 | 20 | $71 |

Miami Beach | Eden Roc Renaissance | 4525 Collins Ave. (W. 41st St.) | 305-674-5594 | www.1500degreesmiami.com

Set in Miami Beach's storied Eden Roc Hotel, this "classy" locale is named for the temperature at which chef Paula DaSilva (*Hell's Kitchen* finalist and 3030 Ocean alum) cooks "juicy", "melt-in-your-mouth" steaks, a "specialty" on the "creative" New American menu; it's expensive and service is "erratic", but diners appreciate being able to "speak without shouting" in the "pretty" dining room or on the "breezy" patio.

Forge Restaurant & Wine Bar *American* | 24 | 26 | 24 | $78 |

Miami Beach | 432 41st St. (Sheridan Ave.) | 305-538-8533 | www.theforge.com

This Miami Beach "landmark" was "reinvented" several years ago with an "over-the-top", "Alice in Wonderland"–esque "makeover" of its many "special rooms" and an updated New American menu bearing the "magic touch" of chef Dewey LoSasso; yet it has "stayed true to its roots" as a playground for "celebrities" and other "monied" types and still boasts a "museumlike wine cellar", so most find it "better than ever" – "bravo!"

Francesco Ⓧ *Peruvian* | 26 | 17 | 23 | $55 |

Coral Gables | 325 Alcazar Ave. (bet. Salzedo St. & SW 42nd Ave.) | 305-446-1600 | www.francescorestaurantmiami.com

According to fans, the "best ceviche in Miami" is to be found at this "first-rate" Peruvian in Coral Gables dishing up "expensive" but "consistently amazing" seafood and other dishes, some "authentic", others with Italian touches; the small space gets "tightly packed" and the "decor could use a refresh", but the "owner is always on-site and it shows" in the overall "welcoming" vibe.

Frankie's Pizza ⓜ↯ *Pizza*

| 26 | 7 | 20 | $14 |

Westchester | 9118 Bird Rd. (92nd Ave.) | 305-221-0221 | www.frankiespizzaonline.com

Since the 1950s, the Pasquarella family has been slinging square (read: "not your standard") pies at this cheap, cash-only pizza joint in Westchester, and folks who've "been going since they were little runts" insist "that should tell you" it's "worth" it; there's a "few picnic tables" in back, but it's "primarily a take-out" spot – indeed, they ship 'half-baked' pies anywhere in the country.

Hakkasan *Chinese*

| 26 | 27 | 24 | $78 |

Miami Beach | Fontainebleau Miami Beach | 4441 Collins Ave. (W. 44th St.) | 786-276-1388 | www.fontainebleau.com

"Wow, so *this* is Chinese food" declare converts whose "eyes are opened" by the "incredible" modern Cantonese fare at the Miami Beach outpost of the London original hidden in the "sprawling" Fontainebleau; assets include "superior" dim sum (most welcome in a city with a "significant shortage"), generally "knowledgeable" service and "chic" environs that are surprisingly "intimate" given the "big" space – just expect to pay "crazy money" to enjoy it all.

Il Gabbiano ●🗷 *Italian*

| 27 | 26 | 27 | $81 |

Downtown | One Miami Tower | 335 S. Biscayne Blvd. (SE 3rd St.) | 305-373-0063 | www.ilgabbianomia.com

From the antipasti to the after-dinner limoncello (both gratis), this Downtown sibling of Il Mulino in NYC (and Sunny Isles Beach) exhibits "true Italian class"; expect an "inspired menu", "extensive" wine list, "stellar" service and "elegant" digs that extend to a "beautiful" outdoor terrace where diners can "gaze at Biscayne Bay or into their companion's eyes" – welcome distractions from tabs that reflect the "top-notch" quality.

J&G Grill *American*

| - | - | - | VE |

Bal Harbour | St. Regis Bal Harbour Resort | 9703 Collins Ave. (96th St.) | 305-993-3333 | www.jggrillmiami.com

Jean-Georges Vongerichten lends a subtle Asian touch to this über-elegant and über-pricey beachfront New American at the stunning St. Regis Bal Harbour, where well-heeled patrons can choose a protein, pair it with a sauce and have it grilled to order; the glass-enclosed dining room mixes city sophistication (cool gray hanging lanterns and linen-wrapped booths) with tropical beauty (palm trees outside every window), while a fairly deep wine list adds extra appeal.

Joe's Stone Crab *Seafood*

| 27 | 20 | 23 | $68 |

South Beach | 11 Washington Ave. (bet. 1st St. & S. Pointe Dr.) | Miami Beach | 305-673-0365 | www.joesstonecrab.com

"Rob a bank, sell the house, [do] whatever it takes" to afford the "succulent" stone crabs that again make this "legendary" SoBe eatery Miami's Most Popular – though "the irony is that everything else on the menu is reasonably priced" and standouts like fried chicken and Key lime pie are equally "to die for"; "looong waits" and "rushed" service from "track-star" waiters racing through the "gigantic" space are

| | FOOD | DECOR | SERVICE | COST |

the norm, but you can "avoid the madness" by heading to the take-out cafe; P.S. closed mid-May to mid-October.

Katsuya by Starck *Japanese*   – | – | – | E

South Beach | SLS Hotel South Beach | 1701 Collins Ave. (17th St.) | Miami Beach | 305-455-2995 | www.sbe.com

The minimalist, black-and-white decor of this pricey Japanese entry in the swanky SLS South Beach, by designer Philippe Starck, deftly show-cases the uniquely personal fare of master sushi chef Katsuya Uechi, who mixes traditional fresh-fish preparations with more eclectic takes; a larger-than-life pair of geisha's eyes gazes seductively from behind the sushi bar, as at the chain's other locations in LA and Houston, while her lips can be found upstairs at the Dragon Room Lounge.

La Dorada *Seafood/Spanish*   26 | 21 | 26 | $77

Coral Gables | 177 Giralda Ave. (Ponce de Leon Blvd.) | 305-446-2002 | www.ladoradamiami.com

This Coral Gables Spaniard offers "elegant, wonderfully simple prepa-rations" of seafood that tastes as fresh as if it were "flown in daily from the Mediterranean" – via "first-class airfare", judging by the cost; however, wallet-watchers say the "awesome" prix fixe lunch is a "great value", while "friendly service", a "good wine selection" and live music on weekends are further pluses.

Makoto *Japanese*   ▽ 25 | 26 | 25 | $60

Bal Harbour | Bal Harbour Shops | 9700 Collins Ave. (96th St.) | 305-864-8600 | www.makoto-restaurant.com

PA powerhouse Stephen Starr pleases Miamians with his "top-class" Japanese sushi and robata effort in chichi Bal Harbour, helmed by chef Makoto Okuwa, a Morimoto protégé; its "sleek", "sedate" setting with a sexy outdoor patio is "so cool you'll forget you're in a mall", but be aware: prices are as posh as the eats.

Matsuri Ⓜ *Japanese*   27 | 20 | 21 | $36

South Miami | 5759 Bird Rd. (bet. Red Rd. & SW 58th Ave.) | 305-663-1615

"Luscious" fish so "fresh" it "tastes like it swam into the restaurant" is the big lure at this longtime South Miami strip-mall mecca for "true sushi aficionados", but it also dishes up "good cooked items" (brush up on your kanji and "ask for the Japanese-language menu" for more "unique" offerings); the "austere" setting isn't always warmed by ser-vice that can swing from "attentive" to "abrupt" – but "who cares with prices like this?"

Michael's Genuine Food & Drink *American*   27 | 20 | 23 | $56

Design District | Atlas Plaza | 130 NE 40th St. (bet. 1st & 2nd Aves.) | 305-573-5550 | www.michaelsgenuine.com

The name of this "trendy" Design District "hot spot" is "a statement of intent that they deliver on" via chef-owner Michael Schwartz's "ambi-tious" yet "down-to-earth" small, medium and large plates of locally sourced New American "comfort" food, backed by "inspired" treats from "genius" pastry chef Hedy Goldsmith and a "well-considered" wine list; staffers can seem "a touch snooty" at times but their "ef-ficiency" compensates, plus there's a "lovely" outdoor courtyard and "decent" prices.

	FOOD	DECOR	SERVICE	COST

Michy's Ⓜ *American/French*   27 | 19 | 25 | $63

Upper East Side | 6927 Biscayne Blvd. (69th St.) | 305-759-2001 | www.michysmiami.com

Chef Michelle Bernstein is "at the top of her game" at this "pricey" Upper East Side "showcase" for "novel takes" on French–New American comfort food; though opinion diverges on the decor – "funky" vs. "Aunt Mildred's living room" – most applaud the staff's "attention to detail"; P.S. those with "commitment issues" can order multiple starters and entrees in half portions.

Naoe Ⓜ *Japanese*   29 | 23 | 28 | VE

Brickell Area | Courvoisier Centre | 661 Brickell Key Dr. (Brickell Ave.) | 305-947-6263 | www.naoemiami.com

"I can't believe this exists in Miami" since it would be "outstanding even in Japan" gush fans of this culinary star, rated the city's tops for Food and Service (recently resettled in bigger digs on Brickell Key, thus outdating the Decor rating); Kevin Cory's "creative" omakase meals include a bento box "revelation" and "impossibly good" sushi, all presented with "warm", "personal" care by "charming" manager Wendy Maharlika and a helper; it's not cheap (price varies according to the day's offerings and how many courses you opt for), but it's so "worth it" – just book "well in advance" (two seatings, Tuesday–Sunday); P.S. a lounge area is in the works.

Nobu Miami Beach *Japanese*   27 | 22 | 22 | $83

South Beach | Shore Club | 1901 Collins Ave. (19th St.) | Miami Beach | 305-695-3232 | www.noburestaurants.com

"Beautiful fish and beautiful people" dazzle at this "über-hip" "pregame warm-up for SoBe's clubs", part of Nobu Matsuhisa's far-flung fusion empire renowned for its "incredible" Japanese-Peruvian cuisine crowned by "sushi to die for" (indeed, the bill alone "may kill you"); the space is "beyond minimalist compared to the rest of the Shore Club's glitz" and critics contend service is "not up to par with the prices", but "have a sake, chill" and "keep your eyes open – you'll be surprised who you might see."

Oishi Thai *Japanese/Thai*   26 | 22 | 24 | $44

North Miami | 14841 Biscayne Blvd. (146th St.) | 305-947-4338 | www.oishithai.com

"Delicious" sushi and other "fabulous" Japanese fare shares billing with "exotic" Thai creations at this North Miami strip-maller, "admirably run" by a onetime Nobu chef; a "cool" modern Asian look, servers who "do everything they can to make for an enjoyable meal" and an optimal "quality/price ratio" further boost its appeal.

OLA *Pan-Latin*   27 | 22 | 25 | $66

South Beach | Sanctuary Hotel | 1745 James Ave. (bet. 17th & 18th Sts.) | Miami Beach | 305-695-9125 | www.olamiami.com

"Ceviche is king" at this "quiet" Pan-Latin respite from the "craziness of South Beach", offering a "superb" culinary "trip from Mexico to Argentina"; set in the boutique Sanctuary Hotel well "off the main drag", it has a "trendy" yet "comfortable" atmosphere, a "thoughtful" selection of wines parsed by a "knowledgeable" crew and a "delightful" terrace.

The Palm *Steak*

| 28 | 20 | 25 | $73 |

Bay Harbor Islands | 9650 E. Bay Harbor Dr. (96th St.) | 305-868-7256 | www.thepalm.com

"Top-quality meat cooked right", "great sides" and "strong drinks" are what you can expect "every time" at this Bay Harbor Islands outpost of the "quintessential NY steakhouse" chain; caricatures line the walls and "local bigwigs" fill the seats of the "clubby" environs, which are overseen by "old-school waiters" and host an "amiable bar scene", but it doesn't come cheap: "my credit card won't allow me near the place."

Palme d'Or 🖹🅼 *French*

| 28 | 27 | 27 | $92 |

Coral Gables | Biltmore Hotel | 1200 Anastasia Ave. (Columbus Blvd.) | 305-913-3201 | www.biltmorehotel.com

"The prize of Coral Gables, if not all of Miami/Dade", is this "superb" New French stunner boasting a "well-considered" wine list and "seamless" service in a "luxurious", "refined" setting, though the recent departure of chef Philippe Ruiz may put the Food rating in question; "not cheap" understates things, especially if you go all out and "stay the night" at the "beautiful" Biltmore for the "ultimate romantic evening."

Pascal's on Ponce 🖹 *French*

| 27 | 20 | 25 | $66 |

Coral Gables | 2611 Ponce de Leon Blvd. (Valencia Ave.) | 305-444-2024 | www.pascalmiami.com

"Creativity abounds" in the "*magnifique*" New French fare at chef-owner Pascal Oudin's "unassuming" storefront bistro "just off the Mile" in Coral Gables; the space is about as "small" as the bills are "big", but "first-rate" service and "soufflés so light that you won't gain a pound" help explain why most find it "always a treat."

Prime One Twelve ⬤ *Seafood/Steak*

| 27 | 23 | 22 | $87 |

South Beach | 112 Ocean Dr. (1st St.) | Miami Beach | 305-532-8112 | www.mylesrestaurantgroup.com

"Super-sexy" yet "serious", this South Beach surf 'n' turfer dishes up "monstrous" portions of "amazing" food, but it's just as well known for hosting the "scene of scenes", with "Bentleys, Ferraris and Lambos" pulling up out front and "wannabes" "rubbing elbows" ("literally: they pack 'em in") with "movie stars", "sports legends" and "models" inside; downsides include "noise", "long waits", variable service and "black-card" tabs, but hey, "you'll have a story to tell."

Pubbelly ⬤🅼 *Asian*

| 24 | 22 | 22 | $38 |

Miami Beach | 1418 20th St. (bet. Bay Rd. & Purdy Ave.) | 305-532-7555 | www.pubbelly.com

"Porktastic!" squeal fans of this pig-centric Miami Beach gastropub that pairs "rich", "creative" Asian fusion fare with a strong selection of craft brews and wine; the "'in' crowd" that throngs the rustic "hole-in-the-wall" digs declares it a "great spot to start, end or make an evening" thanks to its small- and large-plate options, moderate prices and "down-to-earth" service.

Puerto Sagua ⬤ *Cuban*

| 23 | 10 | 18 | $21 |

South Beach | 700 Collins Ave. (7th St.) | Miami Beach | 305-673-1115

"Nothing has changed" at this Cuban diner "landmark" in South Beach since "before the revolution" (or at least since it opened in 1962);

	FOOD	DECOR	SERVICE	COST

waiters in white shirts are still ferrying "rock-solid" comfort food around the "greasy spoon"–style digs "without any fuss", and best of all the bills are still low.

Red Light Little River *American*

	23	12	13	$37

Upper East Side | Motel Blu | 7700 Biscayne Blvd. (76th St.) | 305-757-7116 | www.redlightmiami.com

"Bohemian gourmets" gravitate to this "funky" Upper East Sider attached to a "retro motel", where "awesome chef" Kris Wessel turns out "creative" contemporary Americana with Big Easy spins ("those shrimp!") at "good prices"; the dinerlike digs prompt debate ("enjoyably seedy" vs. a "dive", though there is riverside alfresco seating) and service takes lots of flak ("useless", "slooow"), but for most, the "food makes it all worthwhile"; P.S. closed seasonally from July to mid-August.

Red, The Steakhouse *Steak*

	27	25	24	$83

South Beach | 119 Washington Ave. (1st St.) | Miami Beach | 305-534-3688 | www.redthesteakhouse.com

As the name implies, this "classy" South Beach steakhouse is a true "red meat/red wine lover's paradise" with its "juicy" Angus beef and "extensive wine collection" displayed behind a glass wall – though the "extravagant" price tags require a lot of green; an "attentive" staff, a "cool ambiance" and a "stylish" "contemporary" look complete the "first-rate" experience.

Scarpetta *Italian*

	25	26	23	$79

Miami Beach | Fontainebleau Miami Beach | 4441 Collins Ave. (W. 44th St.) | 305-674-4660 | www.fontainebleau.com

"Spaghetti with oomph", the "best polenta this side of heaven" and other "outstanding" Italian fare make diners "happy to have Scott Conant's talents in Miami" at this Fontainebleau spin-off of the NYC original; yes it's "pricey", but "you get what you pay for", including "thoughtful, efficient" service and a "captivating" setting complete with "fantastic" water views and "*Top Model*"-like patrons.

Sugarcane Raw Bar Grill ● *Eclectic*

	25	24	20	$50

Downtown | 3252 NE First Ave. (32nd St.) | 786-369-0353 | www.sugarcanerawbargrill.com

A "happening scene" unfolds at this Downtowner where the "excellent" menu of Eclectic small plates offers "something for everyone" (raw bar, robata grill, sushi, etc.), and the airy "Key West/Havana" decor transports the "attractive" crowd to an "island paradise"; just know that bills can climb and the "360-degree" indoor-outdoor bar can be a "real meat market."

Timo *Italian/Mediterranean*

	25	19	23	$56

Sunny Isles Beach | 17624 Collins Ave. (bet. 175th Terr. & 178th St.) | 305-936-1008 | www.timorestaurant.com

It's always "worth the schlep" to Sunny Isles Beach to check out the "new surprises" on Tim Andriola's "creative", seasonally changing Italian-Med menu, and "you gotta try" the wood-fired pizzas with "thin, crisp crusts" too; relatively "reasonable prices" and "friendly" servers are more reasons why it's considered a "keeper" despite its sometimes "noisy" setting in a "nondescript shopping mall."

	FOOD	DECOR	SERVICE	COST

Yakko-San ◐ *Japanese*
(fka Hiro's Yakko-San)

| | 27 | - | 21 | $31 |

North Miami Beach | Intracoastal Mall | 3881 NE 163rd St.
(Sunny Isles Blvd.) | 305-947-0064 | www.yakko-san.com

"Feel like Andrew Zimmern" sampling the "unusual" "izakaya-style" small plates and "inspired" sushi at this "adventurous" strip-center Japanese; it's moved post-Survey to a "larger" North Miami Beach space (folks say the modern setting, sporting a large sushi bar, is "fancier" than the old address), but you can expect the same dependable service and "low" prices – especially during the late-night happy hour, 11 PM–close.

Yardbird ◐ *Southern*

| | - | - | - | M |

South Beach | 1600 Lenox Ave. (16th St.) | Miami Beach | 305-538-5220 |
www.runchickenrun.com

Putting the 'South' in South Beach, this newfangled Southern comfort-fooder from exec chef Jeff McInnis (ex Gigi) vends down-home dishes with contemporary twists for not a lot of scratch; the rather large nest is feathered with rustic elements like butcher-block tables and tractor-seat stools and includes a well-stocked bourbon bar.

Zuma ◐ *Japanese*

| | 28 | 27 | 24 | $83 |

Downtown | Epic Hotel | 270 Biscayne Blvd. Way (Brickell Ave.) |
305-577-0277 | www.zumarestaurant.com

"Book way ahead" to secure a seat at the Epic Hotel's "it" spot Downtown because this overseas import (and "international sensation") draws throngs with its "Zen mastery" of modern izakaya-inspired Japanese fare plus sushi, robata grill items and more; "fabulous views" can be had from the terrace overlooking the Miami River, or you can just watch the "beautiful people" burning many "benjamins" in the "stunning" dining room and "vibrant" sake bar/lounge.

Milwaukee

TOP FOOD RANKING

	Restaurant	Cuisine
29	Sanford	American
28	Crazy Water	Eclectic
27	Eddie Martini's	Seafood/Steak
	Ristorante Bartolotta	Italian
	Bacchus	American
	La Merenda	Eclectic
26	Bosley on Brady	Seafood/Steak
	Roots Restaurant*	Californian
	Honeypie	American
	Le Rêve Patisserie*	Dessert/French

OTHER NOTEWORTHY PLACES

Restaurant	Cuisine
Bartolotta's Lake Park	French
Braise	American
Harbor House	Seafood
Hinterland Erie St.	American
Jake's	Steak
Mason St. Grill	American
Maxie's Southern Comfort	Cajun/Creole
Meritage	Eclectic
Odd Duck	Eclectic
Umami Moto	Asian

Bacchus 🗷 *American*   27 | 28 | 26 | $71

Downtown | Cudahy Tower | 925 E. Wells St. (Prospect Ave.) |
414-765-1166 | www.bacchusmke.com
Set in Cudahy Tower, this Downtown New American earns "high
marks all around", from chef Adam Siegel's "top-notch" cuisine to
the "beautiful surroundings" defined by "sophisticated decor" (it
shares top Milwaukee honors), linear lines and windows facing
Lake Michigan; add in "professional" servers who deliver the "signature" "Bartolotta showmanship", and admirers attest it's one of
the "best special-occasion places in town" – with very "expensive"
tabs to match.

Bartolotta's Lake Park Bistro *French*   26 | 27 | 26 | $54

East Side | Lake Park Pavilion | 3133 E. Newberry Blvd. (Lake Park Rd.) |
414-962-6300 | www.lakeparkbistro.com
A "top-of-the-list destination" say aficionados of this spendy East
Side French, where a "beautiful setting" with "spectacular views of
Lake Michigan" provides the backdrop for chef Adam Siegel's "excellent" "classic bistro fare"; a "drool"-worthy wine selection,
"wonderfully helpful staff" and "romantic ambiance" also add appeal for "special occasions."

---

* Indicates a tie with restaurant above

	FOOD	DECOR	SERVICE	COST

Bosley on Brady ⓩ *Seafood/Steak* — 26 | 23 | 24 | $43

East Side | 815 E. Brady St. (bet. Cass & Marshall Sts.) | 414-727-7975 |
www.bosleyonbrady.com

"Key West meets the Brew City" at this "delicious" East Side surf 'n'
turfer where the "interesting" midpriced menu places an "emphasis
on fresh seafood", making it a "rare Milwaukee treat"; the "Florida
Keys theme" carries over to the decor with its "kitschy memorabilia",
and "friendly" staffers contribute to the "upbeat environment", so it's
an overall "wonderful" "escape."

Braise ⓩⓜ *American* — - | - | - | E

Walker's Point | 1101 S. Second St. (Washington St.) | 414-212-8843 |
www.braiselocalfood.com

Local ingredients are the focus of this Walker's Point New American
putting out a daily changing menu of bar nibbles, small plates and
somewhat pricey mains alongside regional brews and global wines; reclaimed materials feature heavily in the casual wood-accented space,
and an open kitchen offers diners a glimpse of the action.

Crazy Water *Eclectic* — 28 | 18 | 24 | $42

Walker's Point | 839 S. 2nd St. (Walker St.) | 414-645-2606 |
www.crazywaterrestaurant.com

With such "inventive", "high-quality" fare on offer, enthusiasts insist you
could "just throw a dart at the menu and be happy" at this "charming"
Walker's Point Eclectic, where "consistently great" service and moderate
tabs contribute to a "relaxed, homey" atmosphere; despite "small",
sometimes "noisy" digs, it's still "always crowded", so "call ahead."

Eddie Martini's ⓩ *Seafood/Steak* — 27 | 24 | 28 | $67

Wauwatosa | 8612 W. Watertown Plank Rd. (86th St.) | 414-771-6680 |
www.eddiemartinis.com

"High-quality white-glove" service "makes you feel like a king" at this
Wauwatosa "classic" turning out "generous portions" of "to-die-for"
chops and "reliably excellent" seafood; the 1940s-style decor is a "real
throwback to the days of the Rat Pack", giving it an "old-fashioned
supper club feel", so though it's not cheap, devotees dub it the "epitome of what the steakhouse is supposed to be."

Harbor House *Seafood* — 23 | 28 | 22 | $60

Downtown | 550 N. Harbor Dr. (Michigan St.) | 414-395-4900 |
www.harborhousemke.com

Set in a "premier location" "looking out over Lake Michigan", this
"trendy" Downtowner from the Bartolotta Restaurant Group offers
"high-quality" seafood-focused fare in "warm surroundings" with
"beautiful decor" (it shares top Milwaukee honors) and "large windows" that provide "spectacular views"; "attentive service" is another
plus, just "bring your paycheck", as it's on the "pricey" side.

Hinterland Erie Street Gastropub ⓩ *American* — 25 | 23 | 24 | $64

Third Ward | 222 E. Erie St. (Water St.) | 414-727-9300 |
www.hinterlandbeer.com

"Imaginative", "seasonal" plates (including housemade charcuterie) are "prepared with flavor and flair" at this Third Ward New
American that's "much higher-end" than its name suggests; "excellent" service and "beautiful" wood-accented surroundings that

FOOD | DECOR | SERVICE | COST

"make you want to stay and linger" help compensate for pricey (some say "overpriced") tabs.

Honeypie *American*
26 | 17 | 22 | $21

Bay View | 2643 S. Kinnickinnic Ave. (Potter Ave.) | 414-489-7437 | www.honeypiecafe.com

A "good spot to fill up" enthuse admirers of this affordable Bay View American where the "creative" comfort food is "better than mama could do" and the sweet offerings include pie that's "in the name for good reason"; solid service and "comfortable" "diner"-like digs further make it "well worth a stop."

Jake's ⑤ *Steak*
▽ 24 | 21 | 23 | $57

Pewaukee | 21445 W. Gumina Rd. (Capitol Dr.) | 262-781-7995 | www.jakes-restaurant.com

Expect reams of red meat and "no better onion rings on the planet" at this "classic" Pewaukee steakhouse, which also offers casual bites in its intimate lounge; "top-notch" service, a lush garden patio and a working fireplace help give the converted century-old barn a "comfortable homestyle feeling."

La Merenda ⑤ *Eclectic*
27 | 18 | 23 | $38

Walker's Point | 125 E. National Ave. (1st St.) | 414-389-0125 | www.lamerenda125.com

Prepare for an "eating adventure" at this "top-notch" yet midpriced Walker's Point Eclectic where "groups share plates, try different things" and "linger" over the "diverse menu" of "outstanding" tapas-style dishes; colorful, casual surroundings and "friendly" staffers contribute to the festive vibe, so be sure to reserve "well in advance" as it can otherwise be "impossible to get into."

Le Rêve Patisserie & Café ⑤ *Dessert/French*
26 | 22 | 22 | $36

Wauwatosa | 7610 Harwood Ave. (Menomonee River Pkwy.) | 414-778-3333 | www.lerevecafe.com

"Traditional and novel" dishes full of "excellent, genuine French flavors" are worth "canceling your flight to Paris" effuse enthusiasts of this midpriced Wauwatosa cafe where the "beautiful" baked goods ("oh, the bread") also win raves; set in a "historic bank building", it has a "charming" vibe further elevated by "consistent" service, leading many to visit "every chance" they get.

Mason Street Grill *American*
25 | 25 | 25 | $57

Downtown | Pfister Hotel | 425 E. Mason St. (Jefferson St.) | 414-298-3131 | www.masonstreetgrill.com

"They can do it all" rave fans of this American in Downtown's historic Pfister Hotel, where "well-flavored" steaks, "to-die-for" seafood and other quality offerings are set down by "helpful" staffers in upscale digs with a "nice atmosphere"; if a few cite "expensive" tabs and leave "underwhelmed", more say it "continues to satisfy", especially since it's "the place to see and be seen in Milwaukee."

Maxie's Southern Comfort *Cajun/Creole*
25 | 20 | 22 | $32

West Side | 6732 W. Fairview Ave. (68th St.) | 414-292-3969 | www.maxies.com

"The cornbread itself is worth the trip" insist fans of this "boisterous" West Side Cajun-Creole turning out "authentic", "top-notch" cooking "honoring the South"; the bi-level space is glitzed up with chandeliers and dark-red walls and service gets solid marks, so it wins "kudos" all around, even if it "can be quite noisy."

Meritage ☒ *Eclectic* 21 | 17 | 22 | $41
West Side | 5921 W. Vliet St. (60th St.) | 414-479-0620 | www.meritage.us
"Farm-to-table in a legitimate sense" swear surveyors of this moderate West Side Eclectic where chef-owner Jan Kelly transforms "local ingredients" into "interesting" plates featuring a "good balance of flavors"; a staff that "attends to you very well" helps hush those who find the contemporary bistro surrounds "not much to look at."

Odd Duck *Eclectic* - | - | - | M
Bay View | 2352 S. Kinnickinnic Ave. (E. Linus St.) | 414-763-5881 | www.oddduckrestaurant.com
Dazzled diners duck into this affordable new Bay View Eclectic for a stellar daily menu of large and small plates (many of them veg-friendly), reflecting the talents of a crafty kitchen staff working with seasonal, local ingredients, topped off with vividly hued cocktails mixed with housemade syrups and tea infusions; aquatic birds figure subtly in the warm, whimsical decor, which leans on reclaimed, sustainable materials.

Ristorante Bartolotta *Italian* 27 | 24 | 25 | $52
Wauwatosa | 7616 W. State St. (Harwood Ave.) | 414-771-7910 | www.bartolottaristorante.com
"Imagination and flair" elevate the "top-notch" Italian cuisine at this "charming" Wauwatosa "gem" where longtime chef Juan Urbieta's "inventive" seasonal menus change often; slightly "pricey" tabs don't deter fans who maintain that its "no-pretensions" (if "noisy") atmosphere and "friendly, knowledgeable" staff make it a "perennial favorite."

Roots Restaurant & Cellar *Californian* 26 | 23 | 22 | $53
Brewers Hill | 1818 N. Hubbard St. (Vine St.) | 414-374-8480 | www.rootsmilwaukee.com
Guided by a "lovely philosophy about fresh, local, seasonal food", this "top" Californian attracts "foodies and vegetarians" alike with "creative cooking" that transforms sustainable, "premium ingredients" (often from the on-site garden) into "something unexpected"; it's somewhat costly, but service gets few complaints and "awesome views" from the "surprisingly cozy" Brewers Hill building (complete with a dual-level patio and pub-style cellar) flavor the "fun vibe."

Sanford ☒ *American* 29 | 26 | 28 | $82
East Side | 1547 N. Jackson St. (Pleasant St.) | 414-276-9608 | www.sanfordrestaurant.com
"Simply exquisite" rave regulars of this East Side New American, where the "unsurpassed creativity" of co-owner and chef Sanford D'Amato results in "innovative", "consistently delicious" cuisine that makes it the "gold standard in Milwaukee" and earns it top Food and Most Popular honors too; staffers (rated No. 1 for Service) are "superb" "without being pretentious" and the storefront setting is "ele-

gant", so pricey tabs are considered a "bargain", especially since a similar experience "would cost double in Chicago."

Umami Moto *Asian*

24 | 27 | 22 | $43

Downtown | 718 N. Milwaukee St. (bet. Mason St. & Wisconsin Ave.) | 414-727-9333 | www.umamimoto.com

"Sleek" and "chic", this "tony" Downtown Asian draws a "see-and-be-seen" crowd with its modern stylings and "elegant" menu featuring "inventive yet classic sushi and sashimi"; it can get "loud at times", service can range from solid to "indifferent" and tabs don't come cheap, but even so, most leave ready to go "back again and again."

Minneapolis/St. Paul

TOP FOOD RANKING

Restaurant	Cuisine
29️ Travail	American
Alma	American
La Belle Vie	French/Mediterranean
28️ Lake Elmo Inn	American
Lucia's	American
Capital Grille	Steak
Craftsman	American
Meritage	American/French
Matt's Bar	Burgers
Manny's Steak	Steak

OTHER NOTEWORTHY PLACES

Axel's	Steak
Bachelor Farmer	Swedish
Big Bowl	Asian
Doolittle's	American
5-8 Club	Burgers
Heidi's	American
Kincaid's	Seafood/Steak
112 Eatery	Eclectic
Saffron	Mediterranean/Mideastern
Victory 44	American

Alma *American* — 29 | 25 | 28 | $55

Dinkytown | 528 University Ave. SE (6th Ave.) | Minneapolis | 612-379-4909 | www.restaurantalma.com

"Alma does the soul good" rave reviewers of this Dinkytown "sleeper" where ingredients from "local farmers" inspire "exceptional" cooking by chef-owner Alexander Roberts that's "always a pleasure" (with "something surprising every time"); "elegant" yet "unpretentious" with a "superb" staff, it's "a bit expensive but worth it" for a "romantic evening", "entertaining business guests" or "just dinner with friends."

Axel's *Steak* — 26 | 23 | 25 | $33

Chanhassen | 560 W. 78th St. (Laredo Dr.) | 952-934-9340
Mendota | 1318 Sibley Memorial Hwy. (D St.) | 651-686-4840
www.axelsrestaurants.com

Fans "love the popovers" and "delicious steaks and seafood" at this "reliable" mini-chain where the plates (ranging from modestly priced to "spendy") are so generous, you can "count on leftovers"; it's "cozy" and kid-friendly with a "helpful" staff, so many dub it a "solid" "favorite."

Bachelor Farmer *Swedish* — 25 | 24 | 25 | $48

Warehouse | 50 Second Ave. N. (Azine Way) | Minneapolis | 612-206-3920 | www.thebachelorfarmer.com

"Eco-friendly local providers" fuel the "clever" "contemporary" Swedish menu at this "hot new" Warehouse District pick with "outstanding" service, "cool digs" and a "hipster-meets-foodie" scene; it's "high-priced" and "hard to get a reservation", though the "secret" Marvel "speakeasy downstairs" is a slightly more accessible option; P.S. those bachelor owners are sons of Minnesota's governor.

Big Bowl *Asian*   25 | 22 | 23 | $21

Edina | Galleria | 3669 Galleria (69th St.) | 952-928-7888
Minnetonka | Ridgedale Ctr. | 12649 Wayzata Blvd. (Plymouth Rd.) | 952-797-9888
Roseville | Rosedale Ctr. | 1705 Hwy. 36 (bet. Fairview & Snelling Aves.) | 651-636-7173
www.bigbowl.com

"Build-your-own stir-fries" packing "loads of fresh veggies" and other "tasty" Chinese and Thai dishes come "as advertised" with "large portions for the right price" at these "contemporary" Asian chain links with "prompt", "efficient" service; offering "unique" cocktails too, they're "pleasing" choices for a "relaxed evening with friends", since "you just can't go wrong" here.

The Capital Grille *Steak*   25 | 24 | 25 | $61

Downtown Mpls | La Salle Plaza | 801 Hennepin Ave. (8th St.) | Minneapolis | 612-692-9000 | www.thecapitalgrille.com

"Exemplary" steak and "all the trimmings" (plus a "great wine list") come with "impeccable" service at this "trusted" Downtown chain link with a "luxurious feel"; sure, you "pay for the quality", but it's "tops" for a "group on business" or a "tête-à-tête with someone special."

The Craftsman *American*   28 | 24 | 26 | $41

South Minneapolis | 4300 E. Lake St. (43rd Ave.) | Minneapolis | 612-722-0175 | www.craftsmanrestaurant.com

"Innovative, "locally grown" New American food meets "cocktails that change with the seasons" at this "neighborhood" "find" set in an Arts and Crafts–style building in South Minneapolis; praising the "well-done" patio and strong service ("couldn't be better"), diners say it's "definitely an experience" that's worth the slightly "high" prices, and might inspire "chefs" in the making.

Doolittle's Woodfire Grill *American*   26 | 24 | 24 | $23

Eagan | 2140 Cliff Rd. (Nicols Rd.) | 651-452-6627
Golden Valley | 550 Winnetka Ave. N. (Golden Valley Rd.) | 763-542-1931
www.doolittlesrestaurants.com

Enticing with a "wonderful aroma", the "chicken on the woodfire grill is outstanding" and the rest of the "diverse menu" also pleases at this "reasonably priced" American duo that's a "frolic" when you want to feel like you're "eating around a campfire"; "friendly" service enhances the "nice ambiance", keeping it a "favorite" for many.

5-8 Club *Burgers*   25 | 16 | 21 | $15

Champlin | 6251 Douglas Ct. (bet. 109th & 110th Aves.) | 763-425-5858
Maplewood | 2289 Minnehaha Ave. (McKnight Rd.) | 651-735-5858
South Minneapolis | 5800 Cedar Ave. (58th St.) | Minneapolis | 612-823-5858
www.5-8club.com

"Unbeatable" burgers are the big draw of this "comfortable" (if slightly "divey") tavern trio, voted Most Popular in Minneapolis, that's "famous" for its "must-have" Juicy Lucy – a half-pounder stuffed with cheese; "service can vary" when "busy", but overall it's "easy on the wallet" with a "neighborly", "working-class atmosphere", and the "food definitely makes up for the decor."

Heidi's *American*   26 | 24 | 23 | $53

Lyn-Lake | 2903 Lyndale Ave. S. (29th St.) | Minneapolis | 612-354-3512 | www.heidismpls.com

Rebuilt following a fire, this "vibrant" New American from Stewart and Heidi Woodman "rocks" say customers who commend the "inventive" plates with "flavor and depth beyond your imagination" served in a "stunning" environment that's as "hip and urban" as the boho Lyn-Lake neighborhood; coming through with "exciting" cocktails and "well-informed" service and delivering "terrific value" for the somewhat "expensive" tabs, it's an all-around "home run."

Kincaid's *Seafood/Steak*   26 | 26 | 26 | $45

Bloomington | 8400 Normandale Lake Blvd. (84th St.) | 952-921-2255
Downtown SP | 380 St. Peter St. (bet. 5th & 6th Sts.) | St. Paul | 651-602-9000
www.kincaids.com

"Classic" chain links in Downtown St. Paul and Bloomington, these meateries "still pull in a lot of power players" for "rewarding" steaks and seafood served in "sharp" surroundings lightened up with large windows; "terrific" service and "wonderful", "twice-daily happy hours" are additional assets, so despite murmurs that it's "a little pricey" and "predictable", its target audience calls it "first-class for business or pleasure."

La Belle Vie *French/Mediterranean*   29 | 27 | 29 | $84

Loring Park | 510 Groveland Ave. (Hennepin Ave.) | Minneapolis | 612-874-6440 | www.labellevie.us

"Just close your eyes" and pick any of the "modern", "exquisite" Med–New French dishes (or go for the "brilliant" tasting menu) at this "wonderful little gem" in Loring Park, "top of the heap when it comes to fine dining", complete with a "formal look" in a "grande dame of an old apartment building", and earning the Twin Cities' No. 1 score for Service ("phenomenal"); sure it's a "splurge", so "bring your best credit card" and get set for a "memorable" evening; P.S. the "gorgeous" bar is "less stuffy" with a more affordable menu.

Lake Elmo Inn *American*   28 | 24 | 27 | $38

Lake Elmo | 3442 Lake Elmo Ave. (Upper 33rd St.) | 651-777-8495 | www.lakeelmoinn.com

The word's out on this "hidden secret" in Lake Elmo (an "agricultural community" on the east side of St. Paul) providing a "first-class", "traditional" yet creative American menu in a "really quaint" setting; service that's "unobtrusive but intuitive" draws returnees for "special occasions", and while it's on the "pricey" side, weekly specials appeal to the "budget-conscious"; P.S. the "fab Sunday brunch with bottomless champagne" is the "best deal."

Lucia's Ⓜ *American*   28 | 23 | 26 | $31

Uptown | 1432 W. 31st St. (Hennepin Ave.) | Minneapolis | 612-825-1572 | www.lucias.com

Praised as a "prairie home-cooking companion", this "pioneering" "Uptown favorite" by chef-owner Lucia Watson follows the "Alice

Waters tradition" of "slow food" based on "locally sourced products", with its "marvelous" "weekly changing" menu that's "short", "well crafted" and an "excellent value"; "relaxing" for an "intimate dinner" (or "lovely" lunch), the "small", "comfortable" room "allows for special attention", leading customers to come back "again and again" (and sample the "well-stocked wine bar" and bakery too).

Manny's Steakhouse Steak   28 | 25 | 27 | $68

Downtown Mpls | W Minneapolis, The Foshay | 825 Marquette Ave. (9th St.) | Minneapolis | 612-339-9900 | www.mannyssteakhouse.com

"A steak man's steakhouse", this "high-rolling" Downtown locale in the W "hits the spot when you need a bludgeon of beef", greeting you with a "meat cart" that lets you "pick your favorite cut", "massive" sides and "stiff" drinks in an "old-time dinner-club" atmosphere; rounded out with a "phenomenal" wine list and "service par excellence", it all adds up to an "A+ meal" that's a "fantastic splurge" – "so if you have $$$ or an expense account, go for it!"

Matt's Bar ⇗ Burgers   28 | 15 | 21 | $13

South Minneapolis | 3500 Cedar Ave. S. (35th St.) | Minneapolis | 612-722-7072 | www.mattsbar.com

"You haven't lived until you try the Juicy Lucy" say fans of the "killer" burger ("cheese on the inside") at this '50s-era South Minneapolis "neighborhood bar" that's "cramped, dark and cheap-looking" (the way "I love it"); though "you'll have a wait during busy times", the servers "know their customers", the "price is right" and everything is "exactly as it should be", "attitude and all."

Meritage ⓜ American/French   28 | 27 | 27 | $49

Downtown SP | Hamm Bldg. | 410 St. Peter St. (6th St.) | St. Paul | 651-222-5670 | www.meritage-stpaul.com

This "little bit of France in the saintly city" of Downtown St. Paul is "tops" for "upscale" brasserie fare with a "delightful", seasonal New American spin, provided with "impeccable" service in a "bistro-style" setting (with "lovely" sidewalk seating) in close proximity to the Ordway Center; the tab is justly "spendy", especially if you opt for an "amazing" tasting menu with wine, though the "outstanding oyster bar" is a more affordable option.

112 Eatery ◐ Eclectic   27 | 23 | 25 | $42

Warehouse | 112 N. Third St. (1st Ave.) | Minneapolis | 612-343-7696 | www.112eatery.com

"Eat where the chefs eat" at this "self-assured" Warehouse District Eclectic by Isaac Becker delivering "pitch-perfect flavor combinations" (including "terrific takes on comfort-food favorites") in a "casual", "convivial" atmosphere with "excellent" service; it's a "tough reservation", but "lucky" diners love that there's a "price point for everyone with top-notch food at every tier" – plus it's "open late."

Saffron Restaurant & Lounge ⓩ Mediterranean/Mideastern   28 | 25 | 26 | $42

Warehouse | 123 N. Third St. (1st Ave.) | Minneapolis | 612-746-5533 | www.saffronmpls.com

"Meze, meze, meze" shout "lucky" lovers of this "contemporary" Warehouse District hang serving "brilliant", "fragrant" and some-

FOOD | DECOR | SERVICE | COST

times "adventurous" Med–Middle Eastern plates that can "change your entire outlook on hummus"; "relaxed yet classy", it also boasts "inventive" cocktails and "cordial" service (including tableside visits by the "extremely nice" owners) that support the upscale tabs.

Travail Kitchen & Amusements 🅂🅼 _American_

29 | 19 | 26 | $41

Robbinsdale | 4154 West Broadway Ave. (bet. 41st & 42nd Aves.) | 763-535-1131

The "stellar", "must-do" tasting menu takes you on a "fascinating" "culinary journey" (touching the "outer edge of molecular gastronomy") at this "unexpected" chef-owned New American in Robbinsdale, voted No. 1 for Food in the Twin Cities, and dubbed one of the "best values" too; "efficient, personalized" service and shared tables add to the "über-cool" vibe, though you need to "line up early" since it "doesn't take reservations" – the only reservation foodies have about the place.

Victory 44 🅼 _American_

26 | 20 | 23 | $28

Northeast | 2203 N. 44th Ave. (Penn Ave.) | Minneapolis | 612-588-2228 | www.victory-44.com

"In a neighborhood that's revitalizing itself", this New American gastropub in a converted Northeast gas station serves "inspired, delicious" dishes (on the "porkcentric" side) listed on a "daily changing" blackboard menu; it's a treat when the "chef brings out your food and talks to you about your meal", and given the "unbelievably low" cost for such "unique", "well-executed" eats, fans only "wish it were in their neighborhood"; P.S. there's an adjoining coffee bar; the kitchen is closed 3–5 PM daily.

Naples, FL

TOP FOOD RANKING

	Restaurant	Cuisine
27	Côte d'Azur	French
	Bleu Provence	French
	USS Nemo	Seafood
26	Truluck's	Seafood
	Capital Grille	Steak
	Escargot 41	French
	Café & Bar Lurcat	American
	Ruth's Chris	Steak
	Veranda	Southern
	Grill	Steak

OTHER NOTEWORTHY PLACES

Alberto's On Fifth	Italian
Angelina's	Italian
Campiello	Italian
Cheesecake Factory	American
Chops City Grill	Seafood/Steak
I. M. Tapas	Spanish
Le Lafayette	French
P.F. Chang's	Chinese
Sale e Pepe	Italian
Strip House	Steak

Alberto's On Fifth *Italian*   – | – | – | E

Naples | 868 Fifth Ave. S. (8th St.) | 239-430-1060 | www.albertosonfifth.com
Alberto Varetto (ex Sale e Pepe) recently hung out his own shingle with this fine-dining Northern Italian in Naples, proffering housemade pastas as well as artfully presented traditional dishes such as osso buco and the like; prices are upscale, in keeping with the capacious white-tablecloth dining room and gracious sidewalk terrace.

Angelina's Ristorante *Italian*   25 | 24 | 23 | $54

Bonita Springs | 24041 S. Tamiami Trail (Pelican Colony Blvd.) | 239-390-3187 | www.angelinasofbonitasprings.com
"Outrageously delicious" Italian fare is ferried by "efficient" servers at this "upscale, classy gem" in Bonita Springs; the "extraordinary surroundings" include "darkish woods", a "signature" wine tower (where a "wonderful selection" of bottles is stored), a "covered patio" and "intimate booths" whose curtains make them "great for that first date" – just remember to "bring your black card" because it's "pricey."

Bleu Provence *French*   27 | 24 | 26 | $57

Naples | 1234 Eighth St. S. (12th Ave.) | 239-261-8239 | www.bleuprovencenaples.com
"*C'est très bon!*" crow enthusiasts of this Naples "labor of love" that "enchants" with "consistent" French fare spanning "many of the tradi-

tional bistro dishes"; "from the moment you walk in, you're welcomed and delighted" by the "exceptional" staff and "handsome" Provençal decor, and while it's "pricey", there's "a fantastic early-bird special"; P.S. "in nice weather", try for the "wonderful" garden.

Café & Bar Lurcat *American*

26 | 24 | 24 | $51

Naples | 494 Fifth Ave. S. (5th St.) | 239-213-3357 | www.cafelurcat.com

Whether you go for the "vibrant" "bar-and-tapas scene downstairs", the "upstairs fine dining", a seat outside at street level or the "magi-cal" balcony, you're in for a "hip" time at this "lovely" "see-and-be-seen place for Naples' beautiful people"; as for the "pricey" New American fare, it's "enticing", "unique", "well prepared" and conveyed via a "friendly, helpful" staff; P.S. "don't miss" the warm cinnamon donuts for dessert.

Campiello Ristorante *Italian*

25 | 25 | 24 | $50

Naples | 1177 Third St. S. (Broad Ave.) | 239-435-1166 | www.campiello.damico.com

Voted the area's Most Popular eatery, this "always crowded" "Naples landmark" offers an "outstanding" Italian menu with "something for everyone" – e.g. "inspired wood-fired pizzas, original pastas, distinc-tive appetizers and delicious wines" – in a "noisy" dining room with an "open kitchen", a "swinging bar" and on "the most happening patio in town"; "service can be rushed at times", but it's mostly "spectacular", and though it's "expensive", if you want to "ogle" the "chichi set", this is the place.

The Capital Grille *Steak*

26 | 25 | 26 | $65

Naples | Mercato | 9005 Mercato Dr. (Tamiami Trail) | 239-254-0640 | www.thecapitalgrille.com

Respondents say this "consistent" Naples link in the "highbrow" na-tional steakhouse chain "gets it right every time", with "outstanding" chops and sides and a "great" wine list (oenophiles suggest you "splurge on one of the big reds") presented by "courteous" servers who "know how to make an evening special"; true, you might have to "take out a second mortgage", but most feel "it's worth every dollar."

Cheesecake Factory *American*

23 | 21 | 22 | $30

Naples | Coastland Ctr. Mall | 2090 Tamiami Trail N. (Golden Gate Pkwy.) | 239-435-1580 | www.thecheesecakefactory.com

"If you leave here hungry, it's your own fault" opine patrons of this Naples national chain link, because not only is there "a lot of variety" on its "dependable" American menu, but the portions are "gigantic" – indeed, you'll probably have "enough for leftovers", especially if you "leave room" for the "sublime" cheesecake; "reasonable prices", "nice ambiance" and "speedy", "observant" staffers complete the picture.

Chops City Grill *Seafood/Steak*

25 | 23 | 24 | $54

Naples | 837 Fifth Ave. S. (bet. 8th & 9th Sts.) | 239-262-4677
Bonita Springs | Brooks Grand Plaza | 8200 Health Center Blvd. (bet. Coconut Rd. & US 41) | 239-992-4677
www.chopscitygrill.com

A "handsome, upscale crowd" creates a "sophisticated buzz" at this "fashionable" Bonita Springs–Naples duo, serving "beautifully plated", "delish" steaks, seafood and some sushi too; although it's "too noisy" for some, most just revel in the "fast-paced" atmosphere, which comes complete with "dynamite drinks", a "huge wine-by-the-glass selection", "sharp service" and "high prices."

Côte d'Azur M French
| 27 | 22 | 26 | $61 |

Naples | 11224 Tamiami Trail N. (bet. Immokalee & Walkerbilt Rds.) | 239-597-8867 | www.cotedazurrestaurant.com
It's "just a storefront in a strip mall", but once inside this "intimate" French bistro, you'll find Provençal fare so "skillfully prepared, artfully presented" and *magnifique* tasting, it earns Naples' No. 1 Food rating; a "superb" staff and setting that, while "not fancy", is "cute" enough, with an "outdoor-cafe" look plus a real patio, are part of the "simply outstanding" package, which is matched by "special-occasion" pricing.

Escargot 41 French
| 26 | 22 | 25 | $63 |

Naples | Park Shore Shopping Ctr. | 4339 Tamiami Trail N. (Morningside Dr.) | 239-793-5000 | www.escargot41.com
"A hidden gem", this Naples bistro does "excellent" renditions of "classic French" fare, with a "delicious" "variety" of the namesake gastropods ("a full page" of the menu is "devoted just to them"), in a "quaint, quiet", "romantic setting" overseen by "friendly" owners; regulars advise "book way in advance during the season", "save room" for a soufflé and be prepared for an "expensive" check (it's "worth it").

The Grill Steak
| 26 | 26 | 28 | $73 |

Naples | Ritz-Carlton Naples | 280 Vanderbilt Beach Rd. (Bay Colony Dr.) | 239-598-6644 | www.ritzcarlton.com
Everything about this Naples "paean to fine dining" is "so very Ritz", from the "remarkable" steaks and "vast wine list" to the "superb service" (voted Naples' best) and "luxurious" "clublike setting" (which takes the top spot for Decor); so even if it's pricey, it's tough to beat for an "elegant" meal.

I.M. Tapas Spanish
| ▽ 25 | 19 | 23 | $47 |

Naples | 965 Fourth Ave. N. (bet. 9th & 10th Sts.) | 239-403-8272 | www.imtapas.com
"Hidden away on a small side street", this Naples "treasure" "wows" with Spanish tapas "lovingly and proudly prepared" with "top-notch ingredients" and a "creative touch"; the simple, intimate setting is a "good place to hang, talk and share", abetted by "great" Iberian wines and "excellent service."

Le Lafayette French
| ▽ 25 | 24 | 23 | $61 |

Naples | 375 13th Ave. (3rd St.) | 239-403-7861 | www.lelafayette.com
Feel "transported to the South of France" at this "charming", "comfortable" venue in Naples, where the "beautiful" patio is the place to be for "excellently prepared" *plats* plus "great wines and desserts"; "but is it worth the price?" – *oui* say fans, "every cent", especially for the "fabulous Sunday brunch."

P.F. Chang's China Bistro Chinese
| 24 | 23 | 24 | $32 |

Naples | Granada Shoppes | 10840 Tamiami Trail N. (Immokalee Rd.) | 239-596-2174

(continued)

P.F. Chang's China Bistro

Ft. Myers | Gulf Coast Town Ctr. | 10081 Gulf Center Dr. (Royal Queen Blvd.) | 239-590-9197
www.pfchangs.com
"Living up to its reputation", this "whimsical, exotic" chain duo's "yummy" "fusion of Chinese and American tastes" makes it a "step above your everyday Asian cuisine" ("love those lettuce wraps!"); there's "sometimes a lengthy wait for a table" and usually lots of "noise", but "well-paced, attentive" service and relatively "low prices" compensate.

Ruth's Chris Steak House *Steak*

26 | 24 | 25 | $65

Estero | Coconut Point Mall | 23151 Village Shops Way (Tamiami Trail) | 239-948-8888 | www.ruthschris.com
What some deem "the standard for an outstanding steak experience", this Estero chain outpost offers its "huge" portions of "sizzling", buttery beef in an "elegant" setting with "attentive service"; "expensive" pricing means it's the kind of place you go "for a celebratory meal", but for "more reasonable" tabs, "try the happy-hour bar menu."

Sale e Pepe Ⓜ *Italian*

24 | 26 | 25 | $75

Marco Island | Marco Beach Ocean Resort | 480 S. Collier Blvd. (Spruce Ave.) | 239-393-1600 | www.sale-e-pepe.com
"Once you've found it, you will want to return often" to this "elegant", "spectacular spot" at Marco Beach Ocean Resort, where "courteous, helpful" staffers proffer "outstanding" Italian cuisine and an "extensive wine list" that suits "every budget" (the fare is across-the-board pricey); many find the "heavily" decorated interior "beautiful", but most prefer the "large patio" for a "fabulous seafront lunch" or a "sunset" dinner.

Strip House *Steak*

▽ 23 | 23 | 20 | $58

Naples | Waldorf Astoria Naples | 475 Seagate Dr. (West Blvd.) | 239-598-9600 | www.striphousenaples.com
"Bringing the Big Apple to Naples", this "dark, adult restaurant" doles out "perfectly cooked steaks and great sides" in a "beautiful room" bedecked with "red velvet drapes, flocked wallpaper" and "classic nude pics"; all in all, it's quite a "surprise for a hotel-lobby restaurant", although the prices are as high as one would expect for the genre.

Truluck's *Seafood*

26 | 24 | 26 | $67

Naples | 698 Fourth Ave. S. (7th St.) | 239-530-3131 | www.trulucks.com
Devotees say they're "truly lucky" to have this Naples chain link specializing in seafood that "couldn't be fresher" (it "has its own fishery") – particularly "best-in-town" stone crabs ("as many as you can devour" on Monday nights in season) – despite the fact that the "deep menu" is "not for the faint of wallet"; "incomparable service" and a "stylish" setting are two more reasons it's so "popular", so be sure to "make a reservation well in advance" or try to sidle up to the bar for the "great happy hour", when "all drinks are half-off."

USS Nemo *Seafood*

27 | 19 | 23 | $49

Naples | 3745 Tamiami Trail N. (Frank Whiteman Blvd.) | 239-261-6366 | www.ussnemorestaurant.com
"Locals" "would go 20,000 leagues" for the "to-die-for" miso sea bass and other "sublime" seafood with "exotic" Pacific Rim "flair", comple-

mented by "delightful" "wine, beer and sake", at this "big hit" in Naples; "don't expect much sizzle" in the "nondescript strip-center" location or "undersea" decor theme ("they want you to feel like you're eating in the cramped quarters of a submarine", and it's "noisy" too), but do count on "friendly service" from the "knowledgeable" staff and "charming owners"; P.S. "make reservations or be prepared to wait."

The Veranda ⓩ *Southern*   26 | 26 | 26 | $46

Ft. Myers | 2122 Second St. (Broadway) | 239-332-2065 | www.verandarestaurant.com

"A wonderfully old-fashioned treat", this Ft. Myers "tradition" for "leisurely" "special occasions" boasts a "plantationlike" feel thanks to its "quaint", "elegant" setting in two early-1900s homes with a "beautiful" dining garden and what may be "the most romantic piano bar in the world" (call for days and times of performances); what's more, "everything is scrumptious" on the "gourmet" Southern menu, "impeccable service" comes from a "professional staff" and it's only "a bit pricey."

New Jersey

TOP FOOD RANKING

	Restaurant	Cuisine
29	Nicholas	American
28	Shumi	Japanese
	Sapori	Italian
	Washington Inn	American
	Lorena's	French
	Chef's Table	French
	Bay Ave. Trattoria	American/Italian
	Saddle River Inn	American/French
27	CulinAriane	American
	A Little Café	Eclectic
	Scalini Fedeli	Italian
	Serenade	French
	Picnic	American
	Drew's Bayshore	American
	Sagami	Japanese
	Restaurant Latour	American
	Andre's	American
	Dino & Harry's	Steak
	Cafe Matisse	Eclectic
	Whispers	American

OTHER NOTEWORTHY PLACES

Restaurant	Cuisine
Amanda's	American
Avenue	French
Cafe Panache	Eclectic
Capital Grille	Steak
Cheesecake Factory	American
Cucharamama	South American
David Burke Fromagerie	American
Elements	American
Fascino	Italian
410 Bank St.	Caribbean/Creole
Frog and the Peach	American
Highlawn Pavilion	American
Luke Palladino	Italian
Maritime Parc	American
Mehndi	Indian
Ninety Acres	American
Peacock Inn	American
Pluckemin Inn	American
Ram's Head Inn	American
Rat's	French
River Palm	Steak

A Little Café 🗷Ⓜ *Eclectic*
27 | 18 | 25 | $39

Voorhees | Plaza Shoppes | 118 White Horse Rd. (Burnt Mill Rd.) | 856-784-3344 | www.alittlecafenj.com

Like the name says, the space is "truly little", but the flavors and portions are "huge" at this "secret" Eclectic BYO in a Voorhees strip mall; though the decor's "too froufrou" for some, there's agreement on the "attentive" service and "pricey-but-worth-it" tabs; P.S. dinner served Wednesday–Saturday only.

Amanda's *American*
26 | 25 | 25 | $49

Hoboken | 908 Washington St. (bet. 9th & 10th Sts.) | 201-798-0101 | www.amandasrestaurant.com

Dining doesn't get much more "civilized" than at this "serene" Hoboken "class act", a "special place" offering a "delectable" American menu served in a "romantic", circa-1895 brownstone; the early-bird dinner is a "real steal", Sunday brunch is "fab" and the service "makes you feel special" – in short, this "quality" experience "does everything right"; P.S. there's validated parking in a nearby lot, but not for early birds.

Andre's 🗷Ⓜ *American*
27 | 21 | 26 | $51

Newton | 188 Spring St. (bet. Adams & Jefferson Sts.) | 973-300-4192 | www.andresrestaurant.com

Chef-owner Andre de Waal's "inventive" seasonal American cooking paired with "terrific" vinos make this "charming", tin-ceilinged storefront a bona fide "destination" in Newton (it also features an on-site wine boutique); throw in "hospitable" service and a "romantic" mood, and the result is a dining experience that's "top-notch on every level"; P.S. open Wednesday–Saturday only.

Avenue *French*
22 | 27 | 21 | $52

Long Branch | Pier Vill. | 23 Ocean Ave. (bet. Chelsea Ave. & Laird St.) | 732-759-2900 | www.leclubavenue.com

"Unusually sophisticated for the Jersey Shore", this "gorgeous" French brasserie in Long Branch's Pier Village boasts "delicious" food, "stylish" decor, "sweeping" ocean views and a "scene-and-a-half" vibe, stoked by a "beautiful", "dressed-up" crowd; "pretty-penny" pricing and "attitude" from the otherwise "professional" staff come with the territory.

Bay Avenue Trattoria Ⓜ *American/Italian*
28 | 13 | 23 | $44

Highlands | 122 Bay Ave. (Cornwall St.) | 732-872-9800 | www.bayavetrattoria.com

"Creative chef" Joe Romanowski and "fabulous host" Maggie Lubcke supply the "magic" at this "unassuming" Italian-American BYO in Highlands where "divinely prepared" dishes and "tiny" dimensions make reservations "a must any night of the week"; though the decor is "nonexistent", few notice since the "emphasis is on the food" here.

Cafe Matisse 🗷Ⓜ *Eclectic*
27 | 26 | 26 | $69

Rutherford | 167 Park Ave. (bet. Highland Cross & Park Pl.) | 201-935-2995 | www.cafematisse.com

"Stunning" says it all about this Rutherford "gem" where the "off-the-charts" Eclectic offerings are available only in three- or four-course grazing menus and served in a "romantic" room decorated with "Matisse

	FOOD	DECOR	SERVICE	COST

prints" – or in an "utterly charming" back garden; the "stratospheric" prices are somewhat alleviated by the BYO policy (there's an on-site wine shop), but given the "stellar" service and "polished ambiance", it's "worth every penny and more."

Cafe Panache ⊠ *Eclectic*

27	23	25	$59

Ramsey | 130 E. Main St. (bet. Island Ave. & Spruce St.) | 201-934-0030 | www.cafepanachenj.com

Chef-owner Kevin Kohler tantalizes the "sophisticated" set with an "exceptional" seasonal menu and "seamless" service at this "top-drawer" Eclectic BYO, the epitome of "big-ticket" dining in Ramsey; a "refreshingly elegant" setting and "friendly but formal" ambiance are further reasons why it can be "hard to get a reservation."

The Capital Grille *Steak*

26	25	25	$62

Cherry Hill | Cherry Hill Mall | 2000 Rte. 38 (Haddonfield Rd.) | 856-665-5252

Paramus | Garden State Plaza | 1 Garden State Plaza (Roosevelt Ave.) | 201-845-7040

www.thecapitalgrille.com

Sure, they're "part of a chain", but these "swank" "meat lover's para-dises" in Cherry Hill and Paramus attract "well-heeled" "movers and shakers" jonesing for slabs of "superb beef"; expect an "extensive wine list", "clubby" atmospherics and service that "makes you feel like royalty", which you may have to be to afford the "prime prices."

Cheesecake Factory *American*

19	19	18	$30

Hackensack | Shops at Riverside | 197 Riverside Sq. (Hackensack Ave.) | 201-488-0330 ●

Short Hills | Short Hills Mall | 1200 Morris Tpke. (John F. Kennedy Pkwy.) | 973-921-0930

Wayne | Willowbrook Mall | 1700 Willowbrook Blvd. (Rte. 46) | 973-890-1400

Bridgewater | Bridgewater Commons | 400 Commons Way (Rte. 206) | 908-252-0399

Edison | Menlo Park Mall | 455 Menlo Park Dr. (Rte. 1) | 732-494-7000

Freehold | Freehold Raceway Mall | 3710 Rte. 9 S. (bet. Rtes. 33 & 537) | 732-462-6544

Cherry Hill | Marketplace at Garden State Park | 931 Haddonfield Rd. (off Rte. 70) | 856-665-7550

www.thecheesecakefactory.com

There are "no surprises" in store at this "wildly popular" American chain, just "steady" food "turned up a notch" and served in "button-bursting portions" from a menu the size of "*War and Peace*"; though critics cite "long waits" and find the "decibels as high as the calorie count", many more call it a "failsafe" choice simply because "you know what you're getting" and it's "always good."

Chef's Table Ⓜ *French*

28	19	26	$52

Franklin Lakes | Franklin Square Shopping Ctr. | 754 Franklin Ave. (Harriet Pl.) | 201-891-6644

"Stellar" traditional French cuisine and "impeccable service" steered by chef Claude and Dolores Baills lend "destination" status to this BYO bistro in a Franklin Lakes strip mall; insiders warn of "small" dimensions, "tight" seating and "tough" weekend reservations, but ultimately this place "still has it" – "why go to NYC?"

	FOOD	DECOR	SERVICE	COST

Cucharamama [M] *S American* — 26 | 22 | 22 | $45

Hoboken | 233 Clinton St. (3rd St.) | 201-420-1700 | www.cucharamama.com
"Unusual", "eye-opening" dishes and "fabulous" breads from a wood-fired oven are paired with "exotic" cocktails at this "exciting" Hoboken South American showcasing the "magic touch" of chef/food historian Maricel Presilla; though the quarters are "super-tight" and "prices can creep up", the "inviting" atmosphere and "top-notch" service make it an "amazing find."

CulinAriane [B][M] *American* — 27 | 20 | 25 | $58

Montclair | 33 Walnut St. (Pine St.) | 973-744-0533 | www.culinariane.com
"Labor-of-love" dining comes to Montclair via this "splendid" New American BYO where chef-owners Ariane and Michael Duarte approach culinary "perfection" with their "superb" menus and "gracious" service; granted, it's "expensive" and rather "tiny", but admirers say it's a bona fide "go-to" for a "special night out"; P.S. dinner only, Wednesday–Saturday.

David Burke Fromagerie [M] *American* — 25 | 24 | 24 | $64

Rumson | 26 Ridge Rd. (Ave. of Two Rivers) | 732-842-8088 | www.fromagerierestaurant.com
Star chef Burke "got his start" at this "upper-crust" Rumson classic and his "modernized" revamp since taking over features "lighter" American "fare with flair" (including his signature spicy lobster cocktail and cheesecake lollipops); though the crowd's as "Waspy" as ever, now its "intimate" rooms are "brighter" and the pricing so "expensive" that "budget-conscious foodies" reserve the experience for a "special occasion" – or go for "Tuesday burger night."

Dino & Harry's *Steak* — 27 | 23 | 24 | $59

Hoboken | 163 14th St. (Garden St.) | 201-659-6202 | www.dinoandharrys.com
"Phenomenal" chops "cooked just right" and "delicious" sides fill out the menu of this "classic" Hoboken steakhouse set in a former 19th-century saloon (and *On the Waterfront* location) replete with vintage stained glass and a tin ceiling; "prompt" service, "lovely" piano music and live jazz make the "over-the-top" tabs easier to stomach.

Drew's Bayshore Bistro [M] *American* — 27 | - | 23 | $42

Keyport | 28 E. Front St. (Division St.) | 732-739-9219 | www.bayshorebistro.com
Admirers are "impressed" with the "remarkable" "craftsmanship" and "honest cooking" of chef Andrew Araneo at this Keyport American BYO that's renowned for its "heartfelt" Cajun-accented eats with a decided "New Orleans kick", served by a "congenial" staff; a 2011 relocation to larger, more upscale digs may help alleviate the "wait" to get in.

Elements *American* — 26 | 25 | 25 | $66

Princeton | 163 Bayard Ln. (bet. Birch & Leigh Aves.) | 609-924-0078 | www.elementsprinceton.com
Finally, there's a "restaurant worth bragging about in Princeton" thanks to this "original" New American showstopper helmed by toque Scott Anderson, whose "haute" menu focuses on "locally grown, sustain-

able products"; "understated" "modern" decor (reminiscent of "Fallingwater"), "well-versed" service and "inventive" cocktails distract from the "Manhattan prices" and strange location on a "busy curve" of Route 206.

Fascino ⊠ *Italian*   26 | 21 | 24 | $56

Montclair | 331 Bloomfield Ave. (bet. Grove & Willow Sts.) | 973-233-0350 | www.fascinorestaurant.com

"Something of a legend", this "classy", family-run BYO in "highly competitive Montclair" fascinates followers with chef Ryan DePersio's "inventive" Italian *cucina* and mom Cynthia's "divine" desserts; despite "limited parking", "hard-to-get" reservations and "expensive" pricing, many feel that this is "as sophisticated as it gets on the other side of the Hudson."

410 Bank Street *Caribbean/Creole*   26 | 21 | 24 | $54

Cape May | 410 Bank St. (bet. Broad & Lafayette Sts.) | 609-884-2127 | www.410bankstreet.com

For most, the "creative" Caribbean-Creole cooking of chef Henry Sing Cheng served by a "cheery" team keeps this longtime Cape May "classic" an "absolute favorite"; sure, it's on the "expensive" side, seating is "tight" and the Victorian setting "not special", but devotees declare it "feels like Key West and tastes like New Orleans"; P.S. reservations are "a must", and you can "bring your best bottle" or opt for the NJ wines offered.

Frog and the Peach *American*   26 | 23 | 24 | $62

New Brunswick | 29 Dennis St. (Hiram Sq.) | 732-846-3216 | www.frogandpeach.com

Bruce Lefebvre's "farm-fresh", "innovative" cuisine "aims to please – and succeeds" – at this "fine-dining" New Brunswick American with an "understated" design and "well-informed" staffers; though a few croak about "small", "expensive" portions, the bar menu is "surprisingly reasonable" and prix fixe options make for a "peachy" experience.

Highlawn Pavilion *American*   25 | 28 | 25 | $64

West Orange | Eagle Rock Reservation | 1 Crest Dr. (Eagle Rock Ave.) | 973-731-3463 | www.highlawn.com

"Wondrous" views of the Manhattan skyline are accompanied by "classically elegant" fare at this "stylish" New American on a West Orange mountaintop that simply "screams special occasion"; "expert" service makes the "NYC prices" easier to swallow, though "good value" at midday makes it "perfect" for a business lunch; P.S. dress code is business casual, but "people still come dressed up."

Lorena's Ⓜ *French*   28 | 22 | 27 | $63

Maplewood | 168 Maplewood Ave. (Highland Pl.) | 973-763-4460 | www.restaurantlorena.com

Close to "perfect", this "spectacular" Maplewood BYO overseen by chef Humberto Campos Jr. offers "sublime" cuisine with such "superb attention to detail" that it's rated NJ's Top French restaurant; granted, it's "unaffordable on a regular basis" and the ultra-"compact" setting means "you'll need to reserve weeks in advance", but given the "flawless" service and "super-romantic" mood, many say it "doesn't get any better" than this.

	FOOD	DECOR	SERVICE	COST

Luke Palladino *Italian* ▽ 26 | 18 | 23 | $49

Northfield | Plaza 9 Shopping Ctr. | 1333 New Rd. (Tilton Rd.) |
609-646-8189 | www.lukepalladino.com

Modern Italian "dining bliss" lands in Northfield via this storefront
BYO from the eponymous chef, where the "beautifully prepared" seasonal menu emerges from an "open kitchen"; though it's so "tiny" that
it's "hard to get a reservation", most are "ecstatic" to get one.

Maritime Parc Ⓜ *American/Seafood* - | - | - | E

Jersey City | Liberty State Park | 84 Audrey Zapp Dr. (bet. Freedom Way &
Phillip St.) | 201-413-0050 | www.maritimeparc.com

Nestled by the marina in Liberty State Park, this high-end Jersey City
eatery features a seasonally oriented New American seafood
menu; the yachtlike, blond-wood design is a match for the drop-dead
views of the Hudson River and Lower Manhattan, best savored from
its outdoor patio.

Mehndi Ⓜ *Indian* 24 | 24 | 22 | $44

Morristown | 88 Headquarters Plaza | 3 Speedwell Ave. (Park Pl.) |
973-871-2323 | www.mehtanirestaurantgroup.com

"Heavenly" Indian fare comes with "real heat if you want it" at this "exotic" spot set in a Morristown mall; "excellent" service and "modern"
decor enhance the "sophisticated" experience, while a $13 lunch buf-
fet is a low-cost alternative to the otherwise "high-end" tabs.

Nicholas Ⓜ *American* 29 | 27 | 28 | $84

Red Bank | 160 Rte. 35 S. (bet. Navesink River Rd. & Pine St.) |
732-345-9977 | www.restaurantnicholas.com

"Hot off its 10th-year anniversary", Nicholas and Melissa Harary's
"fine-tuned" "crown jewel" in Red Bank is again voted New Jersey's
Most Popular restaurant as well as No. 1 for Food and Service; look for
"showstopping", prix fixe–only New American meals served by an
"impeccable" team in an "understatedly elegant", jackets-suggested
setting; it's a "flawless" experience that's "worth every hundred you
spend", though insiders report you can dine for less (and à la carte) at
the "hip", "more relaxed" bar.

Ninety Acres at Natirar Ⓜ *American* 25 | 28 | 23 | $70

Peapack | Natirar Resort & Spa | 2 Main St. (bet. Old Dutch Rd. &
Ramapo Way) | 908-901-9500 | www.ninetyacres.com

Set in a "stunning" restored carriage house on an "idyllic" estate once
owned by the King of Morocco (and winner of Top Decor in New
Jersey), this "sublime" Peapack New American showcases chef David
Felton's "top-notch" "farm-to-table" menu, much of it prepared with
ingredients grown on-site; it's true "destination dining" perfect for
"special occasions", complete with "superb" service and a "see-and-
be-seen" crowd, but don't forget your "trust fund" – you'll need it
when the check arrives.

Peacock Inn Restaurant *American* 26 | 25 | 24 | $71

Princeton | Peacock Inn | 20 Bayard Ln. (bet. Boudinot & Stockton Sts.) |
609-924-1707 | www.peacockinn.com

"Looking great" following a 2010 renovation, this longtime Princetonian
set in a modernized boutique hotel is "making a splash" with "simply

divine" New American creations from a former Nicholas sous-chef; it's a "fine combination of old and new", with "want-to-please" service, a "serene" vibe and, of course, "big-ticket" tabs.

Picnic, the Restaurant ⒮Ⓜ *American* 27 | 24 | 26 | $52

Fair Lawn | Plaza Bldg. | 14-25 Plaza Rd. N. (Fair Lawn Ave.) | 201-796-2700 | www.picnictherestaurant.com

"Word is out" on this "destination-worthy" New American set in a "tiny" storefront in Fair Lawn's historic Radburn section, where the "excellent" menu is "adjusted daily according to market offerings"; BYO makes the "NYC prices" tolerable, and enthusiasts are "wowed" by the "charming" setting, "impeccable" service and "convivial" mood; P.S. wine lockers are available for regular customers.

Pluckemin Inn ⒮ *American* 26 | 26 | 25 | $65

Bedminster | 359 Rte. 206 S. (Pluckemin Way) | 908-658-9292 | www.pluckemininn.com

"Classy but not pretentious", this Bedminster New American "never fails to impress" with "creative" cuisine paired with a "blow-you-away" list of wines stored in an "impressive" three-story tower; its "glitzy" crowd touts the "beautiful" re-created farmhouse setting that exudes "country elegance" and includes "stunning outdoor seating", and though you may need to "dip into the 401k" to settle the tab, the Plucky Tavern offers "more casual" dining in a "preppy" milieu.

Ram's Head Inn Ⓜ *American* 24 | 26 | 25 | $57

Galloway | 9 W. White Horse Pike (bet. Ash & Taylor Aves.) | 609-652-1700 | www.ramsheadinn.com

A "short trek" but light years away from AC, this "elegant" Galloway "class act" (and sibling of The Manor and Highlawn Pavilion) serves "exquisitely presented" Traditional Americana with "wonderful formality" in a jackets-suggested milieu; the "romantic", candlelit digs appeal to "older" folks who think it's "outstanding in all areas" – save for the "not-cheap" tabs – and particularly perfect at "Christmas."

Rat's Ⓜ *French* 24 | 28 | 24 | $60

Hamilton | Grounds for Sculpture | 16 Fairgrounds Rd. (Ward Ave.) | 609-584-7800 | www.ratsrestaurant.org

With its "dazzling" "fairy-tale" setting in a "whimsical" sculpture park inspired by "Monet's garden at Giverny", this "unique" Hamilton "destination" is beloved for its "not-to-be-missed" setting; now managed by Stephen Starr Events, it offers a "creative" country French menu that's less formal than before but still "delicious", while the "attentive" service and "pricey" tabs remain in place.

Restaurant Latour Ⓜ *American* 27 | 26 | 27 | $83

Hamburg | Crystal Springs Resort | 1 Wild Turkey Way (Crystal Springs Rd.) | 973-827-0548 | www.crystalgolfresort.com

Overlooking the Crystal Springs Resort golf course in Hamburg, this "top table" showcases chef Michael Weisshaupt's "incredible" French-accented New American cuisine, prepared from locally sourced ingredients and complemented by an "amazing", 7,000-label wine list; "white-glove" service and an "unhurried" pace enhance the "extraordinary" mood, broken only when the super-"expensive" check arrives; P.S. jackets suggested, open Thursday–Sunday only.

	FOOD	DECOR	SERVICE	COST

River Palm Terrace *Steak*
`25` `20` `22` `$63`

Edgewater | 1416 River Rd. (Palisade Terrace) | 201-224-2013
Fair Lawn | 41-11 Rte. 4 W. (Saddle River Rd.) | 201-703-3500
Mahwah | 209 Ramapo Valley Rd. (Rte. 17) | 201-529-1111
www.riverpalm.com

"Be prepared to spend" big time at this "upscale" chophouse trio where "succulent" steaks and "outstanding" seafood (including sushi at Edgewater and Mahwah) are paired with an "impressive" wine list; some beef that there's "always a wait" and "regulars get preference", but nearly everyone "wants to go back" – as soon as their "cash flow recovers."

Saddle River Inn 🗷Ⓜ *American/French*
`28` `25` `26` `$64`

Saddle River | 2 Barnstable Ct. (Allendale Rd.) | 201-825-4016 | www.saddleriverinn.com

"Superb from beginning to end", this "gold-standard", "big-ticket" grande dame is set in a "casually elegant" 18th-century barn in Saddle River, where "impeccable" Franco-American preparations emerge from the "steady" kitchen; "serious" service and an "inviting" atmosphere burnish the "world-class" experience, and while it certainly "doesn't come cheap", BYO allows one to "indulge more than usual."

Sagami Japanese Restaurant Ⓜ *Japanese*
`27` `14` `21` `$38`

Collingswood | 37 W. Crescent Blvd. (bet. Haddon Ave. & White Horse Pike) | 856-854-9773

"Still rocking" well into its third decade, this Collingswood BYO remains the "barometer to judge" Japanese fare in South Jersey; service is "quick", the decibel level "noisy" and the room "super-crowded", yet "reservations are a must" almost any night of the week at this "best-loved" spot.

Sapori *Italian*
`28` `22` `26` `$40`

Collingswood | 601 Haddon Ave. (Harvard Ave.) | 856-858-2288 | www.sapori.info

A small but "fantastic" "taste of Italy" in Collingswood, this "exceptional" spot via chef Franco Lombardo serves "not-your-usual" fare (e.g. spaghetti with sea urchin) in "lovely" rustic quarters that he designed and constructed himself; a "relaxed" mood and "knowledgeable" servers make this one a "sure hit"; P.S. closed Tuesdays.

Scalini Fedeli 🗷 *Italian*
`27` `25` `26` `$70`

Chatham | 63 Main St. (bet. Parrott Mill Rd. & Tallmadge Ave.) | 973-701-9200 | www.scalinifedeli.com

"Fine dining" gets a "memorable" spin at Michael Cetrulo's "genuine article" in Chatham, where a "perfectly executed" Italian menu is "presented beautifully" by an "outstanding" team; the "romantic" 18th-century farmhouse setting "exudes class" and is "always packed", but for best results "bring your boss or your trust fund" to settle the "high-end" tabs; P.S. dinner is prix fixe only.

Serenade *French*
`27` `26` `26` `$74`

Chatham | 6 Roosevelt Ave. (Main St.) | 973-701-0303 | www.restaurantserenade.com

"Exquisite" cuisine in an "elegant" atmosphere inspires "superlatives all around" for this "upscale" Chatham French where chef

James Laird's "creative" yet "approachable" cooking is paired with a "deep" wine list; granted, the price tags are super-"expensive", but "impeccable" service and the "romantic" mood make for "simply sublime" "celebration" dining.

Shumi ☒ *Japanese*

28	13	24	$51

Somerville | 30 S. Doughty Ave. (Veterans Memorial Dr.) | 908-526-8596
"Experienced palates" tout the "fabulous" sushi at this Somerville BYO that's rated NJ's Top Japanese; true, it's "expensive", the location is "hidden" and there's a decided "lack of decor", but the chef is "dedicated", service is "excellent" and "you get what you pay for" here.

Washington Inn *American*

28	26	27	$57

Cape May | 801 Washington St. (Jefferson St.) | 609-884-5697 | www.washingtoninn.com
Still the "gold standard" for "benchmark" fine dining in Cape May, this "classy" destination is all about "flawless attention to detail", from its "sensational", "artistically presented" Traditional American menu and "nice wine list" to the "gets-everything-right" service and "romantic" setting in a former plantation home; the "pricey" tabs notwithstanding, this one's a natural for "special occasions."

Whispers *American*

27	24	26	$58

Spring Lake | Hewitt Wellington Hotel | 200 Monmouth Ave. (2nd Ave.) | 732-974-9755 | www.whispersrestaurant.com
A bit of "heaven" in Spring Lake's Hewitt Wellington Hotel, this "romantic" BYO is "outstanding in every respect", starting with its "stellar" New American cooking and extending to its "spot-on" service and "elegant" Victorian inn setting; fans murmur it's "as good as it gets" for an "intimate candlelit dinner" with that special someone.

New Orleans

Restaurant	Cuisine
28 Cochon Butcher	Cajun/Sandwiches
Clancy's	Creole
La Provence	Creole/French
Brigtsen's	Contemp. Louisiana
GW Fins	Seafood
Cypress	Creole
Lilette	French
August	French
27 Commander's Palace	Creole
Stella!	American
Bayona	American
Mr. John's	Steak
Boucherie	Southern
Irene's Cuisine	Italian
La Boca	Argentinean/Steak
Sal & Judy's	Creole/Italian
Gautreau's	American/French
Herbsaint	American/French
Chateau du Lac	French
Nine Roses	Chinese/Vietnamese

OTHER NOTEWORTHY PLACES

Acme Oyster House	Seafood
Atchafalaya	Contemp. Louisiana/Creole
Bistro Daisy	American/Southern
Bon Ton Café	Cajun
Café Du Monde	Coffeehouse/Dessert
Cochon	Cajun
Coquette	American
Dickie Brennan's	Steak
Domenica	Italian
Eleven 79	Creole/Italian
Emeril's	Contemp. Louisiana
Galatoire's	Creole/French
Iris	American
K-Paul's Louisiana Kitchen	Cajun
La Petite Grocery	Contemp. Louisiana/French
Martinique Bistro	French/Seafood
Mr. B's Bistro	Contemp. Louisiana
Patois	American/French
Rue 127	American
Upperline	Contemp. Louisiana

	FOOD	DECOR	SERVICE	COST

Acme Oyster House *Seafood*

24 | 18 | 22 | $29

French Quarter | 724 Iberville St. (bet. Bourbon & Royal Sts.) | 504-522-5973
Metairie | 3000 Veterans Memorial Blvd. (Causeway Blvd.) | 504-309-4056
Covington | 1202 N. Hwy. 190 (bet. Crestwood Blvd. & 17th Ave.) | 985-246-6155
www.acmeoyster.com

It's "a shell of a place" hoot fans of this French Quarter seafood centenarian (with suburban spin-offs) that "consistently" delivers "fabulous oysters" and other "out-of-this-world" "Louisiana favorites" with "no pretense" in a "lively", "family-friendly" setting; though it may "seem like a tourist trap" with "lines around the block", even "locals love" this "moderately priced" "mecca of all things oyster"; P.S. "sit at the bar" for the full "shucker experience."

Atchafalaya *Contemp. Louisiana/Creole*

26 | 23 | 23 | $37

Irish Channel | 901 Louisiana Ave. (Laurel St.) | 504-891-9626 | www.atchafalayarestaurant.com

Look for the "giant cast iron pan" outside this Contemporary Louisianan in the Irish Channel where chef Baruch Rabasa pleases "adventurous palates" with "beyond divine" "transformations" of Creole staples and a "delectable" Sunday brunch (with a "do-it-yourself Bloody Mary bar"); the "high-ceilinged" room adorned with "funky art" exudes a "sultry" "New Orleans vibe", and while the staffers may "get bogged down" by crowds of "locals and a few tourists", they always "thank you on the way out."

August *French*

28 | 28 | 27 | $73

Central Business Dist. | 301 Tchoupitoulas St. (Gravier St.) | 504-299-9777 | www.restaurantaugust.com

John Besh's "unforgettable" CBD flagship "glows with his personality" as the "star" chef's "keen sense of flavors" and devotion to "local ingredients" yields "superb" New French fare "presented like works of art"; a "subtly attentive" staff sees to "well-heeled locals" and "Hollywood celebs" in the "stately but not stuffy" space whose "glittering chandeliers and rich wood accents" "demurely whisper class", and even though dinner prices may require "holding up a bank", the weekday lunch is a "steal."

Bayona ☒ *American*

27 | 26 | 26 | $59

French Quarter | 430 Dauphine St. (bet. Conti & St. Louis Sts.) | 504-525-4455 | www.bayona.com

"New Orleans icon" Susan Spicer "continues to inspire" at this French Quarter New American "slice of heaven" where dishes with "creative" Contemporary Louisiana twists are complemented by a "top-notch wine list" and delivered to the table with "grace"; the mood is "festive" inside the "charming old cottage" or its "Garden of Eden" courtyard, and whether for a "special occasion" or a "surprisingly inexpensive" lunch, it's "not to be missed."

Bistro Daisy ☒Ⓜ *American/Southern*

27 | 23 | 26 | $48

Uptown | 5831 Magazine St. (bet. Eleonore St. & Nashville Ave.) | 504-899-6987 | www.bistrodaisy.com

At this "quaint" Uptown "locals' secret" by chef Anton and Diane Schulte, "seasonal ingredients" go into "sophisticated yet unpretentious" takes on New American–Southern fare best enjoyed in tandem with a "wine list that begs you to buy by the bottle"; the "gracious" service ensures guests "never feel crowded or hurried", keeping the "beautiful little cottage" filled with "smiling people."

Bon Ton Café 🅂 *Cajun* | 25 | 22 | 25 | $37

Central Business Dist. | 401 Magazine St. (bet. Natchez & Poydras Sts.) | 504-524-3386 | www.thebontoncafe.com

"Classic", "well-prepared" Cajun (crabmeat au gratin, crawfish étouffée) awaits at this CBD "stalwart" that "fills with lawyers and bankers" who still practice the "three-martini power lunch" in "seersucker suits and skirts"; the "chatty" staff can be "opinionated" but "treats you like family" in a "time capsule" of "exposed-brick walls and beamed ceilings", where "nothing changes except the prices"; P.S. closed weekends.

Boucherie 🅂 🅜 *Southern* | 27 | 22 | 25 | $34

Carrollton | 8115 Jeannette St. (Carrollton Ave.) | 504-862-5514 | www.boucherie-nola.com

At this "quirky" Carrollton cottage, unstoppable chef/co-owner Nathanial Zimet fashions "innovative but never self-indulgent" updates on Southern classics with "unexpected finesse" and offers them at "outrageously reasonable prices"; the "charmingly small" (ok, "cramped") space is "always packed" with "young up-and-comers" ("reservations are a must"), but an "efficient, courteous" staff is quick with "inventive cocktails" and beers from a "thoughtfully curated" list.

Brigtsen's 🅂 🅜 *Contemp. Louisiana* | 28 | 23 | 27 | $54

Riverbend | 723 Dante St. (Maple St.) | 504-861-7610 | www.brigtsens.com

"Feel New Orleans in every bite" of "acclaimed chef" Frank Brigtsen's "rich, upscale" Contemporary Louisiana fare at this "hard-to-find" Riverbend cottage "near the levee"; even if the setting's "not for the claustrophobic", most consider it as "cozy" as a "family dining room", overseen by "warm", "wonderful" servers who are "devoid of attitude even though they could get away with it."

Café Du Monde *Coffeehouse/Dessert* | 26 | 20 | 20 | $11

Central Business Dist. | 500 Port of New Orleans Pl. (Poydras St.) | 504-587-0841

French Quarter | French Mkt. | 800 Decatur St. (St. Ann St.) | 504-525-4544 ◑↻

Gretna | Oakwood Mall | 197 Westbank Expwy. (bet. Terry Pkwy. & Whitney Ave.) | 504-365-8600

Kenner | Esplanade Mall | 1401 W. Esplanade Ave. (Delaware Ave.) | 504-468-3588

Kenner | 3245 Williams Blvd. (bet. 32nd & 33rd Sts.) | 504-469-7699

Metairie | 1814 N. Causeway Blvd. (Melrah Dr.) | 985-951-7474

Metairie | Lakeside Mall | 3301 Veterans Memorial Blvd. (Causeway Blvd.) | 504-834-8694

Metairie | 4700 Veterans Memorial Blvd. (Lime St.) | 504-888-9770

Covington | 70437 S. Tyler St. (Hyacinth Dr.) | 985-893-0453
www.cafedumonde.com

Tourists "from across the world" join locals winding down "a night on the town" at this 24-hour French Quarter "landmark" whose "light-textured" beignets "heaping with powdered sugar" and "smooth"

FOOD DECOR SERVICE COST

chicory coffee satisfy "sweet cravings" in an "open-air" setting; the service can be "uneven" and every surface "sticky", but focus on the "parade of daily life" for an experience that's as New Orleans "as Mardi Gras and humidity"; P.S. suburban branches minimize "the hassle" but lack the "same atmosphere."

Chateau du Lac 🖼 *French* 27 | 23 | 23 | $46
Old Metairie | 2037 Metairie Rd. (Atherton Dr.) | Metairie | 504-831-3773 | www.chateaudulacbistro.com
"Under-the-radar" in Old Metairie, this "excellent" bistro from chef Jacques Saleun provides a roster of "classic" "French country fare" and "creative" specials matched by a "knowledgeably selected" wine list; with the help of a "welcoming" staff, it's a "lively" "neighborhood gem" that lets you "escape to France" even when "surrounded by locals."

Clancy's 🖼 *Creole* 28 | 24 | 26 | $54
Uptown | 6100 Annunciation St. (Webster St.) | 504-895-1111 | www.clancysneworleans.com
"You need a secret decoder ring" to find this Uptown "locals' favorite" whose "mouthwatering" "haute Creole" fare (like smoked soft-shell crab) is "worth the search" and the "expected" prices; "pitch-perfect" servers "make it their career to know and please" the "always cheerful" "old guard" who "table-hop" in the "intoxicatingly loud" downstairs dining room that can feel like a "country club without golf", but still "makes you want to be a regular."

Cochon 🖼 *Cajun* 27 | 23 | 24 | $43
Warehouse District | 930 Tchoupitoulas St. (Andrew Higgins Dr.) | 504-588-2123 | www.cochonrestaurant.com
The "pig never saw it coming" at this "trendy" Warehouse District Cajun where chef-owners Donald Link (Herbsaint, Cochon Butcher) and Stephen Stryjewski fulfill "porky fantasies" (and "tempt a vegetarian" or two) with "sophisticated home cooking like you can't believe", served amid "boisterous", "industrial yet rustic" surroundings; despite seeming "slightly pricey" to some, it's a kick to "get a ringside seat by the kitchen" and chow down among the faithful on a porcine "pilgrimage."

Cochon Butcher *Cajun/Sandwiches* 28 | 21 | 22 | $20
Warehouse District | 930 Tchoupitoulas St. (Andrew Higgins Dr.) | 504-588-7675 | www.cochonbutcher.com
"A must if you dig the pig", Donald Link's "phenomenal" Warehouse District Cajun earns a resounding "oink" of approval and New Orleans' No. 1 Food score for its "daring", "decadent" sandwiches, "atypical" daily sides and "well-curated" wine list; the "small", "laid-back" space (right next to Cochon) has "squashed-together" seating and a "constant crowd", so "plan your time of attack carefully" or let the "ultrafriendly" staff send you home with "superb" charcuterie from the "hard-to-resist" deli case.

Commander's Palace *Creole* 27 | 28 | 28 | $65
Garden District | 1403 Washington Ave. (Coliseum St.) | 504-899-8221 | www.commanderspalace.com
"Step into a grand movie" at this "better-than-ever", unapologetically "over-the-top" Garden District Creole and revel in a "shocking, playful and sinful" "gastronomic experience" worthy of "an Oscar" (or at least

New Orleans' Most Popular, No. 1 Decor and Service ratings); with a "wine list worth the trip itself" and "impeccable" servers who "actually appear to want to serve", it's no wonder that "locals and tourists alike" happily invest in a spendy dinner or "delightful" jazz brunch – after all, this is the "place to bring grandma to assure you're in the will"; P.S. no shorts or T-shirts; jackets suggested for dinner.

Coquette *American*   27 | 26 | 25 | $48

Garden District | 2800 Magazine St. (Washington Ave.) | 504-265-0421 | www.coquette-nola.com
"Farm-to-table without being ostentatious about it", this "chic" Garden District bistro by chef/co-owner Michael Stoltzfus impresses a "young, trendy" clientele with its "ever-changing" New American menu of "ambrosial", "thought-provoking" dishes backed by "sublime" cocktails; an "enthusiastic" staff ensures that whether soaking up the "lively" downstairs ambiance or enjoying the "quieter intimacy" upstairs, fans find it "heavenly on every note"; P.S. the $20 prix fixe lunch is a "great deal."

Cypress ☒Ⓜ *Creole*   28 | 22 | 24 | $40

Metairie | 4426 Transcontinental Dr. (bet. Esplanade Ave. & Murphy Dr.) | 504-885-6885 | www.restaurantcypress.com
Smitten surveyors say this "suburban masterpiece" in Metairie "easily competes" with "New Orleans' finest" thanks to Creole dishes "flavored with a delicate hand" and "specials that never fail to please"; while the "tiny" space "can get noisy", most enjoy the "neighborhood atmosphere" and suggest that ever-"present" owners, chef Stephen and manager Katherine Huth, "don't charge enough for the fabulous food" – no wonder "locals want to keep it their little secret."

Dickie Brennan's Steakhouse *Steak*   27 | 25 | 26 | $63

French Quarter | 716 Iberville St. (bet. Bourbon & Royal Sts.) | 504-522-2467 | www.dickiebrennanssteakhouse.com
"A traditional steakhouse with a New Orleans flair", this Brennan-family beef bastion in the French Quarter "does not disappoint" with its "tender", "immaculate" meat, "perfect sides" and "terrific" drinks served in a "clubby downstairs cavern" (and at the "fun bar"); the "young, attentive" staff "exudes Southern hospitality", rounding out an "extravagant night" that's "worth every dollar."

Domenica *Italian*   27 | 25 | 24 | $39

Central Business Dist. | Roosevelt Hotel | 123 Baronne St. (bet. Canal & Common Sts.) | 504-648-6020 | www.domenicarestaurant.com
At "John Besh's bow to Italy" in the CBD's Roosevelt Hotel, "up-and-coming" chef Alon Shaya "mans the stoves" to create "imaginative" "culinary adventures" starring "exceptional" pizza, "perfect" pasta and "house-cured meats"; the "glam", "glossy" and "high-energy" room is staffed by a "well-trained" team that makes a trip here "worth every penny" – and a "steal" during the "half-price-pie" happy hour.

Eleven 79 ☒ *Creole/Italian*   25 | 23 | 23 | $52

Lower Garden Dist. | 1179 Annunciation St. (bet. Calliope & Erato Sts.) | 504-299-1179 | www.eleven79.com
"Politicians and local celebs" indulge in "rich, garlicky" "upscale" Italian with "Creole touches" at this Lower Garden District "hideaway" by

"New Orleans legend" Joseph Segreto, who "knows his customers" and watches over the "entertaining" staff; devotees of the "hard-to-find" "throwback" suggest you "bring someone you're not supposed to be with", ignore the "elevated" prices and be "enveloped" by "old-world charm" worthy of "Mr. Sinatra."

Emeril's *Contemp. Louisiana*

| 26 | 25 | 25 | $66 |

Warehouse District | 800 Tchoupitoulas St. (Julia St.) | 504-528-9393 | www.emerils.com

"Grand master" Emeril Lagasse "puts on a show" at this "up-to-the-hype" Warehouse District "standard bearer" specializing in "huge portions" of "delectable" Contemporary Louisiana favorites and personal signatures (barbecue shrimp, "sublime" banana cream pie) that will "floor" you with "unexpected flavor"; "gorgeously modern", "jumping with energy" and staffed by "prompt", "intelligent foodies", it's a "high-roller heaven" where "sitting at the chef's bar" is "unforgettable."

Galatoire's Ⓜ *Creole/French*

| 26 | 26 | 27 | $64 |

French Quarter | 209 Bourbon St. (Iberville St.) | 504-525-2021 | www.galatoires.com

"New Orleans wouldn't be New Orleans without" this century-old French Quarter "institution" (now expanding into an adjacent building) where "Southern hospitality" reigns supreme as tux-wearing servers "guide you" to "stellar" seafood and other "pricey" French-Creole "warhorses done with aplomb"; fueled by "copious" drinks, "locals and dignitaries" in "seersucker suits" gather in the "elegantly tiled" main dining room for lunch that's "always a party" – arguably "the most fun you can have over a white tablecloth"; P.S. jackets required after 5 PM and all day Sunday; reservations only accepted upstairs.

Gautreau's Ⓩ *American/French*

| 27 | 25 | 27 | $58 |

Uptown | 1728 Soniat St. (Danneel St.) | 504-899-7397 | www.gautreausrestaurant.com

The "elite meet" at this "secluded" Uptown bistro for chef Sue Zemanick's "elegant", "inspired" New American–New French cooking backed by an "outstanding little wine list"; "wonderful host" Patrick Singley oversees a "cordial" staff in the "jewel box" of a converted pharmacy where the "lighting makes everybody look good" and the "dreamy" dinners are "worth the cost" (and the "search").

GW Fins *Seafood*

| 28 | 26 | 27 | $53 |

French Quarter | D.H. Holmes Apartments | 808 Bienville St. (bet. Bourbon & Dauphine Sts.) | 504-581-3467 | www.gwfins.com

"Simple" yet "beautifully done", "lighter" preparations of fish "flown in from all areas of the oceans" are "accompanied by an extensive wine list" at this "pricey" French Quarter "seafood mecca" set in a "swanky" "open warehouse space"; the "docentlike" staff "bends over backwards" to keep customers happy, so many wonder why it's relatively "under-the-radar" when it's such "a catch"; P.S. no T-shirts or flip-flops.

Herbsaint Ⓩ *American/French*

| 27 | 23 | 25 | $48 |

Warehouse District | 701 St. Charles Ave. (Girod St.) | 504-524-4114 | www.herbsaint.com

Chef/co-owner Donald Link (Cochon) "makes you swoon" with his "refined yet joyous" New American–New French cooking at this

Warehouse District "delight" that "locals swear by" for a "hopping" "business lunch" or "hip", "casually elegant" dinner; there's "gracious service without formality", keeping guests "all smiles" as they share "wonderful small plates", sip "exciting" drinks and watch "passing streetcars on St. Charles Avenue" from the "huge windows."

Irene's Cuisine 🅸 *Italian*   27 | 23 | 25 | $45

French Quarter | 539 St. Philip St. (bet. Chartres & Decatur Sts.) | 504-529-8811

A "glorious" garlic scent wafts from this French Quarter haunt "beloved by locals" for its "fantastic" Southern Italian plates that "make you feel like Caesar himself"; expect the "personable" staff to "usher you to a romantic sitting room" (with a "rockin' piano bar") when you enter, because "even with a reservation", "you will wait" for a table in the "charming" "speakeasy" space.

Iris 🅸 *American*   25 | 22 | 22 | $50

French Quarter | Bienville House Hotel | 321 N. Peters St. (bet. Bienville & Conti Sts.) | 504-299-3944 | www.irisneworleans.com

With a "gentle touch" that lets "each ingredient shine", chef/co-owner Ian Schnoebelen produces "elevated but not stuffy" New American fare at this "chic" "sleeper" in the French Quarter's Bienville House; Laurie Casebonne welcomes the "young, hip clientele" with an "attentive" team and an "infectious laugh" as "amazing" cocktails fuel an experience that "gets better with each visit."

K-Paul's Louisiana Kitchen 🅸 *Cajun*   26 | 22 | 24 | $53

French Quarter | 416 Chartres St. (bet. Conti & St. Louis Sts.) | 877-553-3401 | www.kpauls.com

"The man who brought Cajun into the mainstream", Paul Prudhomme and his "one-of-a-kind" French Quarter kitchen are "still going strong" as exec chef Paul Miller delivers "upscale" eats with "in-your-face flavors" along with a "bargain" "order-at-the-counter" lunch; the "professional" servers are "excellent educators" for "tourists" and "foodies" who make their "pilgrimage" to the "down-home", "comfortable" locale, which "deserves repeat visits, even on the same trip."

La Boca 🅸 *Argentinean/Steak*   27 | 22 | 24 | $55

Warehouse District | 857 Fulton St. (St. Joseph St.) | 504-525-8205 | www.labocasteaks.com

"You are *loca* if you don't try La Boca" say carnivores crazy for this Argentine steakhouse in the Warehouse District specializing in "beautifully executed", "less typical cuts" paired with "full-bodied wines" by a "knowledgeable" team; the "bohemian" look evokes "Buenos Aires", and it's "priced reasonably for the caliber", suiting the crowd of "service-industry folks, young foodies" and others who urge "go for a pisco sour", "go in a group of four and do the tasting menu" or just "go and indulge."

La Petite Grocery 🅼 *Contemp. Louisiana/French*   26 | 24 | 25 | $47

Uptown | 4238 Magazine St. (General Pershing St.) | 504-891-3377 | www.lapetitegrocery.com

At this "quaint"-looking Uptown bistro, "rock-star" chef/co-owner Justin Devillier combines "clean flavors" into "gustatory pleasures" that "lean to French" with a Contemporary Louisiana bent; "congenial" staffers helps make it a "serene" "respite from the busy Magazine Street scene", so even if tabs get "slightly steep" for some, most simply revel in this little "sliver of utopia."

La Provence ☒ *Creole/French* `28` `28` `28` `$56`

Lacombe | 25020 Hwy. 190 (bet. Bremermann & Raymond Rds.) | 985-626-7662 | www.laprovencerestaurant.com

"When you can't fly to Provence, cross the lake" to Lacombe for John Besh's "rustic" yet "upscale" French-Creole made with "fresh, flavorful ingredients" (many of which are "raised on the property") and served in "charming" "country-manor" surroundings; "sublime" service ensures that an "intimate" evening or even just Sunday brunch is "memorable for all the right reasons" – and the "must-try" prix fixe is an "excellent value" to boot.

Lilette ☒☒ *French* `28` `25` `26` `$50`

Uptown | 3637 Magazine St. (Antonine St.) | 504-895-1636 | www.liletterestaurant.com

"Beautiful people", "young professionals" and "movie stars" flock to this "expensive but divine" Uptown "corner bistro" to dine on "artistic", "delicious" French fare "carefully crafted" by chef-owner John Harris and presented with "sexy" drinks by "spot-on" servers; an "understated" "blend of old and modern", the "converted storefront" dining room can "get a little loud", so some raters recommend the patio for a "Parisian" experience.

Martinique Bistro ☒ *French/Seafood* `26` `24` `23` `$47`

Uptown | 5908 Magazine St. (bet. Nashville & State Sts.) | 504-891-8495 | www.martiniquebistro.com

"Savvy locals" love chef Eric LaBouchere's "modern", "high-end" versions of French bistro "classics" (particularly seafood) at this Uptown "gem" showcasing "tantalizing local ingredients" on a "frequently changing" menu; while the "well-trained" staff and "warm" atmosphere transport you to a "small French village", "romantics" say "nothing is better" than the "exquisite" "secret garden" on a "sultry" New Orleans night.

Mr. B's Bistro *Contemp. Louisiana* `26` `25` `25` `$48`

French Quarter | 201 Royal St. (Iberville St.) | 504-523-2078 | www.mrbsbistro.com

Locals "celebrate birthdays" and "impress out-of-towners" at this "lively" French Quarter "staple" from the Brennan family whose "can't-go-wrong" Contemporary Louisiana repertoire includes a "bucket-list-worthy" brunch, an "affordable" lunch and classics like gumbo ya-ya and the "wonderful" if "messy" BBQ shrimp ("wear your bib or you'll be sorry"); with its "accommodating" service and "clubby", "dark-wood" backdrop, it takes you back to a time "when proper manners were still observed" and a restaurant meal was a "rare treat."

Mr. John's Steakhouse ☒☒ *Steak* `27` `24` `26` `$57`

Lower Garden Dist. | 2111 St. Charles Ave. (bet. Jackson Ave. & Josephine St.) | 504-679-7697 | www.mrjohnssteakhouse.com

"Satisfy your steak cravings" at this "pricey but well worth it" Lower Garden District "sleeper" delivering both "superb" Italian specialties

NEW ORLEANS

FOOD   DECOR   SERVICE   COST

and "melt-in-your-mouth" meats that arrive "sizzling"; "professional and precise", the staff tends to a "combination of locals and tourists" in an "old New Orleans" setting that exudes "comfortable elegance" and offers "views of St. Charles Avenue."

Nine Roses *Chinese/Vietnamese*   27 | 19 | 22 | $23
(aka Hoa Hong 9)
Gretna | 1100 Stephens St. (O'Connor St.) | 504-366-7665
"Worth the drive across the bridge", this Gretna "favorite" is prized for "delicious", "authentic" Vietnamese dishes on an "endless" menu that "resembles a novel" (although some suggest you "avoid the Chinese" chapters); service is "friendly", and while the "large venue" lacks luster, the "inexpensive", "generous" portions "never disappoint."

Patois Ⓜ *American/French*   26 | 23 | 24 | $48
Uptown | 6078 Laurel St. (Webster St.) | 504-895-9441 | www.patoisnola.com
There's a "buzz" in a "quiet pocket of Uptown" thanks to this "so cool" French–New American where "talented" chef/co-owner Aaron Burgau crafts a "confident" "farm-to-table" menu bolstered by "eclectic" cocktails, a "standout" brunch and "good value"; generally strong service "makes you want to tip" the "hipsters" overseeing the "adorable" digs, but "boy is it busy" – and "noisy" – with throngs of "in-the-know tourists" and "discerning locals" who declare it New Orleans' "new breed."

Rue 127 Ⓧ *American*   27 | 23 | 25 | $46
Mid-City | 127 N. Carrollton Ave. (Iberville St.) | 504-483-1571 | www.rue127.com
A "loyal following" has discovered this "hidden" Mid-City shotgun house where "greatness" "comes out of the kitchen" in the form of "simply prepared" but "flawlessly executed" New American from chef-owner Ray Gruezke; "well staffed", the "intimate" (and "tiny") quarters foster a "relaxed fine-dining atmosphere" "perfect for a date" or anytime you seek an "exquisite experience" that's somewhat "pricey, but money well spent."

Sal & Judy's Ⓜ *Creole/Italian*   27 | 21 | 25 | $40
Lacombe | 27491 Hwy. 190 (14th St.) | 985-882-9443 | www.salandjudysrestaurant.com
"Be prepared to step back in time" at this "bargain" Creole–Southern Italian in Lacombe where chef-owner Sal Impastato brings "his Italian flair" to "fresh Louisiana produce" in "delicious" dishes that require an "extra car for leftovers"; the "small" setting evokes a "family home" and the staff is "attentive" – though a few feel it caters more to "regulars" who snap up the "hard-to-get reservations."

Stella! *American*   27 | 26 | 27 | $111
French Quarter | Hotel Provincial | 1032 Chartres St. (bet. St. Philip St. & Ursulines Ave.) | 504-587-0091 | www.restaurantstella.com
At this "romantic" "jewel" "tucked away in the Quarter", chef-owner Scott Boswell composes "uncompromising" New American cuisine using "exotic ingredients" and "seemingly kooky combinations" that become "works of art" "begging to be photographed"; each night the staff performs a "dance" that's "a sight to behold", and even if you

"gulp twice when you get the check", acolytes insist the experience warrants the "exclamation point" in the name; P.S. four- and seven-course prix fixe only.

Upperline Ⓜ *Contemp. Louisiana*   27 | 25 | 26 | $51

Uptown | 1413 Upperline St. (bet. Pitt & Prytania Sts.) | 504-891-9822 | www.upperline.com

"Original renditions of traditional favorites" impress at this Uptown "hideaway for locals" that "still hits the mark" with an "unusual" Contemporary Louisiana menu and "unmatched hospitality" via "pure New Orleans" "host with the most" JoAnn Clevenger; set in an 1877 townhouse covered with "art ranging from the beautiful to the bizarre", it's a "treasure of the Big Easy" where a meal feels "like visiting a dear old friend."

New York City

TOP FOOD RANKING

Restaurant	Cuisine
29 Le Bernardin	French/Seafood
Per Se	American/French
28 Bouley	French
Daniel	French
Eleven Madison Park	French
Jean Georges	French
La Grenouille	French
Mas (Farmhouse)	American
Sushi Yasuda	Japanese
Sushi Seki	Japanese
Grocery	American
Gramercy Tavern	American
Marea	Italian/Seafood
Gotham Bar & Grill	American
Annisa	American
27 Peter Luger	Steak
Lucali	Pizza
Saul	American
Picholine	French/Mediterranean
Milos, Estiatorio	Greek/Seafood
Il Mulino	Italian
Scalini Fedeli	Italian
Brooklyn Fare	French
Torrisi Italian	Italian
L'Artusi	Italian

OTHER NOTEWORTHY PLACES

ABC Kitchen	American
Acme	American
Babbo	Italian
Balthazar	French
Beauty & Essex	American
Blue Hill	American
Breslin	British
Del Posto	Italian
Dutch	American
Eataly	Italian
Four Seasons	American
Katz's Deli	Deli
Keens Steakhouse	Steak
Lion	American
Modern	American/French
Nobu	Japanese
Red Rooster	American
River Café	American
Sasabune	Japanese

	FOOD	DECOR	SERVICE	COST

Scalinatella	Italian
Sripraphal	Thai
Tocqueville	American/French
21 Club	American
Union Square Cafe	American
Waverly Inn	American

ABC Kitchen *American*

26 | 24 | 23 | $58

Flatiron | ABC Carpet & Home | 35 E. 18th St. (bet. B'way & Park Ave. S.) | 212-475-5829 | www.abckitchennyc.com

"Farm fresh" is the mantra at Jean-Georges Vongerichten's "killer" Flatiron American in ABC Carpet putting forth "thoughtfully composed" "organic", "sustainable" dishes in white-on-white, "Nordic-chic" digs; "hip, friendly" service adds to the "charming" vibe, though the "tough-to-get reservations" are even tougher now that "Obama has been here."

Acme *American*

– | – | – | M

NoHo | 9 Great Jones St. (Lafayette St.) | 212-203-2121 | www.acmenyc.com

The former Acme Bar & Grill, a Cajun roadhouse on the NoHo scene since 1986, has been completely transformed by Indochine vets into this too-cool-for-school boîte, boasting a cozy, candlelit ambiance and a top toque in the kitchen: chef Mads Refslund (co-founder of Copenhagen's Noma), who's offering a moderately priced, farm-to-table New American menu with some Danish accents; given its modest dimensions and elite scenester target audience, brace yourself for a tough door; P.S. adding to the overall fabulosity, there's a hip lounge in the basement.

Annisa *American*

28 | 24 | 27 | $86

W Village | 13 Barrow St. (bet. 7th Ave. S. & W. 4th St.) | 212-741-6699 | www.annisarestaurant.com

"Adult dining experiences" don't get much more "top-drawer" than Anita Lo's West Village "temple of food" where "adventurous", Asian-accented New Americana is backed up by "polished" service; the "tiny", "minimalist" room is "serene" enough to "hear your dinner companion and no one else's."

Babbo ● *Italian*

27 | 23 | 24 | $81

G Village | 110 Waverly Pl. (bet. MacDougal St. & 6th Ave.) | 212-777-0303 | www.babbonyc.com

The "hype is true" about this 15-year-old Batali-Bastianich "powerhouse" where the "assertive", "adventurous" Italian menu "takes pasta to the next level" and is plied in a "convivial" Village carriage house to the tune of a "loud" rock soundtrack; ignore the "high-end" tabs, "tight" dimensions and "calluses-on-your-redial-finger" reservations: this "exceptional experience" approaches "culinary perfection."

Balthazar ● *French*

24 | 24 | 21 | $57

SoHo | 80 Spring St. (bet. B'way & Crosby St.) | 212-965-1414 | www.balthazarny.com

"What's the point of flying to Paris?" when there's Keith McNally's "always entertaining" SoHo brasserie, where "cut-above" French cooking, "Parisian-cafe-movie-set" decor and a "NY hip" vibe draw a "great mix of humanity" – think "tourists", "Eurotrash", "Victoria Beckham"; "fever-pitch" noise levels and "polite if harried" service show it "hasn't lost its bounce", and insiders tout its "soulful breakfasts" and "manna-from-heaven" bread basket.

Beauty & Essex ● American   23 | 27 | 21 | $59

LES | 146 Essex St. (bet. Rivington & Stanton Sts.) | 212-614-0146 | www.beautyandessex.com

A "scene-and-a-half" hidden behind a "functioning pawn shop", this LES phenom seduces "beautiful" folks with "sexy" Americana served in an "over-the-top", AvroKO-designed duplex; it may come at a "high price", but "free bubbly in the ladies' room" compensates.

Blue Hill American   27 | 24 | 26 | $87

G Village | 75 Washington Pl. (bet. MacDougal St. & 6th Ave.) | 212-539-1776 | www.bluehillfarm.com

A locavore "pioneer", Dan Barber's "sublime" Village American is famed for its "vibrant flavors" and "amazing ingredients" bursting with "straight-from-the-farm" freshness; the "calming" setting, "above-and-beyond" service and "peace-and-quiet" acoustics help mute the "expensive" tabs, though reservations are more "difficult" since "Barack and Michelle" showed up.

Bouley ⊠ French   28 | 27 | 27 | $111

TriBeCa | 163 Duane St. (bet. Greenwich & Hudson Sts.) | 212-964-2525 | www.davidbouley.com

Starting with the "lovely scent of apples in the foyer", David Bouley's TriBeCa "trailblazer" is the epitome of "refined", "grown-up" dining, from the "superlative" New French fare to the "extraordinary" service and "sumptuous", jackets-required setting; granted, it can be "expensive", but in return you get a "priceless", near-"perfection" experience; P.S. the midday $55 prix fixe is "one of the best fancy lunch deals" in town.

The Breslin ● British   24 | 22 | 19 | $49

Chelsea | Ace Hotel | 16 W. 29th St. (bet. B'way & 5th Ave.) | 212-679-1939 | www.thebreslin.com

"Sceney but satisfying", this "dark, woody" Ace Hotel destination from Ken Friedman and April Bloomfield offers "heavenly" "meat in all of its forms" on its "decadent" British menu, but the "beautiful" "hipster" crowd steals the "show"; "noise", "too-cool-for-school" service and no rez–induced "waits" come with the territory.

Brooklyn Fare Kitchen French   27 | 19 | 25 | $293

Downtown Bklyn | 200 Schermerhorn St. (Hoyt St.) | Brooklyn | 718-243-0050 | www.brooklynfare.com

A "must on any foodie's bucket list", this Downtown Brooklyn "gastronomic temple" showcases chef Cesar Ramirez's Japanese-inspired French cooking via 20-plus "out-of-this-world" small plates served in the "spartan" prep kitchen of a gourmet grocery; no question, the $225 prix fixe-only menu is "very expensive", yet it's still the "toughest reservation in the city" with only 18 counterside stools (arranging to "have dinner with the president would be easier"); P.S. it "now has wine" so you needn't BYO.

| | FOOD | DECOR | SERVICE | COST |

Daniel ⊠ French
28 | 28 | 28 | $146

E 60s | 60 E. 65th St. (bet. Madison & Park Aves.) | 212-288-0033 |
www.danielnyc.com

"Haute" puts it mildly at chef Daniel Boulud's 20-year-old East Side
"classic", where the "exceptional" New French fare arrives in an "elegance personified", jackets-required setting; "carefully choreographed"
service distracts from the "lofty", prix fixe–only tabs, making this
"sweep-you-off-your-feet" experience an exercise in "pure pleasure";
P.S. there's "less formal", à la carte dining in the lounge.

Del Posto Italian
26 | 27 | 26 | $110

Chelsea | 85 10th Ave. (bet. 15th & 16th Sts.) | 212-497-8090 |
www.delposto.com

The Batali-Bastianich team "really outdoes themselves" at this "pala-
tial" Chelsea "production" that "sets the bar" with "superlative" Italian
food and wine, "attention-to-detail" service and a "magnificent",
marble-and-mahogany setting replete with balcony seating, private
party spaces and "live piano"; granted, the prices are steep, but this
"special-occasion" magnet is "worth the splurge."

The Dutch ◗ American
24 | 22 | 21 | $62

SoHo | 131 Sullivan St. (Prince St.) | 212-677-6200 |
www.thedutchnyc.com

Andrew Carmellini's "terrific" regional American cooking in "cool"
quarters with an "amazing vibe" make it "hard to get a rez" at this
SoHo "standout"; a skeptical few say it "doesn't live up to the hype" or
the "steep prices", but its "crowded", "happening", "earplug"-worthy
"scene" speaks for itself.

Eataly Italian
24 | 20 | 18 | $40

Flatiron | 200 Fifth Ave. (bet. 23rd & 24th Sts.) | 212-229-2560 |
www.eataly.com

"Disneyland for foodies", this "larger-than-life" Flatiron food hall via
the Batali-Bastianich team celebrates "everything Italian", offering
noshing at counters vending cheese, coffee, fish, gelato, pasta, pizza,
vegetables and wine, all in the "middle of a grocery store" the size of
"Grand Central Station"; the "price of success" includes "extreme
crowds", "no available seats" and "sensory overload", but then again,
there's "nothing else like it anywhere."

Eleven Madison Park ⊠ French
28 | 28 | 28 | $254

Flatiron | 11 Madison Ave. (24th St.) | 212-889-0905 |
www.elevenmadisonpark.com

For years now, chef-owner Daniel Humm has been producing "flawless" New French cooking at this Madison Square Park "temple of fine
dining", where "stunning", "deceptively simple" dishes are served
with "Swiss precision" in a "gorgeous", high-ceilinged setting; a recent
menu change will add elements of showmanship like card tricks and
glass domes filled with smoke.

Four Seasons ⊠ American
27 | 28 | 27 | $102

E 50s | 99 E. 52nd St. (bet. Lexington & Park Aves.) | 212-754-9494 |
www.fourseasonsrestaurant.com

A "calm oasis" in "throbbing Manhattan", this Midtown "icon" draws
"one-percenters" and "seriously famous" folk with "outstanding" New

Americana ferried by a "meticulous" team overseen by owners Alex von Bidder and Julian Niccolini; the "chic-in-a-'50s-way" setting includes the "luminous" Pool Room (best for romance) and the more power lunch–appropriate Grill Room, but no matter where you sit, wear a jacket and bring your checkbook: this "time-honored tradition" is "predictably expensive."

Gotham Bar & Grill   *American*   28 | 26 | 26 | $84

G Village | 12 E. 12th St. (bet. 5th Ave. & University Pl.) | 212-620-4020 | www.gothambarandgrill.com

A "ritual" for many Gothamites, Alfred Portale's "iconic" Village New American offers "standout" dining via "towering plates" of "glorious food", "stellar" service and a "beautiful", "white-linen" setting; nearly 30 years along, "this star shows no sign of dimming", but if the price tags are too "extravagant", there's always the $25 greenmarket lunch for a special "treat."

Gramercy Tavern   *American*   28 | 26 | 27 | $114

Flatiron | 42 E. 20th St. (bet. B'way & Park Ave. S.) | 212-477-0777 | www.gramercytavern.com

"About as perfect as a restaurant can get", Danny Meyer's Flatiron "standard bearer" remains a "great NY institution" thanks to chef Michael Anthony's "exceptional farm-to-fork" New American cuisine coupled with a "soothing", "elegantly rustic" setting and "superior" service that "runs like a well-oiled machine"; granted, the tabs are "quite dear" in the prix fixe–only main dining room, but the non-reserving front tavern offers "cheaper" à la carte options.

The Grocery ☒Ⓜ   *American*   28 | 18 | 27 | $65

Carroll Gardens | 288 Smith St. (bet. Sackett & Union Sts.) | Brooklyn | 718-596-3335 | www.thegroceryrestaurant.com

"Exquisite", "market-driven" fare "imaginatively" rendered has made this "pricey" Carroll Gardens New American a Smith Street standby, as has the "exceptional" service that makes "every diner feel like a VIP"; ok, the "no-frills", "matchbox"-size interior can get "a little claustrophobic", but the "beautiful backyard" offers more elbow room.

Il Mulino   *Italian*   27 | 20 | 24 | $94

G Village | 86 W. Third St. (bet. Sullivan & Thompson Sts.) | 212-673-3783

Il Mulino Uptown ☒   *Italian*

E 60s | 37 E. 60th St. (bet. Madison & Park Aves.) | 212-750-3270 | www.ilmulino.com

"CEOs", "politicians" and "expense-account"–bearing "suits" pile into this "exceptional" Village Italian that's renowned for its "freebie" appetizer "bacchanalia", followed by mega-portioned, "gold-standard" Abruzzi cooking; "old-school" waiters in "black tie", "outdated" decor, "high prices" and "tough" reservations come with the territory; P.S. an UES satellite near Barneys promises more of the same.

Jean Georges ☒   *French*   28 | 27 | 28 | $140

W 60s | Trump Int'l Hotel | 1 Central Park W. (bet. 60th & 61st Sts.) | 212-299-3900 | www.jean-georges.com

"Special event" dining is alive and well at this "hub" of the Jean-Georges Vongerichten "empire", a "well-oiled machine" where "heavenly" New

French "art on a plate" is dispatched by a team that has service "down to a science"; the "lovely", "light-filled" setting burnishes its "gold-standard" aura, but keep in mind that both jackets and deep pockets are "mandatory" here; P.S. the "superb" $38 prix fixe lunch is a NYC "best bet."

Katz's Delicatessen ⏵ *Deli* | 25 | 11 | 14 | $25 |

LES | 205 E. Houston St. (Ludlow St.) | 212-254-2246 | www.katzdeli.com

"Borscht Belt" dining doesn't get more "authentic" than at this LES Jewish deli that's been supplying "skyscraping" pastrami and corned beef sandwiches since 1888; true, it's "cash only" with "low-frills" decor and service, but ultimately it's a "completely NY experience", best known for the immortal line 'I'll have what she's having' from *When Harry Met Sally.*

Keens Steakhouse *Steak* | 26 | 25 | 24 | $74 |

Garment District | 72 W. 36th St. (bet. 5th & 6th Aves.) | 212-947-3636 | www.keens.com

Representing "old NY at its finest", this Garment District "time-traveler's delight" rolls out "superlative" steaks and "brontosaurus-size" mutton chops in a "historic", circa-1885 setting where "Teddy Roosevelt" would feel at home; a "top-flight" single-malt selection and – count 'em – 88,000 clay pipes on the ceiling add to the "unforgettable" feeling; P.S. it also features notable private party rooms.

La Grenouille ⓩ *French* | 28 | 28 | 28 | $114 |

E 50s | 3 E. 52nd St. (bet. 5th & Madison Aves.) | 212-752-1495 | www.la-grenouille.com

Offering "crème de la crème" haute French dining since 1962, Charles Masson's "unsurpassed" Midtown "bastion" of "indulgence" still provides "ethereal" cuisine served by "flawless" staffers amid "exquisite" surroundings with flowers galore; jackets are de rigueur and naturally, all this "perfection" commands high prices, but the $38 upstairs lunch deal is a steal; P.S. it also features some of NYC's best private-party rooms.

L'Artusi *Italian* | 27 | 23 | 24 | $59 |

W Village | 228 W. 10th St. (bet. Bleecker & Hudson Sts.) | 212-255-5757 | www.lartusi.com

Having mastered *l'art* of being "trendy but welcoming", this "beautiful", "lively" bi-level Village Italian from the Dell'anima folks "packs 'em in" for "delectable" small plates and wines conveyed by "delightful" staffers; despite "high prices" and "off-the-charts" noise, most find it "totally satisfying."

Le Bernardin ⓩ *French/Seafood* | 29 | 28 | 29 | $163 |

W 50s | 155 W. 51st St. (bet. 6th & 7th Aves.) | 212-554-1515 | www.le-bernardin.com

Maguy LeCoze and chef Eric Ripert's "best-in-class" Midtown French "seafood shrine" has once again been voted NYC's Most Popular and No. 1 for Food because it embodies a "commitment to excellence" across the board, e.g. "delicate", "impossibly fresh" fish dishes, "efficient-beyond-belief" staffers and a "glorious", "soothing" setting (including the non-reserving "godsend" of a lounge); the prix fixe–only dinner starts at $125, but "you pay for the extraordinary – and you get it."

The Lion ◗ *American* | 22 | 24 | 21 | $67 |

G Village | 62 W. Ninth St. (bet. 5th & 6th Aves.) | 212-353-8400 | www.thelionnyc.com

Chef-owner John DeLucie conjures "old-school" NY at his "swanky" Village American where a "huge skylight, eclectic art and photos" provide the backdrop for a "happening", "celeb"-centric "scene"; the "homey-yet-upscale" fare takes a backseat to the "exciting" "buzz", but it's "delicious" all the same.

Lucali ⌿ *Pizza* | 27 | 19 | 20 | $27 |

Carroll Gardens | 575 Henry St. (bet. Carroll St. & 1st Pl.) | Brooklyn | 718-858-4086

An "unwavering focus on creating the perfect pie" pays off at this "big-league" BYO Carroll Gardens joint that nabs this year's No. 1 Pizza in NYC crown; devotees gladly endure no rez–induced "long waits" and a cash-only policy, 'cause these "brick-oven" beauties are "all they're cracked up to be."

Marea *Italian/Seafood* | 28 | 26 | 26 | $103 |

W 50s | 240 Central Park S. (bet. B'way & 7th Ave.) | 212-582-5100 | www.marea-nyc.com

Chef Michael White presents an "unforgettable fine-dining experience" at this "world-class" CPS "treasure", once again voted NYC's No. 1 Italian thanks to its "incomparable" seafood and housemade pastas, seamless service and "chic", "modern" environs; it's a "definite splurge" – though it's "equally superb and less costly" at lunch, brunch or at the "gorgeous bar", with "celeb" spottings as a bonus.

Mas (Farmhouse) ◗ *American* | 28 | 25 | 27 | $92 |

W Village | 39 Downing St. (bet. Bedford & Varick Sts.) | 212-255-1790 | www.masfarmhouse.com

"Just gets better and better" declare devotees of chef Galen Zamarra's near-"flawless" West Villager where "simple, fresh, immensely satisfying" New American cuisine and a "polished" yet "warm" staff make you "feel like nobility"; factor in moodily lit quarters "quiet" enough for "intimate conversation", and it makes the "perfect" date place – "if you're in the mood to splurge."

Milos, Estiatorio ◗ *Greek/Seafood* | 27 | 24 | 24 | $87 |

W 50s | 125 W. 55th St. (bet. 6th & 7th Aves.) | 212-245-7400 | www.estiatoriomilos.com

"The freshest, most superbly prepared" seafood is the lure at this "exceptional" Midtown Greek whose "gorgeous" whitewashed setting "brings Santorini to NYC"; unless you stick with the "wonderful" apps, you'd best plan on paying "stratospheric" "by-the-pound" pricing – still, you "can't go wrong" with the lunch and pre-theater prix fixe "bargains."

The Modern 🅐 *American/French* | 26 | 26 | 25 | $127 |

W 50s | Museum of Modern Art | 9 W. 53rd St. (bet. 5th & 6th Aves.) | 212-333-1220 | www.themodernnyc.com

Danny Meyer's MoMA "marvel" presents the "ultimate" in museum dining, with chef Gabriel Kreuther's "work-of-art" French–New American cuisine arriving at table via a "terrific" "pro" staff in "beautiful" Bauhaus-influenced confines; it's divided between a "lively", "casual" front barroom offering "less-expensive" à la carte small plates and a "formal" prix fixe–only back room where the "impressive sculpture garden view" is factored into the bill.

Nobu *Japanese* | 27 | 23 | 24 | $83 |
TriBeCa | 105 Hudson St. (Franklin St.) | 212-219-0500
Nobu 57 ● *Japanese*
W 50s | 40 W. 57th St. (bet. 5th & 6th Aves.) | 212-757-3000
Nobu, Next Door *Japanese*
TriBeCa | 105 Hudson St. (bet. Franklin & N. Moore Sts.) | 212-334-4445
www.noburestaurants.com

"Still going strong", Nobu Matsuhisa's "groundbreaking" 1994 TriBeCa flagship draws a "glitzy crowd" to feast on "delectable" Japanese-Peruvian fare in a "stunning" space designed by David Rockwell and at its "cool little brother" next door; at any of the three you're likely to "bump into someone famous", especially at the "sleek", "sexy" (if "more touristy") Midtown outpost; you can also expect to pay "a pretty penny."

Per Se *American/French* | 29 | 28 | 29 | $325 |
W 60s | Time Warner Ctr. | 10 Columbus Circle, 4th fl. (60th St. at B'way) | 212-823-9335 | www.perseny.com

"Elegance at its apex", this "Thomas Keller sensation" in the Time Warner Center is a jackets-required "epic dining event" where an "intricate" French–New American "symphony" is set against "spectacular" Central Park views and delivered by a "second-to-none" staff (once again voted No. 1 in NYC); the prix fixe runs a "heart-stopping" $295, but "world-class food is worth the cost" – and there are always foodies lining up to sample it.

Peter Luger Steak House ⊄ *Steak* | 27 | 16 | 21 | $83 |
Williamsburg | 178 Broadway (Driggs Ave.) | Brooklyn | 718-387-7400 | www.peterluger.com

The "undisputed" steakhouse "champeen" for "eons", this Williamsburg meat-lover's "Valhalla" is "duly famous" for "magnificent", "perfectly aged" porterhouses and "top-flight" sides that devotees "measure others against"; it's "mad-busy all the time" despite the "notoriously" "gnarly" waiters and "throwback-type" German "barroom" setting, not to mention a "cash or house account"–only policy that requires "raiding the ATM" before making the "pilgrimage."

Picholine Ⓜ *French/Mediterranean* | 27 | 25 | 26 | $103 |
W 60s | 35 W. 64th St. (bet. B'way & CPW) | 212-724-8585 | www.picholinenyc.com

A "timeless classic" for "old-fashioned pampering", Terry Brennan's "top-drawer" Lincoln Center–area "destination" is a "refined" "marriage" of "*magnifique*" French-Med fare (concluding with an "unbelievable" cheese course) and "exemplary service" in a "lovely", "adult" setting; "costly" it is, but it's "worth cracking open the piggy bank" for what is always a satisfying experience; P.S. it's temporarily closed for renovations.

Red Rooster *American* | 23 | 23 | 23 | $51 |
Harlem | 310 Lenox Ave. (bet. 125th & 126th Sts.) | 212-792-9001 | www.redroosterharlem.com

"Creative gastronomy" comes to Harlem via "masterful chef" Marcus Samuelsson with his "spirited" New American "hot spot" serving a "fab" menu ranging from Swedish meatballs to "Southern homestyle cooking" to a "vivacious" "mix of demographics" filling "delightful" digs overseen by "eager" staffers; "pizzazz" aside, there are a few grumbles that the food is "secondary" and the waits "nothing to crow about."

River Café *American*

26 | 28 | 26 | $130

Dumbo | 1 Water St. (bet. Furman & Old Fulton Sts.) | Brooklyn | 718-522-5200 | www.rivercafe.com

The "postcard-ready" Lower Manhattan views "dazzle" at Buzzy O'Keefe's "only-in-NY" Dumbo "landmark", where the "tantalizing" New American cuisine and "superlative" service "live up to" the "picturesque", "floral"-enhanced setting; the $100 dinner prix fixe will run up a "hefty bill", but the "unforgettable" "special-occasion" atmosphere more than "justifies the cost."

Sasabune 🗷 Ⓜ *Japanese*

29 | 11 | 23 | $113

E 70s | 401 E. 73rd St. (bet. 1st & York Aves.) | 212-249-8583

Once again rated "NYC's best for sushi", Kenji Takahashi's "sublime" USE Japanese is known for an "incredible culinary journey" of an omakase menu, featuring "clearly superior" fish, "chosen and cut by absolute experts" and sure to induce "swoons" (ditto the tab); the quarters are "spartan" and the "knowledgeable" staff can be "brisk", but finatics hardly notice.

Saul *American*

27 | 21 | 25 | $66

Boerum Hill | 140 Smith St. (bet. Bergen & Dean Sts.) | Brooklyn | 718-935-9844 | www.saulrestaurant.com

"Wonderful from start to finish", chef Saul Bolton's "superb" Boerum Hill "gem" is lauded for "exquisite" New American cuisine brimming with "compelling flavors"; it's "spendy", but to most it's "worth every penny" given the "wonderful" service and "straightforward" but "pleasant" decor – it's "one of Brooklyn's finest."

Scalinatella ● *Italian*

25 | 18 | 22 | $88

E 60s | 201 E. 61st St., downstairs (3rd Ave.) | 212-207-8280

"Superb" Capri-style dishes draw a moneyed "'in' crowd" to this one-of-a-kind Upper East Side Italian "hideaway", "situated downstairs" in an "intimate" grotto; service is as "impressive" as the "incredible" food, but if your server steers you toward the specials, "be prepared for sticker shock."

Scalini Fedeli 🗷 *Italian*

27 | 25 | 27 | $92

TriBeCa | 165 Duane St. (bet. Greenwich & Hudson Sts.) | 212-528-0400 | www.scalinifedeli.com

"You can taste the passion in every dish" at Michael Cetrulo's "gorgeous" TriBeCa Northern Italian, a "powerhouse" where "vaulted-salon" environs, "remarkable wines" and "exemplary service" add up to a "unforgettable", "romantic" experience; yes, its prix fixe–only dinner is $65, but when the food arrives, "little else matters."

Sripraphai ⊭ *Thai*

27 | 14 | 18 | $27

Woodside | 64-13 39th Ave. (bet. 64th & 65th Sts.) | Queens | 718-899-9599 | www.sripraphairestaurant.com

Once again voted NYC's tops-in-genre, you won't find a more "authentic Thai" than this Woodside "mecca", where some of the dishes are "hot and spicy" enough to rate a "fire extinguisher"; just know that "perfunctory" service, "suburban" decor and no rez-induced "long waits" are part of the "incredible bargain."

Sushi Seki ●🖸 *Japanese*

28 | 14 | 22 | $79

E 60s | 1143 First Ave. (bet. 62nd & 63rd Sts.) | 212-371-0238
"Master" chef Seki "does spectacular things with fish" at this "top-notch" East Side Japanese – "you can't go wrong" with his "sublime" omakase; "solid" service helps temper stiff tabs and "tight" quarters – and the 2:30 AM closing time can't be beat.

Sushi Yasuda 🖸 *Japanese*

28 | 22 | 24 | $89

E 40s | 204 E. 43rd St. (bet. 2nd & 3rd Aves.) | 212-972-1001 | www.sushiyasuda.com
Despite losing its eponymous chef, this "stunning" Grand Central-area Japanese standout is still serving sushi that's among "NYC's best"; equally "flawless" service in "simple" blond-wood digs help justify the "expensive" tabs – though the $23 dinner prix fixe "may be the best deal" in town.

Tocqueville 🖸 *American/French*

27 | 26 | 26 | $83

Union Sq | 1 E. 15th St. (bet. 5th Ave. & Union Sq. W.) | 212-647-1515 | www.tocquevillerestaurant.com
A "civilized oasis" off Union Square, this "elegant, understated" French-New American presents the "genius" cuisine of chef Marco Moreira via a "flawless" team that has patrons feeling "like royalty"; yes, it's "expensive", but it's "the place" for a very "special occasion", and the $29 prix fixe lunch is a "steal."

Torrisi Italian Specialties *Italian*

27 | 19 | 23 | $78

NoLita | 250 Mulberry St. (bet. Prince & Spring Sts.) | 212-965-0955 | www.torrisinyc.com
"Now that it takes reservations", there's "no excuse not to go" to this NoLita "standout" that "lives up to the hype" with its "clever, delightful" takes on the Italian-American classics "mom made", offered in a seven-course, $65 prix fixe–only format; the basic digs are "tiny", but "nimble" staffers keep the feel "friendly"; P.S. it's dinner-only, but its next-door sibling, Parm, does lunch.

21 Club 🖸 *American*

24 | 25 | 25 | $74

W 50s | 21 W. 52nd St. (bet. 5th & 6th Aves.) | 212-582-7200 | www.21club.com
Bringing the "glory of yesteryear to the modern day", this "timeless" Midtown "sentimental favorite" parlays *Mad Men*–era dining via a "man's-man" American menu, eclectic "memorabilia hanging from the ceiling" and "efficient, unobtrusive" service from "career waiters"; jackets are required, as is a full wallet – though the $35 prix fixe lunch is a true "bargain"; "extraordinary private rooms" upstairs ice the cake.

Union Square Cafe *American*

27 | 23 | 26 | $71

Union Sq | 21 E. 16th St. (bet. 5th Ave. & Union Sq. W.) | 212-243-4020 | www.unionsquarecafe.com
"Danny Meyer's original flagship" in Union Square has locked up "forever-favorite" status, accruing perennial "accolades" for its "expertly prepared" "Greenmarket"-driven New American cuisine, "affable,

	FOOD	DECOR	SERVICE	COST

unpretentious" service and "subdued, stylish" digs; the experience is "worth every penny", and while scoring a rez "isn't always easy", you can always "eat at the bar."

Waverly Inn ◐ *American*   22 | 24 | 21 | $67

W Village | 16 Bank St. (Waverly Pl.) | 917-828-1154

Maybe "the celebrity buzz has slowed", but Graydon Carter's "clubby", historic West Village American remains a "lively scene" where "beautiful" types nibble "high-end spins" on "home-cooking" favorites; some say its "elegant", "fireplace"-enhanced confines (complete with Edward Sorel mural) even exude a "neighborly charm" of late – fortunately the neighbors are mostly well-off.

Orange County, CA

TOP FOOD RANKING

Restaurant	Cuisine
29 Bluefin	Japanese
Marché Moderne	French
28 Basilic	French/Swiss
Blake's Place	BBQ
Gabbi's Mexican	Mexican
Park Ave	American
27 Il Barone	Italian
La Sirena*	Mexican
Napa Rose	Californian
Ramos House	American

OTHER NOTEWORTHY PLACES

Anaheim White House	Italian
Broadway by Amar Santana	American
Charlie Palmer	American
In-N-Out	Burgers
Mastro's Ocean	Seafood/Steak
Ranch	American
South of Nick's	Mexican
3Thirty3 Waterfront	American
21 Oceanfront	Seafood
230 Forest Avenue	Californian

Anaheim White House *Italian*   `25` `24` `25` `$57`
Anaheim | 887 S. Anaheim Blvd. (Vermont Ave.) | 714-772-1381 | www.anaheimwhitehouse.com
"The staff treats you like royalty" at this "regal" Anaheim landmark "just down the road from the land of Mickey and Donald", where chef-owner Bruno Serato is lauded for both his "beautifully pre-pared" Italian fare and community work with needy kids; critics may find the decor "dated" and "stuffy", but an "older clientele" appreciates the "formal" yet "festive" ambiance that makes it "great for celebrations."

Basilic 🚫 Ⓜ *French/Swiss*   `28` `22` `27` `$53`
Newport Beach | 217 Marine Ave. (Park Ave.) | 949-673-0570 | www.basilicrestaurant.com
Intrepid eaters say "you'll never forget" the "superb", "pricey" French-Swiss cuisine that "deserves its reputation" at this "hard-to-find" Balboa Island "jewel box" overseen by chef-owner Bernard Althaus; a "thoughtful" wine selection, "wonderful" service and a "quaint, ro-mantic" atmosphere are further assets, though since it only seats 24 people, "definitely make reservations"; P.S. "Raclette Night is a must-do."

---

* Indicates a tie with restaurant above

Blake's Place *BBQ*

28 | 19 | 25 | $15

Anaheim | 2905 E. Miraloma Ave. (N. Red Gum St.) | 714-630-8574 | www.blakesplacebbq.com

This "bustling local favorite" in Anaheim has an "IQ for BBQ" say carnivores who "crave" its "tender" brisket and ribs with "real wood-smoke pit flavor", slathered in "incredible" sauce and conveyed by an "on-the-ball" crew; those indulging off-site say it's "even better as take-out" and the catering's "well worth it."

Bluefin *Japanese*

29 | 23 | 26 | $53

Newport Coast | Crystal Cove Promenade | 7952 E. PCH (Reef Point Dr.) | 949-715-7373 | www.bluefinbyabe.com

"Way beyond a sushi bar", this "busy" Newport Coast Japanese – voted Orange County's No. 1 for Food – showcases chef-owner Takashi Abe's "phenomenal" fish and other "yummy" creations for a mostly local clientele; the "fast" service and "fabulous", waterfall-enhanced modern decor make the most of the Crystal Cove Promenade space, and though some think it's "pricey", the omakase lunch is still a "deal."

Broadway by
Amar Santana ● *American/Eclectic*

26 | 27 | 29 | $57

Laguna Beach | 328 Glenneyre St. (Forest Ave.) | 949-715-8234 | www.broadwaybyamarsantana.com

"Laguna Beach has a new star" in chef-owner Amar Santana's "swanky", Manhattan-themed New American–Eclectic "oasis" – rated tops for Service in OC – where an "impeccable" staff ferries tasting menus and small plates (plus "unique" cocktails and a Cal-heavy wine list) into the night while navigating a "lively" space featuring chef's-table seats overlooking the kitchen; costs are proportionate, and some cite a "noisy" scene, but to most, it's "raised the bar."

Charlie Palmer at Bloomingdale's
South Coast Plaza *American*

22 | 25 | 23 | $62

Costa Mesa | South Coast Plaza | 3333 Bristol St. (Anton Blvd.) | 714-352-2525 | www.charliepalmer.com

When the "beautiful" people crave a "classy respite" from South Coast Plaza, Charlie Palmer's "elegant" New American comes through with an "inventive and delicious" menu served amid "soothing", "modern decor"; "top-notch" service adds to the "highly civilized" air that suits "expense accounts", while shallow pockets adore the "bargain"-priced "three course lunch." P.S. oenophiles can take home bottles from the "incredible" wine list at the adjacent Next Vintage shop.

Gabbi's Mexican Kitchen *Mexican*

28 | 24 | 23 | $33

Orange | 141 S. Glassell St. (bet. Almond & Chapman Aves.) | 714-633-3038 | www.gabbipatrick.com

Those "in the know" head to this upmarket, "rustic" hacienda (with "no sign outside") for the "haute" side of Mexican cuisine in Old Town Orange, where the "next-level" plates by chef/co-owner Gabbi Patrick are not only "delightful" but "works of art", and the desserts are "delicious" too; long waits are "accurate indicators" of its popularity, and while it's slightly "pricey" for the genre, guests assure "you'll go away loving every bit."

	FOOD	DECOR	SERVICE	COST

Il Barone Ristorante 🖾 *Italian* — 27 | 22 | 24 | $41

Newport Beach | 4251 Martingale Way (Corinthian Way) | 949-955-2755 | www.ilbaroneristorante.com

The "chef's specials" alone are "well worth the drive" to this Newport Beach Italian where presiding couple chef Franco Barone and manager Donatella Barone treat guests to "superb", slightly "pricey" fare in a "lovely" ambiance; given the "warm, gracious hospitality" and "over-the-top" service, fans say it's "spot-on" when you're "celebrating."

In-N-Out Burger ● *Burgers* — 26 | 16 | 23 | $10

Costa Mesa | 594 W. 19th St. (bet. Anaheim & Maple Aves.)
Huntington Beach | 18062 Beach Blvd. (Talbert Ave.)
Laguna Niguel | 27380 La Paz Rd. (Avila Rd.)
Tustin | Tustin Mktpl. | 3020 El Camino Real (Jamboree Rd.)
800-786-1000 | www.in-n-out.com

"The double-double animal style is the eighth wonder of the world" proclaims the "fanatical following" of this "iconic" burger chain, perfecting "what fast food should be" with its "simple", "mind-blowing" patties and "real shakes" served in bright "vintage" settings manned by a "smiling", "organized" team; no visit to Southern California is complete "without a stop", now "if only there were a way to make the lines shorter."

La Sirena Grill *Mexican* — 27 | 17 | 22 | $18

Irvine | 3931 Portola Pkwy. (Culver Dr.) | 714-508-8226
Laguna Beach | 347 Mermaid St. (Park Ave.) | 949-497-8226 🖾
www.lasirenagrill.com

"Eat without the guilt" at this casual "fresh-Mex" chainlet offering "bold takes" on the classics crafted from local, organic and sustainable ingredients like a "not-to-be-missed" blackened-salmon burrito; though the tabs are higher than the competition, allies appreciate the "quality" eats as well as the "friendly" crew that dishes it out; P.S. the Laguna Beach location has outdoor seating only.

Marché Moderne *French* — 29 | 25 | 27 | $61

Costa Mesa | South Coast Plaza | 3333 Bristol St. (Anton Blvd.) | 714-434-7900 | www.marchemoderne.net

"*C'est magnifique!*"exclaim fans of this "expensive" "gem" in South Coast Plaza (OC's Most Popular restaurant) featuring such "exquisite" French fare – from "decadent" classics to "inventive" small plates – that "you almost want a reverse gastric banding so you can eat the entire menu"; add in a "charming" staff and "gorgeous" setting with a patio and "a view of the Christian Louboutin store across the way", and "what more could you ask for?"; P.S. the three-course prix fixe lunch is a "flat-out steal."

Mastro's Ocean Club *Seafood/Steak* — 26 | 26 | 23 | $78

Newport Coast | Crystal Cove Promenade | 8112 E. PCH (Reef Point Dr.) | 949-376-6910 | www.mastrosrestaurants.com

"If you're going to 'do it up', do it here" at this "flashy" "high-end" Crystal Cove chophouse where "excellent" steaks and seafood are paired with "appropriately old-school service and strong martinis" in luxe digs packed with "beautiful people"; it's a tad "superficial" to some, and "unless your bank account is in the six figures" it can be way "too expensive" to boot; P.S. don't miss the serious "pick-up action" at the bar.

| | FOOD | DECOR | SERVICE | COST |

Napa Rose *Californian* 27 | 26 | 28 | $68

Anaheim | Disney's Grand Californian Hotel & Spa | 1600 S. Disneyland Dr. (bet. Ball Rd. & Katella Ave.) | 714-300-7170 | www.disneyland.com
Offering an "elegant escape" within the Disneyland theme park, this "special-occasion" dining room spotlights Andrew Sutton's "breathtaking" seasonal Californian cuisine and "amazing" wines from "the best list within a walk of the Matterhorn"; the Craftsman-style setting boasts "exceptional" service and a surprisingly "kid-friendly" vibe – just "bring two checkbooks" to foot the bill.

Park Ave Ⓜ *American* 28 | 24 | 27 | $41

Stanton | 11200 Beach Blvd. (bet. Katella & Orangewood Aves.) | 714-901-4400 | www.parkavedining.com
A "gem" in Stanton, this "sophisticated" American from David Slay supplies "simple comfort food done perfectly", crafted from "fresh" ingredients from the "lovely" garden out back and matched with "phenomenal" cocktails; adding to the charm is the "swank" "midcentury Googie setting", "superb" hospitality and "reasonable" pricing.

Ramos House Café Ⓜ *American* 27 | 24 | 25 | $38

San Juan Capistrano | 31752 Los Rios St. (Ramos St.) | 949-443-1342 | www.ramoshouse.com
Set in a "beautiful" old cottage on the train tracks in Old San Juan Capistrano, this New American is a "treasure" serving "elaborate", "incredible" Southern-style lunches and brunches from chef John Q. Humphreys, along with massive Bloody Marys on the tree-shaded patio; "knowledgeable" service cements the "pleasurable", albeit "pricey", experience; P.S. the buttermilk biscuits alone are "worth the drive."

The Ranch *American* ∇ 28 | 29 | 28 | $45

Anaheim | 1025 E. Ball Rd. (S. Lewis St.) | 714-687-6336 | www.theranch.com
Fine dining meets "country western" at this "upscale ranch" in Anaheim serving "incredibly creative" rustic American cuisine and "impressive" wines in an abode of dark woods and Texas touches; "yes, it's in an industrial area", but the ambiance and service are "excellent", and it's especially "fun" for a date; P.S. an attached saloon features live and DJ'd country music and dancing Wednesday–Sunday.

South of Nick's *Mexican* ∇ 24 | 24 | 24 | $32

San Clemente | 110 N. El Camino Real (Avenida Del Mar) | 949-481-4545 | www.thenicko.com
One of the latest additions to San Clemente is this sib of Nick's, a redo of a historic Spanish-tiled casita featuring "creative, modern" spins on Mexican classics and a busy bar with an elite list of sipping tequilas; weekend breakfasts are welcome hangover fare.

3Thirty3 Waterfront ◑ *American* 23 | 23 | 21 | $38

Newport Beach | 333 Bayside Dr. (PCH) | 949-673-8464 | www.3thirty3nb.com
This "trendy" Newport Beacher is where "cougars", "sugar daddies" and young ones collide for "tasty" New American small plates and cocktails served against a backdrop of "knock-your-socks-off" waterfront vistas; some quibble about "slow" service and "loud" acoustics, but most don't mind since prices are moderate and it's mostly "about the scene."

	FOOD	DECOR	SERVICE	COST

21 Oceanfront *Seafood*
25 | 23 | 23 | $54

Newport Beach | 2100 W. Oceanfront (21st St.) | 949-673-2100 |
www.21oceanfront.com

"Gorgeous views" of the ocean set the scene at this lavish, long-established Newport Beach seafooder where "superb" servers ferry "fabulous" fish and steaks to a deep-pocketed crowd; although a few find fault with the "old-school" looks and "no-surprises" menu, on the whole most deem it "worth a try" for a "special occasion."

230 Forest Avenue *Californian*
25 | 20 | 22 | $42

Laguna Beach | 230 Forest Ave. (PCH) | 949-494-2545 |
www.230forestavenue.com

Chef-owner Marc Cohen's "lively" Californian in the heart of Laguna Beach is "frequented by locals" and tourists who come for the "unique", "delicious" menu abetted by "top-notch" service and "great people-watching" in "trendy" surroundings; despite the "cramped quarters" ("be prepared to sit in the laps of the couple next to you"), "fair prices" make it a "winner."

Orlando

TOP FOOD RANKING

	Restaurant	Cuisine
29	Cress	Eclectic
	Victoria & Albert's	American
28	Nagoya Sushi	Japanese
	Chatham's Place	Continental
	Norman's*	New World
	Christner's Del Frisco's	Steak
	Viet Garden	Thai/Vietnamese
	Jiko – The Cooking Place	African
	Texas de Brazil	Brazilian
	Lee & Rick's Oyster Bar	Seafood
27	Ruth's Chris	Steak
	Seito Sushi	Japanese
	Pho 88	Vietnamese
	4 Rivers Smokehouse	BBQ
	Prato	Italian
	The Palm	Steak
	Black Bean Deli	Cuban
	Fleming's Prime	Steak
	Ming Bistro	Chinese
	Capital Grille	Steak

OTHER NOTEWORTHY PLACES

Bahama Breeze	Caribbean
Boma	African
Bosphorous	Turkish
Charley's	Steak
Cheesecake Factory	American
Chef's Table at Edgewater	American
Christini's Ristorante	Italian
Dragonfly	Japanese
Enzo's Restaurant	Italian
Flying Fish Café	Seafood
K Restaurant	American
Luma on Park	American
Primo	Italian/Mediterranean
Roy's	Hawaiian
Rusty Spoon	American
Sanaa	African/Indian
Seasons 52	American
Todd English's Bluezoo	Seafood
Venetian Room	Continental
Vines Grille & Wine Bar	Steak

* Indicates a tie with restaurant above

ORLANDO

	FOOD	DECOR	SERVICE	COST

Bahama Breeze M *Caribbean* | 24 | 25 | 24 | $29 |

International Drive | 8849 International Dr. (Austrian Row) |
407-248-2499 ●
East Orlando | 1200 N. Alafaya Trail (Ashton Manor Way) |
407-658-6770
Lake Buena Vista | 8735 Vineland Ave. (Apopka Vineland Rd.) |
407-938-9010
Altamonte Springs | Altamonte Mall | 499 E. Altamonte Dr.
(Palm Springs Dr.) | 407-831-2929
Kissimmee | 8160 W. Irlo Bronson Memorial Hwy. (Orange Lake Rd.) |
407-390-0353
www.bahamabreeze.com

"Step away from the everyday" at this "top-quality" chain – voted Most
Popular in the Orlando survey – where the "music will whisk you to the
islands" and the "fruity" tropical cocktails, "delicious" Caribbean
cooking and "beautiful" "resort"-like surroundings will keep you there;
the "prices are reasonable" and "service is usually attentive", making
the fittingly "breezy" atmosphere that much more "enjoyable."

Black Bean Deli ⊠ *Cuban* | 27 | 13 | 23 | $11 |

Winter Park | 325 S. Orlando Ave. (Fairview Ave.) | 407-628-0294 |
www.blackbeandeli.com

For "Cuban done right", diners point to this Winter Park "hole-in-the-
wall" where the "kitchen creates miracles", sending out "outstanding"
fare, including some of the "best black beans" (of course); it's an
"excellent value for the dollar", and since the "tiny" digs have limited
seating, most suggest you "get it to go", adding "timely" service makes it
"delicious for a quickie."

Boma – Flavors of Africa *African* | 27 | 27 | 26 | $39 |

Animal Kingdom Area | Disney's Animal Kingdom Lodge |
2901 Osceola Pkwy. (Sherberth Rd.) | Lake Buena Vista |
407-938-4722 | www.disneyworld.com

"You can eat yourself into a coma" at this "popular" "fine-dining
buffet" set in the Animal Kingdom Lodge, where the "wide assort-
ment of African delicacies", like "wonderful roasted meats", "outstanding vegetarian options" and "some of the best desserts at
Disney", features "loads of unusual spices and flavors"; also cementing its "must-do" status are "excellent" service and "realisti-
cally themed", marketlike surroundings that add to the "feeling of
being in Africa."

Bosphorous Turkish Cuisine *Turkish* | 25 | 23 | 21 | $30 |

Bay Hill/Dr. Phillips | The Marketplace | 7600 Dr. Phillips Blvd.
(Sand Lake Rd.) | 407-352-6766 | www.anatoliaorlando.com
Winter Park | 108 S. Park Ave. (Morse Blvd.) | 407-644-8609 |
www.bosphorousrestaurant.com

"Save the airfare to Istanbul" and head instead to this moderate Winter
Park Turkish (with a new Dr. Phillips sequel), where the "delicious",
"well-prepared" fare, like "incredible", "puffy" lavosh bread and "or-
gasmically good" hummus, is "perfect for sharing"; the casual dining
room is pleasant, and sidewalk seating is "nice too", so though
"friendly" service can be "somewhat slow", fans suggest you simply
appreciate that there's "no rush."

	FOOD	DECOR	SERVICE	COST

The Capital Grille *Steak* 27 | 25 | 26 | $70

International Drive | Pointe Orlando | 9101 International Dr.
(Pointe Plaza Ave.) | 407-370-4392 | www.thecapitalgrille.com
"Done-to-perfection" steaks and "well-prepared sides" result in "deliciously crafted meals" at this "special-occasion" chophouse chain link in International Drive; "professional" service and "classy surroundings" further make it "upscale in every regard", so "expense-account" tabs are to be expected.

Charley's Steak House *Steak* 26 | 23 | 25 | $59

International Drive | 8255 International Dr. (Sand Lake Rd.) | 407-363-0228
Kissimmee | 2901 Parkway Blvd. (Irlo Bronson Memorial Hwy.) | 407-239-1270

Charley's Wildfire Grille *Steak*

South Orlando | 6107 S. Orange Blossom Trail (bet. Lancaster & Oak Ridge Rds.) | 407-851-7130
www.charleyssteakhouse.com
"Come hungry" to this chophouse triumvirate where the "cooked-to-perfection" cuts are "as tender as butter" and served in portions so "huge" you'll leave "feeling stuffed"; "the staff delivers on service even when stretched thin", and "classy", white-tablecloth surrounds boost the "special-occasion" appeal, all of which makes "expensive" tabs easier to digest; P.S. the Orlando branch has been reconcepted into Charley's Wildfire Grille, offering a smaller but less pricey menu in a brighter setting.

Chatham's Place ⊠ *Continental* 28 | 24 | 27 | $61

Bay Hill/Dr. Phillips | 7575 Dr. Phillips Blvd. (Sand Lake Rd.) | 407-345-2992 | www.chathamsplace.com
A "charming little hideaway", this spendy Dr. Phillips Continental is "well attended by locals" who savor "carefully prepared", "top-notch" dishes featuring produce from the chef's own garden and enjoy wine from an "excellent selection"; "impeccable" service and a "classy", "romantic" dining room further justify its status as an "all-time favorite."

Cheesecake Factory *American* 25 | 24 | 24 | $30

Millenia | Mall at Millenia | 4200 Conroy Rd. (Millenia Blvd.) | 407-226-0333
Winter Park | Winter Park Village | 520 N. Orlando Ave. (Gay Rd.) | 407-644-4220
www.thecheesecakefactory.com
"Bring your appetite and your sweet tooth" to these "moderately priced" chain link twins in Millenia and Winter Park best known for "enormous portions (think tomorrow's lunch")" of "delicious", "well-seasoned" fare off a "huge, book-size menu"; "dependable" service and an "upbeat", "inviting" scene – plus "out-of-this-world" cheesecake, of course – help most overlook "noisy" conditions and "huge waits to get in."

Chef's Table at the Edgewater Hotel & Tasting Room ⊠Ⓜ *American* 28 | 23 | 28 | $84

Winter Garden | Edgewater Hotel | 99 W. Plant St. (bet. Boyd & Main Sts.) | 407-230-4837 | www.chefstableattheedgewater.com
A "true dining experience" awaits at this "quaint" Winter Garden New American where chef Kevin Tarter "describes all menu items table-

side" and "puts his heart" into the "outstanding" seasonal prix fixes; his sommelier wife Laurie adds even more "personal touches" and service is "astonishingly good" overall, so fans suggest you "settle in" and "plan to spend several hours" enjoying an "intimate" meal; P.S. the adjoining Tasting Room is a less costly alternative with small plates and a "great bar."

Christini's Ristorante Italiano *Italian*   26 | 23 | 25 | $71
Bay Hill/Dr. Phillips | The Marketplace | 7600 Dr. Phillips Blvd. (Sand Lake Rd.) | 407-345-8770 | www.christinis.com
After more than 25 years this Dr. Phillips Italian still "doesn't miss a beat", turning out "excellent" "traditional favorites" in "charming" marble-accented surrounds with a "grown-up" vibe; "attentive" service garners praise too, and while a few critics contend it's "overpriced and overrated", more say you're in for a "fantastic experience" – just "be prepared to drop a bundle."

Christner's Del Frisco's Prime Steak &   28 | 23 | 26 | $65
Lobster ⊠ *Steak*
Winter Park | 729 Lee Rd. (Alloway St.) | 407-645-4443 | www.delfriscosorlando.com
"Top-of-the-line" say fans bedazzled by the "high-quality", "mouthwatering" cuts "served on a sizzling plate" at this "popular" Winter Park chophouse also known for its "prime" lobster, "expansive" wine list and "old-fashioned", "supper club"–like surrounds; with "first-class" service, "expense-account" tabs are a given, so many suggest saving it for "when you want to impress someone."

Cress ⊠ Ⓜ *Eclectic*   29 | 26 | 28 | $41
Deland | 103 W. Indiana Ave. (Cypress Ave.) | 386-734-3740 | www.cressrestaurant.com
"Incredible talent" Hari Pulapaka ("geeky math professor" by day, chef-owner by night) "never fails to delight" at this "rare jewel in Deland", wowing with "innovative" "globally inspired" cooking that highlights "crazy refined flavors" and earns No. 1 Food honors in the Orlando area; servers who "know their menu" work the "intimate", "romantic" space, and while it's not cheap, it's labeled "one of the best" around.

Dragonfly *Japanese*   27 | 26 | 24 | $38
Bay Hill/Dr. Phillips | Dellagio Plaza | 7972 Via Dellagio Way (Della Dr. & Sand Lake Rd.) | 407-370-3359 | www.dragonflysushi.com
"Mingle with the hip crowd" at this Japanese izakaya on Dr. Phillips' Restaurant Row that "hits the spot" with a "variety" of "interesting" "tapas-style" dishes, including "excellent sushi rolls" and "flavorful" specialties from the robata grill; "modern" environs with cork floors and dark wood tables appeal, as does generally "attentive" service, and though what's "reasonable" to some is "expensive" to others, all appreciate the "great happy hour."

Enzo's Restaurant on the Lake ⊠ Ⓜ *Italian*   27 | 24 | 26 | $49
Longwood | 1130 U.S. 17 (bet. Laura St. & Wildmere Ave.) | 407-834-9872 | www.enzos.com
"Upscale dining with down-home flavors" sums up this "romantic" Longwood "fixture", a "wonderful celebration place" that "captures

the essence of Italian cuisine" in "excellent" cooking from a "kitchen that doesn't seem capable of sending out a bad meal"; "friendly yet professional servers" further sweeten the "scenic" lakeside setting, making "pricey" tabs less than surprising.

Fleming's Prime Steakhouse & Wine Bar *Steak*

| 27 | 25 | 27 | $63 |

Bay Hill/Dr. Phillips | Dellagio Plaza | 8030 Via Dellagio Way (Della Dr. & Sand Lake Rd.) | 407-352-5706
Winter Park | 933 N. Orlando Ave. (Lee Rd.) | 407-699-9463
www.flemingssteakhouse.com

Diners "indulge" in "top-notch" steaks and one of the "best burgers in town" at this "reliable" Dr. Phillips and Winter Park chophouse chain duo, where a "modern" and "less stodgy" vibe makes it a "far hipper destination" than some of its kin; "professional, friendly" service adds to the "high-end" experience, and if tabs seem too "expensive", "try the bar menu for a lower-priced option."

Flying Fish Café *Seafood*

| 26 | 24 | 26 | $57 |

Epcot Area | Disney's BoardWalk Inn | 2101 Epcot Resorts Blvd. (Buena Vista Dr.) | Lake Buena Vista | 407-939-3463 | www.disneyworld.com

An "oasis in the middle of chaos", this spendy Disney BoardWalk sea-fooder has diners "flying high" with "innovative", "well-prepared" plates, including the "memorable" potato-wrapped snapper, plus "se-lections for landlubbers" too; also winning praise are "experienced", "accommodating" staffers who "add to the evening" and a "welcoming (if sometimes noisy) atmosphere."

4 Rivers Smokehouse ⊠ *BBQ*

| 27 | 20 | 24 | $19 |

Longwood | Longwood Village Shopping Ctr. | 1869 W. State Rd. 434 (bet. Raymond Ave. & Springwood Circle) | 407-474-8377
Winter Garden | Tri-City Shopping Ctr. | 1047 S. Dillard St. (Colonial Dr.) | 407-474-8377
Winter Park | 1600 W. Fairbanks Ave. (Formosa Ave.) | 407-474-8377
www.4rsmokehouse.com

'Cue fans "go gaga" over the "heavenly" Texas-style BBQ at this counter-serve trio, an Orlando-area "sensation" thanks to "humongous" por-tions of "smoked-to-perfection brisket", "simply divine" pulled pork and a "variety of delicious sides" all washed down with "retro sodas" ("no booze"); yes, "lines can be long" and it's often "crowded", but "reasonable" tabs and "gracious" service help, so most still give it a "definite thumbs-up."

Jiko – The Cooking Place *African*

| 28 | 28 | 28 | $59 |

Animal Kingdom Area | Disney's Animal Kingdom Lodge | 2901 Osceola Pkwy. (Sherberth Rd.) | Lake Buena Vista | 407-938-4733 | www.disneyworld.com

The "diverse", "African-inspired specialties" are "crazy good" say fans of this "must-visit" in Disney's Animal Kingdom Lodge, where the of-ferings are "exotic enough to be original" but still "accessible" enough for "picky eaters" and are augmented by a "fantastic" South African-focused wine list; a wall that "changes colors like a sunset" makes the "beautifully designed", "transportive setting" "even more magical", and service is "terrific" too, so it comes "highly recommended" – "if you have the money", of course.

K Restaurant 🖾 *American* | 26 | 21 | 24 | $49 |

College Park | 1710 Edgewater Dr. (bet. New Hampshire & Yates Sts.) | 407-872-2332

"Creative", "cleanly crafted" plates prepared with "locally sourced ingredients" (including some from the backyard garden) result in a "joy-of-eating experience" at this College Park New American from "experimental" chef-owner Kevin Fonzo; the "remodeled house" setting is "inviting", and "attentive" staffers make even out-of-towners "feel like they live in the neighborhood", so "high" prices don't deter devotees who vow they'll "definitely be back."

Lee & Rick's
Oyster Bar *Seafood* | 28 | 12 | 24 | $26 |

Kirkman Road | 5621 Old Winter Garden Rd. (Kirkman Rd.) | 407-293-3587 | www.leeandricksoysterbar.com

"Food of the gods" comes in the form of "awesome" "shucked-to-order" oysters at this Kirkman Road seafooder, where diners who "sit at the concrete bar" are rewarded by "buckets (that's right, buckets)" of the bivalves (served by the dozen at tables) and the opportunity to "BS" with the "friendly" staffers; "don't get dressed up" because the "dive" digs have "all the charm of a men's washroom", but hey, "that's how they keep the numbers manageable."

Luma on Park *American* | 25 | 27 | 25 | $48 |

Winter Park | 290 S. Park Ave. (bet. Lyman & New England Aves.) | 407-599-4111 | www.lumaonpark.com

A "chic", "ultramodern" dining room with a "buzzy atmosphere" provides the backdrop for "innovative", "beautifully crafted" New American plates at this "high-end" Winter Park "hot spot", where the "always changing" seasonal menu gets a boost from "delicious" cocktails and an "extensive wine list"; add in "knowledgeable" staffers who make you their "number-one priority" and it's no surprise many make it a "special-occasion" destination.

Ming Bistro *Chinese* | 27 | 14 | 21 | $19 |

Mills 50 | 1212 Woodward St. (Colonial Dr.) | 407-898-9672
"Hungry locals" converge on this Mills 50 Chinese for "incredible" "authentic" fare, including some of "the best dim sum in town"; the "minimal" decor verges on "shabby", but "service is pleasant", and with "easy-on-the-wallet" tabs, most leave "with smiles on their faces."

Nagoya Sushi *Japanese* | 28 | 22 | 26 | $35 |

Bay Hill/Dr. Phillips | The Marketplace | 7600 Dr. Phillips Blvd. (Sand Lake Rd.) | 407-248-8558
Winter Springs | Willa Springs Shopping Ctr. | 5661 Red Bug Lake Rd. (Tuskawilla Rd.) | 407-478-3388 🖾 Ⓜ
www.nagoyasushi.com

"Don't give up" trying to locate this "hard-to-find" Dr. Phillips Japanese (with a Winter Springs sib) advise admirers who say the reward is "fresh", "outstanding sushi and bento" "well served" by "friendly" staffers; moderate tabs are a further plus, so the only complaint is that the "hole-in-the-wall" digs seem a bit "too small" given its "popularity."

Norman's New World
28 | 27 | 28 | $94

South Orlando | Ritz-Carlton Grande Lakes | 4012 Central Florida Pkwy. (John Young Pkwy.) | 407-393-4333 | www.normans.com

"Impeccable" service will make you "feel like a queen" at this high-end dining room in South Orlando's "impressive" Ritz-Carlton Grande Lakes where chef Norman Van Aken sends out "exquisite" New World cuisine; elegant, marble-walled surroundings further contribute to the "world-class" experience, making it easy to "forget Mickey, Donald and a million screaming kids are just a few blocks away."

The Palm Steak
27 | 24 | 26 | $71

Universal Orlando | Hard Rock Hotel | 5800 Universal Blvd. (Major Blvd.) | 407-503-7256 | www.thepalm.com

"Tender" "perfectly cooked" chops, "juicy" lobsters and some of the "best cocktails in town" bring an "upper-crust" crowd to this "high-end" NY-based steakhouse set in Universal's Hard Rock Hotel; the caricature-enhanced space has a "pleasant atmosphere" and the "attentive" staff is there when "you want to be pampered", so it fits the bill on "splurge nights."

Pho 88 Vietnamese
27 | 16 | 21 | $16

Mills 50 | 730 N. Mills Ave. (Park Lake St.) | 407-897-3488 | www.pho88orlando.com

"Authentic" offerings mean there's "no faux pho" at this Mills 50 Vietnamese say fans cheering the "kick-butt" eats; the casual space may not inspire the same praise, but service gets few complaints, and with "wallet-friendly" prices, it's considered an overall "find."

Prato Italian
27 | 28 | 26 | $37

Winter Park | 124 N. Park Ave. (Morse Blvd.) | 407-262-0050 | www.prato-wp.com

The "meatballs deserve a standing ovation" rave fans of this "beautifully decorated" Park Avenue Italian that's heralded as one of the "best new restaurants in Winter Park" for its "hearty, rustic" "foodie cuisine"; the "cool, hip atmosphere" makes it feel like a "real Manhattan-style joint", service gets high marks too and with approachable prices, it's quickly becoming a "favorite."

Primo Italian/Mediterranean
28 | 24 | 26 | $63

South Orlando | JW Marriott Grande Lakes | 4040 Central Florida Pkwy. (John Young Pkwy.) | 407-393-4444 | www.grandelakes.com

"Not a typical hotel restaurant" attest admirers of this "upscale" Italian-Med inside South Orlando's JW Marriott Grande Lakes, where the "excellent", "inventively prepared" cuisine highlights local ingredients; further incentives include a "warm, knowledgeable" staff and "beautiful" Tuscan-style dining room, leaving some wondering why "no one seems to know about it."

Roy's Hawaiian
27 | 26 | 27 | $54

Bay Hill/Dr. Phillips | Plaza Venezia | 7760 W. Sand Lake Rd. (bet. Della Dr. & Dr. Phillips Blvd.) | 407-352-4844 | www.roysrestaurant.com

"Aloha at its finest" can be found at this Restaurant Row link in Roy Yamaguchi's upscale Hawaiian chain, a "special-event favorite" that "never disappoints", from the "flavorful" and "innovative" fusion fare to the "gracious", "accommodating" staffers; sure, it's "on the pricey side", but the "festive", "friendly atmosphere" helps ease the pain.

Rusty Spoon *American* | 25 | 22 | 25 | $36 |

Downtown Orlando | 55 W. Church St. (Orange Ave.) | 407-401-8811 | www.therustyspoon.com

"Fine dining without the stuffiness or price" brings chowhounds to this Downtown Orlando gastropub where the "rustic, inspired" New American offerings are made with "local, fresh ingredients"; further pluses include "personable" staffers and a "cozy" earth-toned setting.

Ruth's Chris Steak House *Steak* | 27 | 25 | 26 | $72 |

Bay Hill/Dr. Phillips | Fountains Plaza | 7501 W. Sand Lake Rd. (bet. Dr. Phillips Blvd. & Turkey Lake Rd.) | 407-226-3900
Lake Mary | 80 Colonial Center Pkwy. (County Rd. 46A) | 407-804-8220
Winter Park | Winter Park Vill. | 610 N. Orlando Ave. (Webster Ave.) | 407-622-2444
www.ruthschris.com

"*Magnifique*" proclaim fans of this "special-occasion" chophouse chain known for "melt-in-your-mouth delicious" steaks and a "classy", "clubby atmosphere"; "pampering" service is another part of the package – as are prices considered "reflective" of the "high-class" experience.

Sanaa *African/Indian* | 25 | 26 | 27 | $36 |

Animal Kingdom Area | Disney's Animal Kingdom Villas | 2901 Osceola Pkwy. (Epcot Center Dr.) | Lake Buena Vista | 407-939-3463 | www.disneyworld.com

"Get a seat by the window" for "fantastic views" of the "exotic animals" roaming right outside at this midpriced eatery in Disney's Animal Kingdom Lodge, where the "exciting ambiance" is matched by "well-prepared" African-Indian fare that offers an "adventure in flavors"; "impeccable" service further "adds to the experience", ensuring a "wonderful meal all around."

Seasons 52 *American* | 27 | 26 | 26 | $40 |

Bay Hill/Dr. Phillips | Plaza Venezia | 7700 W. Sand Lake Rd. (bet. Della Dr. & Dr. Phillips Blvd.) | 407-354-5212
Altamonte Springs | 463 E. Altamonte Dr. (Palm Springs Dr.) | 407-767-1252
www.seasons52.com

"Even the most season-ed diners" "rave" about these Dr. Phillips and Altamonte chain links, where the "well-presented" New American dishes are all 475 calories or fewer (including the "perfectly sized" shot-glass sweets) so you can "enjoy a delicious dinner and dessert" "without breaking the nutrition bank"; the "inviting" dining rooms have a "very Frank Lloyd Wright feel" and service is "professional", so even if a few heartier eaters may "want to stop by Burger King on the way home", most deem it a "winner."

Seito Sushi *Japanese* | 27 | 23 | 24 | $33 |

Baldwin Park | 4898 New Broad St. (Jake St.) | 407-898-8801 🖪 Ⓜ
Bay Hill/Dr. Phillips | Phillips Crossing | 8031 Turkey Lake Rd. (Sand Lake Rd.) | 407-248-8888 | www.seitosushi.com

Some of the "freshest sushi and sashimi" is offered alongside "excellent hot dishes" at this "happening" Dr. Phillips Japanese (with a

Baldwin Park twin); "knowledgeable" staffers tend the "trendy", "modern" digs, and while it's not cheap, it's "not crazy expensive" either, all of which makes it pretty "hard to beat."

Texas de Brazil *Brazilian*

28 | 25 | 27 | $63

International Drive | 5259 International Dr. (Touchstone Dr.) | 407-355-0355 | www.texasdebrazil.com
Expect to be "rolled out" of this I-Drive link of the Brazilian churrascaria chain, a "high-end" "meat lovers paradise" where "strolling gauchos" deliver a "never-ending selection" of "deliciously prepared", "mouthwatering" meat "until you scream '*no mas*'"; the "huge", "heavenly" salad bar completes the "pig-out" experience, and while it doesn't come cheap, most are satisfied since you get "lots of food for lots of bucks."

Todd English's Bluezoo *Seafood*

25 | 25 | 24 | $59

Epcot Area | Walt Disney World Swan and Dolphin | 1500 Epcot Resorts Blvd. (Buena Vista Dr.) | Lake Buena Vista | 407-934-1111 | www.thebluezoo.com
A "stunning restaurant with food to match", this "hip" seafooder in Disney World's Dolphin resort wins kudos for its "elegant but not stuffy" setting and "creative", "delicious" offerings from celeb chef Todd English; other pros include "attentive" staffers, an "extensive wine list" and "top-shelf ambiance", all of which help make "expensive" tabs easier to swallow.

Venetian Room Ⓢ Ⓜ *Continental*

28 | 25 | 28 | $85

Lake Buena Vista | Caribe Royale | 8101 World Center Dr. (bet. Apopka Vineland Rd. & International Dr.) | 407-238-8060 | www.thevenetianroom.com
For the "ultimate dining experience", big spenders head to this "hidden jewel" in Lake Buena Vista's Carib Royale Hotel, where "memorable" Continental dishes are "artfully presented" by a team of "first-class" servers; the "romantic" white-tablecloth surroundings further ensure an "elegant" dinner that's just right for "special occasions."

Victoria & Albert's *American*

29 | 28 | 29 | $136

Magic Kingdom Area | Disney's Grand Floridian Resort & Spa | 4401 Floridian Way (bet. Maple Rd. & Seven Seas Dr.) | Lake Buena Vista | 407-939-3862 | www.victoria-alberts.com
A "once-in-a-lifetime experience", this Grand Floridian "celebration destination" earns "superlatives all around", from chef Scott Hunnel's "exquisite", "beautifully presented" New American prix fixes to "impeccable" service – voted No. 1 in Orlando – and an "über-romantic, high-end" setting where "elegance rules" (jackets are required for men); you may "need to hock one of your kids" to pay, but those "trying to impress" say there's "no finer place."

Viet Garden *Vietnamese/Thai*

28 | 16 | 23 | $17

Mills 50 | 1237 E. Colonial Dr. (Shine Ave.) | 407-896-4154 | www.vietgardenorlando.com
Take an "enjoyable adventure" abroad courtesy of "excellent" "traditional" dishes at this Mills 50 Vietnamese-Thai, where highlights include "the best peanut sauce" and "crave"-worthy garden rolls; "plain

surroundings" are boosted by "attentive" servers and it's "well priced", both of which help it "stand out from the competition."

Vines Grille & Wine Bar *Steak* 25 | 24 | 22 | $54

Bay Hill/Dr. Phillips | Fountains Plaza | 7533 W. Sand Lake Rd. (bet. Dr. Phillips Blvd. & Turkey Lake Rd.) | 407-351-1227 | www.vinesgrille.com

"Delicious" steaks and "can't-beat" live music (nightly) make this Dr. Phillips chophouse a "first-rate" choice say regulars also singling out the "great wine selections"; LED fireplaces and dark-wood walls enhance the upscale-casual space, and though it's on the "expensive" side, fans still make it a "standard dining-out place."

	FOOD	DECOR	SERVICE	COST

Palm Beach

TOP FOOD RANKING

	Restaurant	Cuisine
28	Marcello's La Sirena	Italian
	Chez Jean-Pierre	French
27	11 Maple Street	American
	Captain Charlie's	Seafood
	Café L'Europe	Continental
	Casa D'Angelo	Italian
26	Abe & Louie's	Steak
	Trattoria Romana	Italian
	Café Boulud	French
	Chops Lobster Bar	Seafood/Steak

OTHER NOTEWORTHY PLACES

Bonefish Grill	Seafood
Buccan	Eclectic
Café Chardonnay	American
Four Seasons	Seafood
Kee Grill	Seafood/Steak
Little Moir's	Seafood
Max's Harvest	American
Seasons 52	American
32 East	American
Tides	Floridian

Abe & Louie's *Steak*　　26 | 24 | 25 | $66

Boca Raton | 2200 W. Glades Rd. (NW Sheraton Way) | 561-447-0024 | www.abeandlouies.com

The bone-in filet is "as good as it gets" ("you could cut it with a fork"), the "sides are a great match" and the wine list is "impressive" at this Boston-bred beef palace in Boca favored for "power lunches" and "special occasions"; the "clubby" environs are "comfy" and "well managed" by "experienced" pros – "when you have a reservation for 8 PM, you sit down at 8 PM" – so while it costs "big bucks", most feel it delivers big-time.

Bonefish Grill *Seafood*　　22 | 19 | 21 | $36

Stuart | Stuart Ctr. | 2283 SE Federal Hwy. (Monterey Rd.) | 772-288-4388
Lake Worth | 9897 Lake Worth Rd. (Woods Walk Blvd.) | 561-965-2663
Palm Beach Gardens | 11658 U.S. 1 (PGA Blvd.) | 561-799-2965
Boca Raton | Shops at Boca Grove | 21065 Powerline Rd. (bet. Glades Rd. & W. Palmetto Park Rd.) | 561-483-4949
Boynton Beach | 1880 N. Congress Ave. (Gateway Blvd.) | 561-732-1310
www.bonefishgrill.com

"Just-out-of-the-water fish in many forms" "draws droves" to these "delightful", "easygoing" seafooders ("hard to believe it's a chain"); "longish waits, even with a reservation" and "noise" are balanced by "prompt, courteous" service and "competitive prices"; P.S. the "Bang Bang Shrimp is bang-on."

Buccan *Eclectic*

25	23	21	$52

Palm Beach | 350 S. County Rd. (Australian Ave.) | 561-833-3450 | www.buccanpalmbeach.com

"An instant hit", this "utterly hip" Eclectic helmed by Clay Conley (ex Miami's Azul) is "exactly what Palm Beach needed", drawing a "beautiful" "young crowd" that makes it a "zoo on weekend nights"; the mix of "imaginative" small bites (think hot dog panini, bacon-wrapped Florida peaches), wood-fired pizzas and entrees can add up, but that doesn't faze many since it's "not easy to snag a prime-time table" or happy-hour berth at the bar.

Café Boulud *French*

26	26	26	$75

Palm Beach | Brazilian Court Hotel | 301 Australian Ave. (Hibiscus Ave.) | 561-655-6060 | www.danielnyc.com

"Beautiful people" "break out their diamonds and gold" at this "un-Florida" "class act" in the Brazilian Court Hotel that's voted Palm Beach's Most Popular thanks to "sophisticated" French fare that "does Daniel [Boulud] proud", backed by "excellent" wines and a staff operating at "the peak of hospitality" in the "casually elegant" interior or on the "lush" terrace; sure it's "pricey", but the prix fixe lunch and weekend brunch are "bargains"; P.S. there was a post-Survey chef change.

Café Chardonnay *American*

25	22	23	$59

Palm Beach Gardens | Garden Square Shoppes | 4533 PGA Blvd. (Military Trail) | 561-627-2662 | www.cafechardonnay.com

This "classy" American in a "nondescript" Palm Beach Gardens strip mall "must be doing something right" because after more than 25 years it's still many folks' "first choice" for a "night on the town"; the "innovative" food is served by "skilled" staffers, the "quiet", "charming" space is conducive to "conversations" and there's a "wonderful wine list" to boot, key ingredients for those celebrating "special occasions."

Café L'Europe Ⓜ *Continental*

27	27	27	$78

Palm Beach | 331 S. County Rd. (Brazilian Ave.) | 561-655-4020 | www.cafeleurope.com

"Bump elbows with the country's wealthiest people" at this "fine-dining icon" that's "still hitting all the right notes" after three decades with its "scrumptious" Continental cuisine, 2,000-bottle wine list and "superb" staff – rated tops in Palm Beach – that treats diners "like royalty"; add in an "old-world" setting filled with fresh flowers and "lovely" music via a "magical pianist", and even if tabs are "astronomical", it's "worth it."

Captain Charlie's Reef Grill *Seafood*

27	14	23	$36

Juno Beach | Beach Plaza | 12846 U.S. 1 (bet. Juno Isles Blvd. & Olympus Dr.) | 561-624-9924

"Don't be put off by the dumpy strip-mall exterior" or no-reservation policy – this "wildly popular" Juno Beach seafooder is a "classic not to be missed" on account of its "strikingly fresh fish" in "creative" preparations; "professional" service and a "large" list of wines "at ridiculously low prices" offset the "spartan surroundings and noise"; P.S. try its takeout-oriented sibling 3 Doors Up in the same strip.

Casa D'Angelo *Italian*

27 | 22 | 24 | $61

Boca Raton | 171 E. Palmetto Park Rd. (bet. Mizner Blvd. & N. Federal Hwy.) | 561-996-1234 | www.casa-d-angelo.com

Chef-owner Angelo Elia's "outstanding" Northern Italian fare, including a "wide variety of homemade pasta", takes diners on a "delightful" "journey to Italy" without leaving Boca; it's "expensive" (i.e. an excuse to "wear your Valentino") and tables are "a tad too cozy" in the "bustling" space, but "warm" service and a "wine room that has to be seen to be believed" help explain why it's "beloved" by many – reservations are highly recommended.

Chez Jean-Pierre Bistro ⊠ *French*

28 | 22 | 26 | $74

Palm Beach | 132 N. County Rd. (bet. Sunrise & Sunset Aves.) | 561-833-1171 | www.chezjean-pierre.com

"*Mais oui*" exclaims the "very Palm Beach" crowd that flocks to this "family-run" "country kitchen" for chef Jean-Pierre Leverrier's "consistently awesome" French fare including "outstanding Dover sole" and profiteroles with "chocolate sauce worth drowning in"; the "elegant" space is lined with "unique" modern art and warmed by "attentive" service, and while it helps to have "money to burn", most say it "always delivers"; P.S. closed July through mid-August.

Chops Lobster Bar *Seafood/Steak*

26 | 25 | 26 | $71

Boca Raton | Royal Palm Pl. | 101 Plaza Real S. (1st St.) | 561-395-2675 | www.chopslobsterbar.com

From "excellent steaks" and "fabulous" "flash-fried lobster" to "top-notch" service, this "happening" Boca branch of an Atlanta-based surf 'n' turfer "rarely misses"; the full menu is offered in both the "clubby" steakhouse side and in the replica of NYC's famed Oyster Bar complete with vaulted, tiled ceiling, and there's a lively "bar scene" with live music most nights; of course, some balk at "billfold-fracturing" tabs, but most feel it's "worth it."

11 Maple Street Ⓜ *American*

27 | 22 | 25 | VE

Jensen Beach | 3224 NE Maple Ave. (Jensen Beach Blvd.) | 772-334-7714 | www.11maplestreet.net

This "out-of-the-way" New American in "funky" Jensen Beach is a place to "escape the hustle" while enjoying chef-owner Mike Perrin's "inventive" seafood-strong menu, featuring mostly small plates presented like "works of art" and "costing about the same"; set in a "quaint" "Old Florida house", it has a "lovely" vibe and "friendly" staffers who are "knowledgeable" about the food and substantial wine list.

Four Seasons – The Restaurant *Seafood*

25 | 26 | 26 | $77

Palm Beach | Four Seasons Resort | 2800 S. Ocean Blvd. (Lake Ave.) | 561-533-3750 | www.fourseasons.com

"It's the Four Seasons – that's all you need to know" aver fans who declare this "delightful" grande dame in Palm Beach is "hotel dining done right", from Darryl Moiles' "sensational seafood" to the "pampering" treatment; the "pretty" room is enhanced by water views, but be aware that "special evenings" like this "don't come cheap."

Kee Grill *Seafood/Steak*

24 | 21 | 22 | $47

Juno Beach | 14020 U.S. 1 (Donald Ross Rd.) | 561-776-1167

(continued)

Kee Grill

Boca Raton | 17940 N. Military Trail (Clint Moore Rd.) | 561-995-5044
"Consistent quality and value" are the hallmarks of this Boca–Juno Beach duo offering "finely prepared fish dishes" along with land-based options and "wonderful sides" like spinach soufflé ("heaven in a rame-kin"); the "tropical island" digs get "jammed" by an "older crowd" so "don't linger" because the staff, though "friendly", will "take the water glass out of your hand", leading insiders to recommend the "terrific" early-bird hour's more "relaxed pace" (call for times and availability).

Little Moir's Food Shack ⊠ *Seafood* | 26 | 15 | 21 | $36 |

Jupiter | Jupiter Sq. | 103 U.S. 1 (E. Indiantown Rd.) | 561-741-3626

Little Moir's Leftovers Café ⊠ *Seafood*

Jupiter | Abacoa Bermudiana | 451 University Blvd. (Military Trail) | 561-627-6030
www.littlemoirsfoodshack.com
Fish fanciers "queue up" at these "funky", "colorful" seafood "shacks" in different Jupiter malls for "a wide array" of "killer" Florida catch at "reasonable" prices; the original looks a bit "run-down" while the bigger Abacoa locale has a slightly "more grown-up atmosphere", but both have a "laid-back" charm enhanced by an "eclectic collection of craft beer" and "friendly" service.

Marcello's La Sirena ⊠ *Italian* | 28 | 19 | 26 | $66 |

West Palm Beach | 6316 S. Dixie Hwy. (bet. Franklin & Nathan Hale Rds.) | 561-585-3128 | www.lasirenaonline.com
There are "no surprises" at this 25-year-old West Palm Beach "icon", just "unforgettable" Italian "soul food" – which rates as the No. 1 meal in the county – accompanied by a wine list full of "character" and "professional" service, making it perfect for "special occasions"; its "old-style, white-tablecloth" setting can get "crowded", but tables are in better supply if you "eat later than the senior set"; P.S. closed in summer.

Max's Harvest *American* | – | – | – | M |

Delray Beach | Pineapple Grove | 169 NE Second Ave. (bet.1st & 2nd Sts.) | 561-381-9970 | www.maxsharvest.com
Restaurateur Dennis Max brings a modern American menu tuned to local and heritage foods with smart wine pairings to Delray's Pineapple Grove; reservations are prudent for dinner in season, regardless of where you want to sit in the four-part space: lush back patio and bar, front sidewalk tables or a pair of inner rooms, one with views of an open kitchen.

Seasons 52 *American* | 23 | 24 | 23 | $42 |

Palm Beach Gardens | 11611 Ellison Wilson Rd. (PGA Blvd.) | 561-625-5852
Boca Raton | 2300 NW Executive Center Dr. (Glades Rd.) | 561-998-9952
www.seasons52.com
"Guilt-free" food (all items are under 475 calories) that "actually tastes exciting" – like "out-of-this-world" flatbreads and "cute" desserts in shot glasses – is the "unique concept" behind this "health-oriented but not health-nutty" New American chain; "warm decor", "well-trained" servers, "interesting" wines and "active" bar scenes with nightly live piano further explain why it's so "popular."

	FOOD	DECOR	SERVICE	COST

32 East *American* | 25 | 21 | 23 | $55 |

Delray Beach | 32 E. Atlantic Ave. (bet. 1st & Swinton Aves.) |
561-276-7868 | www.32east.com

Chef Nick Morfogen "continues to surprise and impress" with his
"nightly changing" dinner menu featuring "fresh, local ingredients" at
this New American "favorite" in Delray Beach; service is "above par",
and though tabs are "on the pricey side", it draws a "young, energetic"
crowd that turns the inside into a "festive" "zoo" – those who prefer
not to "scream" can sit outside and watch "*tout* Delray" stroll by on
"fashionable" Atlantic Avenue.

The Tides Ⓩ *Floridian* | 24 | 23 | 23 | $51 |

Vero Beach | 3103 Cardinal Dr. (Camelia Ln.) | 772-234-3966 |
www.tidesofvero.com

Loyalists laud this "fine"-dining destination in a "small" "converted
house" in Vero Beach, where the "talented" chef-owner offers up "interesting" Floridian fare à la carte or via a multicourse chef's table option; "excellent" customer service and an "elegant" dining room make
up for "pricey" tabs.

Trattoria Romana *Italian* | 26 | 21 | 22 | $63 |

Boca Raton | 499 E. Palmetto Park Rd. (NE 5th Ave.) | 561-393-6715 |
www.trattoriaromanabocaraton.com

A real "class act", this Boca Italian puts out "terrific" "old-fashioned"
fare (with a "don't-miss" antipasto bar) that keeps it perpetually
"crowded"; a recent renovation added a "much-needed" bar pouring
cocktails and wine that "makes waits a lot more enjoyable", although
some still take issue with "expensive" prices and service that seems
to "favor regulars."

Philadelphia

TOP FOOD RANKING

	Restaurant	Cuisine
29	Fountain	Continental/French
	Vetri	Italian
	Birchrunville Store	French/Italian
	Bibou	French
28	Sycamore	American
	Fond	American
	Paloma	French/Mexican
	Bluefin	Japanese
	Vedge	Vegetarian
	Sketch	Burgers
	Talula's Table	European
	Morimoto	Japanese
	Amada	Spanish
	Sovana Bistro	Mediterranean
	Little Fish	Seafood
	Domani Star	Italian
	Ela	American
	Capogiro	American/Dessert
	Majolica*	American
27	Zahav	Israeli

OTHER NOTEWORTHY PLACES

Restaurant	Cuisine
Alma de Cuba	Latin
Barbuzzo	Mediterranean
Barclay Prime	Steak
Buddakan	Asian
Capital Grille	Steak
Chickie's & Pete's	Pub Food
Dmitri's	Greek
Han Dynasty	Chinese
Il Pittore	Italian
Iron Hill Brewery	American
Le Virtu	Italian
Lolita	Mexican
Modo Mio	Italian
Osteria	Italian
Rittenhouse Tavern	American
Sbraga	American
Talula's Garden	American
Tashan	Indian
Tinto	Spanish
Vernick Food & Drink	American

* Indicates a tie with restaurant above

Alma de Cuba   *Nuevo Latino*

25	26	24	$50

Rittenhouse | 1623 Walnut St. (bet. 16th & 17th Sts.) | 215-988-1799 |
www.almadecubarestaurant.com

You almost "expect Papa Hemingway" to appear at Stephen Starr and Douglas Rodriguez's "upscale", "special-occasion" Nuevo Latino, still "trendy" after a decade-plus in Rittenhouse; brace yourself for "invasive noise levels" generated by "high rollers" who "come for the mojitos" in the "dim" lounge but stay for the "bold flavors" "from land and sea" (e.g. "amazing" ceviche) and "world-class" desserts, all served by a "prompt, attentive" staff in the sleek, contemporary space.

Amada   *Spanish*

28	25	25	$53

Old City | 217-219 Chestnut St. (bet. 2nd & 3rd Sts.) | 215-625-2450 |
www.amadarestaurant.com

Iron Chef Jose Garces' "rustic yet swanky" Spanish "crown jewel" in Old City "still gets a big *olé*" for its "fabulous" tapas, "perfectly crafted" sangria and "attentive" service, though it also gets a few jeers for "noise levels" approaching a "soccer match"; fans recommend "bringing a group to justify over-ordering", and since "noshing" makes you "run up a bill", consider the "pig roast" (which must be ordered in advance) or "tasting menus."

Barbuzzo ● *Mediterranean*

27	21	24	$43

Washington Square West | 110 S. 13th St. (Sansom St.) | 215-546-9300 |
www.barbuzzo.com

You'd get "fresher" produce only "in the middle of a farmer's field" gush fans of Marcie Turney and Valerie Safran's Med "gem" in Washington Square West, offering "beautiful" fare featuring "locally cultivated ingredients" and "knowledgeable" service; you'll "eat sardines and feel like one too" in the "cramped" space, but for most, it's "well worth it", especially the budino dessert, which is "so good it should be illegal."

Barclay Prime   *Steak*

26	25	26	$76

Rittenhouse | The Barclay | 237 S. 18th St. (Locust St.) | 215-732-7560 |
www.barclayprime.com

"Big-business types on expense accounts" and other high rollers head to Stephen Starr's "meat mecca" on Rittenhouse Square, where "mouthwatering steaks" are served by "professional" servers in a "hip library" setting, and bartenders pour "terrific drinks" at the "chic bar"; while some decry "overpriced" wines and the "gimmicky $100 cheesesteak", really, "any place where you can pick out your own knife is automatically awesome."

Bibou �{M}⌷ *French*

29	21	27	$55

Bella Vista | 1009 S. Eighth St. (Kimball St.) | 215-965-8290 |
www.biboubyob.com

Go ahead and "bring your best bottle" to this "intimate" BYO bistro housed in a former row house in Bella Vista, where Pierre Calmels creates "soulfully designed" French fare boasting flavors both "subtle and bold", while his wife, Charlotte, will "treat you like mom" did; it's almost "impossible to get a reservation", especially on Sundays, when it offers an "amazing" $45 prix fixe, and remember it's cash only.

	FOOD	DECOR	SERVICE	COST

Birchrunville Store Cafe 🖼️Ⓜ️⇗ *French/Italian* | 29 | 25 | 28 | $57

Birchrunville | 1403 Hollow Rd. (Flowing Springs Rd.) | 610-827-9002 | www.birchrunvillestorecafe.com

"Take a GPS" and head into the "rolling hills of Chester County's horse country", home to Francis Trzeciak's French-Italian "gem" that's "hard to find and harder to forget", thanks to his "inspired" cuisine that was "farm-to-fork before it was cool", served by an "excellent" staff in an "intimate", high-ceilinged setting that lets you "pretend you are in Provence"; BYO makes the "steep" tabs "more palatable" (just don't forget to bring cash).

Bluefin 🖼️ *Japanese* | 28 | 19 | 23 | $43

East Norriton | 2820 Dekalb Pike (Germantown Pike) | 610-277-3917 | www.restaurantbluefin.com

Even after a move into larger, more "engaging new digs" in an East Norriton strip mall, it's "still hard to get a reservation" at Yong Kim's Japanese BYO, thanks to what many say is the "freshest, most creative sushi in the 'burbs", including "insanely delicious" rolls that "melt like butter"; "smiling", "friendly" service is another plus, and given the "awesome" fare and "reasonable" prices, many "can't help but over-order."

Buddakan ⚫ *Asian* | 27 | 27 | 25 | $57

Old City | 325 Chestnut St. (4th St.) | 215-574-9440 | www.buddakan.com

Still "buzzing" after 15 years, Stephen Starr's "sexy", "swanky" Old City Asian earns Philadelphia's Most Popular title thanks to "creative", "exceptionally flavorful" food (oh those "amazing" edamame ravioli) served by a "professional" staff in a "beautiful", "Buddhist-chic" setting; sure, the "lively crowd" and "thumping" "techno-beats" prompt some to "pray to Buddha for peace" and your wallet will end up "significantly lighter", but most agree the experience is "well worth it."

The Capital Grille *Steak* | 26 | 25 | 26 | $65

Avenue of the Arts | 1338 Chestnut St. (Broad St.) | 215-545-9588
King of Prussia | 236 Mall Blvd. (Goddard Blvd.) | 610-265-1415
www.thecapitalgrille.com

An "upscale crowd" indulges its "carnivorous cravings" at this "clubby" national steakhouse chain, a "slice of red meat heaven" where the "awesome" steaks are "expertly prepared", "superb" bartenders pour "terrific" drinks and the "service is always stellar"; most agree it's "worth the splurge", so "bring lotsa money" for a "night to remember."

Capogiro Gelato Artisans *American/Dessert* | 28 | 16 | 21 | $9

East Passyunk | 1625 E. Passyunk Ave. (Morris St.) | 215-462-3790
Rittenhouse | 117 S. 20th St. (Sansom St.) | 215-636-9250 ⚫
University City | Radian | 3925 Walnut St. (40th St.) | 215-222-0252 ⚫
Washington Square West | 119 S. 13th St. (Sansom St.) | 215-351-0900 ⚫
www.capogirogelato.com

Surveyors swoon over this dessert chain's "decadent", "silky rich" gelato made with "fresh, local" and "seasonal" ingredients, served by a "congenial" staff "generous with samples" of the "myriad flavors"; many tout it as a post-dinner stop to "really impress a date" (though it also serves a limited menu of New American fare), and while a few carp about "pricey", "small portions", for most it's a "treat" well worth the "extra time on the treadmill."

	FOOD	DECOR	SERVICE	COST

Chickie's & Pete's ❶ *Pub Food* — 23 | 22 | 22 | $26

Eastwick | 8500 Essington Ave. (Arrivals Rd.) | 215-492-0569
Northeast Philly | 4010 Robbins Ave. (bet. Charles & Mulberry Sts.) | 215-338-3060
South Philly | 1526 Packer Ave. (15th St.) | 215-218-0500
Bensalem | Parx Casino | 2999 Street Rd. (Tillman Dr.) | 267-525-7333
Warrington | 500 Easton Rd. (bet. Elm & Garden Aves.) | 215-343-5206

Chickie's & Pete's Cafe ❶ *Pub Food*

Northeast Philly | Roosevelt Plaza | 11000 Roosevelt Blvd. (bet. Red Lion & Woodhaven Sts.) | 215-856-9890
www.chickiesandpetes.com

"Crab fries rule" at this "high-decibel", Philadelphia-centric sports-bar chain (ranked the city's Most Popular chain), which is "loaded with TVs" to "yell at" and "decent" fried food to douse with "beer, beer, beer"; though critics dismiss it as a "Chuck E. Cheese's for adults", with takes on the service ranging from "friendly" to "subpar", most consider it a "great place to get together with friends" – as long as they're "Philly fans."

Dmitri's *Greek* — 25 | 16 | 21 | $33

Northern Liberties | 944 N. Second St. (Laurel St.) | 215-592-4550
Queen Village | 795 S. Third St. (Catharine St.) | 215-625-0556 ⌿
Rittenhouse | 2227 Pine St. (23rd St.) | 215-985-3680
www.dmitrisrestaurant.com

Afishionados gladly sit "elbow-to-elbow" to savor "awesome seafood" "prepared as simply as possible" at these "informal" Med taverns, whose prices are "friendly to the wallet" and help most overlook what some describe as "consistently inconsistent" service from a "hipster" staff; the Queen Village original is BYO and cash-only, while Northern Liberties is also BYO but accepts credit cards and Fitler Square takes plastic and has a liquor license (got that?).

Domani Star *Italian* — 28 | 19 | 25 | $35

Doylestown | 57 W. State St. (bet. Hamilton & Main Sts.) | 215-230-9100 | www.domanistar.com

While the meatballs may be "to die for", "every dish on the menu is a hit" at this "convivial" Italian BYO in Downtown Doylestown, where the "fresh", "tasty" fare is "served with a smile" and "lives up to the prices" (especially the Sunday–Thursday dinner prix fixe, a "steal" of a deal); some report "cramped", "noisy" environs, but most declare it a "winner."

Ela ❶ Ⓜ *American* — 28 | 24 | 25 | $50

Queen Village | 627 S. Third St. (Bainbridge St.) | 267-687-8512 | www.elaphilly.com

Jason Cichonski (ex Lacroix) is "wowing everyone" at his upscale-casual Queen Village New American with "inventive", "molecular cuisine" featuring "interesting pairings of textures and flavors" (the "liquid cookie dough dessert is to die for"); while some caution that "small plates lead to expensive dinners", it's nonetheless a "great neighborhood spot" that impresses "without trying to be too cool for school."

	FOOD	DECOR	SERVICE	COST

Fond 🗓️Ⓜ️ *American*   28 | 20 | 27 | $49

East Passyunk | 1617 E. Passyunk Ave. (Tasker St.) | 215-551-5000 | www.fondphilly.com

"Over-the-top terrific" sums up surveyors' sentiments about this high-end BYO on the East Passyunk strip, where "every bite" of Lee Styer's New American cooking and Jessie Prawlucki's "heavenly desserts" "takes your breath away", while Tory Keomanivong's "enthusiastic" servers are "genuinely caring"; it's an overall "memorable" experience, and a move to a new location (with a bar) later in 2012 may resolve the "space issue."

Fountain Restaurant *Continental/French*   29 | 28 | 28 | $82

Logan Square | Four Seasons Hotel | 1 Logan Sq. (Benjamin Franklin Pkwy.) | 215-963-1500 | www.fourseasons.com

Philadelphia's No. 1 for Food, Decor and Service, the Four Seasons' "formal but comfortable" French-Continental standout makes you "feel like royalty" with "fabulous" "feasts" of "succulent, creative" fare and "impeccable" service in a "beautiful" setting; "you feel rich just being there", though maybe less so after you leave – but "go ahead and splurge" since most agree it's the "standard by which all other restaurants should be judged."

Han Dynasty *Chinese*   25 | 15 | 19 | $26

Manayunk | 4356 Main St. (bet. Grape & Levering Sts.) | 215-508-2066
Old City | 108 Chestnut St. (Front St.) | 215-922-1888
University City | 3711 Market St. (38th St.) | 215-222-3711
Exton | 260 N. Pottstown Pike (Waterloo Blvd.) | 610-524-4002
Royersford | Limerick Square Shopping Ctr. | 70 Buckwalter Rd. (Rte. 422) | 610-792-9600
www.handynasty.net

Aficionados advise be sure to "grab your water" and "take extra tissues" to cope with the "tongue-numbing", dial-by-number "heat" at Han Chiang's five "affordable" Sichuan destinations, where some fans would "probably trade" their "first-born child" for the "ecstasy-inducing" dan dan noodles; while the contemporary surroundings leave little impression, opinions of the owner range from "amusing to annoying."

Il Pittore *Italian*   26 | 24 | 25 | $63

Rittenhouse | 2025 Sansom St. (bet. 20th & 21st Sts.) | 215-391-4900 | www.ilpittore.com

"Bring your bonus check" to experience chef Chris Painter's "inventive" takes on modern Italian cuisine at his and Stephen Starr's "intimate" storefront "splurge" in Rittenhouse; the "portions are small to allow for several courses" (you may find yourself "ordering more than you should"), and meals are enhanced by "smooth wine pairings" provided by a "lovely" staff that keeps an eye on you "without going overboard."

Iron Hill
Brewery & Restaurant *American*   22 | 21 | 22 | $28

Chestnut Hill | 8400 Germantown Ave. (bet. Gravers Ln. & Highland Ave.) | 215-948-5600 ☣

(continued)

(continued)

Iron Hill Brewery & Restaurant

Phoenixville | 130 Bridge St. (Starr St.) | 610-983-9333
West Chester | 3 W. Gay St. (High St.) | 610-738-9600
Media | 30 E. State St. (bet. Jackson & Monroe Sts.) | 610-627-9000
North Wales | Shoppes at English Vill. | 1460 Bethlehem Pike (Welsh Rd.) | 267-708-2000
Lancaster | 781 Harrisburg Ave. (bet. College & Race Aves.) | 717-291-9800
www.ironhillbrewery.com

"There's no better place to be Friday at 5" than these "always busy" local brewpubs whose "bright, open" (maybe a little "corporate") settings permit prime viewing of the brewing process while amping the "noise"; surveyors tout the "inventive" "comfort food" "for the masses" and "down-to-earth" service but add "the beer alone is worth the trip" – so "make sure to get the sampler and a designated driver."

Le Virtù *Italian*　　27 | 22 | 23 | $49

East Passyunk | 1927 E. Passyunk Ave. (bet. McKean & Mifflin Sts.) | 215-271-5626 | www.levirtu.com

"Craveable fresh pasta", "housemade salumi" – "you cannot wrong with anything" on the "rustic" menu at this "casual" yet "elegant" Abruzzese "destination" in East Passyunk where "the pig head sits in the kitchen in full view" to remind that this is "not your standard red-sauce Italian"; while some think the "servers need more personality", others "feel well cared for", and the "lovely" outdoor garden is an added bonus.

Little Fish BYOB *Seafood*　　28 | 16 | 23 | $44

Bella Vista | 746 S. Sixth St. (Fitzwater St.) | 267-455-0172 | www.littlefishbyob.com

Making a big "splash" despite its "tiny" (22 seats) dimensions, Chadd Jenkins' "solid" BYO Bella Vista seafooder hooks fish lovers with its "creative" chalkboard menu and a "superior" Sunday tasting menu full of "fabulous surprises"; fans describe it as a "perfect little hole-in-the-wall" with a "quaint" "Village feel" and "helpful" staff, urging "make reservations early" – "you won't be sorry, if you can get in."

Lolita ⊘ *Mexican*　　26 | 19 | 20 | $39

Washington Square West | 106 S. 13th St. (bet. Chestnut & Sansom Sts.) | 215-546-7100 | www.lolitabyob.com

"Bring your own tequila", order housemade mixers and watch "the fun begin" at this "scene-driven", cash-only Mex BYO in Wash West proffering "well-prepared" carne asada and other delights, served by an "efficient", though some say "unfriendly", staff; it gets "packed" and "loud" in the "tight space", but for fans, that "just makes the party better"; P.S. there's an $18-per-person food minimum and automatic 20% tip on parties of five or more.

Majolica Ⓜ *American*　　28 | 21 | 25 | $49

Phoenixville | 258 Bridge St. (bet. Gay & Main Sts.) | 610-917-0962 | www.majolicarestaurant.com

Cognoscenti urge you to "let your bouche be amused" by chef Andrew Deery's "artistic" treatment of New American cuisine – "amazing flavors not usually found in the suburbs" – at the pricey, "trendsetting"

Phoenixville BYO he runs with his wife, Sarah Johnson; between the "lovely, intimate" dining room and "warm" service with "no rush", most say it's an "unpretentious indulgence" that's "worth the trip" for a "special night out."

Modo Mio ☑⇄ *Italian*   27 | 17 | 24 | $40
Northern Liberties | 161 W. Girard Ave. (Hancock St.) | 215-203-8707 | www.modomiorestaurant.com

"Every dish pops with flavor" on the $35, four-course Italian 'turista' menus at Peter McAndrews' "modest" BYO trattoria near Northern Liberties, which many deem one of the "best deals in the city"; the service is "knowledgeable", although a few find it "quirky", while others complain that the space's "horrific acoustics" make "lip-reading" necessary; P.S. don't forget cash, and "reservations are a must."

Morimoto *Japanese*   28 | 27 | 26 | $74
Washington Square West | 723 Chestnut St. (bet. 7th & 8th Sts.) | 215-413-9070 | www.morimotorestaurant.com

"Omakase: just do it" urge boosters of this "one-of-a-kind" Japanese from Stephen Starr and Iron Chef Masaharu Morimoto in Washington Square West, where legions are tempted to "close their eyes in rapturous delight" over the "heavenly" fare – but if they did, they'd miss the "color-changing", "postmodern" setting; "knowledgeable" service is another plus, and despite "splurge" pricing, many leave "screaming 'I want Mor-imoto!'"

Osteria *Italian*   27 | 25 | 26 | $55
North Philly | 640 N. Broad St. (Wallace St.) | 215-763-0920 | www.osteriaphilly.com

"Tuscany" is just a "cab ride" away courtesy of this "pricey" North Philly "treasure" where the "bustle and warmth" is "conducive to conversation" and chef Jeff Michaud's "robust", "inventive" Italian cooking makes "every mouthful a delight", from "savory, crispy" pizzas and "house-cured" salumi to "creative" handmade pastas matched with a "mouthwatering wine list"; "knowledgeable" service orchestrates a "fantastico" experience in which the Vetri Family's "golden touch is apparent."

Paloma Mexican   28 | 21 | 25 | $54
Haute Cuisine ☒☑ *French/Mexican*
Bella Vista | 763 S. Eighth St. (Catharine St.) | 215-928-9500 | www.palomafinedining.com

Fans predict "you'll keep coming back" to this "cozy", white-tablecloth Bella Vista BYO for chef-owner Adán Saavedra's "inventive" "haute" French fare "laced" with the "flavors and spices of Mexico" and topped off with his "charming" wife Barbara's "homemade desserts" (the "spicy sorbets alone are worth the visit" to some); "charming" service, "reasonable" prices and a "quiet" setting with "ample room" "between tables" seal the deal.

Rittenhouse Tavern ☑ *American*   - | - | - | E
Rittenhouse | Philadelphia Art Alliance | 251 S. 18th St. (Manning St.) | 215-732-2412 | www.rittenhousetavern.com

'Approachable elegance' is the theme at this upscale American brasserie in the historic Art Alliance mansion/exhibition hall on Rittenhouse

Square, where chefs Nicholas Elmi (Le Bec-Fin) and Ed Brown are plating refined, locally sourced modern fare; in addition to the baroquely styled, business-appropriate dining room, there's a transporting outdoor garden for warm-weather dining.

Sbraga *American*   27 | 24 | 24 | $64

Avenue of the Arts | 440 S. Broad St. (Pine St.) | 215-735-1913 | www.sbraga.com

A "*Top Chef* creates a top restaurant" is the story line of Kevin Sbraga's New American located "steps from the Kimmel Center", where the TV "winner" provides "affordable fine dining" with a "bargain" prix fixe of "mind-bending" small plates; an open kitchen anchors the "trendy" rustic space (which can get "noisy"), while the "friendly", "knowledgeable" staff works hard to ensure a "memorable evening."

Sketch *Burgers*   28 | 20 | 24 | $15

Fishtown | 413 E. Girard Ave. (Columbia Ave.) | 215-634-3466 | www.sketch-burger.com

"Super-messy burgers" and other "comfort-food" classics are "worth the hike" to this Fishtown "joint" where diners doodle while they wait and seating options include "vintage church pews"; Kobe beef and even vegan patties plus sauces that add "the right amount of sloppy, fatty goodness" are a testament to the kitchen's "creativity", and while it all "might cost a few bucks more", "personal, passionate" service seals the deal.

Sovana Bistro Ⓜ *French/Mediterranean*   28 | 23 | 26 | $53

Kennett Square | 696 Unionville Rd. (Rte. 926) | 610-444-5600 | www.sovanabistro.com

Enthusiasts encourage city folk to "get in your Zipcars", pronto, because this "contemporary" Kennett Square destination is "worth the ride into the country" for "surprising, original" French-Med fare that reflects "great use of locally grown or raised" ingredients – predictably, the "tiny tables" are "packed at all hours"; accounting for the "quality" eats, "first-class" service and optional BYO, "prices are not bad", but "bring extra cash" anyway.

Sycamore Ⓜ *American*   28 | 22 | 25 | $45

Lansdowne | 14 S. Lansdowne Ave. (Baltimore Ave.) | 484-461-2867 | www.sycamorebyo.com

"Local ingredients" shine on chef Sam Jacobson's "wonderfully inventive" New American tasting and prix fixe menus at this BYO "gem" in a "low-key" Lansdowne storefront where the "owner's belief in service is inspiring"; a "first-class" cheese course, "wonderful" sticky toffee pudding dessert and "incredible" "cocktail mixers" are pluses, leaving "high prices" as the only complaint.

Talula's Garden *American*   27 | 27 | 25 | $63

Washington Square West | 210 W. Washington Sq. (Walnut St.) | 215-592-7787 | www.talulasgarden.com

"Oohs and ahs" fill the "farmhouse-chic" confines of this "spectacular" collaboration between Aimee Olexy (Talula's Table) and Stephen Starr, where the "wonderfully inventive" American cuisine showcases the "best ingredients the season has to offer", including a "can't-miss cheese plate"; "impeccable" servers "lead you to exactly what you want", and in summer the "gorgeous garden" is "perfect" for a "magical meal" that's "well worth" the "high price."

Talula's Table *European* | 28 | 24 | 28 | $92 |

Kennett Square | 102 W. State St. (Union St.) | 610-444-8255 | www.talulastable.com

"The tough part is getting in" to Aimee Olexy's "outstanding" European BYO in a Kennett Square market, where groups of eight to 12 sit at the sole table for the "superb" eight-course prix fixe that delivers an "educating experience for the taste buds"; you'll need "deep pockets" and reservations "a year in advance", but the "staff couldn't be friendlier" and most agree it "deserves all the accolades it receives."

Tashan *Indian* | 25 | 25 | 23 | $51 |

Avenue of the Arts | 777 S. Broad St. (Catharine St.) | 267-687-2170 | www.mytashan.com

"Bollywood buzz with upscale Indian" fare sums up this Tiffin offshoot on Avenue of the Arts that "could make an Indian foodie out of anyone" with its "creative spin" and nontraditional approach; far from "lamb vindaloo territory", this is fusion gone "to nirvana" in a "snazzy" setting where servers who are "excited to share their knowledge" help make the "pricey" experience "worth every penny."

Tinto *Spanish* | 27 | 24 | 24 | $56 |

Rittenhouse | 114 S. 20th St. (Sansom St.) | 215-665-9150 | www.tintorestaurant.com

This "impeccable" Rittenhouse Basque is Iron Chef "Jose Garces at his best", showcasing "innovative" *pintxos* (small plates) that are "huge in flavor" and "remain true to Spanish spirit", enhanced by selections from an "amazing wine list" and served in an "intimate", "comfortable" cellarlike space; "informed" staffers help create a "convivial", "more personal" vibe than at some of his other operations, and though it's "not cheap", most consider it a "winner."

Vedge ☒ *Vegan* | 28 | 28 | 28 | $47 |

Washington Square West | 1221 Locust St. (Camac St.) | 215-320-7500 | www.vedgerestaurant.com

Rich Landau and Kate Jacoby make you "forget images of hippies and heavy-handed meat substitutes" with "inventive, delectable" vegan and vegetarian small plates featuring "astoundingly fresh" veggies at their "elegant" successor to Horizons, set in a "charming old mansion" in Washington Square West; "gorgeous" decor and "excellent" service add to its allure, and while a few gripe about "pricey" "small portions", the "extraordinary" fare makes even "hard-core carnivores" "consider giving up meat."

Vernick Food & Drink Ⓜ *American* | - | - | - | E |

Rittenhouse | 2031 Walnut St. (21st St.) | 267-639-6644 | www.vernickphilly.com

Returning to his hometown after years with Jean-Georges Vongerichten, chef Gregory Vernick has set up a bi-level American in a Rittenhouse brownstone, serving a pricey menu of simple, polished classics (roasted Amish chicken, braised beef cheek); the chic, Euro-inspired setting includes a seven-seat counter at the open kitchen and sunny window seating on the second floor.

	FOOD	DECOR	SERVICE	COST

Vetri ⌧ *Italian*

29 | 25 | 28 | $202

Washington Square West | 1312 Spruce St. (bet. Broad & 13th Sts.) | 215-732-3478 | www.vetriristorante.com

Acolytes attest "heaven on earth" can be found in an "unassuming" townhouse in Washington Square West, home of Marc Vetri's flagship Italian, a "gastronomic tour de force" that's "high-end" "without being ostentatious", offering "sublime" cuisine and "professional" service; while you may have to "raid your 401(k)" given a prix fixe–only menu that starts at $155, it's on just about "everyone's bucket list."

Zahav *Israeli*

27 | 24 | 26 | $51

Society Hill | 237 St. James Pl. (2nd St.) | 215-625-8800 | www.zahavrestaurant.com

A "breath of fresh international air", Michael Solomonov's "one-of-a-kind" Society Hill Israeli "blends traditional food" (think "heavenly hummus") with "modern techniques" for "delectable combinations" to "keep your tongue guessing"; a "responsive" staff elevates the "casual" setting and guides diners through the journey – a "splurge", but an "adventure" that acolytes assert "everyone must try."

Phoenix/Scottsdale

TOP FOOD RANKING

Restaurant	Cuisine
_28_ Kai	Eclectic
Binkley's	American
Quiessence	American
Noca	American
_27_ Barrio Cafe	Mexican
Tarbell's	American
Eddie V's	Seafood/Steak
FnB*	American
Hana*	Japanese
Vincent's/Camelback	French/Southwestern

OTHER NOTEWORTHY PLACES

Atlas Bistro	American
Fleming's Prime	Steak
Lon's/Hermosa	American
Mastro's City Hall	Steak
Nobuo/Teeter House	Japanese
P.F. Chang's	Chinese
Pizzeria Bianco	Pizza
Rancho Pinot	American
Shinbay	Japanese
T. Cook's	Mediterranean

Atlas Bistro ⌾Ⓜ _American_   26 | 17 | 22 | $50

South Scottsdale | Wilshire Plaza | 2515 N. Scottsdale Rd. (Wilshire Dr.) | Scottsdale | 480-990-2433 | www.atlasbistrobyob.com

"Some of the most imaginative and delicious food in the valley", listed on an "ever-changing menu", is found at this "intimate" New American whose "welcoming" service offsets its "not much to look at" setting in a South Scottsdale strip mall; you can BYO or buy a bottle at the "big wine shop" attached, and the corkage is only $10 – an "amazing" boon for "wine lovers" and dollar-watchers alike.

Barrio Cafe Ⓜ _Mexican_   27 | 19 | 23 | $34

Phoenix | 2814 N. 16th St. (Thomas Rd.) | 602-636-0240 | www.barriocafe.com

"This ain't yo' mama's Taco Bell" crow fans of chef-owner Silvana Salcido Esparza's "upbeat", "funky", "colorful" Southern Mexican spot in Central Phoenix, where the "innovative, superbly prepared" "haute" meals come with "fantastic" guacamole prepared tableside, an "amazing selection of tequilas" (over 200), "delectable margaritas" and "warm, attentive" service; its location in a "somewhat dicey area" doesn't prevent it from being "always crowded", and with no reservations accepted, "come early or come late or you certainly will wait."

---

* Indicates a tie with restaurant above

	FOOD	DECOR	SERVICE	COST

Binkley's Restaurant 🎇 Ⓜ️ *American* | 28 | 22 | 27 | $84 |

Cave Creek | 6920 E. Cave Creek Rd. (Tom Darlington Dr.) | 480-437-1072 |
www.binkleysrestaurant.com

"Every meal is a revelation" at "genius" chef-owner Kevin Binkley's
"world-class" restaurant in an "aging strip mall" in "the boondocks" of
Cave Creek, where the French-inspired New American fare is available
in "elaborate", "cutting-edge" tasting menus whose "locally sourced"
courses are "interspersed with tastings and palate-clearers that are
equally imaginative" and "beautifully presented" by "polite" staffers;
it may require "three hours" and "a second mortgage", but for a "wonderful treat for the soul and stomach", "it's worth every penny."

Eddie V's Prime Seafood *Seafood/Steak* | 27 | 26 | 25 | $58 |

North Scottsdale | Scottsdale Quarter | 15323 N. Scottsdale Rd.
(Greenway Hayden Loop) | Scottsdale | 480-730-4800 | www.eddiev.com

With a "fabulous location" in the Scottsdale Quarter, this "glitzy" "desert
oasis" "bustles all week" with "beautiful people" "young" and "older"
sampling the "wide variety" of "succulent seafood" and "never-go-
wrong" steaks that, while "expensive", are nonetheless "a good
value"; "responsive service" is a plus, but "at peak hours", the "loud" din,
especially from the "happening bar", can grate – though that's to be expected considering the scene is as "hot, hot, hot" as "Arizona in July."

Fleming's Prime Steakhouse & | 26 | 24 | 25 | $61 |
Wine Bar *Steak*

Chandler | 905 N. 54th St. (West Ray Rd.) | 480-940-1900
North Scottsdale | Market St. at DC Ranch | 20753 N. Pima Rd.
(Thompson Peak Pkwy.) | Scottsdale | 480-538-8000
Scottsdale | 6333 N. Scottsdale Rd. (Lincoln Dr.) | 480-596-8265
www.flemingssteakhouse.com

"Perfectly aged beef" "cooked just right" may be the raison d'être for this
"classy", "clubby", "consistent" steakhouse chain, but respondents are
equally enthusiastic about the "superb" wine program, featuring "100
wines by the glass", not to mention the "generous portions" and "oblig-
ing staff"; prices are "amped-up", so budgeters should consider the
"killer happy-hour deals", including a burger that "can't be beat."

FnB Restaurant Ⓜ️ *American* | 27 | 20 | 26 | $52 |

Old Town | 7133 E. Stetson Dr. (Scottsdale Rd.) | Scottsdale |
480-425-9463 | www.fnbrestaurant.com

At this "teeny" "treat" in Old Town, "extremely creative" chef-owner
Charleen Badman "lovingly prepares" "magnificent" "farm-to-table"
New American cuisine – served in "great portions for the money" alongside an "all-Arizona wine list" ("it works") – while her "host-with-the-
most" partner, Pavle Milic, oversees the "impeccable service"; there are
a few tables in the space bedecked with multicolored floor tiles, but insiders suggest you "sit at the counter" to watch the "magic" – either way,
"call far in advance for a reservation"; P.S. closed Monday–Tuesday.

Hana Japanese Eatery Ⓜ️ *Japanese* | 27 | 17 | 23 | $35 |

Phoenix | 5524 N. Seventh Ave. (Missouri Ave.) | 602-973-1238 |
www.hanajapaneseeatery.com

"Big pieces" of "reasonably priced" sashimi and "amazing sushi" made
from "the freshest fish in town" keep this family-owned Japanese

"neighborhood gem" in Phoenix "always crowded"; though the digs are "charmless" and "cramped", no one really minds, especially in light of the "friendly, efficient" service and no-corkage BYO policy; P.S. "for a real treat", "try the shabu-shabu on Sunday nights" or order it 24 hours in advance other days.

Kai 🖼️Ⓜ️ *Eclectic* | 28 | 27 | 29 | $80 |

Chandler | Sheraton Wild Horse Pass Resort & Spa | 5594 W. Wild Horse Pass Blvd. (Loop Rd.) | 602-225-0100 | www.wildhorsepassresort.com

"Prepare to be dazzled" by this "ultimate dining experience" in a resort restaurant on a Chandler reservation, where the "incredible", "unique" Native American–inflected Eclectic fare earns Phoenix/Scottsdale's No. 1 Food rating – plus the service is "remarkable", the decor is "lovely" and the views are "stunning", especially from the patio at sunset; true, it's "in the middle of nowhere" and "very expensive", but for "romantic" "special occasions", you "can't beat it."

Lon's at the Hermosa *American* | 26 | 28 | 26 | $60 |

Paradise Valley | Hermosa Inn | 5532 N. Palo Cristi Rd. (Stanford Dr.) | 602-955-7878 | www.lons.com

"Impress out-of-town friends", a "date" or "clients" at this "quintessential" "Arizona experience" in a "beautifully remodeled 1920s Southwestern resort" in Paradise Valley, serving "exciting", "superb" New American cuisine in a "warm interior" and on an "extraordinary" patio with "mature trees, colorful flowers" and a fire pit; "gracious service" and an "admirable" wine list are two more reasons it's "a place you will go back to", one that's "extra nice if someone else is buying."

Mastro's City Hall Steakhouse *Steak* | 26 | 24 | 25 | $69 |

Scottsdale | 6991 E. Camelback Rd. (Goldwater Blvd.) | 480-941-4700 | www.mastrosrestaurants.com

"Melt-like-butter" beef and a "hot", "celeb"-centric clientele, including plenty of "eye candy" at the "action"-packed bar, are the two specialties of this "posh" Scottsdale "destination steakhouse" boasting a "sophisticated", "flashy setting" and "impeccable service"; additionally, "the wine list is fit for a king and food portions are fit for an army" – which somewhat mitigates the fact that it "costs a ton" to dine here (most feel it's "worth the extra dollars").

Nobuo at Teeter House Ⓜ️ *Japanese* | ▽ 28 | 25 | 25 | $49 |

Downtown Phoenix | Heritage Sq. | 622 E. Adams St. (Monroe St.) | Phoenix | 602-254-0600 | www.nobuofukuda.com

"Nothing like it anywhere" say supporters of "genius" chef Nobuo Fukuda's "relaxed" Japanese izakaya, a "treasure" ensconced in a "charming old house" in Downtown Phoenix's Heritage Square; staffed by an "on-point" crew, it provides "artfully prepared", "fabulous small plates" ("spend a little or a lot" depending how much you order) as well as a tasting menu on weekends, delivering "creativity in each bite."

Noca Ⓜ️ *American* | 28 | 20 | 24 | $57 |

Camelback Corridor | 3118 E. Camelback Rd. (32nd St.) | Phoenix | 602-956-6622 | www.restaurantnoca.com

A "wonderful surprise in a strip mall", this Camelback Corridor spot creates "original", "exciting" seasonal New American savories that are so "ultradelicious", you'll "want to lick the plate" clean before the "personable staff" replaces them with the "fabulous" complimentary cotton candy; "gracious owner" Eliot Wexler helps craft a "big-city vibe" that works for a "special occasion or just a nice night out" – "so long as you aren't strapped for cash"; P.S. a post-Survey renovation is not reflected in the Decor score.

P.F. Chang's China Bistro *Chinese*

| 22 | 22 | 22 | $30 |

Chandler | Chandler Fashion Ctr. | 3255 W. Chandler Blvd. (bet. Chandler Village Dr. & Rte. 101) | 480-899-0472
Fashion Square | The Waterfront | 7135 E. Camelback Rd. (Scottsdale Rd.) | Scottsdale | 480-949-2610
Mesa | 6610 E. Superstition Springs Blvd. (Power Rd.) | 480-218-4900
North Scottsdale | Kierland Commons | 7132 E. Greenway Pkwy. (Scottsdale Rd.) | Scottsdale | 480-367-2999
Tempe | 740 S. Mill Ave. (bet. 7th St. & University Dr.) | 480-731-4600
www.pfchangs.com

Though many voters are "not sure the Chinese would recognize" the "Americanized" Sino fare served at this chain, "who cares?" – it's "safe" and "scrumdiddlyumptious" enough to "please" "everyone", hence it earns Phoenix/Scottsdale's Most Popular restaurant rating; what's more, the price point is "reasonable", the setting is "classy" and the staff is "pleasant", so most forgive the sometimes "long waits to get in" and the "loud" "noise."

Pizzeria Bianco *Pizza*

| 26 | 19 | 21 | $29 |

Downtown Phoenix | Heritage Sq. | 623 E. Adams St. (7th St.) | Phoenix | 602-258-8300 | www.pizzeriabianco.com

"Believe the hype" say surveyors of this "cult legend" in Heritage Square, which cranks out Neapolitan wood-fired pizzas so "extraordinary" (thanks in part to locally sourced ingredients), they could very well be the "best on the planet"; though you should prepare for a "long wait" ("absolutely worth" it) to get into the "quaint", brick-walled dining room at dinnertime, things have "greatly improved" now that hours have been "expanded" to include lunch, when "lines are almost nil."

Quiessence Restaurant & Wine Bar 🅢🅜 *American*

| 28 | 26 | 25 | $64 |

South Phoenix | Farm at South Mountain | 6106 S. 32nd St. (Southern Ave.) | Phoenix | 602-276-0601 | www.quiessencerestaurant.com

"Farmhouse meets gourmet" at this "bucolic", "romantic" "magnet for foodies" at the Farm at South Mountain, where the "sumptuous", "inventive" seasonal New American fare is "beautifully presented" alongside "superb" wines in a "lovely, romantic" interior and on a "wonderful" patio; "gracious", "professional service" abets the "unique experience", and while it's "expensive", "this is a place where you get what you pay for."

Rancho Pinot 🅢🅜 *American*

| 26 | 22 | 24 | $55 |

Scottsdale | Lincoln Vlg. | 6208 N. Scottsdale Rd. (bet. Lincoln & McDonald Drs.) | 480-367-8030 | www.ranchopinot.com

Chef-owner Chrysa Robertson continues to prove she's the "Alice Waters" of Scottsdale by making "inspired use of local, seasonal ingredients" in her "sophisticated" American cuisine at this "terrific" "high-end neighborhood place" with "cowboy-chic" decor (some say it's "fabulous", others call it "creaky"); "charming" servers are on hand to ferry the "carefully crafted cocktails" and "superb" wines, all of which makes for a "must-visit", particularly when entertaining "out-of-town guests"; P.S. open nightly November–April.

ShinBay ☒ Japanese
- | - | - | VE

Scottsdale | Scottsdale Seville | 7001 N. Scottsdale Rd. (E. Indian Bend Rd.) | 480-664-0180 | www.shinbay.com

There's nothing flashy about chef-owner Shinji Kurita or his modern Japanese digs, simply designed with wood and polished stone, in the Scottsdale Seville, but his meticulously sourced, painstakingly crafted (and pricey) omakase dinners – featuring wild-caught fish from Japan, giant Madagascar prawns, Kumamoto oysters and perfect uni – are spectacular; though a small à la carte selection is available, the full five- or seven-course dinner is the only way to go.

Tarbell's American
27 | 22 | 26 | $52

Camelback Corridor | Camelback East Shops | 3213 E. Camelback Rd. (32nd St.) | Phoenix | 602-955-8100 | www.tarbells.com

Experience a "deft" "synergy of wine and food" at this "lively" Camelback Corridor "shining beacon" where "culinary celebrity" and oenophile Mark Tarbell pairs "wonderful" American fare with "fantastic" wines among "pleasant" trappings; he "runs a tight ship" in the service department too, with "helpful", "personable" staffers to attend to a crowd filled with "important people" – the kind who have no trouble paying slightly "high-end" tabs.

T. Cook's Mediterranean
26 | 28 | 27 | $66

Phoenix | Royal Palms Resort & Spa | 5200 E. Camelback Rd. (bet. Arcadia Dr. & 56th St.) | 602-808-0766 | www.royalpalmshotel.com

"Have anything, you'll love it all" assure acolytes of this Phoenix "jewel" in a "boutique resort" whose "exceptional" Mediterranean fare and "excellent wine list" are served by "stellar" staffers in "romantic" digs with "fireplaces everywhere" and "lush", "impressive grounds"; the "expensive" tabs are unsurprising given the "one-of-a-kind" "dining experience", but you need not "wait for a special occasion", what with the "incredible" breakfasts, lunches and brunches whose slogan could well be "same quality, lower price."

Vincent's on Camelback ☒ French/Southwestern
27 | 24 | 25 | $60

Camelback Corridor | 3930 E. Camelback Rd. (40th St.) | Phoenix | 602-224-0225 | www.vincentsoncamelback.com

"Year after year", this Camelback Corridor "institution" is "never a disappointment" thanks to chef Vincent Guerithault's "remarkable", "creative" "fusion of Classic French and Southwest cuisines" plus "gracious" service; the "deep wine list" pleases oenophiles, and if aesthetes lament "dated decor", most find the setting "comfortable", "romantic" and as suited to "special occasions" as the "pricey" tabs suggest.

FOOD　DECOR　SERVICE　COST

Portland, OR

TOP FOOD RANKING

Restaurant	Cuisine
29 Painted Lady	Pacific NW
28 Le Pigeon	French
Genoa	Italian
Evoe	European/Sandwiches
Cabezon	Seafood
Lardo	Sandwiches
Andina	Peruvian
Noho's	Hawaiian
Lovely's Fifty Fifty	Pizza
Nostrana	Italian

OTHER NOTEWORTHY PLACES

Flying Pie	Pizza
Gustav's	German
Heathman	French/Pacific NW
Higgins	Pacific NW
Jake's Famous Crawfish	Seafood
Laurelhurst Market	Steak
Little Bird	French
McMenamins	Pub Food
Paley's Place	Pacific NW
Woodsman Tavern	Pacific NW

Andina *Peruvian*　　　　　28 | 26 | 26 | $40

Pearl District | Pennington Bldg. | 1314 NW Glisan St. (bet. 13th & 14th Aves.) | Portland | 503-228-9535 | www.andinarestaurant.com

An array of "lovely flavors" "tickle your taste buds" at this Pearl District "destination", where "adventurous" eaters tuck into "delicious, modern" Peruvian fare – plus a "huge selection" of "inventive, colorful" tapas – and wash it down with "amazing" "regional cocktails" (the "spicy" Sacsayhuáman concoction, pronounced 'sexy woman', is a "must"); "warm" service matches the "boisterous", "gorgeous" environs , and though "pricey", there's no denying it's the "real deal."

Cabezon 🗷 *Seafood*　　　　28 | 25 | 27 | $36

Hollywood | 5200 NE Sacramento St. (52nd Ave.) | Portland | 503-284-6617 | www.cabezonrestaurant.com

Tucked on a Hollywood side street, this "family-run" "neighborhood gem" offers a "wonderful", daily changing menu of "fresh", "creative" fin fare, as well as a number of "options for those who don't want seafood"; a "friendly" staff makes you "feel welcome" in the wooden-raftered interior (and, seasonally, at the sidewalk tables), and if some reviewers find the bill a tad "spendy", most agree it's "worth it."

	FOOD	DECOR	SERVICE	COST

Evoe ⓜ *European/Sandwiches* — 28 | 21 | 25 | $21

Hawthorne | 3731 SE Hawthorne Blvd. (bet. 37th & 38th Aves.) |
Portland | 503-232-1010 | www.pastaworks.com/evoe
"Every bite" of chef Kevin Gibson's "unusual, creative" sandwiches
and small plates is a "burst of flavor" insist insiders who "sit at the
counter" of this Hawthorne "gem" and watch as the European-inspired
dishes "come together"; it's set in a "simple, small" space in an "odd
location" (inside the gourmet grocery Pastaworks), but a "large collection" of wines by the glass, modest prices and that "exquisite" chow
overcome all; P.S. closes at 7 PM; closed Monday–Tuesday.

Flying Pie *Pizza* — 27 | 21 | 24 | $21

Lake Oswego | 3 Monroe Pkwy. (Boones Ferry Rd.) | 503-675-7377
Milwaukie | 16691 SE McLoughlin Blvd. (Naef Rd.) | 503-496-3170
Montavilla | 7804 SE Stark St. (78th Ave.) | Portland |
503-254-2016
Gresham | 1600 NW Fairview Dr. (Burnside Rd.) | 503-328-0018
www.flying-pie.com
"You'll never leave hungry" from this "quality" pizza chainlet, where
the "out-of-this-world" pies "heaped high" with "fresh" meat and veggies are "not a solo" venture ("bring friends") – and come at tabs that
lead frequent flyers to advise "you get way more than you pay for";
they skew "noisy", but the "smiling service is always a plus", as is the
"laid-back", "family-oriented" vibe and "offbeat" video games.

Genoa *Italian* — 28 | 18 | 21 | $85

Belmont | 2832 SE Belmont St. (bet. 28th & 29th Aves.) | Portland |
503-238-1464 | www.genoarestaurant.com
A "beloved" Belmont "institution" for "romantic", "unhurried" evenings
full of "food artistry", this "formal" Italian "wows" with an "exquisite"
five-course prix fixe menu of "imaginatively prepared", "consistently
superb" plates; the "impeccable service" includes a sommelier at the
"top of his game", and while it's "expensive", it's "well worth it"; P.S. it
shares space with "casual cousin" Accanto next door.

Gustav's *German* — 25 | 24 | 24 | $25

Clackamas | 12605 SE 97th Ave. (Sunnyside Rd.) | 503-653-1391
Hollywood | 5035 NE Sandy Blvd. (50th Ave.) | 503-288-5503
Tigard | 10350 SW Greenburg Rd. (Oak St.) | 503-639-4544
www.gustavs.net
"*Wunderbar!*" declare devotees of this "busy" local chainlet revered for
its "gut-busting" platters of "hearty", "full-flavored" German fare, "awesome deals" ("happy hour? yes, please") and "some of the best im-
ported beers" on tap; the "festive" atmosphere is enhanced by "yodeling
servers" in "authentic" garb who somehow "make you want to wear le-
derhosen" too – no wonder it's voted the Most Popular spot in Portland.

Heathman Restaurant *French/Pacific NW* — 26 | 25 | 26 | $47

Downtown | Heathman Hotel | 1001 SW Broadway (Salmon St.) |
Portland | 503-790-7752 | www.heathmanrestaurantandbar.com
"Elegance without pretense" takes center stage at this "romantic" destination in Downtown's "beautiful" Heathman Hotel, where "inventive"
"French-inflected" Pacific NW fare is prepped with a "commitment to
fresh, farm-to-table quality" – and whose "terrific" breakfasts, high
tea and "cool happy hours" also have a legion of fans; "impeccable"

service and a seemingly "bottomless" wine cellar supplement the "high-end enjoyment"; P.S. the post-Survey departure of culinary director Philippe Boulot may outdate the Food score.

Higgins Restaurant & Bar ● *Pacific NW* | 27 | 24 | 27 | $46 |

Downtown | 1239 SW Broadway (Jefferson St.) | Portland | 503-222-9070 | www.higginsportland.com

"Uniformly superb" NW dishes comprising the "freshest local ingredients" have kept "godfather of sustainability" Greg Higgins and his Downtown bistro near the "top of the Portland food chain" for nearly two decades; "outstanding" Oregon wines "add another dimension to meals", while the "classy" yet "relaxed" vibe in the "always busy" dining room ("make reservations!") is echoed by a staff of "total pros"; P.S. the "lively" bar boasts an "astonishing beer list" – and "less expensive" tabs.

Jake's Famous Crawfish *Seafood* | 27 | 24 | 26 | $38 |

Downtown | 401 SW 12th Ave. (Stark St.) | Portland | 503-226-1419 | www.jakesfamouscrawfish.com

This "legendary Portland seafood palace" is "still delivering the goods" after 100-plus years in its "clubby" Downtown digs, where "fresh, delicious" fish comes accompanied by "professional" service; it gets a "little pricey", which explains why the "bargain" lunch specials and "amazing" happy hours are especially "popular" – and that's when you'll see a "healthy amount of locals" among a "lot of tourists" in the eatery that spawned the McCormick & Schmick's chain.

Lardo Ⓜ *Sandwiches* | 28 | 21 | 27 | $17 |

Hawthorne | 1212 SE Hawthorne Blvd. (12th Ave.) | Portland | 503-234-7786 | www.lardopdx.com

Having originally peddled his "melt-in-your-mouth" pork products and "delicious" fries from one of the "cutest" food trucks, "talented" chef Rick Gencarelli has moved to solid ground with the post-Survey opening of this brick-and-mortar Hawthorne sandwich shop (not reflected in the Decor score); expect the same "awesome" pig-centric sammies, plus plenty of indoor/outdoor seating and a dozen-plus beers on tap.

Laurelhurst Market *Steak* | 26 | 21 | 24 | $43 |

Kerns | 3155 E. Burnside St. (32nd Ave.) | Portland | 503-206-3097 | www.laurelhurstmarket.com

"It's all about the meat" at this "lively" Kerns steakhouse/butcher shop, a "carnivore's delight" proffering "unusual" cuts "aged to perfection (and cooked even better)" plus "awesome" sides to go with; tabs can be a "little pricey" and toe-tappers lament "excruciating" waits for a table in the "industrial" space, but "exquisite" cocktails from some of the "best bartenders in town" and "professional" service help quell most beefs.

Le Pigeon *French* | 28 | 22 | 25 | $46 |

Lower Burnside | 738 E. Burnside St. (8th Ave.) | Portland | 503-546-8796 | www.lepigeon.com

"Impeccable" French cuisine that blends "whimsy, precision and inventiveness" attracts an "eclectic crowd" to this "snug joint" in Lower Burnside, where "loyal minions" snag seats at communal tables or at the counter to watch "highly skilled" (and "tattooed") chef Gabriel Rucker turn out "genius dishes" from an "ever-changing menu"; while some find it "pricey" for the tight fit, most are "drooling to go back."

	FOOD	DECOR	SERVICE	COST

Little Bird *French*

27 | **24** | **25** | **$35**

Downtown | 219 SW Sixth Ave. (Oak St.) | Portland | 503-688-5952 |
www.littlebirdbistro.com

"If you like Le Pigeon, you'll love" this "superb" Downtown bistro since
both share "*wunderkind*" chef Gabriel Rucker, who here helms an "interesting" menu of "country French" fare at "friendlier prices" (including a
duck confit that "will make a Frenchman cry"); the "just right", "foxy"
setting with dark red banquettes and an upstairs mezzanine are "usually
crowded" and overseen by a staff that "works as an amazing team."

Lovely's Fifty Fifty Ⓜ *Pizza*

28 | **22** | **26** | **$25**

Mississippi | 4039 N. Mississippi Ave. (bet. Mason & Shaver Sts.) |
Portland | 503-281-4060 | www.lovelysfiftyfifty.com

At this "cute, kitschy" Mississippi joint, "gorgeous" wood-fired pizzas
with "unconventional", locally sourced toppings share space on a gently priced menu with "delicious" salads and "killer" housemade ice
cream (including salted caramel – "OMG!") made all the better by "great
service"; naturally, it's almost "always jammed" with a "lively" crowd,
but no matter: loyalists just "love this place."

McMenamins Bagdad *Pub Food*

24 | **23** | **22** | **$22**

Hawthorne | 3702 SE Hawthorne Blvd. (37th Ave.) | Portland |
503-236-9234

McMenamins Barley Mill Pub *Pub Food*

Hawthorne | 1629 SE Hawthorne Blvd. (17th Ave.) | Portland |
503-231-1492

McMenamins Black Rabbit Restaurant *Pub Food*

Troutdale | Edgefield | 2126 SW Halsey St. (244th Ave.) |
503-669-8610

McMenamins Blue Moon *Pub Food*

Northwest Portland | 432 NW 21st Ave. (Glisan St.) | Portland |
503-223-3184

McMenamins Chapel Pub *Pub Food*

Humboldt | 430 N. Killingsworth St. (Commercial Ave.-Haight Ave. Alley) |
Portland | 503-286-0372

McMenamins Kennedy School
Courtyard Restaurant *Pub Food*

Concordia | Kennedy School | 5736 NE 33rd Ave. (bet. Jessup &
Simpson Sts.) | Portland | 503-249-3983

McMenamins Ringlers Annex *Pub Food*

Downtown | 1223 SW Stark St. (Burnside St.) | Portland | 503-384-2700

McMenamins Ringlers Pub *Pub Food*

Downtown | 1332 W. Burnside St. (bet. 13th & 14th Aves.) | Portland |
503-225-0627

McMenamins St. Johns *Pub Food*

St. Johns | 8203 N. Ivanhoe (Richmond Ave.) | Portland | 503-283-8520
www.mcmenamins.com

McMenamins Zeus Café *Pub Food*

Downtown | McMenamins Crystal Hotel | 303 SW 12th Ave. (bet. Burnside &
Stark Sts.) | Portland | 503-384-2500 | www.zeuscafepdx.com
Additional locations throughout the Portland area

The "solid" if "basic" pub fare "goes down easy" with the "hearty",
housemade craft beer at this "reliable" tavern family (ranked Most
Popular chain in Portland) owned by the McMenamin brothers, who

specialize in restoring notable buildings and decking them out with "eclectic" furnishings and colorful murals; opinions on service run the gamut ("swell" to "slow"), but many agree that the environs are "mellow" and the inexpensive menu offers "something for everyone."

Noho's *Hawaiian*   28 | 22 | 25 | $18

Beaumont | 4627 NE Fremont St. (47th Ave.) | Portland | 503-445-6646
Clinton | 2525 SE Clinton St. (26th Ave.) | Portland | 503-233-5301
www.nohos.com

It's "like a mini-vacation to the islands" at this "authentic" Hawaiian duo, where the "brilliant" barbecue "always hits the spot" ("Kahlua pig makes for a mighty fine Friday night"), as do the "not too expensive" prices; while "helpful" servers and surfer-abilia can be expected at both, Beaumont features a "great patio", while alcohol-free Clinton can feel a bit "crowded" – though "the food really makes up for it."

Nostrana *Italian*   28 | 24 | 23 | $37

Buckman | 1401 SE Morrison St. (14th Ave.) | Portland | 503-234-2427 | www.nostrana.com

"Wonderful" thin-crust pizza "baked to blistered perfection" in a wood-fired oven attracts acolytes to this "unpretentious" (some say "pricey") Buckman Italian that also wins converts for "authentic" dishes constructed from "high-quality ingredients handled simply"; though the oft-"crowded" digs can get "noisy at times", the "welcoming, knowledge-able" staff lends the "soaring", "lodge"-like space a "convivial" vibe.

Painted Lady Ⓜ *Pacific NW*   29 | 28 | 29 | $85

Newberg | 201 S. College St. (2nd St.) | 503-538-3850 | www.thepaintedladyrestaurant.com

"You're in for a remarkable" evening (and the Portland area's No. 1–rated Food) the "minute you step inside the picket fence" at this wine-country "jewel" set in a "romantic" Newberg Victorian, where the "world-class" Pacific NW tasting menus are "fascinating in their variety, seasonality and freshness"; "well-orchestrated" service and "fabulous" local vinos add to the "stellar" experience; P.S. rezzies required.

Paley's Place Bistro & Bar *Pacific NW*   27 | 24 | 26 | $58

Northwest Portland | 1204 NW 21st Ave. (Northrup St.) | Portland | 503-243-2403 | www.paleysplace.net

With the "intimate" confines of a "charming" Victorian dwelling serving as his backdrop, "master chef" Vitaly Paley prepares "sophisticated", "always surprising" Pacific NW fare replete with European flourishes and made from the "freshest" local ingredients in NW Portland; happily, he's backed by a "professional" staff and a "consummate hostess" "running the front of the house with ease" – his wife, Kimberly; P.S. reservations are "essential", especially for seats on the "gracious veranda."

The Woodsman Tavern *Pacific NW*   24 | 23 | 24 | $36

Division | 4537 SE Division St. (46th Ave.) | Portland | 971-373-8264 | www.woodsmantavern.com

Stumptown Coffee founder Duane Sorenson is the brains behind this Division "source of hyper-buzz", where a "professional" staff of "hairy guys and pretty gals" proffers "delicious" Pacific NW plates and inventive cocktails at modest tabs; the "cavernous" space features dark woods and vintage mountain landscapes that feed the rustic vibe.

Sacramento

TOP FOOD RANKING

	Restaurant	Cuisine
29	Taste	American
	Ambience	American
	Mulvaney's	American
	Kitchen	American
	Sunflower Drive-In	Health Food
28	Hawks	American
	Taylor's Kitchen	American
	Waterboy	Californian
27	Biba	Italian
	Ella	American

OTHER NOTEWORTHY PLACES

Blackbird Kitchen	Seafood
Cheesecake Factory	American
Firehouse	Continental
Frank Fat's	Chinese
Grange	Californian
Kru	Japanese
Lemon Grass	Thai/Vietnamese
Magpie Café	American
Mikuni	Japanese
Press Bistro	American

Ambience ◪ *American*   29 | 25 | 26 | $72
Carmichael | 6440 Fair Oaks Blvd. (Marconi Ave.) | 916-489-8464 |
www.ambiencerestaurantsac.com
"Don't let the location put you off" this hushed New American destination (with French touches) in a Carmichael "suburban strip
mall" – it's actually a "dining diamond" boasting "eye-catching"
presentations of "fabulous, inventive" prix fixe–only cuisine and
"architectural" desserts complemented by a "solid" selection of
bottles; some customers say it's "a bit pricey", but it's worth the
"splurge" for a "romantic" "special occasion", abetted by "semi-private
niches" and "professional" service.

Biba ◪ *Italian*   27 | 23 | 26 | $49
Midtown | 2801 Capitol Ave. (28th St.) | 916-455-2422 |
www.biba-restaurant.com
Chef-owner Biba Caggiano reigns as "the queen of Italian food" at
this "consistently excellent" Midtown "institution", where the "exceptional" fare is "beautifully presented" by "knowledgeable, attentive"
staffers (and accompanied by live piano most nights); a post-
Survey "full interior renovation" outdates the Decor score and makes
the prices, which are "geared toward lobbyist budgets", even more
"worth it"; P.S. the "legendary" "lasagna is a must", but alas, available
only Thursday and Friday.

	FOOD	DECOR	SERVICE	COST

Blackbird Kitchen & Bar 🗷 Ⓜ *Seafood*   - | - | - | M

Downtown | 1015 Ninth St. (J St.) | 916-498-9224 |
www.blackbird-kitchen.com

Hatched in April 2012, this highly personal American has taken wing,
enticing a hip young Downtown crowd with a quirkily stylish bi-level
dining room, local art and a hopping downstairs bar - think craft cocktails, a tight, affordable beer and wine list and an extended happy
hour; the frequently changing menu emphasizes locally farmed produce and sustainable seafood, offered raw in delicate composed plates
or inventively seasoned and cooked.

Cheesecake Factory *American*   22 | 22 | 21 | $26

Arden-Arcade | Market Sq. | 1771 Arden Way (Heritage Ln.) | 916-567-0606
Roseville | Galleria at Roseville | 1127 Galleria Blvd. (Roseville Pkwy.) |
916-781-3399
www.thecheesecakefactory.com

"Huge portions" of "affordable" American grub, a "long-as-a-book"
menu offering "something to please almost every craving" and "scrumptious cheesecake" are the reasons why surveyors rate these Arden-
Arcade and Roseville branches of the national chain Sacramento's
Most Popular restaurants; though there are complaints about the
"long waits", "out-there" decor and "high calorie" counts, the majority
overlooks them because the eateries are "fun" for "friends and family
get-togethers" and even "a date."

Ella Dining Room & Bar 🗷 *American*   27 | 27 | 26 | $56

Downtown | The Cathedral Bldg. | 1131 K St. (12th St.) | 916-443-3772 |
www.elladiningroomandbar.com

At this Downtown "charmer", local-star restaurateur Randall Selland
presents "genius" seasonal New American fare featuring "exciting
small plates", paired with "creative artisan cocktails" and "superb
wines" in an "airy", "breathtakingly beautiful" setting festooned with
hundreds of shutters; some respondents "'shutter' at the prices", but
with "outstanding service" thrown into the mix, most deem it a "nice
splurge" "for that special dinner" or a "power lunch"; P.S. a post-
Survey chef change is not reflected in the Food score.

Firehouse *Continental*   25 | 24 | 25 | $54

Old Sacramento | 1112 Second St. (bet. K & L Sts.) | 916-442-4772 |
www.firehouseoldsac.com

This Old Sacramento Continental in a converted firehouse ("with
brass pole and all") plies "traditional" appetites with "outstanding"
"old-line haute cuisine" and a "stellar wine list" in a "gentleman's
club"–like interior and "beautiful" courtyard, all benefiting from "fantastic service"; yes, it's "expensive", but admirers say "you feel like
you get your money's worth", so "do try it, and do save room for the
scrumptious desserts"; P.S. the Monday–Wednesday lunch special is
an affordable way to go.

Frank Fat's *Chinese*   24 | 22 | 24 | $34

Downtown | 806 L St. (8th St.) | 916-442-7092 | www.fatsrestaurants.com
A Downtown "institution" that has "kept up its quality" since 1939,
this "power joint" popular among the "state's movers and shakers" offers "excellent upscale Chinese food" like "must-try" honey walnut

prawns, "elegantly prepared and served" by a "prompt" staff; the "sexy" Asian "deco" setting features an "elegant bar and cool booths", and the prices are mostly moderate; P.S. "don't miss the iconic banana cream pie for dessert."

Grange *Californian*   25 | 25 | 23 | $46

Downtown | Citizen Hotel | 926 J St. (bet. 9th & 10th Sts.) | 916-492-4450 | www.grangesacramento.com
"Locavore heaven" is "located in a charming hotel" say fans of this Downtown Californian whose "superb farm-to-table philosophy" yields "exciting", "amazing" dishes that change daily; a "wonderful", architecturally "sophisticated" setting, "attentive" service and "expensive" pricing, not to mention "impressive wines" and "complex cocktails", all shore up its standing as a "hot spot"; P.S. a post-Survey chef change may outdate the Food score.

Hawks ⓜ *American*   28 | 27 | 27 | $48

Granite Bay | Quarry Ponds Town Ctr. | 5530 Douglas Blvd. (bet. Barton Rd. & Berg St.) | 916-791-6200 | www.hawksrestaurant.com
This "lovely little" Granite Bay American attracts a flock of followers who "always feel well taken care of", with "satisfying" fare that's "marvelous" "from amuse-bouche to dessert" and "unpretentious professional" service; an "outstanding wine list" and "great" patio further make it "worth the drive from Downtown", and if it's a bit of a "splurge", the prix fixe Sunday supper is "a deal that can't be beat."

The Kitchen ⓜ *American*   29 | 25 | 27 | $163

Arden-Arcade | 2225 Hurley Way (Howe Ave.) | 916-568-7171 | www.thekitchenrestaurant.com
Randall Selland and crew present "dinner theater with the chefs as the stars" at this Arden-Arcade New American, and acolytes rave about the "unparalleled", "interactive event" where "outstanding" multicourse, multihour prix fixes are made with "the freshest, most exotic ingredients" alongside "entertaining" "commentary"; with such a "small server-to-table ratio", you're "treated like royalty", adding to a "special night out" for which you should prepare to pay a "steep" price.

Kru *Japanese*   27 | 20 | 23 | $30

Midtown | 2516 J St. (bet. 25th & 26th Sts.) | 916-551-1559 | www.krurestaurant.com
"When they want sushi", toques from other eateries hit this Midtown Japanese where "fun, interactive" chefs prepare and "beautifully plate" "inspiring" creations, which can be paired with "unique sakes"; the "cosmopolitan, minimalist" setting also pleases, as do the moderate prices and "professional, friendly" table service.

Lemon Grass ⓩ *Thai/Vietnamese*   25 | 20 | 24 | $31

Arden-Arcade | 601 Munroe St. (Fair Oaks Blvd.) | 916-486-4891 | www.starginger.com
"As good as ever" rave loyalists of chef-owner Mai Pham's Arden-Arcade "institution" where the "pioneer" "beautifully prepares" her "zippy", "aromatic", "refined" Thai-Vietnamese recipes; a "warm, upscale ambience", "affordable" prices and "knowledgeable" service are part of the package, so if you haven't been, "go" – and prepare to "get addicted."

FOOD DECOR SERVICE COST

Magpie Café ☒ *American* | 27 | 18 | 22 | $24 |

Downtown | 1409 R St. (14th St.) | 916-452-7594 |
www.magpiecafe.com

"Wow" marvel mavens of this Downtown cafe that "carefully chooses" local, seasonal, "quality ingredients" for its "fantastic", "inspiring" American fare, including "amazing" baked goods and desserts; the prices are as "unfancy" as the "small", "urban" setting, which features counter service during the day and table service for dinner, both performed by "friendly", "attentive" staffers.

Mikuni *Japanese* | 25 | 21 | 22 | $30 |

Arden-Arcade | 1735 Arden Way (Challenge Way) | 916-564-2114
Davis | 500 First St. (bet. D & E Sts.) | 530-756-2111
Elk Grove | 8525 Bond Rd. (bet. Elk Crest Dr. & Stockton Blvd.) | 916-714-2112
Fair Oaks | 4323 Hazel Ave. (bet. Lake Nimbus Dr. & Winding Way) | 916-961-2112
Midtown | 1530 J St. (bet. 15th & 16th Sts.) | 916-447-2112
Roseville | 1017 Galleria Blvd. (Roseville Pkwy.) | 916-780-2119
www.mikunisushi.com

"Trendy", "heavenly, fresh sushi" with "divine sauces" prepared with "flair and zest" are the stars of the "book-length menu" at this Japanese mini-chain that's "always packed" and "noisy", especially the "hip" Midtown outlet (the "'burbs sites offer more family atmosphere"); as for decor and service, they're "adequate for the price they charge", although a number of folks find that price "a bit expensive" – thankfully, the "quality" is "consistent."

Mulvaney's B&L ☒ Ⓜ *American* | 29 | 24 | 27 | $50 |

Midtown | 1215 19th St. (bet. Capitol Ave. & L St.) | 916-441-6022 |
www.mulvaneysbl

"Praise the lard!" exalt disciples of this "Midtown gem" and its "ingenious" chef, Patrick Mulvaney, "a serious fan of the whole hog" who crafts a "sophisticated", daily changing menu of "luscious", "adventurous" "farm-to-table" New American dishes in a "quaint, old fire station" with a "lovely patio"; "sharp" staffers "can match" the fare with the "outstanding wine list", and while "a hog-wild dinner for two could set you back", it's "worth it" for "a special night out", especially "if you want to impress out-of-town guests."

Press Bistro Ⓜ *American* | 26 | 24 | 25 | $36 |

Midtown | 1809 Capitol Ave. (18th St.) | 916-444-2566 |
www.thepressbistro.com

Stop the presses! – it's "raves" all around for this "lively, affordable" New American arrival in Midtown whose "innovative concoctions" include "yummy" tapas, "impressive entrees" and "incredible" cocktails; "comfortably chic decor" and "relaxed lighting" also please, as does the "stellar service", which is overseen by the "delightful" chef-owner.

Sunflower Drive-In *Health Food/Vegan* | 29 | 9 | 18 | $12 |

Fair Oaks | 10344 Fair Oaks Blvd. (Main St.) | 916-967-4331 |
www.sunflowernaturalrestaurant.com

Fanatics are so "nuts for the nutburger" at this Fair Oaks purveyor of "awesome"-tasting, "good-value" vegan health food, they'll "drive miles out of their way to eat there"; just know that "there is no decor" and "service is at the window – and you better have your order ready 'cuz they don't have time for chitchat"; P.S. when the weather allows, eat at "one of the picnic tables outside" where chickens roam free.

Taste *American*

29 | 26 | 28 | $43

Plymouth | 9402 Main St. (Mineral St.) | 209-245-3463 | www.restauranttaste.com

"Surprise!" – "the finest dining experience in the greater Sacramento area" is found at this "unbelievable jewel" in "tiny", "rural" Plymouth, whose "superb", "high-end" American fare earns the No. 1 Food rating; the "wonderful, welcoming service" and setting that "oozes simple charm, character and class" make it a natural for "a special occasion" and a particularly "perfect ending to a day of wine tasting" in the "nearby Shenandoah Valley of Amador County."

Taylor's Kitchen Ⓜ *American*

28 | 22 | 24 | $46

Land Park | 2900 Freeport Blvd. (4th Ave.) | 916-443-6881 | www.taylorsmarket.com

"Magically skilled chefs", an "inventive, ever-changing menu" and a "well-chosen" vino list make this "casual", "inconspicuous" American next door to Land Park "specialty grocer" Taylor's Market a "destination for serious lovers of food and wine"; "great service and lovely decor" abet a "fun and deliciously satisfying evening" that's worth a "pricey" tab.

Waterboy *Californian*

28 | 23 | 26 | $49

Midtown | 2000 Capitol Ave. (20th St.) | 916-498-9891 | www.waterboyrestaurant.com

"Lovingly prepared", "world-class" modern Californian cuisine with Southern French–Northern Italian influences "to delight the foodie" pours out of Rick Mahan's kitchen at this "classy", "light and airy" Midtown "standout" that also features an "awesome wine list" and a "warm", "unobtrusive but ever-observant" staff; what's more, the cost is what you might "expect at a much lesser establishment", which means it works "for everything from family get-togethers to special occasions to a treat for out-of-town friends."

Salt Lake City & Mountain Resorts

TOP FOOD RANKING

Restaurant	Cuisine
28 Foundry Grill	American
Mariposa	American
Takashi	Japanese
Talisker on Main	American
Tiburon	American
Ruth's Chris	Steak
Communal	American
Chanon	Thai
Settebello	Italian
Franck's	American/French

OTHER NOTEWORTHY PLACES

Blue Iguana	Mexican
Cheesecake Factory	American
Copper Onion	American
Forage	American
Lion House Pantry	American/Dessert
Market Street Grill	Seafood
Mazza	Mideastern
Pago	American
Red Iguana	Mexican
Rodizio Grill	Brazilian/Steak

Blue Iguana *Mexican*   23 | 20 | 22 | $23

Downtown | 165 S. West Temple (100 S.) | Salt Lake City | 801-533-8900
Park City | 628 Park Ave. (Heber Ave.) | 435-658-9830
www.blueiguanarestaurant.net

"Mouthwatering moles" are the standout at this "accommodating", "affordable" duo that "fills your plate" with "excellent" Mexican food and tops it off with "strong, tasty" margaritas; the "slightly rough-around-the-edges" subterranean locale in Downtown Salt Lake has a "cool bohemian vibe", while Park City is a bit more refined with "old-miner historic-chic" decor and a deck overlooking Main Street.

Chanon Thai Cafe Ⓜ *Thai*   28 | 14 | 17 | $19

Eastside | 278 E. 900 South (300 E.) | Salt Lake City | 801-532-1177 | www.chanonthai.com

Heat hounds find some of the most "authentic, light-your-mouth-on-fire Thai in the Valley" at this "hole-in-the-wall" Eastsider serving "fantastic" curries and other "sweet, savory, complex" dishes that "satisfy" for "inexpensive" tabs; "you don't go for the atmosphere" or the service, but the "line outside" means "food is the top priority" here.

Cheesecake Factory *American*   25 | 24 | 23 | $29

Downtown | City Creek Ctr. | 65 Regent St. (100 S.) | Salt Lake City | 801-521-1732

(continued)

Cheesecake Factory

Murray | Fashion Place Mall | 6223 S. State St. (E. Winchester St.) | 801-266-9100 ●
www.thecheesecakefactory.com

"Delicious cheesecake, as expected, but some darn good entrees as well" hook customers at this "awesome" American with Downtown and Murray mall branches (Salt Lake City's Most Popular chain), where the food is "served with a smile" from a "menu so large it's bordering on obnoxious"; dubbed both "marvelous" and "kitschy", the surroundings generate "lots of hustle and bustle" (i.e. "long waits"), and while prices run a little "high", the "eye-popping" portions encourage you to "plan on leftovers."

Communal ⓈⓂ *American*   28 | 27 | 26 | $31

Provo | 100 N. University Ave. (100 N.) | 801-373-8000 | www.communalrestaurant.com

Part of a "revitalizing urban scene", this "stellar" Provo American delivers "incredible" "locavore" fare that "changes with the seasons", providing "needed relief from the chains and kitschy eateries of Utah Valley"; service is "top-notch" and the room's "hip to boot", "attractively" furnished with a "surprisingly comfortable" communal table and a few counter seats, so those who squeeze in say it's "100% worth the price"; P.S. the "fabulous" biscuits are a Saturday brunch treat.

Copper Onion *American*   25 | 20 | 22 | $31

Downtown | 111 E. Broadway (State St.) | Salt Lake City | 801-355-3282 | www.thecopperonion.com

"You had me at bone marrow" sigh "bon vivants" who marvel at the "magnificent flavors and creativity" abounding at this "bustling" Downtown New American, a "far-and-away favorite" for its "robust", "exciting" (and "reasonable") menu of small and large plates served in a "rustic/modern" room with an "indie film theater right next door"; it's a kick to "sit at the counter and watch the kitchen crew", so even if a few detect some "attitude", most find it a "must-dine."

Forage ⓈⓂ *American*   27 | 23 | 27 | $109

Downtown | 370 E. 900 South (400 E.) | Salt Lake City | 801-708-7834 | www.foragerestaurant.com

"No pedestrian fare here", just an "unforgettable culinary experience" of many "tiny", "artful" (and sometimes "bizarre") dishes at this "intimate" Downtown New American incorporating "formal, molecular gastronomy" into a prix fixe meal often lasting "three hours"; "service is flawless", the ambiance "subtle" and "wonderful extras" appear throughout the evening, so it's "pricey, but worth saving up for."

Foundry Grill *American*   28 | 27 | 24 | $36

Provo | Sundance Resort | 8841 N. Alpine Loop Rd. (Stewart Rd.) | 801-223-4220 | www.sundanceresort.com

"Simplicity" in the kitchen lends itself to "delicious", "satisfying" fare – earning the No. 1 Food score in the Salt Lake City/Mountain Resorts Survey – at this "rustic" American with a "cabin feel" at Robert Redford's Sundance Resort, where tourists as well as Provo and Park City locals "cozy up to the fireplace" in winter or "dine on the patio with the river and beautiful mountains in the background" in summer; rounded out by "good service" and midpriced menus, it's a "rewarding" experience that "makes you want to linger", perhaps for a "longer stay."

Franck's 🅢🅜 *American/French*   **28 | 24 | 27 | $49**

Cottonwood | 6263 Holladay Blvd. (6200 South) | Salt Lake City | 801-274-6264 | www.francksfood.com

"Exciting, daring and delicious" French-American fare in "whimsical interpretations" rates raves for chef Franck Peissel, who's "always in the kitchen" of this Cottonwood "standout" (check out the "kitchen cam"); "attentive", "informed" servers staff the "romantic" dining room and "lovely" patio, so while it's "a bit pricey", most find it a "marvelous" experience all around.

Lion House Pantry 🅢 *American/Dessert*   **25 | 22 | 24 | $17**

Downtown | 63 E. South Temple St. (bet. Main & State Sts.) | Salt Lake City | 801-363-5466 | www.lion-house.com

The "rolls with honey butter" are "heaven" in the house that Brigham Young built near Downtown's Temple Square, where American "down-home cooking" and "delicious desserts" come "cafeteria-style" with a "side of history"; it's "great for a family gathering" and for "tourists who want to see what Mormon food is all about", even if the "bakery items" tend to outshine the rest; P.S. no alcohol.

The Mariposa 🅜 *American*   **28 | 27 | 29 | $74**

Deer Valley | Silver Lake Lodge, Deer Valley Resort | 7600 Royal St. (Rte. 224) | 435-645-6715 | www.deervalley.com

"You're in for a treat" at this "unbelievable" Deer Valley destination where the "outstanding" (and expensive) New American fare and "fantastic wine list" are provided by a "remarkable" staff, earning it the No. 1 Service score in the Salt Lake City/Mountain Resorts Survey; with an "intimate", "lovely" setting at the winter-only Silver Lake Lodge, it's dubbed the "pinnacle" of dining among the Park City ski set.

Market Street Grill *Seafood*   **25 | 24 | 25 | $36**

Cottonwood | 2985 E. Cottonwood Pkwy. (3000 E.) | Salt Lake City | 801-942-8860
Downtown | 48 W. Market St. (Main St.) | Salt Lake City | 801-322-4668
South Jordan | 10702 S. River Front Pkwy. (700 W.) | 801-302-2262
www.gastronomyinc.com

"Superior" "fresh fish in land-locked Salt Lake City" (including "cold seafood platters that make your eyes pop") is the hallmark of this "lively, bustling" trio voted Most Popular in the metro area, with an airy Cape Cod style in South Jordan and "still-hip" "brasserie" vibe in Cottonwood and Downtown (where the breakfast "rocks" too); "wonderful" service is another plus, and while opinions vary on whether prices are fair or "fairly steep", most say it's still "buzzing" for a reason.

Mazza 🅢 *Mideastern*   **27 | 22 | 23 | $22**

Eastside | 912 E. 900 South (900 E.) | Salt Lake City | 801-521-4572
Eastside | 1515 S. 1500 East (bet. Emerson & Kensington Aves.) | Salt Lake City | 801-484-9259
www.mazzacafe.com

"Shawarma, kebabs and deliciousness" reign at this "decently priced" Eastside Middle Eastern duo that also excels with "vegan and vegetar-

| | FOOD | DECOR | SERVICE | COST |

ian" choices and "excellent" Lebanese wines in a "fun neighborhood" atmosphere; you're likely to see chef-owner Ali Sabbah "cruising the restaurant in his white shirt", overseeing a "happy, helpful" staff and "ensuring a great meal"; P.S. 15th East is the original "casual" charmer, while the 9th South location is larger with a "neat design."

Pago Ⓜ *American* | 26 | 23 | 24 | $38 |

Eastside | 878 S. 900 East (900 S.) | Salt Lake City | 801-532-0777 | www.pagoslc.com

"Put on your best jeans" and dig into "inventive" New American with a focus on "local" at this "fabulous little" Eastsider where "exposed brick, polished hipsters and flavorful food fuse" into a "snug" package, complete with a "top-notch" wine list; servers are "knowledgeable and efficient", and though "hefty" prices put some off, supporters say it's a real "value"; P.S. "make reservations."

Red Iguana *Mexican* | 27 | 19 | 24 | $20 |

Downtown | 736 W. North Temple St. (800 West) | Salt Lake City | 801-322-1489

Red Iguana 2 *Mexican*

Downtown | 866 W. South Temple (900 West) | Salt Lake City | 801-214-6050
www.rediguana.com

"If mole is the food of the gods, this place is heaven" avow converts who crave the "magnificent" sauces accenting the "unique", "stellar" Mexican with "regional" flavor at these "festive little cantinas" west of Downtown (North Temple is the original, funkier locale); there's "always a wait" given the "packed" quarters, but service is "amazingly fast and helpful", and it's "cheap too."

Rodizio Grill *Brazilian/Steak* | 26 | 23 | 25 | $35 |

Eastside | 459 Trolley Sq. (bet. 600 S. & 700 E.) | Salt Lake City | 801-220-0500 | www.rodiziogrill.com

Experience a Brazilian "meat-a-palooza" at this Eastside fave where the "delectable", "fresh-off-the-fire" steak and other skewers (including "irresistible" glazed pineapple) "keep on coming", so it's "definitely worth the money" – whether or not you indulge at the "exceptional" salad bar; the staff is "fun and personable" and the "beautiful" second-floor setting on Trolley Square offers "lots of windows to view the city", all the more reason "carnivores of the world celebrate here."

Ruth's Chris Steak House *Steak* | 28 | 25 | 27 | $67 |

Downtown | 275 S. West Temple (W. Broadway) | Salt Lake City | 801-363-2000

Park City | Hotel Park City | 2001 Park Ave. (Thaynes Canyon Dr.) | 435-940-5070
www.ruthschris.com

"Mouthwatering steaks and sides" conjure "Shangri-la" for champions of these "high-end" links in the national chophouse chain, counted on for "quality and consistency" when it comes to delivering "out-of-this-world" beef; add in "meticulous" service and "beautiful" decor – including a swank bar in the Salt Lake location and a swell deck in Park City – and the "exquisite" experience is "spendy but worth it."

Settebello *Italian* | 28 | 19 | 22 | $22 |

Downtown | 260 S. 200 West (Broadway) | Salt Lake City | 801-322-3556 | www.settebello.net

"Made before your eyes" with "pure, fresh" ingredients and a "charred" thin crust, the "savory", "real Neapolitan" pies at this "casual" Downtown brick-oven pizzeria (with a newish Farmington outpost) are rated the "hands-down best" in town; "terrific" salads and "tasty" gelato round out the offerings, so despite a "cafeteria"-like atmosphere, loyalists would choose it for a "last meal."

Takashi Ⓩ *Japanese* | 28 | 25 | 23 | $37 |

Downtown | 18 W. Market St. (bet. 300 & 400 S.) | Salt Lake City | 801-519-9595

"Prepare to be blown away" by Takashi Gibo's "phenomenal" sushi and other "spectacular" Japanese dishes (with a little "Peruvian flair") that are a "feast for the eyes as well as the palate" at this Downtown "hot spot" with "terrific", art-adorned surroundings, "excellent" service and a "lively, youthful" following; diners don't mind "dropping some coin" on the "finest" catches, though "long waits" are a "downside" so be sure to "go early."

Talisker on Main *American* | 28 | 27 | 26 | $62 |

Park City | 515 Main St. (Herber Ave.) | 435-658-5479 | www.taliskeronmain.com

"Unique, seasonal creations" shine at this "sophisticated" Park City American offering "first-class dining on Main Street", with its daily changing menu and "cozy", "welcoming" atmosphere that's "perfect for a night with friends or a romantic date" (especially in the intimate wine room); praising "unparalleled" dinners capped off by "exceptional" service, fans barely blink at the tall bill; P.S. closed from mid-April to early June.

Tiburon *American* | 28 | 24 | 26 | $47 |

Sandy | 8256 S. 700 East (9000 S.) | 801-255-1200 | www.tiburonfinedining.com

"Every dish is a winner" bolstered by "vegetables and herbs from the garden" on-site, but "the elk tenderloin cannot be beat" say lovers of this "rare" American offering "fine dining in a suburban setting" south of Salt Lake in Sandy; fans also "love the patio", "great atmosphere" and "cordial", "down-to-earth" staff, recommending it "for a date" or "special occasion."

San Antonio

TOP FOOD RANKING

	Restaurant	Cuisine
28	Bistro Vatel	French
27	Sorrento	Italian
	Bohanan's	American
	Dough	Pizza
	Silo	American
	Il Sogno	Italian
	Gourmet Burger	Burgers
	Sandbar	Seafood
26	Grey Moss Inn	American
	Biga on the Banks	American

OTHER NOTEWORTHY PLACES

Restaurant	Cuisine
Bliss	American/Eclectic
Boudro's	Seafood/Steak
Citrus	American/Eclectic
Feast	American/Eclectic
La Gloria	Mexican
Lüke	French/German
Monterey	American
NAO	Pan Latino
Rudy's Country Store	BBQ
Sustenio	American/Southwestern

Biga on the Banks *American*   26 | 26 | 25 | $50

River Walk | 203 S. St. Mary's St. (Market St.) | 210-225-0722 |
www.biga.com

"First-rate all the way" – and San Antonio's Most Popular restaurant –
this "sophisticated" River Walk respite puts out an "excellent", "innovative" mix of New American and Southwest fare from chef-owner Bruce
Auden in "industrial-chic" surroundings; add an "accommodating" staff
and it's worth the "splurge"; P.S. look for pre- and post-theater prix
fixe dinners as well as half-price options on entrees on weekends.

Bistro Vatel Ⓜ *French*   28 | 20 | 25 | $46

Olmos Park | 218 E. Olmos Dr. (McCullough Ave.) | 210-828-3141 |
www.bistrovatel.com

It may be a "low-key" bistro in an Olmos Park strip mall but its "lovely"
fish, hanger steaks and other "super", "high-quality" French fare from
Damien Watel earn it San Antonio's No. 1 Food rating; a "cozy atmosphere" and "good-value" pricing further inspire repeat visits; P.S. the
$45 prix fixe menu is "a deal."

Bliss Ⓩ Ⓜ *American*   - | - | - | E

Southtown | 926 S. Presa St. (Eager St.) | 210-225-2547 |
www.foodisbliss.com

The first solo venture of well-respected chef Mark Bliss (Silo), this
stylishly updated filling station in Southtown fuels appetites with

high-octane, high-end New American dishes like chicken-fried oysters and seared scallops on cheesy grits, as well as daily creative extras; the space is enhanced with modern art and natural light, and the stove-side chef's table offers a glimpse of the calm control a kitchen can be.

Bohanan's Prime Steaks & Seafood *Steak*   27 | 23 | 26 | $72

Downtown | 219 E. Houston St., 2nd fl. (bet. Navarro & St. Mary's Sts.) | 210-472-2600 | www.bohanans.com

A "classic steakhouse done right", this "much-loved" Downtown entry "exceeds expectations" with "outstanding" beef, a "stellar bar with well-made cocktails" and an "old-school" vibe; "expensive" tabs hardly faze the "expense-account" clientele; P.S. the bar is on the ground floor and stays open later with a light menu.

Boudro's on the Riverwalk *Seafood/Steak*   24 | 22 | 22 | $40

River Walk | 421 E. Commerce St. (bet. Losoya & Presa Sts.) | 210-224-8484 | www.boudros.com

It's always a "party" at this River Walk spot where "tourists and locals" angle for an outside seat for "mouthwatering" seafood and steaks with Texas touches, "famous" tableside guac and "strong drinks" that "will have you down for the count"; "exceptional people-watching" and "attentive service" seal the deal; P.S. "make reservations."

Citrus *American/Eclectic*   ▽ 26 | 24 | 24 | $45

Downtown | Hotel Valencia | 150 E. Houston St. (St. Mary's St.) | 210-230-8412 | www.hotelvalencia.com

"More than a hotel restaurant", this "chic" entry in Downtown's Valencia proves a "wonderful choice" for business or a date thanks to its "excellent" Eclectic–New American menu that changes with the seasons; the "upscale" setting also boasts River Walk views from the upper deck; P.S. breakfast and paella lunches are also popular.

Dough *Pizza*   27 | 21 | 24 | $26

North Central | Blanco Junction Shopping Ctr. | 6989 Blanco Rd. (Loop 410) | 210-979-6565 | www.doughpizzeria.com

"Mamma mia!", there are "lines out the door every night" at this otherwise unassuming North Central pizzeria plying "superlative", "thin-crust" Neapolitan pies and other "fab" Italian items "done with panache" including a "not-to-be-missed" housemade burrata; there's also "terrific" service, "generous wine pours" and modest bills, making it a "definite must-go."

Feast *American*   - | - | - | M

Southtown | 1024 S. Alamo St. (bet. Cedar & Mission Sts.) | 210-354-1024 | www.feastsa.com

Tongues are wagging about Southtown's latest player in the small-plates dining scene, this hip New American delivering fanciful dishes (categorized as hot/chilled/grilled/crispy/melted) and inspired takes on classic cocktails; it has a cool, ethereal look with crystal chandeliers and acrylic furniture set against white walls; pricing, however, is decidedly down-to-earth.

Gourmet Burger Grill *Burgers*   27 | 17 | 21 | $15

North | CityView | 11224 Huebner Rd. (McDermott Frwy.) | 210-558-9200

(continued)

Gourmet Burger Grill

North Central | The Legacy | 18414 Hwy. 281 N. (Loop 1604) |
210-545-3800
www.gourmetburgergrill.com

"Perfectly seasoned" lamb, bison, tuna and veggie patties add zest to
the usual burger grind at these "gourmet" grills in San Antonio, also
slinging more "traditional" varieties; prices are pleasing, but the looks
are strictly "strip-mall chic" with a spare, functional design.

Grey Moss Inn *American*

27 | 26 | 26 | $45

Helotes | 19010 Scenic Loop Rd. (Blue Hill Dr.) | 210-695-8301 |
www.grey-moss-inn.com

With "all the charm of a country inn a short distance from San Antonio",
this "delightful hideaway" in Helotes hosts "romantic dinners" galore
in its "rustic" interior or its "beautiful" courtyard; the "unique" Texas-
accented American menu features "delicious" steaks cooked on an
outdoor grill, although some find the bills a touch costly.

Il Sogno Ⓜ *Italian*

27 | 23 | 25 | $48

Near North | Pearl Brewery | 200 E. Grayson St. (Karnes St.) |
210-223-3900 | www.pearlbrewery.com

A "don't-miss" antipasti table "tempts" on arrival and leads to "expertly
prepared", "innovative" Italian plates from chef Andrew Weissman
(Sandbar) at this Near Northerner in the Pearl Brewery complex; it's
"pricey", but service is "impeccable", making entree into the "always"
a-"buzz" industrial dining room "worth waiting" for.

La Gloria *Mexican*

23 | 21 | 16 | $20

Near North | Pearl Brewery | 100 E. Grayson St. (Elmira St.) | 210-267-9040 |
www.lagloriaicehouse.com

"Funky" and "informal", this Near North cantina in the Pearl Brewery
from Johnny Hernandez specializes in "wonderful", "fantastically
spiced" Mexican street food in small plates that are "fun to share";
admirers overlook uneven service and "not cheap" à la carte pricing and focus on the "picturesque" views from the quieter end of
the River Walk.

Lüke *French/German*

22 | 20 | 19 | $39

Downtown | Embassy Suites | 125 E. Houston St. (Soledad Ave.) |
210-227-5853 | www.lukesanantonio.com

This "delicious respite" Downtown comes from New Orleans chef
John Besh (August, La Provence) and is set in a somewhat "odd location" inside a new Embassy Suites (though it's not the hotel restaurant); it serves a mostly "excellent" French-German brasserie menu
that's "not just the same old, same old" backed by "fantastic local and
Belgian beers"; despite "inconsistent" service, its reasonable bills,
"old-style bar" and quiet River Walk patio make it a popular pre- or
post-theater treat.

The Monterey ◑ *American*

- | - | - | I

Southtown | 1127 S. St. Mary's (bet. Pereida & Stieren Sts.) |
210-745-2581 | www.themontereysa.com

"Incredibly inventive" American snacks grab the spotlight at this
Southtown spot, a renovated gas station with "limited inside seating"

and three times the space on the "great" patio; like the food menu, the considerable wine and beer selection is "affordably priced", just as you would expect from such an "eclectic, casual" environment.

NAO ⊠Ⓜ *Latin American*

| – | – | – | M |

Near North | Culinary Institute of American | 312 Pearl Pkwy. (Karnee St.) | 210-554-6481 | www.ciarestaurants.com

Latin ingredients, ancient techniques and student learning are woven into fascinating dishes boasting the elite distinction of the Culinary Institute of America at this moderately priced Near North arrival; dinner entrees, small plates and cocktails showcase unusual yet familiar components from Latin American and Caribbean cultures, turning the dining experience into a flavorful, boundary-expanding excursion; P.S. limited seating demands advance reservations.

Rudy's *BBQ*

| 25 | 16 | 20 | $16 |

Selma | 15560 I-35 N. (Evans Rd.) | 210-653-7839
Leon Springs | 24152 I-10 W. (Boerne Stage Rd.) | 210-698-2141
Westside | 10623 Westover Hills Blvd. (Hwy. 151) | 210-520-5552
www.rudys.com

You can smell the smoke from "a mile away" at these "solid-as-a-rock" chain pit stops doling out "tender" BBQ brisket ("go for the extra moist") and "mouthwatering ribs" sided with "amazing" "signature creamed corn"; most are set in refurbished gas stations, so you can line up "cafeteria-style", "order by the pound" and fill up your tank on the way out – talk about "true fast food."

Sandbar Fish House & Market ⊠Ⓜ *Seafood*

| 27 | 23 | 23 | $41 |

Near North | Pearl Brewery | 200 E. Grayson St. (Karnes St.) | 210-212-2221 | www.sandbarsa.com

"Every single dish is crafted with total precision" and tastes "superb" at this Near North seafooder overseen by Andrew Weissman (Il Sogno); its steel-and-white-tile locale in the Pearl Brewery complex is "a little stark" and the tabs are a bit "pricey", but don't let that deter you – it's unquestionably "worth it."

Silo Elevated Cuisine *American*

| 27 | 25 | 26 | $41 |

Alamo Heights | 1133 Austin Hwy. (Mt. Calvary Dr.) | 210-824-8686

Silo 1604 *American*

Loop 1604 | Ventura Plaza | 434 N. Loop 1604 NW (off Access Rd. 1604) | 210-483-8989
www.siloelevatedcuisine.com

Admirers attest it's "impossible to go wrong" at this Alamo Heights bistro or its Loop 1604 spin-off serving up a "surprising" roster of New American dishes in "chic" surroundings blessed with "cool" bar scenes; tabs are "pricey, but not outrageous" – no wonder both are so "popular."

Sorrento ⊠ *Italian*

| 27 | 17 | 23 | $29 |

Alamo Heights | 5146 Broadway St. (Grove Pl.) | 210-824-0055 | www.sorrentopizzeria.com

"Great" pizza is the highlight of this Alamo Heights Italian with a ristorante component preparing antipasti, pastas and entrees; wallet-friendly prices match the "homey, comfortable" environment, with red-checkered tablecloths and "families" galore.

Sustenio *Southwestern* | - | - | - | M |

Northeast | Eilan Hotel | 17103 La Cantera Pkwy. (I-10 Frontage Rd.) | 210-598-2900 | www.eilan.com

Dallas legend Stephan Pyles makes a splash in San Antonio with this upscale Southwestern newcomer set in an airy space in the Eilan Hotel; it features his signature ceviche bar along with some classics from his eponymous flagship like a dressed-up Caesar salad and cowboy rib-eye, plus new twists on local ingredients courtesy of executive chef David Gilbert; P.S. there's also an impressive cocktail menu.

San Diego

TOP FOOD RANKING

	Restaurant	Cuisine
29	Sushi Ota	Japanese
28	Tao	Asian/Vegetarian
	Market Restaurant	Californian
	Tapenade	French
27	Pamplemousse	American/French
	Ruth's Chris	Steak
	Donovan's Steak	Steak
	West Steak	Steak/Seafood
	Blue Water	Seafood
	Mille Fleurs	French

OTHER NOTEWORTHY PLACES

Restaurant	Cuisine
Addison	French
Anthony's Fish	Seafood
A.R. Valentien	Californian
Brigantine Seafood	Seafood
George's Cal. Modern/Ocean	Californian
In-N-Out	Burgers
Island Prime/C Level Lounge	Seafood/Steak
94th Aero Squadron	American/Steak
Phil's BBQ	BBQ
Wine Vault	Eclectic

Addison Ⓢ Ⓜ *French*   27 | 27 | 27 | $130

Carmel Valley | Grand Del Mar | 5200 Grand Del Mar Way (Del Mar Way) | 858-314-1900 | www.addisondelmar.com

"First class in every respect", this "extravagant" New French draws seekers of "ethereal flavors" to Carmel Valley's "ultraposh" Grand Del Mar resort, where chef William Bradley's "superior" dinners (with "astounding" wine pairings) rank among "SoCal's best"; the food is matched by "opulent villa" surroundings where you're "treated like royalty" by a "formal but warm" staff that earns the No. 1 score for Service in San Diego – though you may have to "pawn the family jewels to afford it."

Anthony's Fish Grotto *Seafood*   24 | 20 | 22 | $31

Downtown | 1360 N. Harbor Dr. (Ash St.) | 619-232-5103
La Mesa | 9530 Murray Dr. (Water St.) | 619-463-0368

Anthony's Fishette *Seafood*

Downtown | 1360 N. Harbor Dr. (Ash St.) | 619-232-2175
www.gofishanthonys.com

"Around for decades", these "classic" midpriced seafooders, voted Most Popular in San Diego, still turn out "famous" chowder and other "delicious" daily catches for "tourists and locals" alike; service is "family-friendly", and though critics call them fairly "dated", they're won over by the "completely unpretentious" feel and "fresh ocean breezes" at the Downtown locale's more "casual" Fishette adjunct.

A.R. Valentien *Californian*
26 | 26 | 26 | $67

La Jolla | Lodge at Torrey Pines | 11480 N. Torrey Pines Rd. (Callan Rd.) | 858-777-6635 | www.arvalentien.com

Chef Jeff Jackson "works wonders" with the "freshest" of "farm-to-table" ingredients to create a "constantly changing" menu of "incomparable" Cal cuisine at this "unique destination" in La Jolla's Lodge at Torrey Pines; "impeccable" service that's "gracious yet unobtrusive" and a "beautiful, Craftsman-style" setting with "majestic" golf-course views make it a "gift to San Diego" – albeit a "pricey" one.

Blue Water Seafood *Seafood*
27 | 15 | 20 | $21

India Street | 3667 India St. (bet. Chalmers & Washington Sts.) | 619-497-0914 | www.bluewaterseafoodsandiego.com

Fish doesn't get any "fresher" than this "unless you catch it yourself" say fans of this "bang-for-the-buck" India Street restaurant/market serving "delicious, customizable seafood" via counter service with "long lines"; there's "no pretension – or ambiance", so "dive buddies" and others can "cruise in wearing drenched wet suits" and dine on "paper plates with plastic utensils."

Brigantine Seafood *Seafood*
24 | 22 | 23 | $35

Coronado | 1333 Orange Ave. (Adella Ave.) | 619-435-4166
La Mesa | 9350 Fuerte Dr. (bet. Grossmont Blvd. & Severin Dr.) | 619-465-1935
Escondido | 421 W. Felicita Ave. (Centre City Pkwy.) | 760-743-4718
Point Loma | 2725 Shelter Island Dr. (Shafter St.) | 619-224-2871
Poway | 13445 Poway Rd. (Community Rd.) | 858-486-3066
Del Mar | 3263 Camino Del Mar (Via De La Valle) | 858-481-1166
www.brigantine.com

For "flavorful, simple" fare that "satisfies your seafood cravings" – think "favorite" fish tacos and "perfectly cooked" fillets – this "upscale chain" meets "high expectations", especially during the "vibrant", "affordable" happy hour; the "polite" staff is "speedy" even when there's a "huge crush" of customers, and though the "dust needs to be blown off" some locations, Del Mar is "newly renovated."

Donovan's Steak & Chop House *Steak*
27 | 25 | 26 | $68

Gaslamp Quarter | 570 K St. (6th Ave.) | 619-237-9700
Golden Triangle | 4340 La Jolla Village Dr. (Genesee Ave.) | 858-450-6666 🛇
www.donovanssteakhouse.com

Beef eaters boast "you'll never have a better steak" than at these Golden Triangle and Gaslamp "temples of red meat" where a "superb" team proffers "generous" plates of "tender", "top-quality" cuts "with all the fixin's" and "smooth" martinis at "through-the-roof" prices; the "dark, clubby" decor pleases, though "noisy, upscale crowds" make an "intimate dinner" unlikely.

George's California Modern *Californian*
27 | 27 | 26 | $51

La Jolla | 1250 Prospect St. (bet. Cave St. & Ivanhoe Ave.) | 858-454-4244

George's Ocean Terrace *Californian*

La Jolla | 1250 Prospect St. (bet. Cave St. & Ivanhoe Ave.) | 858-454-4244
www.georgesatthecove.com

With "fantastic" Californian fare from chef Trey Foshee, an "eclectic, extensive" wine list and a "one-of-a-kind" setting boasting "unsurpassed" ocean views, it's no wonder proprietor George Hauer's "tried-and-true performer" in La Jolla "endures with consistency"; the "accommodating" staff "operates like a well-oiled machine", plus the "relaxed" rooftop terrace offers a less "pricey" option for equally "enjoyable" meals.

In-N-Out Burger ● *Burgers* 26 | 18 | 24 | $10

El Cajon | 1541 N. Magnolia Ave. (Bradley Ave.)
Kearny Mesa | 4375 Kearny Mesa Rd. (Armour St.)
Mira Mesa | 9410 Mira Mesa Blvd. (Westview Pkwy.)
Mission Valley | 2005 Camino Del Este (Camino Del Rio)
Carlsbad | 5950 Avenida Encinas (Palomar Airport Rd.)
Rancho Bernardo | 11880 Carmel Mountain Rd. (Rancho Carmel Dr.)
Pacific Beach | 2910 Damon Ave. (Mission Bay Dr.)
Chula Vista | 1725 Eastlake Pkwy. (Dawn Crest Ln.)
Sports Arena | 3102 Sports Arena Blvd. (Rosecrans St.)
800-786-1000 | www.in-n-out.com

Rated Most Popular chain and top Bang for the Buck in San Diego, this "classic-Cal" burger chain is "beloved" for "fresh-cut fries, fresh-cut produce and fresh beef" that all add up to "heaven on a bun" and can be complemented with grilled cheese, Neapolitan milkshakes and saucy "animal-style" patties from the "secret menu"; a "chipper" counter crew and "extra-clean" locations help offset "long waits" and a sometimes "slow drive-thru."

Island Prime/C Level Lounge *Seafood/Steak* 26 | 27 | 25 | $46

Harbor Island | 880 Harbor Island Dr. (Harbor Dr.) | 619-298-6802 | www.cohnrestaurants.com

"Show off your hometown" at this Harbor Island waterfronter from Cohn Restaurant Group, with "spectacular" skyline views ("what more decor do you need?") and "well-crafted, flavorful" steak and seafood dishes from chef Deborah Scott; whether in the "upscale" Island Prime or "more casual, less costly" C-Level Lounge, the staff lends a "pleasant" touch.

Market Restaurant & Bar *Californian* 28 | 23 | 26 | $69

Del Mar | 3702 Via de la Valle (El Camino Real) | 858-523-0007 | www.marketdelmar.com

"Everything is spectacular" on "genius" chef-owner Carl Schroeder's "fresh, irresistible" menu (including sushi) at this "expensive but worth-it" Del Mar "must", where "inventive" Californian dishes drawing on "many cultures" pair with "unknown gems" from a "thoughtful" wine list; you may need to "borrow a Ferrari" to fit in, but most say the "super-relaxed" surrounds and "pro" servers who are "anxious to please" complete the "flawless" night.

Mille Fleurs *French* 27 | 26 | 27 | $76

Rancho Santa Fe | Country Squire Courtyard | 6009 Paseo Delicias (Avineda De Acasias) | 858-756-3085 | www.millefleurs.com

"Mon dieu!" exclaim "stylish" fans of chef Martin Woesle's "delightful" New French creations at this "epitome of culinary indulgence" in Rancho Santa Fe, where "extraordinary" service bolsters the "first-class" (a few say "stuffy") atmosphere in a Provençal "country-home" setting; there's also a "special" patio and "welcoming" piano bar, where those not up for "investment dining" can enjoy a more "accessible" menu.

	FOOD	DECOR	SERVICE	COST

94th Aero Squadron
Restaurant *American/Steak* | 22 | 22 | 22 | $32 |

Kearny Mesa | 8885 Balboa Ave. (Ponderossa Ave.) | 858-560-6771 |
www.94thaerosquadron.signonsandiego.com

Offering "predictable but always tasty" surf 'n' turf, a "great" Sunday
brunch and solid service, this Kearny Mesa "standby" near Montgomery
Field invites high-flying fans to dine then "walk to their private plane
and take off"; those who find the antiques-packed interior "faded" can
enjoy a "lovely landscaped outdoor area", where they can watch jets
disembark "with the wind in their hair."

Pamplemousse Grille *American/French* | 27 | 22 | 26 | $71 |

Solana Beach | 514 Via de la Valle (I-5) | 858-792-9090 |
www.pgrille.com

Even those "not easily impressed" will be "blown away" by the French-
New American "masterpieces", "magisterial" wine list and "sticker-
shock prices" at this "class act" in a Solana Beach office complex;
"bigger-than-life" chef-owner Jeffrey Strauss is a "great host", guiding
"warm yet not intrusive" service in an "elegant, comfortable" space
(decorated with "farm paintings") that attracts a "winning" crowd
from the nearby racetrack.

Phil's BBQ Ⓜ *BBQ* | 26 | 20 | 22 | $22 |

San Marcos | 579 Grand Ave. (San Marcos Blvd.) | 760-759-1400
Sports Arena | 3750 Sports Arena Blvd. (Hancock St.) | 619-226-6333
www.philsbbq.net

"Wonderful aromas" of "scrumptious", "exceedingly tender" ribs and
pulled pork draw lines "longer than Disneyland" to these "affordable"
Sports Arena and San Marcos "benchmark BBQ" spots where an
"eager-to-please" counter staff makes sure queues "move fast"; diners dig in at "family-style picnic tables" equipped with "plenty of paper
towels" to mop up the "finger-lickin'" feast.

Ruth's Chris Steak House *Steak* | 27 | 24 | 26 | $71 |

Del Mar | 11582 El Camino Real (Carmel Valley Rd.) | 858-755-1454
Downtown | 1355 N. Harbor Dr. (Ash St.) | 619-233-1422
www.ruthschris.com

Unleash your inner "caveman" on the "buttery" steaks "cooked to perfection" and complemented by "gargantuan" sides, "sinful" desserts
and "potent" cocktails at these Downtown and Del Mar links in the
"high-end" national chain; "superior" service and "fantastic" views from
the "contemporary" dining room further support the "splurge" prices.

Sushi Ota *Japanese* | 29 | 16 | 21 | $49 |

Pacific Beach | 4529 Mission Bay Dr. (Bunker Hill St.) | 858-270-5670 |
www.sushiota.com

"Sushi purists" will "cry" tears of "pleasure" when "lucky enough" to
snag a seat at this "incomparable" Pacific Beach Japanese, where "extremely gracious" chef-owner Yukito Ota and his talented "army"
earn the No. 1 Food score in San Diego with "simply magnificent" seafood "delicacies" and an "innovative" omakase tasting; frequently
"hurried" service, a "random" strip-mall location and "shabby" interior certainly don't match the "phenomenal" fare and "pricey" tabs,
but guests still need to make a reservation "well in advance."

	FOOD	DECOR	SERVICE	COST

Tao ☒ *Asian/Vegetarian* | 28 | 21 | 24 | $19 |

Normal Heights | 3332 Adams Ave. (Felton St.) | 619-281-6888

Even though you're allowed to "write on the walls" with markers, don't be deceived by the "quirky" setting of this Normal Heights Asian joint – an affordable new "favorite" for its "generous", "spicy" and "always-fresh" dishes that appeal to carnivores and vegetarians alike; what's more, the staff "always greets you warmly" and is "very willing to accommodate" any special requests.

Tapenade *French* | 28 | 21 | 26 | $61 |

La Jolla | 7612 Fay Ave. (bet. Kline & Pearl Sts.) | 858-551-7500 | www.tapenaderestaurant.com

Francophiles say "*merci*" to "brilliant" chef Jean-Michel Diot for his "creative" dishes with "fantastically layered" flavors and "delightful presentations", complemented by a "well-balanced" wine list, at this "pricey" French destination in La Jolla; the atmosphere is "bright" and "serene", and though a few detect a "mildly pretentious" air, most report "first-rate" service attuned to the "classy" clientele.

West Steak & Seafood *Seafood/Steak* | 27 | 25 | 26 | $64 |

Carlsbad | 4980 Avenida Encinas (Cannon Rd.) | 760-930-9100 | www.weststeakandseafood.com

"Terrific fine dining" thrives at this Carlsbad surf 'n' turfer, where "perfectly prepared" steaks and "outstanding" seafood – sided with seasonal produce from the restaurant's private farm – earn raves; upscale decor and "attentive" servers reinforce its "special-occasion" status, though the happy-hour bar menu is an "excellent" deal.

Wine Vault & Bistro ☒☒ *Eclectic* | 27 | 22 | 25 | $45 |

India Street | 3731 India St. (Washington St.) | 619-295-3939 | www.winevaultbistro.com

With "scrumptious, thoughtfully prepared" Eclectic fare, "well-chosen" wine pairings and "bargain" prix fixe meals, "you can't go wrong" at this "hidden treasure" in Mission Hills; the "simple" space holds "large communal tables" that create "great camaraderie with fellow guests", overseen by "dedicated" owners who "truly care about their patrons"; P.S. open Thursday–Saturday only (with winemaker dinners on other nights).

San Francisco Bay Area

	Restaurant	Cuisine
29	Gary Danko	American
	French Laundry	American/French
28	Kiss Seafood	Japanese
	Seven Hills	Italian
	Acquerello	Italian
	Erna's Elderberry	Californian/French
	Marinus	Californian/French
	Kokkari Estiatorio	Greek
	Sierra Mar	Californian/Eclectic
	Evvia	Greek
	Redd	Californian
	Commis	American
	Chez Panisse Café	Californian/Mediterranean
	Rivoli	Californian/Mediterranean
	Chez Panisse	Californian/Mediterranean
	Cafe Gibraltar	Mediterranean
27	Sushi Zone	Japanese
	Cucina Paradiso	Italian
	Ichi Sushi*	Japanese
	Boulevard	American

OTHER NOTEWORTHY PLACES

Absinthe	French/Mediterranean
A16	Italian
Atelier Crenn	French
Aziza	Moroccan
Benu	American
Cheesecake Factory	American
Cotogna	Italian
Delfina	Italian
Frances	Californian
House of Prime Rib	American
La Folie	French
Manresa	American
Masa's	French
Meadowood	Californian
Michael Mina	American
Quince	Italian
Saison	American
Slanted Door	Vietnamese
State Bird Provisions	American
Zuni Café	Mediterranean

* Indicates a tie with restaurant above

Absinthe ●🅼 *French/Mediterranean* — 24 | 23 | 22 | $49

Hayes Valley | 398 Hayes St. (Gough St.) | San Francisco | 415-551-1590 | www.absinthe.com

You'll feel like you're "in Paris" at this "ravishing, romantic" brasserie that's "deservedly popular" with "young hipsters" and "opera-goers" alike; this "longtime Hayes Valley gem" has "kept its wow factor" thanks to "lovely cocktails" crafted by "expert mixologists" and "fabulous" French-Med fare served by a "professional staff", even if it's "a bit pricey" and "noisy" for some.

Acquerello 🆉🅼 *Italian* — 28 | 26 | 28 | $98

Polk Gulch | 1722 Sacramento St. (bet. Polk St. & Van Ness Ave.) | San Francisco | 415-567-5432 | www.acquerello.com

When you're "in the most romantic of moods", this Polk Gulch "old-world" "shrine" "to haute cuisine à la Italia" is "superlative in every sense", from the "superior" wine list to the "very current" Italian prix fixe menus that are "perfection on a plate"; "well-dressed" patrons populate the "elegant", "hushed" setting in a former chapel, where "gracious" servers "anticipate" your "every need" ("the ballet should be this well choreographed"); and if it's undoubtedly "expensive", "who could put a price" on such an "exquisite" experience?

A16 *Italian* — 25 | 21 | 22 | $46

Marina | 2355 Chestnut St. (bet. Divisadero & Scott Sts.) | San Francisco | 415-771-2216 | www.a16sf.com

"So good" they could rename it "A-1" say fans of this ever-"trendy" Marina trattoria popular for the likes of "blistered", "wood-fired" Neapolitan pizza, "astounding salumi" and "rustic" housemade pastas; the "narrow" room is "about as fast-paced, noisy and crowded as its namesake" Italian highway, but "knowledgeable" staffers help decipher the "lesser-known labels from Southern Italy", while an "open kitchen" provides "theatrical flair"; P.S. lunch is served Wednesday–Friday.

Atelier Crenn 🆉🅼 *French* — 27 | 24 | 26 | $134

Marina | 3127 Fillmore St. (bet. Filbert & Greenwich Sts.) | San Francisco | 415-440-0460 | www.ateliercrenn.com

"For that special night out", "soulful host" Dominique Crenn's "groundbreaking" Marina atelier truly "shines" presenting "mind-blowing", "visually beautiful" French tasting menus that employ all "the latest bells and whistles" of "molecular gastronomy" and "push culinary boundaries" while still "tasting divine"; service is "impeccable", and although the "minimalist" decor and "small portions with high price" are "not for the meat-and-potatoes crowd", smitten surveyors insist the chef's "scope and ambition" "leaves everyone" else in town behind.

Aziza *Moroccan* — 26 | 22 | 25 | $58

Outer Richmond | 5800 Geary Blvd. (22nd Ave.) | San Francisco | 415-752-2222 | www.aziza-sf.com

"Genius" chef Mourad Lahlou takes Moroccan cooking "to the next level" at this somewhat "pricey" Outer Richmond "favorite", where the "exquisitely flavored" plates showcase "innovative" "Californian touches" and the "delicately concocted" cocktails "rock the casbah"; add to that "attentive but not smothering" service and "dark", "romantic" environs and devotees dub it a "nonstop wow"; P.S. closed Tuesday.

FOOD | DECOR | SERVICE | COST

Benu ☒Ⓜ *American*

27 | 24 | 28 | $160

SoMa | 22 Hawthorne St. (bet. Folsom & Howard Sts.) | San Francisco | 415-685-4860 | www.benusf.com

"French Laundry alumnus" Corey Lee has "come into his own" at this SoMa New American where the "exquisite", "innovative" cuisine "seems more like art than food" and the "Asian-inspired tasting menu" with "terrific wine pairings" is a "culinary extravaganza" (with "eye-popping prices" to match); impressions of the decor range from "minimalist/beautiful" to overly "stark", but that doesn't overshadow the all-around "memorable experience", complete with "outstanding" service and "kitchen views" that are a treat.

Boulevard *American*

27 | 26 | 27 | $69

Embarcadero | Audiffred Bldg. | 1 Mission St. (Steuart St.) | San Francisco | 415-543-6084 | www.boulevardrestaurant.com

Chef-owner Nancy Oakes remains the "boss of fine dining" at her "dress-to-impress" "belle epoque" Embarcadero flagship (with a "Bay view to boot"), which "works like a fine Swiss watch", proffering "magnificent, refined" American fare and "superb" wines via a "top-notch" staff; everyone from lunching "conventioneers" to "celebrities" assures it's "always crowded" and "noisy", while "year in and year out" it serves as a "go-to" for "power dinners or a romantic night out" – yes, it's "expensive, but oh so worth it."

Cafe Gibraltar Ⓜ *Mediterranean*

28 | 23 | 26 | $43

El Granada | 425 Ave. Alhambra (Palma St.) | 650-560-9039 | www.cafegibraltar.com

Chef/co-owner and "perfectionist" Jose Luis Ugalde's "inventive" "seasonal organic" Mediterranean cuisine, paired with "unusual wines to match", makes for a "treat" "altogether much better than" little El Granada "has any right to" say appreciative fans who find it "unforgettable"; add in "knowledgeable service that allows the fabulous food to star" and a "serene" atmosphere (replete with a peekaboo "view to die for") and you see why it's "so worth the trip."

Cheesecake Factory *American*

21 | 21 | 20 | $28

Downtown | Macy's | 251 Geary St., 8th fl. (bet. Powell & Stockton Sts.) | San Francisco | 415-391-4444
Pleasanton | Stoneridge Mall | 1350 Stoneridge Mall Rd. (Foothill Rd.) | 925-463-1311
Corte Madera | The Village at Corte Madera | 1736 Redwood Hwy. (Hwy. 101) | 415-945-0777
Palo Alto | 375 University Ave. (bet. Florence & Waverly Sts.) | 650-473-9622
San Jose | 925 Blossom Hill Rd. (bet. Santa Teresa & Winfield Blvds.) | 408-225-6948
Santa Clara | Westfield Shoppingtown Valley Fair | 3041 Stevens Creek Blvd. (Santana Row) | 408-246-0092
www.thecheesecakefactory.com

With a menu that "competes in length with *War and Peace*", this "always packed" go-to – SF's No. 1 chain – dishes out "flavorful" midpriced American fare in portions so "gargantuan", many take their "scrumptious" signature cheesecake "home in a bag"; "long" waits and "over-the-top" decor deter detractors, who call the "calorific" eats "uninspired", but they're outnumbered by "crowds" of admirers dubbing it a "satisfying" and "fun" "family fave" with "friendly" service.

Chez Panisse ⑧ *Californian/Mediterranean*   28 | 25 | 27 | $87

Berkeley | 1517 Shattuck Ave. (bet. Cedar & Vine Sts.) | 510-548-5525 |
www.chezpanisse.com

"After 40 years", Alice Waters' "iconic" Berkeley "landmark" is "maybe
not cutting-edge" anymore and the "high priestess" herself is "seldom
seen", but it remains a "mecca" for "ethereal locavore" Cal-Med meals
"served simply and without ego", accompanied by "fantastic wines"
and "outstanding service"; while the "adherence to purity" strikes
some as "almost comical" at times, and the "very expensive", "limited
daily menus make it a gamble for picky eaters", devotees insist "you
owe it to yourself" to "stroll through" the kitchen of this "understated"
Craftsman bungalow "where it all began", to "find out why."

Chez Panisse Café ⑧ *Californian/Mediterranean*   28 | 24 | 26 | $54

Berkeley | 1517 Shattuck Ave. (bet. Cedar & Vine Sts.) | 510-548-5049 |
www.chezpanisse.com

"Incredible" "farm-to-table" Cal-Med meals ("including pizza") built
on produce that tastes "like it was picked that morning" (and "it was!")
draw "budget-conscious" food lovers to this "more-relaxed", "easier"-
to-access sibling of Alice Waters' Berkeley "high temple" downstairs,
where an à la carte menu is served "with the same care and commitment", but at a more "earthly price"; the "homey" "Craftsman setting"
and "gracious" staff add to the experience of an "enjoyable" lunch or
"casual" dinner, and groupies can still take a spin "through the kitchen."

Commis Ⓜ *American*   28 | 21 | 26 | $98

Oakland | 3859 Piedmont Ave. (Rio Vista Ave.) | 510-653-3902 |
www.commisrestaurant.com

Buckle in for a "gastronomical ride" at this "unmarked" Oakland New
American from "genius" chef-owner James Syhabout, whose "adventurous" "molecular gastronomy–imbued" prix fixes are chock-full of
"unbelievably delicious" "oddball combinations" that fans dub "world-
view-altering"; "first-class" service helps elevate the "tiny", "spartan"
digs, and while reservations are "hard to get", diners with an "open
mind" (and deep bank account) are in for one of "the best high-end
dining experiences in the area."

Cotogna *Italian*   26 | 22 | 24 | $52

Downtown | 490 Pacific St. (Montgomery St.) | San Francisco |
415-775-8508 | www.cotognasf.com

Lindsay and Michael Tusk have "done it again" at this "weekday lunch
spot" and "late-night" Downtown dinner destination that "shares a
kitchen" with big sis Quince, offering equally "unreal pastas" and other
Italian fare such as "marvelous" roasted meats and "wood-fired" pizzas (plus family-style Sunday suppers) in more "rustic" digs at a "fraction of the price"; it's also about "twice as loud" and a tough rez, but
with wine for "$40" a bottle and a "cheerful" staff, "what's not to love?"

Cucina Paradiso ⑧ *Italian*   27 | 23 | 26 | $37

Petaluma | 114 Petaluma Blvd. N. (bet. Washington St. & Western Ave.) |
707-782-1130 | www.cucinaparadisopetaluma.com

"Lots of regulars" call this Petaluma Italian a "favorite", praising its
"sophisticated flavors" and "well-executed" dishes, especially the
"exceptional homemade pastas"; the trattoria-style space can get a

"bit noisy", but service is "welcoming" and with such "reasonable prices", most consider it an "amazing deal."

Delfina *Italian*   27 | 20 | 23 | $49

Mission | 3621 18th St. (bet. Dolores & Guerrero Sts.) | San Francisco | 415-552-4055 | www.delfinasf.com

Visiting the Mission without trying Craig and Anne Stoll's "first restaurant" that started it all is "like being in Egypt and not seeing the pyramids" say the "hipsters and well-heeled boomers" who frequent this "unpretentious" trattoria for its "simple, soulful" Northern Italian cuisine "paired with great wines" by "knowledgeable" staffers; just reserve "well in advance" as it's often "crowded" (and "noisy" to boot), or you might wind up at their "pizzeria next door."

Erna's Elderberry House *Californian/French*   28 | 28 | 28 | $96

Oakhurst | Château du Sureau | 48688 Victoria Ln. (Hwy. 41) | 559-683-6800 | www.elderberryhouse.com

"Anyone visiting Yosemite" "must" stop by this Oakhurst "special-occasion" spot for a "taste of Europe in the Sierras" by way of the "fantastic" New French–Californian prix fixes often proffered by the "charming" "Erna herself" in an "elegant" "fairy-tale" setting; it's "very expensive", but "nothing compares" for miles around, and if you stay overnight at the "adjacent château", Sunday brunch is "exquisite" too.

Evvia *Greek*   28 | 25 | 26 | $55

Palo Alto | 420 Emerson St. (bet. Lytton & University Aves.) | 650-326-0983 | www.evvia.net

The "upscale Greek cuisine" at this "top-tier" Palo Altan (little sis of SF's Kokkari) is "blessed by the gods of Mount Olympus" cheer fans touting the "otherworldly" lamb, "expertly grilled fish" and other "succulent" specialties, all delivered via "friendly", "engaging" servers; its "lively atmosphere is pleasure-enhancing" too, and though it gets "noisy and densely packed in" at "prime hours", most agree it's "always a favorite – especially if someone else is picking up the tab."

Frances Ⓜ *Californian*   27 | 20 | 25 | $58

Castro | 3870 17th St. (Pond St.) | San Francisco | 415-621-3870 | www.frances-sf.com

Chef-owner "Melissa Perello knows how to make her beautiful fresh ingredients speak for themselves" at this "amazing" Castro Californian showcasing her "culinary virtuosity" for "totally reasonable" prices; "getting a reservation" is as elusive as snagging a "Wonka golden ticket" (though if you're lucky, you'll find "room at the bar"), and the "cramped" space gets "way too loud", but a "friendly", "dedicated" staff along with a "brilliant" "wines-by-the-ounce" offer keeps the place "full of smiling faces."

French Laundry *American/French*   29 | 27 | 28 | $297

Yountville | 6640 Washington St. (Creek St.) | 707-944-2380 | www.frenchlaundry.com

"Words can't even describe" the "experience of a lifetime" say food lovers who've had the "thrill" of landing a reservation and making "the trek" to Thomas Keller's "culinary Everest" in Yountville where the "heavenly" New American–French tasting menus "feature ingredients treated with the utmost respect and care" and the "impeccable" service is "like a coordinated dance"; it's all "too precious" for some and wines cost "a fortune", but acolytes insist "you'll go to your grave (in a pauper's field) remembering this meal" and the "exquisite" "gardens outside the stone building."

Gary Danko *American*   29 | 27 | 29 | $110
Fisherman's Wharf | 800 N. Point St. (Hyde St.) | San Francisco | 415-749-2060 | www.garydanko.com
It's "tough enough to get to No. 1 and even harder to stay there", but Gary Danko (the man and his "truly American classic" on the Wharf) "remains the reigning and undefeated champ" for Food, Service and Popularity in the Bay Area Survey, offering "the epitome of white-tablecloth fine dining" without the "stuck-up feeling" via "exceptional", "flexible prix fixe" options and "marvelous" "custom pairings" of wine (plus an "astounding" cheese cart); it's all delivered in a "gorgeous" "jewel-box" setting by a "most gracious" staff that "treats everyone like a millionaire", and naturally, it comes "at a price", but it's widely considered a "relative bargain" compared to other "temples of gastronomy."

House of Prime Rib *American*   26 | 22 | 25 | $56
Polk Gulch | 1906 Van Ness Ave. (Washington St.) | San Francisco | 415-885-4605 | www.houseofprimerib.net
"If you have anything other than prime rib" at this "reasonably priced" Polk Gulch "blast from the past" "you're missing the point", as they've got its "preparation and presentation" "down to a science", with "courteous" servers carving "generous" slabs from big "shiny" "metal zeppelins"; paired with "unparalleled" sides and an "irresistible" martini "delivered in its own shaker", it's an "old-school indulgence" in a "handsome English steakhouse" setting.

Ichi Sushi ⓩ *Japanese*   27 | 18 | 23 | $46
Bernal Heights | 3369 Mission St. (Godeus St.) | San Francisco | 415-525-4750 | www.ichisushi.com
"Magnificent" sashimi and "traditional, superbly prepared nigiri" featuring fish that you might've "never had before", particularly if you "go with the omakase", are sold for relatively "reasonable prices" at this "friendly" Japanese "hole-in-the-wall" in Bernal Heights; it's "really tiny", so "get there early", especially if you "want a seat at the bar."

Kiss Seafood ⓩⓜ *Japanese*   28 | 18 | 25 | $83
Japantown | 1700 Laguna St. (Sutter St.) | San Francisco | 415-474-2866
"For the real thing" without the airfare, foodies trek to this "secret sushi spot" in Japantown where "divinely executed sushi" ("any fresher and you'd be eating underwater") and "amazingly authentic" omakase dinners are served in "living room"–sized digs; with only "12 seats" overseen by "the chef and his wife", it feels like an "honor to eat here" for guests who gush it's "well worth the money and the effort" and "virtually impossible not to leave happy."

Kokkari Estiatorio *Greek*   28 | 27 | 27 | $59
Downtown | 200 Jackson St. (bet. Battery & Front Sts.) | San Francisco | 415-981-0983 | www.kokkari.com
"Politicos", "power execs" and "special-occasion" celebrants frequent this "happening" Downtown Greek for "incredible" cuisine featuring

"impressive" meats spit-roasted on an open fire and "to-die-for" desserts, all brought by a "talented staff"; a "beautiful" dining room and "always-busy bar" that "retain the warmth and coziness of a taverna" add to what fans deem a "grand" "fine-dining experience" – with "a price tag that matches" (it's "worth the splurge").

La Folie 🅰 *French* — 27 | 25 | 27 | $107

Russian Hill | 2316 Polk St. (bet. Green & Union Sts.) | San Francisco | 415-776-5577 | www.lafolie.com

For that "special night" "splurge", Francophiles never "pass up an opportunity to dine" at "master chef" Roland Passot's Russian Hill "jewel box", where he "continues to keep his hand" "in the kitchen" and in the "ornate" dining room proffering "beautifully presented" "haute cuisine" prix fixe French dinners; it's a "lyrical experience" from the "amuse-bouche" to "*le digestif*", enhanced by "superb", "unpretentious" service and brother George's "gorgeous wine list"; P.S. the adjacent lounge serves "unique" drinks and appetizers.

Manresa 🅼 *American* — 27 | 25 | 27 | $163

Los Gatos | 320 Village Ln. (bet. N. Santa Cruz & University Aves.) | 408-354-4330 | www.manresarestaurant.com

It "doesn't get more farm-to-table" than at this "crown jewel on the Peninsula" where "thought-provoking" New American fare emerges from chef-owner David Kinch's Los Gatos "atelier/kitchen" in the form of "innovative" tasting menus built around "pristine ingredients" from a biodynamic farm; the newly "remodeled" dining room and cocktail lounge have a "modern" atmosphere that "befits" the "three-hour" "ultra-high-end" "extravaganza", and when you add in the "superbly choreographed service", diners say it's "no wonder it costs so much."

Marinus 🅼 *Californian/French* — 28 | 28 | 27 | $93

Carmel Valley | Bernardus Lodge | 415 W. Carmel Valley Rd. (Laureles Grade Rd.) | 831-658-3595 | www.bernardus.com

Way beyond the typical "hotel restaurant", this Carmel Valley "gem" at Bernardus Lodge boasts a "beautiful" setting and "inviting" revamped decor as a backdrop for Cal Stamenov's "impeccable" Cal–New French menus that "push the envelope" while pleasing vegetarians, locavores and omnivores alike; service is "top-of-the-line" and the wine list is "staggering" (with "prices to match"), so overall it's "well worth the trip for a special occasion" and even better to "stay the night so you can savor every glass."

Masa's 🅱🅼 *French* — 27 | 26 | 27 | $127

Downtown | Hotel Vintage Ct. | 648 Bush St. (bet. Powell & Stockton Sts.) | San Francisco | 415-989-7154 | www.masasrestaurant.com

"Exquisite in every way", this Downtown fine-dining "landmark" continues to "dazzle" with chef Gregory Short's "sublime" New French tasting menus enlivened by "local ingredients" and "playful wine pairings", all capped off with "the best cheese and candy carts in the city"; it's all delivered with "superb service" in a "quiet", "elegant" setting for a "special-occasion experience" that's so "fabulous" there's "no other word for it – except perhaps expensive"; P.S. jackets suggested.

Meadowood, The Restaurant ⌧ *Californian*   27 | 26 | 27 | $150
(aka The Restaurant at Meadowood)
St. Helena | Meadowood Napa Valley | 900 Meadowood Ln. (Silverado Trail) | 707-967-1205 | www.meadowood.com

Hidden in a "high-end" St. Helena "country club"-like resort with "serene views of forest" and "croquet fields", this gourmet "delight" is "a shrine to cuisine" under the helm of chef Christopher Kostow, who displays "pure artistry" with his "stellar" Californian tasting menus (and "whimsical presentations"); "fantastic premium" wines add to the "great experience", as does a "perfectly" coordinated "small army of servers" at your "every beck and call" in the revamped dining room (reopened post-Survey); it's definitely a "sky-is-the-limit" tab, but "worth the splurge."

Michael Mina   *American*   27 | 25 | 27 | $105
Downtown | 252 California St. (Battery St.) | San Francisco | 415-397-9222 | www.michaelmina.net

Michael Mina "got it right" again at his more "casual" Downtown namesake offering "distinctive" Japanese-accented New American cuisine (plus "old favorites" "prepared in new ways") and "fantastic" service in a "gorgeous setting" "retained from its predecessor, Aqua"; the "no-tablecloth" vibe is more "party bistro than fine dining" – especially at the "noisy" bar filled with "suits" at lunch and a "younger crowd" later on – and the tasting menu with "spectacular" wine pairings is "pricey", but "outrageously good."

Quince ⌧ *Italian*   26 | 26 | 26 | $124
Downtown | 470 Pacific Ave. (bet. Montgomery St. & Pacific Ave.) | San Francisco | 415-775-8500 | www.quincerestaurant.com

"Pasta magician" Michael Tusk and his wife, Lindsay, "wow" at their "fancy" Downtown Cal-Italian that's filled with "movers and shakers" "wining and dining" on "compelling", "high-end" tasting menus and "fabulous" (albeit "expensive") vintages delivered with "thoughtful service"; it's "fantastic in every way" with a "palace"-like interior and "a bill to match", so while some "tsk" it's all "a bit precious", to others it's the stuff of "dreams."

Redd   *Californian*   28 | 23 | 26 | $70
Yountville | 6480 Washington St. (Oak Circle) | 707-944-2222 | www.reddnapavalley.com

Richard Reddington's "upscale without being stuffy" "special-occasion restaurant" is "a standout in Yountville's sea of greats", only with far "less show" and at "a fraction of the cost", presenting "brilliant" Californian cuisine (with "playful" East-meets-West "combinations") that's as "pleasing to the eye as to the palate"; the "simple, modern" indoor/outdoor digs may be "too cool" for some, but "impeccable without hovering" service plus a "deep wine list" (along with cheaper options for lunch or at the bar) leave most "with a foodie glow."

Rivoli   *Californian/Mediterranean*   28 | 24 | 25 | $51
Berkeley | 1539 Solano Ave. (bet. Neilson St. & Peralta Ave.) | 510-526-2542 | www.rivolirestaurant.com

"Still great after all these years", this "exceptional" "neighborhood standby" "on the outskirts of Berkeley" is run by a husband-and-wife team who know how to "keep it simple" but still wow, delivering "consistently scrumptious" Cal-Med fare paired with well-curated wines and "fantastic" service; the "petite" but "romantic setting" overlooking a "secret garden" "never fails to impress", leading fans to say this "gem" "equals or surpasses" some "more expensive" rivals.

Saison ⬛Ⓜ *American* — 27 | 23 | 26 | $257

Mission | 2124 Folsom St. (17th St.) | San Francisco | 415-828-7990 | www.saisonsf.com

Experience "epic" dining at this 18-seat "temple of gastronomy" in the Mission where chef Joshua Skenes "wows" in his "open kitchen" preparing "off-the-charts" New American tasting menus matched with "sublime wine pairings"; don't be fooled by the "unpretentious" service and blaring "rock music" – despite "tiny portions", "you and your date can drop a grand here" (at the chef's counter); P.S. prepaid online reservations required.

Seven Hills Ⓜ *Italian* — 28 | 22 | 26 | $47

Nob Hill | 1550 Hyde St. (Pacific Ave.) | San Francisco | 415-775-1550 | www.sevenhillssf.com

"Creative" farm-to-table cuisine inspired by Rome (a seven-hilled city like SF) includes "amazing" "housemade giant raviolis" at this "darling", "intimate" Nob Hill trattoria that also offers an "interesting" selection of "well-priced" wines chosen by "two master sommeliers"; "the caliber of cooking is comparable to more expensive places", plus a "lively" noise level and "welcoming" servers help create a "friendly" atmosphere.

Sierra Mar *Californian/Eclectic* — 28 | 29 | 27 | $93

Big Sur | Post Ranch Inn | Hwy. 1 (30 mi. south of Carmel) | 831-667-2200 | www.postranchinn.com

Diners have their heads in the clouds, almost literally, as they gaze out over the "seemingly infinite horizon" through the "floor-to-ceiling windows" of this "exclusive" locale perched "on the edge of a cliff overlooking the ocean" in Big Sur's Post Ranch Inn; voted the Bay Area's No. 1 for Decor, it's a truly "amazing setting" for "sensational" Cal-Eclectic meals paired with "world-class" wines, but while "the view is priceless" and service is "outstanding", tabs match the sky-high location.

Slanted Door *Vietnamese* — 26 | 23 | 23 | $53

Embarcadero | Ferry Bldg. Mktpl. | 1 Ferry Bldg. (The Embarcadero) | San Francisco | 415-861-8032 | www.slanteddoor.com

At this "picture-perfect" location on the Embarcadero waterfront, Charles Phan's "legendary", "modern" Vietnamese "masterpiece" presents "off-the-charts delicious" small plates and "unique" wines "beautifully" paired by the "hip" (albeit "slammed") staff in a "stunning" "glass setting"; yes, it's "loud" and "pricey", but the "fab Bay views" alone are worth "every penny" and the "fight through the crowds at the Ferry Building", if only for a "late lunch" or to "sit at the bar" "with the locals."

State Bird Provisions ⬛ *American* — 27 | 18 | 23 | $50

Western Addition | 1529 Fillmore St. (bet. Geary Blvd. & O'Farrell St.) | San Francisco | 415-795-1272 | www.statebirdsf.com

Rubicon alums Stuart Brioza and Nicole Krasinski are behind this American newcomer in an urban-cozy Western Addition storefront that's "spinning heads" with "clever" "small plates" and larger dishes served "dim-sum style"; because enthusiasts "order so many plates" from the "knowledgeable" staff, the tab can creep up, still, there's a reason it's "packed" with chefs "on their day off"; P.S. dinner only Monday–Thursday, closed Sundays.

Sushi Zone 🔊⇥ *Japanese*

27 | 15 | 18 | $32

Castro | 1815 Market St. (bet. Guerrero St. & Octavia Blvd.) | San Francisco | 415-621-1114

Like those "tiny Tokyo restaurants", this "crazy-packed" Castro Japanese with just a "few seats" delivers "fantastically fresh" sushi, a "ridiculously long sake list" and "a whole lot of character" for a reasonable price; the sushi "isn't exactly authentic" ("mango and macadamia nuts") but they "don't skimp on portions", just "prepare yourself" for a "long wait."

Zuni Café Ⓜ *Mediterranean*

26 | 22 | 23 | $52

Hayes Valley | 1658 Market St. (bet. Franklin & Gough Sts.) | San Francisco | 415-552-2522 | www.zunicafe.com

Everyone from theatergoers to the "digerati" "buzz" about "the roast chicken" (and the burgers "if you can get there for lunch or after 10 PM") at Judy Rodgers' "quintessential San Francisco bistro" in Hayes Valley that has turned out "satisfying" "wood-fired" Med meals "since the '70s"; the "bustling" zinc bar is still the "best place for oysters", a "well-mixed cocktail" and "people-watching", so despite murmurs of occasional "attitude" from the servers, "wild horses couldn't keep" fans away.

Seattle

	Restaurant	Cuisine
29	Rover's	French
	Nishino	Japanese
	Staple & Fancy Mercantile*	Italian
	Il Terrazzo Carmine	Italian
28	Herbfarm	Pacific NW
	Paseo	Cuban
	Tat's Deli	American
	Shiro's Sushi	Japanese
	La Medusa	Italian/Mediterranean
	Le Reve Bakery*	Bakery/French
	Canlis	Pacific NW
	Nell's	American
	Spinasse	Italian
	Buffalo Deli	Deli
	Facing East	Taiwanese
	Corson Building	Eclectic
	Salumi*	Italian/Sandwiches
27	Metropolitan Grill	Steak
	Lark	American
	Daniel's Broiler	Steak

OTHER NOTEWORTHY PLACES

Anthony's HomePort	Pacific NW/Seafood
Aqua by El Gaucho	Seafood
Blind Pig Bistro	Eclectic
Blue C Sushi	Japanese
Book Bindery	American
Cafe Juanita	Italian
Crush	American
Dahlia Lounge	Pacific NW
Dick's Drive-In	Burgers
Georgian	French/Pacific NW
Harvest Vine	Spanish
Kisaku Sushi	Japanese
La Carta/Mezcaleria Oaxaca	Mexican
Mashiko	Japanese
Revel	American/Korean
Seastar	Seafood
Serious Pie	Pizza
Szmania's	Steakhouse
13 Coins	Italian
Wild Ginger	Pacific Rim

* Indicates a tie with restaurant above

	FOOD	DECOR	SERVICE	COST

Anthony's HomePort *Pacific NW/Seafood*   25 | 24 | 24 | $37

SeattleTacoma International | Sea-Tac International Airport | 17801 International Blvd. (176th St.) | 206-431-3000
Shilshole | 6135 Seaview Ave. NW (61st St.) | 206-783-0780
Kirkland | Moss Bay Marina | 135 Lake St. S. (Kirkland Ave.) | 425-822-0225
Des Moines | Des Moines Marina | 421 S. 227th St. (Marine View Dr.) | 206-824-1947
Edmonds | Edmonds Marina | 456 Admiral Way (Dayton St.) | 425-771-4400
Everett | Everett Marina Vill. | 1726 W. Marine View Dr. (18th St.) | 425-252-3333
Tacoma | 5910 N. Waterfront Dr. (Trolley Ln.) | 253-752-9700
Gig Harbor | 8827 N. Harborview Dr. (Peacock Hill Ave.) | 253-853-6353
Bellingham | 25 Bellwether Way (Roeder Ave.) | 360-647-5588
Olympia | Marina | 704 Columbia St. NW (Capitol Way) | 360-357-9700
www.anthonys.com
Additional locations throughout the Seattle area
A "wonderful representation of Washington", this "dependable" fleet of seafooders (Seattle's Most Popular chain) reels 'em in with "fresh, local" fin fare and shellfish along with "waterfront settings" that provide "unbeatable" views; though a few carp about "tired" decor needing a "revamp", a "congenial", "well-informed" staff keeps things swimming smoothly, and budget-watchers praise the "affordable prices" and "sunset dinners" ("a heck of a deal").

Aqua by El Gaucho ● *Seafood*   27 | 26 | 25 | $55
(fka Waterfront Seafood Grill)
Seattle Waterfront | Pier 70 | 2801 Alaskan Way (Broad St.) | 206-956-9171 | www.elgaucho.com
"Succulent seafood" takes center stage at this El Gaucho group reboot of the former Waterfront Seafood Grill, supported by servers who "know their stuff", a wine list with bottles at "all price levels" and "spectacular" floor-to-ceiling views of Elliott Bay; though bargain-hunters say you won't find any here ("it's pretty spendy"), the "bright, airy" modern room is a "great place" for "business dinners" or "special occasions."

Blind Pig Bistro *American*   27 | 20 | 24 | $38
Eastlake | 2238 Eastlake Ave. E. (Lynn St.) | 206-329-2744 | www.blindpigbistro.com
"Go here *now*" urge advocates of this "real foodie restaurant", a recent addition to the Eastlake scene serving an ever-changing lineup of "imaginative" midpriced American small plates; the trendy space (formerly Sitka & Spruce, then Nettletown) features a taxidermied head and blood-red walls, though more accolades are reserved for the "wines under $10" and "steal" of a tasting menu; P.S. the 22-seater doesn't take reservations, so "come early or late" or on a weeknight.

Blue C Sushi *Japanese*   21 | 21 | 20 | $21
Downtown | Grand Hyatt Hotel | 1510 Seventh Ave. (bet. Pike & Pine Sts.) | 206-467-4022
Fremont | 3411 Fremont Ave. N. (34th St.) | 206-633-3411
University Village | University Vill. | 4601 26th Ave. NE (University Village St.) | 206-525-4601
Bellevue | Bellevue Sq. | 503 Bellevue Sq. (bet. 4th & 8th Sts.) | 425-454-8288
Lynnwood | Alderwood Mall | 3000 184th St. SW (bet. Alderwood Mall Pkwy. & 33rd Ave.) | 425-329-3596

(continued)

Blue C Sushi

Tukwila | Westfield Southcenter | 468 Southcenter Mall
(bet. Strander Blvd. & Tukwila Pkwy.) | 206-277-8744
www.bluecsushi.com

Fans of "decent, tasty sushi" and "convenience" like to sit down in
front of the "entertaining" "conveyor belt", grab what looks good and
"immediately start eating" at these "busy" Japanese joints; "modern"
decor featuring "huge screens" playing "anime" and other clips make
it a "hit with the family", but the budget-minded "pay attention to the
plate colors" that determine prices to "avoid a giant bill."

Book Bindery *American*   27 | 27 | 25 | $61

Queen Anne | 198 Nickerson St. (Etruria St.) | 206-283-2665 |
www.bookbinderyrestaurant.com

Virtuoso chef Shaun McCrain (ex Per Se) shapes a "stunning" American
menu with "subtle" and "intriguing combinations" at this Queen Anne
addition, where a "knowledgeable" staff works "beautiful" modern
spaces that reveal views of the Lake Washington Ship Canal and the
aging barrels of the adjacent Almquist Family Vintners winery; sure,
it's a "bit pricey", but insiders insist a "special evening" here that
"helps you forget your cares" is worth it.

Buffalo Deli ☒ *Deli*   28 | 21 | 22 | $21

Belltown | 2123 First Ave. (bet. Blanchard & Lenora Sts.) | 206-728-8759 |
www.thebuffalodeli.com

"It's like being in Buffalo" swear supporters of this "super-friendly"
Belltown deli, where "high-quality" lunches include "incredible matzo
ball" soup and "great, creative" sandwiches (e.g. the famed "beef on
weck"), all at a "reasonable price"; since the no-frills place "can get
busy", those in the know "call their orders in."

Cafe Juanita ☒ *Italian*   27 | 24 | 26 | $64

Kirkland | 9702 NE 120th Pl. (97th Ave.) | 425-823-1505 |
www.cafejuanita.com

"Inventive", "delectable" Northern Italian cuisine that makes the
most of "whatever is local and fresh" lures loyalists to chef-owner
Holly Smith's Kirkland "gem", where an "impeccable" staff expertly
guides diners through the "small" but "surprise"-filled menu and
"excellent" wine list (so "listen to your server"); the "intimate",
"minimalist" dining room is "nestled" in an "unassuming" building
that "sits among trees", a "low-key" setting for an "expensive" but
altogether "unforgettable" meal.

Canlis ☒ *Pacific NW*   28 | 28 | 28 | $84

Lake Union | 2576 Aurora Ave. N. (Westlake Ave.) | 206-283-3313 |
www.canlis.com

The "next generation of Canlis sons" makes sure that "everything's
perfect" at this circa-1950 "Seattle institution", where chef Jason
Franey (ex NYC's Eleven Madison Park) reinterprets Pacific NW classics and turns out "perfectly executed" meals that are "outstanding
from beginning to end"; in the midcentury yet modern room framing a
"gorgeous Lake Union View", service that's "like choreography" antic-
ipates your every need, and while it's all "brutally pricey", you "definitely get what you pay for."

	FOOD	DECOR	SERVICE	COST

Corson Building ⓜ *Eclectic* | 28 | 22 | 26 | $66 |

Georgetown | 5609 Corson Ave. S. (Airport Way) | 206-762-3330 | www.thecorsonbuilding.com

Chef-owner Matthew Dillon (Sitka & Spruce, Bar Ferd'nand) "showcases the freshest ingredients" in "magnificent", "family-style" dinners served at communal tables at this "swoon"-worthy Georgetown Eclectic, which is set in a "funky" 1910 Spanish-style building reminiscent of a European country house; though the "romantic" room can get "noisy" and "it's definitely pricey", the staff's "genuine hospitality" help make it "worth the splurge"; P.S. hours and menus vary.

Crush ⓜ *American* | 27 | 23 | 25 | $56 |

Madison Valley | 2319 E. Madison St. (23rd Ave.) | 206-302-7874 | www.crushonmadison.com

Set in a "revamped" Craftsman house with a "modern" vibe, this "gem" in "up-and-coming" Madison Valley features "fresh, original" takes on American cuisine from chef-owner Jason Wilson, who provides "delicious thrills every time"; the "prompt" staff is "knowledgeable" about the "locally sourced" fare and "impressive" wine pairings, and while a meal here is "memorable", so is the large bill that goes with it.

Dahlia Lounge *Pacific NW* | 27 | 24 | 25 | $47 |

Downtown | 2001 Fourth Ave. (Virginia St.) | 206-682-4142 | www.tomdouglas.com

"After all these years", Tom Douglas' first venture is still an "absolute favorite" among fans of this Downtowner's "outstanding", "Asian-infused" Pacific NW cuisine that includes a "rock-your-world" coconut cream pie (get one to go at the bakery next door); the contemporary room's "happy" vibe and "dependable, pleasant" staff are part of the "iconic" (if "a tad pricey") experience.

Daniel's Broiler *Steak* | 27 | 26 | 26 | $58 |

Leschi | Leschi Marina | 200 Lake Washington Blvd. (Alder St.) | 206-329-4191
South Lake Union | 809 Fairview Pl. N. (Valley St.) | 206-621-8262
Bellevue | Bank of America Bldg., Bellevue Pl. | 10500 NE Eighth St., 21st fl. (bet. Bellevue Way & 106th Ave.) | 425-462-4662
www.schwartzbros.com

"Perfectly cooked" prime cuts of meat come with sides of "unbeatable views" and "VIP"-worthy service at this "class-act" steakhouse trio; the bill comes with some "sticker shock", so the "busy" room is the spot for a "business dinner" or "special occasion", while the budget-minded put away "delicious, filling" appetizers at the "amazing" happy hour.

Dick's Drive-In ◐⊭ *Burgers* | 24 | 15 | 22 | $9 |

Capitol Hill | 115 Broadway E. (bet. Denny Way & John St.) | 206-323-1300
Crown Hill | 9208 Holman Rd. NW (bet. 12th & 13th Aves.) | 206-783-5233
Wallingford | 111 NE 45th St. (bet. 1st & 2nd Aves.) | 206-632-5125
Lake City | 12325 30th Ave. NE (Lake City Way) | 206-363-7777
Queen Anne | 500 Queen Anne Ave. N. (Republican St.) | 206-285-5155
Edmonds | 21910 Hwy. 99 (220th St.) | 425-775-4243
www.ddir.com

"Unchanged" since the '50s, this "legendary" Seattle chain of "fast-food joints" earns its "cult following" with "always-fresh" burgers, "homemade french fries" and "hand-dipped shakes", made with "lightning-fast" speed and for prices that "don't break the bank"; since "everyone goes here", lines can be "long", even up to the 2 AM closing time; P.S. cash only.

Facing East *Taiwanese*   28 | 21 | 22 | $19

Bellevue | Belgate Plaza | 1075 Bellevue Way NE (bet. 10th & 12th Sts.) | 425-688-2986 | www.facingeastrestaurant.com

"Don't worry about the long lines" at this Bellevue strip-mall "favorite": expats and locals alike say it's just part of the "pre-dinner ritual" for those who want to indulge in "interesting", "authentic" Taiwanese fare "not found anywhere" else in town; "reasonable" prices and "fast", "super-friendly" servers help keep the "unpretentious", modern room "packed."

The Georgian *French/Pacific NW*   27 | 29 | 28 | $53

Downtown | Fairmont Olympic Hotel | 411 University St. (bet. 4th & 5th Aves.) | 206-621-7889 | www.fairmont.com

The "old-world surroundings" in this 1924 Italianate dining room in Downtown's Fairmont Olympic Hotel make it a "special place for a special night", with "crystal chandeliers", "high, high ceilings", 11 tints of buttercream paint on the walls and the No. 1 ranking for Decor in Seattle; the "elegant", "outstanding" Pacific Northwest–French fare is delivered by "gracious, welcoming" servers, and while "you pay for the spectacular" experience, fans say it's "worth the splurge"; P.S. the prix fixe lunch is an "unbelievable deal."

Harvest Vine *Spanish*   27 | 23 | 24 | $45

Madison Valley | 2701 E. Madison St. (27th Ave.) | 206-320-9771 | www.harvestvine.com

At this "quaint" Madison Valley *cocina,* fans feel as if they're "being entertained at a great dinner party" when they "sit at the bar" and watch the chefs "work their magic" whipping up "unusual, authentic" (and "expensive") Basque tapas; "unobtrusive" servers patrol an "in-timate" space that gets "crowded" and "noisy", though the "romantic" wine cellar filled with "carefully chosen" Spanish bottles provides a "quieter" dining experience.

The Herbfarm 🅼 *Pacific NW*   28 | 26 | 28 | $167

Woodinville | 14590 NE 145th St. (Woodinville-Redmond Rd.) | 425-485-5300 | www.theherbfarm.com

The "world-class" tasting menu at this Woodinville "culinary re-treat" highlights "subtle herbs" and other esoteric Pacific NW in-gredients, along with "free-flowing" wine pairings; starting with a "garden tour", an "enchanted evening" here includes a "story" about the night's offerings, "impeccable" service and an "astronomically ex-pensive" bill to match the "unforgettable" experience; P.S. since the "adventure" can last more than four hours, some "stay the night" in the restaurant's suites.

Il Terrazzo Carmine 🅼 *Italian*   29 | 27 | 28 | $56

Pioneer Square | 411 First Ave. S. (bet. Jackson & King Sts.) | 206-467-7797 | www.ilterrazzocarmine.com

Impresario Carmine Smeraldo passed away in early 2012, but his "leg-endary" Pioneer Square Italian is still "a must" among "movers and shakers" who dig into "solid, traditional" entrees and sip "grand martinis" or pours from the "extensive" wine list; "hidden" in an office building, the "charming dining room" has a "warm, inviting atmosphere" and features "top-notch" service that's "reminiscent of New York" (as are the "expensive" prices).

Kisaku Sushi *Japanese*　27 | 20 | 24 | $35
Wallingford | 2101 N. 55th St. (Meridian Ave.) | 206-545-9050 | www.kisaku.com
The "secret" is out about this Wallingford Japanese, a "neighborhood treasure" where "master" chef Ryuichi Nakano sates locals with "melt-in-your-mouth" sushi and "superb" contemporary dishes; while families appreciate the "kid-friendly" service and "reasonable prices", the cognoscenti ask for the "off-menu" special rolls or sit at the bar and order the "impeccable" omakase; P.S. closed Tuesdays.

La Carta de Oaxaca ☒ *Mexican*　26 | 21 | 21 | $23
Ballard | 5431 Ballard Ave. NW (22nd Ave.) | 206-782-8722
Mezcaleria Oaxaca ☒ *Mexican*
Queen Anne | 2123 Queen Anne Ave. N. (bet. Boston & Crockett Sts.) | 206-216-4446
www.lacartadeoaxaca.com
So "authentic" there's an *abuela* "in the kitchen making the tortillas", these "friendly" Ballard and Queen Anne twins turn out "killer mole" and other Oaxacan specialties; arty "black-and-white images of Mexico" make the "hopping" spots feel a cut above "typical" taquerias, while "reasonable prices" and "must-try" margaritas explain the "long waits" for a table; P.S. the newer Queen Anne Avenue location specializes in cocktails made from its mezcal namesake.

La Medusa ☒☒ *Italian/Mediterranean*　28 | 21 | 25 | $37
Columbia City | 4857 Rainier Ave. S. (Edmunds St.) | 206-723-2192 | www.lamedusarestaurant.com
At this "casual" Italian in Columbia City, "creative foodie globe-trotters" in an "open kitchen" concoct some of the "best Sicilian soul food this side of Palermo"; "friendly" servers contribute to the "warm, welcoming" ambiance in the "vibrant" (and "often crowded") storefront space, where the "reasonably priced" menu on a "large chalkboard" gets updated regularly; P.S. Wednesdays May–October, a $30 prix fixe highlights farmer's-market finds.

Lark ☒ *American*　27 | 22 | 25 | $51
Capitol Hill | 926 12th Ave. (bet. Marion & Spring Sts.) | 206-323-5275 | www.larkseattle.com
In the heart of Capitol Hill, John Sundstrom's American "standout" enchants with "inventive", "locally sourced" small plates that are "fun to share"; "professional" yet "personal" service and a "relaxing" vibe make the "tasteful", "rustic" room "feel like it's full of friends", and while all those "incredibly tasty dishes" can make the bill "pricier than expected", most agree the "serious culinary experience" is "worth every penny."

Le Reve Bakery *Bakery/French*　28 | 22 | 24 | $11
Queen Anne | 1805 Queen Anne Ave. N. (Blaine St.) | 206-623-7383 | www.lerevebakery.com
"*Incroyable!*" say *amis* who "love" this "amazing bakery", a 2010 arrival in a "quaint", "little old house" in Queen Anne where "great pastries",

	FOOD	DECOR	SERVICE	COST

"to-die-for" cakes and other reasonably priced goodies are "not only pretty to look at" but "melt-in-your-mouth good"; though service isn't "super-fast", it's "cozy" inside, and the patio is the place to sip a "yummy coffee" and watch locals "stroll by on a sunny day."

Mashiko *Japanese*
27 | 18 | 24 | $40

West Seattle | 4725 California Ave. SW (bet. Alaska & Edmunds Sts.) | 206-935-4339 | www.sushiwhore.com
West Seattle's "sassiest" sushi joint gets environmental props for matching "sustainable fish" with other "high-quality ingredients" in "creative", "tasty" (and "pricey") combos that'll "blow you away"; in the "arty" (some say slightly "out-of-date") room, the "savvy" staff happily recommends favorite rolls and cooked dishes, but purists opt for chef-owner Hajime Sato's "meal-of-your-life" omakase menu; P.S. sit at the bar to appear on the video streamed live on the restaurant's website.

Metropolitan Grill *Steak*
27 | 25 | 27 | $69

Downtown | 820 Second Ave. (2nd Ave.) | 206-624-3287 | www.themetropolitangrill.com
This "old-school" Downtown meatery is a "staple" with the "power lunch" crowd for its "amazing cuts" of dry-aged beef ("don't tell your cardiologist") and "classic sides" such as "to-die-for" mashed potatoes; the "retro steakhouse atmosphere" extends to "comfy booths", "wood and brass" furnishings and "insightful" staffers – just expect a "big bill to go with it" all.

Nell's *American*
28 | 20 | 27 | $44

Green Lake | 6804 E. Green Lake Way N. (2nd Ave.) | 206-524-4044 | www.nellsrestaurant.com
In a "hidden storefront" across from Green Lake, chef Philip Mihalski's "oasis of serenity" wins accolades for "imaginative" American creations made from the "best local, seasonal ingredients" and paired with a "killer wine list"; the basic room looks a tad "tired" to some, but to those who appreciate "relaxed" yet "food-savvy" servers and a "quiet atmosphere", it's a "happy place."

Nishino *Japanese*
29 | 23 | 27 | $54

Madison Park | 3130 E. Madison St. (Lake Washington Blvd.) | 206-322-5800 | www.nishinorestaurant.com
Kyoto-born Nobu alum Tatsu Nishino conceives "delicate, inventive" and altogether "amazing" sushi for deep-pocketed fin fans at his "low-key" Madison Park Japanese; "expert" service and "masterpieces on the walls" by local artist Fay Jones put diners "in a Zen state", but those who want a truly transporting experience know "it's all about" the "straight-from-heaven" omakase menu (just be sure to "order a few days ahead").

Paseo ⌦Ⓜ⇴ *Cuban*
28 | 12 | 20 | $13

Shilshole | 6226 Seaview Ave. NW (62nd St.) | 206-789-3100
Fremont | 4225 Fremont Ave. N. (bet. 42nd & 43rd Sts.) | 206-545-7440
www.paseoseattle.com
"Man oh man" moan enthusiasts enamored of the "chin-dripping-delicious" Cuban sandwiches "bursting with tender, slow-cooked pork" at this pair of "tiny", "tumbledown" shacks; there's "limited seating" and they often "run out of the most popular items", but that

doesn't stop lines that "go out the door"; P.S. cash only, though you won't need much.

Revel *American/Korean* | 27 | 22 | 22 | $33 |

Fremont | 403 N. 36th St. (Phinney Ave.) | 206-547-2040 | www.revelseattle.com

Iron Chef team Rachel Yang and Seif Chirchi's "fusion of French" technique, American flavors and "Korean street food" yields revel-atory results in the form of "spicy", full-flavored and "reasonably priced" small plates at this "urban party experience" in Fremont; the industrial-chic interior can get "noisy" when full, while "custom" drinks at Quoin, the adjacent 21-and-over lounge, help ease "long waits" for a table.

Rover's ⓜ *French* | 29 | 26 | 29 | $105 |

Madison Valley | 2808 E. Madison St. (28th Ave.) | 206-325-7442 | www.thechefinthehat.com

"Seattle icon" Thierry Rautureau gives Pacific NW fare an "haute cuisine" boost with "outstanding" prix fixe menus (and some à la carte options) at his "truly indulgent" French "slice of heaven" in Madison Park, voted No. 1 for Food and Service in Seattle; inside the flower-filled cottage, you'll "feel like you're dining in the chef's own home", though one where a "well-oiled" team of nearly "flawless" servers helps make the "breathtakingly expensive" meals "don't-miss special events."

Salumi 🅂ⓜ *Italian/Sandwiches* | 28 | 14 | 20 | $17 |

Pioneer Square | 309 Third Ave. S. (bet. Jackson & Main Sts.) | 206-621-8772 | www.salumicuredmeats.com

Gina Batali (yep, "Mario's sister") "knows what she's doing" at her Pioneer Square "Italian paradise", where fans wait in "long lines" for "massive sandwiches" of "insanely good" house-cured salami in addition to other "delicious" deli specialties; just know there's "limited" "communal seating", making "takeout" a popular option; P.S. open Tuesday–Friday until 4 PM, but "get there early" since popular items can "run out."

Seastar Restaurant & Raw Bar *Seafood* | 27 | 25 | 25 | $52 |

South Lake Union | 2121 Terry Ave. (bet. Denny Way & Lenora St.) | 206-462-4364

Bellevue | Civica Office Commons | 205 108th Ave. NE (2nd St.) | 425-456-0010

www.seastarrestaurant.com

John Howie's "outstanding", "upscale" seafooders are "definitely keepers" to admirers of his "stellar" takes on the "freshest" fin fare; though prices are "expensive", the oyster shucking and sushi making at the raw bars is a "show in itself", while "high-end service" and "airy", modern spaces filled with "swells" complete the package; P.S. Bellevue gets props for "power dinners", while the newer South Lake Union outpost is in an up-and-coming area.

Serious Pie *Pizza* | 26 | 19 | 21 | $26 |

Downtown | 316 Virginia St. (bet. 3rd & 4th Aves.) | 206-838-7388 | www.tomdouglas.com

South Lake Union | 401 Westlake Ave. N. (Harrison St.) | 206-436-0050 | www.seriouspiewestlake.com

"The name says it all" at this "transformational" pizzeria pair, where "wood-fired" "cracker-thin" crusts sport "seriously inventive" toppings of "fresh artisanal ingredients"; servers are "attentive", and though there are "long waits" and some find the tabs a tad "pricey", it's all "worth it" to savor "what pizza is supposed to be"; P.S. the "tiny" Downtown original's "communal tables" mean "you'll get cozy with your neighbors", while newer South Lake Union is larger.

Shiro's Sushi *Japanese*   28 | 20 | 25 | $53

Belltown | 2401 Second Ave. (Battery St.) | 206-443-9844 | www.shiros.com
Shiro Kashiba is semi-retired now, but the "true master" still pops in at his Belltown stalwart, where "purists" say his omakase is one of the "best sushi experiences" and the "lavish" à la carte menu is "as good as it gets"; sure, it can be "a little spendy", but the "professional" staff is "attentive", and the "spartan" room full of Japanese "expats" attracts celebs too, helping make dinner here a "night of entertainment."

Spinasse *Italian*   28 | 21 | 25 | $54

Capitol Hill | 1531 14th Ave. (bet. Pike & Pine Sts.) | 206-251-7673 | www.spinasse.com
Chef Jason Stratton turns to the Piedmont region for inspiration at his "must-try" Capitol Hill trattoria, where "attentive" servers deliver "delicate, sublime" (and "pricey") pastas paired with "light" sauces and "rustic", meaty ragùs; savvy surveyors who say the "small" space can get "noisy and crowded" opt for seats at the "kitchen-view" bar so they can "feel like they're cooking with the chef"; P.S. hit adjacent Bar Artusi for a "drink while you wait."

Staple & Fancy Mercantile *Italian*   29 | 25 | 26 | $48

Ballard | Kolstrand Bldg. | 4739 Ballard Ave. NW (17th Ave.) | 206-789-1200 | www.ethanstowellrestaurants.com
Ethan Stowell's "spectacular" Italian elicits "OMG"s for the "smashingly good" four-course tasting menu, as well as the "constantly changing dishes" among the "incredible" à la carte options, all at relatively "low" prices; the "great location" on "gentrifying" Ballard Avenue adds to the "adventure", and though the namesake former grocer's space has brick walls, the room is quiet enough to "carry on a conversation."

Szmania's *Steakhouse*   27 | 24 | 25 | $40

Magnolia | 3321 W. McGraw St. (34th Ave.) | 206-284-7305 | www.szmanias.com
Ludger Szmania gave his Magnolia spot a steakhouse reboot in 2011, but the influence of the "talented" Austrian-born chef's native cuisine remains in dishes like the "terrific" jäger schnitzel; "reasonable prices", a "contemporary" space and "friendly" servers who make "knowledgeable" recommendations help cement a rep as a "great neighborhood restaurant"; P.S. special menus include BBQ Sundays, wine and movie nights and Oktoberfest.

Tat's Deli ⊠ *American*   28 | 15 | 22 | $12

Pioneer Square | 159 Yesler Way (2nd Ave.) | 206-264-8287 | www.tatsdeli.com
"Eat these with your sleeves rolled up" warn advocates of the "huge", "sloppy", "yummy" sandwiches at this "piece of the East Coast" in Pioneer Square; there can be "long lines at lunch" (a web cam helps gauge wait times), but the price is right for "satisfying" fare that's "so much better than chains."

13 Coins ● *Italian*

24 | 21 | 23 | $34

South Lake Union | 125 Boren Ave. N. (Denny Way) | 206-682-2513
SeaTac | 18000 International Blvd. (bet. 180th & 182nd Sts.) |
206-243-9500
www.13coins.com

Enter a "time warp" at these "funky" SeaTac and South Lake Union 24/7
"landmarks" – voted Most Popular in Seattle – featuring an "extensive
menu" of "yummy" Italian classics, standard lunch fare and "hangover-
cure" breakfasts, in addition to "no-fuss service" and "great people-
watching" ("especially in the wee hours"); while the "high-backed
booths" provide "privacy", regulars often prefer the "swivel seating"
at the bar, where they can banter with "witty" chefs who fire up "off-
the-menu" requests.

Wild Ginger *Pacific Rim*

25 | 24 | 23 | $38

Downtown | Mann Bldg. | 1401 Third Ave. (Union St.) | 206-623-4450
Bellevue | The Bravern | 11020 NE Sixth St. (110th Ave.) | 425-495-8889
www.wildginger.net

Proffering "exceptional" Pacific Rim fare – think rave-worthy "duck
buns" and other "creative", "rather expensive" dishes with housemade sauces – this "must-go" Downtown and Bellevue duo remains
"super busy", though the "attentive" staff ably handles the "business
lunches" and "pre-symphony crowds" in the "sleek", "sexy" dining
room; P.S. the newer, larger Sixth Street location features "happy-hour
bargains" and weekend dim sum brunches.

St. Louis

TOP FOOD RANKING

Restaurant	Cuisine
29 Bogarts Smokehouse	BBQ
28 Citizen Kane's Steak	Steak
Pappy's Smokehouse	BBQ
Sidney Street Cafe	American
Niche	American
Anthony's	American/Italian
Crossing	French/Italian
27 Tony's	Italian
Blues City Deli	Deli
Acero	Italian

OTHER NOTEWORTHY PLACES

Annie Gunn's	American/Steak
Blueberry Hill	American
Charlie Gitto's	Italian
Farmhaus	American
Five Bistro	American
Home Wine Kitchen	American
Mai Lee	Chinese/Vietnamese
Tavern Kitchen	American
Ted Drewes	Ice Cream
Three Sixty	American

Acero ◪ *Italian*   27 | 23 | 25 | $39

Maplewood | 7266 Manchester Rd. (Southwest Ave.) | 314-644-1790 | www.fialafood.com

"Clever plates with superb ingredients" "reward the adventurous" at this "unforgettable" Maplewood Italian from Jim Fiala (The Crossing, Liluma), where "exquisite" polentas and housemade pastas that "deserve a standing ovation" are standouts on the small yet "inventive" menu; an "accommodating" staff adds to the "laid-back" bistro vibe, as does the "fantastic people-watching" in the lively bar and out on the patio; P.S. the popular prix fixe option is a real "bargain."

Annie Gunn's Ⓜ *American/Steak*   27 | 23 | 25 | $51

Chesterfield | 16806 Chesterfield Airport Rd. (Baxter Rd.) | 636-532-7684 | www.anniegunns.com

Reviewers advise "make a reservation weeks in advance" for this "deservedly popular" Chesterfield American (spun off from the adjoining Smokehouse Market), "renowned" for its "superb" steaks, "phenomenal" seafood and "incredible" seasonal specials by "imaginative" chef Lou Rook, all matched by an "exceptional" wine selection; the service "soars" too, and while the "rustic" setting has a "casual" "tavern atmosphere", it "lives up to its reputation" as a "top-notch culinary experience."

Anthony's 🔒 *American/Italian* | 28 | 24 | 29 | $55 |
Downtown | 10 S. Broadway (Market St.) | 314-231-7007 |
www.tonysstlouis.com

Voted No. 1 for Service in the city, this "lower-priced, more casual sib" to next-door Tony's boasts a "splendid", "old-school" staff providing a "superior" menu of "fantastic" burgers and other traditional American-Italian fare in a "soigné" Downtown room where "you never know what famous St. Louisan or power broker you'll see at the bar"; at dinner it shows a slightly "more adventurous side" (while offering all the costly "signatures" from Tony's kitchen as well), and the location "across from the stadium" makes it a popular "pre-game stop."

Blueberry Hill *American* | 22 | 25 | 20 | $21 |
Loop | 6504 Delmar Blvd. (bet. Melville & Westgate Aves.) |
314-727-4444 | www.blueberryhill.com

"Elvis has not left the building", as shown in the "legendary" collection of "offbeat" "pop culture paraphernalia" at this Loop "institution" with an "always happening", "youthful" atmosphere for chowing down on "tasty" American "pub grub" ("can't beat the burgers") and "excellent draft beers", served by a "laid-back" staff with "piercings and multiple tattoos"; leave time to "find your thrill" with "darts, pinball" and "live music", sometimes from the "father of rock 'n' roll", Chuck Berry himself.

Blues City Deli *Deli* | 27 | 22 | 25 | $11 |
Benton Park | 2438 McNair Ave. (Victor St.) | 314-773-8225 |
www.bluescitydeli.com

"Excellent" deli sandwiches, Italian po' boys and other house "creations" "piled high" with "savory" ingredients are accompanied by hard-to-find sodas and a "bigger variety of chips than an '80s cop show" at this "funky" Benton Park "gem"; despite "lines out the door", a "friendly" team keeps counter service "fast", while lots of "vintage" memorabilia and frequent "live music" make the short wait pleasant.

Bogarts Smokehouse 🔒🅼 *BBQ* | 29 | 19 | 25 | $16 |
Soulard | 1627 S. Ninth St. (Lafayette Ave.) | 314-621-3107 |
www.bogartssmokehouse.com

The BBQ "will change your life" declare devotees of this "jewel" across from Soulard Market, voted No. 1 for Food in the city for its "smokin' good" Memphis and St. Louis specialties ("apricot-glazed ribs caramelized with a blow torch") delivering an "amazing" "complexity of flavors"; expect a "laid-back atmosphere" and "line out the door", though it "goes pretty quickly when you're licking your fingers" from the "free samples provided by the friendly owner."

Charlie Gitto's at Harrah's Casino *Italian* | 26 | 23 | 25 | $38 |
Maryland Heights | Harrah's Casino | 777 Casino Center Dr. (Roadway) |
314-770-7663
Charlie Gitto's From the Hill *Italian*
Chesterfield | 15525 Olive Blvd. (Chesterfield Pkwy.) | 636-536-2199
Charlie Gitto's on The Hill *Italian*
The Hill | 5226 Shaw Ave. (Marconi Ave.) | 314-772-8898
www.charliegittos.com

"Rich, flavorful and satisfying" "red-sauce Italian" and "exemplary" service that's "prompt without being pushy" have surveyors hailing this slightly "pricey" "old-world gem" on The Hill as "a place a Soprano would love"; some relish the original's "elegant", "step-back-in-time" atmosphere (with an "enjoyable" patio), but two new outposts in Chesterfield and Harrah's Casino accommodate those looking for "classic Gitto cuisine in a fresh, modern environment."

Citizen Kane's Steakhouse 🅜 *Steak*   28 | 22 | 27 | $50

Kirkwood | 133 W. Clinton Pl. (Clay Ave.) | 314-965-9005 | www.citizenkanes.com

"Steak lovers" relish the "straightforward" menu of "quality" cuts at this unassuming locale in quaint Kirkwood, a "vintage house" that's "not big on ambiance" but "relaxed", "homey" and welcoming to all – whether in "suits or shorts and flip-flops"; the "high cost" strikes most as "reasonable", though some reserve it mainly for a "special night out."

The Crossing 🅇 *American*   28 | 22 | 27 | $52

Clayton | 7823 Forsyth Blvd. (Central Ave.) | 314-721-7375 | www.fialafood.com

This "stellar" Clayton kitchen by chef-owner Jim Fiala blends French and Italian influences to provide "imaginative" yet "elegant" high-end New American cuisine in a "cozy" setting tended by a staff that "shines"; meanwhile, the "star-of-the-show" tasting menus and wine flights are the "way to go" for a "sublime" experience that's a "fantastic value" too.

Farmhaus 🅇 *American*   27 | 20 | 25 | $36

South City | 3257 Ivanhoe Ave. (Bradley Ave.) | 314-647-3800 | www.farmhausrestaurant.com

The "flavor just pops" at this "brilliant new addition" to South City by rising-star chef Kevin Willmann, showcasing "locally grown" ingredients in "unique takes on traditional" New American dishes that are often "extraordinary" (and sometimes "bizarre"); "casual" in feel with "helpful" service, it's a little "pricey" for "small portions", but the "wonderful" "$10 blue-plate special" for lunch brings serious "bang for the buck."

Five Bistro 🅇🅜 *American*   27 | 25 | 28 | $39

The Hill | 5100 Daggett Ave. (Hereford St.) | 314-773-5553 | www.fivebistro.com

A "farm-to-table" "favorite", this New American on The Hill boasts an "eclectic", daily changing menu by chef-owner Anthony Devoti, who has an "excellent way with local ingredients" and crafting "special dinners" that are "worth every dime"; "top-notch" servers let diners "set the pace of the meal", while adept wine pairings and "nice decor" round out the "relaxed" experience; P.S. dig into some of the "best burgers in town" on the late-night menu Thursday–Saturday.

Home Wine Kitchen *American*   23 | 22 | 24 | $31

Maplewood | 7322 Manchester Rd. (bet. Marshall Ave & Sutton Blvd.) | 314-802-7676 | www.homewinekitchen.com

"Imaginative" weekly changing American menus with a rustic edge are matched by an innovative, well-chosen wine list (all selections are priced the same) at this Maplewood locale delivering an "upscale dining experience" with "lovely" service in a "small", "homey" setting; "brave" customers say the "no-menu Mondays rock", since the "surprising" three-course chef's-choice meal "turns dinner into true entertainment."

Mai Lee Ⓜ *Chinese/Vietnamese* 26 | 19 | 23 | $21
Richmond Heights | 8396 Musick Memorial Dr. (Hanley Rd.) | 314-645-2835 | www.maileerestaurant.com
"Heaping portions" of "authentic", "fresh" and "flavorful" Vietnamese and Chinese dishes from a "massive" menu keep this "foodie's-value" pick in Richmond Heights "packed" day and night; a "cheerful" staff is ready to help newcomers, so forget the "odd location" and "sparse" room, and just tuck into the "inexpensive", "quality" eats.

Niche *American* 28 | 25 | 26 | $59
Benton Park | 1831 Sidney St. (I-55) | 314-773-7755 | www.nichestlouis.com
Admirers advise "trust Gerard Craft and go with the tasting menu" at this "inspired", "locally driven" American where the chef-owner's "finesse and artistry" give shape to "sublime" dinners, and "even dubious combinations amaze the senses"; wine pairings are "perfect", the staff "knows its stuff" and the "tiny" space packs "tremendous ambiance", but just remember "reservations are essential" to partake of the "expensive, original" and "modern" cuisine; P.S. a move to Clayton is in the works.

Pappy's Smokehouse *BBQ* 28 | 18 | 23 | $18
Midtown | 3106 Olive St. (Cardinal Ave.) | 314-535-4340 | www.pappyssmokehouse.com
Devotees of the "remarkable", "fall-off-the-bone" Memphis-style BBQ at this "informal" Midtown "standout" say "don't let the long lines scare you", as they "move quickly" and the resulting "generous portions" at "competitive" prices will have you in "hog heaven"; fair warning: the house-smoked 'cue does "frequently sell out" by mid-afternoon, and "when they run out, that's it for the day"; P.S. no alcohol.

Sidney Street Cafe Ⓢ Ⓜ *American* 28 | 25 | 27 | $53
Benton Park | 2000 Sidney St. (Salena St.) | 314-771-5777 | www.sidneystreetcafe.com
Customers commend chef Kevin Nashan's "artistry of the highest order" in crafting "outstanding" seasonal "chalkboard menus" at this Benton Park "treasure", dubbed the city's "gold standard" for New American fine dining; exposed brick, "soft lights and intimate booths" make it a popular "romantic" choice, while a longtime, "extremely professional" staff creates an experience at once sophisticated and "comfortable" for "special occasions" and "casual" dinners alike.

Tavern Kitchen & Bar *American* 26 | 23 | 26 | $38
Kirkwood | 2961 Dougherty Ferry Rd. (Country Stone Dr.) | 636-825-0600 | www.tavernstl.com
"Artfully presented", "excellent food and drink" and "impeccable" service have surveyors hailing this "up-and-comer" as an "unexpected gem" for American "fine dining" in a Kirkwood strip mall; it's "casual" (though "not cheap") and "usually crowded", but try to nab one of the open kitchen's countertop seats for a unique, stove-side experience.

	FOOD	DECOR	SERVICE	COST

Ted Drewes Frozen Custard *Ice Cream* | 28 | 17 | 26 | $8 |

South City | 6726 Chippewa St. (Devonshire Ave.) | 314-481-2652
South Grand | 4224 S. Grand Blvd. (bet. Bingham Ave. & Kingsland Ct.) |
314-352-7376
www.teddrewes.com

Fanatics "can't imagine St. Louis without" this "iconic" South Grand and
South City "national treasure", voted Most Popular in the city for its
"smooth", "tantalizing" "concretes" ("lots of varieties" of frozen cus-
tard) satisfying sweet tooths for over 80 years; while both locations are
just "walk-up windows" that attract "long lines", "waits are minimal"
thanks to "workers who really hustle", plus it's "always a party" outside.

Three Sixty *American* | 22 | 29 | 23 | $30 |

Downtown | Hilton St. Louis at the Ballpark | 1 S. Broadway (Market St.) |
314-241-8439 | www.360-stl.com

"Location, location, location!" cheer fans of this "rooftop-patio"
"hot spot" 400 feet above Downtown, whose "swanky", eye-popping
setting, voted No. 1 for Decor in St. Louis, creates a "vibrant" atmosphere, with floor-to-ceiling glass walls that let guests "sit in the
clouds" to sip "specialty cocktails" and dine on "delicious", "diverse" American small plates and entrees; with Busch Stadium
next door it allows a tip-top glimpse of "ball-game action", but be
sure to check out all 360 degrees of "magnificent views."

Tony's 🅱 *Italian* | 27 | 25 | 27 | $75 |

Downtown | 410 Market St. (B'way) | 314-231-7007 | www.tonysstlouis.com

From "melt-in-your-mouth" carpaccio to "ethereal zabaglione", "elegance abounds" at this Downtown Italian "landmark" (and "celebration" magnet) where "tableside preparations" are a highlight of the
"luxurious" service, lending it an "old-world" feel despite its somewhat "modern" look; a few suggest it could use a "dose of excitement", but most agree the kitchen "continues to deliver", keeping it
"the place to go" for "classic fine dining" that's a "worthwhile splurge."

Tampa/Sarasota

TOP FOOD RANKING

Restaurant	Cuisine
28 Beach Bistro	Floridian
Pané Rustica	Eclectic
27 Bern's	Steak
Cafe Ponte	American
Maison Blanche	French
Restaurant BT	French/Vietnamese
Armani's	Italian
Mise en Place	American
26 Bijou Café	Continental
Ruth's Chris	Steak

OTHER NOTEWORTHY PLACES

Boca Kitchen	Californian/Mediterranean
Bonefish Grill	Seafood
Cevíche	Spanish
Ciro's Speakeasy	American
Columbia	Cuban/Spanish
Derek's Culinary Casual	American
Indigenous	American
Michael's On East	American
Refinery	American
SideBern's	Mediterranean

Armani's 🖥 Ⓜ *Italian*　　　27 | 27 | 27 | $65

Tampa | Grand Hyatt Tampa Bay | 2900 Bayport Dr., 14th fl. (Hwy. 60) | 813-207-6800 | www.grandtampabay.hyatt.com

"Everything it's hyped up to be", this "classy" longtime "destination" atop the Hyatt serves its "excellent, cutting-edge" Northern Italian cuisine, featuring a "fabulous antipasti bar", amid "million-dollar views" of Tampa Bay and "gorgeous sunsets"; though the bill can seem as "high" as the setting, it's "worth it" for "a true treat" that includes "impeccable service", a "terrific wine list" and a cocktail lounge that "feels high-end and exclusive" (with live piano Friday–Saturday).

Beach Bistro　*Floridian*　　　28 | 24 | 27 | $68

Holmes Beach | 6600 Gulf Dr. (66th St.) | 941-778-6444 | www.beachbistro.com

The "exciting", "sophisticated", "exquisitely prepared" Floridian cuisine earns Tampa/Sarasota's No. 1 Food score at this "evergreen" beachfront bistro on Anna Maria Island, where guests are "waited on hand and foot" by "personable" owner Sean Murphy and his "unerring" staff; the art-adorned interior is "a bit too cozy" for some, so try to "get a table outside" for more breathing room and the most "glorious view of the water", especially at sunset; P.S. prices can be "stratospheric", though bargains are to be found in the 'smaller-plates' selection and Murphy's Bar menu.

	FOOD	DECOR	SERVICE	COST

Bern's Steak House *Steak*

| 27 | 22 | 27 | $68 |

Tampa | 1208 S. Howard Ave. (bet. Marjory & Watrous Aves.) | 813-251-2421 | www.bernssteakhouse.com
Voted the region's Most Popular restaurant, this "Tampa institution" from 1956 is a "one-of-a-kind experience", with "incredible", "perfectly cooked" (and "pricey") dry-aged steaks, a "telephone-directory-sized wine list", "old-school", "well-trained" servers who "can't do enough for you" and "decor like a fancy bordello"; after dinner, "don't miss the tour of the kitchen and wine cellar" ("a blast"), then settle in for "marvelous" sweets in the "awesome" dessert room upstairs, featuring booths "shaped like wine casks" ("requires separate reservations").

Bijou Café Ⓩ *Continental*

| 26 | 26 | 26 | $57 |

Sarasota | 1287 First St. (Pineapple Ave.) | 941-366-8111 | www.bijoucafe.net
"Across from the beautifully restored opera house and library" – thus a "great choice" for "pre-theater" as well as "special occasions" – this Sarasota spot imbues "traditional Continental" cuisine with "modern style", and the results are "to die for"; an "extensive list of South African wines" and "professional, friendly" service add to the "delight", so while it's "a little pricier than competitors", it's also "more elegant than most."

Boca Kitchen Bar
Market Ⓩ Ⓜ *Californian/Mediterranean*

| – | – | – | M |

Tampa | 901 Platt St. (South Blvd.) | 813-254-7070 | www.bocatampa.com
This newcomer has taken local and sustainable to new levels in Tampa, employing two 'runners' who source ingredients – from local farms and artisanal purveyors as well as the garden of co-owner Gordon Davis (Ciro's, Samba Room) – which are crafted by chef Ted Dorsey into shareable Cal-Med small plates; a savvy, food-obsessed service team oversees the lively yet intimate warren of rooms in a former 1928-vintage gas station.

Bonefish Grill *Seafood*

| 24 | 21 | 22 | $35 |

Bradenton | 7456 W. Cortez Rd. (75th St.) | 941-795-8020
Sarasota | 3971 S. Tamiami Trail (Bee Ridge Rd.) | 941-924-9090
Sarasota | 8101 Cooper Creek Blvd. (University Pkwy.) | 941-360-3171
Bellaire Bluffs | 2939 W. Bay Dr. (Indian Rocks Rd.) | 727-518-1230
Clearwater | Kash 'N Karry Plaza | 2519 McMullen Booth Rd. (Enterprise Rd.) | 727-726-1315
St. Petersburg | Tyrone Square Mall | 2408 Tyrone Blvd. (66th St.) | 727-344-8600
St. Petersburg | 5062 Fourth St. N. (51st. Ave.) | 727-521-3434
Brandon | 1015 Providence Rd. (Lumdsen St.) | 813-571-5553
Tampa | 13262 N. Dale Mabry Hwy. (Fletcher Ave.) | 813-969-1619
Tampa | 3665 Henderson Blvd. (Sterling St.) | 813-876-3535
www.bonefishgrill.com
Additional locations throughout the Tampa/Sarasota area
"The Bang Bang Shrimp is everybody's favorite" but all of the seafood is "terrific" at this "casual", "comfortable", "dependable" chain where the "wait can be long" because it's "always crowded" (and "noisy, but fun", especially at the "hopping bar"); the "competitive price" helps to keep it "kid-friendly", while the "solid cocktails" and "nice wine selection" make it an "impressive date-night" spot too, abetted by largely "pleasant", "attentive" staffers.

	FOOD	DECOR	SERVICE	COST

Cafe Ponte ⌧ *American* — 27 | 23 | 26 | $55

Clearwater | Icot Ctr. | 13505 Icot Blvd. (Ulmerton Rd.) | 727-538-5768 |
www.cafeponte.com
"Don't let the strip-mall location fool you", for this Clearwater eatery is a
"masterpiece" thanks to "creative, skilled" chef-owner Chris Ponte's
"outstanding" New American dishes highlighting "Asian and
Mediterranean flavors", "skillfully served" by a "sharp" staff in "comfy",
"supper club"–like environs; it's in the "splurge category" for many,
but there's an early-bird prix fixe that offers "excellent value."

Ceviche Tapas Bar & Restaurant ❶ *Spanish* — 23 | 23 | 20 | $35

Sarasota | 1216 First St. (Tamiami Trail) | 941-952-1036 Ⓜ
Clearwater | 2930 Gulf to Bay Blvd. (bet. McMullen Booth Rd. & Rte. 19) |
727-799-3082
St. Petersburg | Ponce de Leon Hotel | 10 Beach Dr. (Central Ave.) |
727-209-2299
Tampa | 2500 W. Azeele St. (Hills Ave.) | 813-250-0203
www.ceviche.com
"It's fun, it's delicious, it's adventurous, it's about sharing" rhapsodize
respondents smitten by this "popular" regional chain whose menu
lists "over 100" "stylish and interesting" Spanish tapas, plus "fabulous
sangria" and "decent" wines; with "dim lighting" and "live music on
some evenings", both the interior and patio are reliably "romantic" –
it's just the service that's "hit-or-miss."

Ciro's Speakeasy & Supper Club ❶⌧Ⓜ *American* — ▽ 22 | 28 | 26 | $53

Tampa | 2109 Bayshore Blvd. (Harvard Ave.) | 813-251-0022 |
www.cirosspeakeasy.com
"Shhh" – surveyors beg you to keep "Tampa's best-kept secret", this
"pricey" New American speakeasy from the folks behind Ceviche and
others, where there's no sign, a doorbell and a "secret password to get
in" (don't worry if you don't have it); once inside, the "well-trained"
servers, dressed in Prohibition garb, "stay in character" while dispensing the "creative", "delicious" dishes, while "knowledgeable, gracious"
bartenders concoct "amazing" classic cocktails out of "several different kinds of absinthe and a huge whiskey collection."

Columbia *Cuban/Spanish* — 23 | 23 | 22 | $37

Sarasota | 411 St. Armands Circle (Blvd. of Presidents) | 941-388-3987
Clearwater | 1241 Gulf Blvd. (½ mi. south of Sand Key Bridge) |
727-596-8400
St. Petersburg | St. Petersburg Pier | 800 Second Ave. NE (Beach Dr.) |
727-822-8000
Ybor City | 2117 E. Seventh Ave. (bet. 21st & 22nd Sts.) | 813-248-4961
Tampa International | 4100 George J. Bean Pkwy. (Memorial Hwy.) |
Tampa | 813-870-8700
Columbia Café *Cuban/Spanish*
Tampa | Tampa Bay History Ctr. | 801 Old Water St. (Channelside Dr.) |
813-229-5511
www.columbiarestaurant.com
The oldest and largest restaurant in the state, the Ybor City original of
this Cuban-Spanish mini-chain offers "the best experience, combining
incredible food with turn-of-the-20th-century architecture and furnishings"; but all locations are "consistent" in terms of the "classic"

dishes (in particular, "the paella is to die for" and "the 1905 salad knocks it out of the park"), "fantastic sangria", "stellar service" and "reasonable" prices; P.S. the flamenco dancers at the flagship are "amazing", and the Tampa cafe serves a limited menu; the St. Petersburg location is closing in 2013.

Derek's Culinary Casual 🍴Ⓜ️ *American*   25 | 19 | 24 | $55

Sarasota | 514 Central Ave. (bet. 5th & 6th Sts.) | 941-366-6565 | www.dereks-sarasota.com

Derek Barnes, "a chef with an original point of view", "sources ingredients locally" and crafts "innovative" "mixes of taste and texture" for his "superb" New American dishes, which are "presented artistically" at this "soul-satisfying experience" in Sarasota; while there's no hard liquor, beer and wine are on offer, along with "terrific service" and a "metropolitan" setting befitting the "upscale" tabs.

Indigenous 🍴Ⓜ️ *American*   – | – | – | M

Sarasota | 239 S. Links Ave. (Adams Ln.) | 941-706-4740 | www.indigenoussarasota.com

In a lovely old bungalow with indoor and outdoor dining areas as well as a lovely 'wine cottage', chef-owner Steve Phelps charms Sarasotans with a seasonally changing American menu highlighting the best of what's local – be that Florida grass-fed beef, Gulf fish and shrimp, or oranges from a nearby backyard – in preparations accented with architectural showmanship and whimsy; warm service and a short, thoughtful wine list (plus a 'captain's list' of big-time bottlings) complement the cuisine.

Maison Blanche Ⓜ️ *French*   27 | 25 | 27 | $80

Longboat Key | 2605 Gulf of Mexico Dr. (Ave. of the Flower) | 941-383-8088 | www.maisonblancherestaurants.com

Chef-owner Jose Martinez "lovingly prepares" "exquisite" "classic French cuisine with a modern twist" at this "charmer" on Longboat Key, where the "simple but elegant setting" allows you to "concentrate on the flavors"; some grouse about the "astronomical prices", but for a "fabulous fancy night out" with "impeccable service" to match, it delivers (except in summer, when it's closed).

Michael's On East 🍴 *American*   25 | 24 | 25 | $61

Sarasota | Midtown Plaza | 1212 East Ave. S. (Bahia Vista St.) | 941-366-0007 | www.michaelsoneast.com

A "standby" "for lunch, dinner and after-theater drinks", this "relaxing" yet "happening", "sophisticated" Sarasotan augments its "outstanding" regular New American menu ("high end, but well worth it") with monthly three-course 'epicurean adventures' that are "wonderful as well as inexpensive"; "smart, modern decor", an "enjoyable" piano bar and "accommodating, friendly" service are additional draws.

Mise en Place 🍴Ⓜ️ *American*   27 | 23 | 25 | $55

Tampa | 442 W. Kennedy Blvd. (Hyde Park Ave.) | 813-254-5373 | www.miseonline.com

"Even after 25 years", chef/co-owner Marty Blitz "continues to reach for higher levels of excellence" (and "delights in creating new dishes") at his University of Tampa–area New American, where the fare is "prepared with attention to detail" and "presented in an unpretentious manner" alongside "carefully selected wines" by "polished" staffers in "a lovely, elegant setting"; prices may "fall into the 'big night out' category", but surveyors assert it's "worth every penny" for such a "dependable, innovative" experience.

Pané Rustica ⓜ *Eclectic* | 28 | 21 | 23 | $33 |

Tampa | 3225 S. MacDill Ave. (Bay to Bay Blvd.) | 813-902-8828 | www.panerusticabakery.com

Though it "started primarily as a [breakfast and] lunch destination", this "classy yet casual" South Tampa purveyor of "awesome artisan breads", "amazing thin-crust specialty pizzas", "fantastic" sandwiches and other "delectable baked goods" has added a "lovely bar", causing the Wednesday–Saturday Eclectic dinner service to really "take off"; so while it's now "more chic by night", it remains as "fairly priced" as ever, with "friendly service" thrown into the mix.

The Refinery ⓜ *American* | 25 | 18 | 20 | $29 |

Tampa | 5137 N. Florida Ave. (Frierson Ave.) | 813-237-2000 | www.thetamparefinery.com

"A foodie's dream", this Tampa "pioneer" presents a "delightful", "inspired farm-to-table" American menu that "changes every Thursday", featuring "adventuresome" "twists" and "organic, local" ingredients chosen by a chef who's "truly an artisan"; though some deem the setting "sub-great", others dig its "down-to-earth ambiance" – everyone, meanwhile, appreciates the "excellent value."

Restaurant BT Ⓩ *French/Vietnamese* | 27 | 21 | 22 | $50 |

Tampa | 2507 S. MacDill Ave. (bet. Palmira Ave. & San Jose St.) | 813-251-1916 | www.restaurantbt.com

"Flavor genius" B.T. Nguyen now offers her "creative", "exquisitely prepared" French-Vietnamese fusion dishes "using local ingredients" in a "stylish", "contemporary", "smaller" new Tampa setting featuring an "intimate" patio laden with "big pots of plants and herbs"; what's more, the staff is "knowledgeable" about the "expensive" menu.

Ruth's Chris Steak House *Steak* | 26 | 23 | 26 | $60 |

Sarasota | 6700 S. Tamiami Trail (Stickney Point Rd.) | 941-924-9442
Tampa | 1700 N. Westshore Blvd. (Spruce St.) | 813-282-1118
www.ruthschris.com

Both the scene and the steaks are "still sizzling" (the latter in butter) at these "elegant", "inviting" Tampa and Sarasota iterations of the national chain, where the "cordial", "professional" staffers also dole out "superb sides" and "well-prepared martinis"; true to its ilk, full meals here are usually "costly", but bargain-hunters reveal a "best-kept secret": the bar menu, where the "excellent" fare comes in "smaller portions."

SideBern's Ⓩ *Mediterranean* | 26 | 23 | 24 | $55 |

Tampa | 2208 W. Morrison Ave. (Howard Ave.) | 813-258-2233 | www.sideberns.com

A "more daring" yet "relaxed alternative to big brother" Bern's Steak House down the street, this Tampa "powerhouse" "artistically presents" "innovative seasonal" Mediterranean cuisine alongside "over-the-top drinks" and bottles from the "excellent attached wine store"; a "cool" "upscale atmosphere" that includes "great outdoor dining" is a boon, as are prices that seem "worth every penny."

Tucson

TOP FOOD RANKING

	Restaurant	Cuisine
28	Fleming's Prime	Steak
27	Vivace	Italian
	Dish	American
	Le Rendez-Vous	French
	Cafe Poca Cosa	Mexican
26	Athens on Fourth	Greek
	Grill at Hacienda del Sol	American
	Beyond Bread	Sandwiches
25	El Güero Canelo	Mexican
	Vero Amore	Italian/Pizza

OTHER NOTEWORTHY PLACES

Restaurant	Cuisine
Abbey	American
Agustín Brasserie	French
Arizona Inn	Continental
DOWNTOWN Kitchen	Eclectic
El Charro	Mexican
Feast	Eclectic
Maynards	French
P.F. Chang's	Chinese
Tavolino	Italian
Zinburger	American

The Abbey Ⓜ *American*　　　　　　　|　24 | 22 | 24 | $33 |

Foothills | Shops at Ventana Canyon | 6960 E. Sunrise Dr. (Kolb Rd.) | 520-299-3132 | www.theabbeytucson.com

Culinary "nirvana" is found at this "hip", "welcome addition to the Foothills", where the "small menu" of "rib-sticking" American "comfort food" is "different", "delicious" and "fairly priced" (the happy hours, 4–6 PM and after 8 PM, feature "incredible bargains"); what's more, service is "relaxed" and the setting, with garage doors you can peer through to "watch the mountains blush at sunset", is a whole lot of "fun."

Agustín Brasserie Ⓢ Ⓜ *French*　　　　　|　– | – | – | M |

Downtown | Mercado San Agustín | 100 S. Avenida del Convento (Congress St.) | 520-398-5382 | www.agustinbrasserie.com

A Francophile enclave in Downtown's Mexican-style Mercado San Agustín complex, this midpriced brasserie serves bistro classics in a high-ceilinged room that's a study in black-and-white with tiny tiles and hanging globe lights; both couples and singles like the sophisticated (but not snooty) vibe, not to mention the lively bar serving perfect Bellinis.

Arizona Inn Restaurant ◗ *Continental*　　|　23 | 26 | 25 | $51 |

Midtown | Arizona Inn | 2200 E. Elm St. (bet. Campbell Ave. & Tucson Blvd.) | 520-325-1541 | www.arizonainn.com

"Step back in time" to a "gentler", more "elegant" era "when gracious service was the norm" at this Continental in a "historic" Midtown inn with "gorgeous Spanish Colonial" decor and "luxuriant gardens"; since it's "a bit spendy", the "fine", "conservative" fare works best for "special occasions", "business lunches" and folks who enjoy "patterned china, real silver utensils" and finger bowls – the sort "who are unlikely to be texting" at the table.

Athens on Fourth ☒ *Greek* 26 | 19 | 25 | $27

University/4th Ave | 500 N. Fourth Ave. (6th St.) | 520-624-6886 | www.athensonfourth.com

You're "guaranteed to go home satisfied" at this "wonderful", "popular" Greek near U of A, where the "wide" "variety" of fare is augmented by Hellenic wines and the "moderate prices" make it a "great value"; add "outstanding service" and an "upscale, elegant" atmosphere, and it's clear why surveyors say it's "not at all your standard souvlaki joint."

Beyond Bread *Sandwiches* 26 | 18 | 22 | $13

Midtown | 3026 N. Campbell Ave. (Blacklidge Dr.) | 520-322-9965
Midtown | Monterey Vlg. | 6260 E. Speedway Blvd. (Wilmot Rd.) | 520-747-7477
Northwest | 421 W. Ina Rd. (Oracle Rd.) | 520-461-1111
www.beyondbread.com

"Man could truly live by bread alone" at these "great-value" bakery/cafes where the "freshly made" loaves are used in a "dazzling array" of "inventive", "über-delish" sandwiches that are so "massive", many find it "a feat to finish" one – indeed, saving room for the "fabulous desserts" "might be an issue"; the daytime atmosphere is often "frenetic", but "service is quick", while in the off hours, it can feel more "relaxing."

Cafe Poca Cosa ☒Ⓜ *Mexican* 27 | 24 | 24 | $34

Downtown | 110 E. Pennington St. (Scott Ave.) | 520-622-6400 | www.cafepocacosatucson.com

"Nothing leaves the kitchen" of chef-owner Suzana Davila unless it's "amazingly, perfectly delicious" at this "chic" Downtowner whose "magical" regional Mexican fare and "remarkably reasonable prices" earn it Tucson's Most Popular restaurant honors; the "friendly" servers are "knowledgeable" about "the twice-daily changing" "chalkboard menu", but fans "strongly recommend the chef's-choice plate", a "colorful" "sampling of three entrees"; P.S. don't forget the "awesome margaritas."

The Dish ☒Ⓜ *American* 27 | 20 | 25 | $44

Midtown | 3131 E. First St. (Country Club Rd.) | 520-326-1714 | www.dishbistro.com

You "can't dis The Dish" assert respondents who rave about this "upscale" yet "reasonably priced" Midtown New American's "scrumptious", "innovative" cuisine as much as its "fantastic" wine program in which you select any bottle from the surrounding liquor store, The RumRunner, and pay corkage; with only 34 seats, the setting can feel "a bit cramped", but "warm" and "convivial" vibes rule the day thanks in part to the "knowledgeable", "attentive service."

DOWNTOWN Kitchen + Cocktails *Eclectic* 24 | 23 | 24 | $38

Downtown | 135 S. Sixth Ave. (Broadway Blvd.) | 520-623-7700 | www.downtownkitchen.com

Chef Janos Wilder "has done it again" at this Downtown Eclectic addition where the "heavenly" "multicultural" "creations" are based on "sustainable and local" ingredients and sold for relative-"bargain prices"; "excellent service" helps make it "perfect" for a pre- or post-"theater/concert meal", but keep in mind that the "hip, urban" digs get "noisy" – fueled no doubt by the "amazing" cocktails, especially during the "unbelievable happy hour"; P.S. a sidewalk patio opened up post-Survey.

El Charro Café *Mexican*
23 | 22 | 21 | $23

Downtown | 311 N. Court Ave. (Council St.) | 520-622-1922
Foothills | 6910 E. Sunrise Dr. (Kolb Rd.) | 520-514-1922
Midtown | El Mercado | 6310 E. Broadway Blvd. (Wilmot Rd.) | 520-745-1922
Northwest | 7725 N. Oracle Rd. (bet. Ina & Magee Rds.) | 520-229-1922
Sahuarita | 15920 S. Rancho Sahuarita Blvd. (Helmet Peak Rd.) |
520-325-1922
www.elcharrocafe.com

"Family-owned since Tucson was very small" (1922), this "quintes-sential" Mexican restaurant in "an old house with wooden floors" Downtown is known for "darn-yummy" Sonoran-style eats like "not-to-be-missed" carne seca ("sun-dried on the roof") and possibly hav-ing "invented the chimichanga"; though not as "picturesque", its off-spring offer a similarly "lively atmosphere", "pretty good service" and, more importantly, "great value."

El Güero Canelo *Mexican*
25 | 12 | 19 | $9

Eastside | 5802 E. 22nd St. (bet. Sahuara & Van Buren Aves.) | 520-790-6000
Midtown | 2480 N. Oracle Rd. (Alturas St.) | 520-882-8977
South Tucson | 5201 S. 12th Ave. (Utah St.) | 520-295-9005
www.elguerocanelo.com

"Powerhouse" Sonoran hot dogs set in "fluffy rolls" and "slathered" with your choice of "toppings and sauces" are the prime reasons to seek out this "quick" and "inexpensive" Mexican trio, but "don't miss out on the rest of the menu", featuring "excellent tacos"; also, "don't let yourself be put off by the decor", especially at the South Tucson original, "a rustic assemblage of trailers" with "loud music."

Feast ☒ *Eclectic*
24 | 20 | 24 | $33

Midtown | 3719 E. Speedway Blvd. (bet. Country Club & Alvernon Rds.) |
520-326-9363 | www.eatatfeast.com

It's a "feast for the senses" at this affordable bistro featuring a "monthly changing" menu (with "a core of yummy staples") of "quirky-in-a-good-way" Eclectic fare from "charming" chef-owner-oenophile Doug Levy, who "puts his heart and soul into his food" as well as the "excep-tional", "extensive list of moderately priced wines"; devotees have embraced the new Midtown location (just a mile from the original) for its "friendly, low-key atmosphere" and ability to "accommodate more folks" while praising service that's as "terrific" as ever.

Fleming's Prime Steakhouse & Wine Bar *Steak*
28 | 26 | 27 | $53

Foothills | 6360 N. Campbell Ave. (Skyline Dr.) | 520-529-5017 |
www.flemingssteakhouse.com

"Bring your wallet" and a "big appetite" to this "clubby", "pricey" Foothills chophouse chain link, winner of Tucson's No. 1 Food score for its "outstanding" steaks "prepared to exacting standards", plus "solid sides", "delicious breads and spreads" and "great sweet endings"; tipplers toast the "fine wine list", featuring an "extensive by-the-glass" selection, and "superb martinis", while all applaud the "flawless service."

Grill at Hacienda del Sol American   26 | 28 | 25 | $54

Foothills | Hacienda del Sol | 5501 N. Hacienda del Sol (bet. River Rd. & Sunrise Dr.) | 520-529-3500 | www.haciendadelsol.com
With its "stunning", "romantic" perch "above the lights of the city", "old Southwestern" ambiance and "creative, well-executed menu", this New American in a "historic" Foothills resort is a "jewel in the desert"; "professional, knowledgeable service" and "fantastic wine selection" cement its reputation as "ideal for special occasions" and a "must" with "out-of-town guests", and though it's "pricey", most deem it "worth the splurge" (though Sunday brunch is "more affordable", and "out of this world" to boot).

Le Rendez-Vous M French   27 | 22 | 24 | $50

Midtown | 3844 Fort Lowell Rd. (Alvernon Way) | 520-323-7373 | www.lerendez-vous.biz
For "well-prepared, outstandingly presented" "classic French cooking in the desert", look no further than this Midtowner where dinners are "pricey but worth the extra expense" and lunchtime features some "great values"; bolstered by a "carefully selected" wine list and "excellent" staff (performing "tableside service for many dishes"), it feels a bit like a "romantic" place on "the Left Bank of Paris" – a "treat" for "celebrating" "special occasions"; P.S. the post-Survey addition of a bistro in the front room, serving inexpensive small plates, is not reflected in the ratings.

Maynards Market & Kitchen French   24 | 25 | 23 | $37

Downtown | Historic Train Depot | 400 N. Toole Ave. (Congress St.) | 520-545-0577 | www.maynardsmarkettucson.com
"The sound of freight trains rumbling by" this "hip", midpriced venue in Downtown's historic railway depot "adds excitement to a fine meal" of "fabulous", "creative" French bistro dishes, available in a room that resembles a "vintage first-class dining car" or on the "platform-cum-patio", all monitored by "professional" staffers; "well-selected" wines are available (for a corkage fee) from the neighboring gourmet market, as are more casual, counter-served eats.

P.F. Chang's China Bistro Chinese   23 | 23 | 23 | $28

Foothills | Joesler Vlg. | 1805 E. River Rd. (bet. Camino Luz & Campbell Ave.) | 520-615-8788 | www.pfchangs.com
"Forget authenticity and go for the flash" at this Foothills branch of the national chain whose "terrific" "Americanized" Chinese fare is priced for "value", particularly the "great happy-hour specials" ("don't miss the lettuce wraps"); it's often "crowded" and "noisy", but it's also "quick, friendly", "lushly decorated" and "consistent" whether you go for "business lunches", dinner with "the whole family" or "a fun night with friends" and "froufrou Asian cocktails."

Tavolino Ⓩ Italian   24 | 23 | 22 | $39

Foothills | 2890 E. Skyline Dr. (Ina Rd.) | 520-531-1913 | www.tavolinoristorante.com
Ensconced in "stylish" digs with a "lovely patio", this frequently "packed" Italian in the Foothills delivers "sumptuous" Northern cui-

sine like "ethereal" housemade pastas and wood-fired pizzas and meats; service is "attentive" and "efficient", though a few just "wish it were $5 cheaper."

Vero Amore *Italian/Pizza* | 25 | 19 | 24 | $23 |

Marana | 12130 N. Dove Mountain Blvd. (W. Tangerine Rd.) | 520-579-2292

Midtown | 3305 N. Swan Rd. (E. Ave Rio Bruza) | 520-325-4122
www.veroamorepizza.com

"First-class gourmet" Neapolitan pizza is the star at both the original Midtown locale and its more expansive Marana offshoot, the latter offering a larger menu of Italian entrees; some say the "casual" setting's rather "uninspired", but "terrific Chiantis" and reasonable prices are other reasons to come.

Vivace Ⓩ *Italian* | 27 | 23 | 26 | $42 |

Foothills | St. Philip's Plaza | 4310 N. Campbell Ave. (E. River Rd.) | 520-795-7221 | www.vivacetucson.com

Chef-owner Daniel Scordato sends out "consistently wonderful", "well-priced" Italian fare while "closely supervising" "some of the most professional servers in town" at this "welcoming" Foothills stalwart in St. Philip's Plaza; an "extensive wine list", "elegant, comfortable" interior and "lovely patio" are three more boons for its "broad, loyal customer base", and if you want to join it, be sure to "make reservations well ahead."

Zinburger *Burgers* | 24 | 19 | 22 | $22 |

Foothills | Joesler Vlg. | 1865 E. River Rd. (Campbell Ave.) | 520-299-7799

Midtown | 6390 E. Grant Rd. (Wilmot Rd.) | 520-298-2020 Ⓢ Ⓜ
www.foxrc.com

"Zinfully wonderful" burgers with "creative" toppings, "fabulous fries", "thick milkshakes" and "terrific wines" keep customers coming to this "cool", "upscale" duo in the Foothills and Midtown by restaurateur Sam Fox; "crowded" conditions are overcome by "fast-paced" service, and if it can feel a bit "expensive", at least happy hour offers "special deals."

Washington, DC, Metro Area

TOP FOOD RANKING

Restaurant	Cuisine
28 Rasika	Indian
L'Auberge Chez François	French
Komi	American/Mediterranean
Marcel's	Belgian/French
Prime Rib	Steak
Corduroy	American
Obelisk	Italian
Little Serow	Thai
Peking Duck	Chinese
27 CityZen	American
Eve	American
Makoto	Japanese
Russia House Rest.	Russian
Palena	American
Ray's The Steaks	Steak
Blue Duck Tavern	American
Tosca	Italian
BlackSalt	American/Seafood
Fiola	Italian
Ruan Thai	Thai

OTHER NOTEWORTHY PLACES

Birch & Barley	American
Bourbon	Steak
Bread Line	Bakery/Sandwiches
Clyde's	American
Cork	American
Equinox	American
Five Guys	Burgers
Inn at Little Washington	American
J&G Steakhouse	American/Steak
Johnny's Half Shell	American/Seafood
Mintwood Place	American
Pizzeria Paradiso	Pizza
Ray's Hell Burger	Burgers
Ris	American
1789	American
Source	American
2 Amys	Pizza
Vidalia	American
Volt	American
Zaytinya	Mediterranean/Mideastern

	FOOD	DECOR	SERVICE	COST

Birch & Barley ⓜ *American* — 24 | 23 | 24 | $41

Logan Circle | 1337 14th St. NW (bet. P St. & Rhode Island Ave.) |
202-567-2576 | www.birchandbarley.com

Pairing "super-creative" New American food with beer is the mission
of this somewhat spendy Logan Circle gastropub, whose "chipper"
servers are "great guides" to the "tremendous" brew list (50 on
tap, 500 bottles); it's easy to "impress a date" in the "beautiful" "dark"
and distressed digs that are "cool" "without being obnoxious about it",
and its "indulgent" Sunday brunch is also popular; P.S. sister bar/lounge
Churchkey is upstairs.

BlackSalt *American/Seafood* — 27 | 21 | 23 | $55

Palisades | 4883 MacArthur Blvd. NW (U St.) | 202-342-9101 |
www.blacksaltrestaurant.com

"Inventive, gorgeous and impeccably executed" New American seafood at "not-quite lobbyist prices" is served with "care" at the Black
Restaurant Group's "popular" Palisades flagship; if the "decor is not up
to the quality of the food", it's not apparent from the "sit-and-be-
seen" hordes always packing the "fun bar", "lively" main dining room
and somewhat more "intimate" and "elegant" back room; P.S. it's
"hard to resist" the "terrific" on-site market for "fresh, fresh, fresh"
fish "on your way out."

Blue Duck Tavern *American* — 27 | 25 | 26 | $64

West End | Park Hyatt | 1201 24th St. NW (bet. M & N Sts.) |
202-419-6755 | www.blueducktavern.com

Birds of a feather are "wowed every time" by the elevated, "beautifully
crafted" "comfort food" at this "elegant" West End New American;
just as ducky: it's "high on style and low on pretension", with an "extremely gracious" staff that "knows how to show you a good time" in
"modern", "Shaker-inspired" environs that are often graced by "famous" faces; P.S. should the bill "make you 'blue'", there are "lower
prices" at lunch, and in the bar/lounge.

Bourbon Steak *Steak* — 25 | 25 | 25 | $70

Georgetown | Four Seasons Hotel Washington DC |
2800 Pennsylvania Ave. NW (28th St.) | 202-944-2026 |
www.bourbonsteakdc.com

"Of course the steaks are superb" at Michael Mina's DC chophouse, but
"trust the chefs" to take you on an "amazing adventure" via the rest of
the "inventive" New American menu at this "popular" Four Seasons
venue – "the place to see, be seen and spend money in Georgetown";
"impeccable service" is de rigueur and "celebrity sightings" are common
in the "modern and polished" dining room, as well as the bar that's
"rife with power-sippers (and those looking to get attached to them)."

Bread Line ⓩ *Bakery/Sandwiches* — 23 | 12 | 17 | $15

World Bank | 1751 Pennsylvania Ave. NW (bet. 17th & 18th Sts.) |
202-822-8900 | www.breadline.com

"It's the bread, stupid", and the way this gently priced bakery/cafe
"down the block" from the White House and World Bank can "pack so
many flavors and textures" into one "delicious" sandwich makes for an
"unmatched" lunch; at midday, an "efficient" crew moves the "long"
queue "fast", though many leave the "stark" industrial premises to sit

outside or go "picnicking"; P.S. it's line-free at breakfast, or go for "fine pastry and coffee" in the afternoon.

CityZen 🖼 Ⓜ *American* | 27 | 27 | 27 | $115 |

SW | Mandarin Oriental | 1330 Maryland Ave. SW (12th St.) | 202-787-6006 | www.mandarinoriental.com

Chef Eric Ziebold "delivers taste, imagination and fun" via a multicourse menu that adds up to a "fabulous meal full of pleasant surprises" at this "stunningly beautiful" "Nouvelle American" "destination" in the Mandarin Oriental; a "personal touch from the minute you walk in the door" enhances the experience, which leads flush foodies to exult "fine dining is still alive and worth every cent"; P.S. the "very hip" bar offers a "real-bargain" tasting menu.

Clyde's ● *American* | 22 | 23 | 22 | $33 |

Chinatown | Gallery Pl. | 707 Seventh St. NW (bet. G & H Sts.) | 202-349-3700
Georgetown | Georgetown Park Mall | 3236 M St. NW (bet. Potomac St. & Wisconsin Ave.) | 202-333-9180
Chevy Chase | 5441 Wisconsin Ave. (bet. Montgomery St. & Wisconsin Circle), MD | 301-951-9600
Rockville | 2 Preserve Pkwy. (bet. Tower Oaks Blvd. & Wootton Pkwy.), MD | 301-294-0200
Greater Alexandria | Mark Ctr. | 1700 N. Beauregard St. (bet. Rayburn Ave. & Seminary Rd.) | Alexandria, VA | 703-820-8300
Reston | Reston Town Ctr. | 11905 Market St. (bet. Reston & Town Ctr. Pkwys.), VA | 703-787-6601
Tysons Corner | 8332 Leesburg Pike (Rte. 123) | Vienna, VA | 703-734-1901
Broadlands | Willow Creek Farm | 42920 Broadlands Blvd. (bet. Belmont Ridge Rd. & Claiborne Pkwy.), VA | 571-209-1200
www.clydes.com

"Nostalgic" themes (old farmhouse, Adirondack lodge, the Golden Age of Travel) make each location of this homegrown American saloon feel like a "unique" "adventure", so it's no wonder they're "popular" stops for everyone from "kids" to "grandma" – indeed, they're Greater DC's Most Popular places to dine; "upbeat" service also plays a role, along with the fact that diners are sure to "get their money's worth" via a "value"-packed menu of "solidly appealing", "honest" eats.

Corduroy 🖼 *American* | 28 | 25 | 26 | $68 |

Mt. Vernon Square/Convention Center | 1122 Ninth St. NW (bet. L & M Sts.) | 202-589-0699 | www.corduroydc.com

"Every morsel from the kitchen is a thing of beauty", and matched by "excellent" wines, at Tom Power's "civilized" New American in a townhouse opposite the Convention Center; service that's "polished yet the antithesis of stuffy" and "clean-lined", "modern" decor both strike a balance between "elegant" and "casual", adding up to an "expensive but worth it" experience; P.S. the "hideaway upstairs bar" offers what may be the "best" three-course "bar bargain" in town.

Cork Ⓜ *American* | 25 | 22 | 23 | $44 |

Logan Circle | 1720 14th St. NW (bet. R & S Sts.) | 202-265-2675 | www.corkdc.com

At this über-trendy Logan Circle wine bar, "a huge array of wines by the glass without an outrageous markup" is paired with "delightful" New American small plates with an "extra edge of creativity" courtesy of chef Robert Weland (ex Poste); the "well-informed" staff doubles as "eye candy" in the "stylish", brick-walled, "dimly lit" space that gets "loud" and "crowded" late, so best come "early."

Equinox *American*

25 | 22 | 24 | $68

Golden Triangle | 818 Connecticut Ave. NW (bet. H & I Sts.) | 202-331-8118 | www.equinoxrestaurant.com

Chef/co-owner Todd Gray (and executive chef Karen Nicholas) "can just plain cook", using "locally sourced" ingredients in "creative" ways in the "outstanding" New American dishes that grace the tables at this "pricey" fine-dining spot steps from the White House; "polished" service is "worthy of that special night" out but "also establishment enough for business lunches", when one spots famous faces in the "sleek", contemporary rooms.

Eve, Restaurant ⊠ *American*

27 | 25 | 26 | $86

Old Town | 110 S. Pitt St. (bet. King & Prince Sts.) | Alexandria, VA | 703-706-0450 | www.restauranteve.com

"You don't just dine" at Cathal Armstrong's "pitch-perfect" Old Town New American, you get a taste of "perfection" as you are "cosseted" in "plush" banquettes in the "romantic" tasting room, where "personalized" multicourse menus evince the chef's "passion" and "attention to detail"; or head to the connecting bistro and bar to "savor the delicious food" on the cheap – it offers à la carte choices and, at lunch, there's a two-course "bargain" prix fixe for around $15.

Fiola ⊠ *Italian*

27 | 25 | 26 | $68

Penn Quarter | 601 Pennsylvania Ave. NW (entrance on Indiana Ave. bet. 6th & 7th Sts.) | 202-628-2888 | www.fioladc.com

"Wow", Fabio Trabocchi's "sensational" Penn Quarter venue offers the "complete package" – "his elegant magic touch" with rustic Italian cuisine, a "fabulous" (and "unstuffy") villalike ambiance plus "extremely engaging" help; aim for a table in the rear to "ogle" the objets d'art and the "lively crowd", and though it's not cheap, tabs are an "unbelievable" value given the "truly wonderful dining experience."

Five Guys *Burgers*

24 | 14 | 21 | $12

Chinatown | 808 H St. NW (bet. 8th & 9th Sts.) | 202-393-2900
Georgetown | 1335 Wisconsin Ave. NW (Dumbarton St.) | 202-337-0400
Bethesda | 4829 Bethesda Ave. (bet. Arlington & Clarendon Rds.), MD | 301-657-0007
Frederick | Shops at Monocacy | 1700 Kingfisher Dr. (Rte. 26), MD | 301-668-1500
Greater Alexandria | 4626 King St. (Beauregard St.) | Alexandria, VA | 703-671-1606
Greater Alexandria | 7622 Richmond Hwy. (Boswell Ave.) | Alexandria, VA | 703-717-0090
Old Town | 107 N. Fayette St. (King St.) | Alexandria, VA | 703-549-7991
Herndon | Fox Mill Ctr. | 2521 John Milton Dr. (Fox Mill Rd.), VA | 703-860-9100
Springfield | 6541 Backlick Rd. (Old Keene Mill Rd.), VA | 703-913-1337
Manassas | Manassas Corner | 9221 Sudley Rd. (Centerville Rd.), VA | 703-368-8080
www.fiveguys.com
Additional locations throughout the DC area

"Hot, juicy and smothered in whatever your heart desires", this is "the way a burger should be" say fans of these über-"popular" counters, rated the DC area's Most Popular chain; while the "sparse" white-and-red-tiled settings earn few raves, "who cares" when "the prices are right" and there are free peanuts to shell while you wait – which won't be long since the "hard-working" crews fill orders "fast."

Inn at Little Washington *American*   `29` `29` `29` `$205`
Washington | Inn at Little Washington | 309 Middle St. (Main St.), VA | 540-675-3800 | www.theinnatlittlewashington.com
"Simply the best", Patrick O'Connell's hunt-country New American "cit-adel" delivers a "life-altering experience" as guests get "pampered" in an "intimate", richly embroidered setting, where "revelatory" multicourse repasts are "prepared with extraordinary skill" and seasoned with a "touch of whimsy"; in short, it's "worth every penny . . . and that's a lot of pennies!"; P.S. "spend the night for the ultimate indulgence."

J&G Steakhouse *American/Steak*   `24` `24` `23` `$68`
Downtown | W Hotel | 515 15th St. NW (bet. F St. & Pennsylvania Ave.) | 202-661-2440 | www.jgsteakhousewashingtondc.com
Jean-Georges Vongerichten's "modern take" on the steakhouse genre brings some of the "best" "juicy" cuts to Downtown, though often the "stars of the meal" are his "transcendent" New American dishes; just off the W Hotel's "disco-feeling lobby", the dining room, with its high ceilings and suave appointments, exudes an "understated" "chic" matched by its "polite" servers; P.S. the less pricey "hidden wine bar" downstairs is "perfect for an illicit tryst."

Johnny's Half Shell 🛇 *American/Seafood*   `21` `20` `20` `$47`
Capitol Hill | 400 N. Capitol St. NW (Louisiana Ave.) | 202-737-0400 | www.johnnyshalfshell.net
Super-"fresh" seafood, seasoned with the "Congressional or Supreme Court gossip" that can be overheard at this Capitol Hill New American's "active bar" or in its "more reserved" dark-wood dining area, powers Ann Cashion and John Fulchino's "tightly run ship"; time-honored Gulf and Chesapeake recipes are "prepared with skill and served with speed", and live jazz enlivens the weekends.

Komi 🛇Ⓜ *American/Mediterranean*   `28` `22` `28` `$176`
Dupont Circle | 1509 17th St. NW (P St.) | 202-332-9200 | www.komirestaurant.com
Johnny Monis leads diners on a "gastro-adventure" at his Dupont Circle American-Med "temple" offering a "dazzling variety of dishes beautifully prepared and executed" in a "subdued", "understated" setting, made more "relaxing" by a staff that's "detail-oriented without being uptight"; "expect to spend the evening" as they "serve and serve and serve" a fixed-price "parade" of plates along with "witty wine pairings" – and while the "high price" and "hard-to-get reservations" give "mere eaters" pause, food fanatics chant "just go."

L'Auberge Chez François Ⓜ *French*   `28` `27` `28` `$81`
Great Falls | 332 Springvale Rd. (Beach Mill Rd.), VA | 703-759-3800
Jacques' Brasserie Ⓜ *French*
Great Falls | 332 Springvale Rd. (Beach Mill Rd.), VA | 703-759-3800
www.laubergechezfrancois.com
This "fairy-tale destination" in Great Falls, VA, is "like a fine wine that ages beautifully", eternally providing visitors with "wonderful", "ge-

mütlich" Alsatian cuisine that's in perfect harmony with its "charming", "rustic" farmhouse setting; the "unstuffy" staff "pampers" diners during "long and leisurely" multicourse repasts, and though the air is "rarefied", the prix fixe menu means there's "no wincing" over surprises on the bill; P.S. thrifty types may prefer the more "casual ambiance" of the cellar brasserie, whose à la carte menu has "less impact on your wallet."

Little Serow *Thai*

| 28 | 19 | 27 | $60 |

Dupont Circle | 1511 17th St. NW (bet. P & Q Sts.) | www.littleserow.com
"Small in size but packed with flavor and flair", chef-owner Johnny Monis' new Issan-style Thai in Dupont Circle (DC's top-rated newcomer) "transports" taste buds with "intense and unusual", "kick-your-ass spicy" fare; it's "easier on the pocket" than his celebrated Komi (upstairs next door), and you should "check your control freak at the door" of this "super-dark" cave and let the "incredibly knowledgeable" staff guide you through the "delicious" set-menu journey.

Makoto Ⓜ *Japanese*

| 27 | 19 | 23 | $78 |

Palisades | 4822 MacArthur Blvd. NW (U St.) | 202-298-6866
"Leave your shoes – and your ego – at the door" of this tiny Palisades Japanese temple where the "exquisite jewel-box plates" on its multicourse omakase menu come to the table the "chef's way"; the setting is simple and traditional, with "hard" bench seating, but it's "unparalleled in DC" say those who "know the difference", so a little patience and a thick wallet will transport you "half a world away."

Marcel's *Belgian/French*

| 28 | 26 | 28 | $95 |

West End | 2401 Pennsylvania Ave. NW (24th St.) | 202-296-1166 | www.marcelsdc.com
"Build your own feast" at this "refined" West End modern French-Belgian by choosing from its "expansive" prix fixe menu selections, all of which showcase the "intricacy" and "subtlety" of Robert Wiedmaier's "brilliant" cuisine; factor in "pampering" service and an "elegant", "special-occasion" atmosphere and you get "full value" for the "expensive" tab; P.S. for a real deal, there's a pre-theater option that includes shuttle service to the Kennedy Center.

Mintwood Place Ⓜ *American*

| – | – | – | M |

Adams Morgan | 1813 Columbia Rd. NW (Biltmore St.) | 202-234-6732 | www.mintwoodplace.com
There's a been-here-forever feel about this convivial, midpriced addition to Adams Morgan, showcasing Cedric Maupillier's (ex Central Michel Richard) French-accented American cooking, much of it done in a wood-burning oven; the farmhouse-moderne look (pale wainscoting, antique implements) instills an easygoing ambiance, and there's a sidewalk patio for watching the neighborhood pass by.

Obelisk Ⓩ Ⓜ *Italian*

| 28 | 20 | 26 | $98 |

Dupont Circle | 2029 P St. NW (bet. 20th & 21st Sts.) | 202-872-1180
From the antipasto "spectrum of delights" to sweet endings like "candied fennel ice cream", a "stellar" prix fixe dinner (no à la carte) at Peter Pastan's Dupont Circle Italian soars to "heights taller than the Washington Monument", DC's other obelisk; the "intimate", "informal" townhouse setting allows diners to focus on "what Italian cook-

FOOD   DECOR   SERVICE   COST

ing is really about": "simple but expertly prepared food served by pros", which along with "superb" wines, is "worth every euro."

Palena *American*   27 | 22 | 24 | $98

Cleveland Park | 3529 Connecticut Ave. NW (bet. Ordway & Porter Sts.) | 202-537-9250 | www.palenarestaurant.com

"Ambrosia fit for the gods" is on the menus at Frank Ruta's Cleveland Park New American, and fans swear the "quiet", "dimly lit" back room's prix fixe (no à la carte) is "worth" the "expense", while noting the "casual" front cafe is "one of the best bargains in town", with its "succulent" burgers, entrees and a bread basket "worth paying for" – and, indeed, they do charge for it; service throughout matches the kitchen's "high competency", and a market annex sells "superb" desserts and savories.

Peking Duck Restaurant Ⓜ *Chinese*   28 | 18 | 23 | $35

Greater Alexandria | 7531 Richmond Hwy. (Woodlawn Trail) | Alexandria, VA | 703-768-2774 | www.pekingduck.com

No canard, "authentic barely begins to describe" this venerable but unassuming-looking Peking duck specialist "all the way out" near Fort Belvoir in Greater Alexandria, where the roasted fowl is sliced "in front of you" just "like in Peking" (er, Beijing); if that doesn't sound ducky, ask the "superb" staff for "suggestions" (hint: "delicious" soups), and have no fear of the bill – it won't bite.

Pizzeria Paradiso *Pizza*   23 | 17 | 19 | $26

Dupont Circle | 2003 P St. NW (bet. Hopkins & 20th Sts.) | 202-223-1245
Georgetown | 3282 M St. NW (bet. Potomac & 33rd Sts.) | 202-337-1245
Old Town | 124 King St. (bet. Lee & Union Sts.) | Alexandria, VA | 703-837-1245
www.eatyourpizza.com

These midpriced "pizza nirvanas" in Dupont Circle, Georgetown and Old Town Alexandria are "delicious enough for serious foodies but still casual enough for an outing with family and friends"; service is generally "ok" in the "pleasant", "cosmopolitan" brick-walled settings, and if they tend to get "crowded" and "loud" at times, "beer geeks" recommend the "ameliorating" powers of the "impressive" brew list.

Prime Rib Ⓩ *Steak*   28 | 26 | 28 | $71

Golden Triangle | 2020 K St. NW (bet. 20th & 21st Sts.) | 202-466-8811 | www.theprimerib.com

Do as they do in *Mad Men* – "dress up, have a martini, take it easy and smile" – at this "classic" Golden Triangle steakhouse that's still operating at the very "top of its game", delivering "fantastic" "slabs of meat" and "masterful seafood"; from the "sophisticated", "1940s supper-club vibe" to the "sublime" tuxedoed service, it's a "perfect evening out"; P.S. business-casual dress (with jackets required after 5 PM).

Rasika Ⓩ *Indian*   28 | 25 | 26 | $51

Penn Quarter | 633 D St. NW (bet. 6th & 7th Sts.) | 202-637-1222
West End | 1190 New Hampshire Ave. NW (M St.) | 202-466-2500
www.rasikarestaurant.com

"Only superlatives" describe the "mind-blowing" "modern Indian" food that gives diners a "mouthgasm" at this "wildly popular", "classy" Penn Quarter destination (and its new, cosmopolitan West End sister)

FOOD | DECOR | SERVICE | COST

that has diners "salivating" for dishes like its crispy spinach; "luxuri-ous" appointments, a "knowledgeable" wait staff and a sommelier "savant" create a "sophisticated" environment that further makes it a "bargain for the quality" – translation: "plan early" for a reservation, or "eat at the bar."

Ray's Hell Burger 🚫 *Burgers*
(aka Ray's Butcher Burgers)

26 | 10 | 16 | $16

Courthouse | Colonial Vill. | 1725 Wilson Blvd. (bet. Quinn & Rhodes Sts.) | Arlington, VA | 703-841-0001 | www.rayshellburger.com

"In the world of burgers", there's simply "no comparison" to this "in-credibly well-priced" Courthouse paragon, its "epic" patties made from "quality" "steak cuttings", with "juices dripping down your forearm"; "fanatics" will stand on line with "everyone from union members to heads of state" for the "hectic" ordering experience in this "no-frills" counter-serve "hole-in-the-wall", and remember to "bring cash", since it doesn't take cards.

Ray's The Steaks *Steak*

27 | 18 | 22 | $46

Courthouse | Navy League Bldg. | 2300 Wilson Blvd. (Adams St.) | Arlington, VA | 703-841-7297 | www.raysthesteaks.com

"No-frills deliciousness" sums up Mike 'Ray' Landrum's Courthouse beefeteria that "rays-es the bar on great steaks" at "bargain-basement prices" – the "breathtaking" hunks are served with two sides along with "affordable" wines in "sparse" white surroundings by "knowledgeable", "efficient" servers; "why pay for decor and snooti-ness at 'fine' steakhouses?" ask acolytes who appreciate "not being nickeled, dimed and dollared", saying this may be the "best restaurant idea in history."

Ris *American*

25 | 22 | 24 | $57

West End | 2275 L St. NW (23rd St.) | 202-730-2500 | www.risdc.com

If only the "government was run as well as" Ris Lacoste's West End New American bistro sigh surveyors, citing "gold-star" service and a "polished kitchen" turning out "exciting" "market-fresh" dishes in a "sophisticated", "modern" setting; various deals offer a way around high prices, so whether headed for Kennedy Center, meeting "friends and family" or hanging at the bar, it suits the whole neighborhood.

Ruan Thai *Thai*

27 | 15 | 21 | $22

Wheaton | 11407 Amherst Ave. (University Blvd.), MD | 301-942-0075 | www.ruanthaiwheaton.com

"Everything is just so good" on the menu – notably "not-to-be-missed" deep-fried watercress – at this Wheatonite known for its "real" Thai cuisine "priced well"; "fast", "friendly service keeps the "bustling" scene and "very busy carry-out" operation under control, so who cares if the digs are "sparse", since you "don't go for the ambiance."

Russia House Restaurant *Russian*

27 | 23 | 25 | $51

Herndon | 790 Station St. (bet. Elden St. & Park Ave.), VA | 703-787-8880 | www.russiahouserestaurant.com

"Someone in the kitchen truly knows how to cook" say fans of this high-end Herndon spot's "superb" French-influenced Russian special-ties that naturally don't come cheap; cocktails get a boost from the "welcoming" owners' "excellent stash of Russian vodka" ("flavored shots" work too), enhancing the "unique charm" of a "delightful" meal in formal surroundings.

1789 *American*   26 | 25 | 26 | $70

Georgetown | 1226 36th St. NW (Prospect St.) | 202-965-1789 | www.1789restaurant.com

"White gloves and pearls" might suit this "distinguished" Georgetown "classic" with a "refined", "historic" townhouse setting and "expertly prepared" "farm-to-table" New American cooking that together make it a "special place to impress or luxuriate"; politicians and parents visiting their kids at the university mean that the "people-watching" (and "eavesdropping") is as good as the food, while a "personable" staff makes diners feel so like "landed gentry" that it's "worth every penny" of its very contemporary prices.

The Source ⓩ *Asian*   27 | 24 | 24 | $68

Penn Quarter | Newseum | 575 Pennsylvania Ave. NW (6th St.) | 202-637-6100 | www.wolfgangpuck.com

"Brilliant East-meets-West fare" is the lead story (with a sidebar on "outstanding" bar bites) at this "hip" Wolfgang Puck destination adjacent to Penn Quarter's Newseum, sporting a "sleek" multilevel setting; "friendly but not intrusive" servers are another reason why subscribers place it in the "expensive-but-worth-it" column.

Tosca ⓩ *Italian*   27 | 24 | 26 | $68

Penn Quarter | 1112 F St. NW (bet. 11th & 12th Sts.) | 202-367-1990 | www.toscadc.com

"Fine dining gets no finer" say fans, than at this "sophisticated" Penn Quarter Italian where the "flawless", uniformed waiters deliver near-"perfect" food as "ex-senators and lobbyists swap business cards" in the "elegant" neutral-toned setting; it's a perfect place for observing "how Washington really works", and the relatively "affordable" pre-theater dinner menu is ideal "for those not on an expense account."

2 Amys *Pizza*   25 | 17 | 20 | $25

Cleveland Park | 3715 Macomb St. NW (Wisconsin Ave.) | 202-885-5700 | www.2amyspizza.com

"Dough my god, the crust!" gush groupies wowed by the "ambrosial" DOC-certified Neapolitan pies at this "popular" Cleveland Park pizzeria (some tout the "exceptional" small plates too); the scene inside the "sunny", white-tiled premises can be "mayhem" – it's a "yuppies-with-kids" magnet – but once the "friendly" staff delivers the "excellent-for-the-price" food, most "everyone is happy" – especially after swigging one of the "treasures on tap" or something from the quieter wine bar's "adventurous selection."

Vidalia *Southern*   26 | 24 | 25 | $63

Golden Triangle | 1990 M St. NW (bet. 19th & 20th Sts.) | 202-659-1990 | www.vidaliadc.com

"Southern roots" sprout "undeniably cosmopolitan" blossoms on the "inspired" New American menu at this fine-dining "favorite" in Golden Triangle, where the "impeccable" staff makes each meal "an event in itself"; hidden underground, the "comfortably" "elegant" setting is "just right" for "intimate moments" and "special events", with "witty" cocktails and happy-hour specials in the lounge; P.S. for around $20, the three-course lunch is a "fantastic deal."

Volt Ⓜ *American*   28 | 26 | 28 | $104

Frederick | Houck Mansion | 228 N. Market St. (bet. 2nd & 3rd Sts.), MD | 301-696-8658 | www.voltrestaurant.com

An "evening in foodie heaven" awaits at this true "dining destination" in a "beautiful", contemporized 1890s mansion in Frederick, where chef/co-owner Bryan Voltaggio "evokes a sense of wonder" with his "exotically scrumptious" New American meals based on seasonal ingredients; choose from several prix fixe options for dinner, including a "well-choreographed" 21-course "culinary adventure", then let the "incredibly friendly", "top-notch" servers take it from there; "is it expensive? yes – is it really worth it? yes."

Zaytinya *Mediterranean/Mideastern*   26 | 24 | 22 | $43

Penn Quarter | Pepco Bldg. | 701 Ninth St. NW (G St.) | 202-638-0800 | www.zaytinya.com

"Who can resist" the "wonders" of chef José Andrés' "unbelievably tasty" Eastern Mediterranean meze, especially when paired with "phenomenal" regional wines in a "beautiful, light and airy" setting close to everything in the Penn Quarter; the city's "enduring" "love affair" with this "crazy, loud" stunner means reservations are "highly recommended", but once your "culinary tour" is booked, a "helpful staff" will be your "guide" – just beware: it's "hard to keep the bill down with so many tempting small plates."

Westchester/Hudson Valley

TOP FOOD RANKING

Restaurant	Cuisine
29 Sushi Nanase	Japanese
28 Xaviars at Piermont	American
Il Cenàcolo	Italian
Freelance Cafe	American
Buffet de la Gare	French
Blue Hill/Stone Barns	American
27 Escoffier	French
La Crémaillère	French
Caterina de Medici	Italian
La Panetière	French
Rest. X/Bully Boy Bar	American
X2O Xaviars	American
Ocean House	Seafood
Arch	Eclectic
Iron Horse Grill	American
Serevan	Mediterranean
Il Barilotto	Italian
No. 9	American
26 Big W's Roadside	BBQ
Aroma Osteria	Italian

OTHER NOTEWORTHY PLACES

A Tavola	Italian
Bedford Post/Farmhouse	American
Cookery	Italian
Crabtree's Kittle House	American
Crimson Sparrow	American
Cucina	Italian
Equus	American/French
42	American
Glenmere	American
Harvest on Hudson	Mediterranean
Mercato	Italian
Nina	Eclectic
Peter Pratt's Inn	American
Plates	American
Restaurant North	American
Sonora	Nuevo Latino
Swoon	American
Tarry Lodge	Italian
Wasabi	Japanese
Zephs'	American/Eclectic

WESTCHESTER/HUDSON VALLEY

	FOOD	DECOR	SERVICE	COST

The Arch ⓂEclectic
27 | 25 | 27 | $71

Brewster | 1292 Rte. 22 (end of I-684) | 845-279-5011 |
www.archrestaurant.com

"A golden oldie that never loses its luster", this "delightful" Brewster Eclectic "changes just enough to keep up with the times", offering "exceptional", "refined" "classics" and "amazing soufflés" in a "pretty" stone house where "fireplaces, well-spaced tables" and "charming", "never-stuffy" service make "romantic evenings a natural"; of course, it's "not cheap" (although "Sunday brunch is a relative bargain"), but "worth every penny" for something "special"; P.S. jackets suggested at dinner.

Aroma Osteria Ⓜ Italian
26 | 25 | 25 | $49

Wappingers Falls | 114 Old Post Rd. (Rte. 9) | 845-298-6790 |
www.aromaosteriarestaurant.com

"Bountiful servings" of *molto delizioso* Southern Italian fare and a "spectacular wine list" earn "high marks" for Eduardo Lauria's Wappingers Falls "gem", where the "polite", "well-trained staff" serves in a "sensual", "pretty" space done up like "a Tuscan villa"; one "turn-off for romantics": it's "acoustically challenged, so be prepared to talk with your hands", or eat "outside in the grape arbor" in summer.

A Tavola Italian
- | - | - | M

New Paltz | 46 Main St. (Chestnut St.) | 845-255-1426 |
www.atavolany.com

Ensconced in the New Paltz space that once housed Beso, this stylish Italian launched by Bonnie and Nathan Snow (alumni of Manhattan's Sfoglia) is drawing raves with creative takes on regional dishes like octopus with chickpeas and pappardelle Bolognese, plus housemade gelato; a large wine rack forms a centerpiece downstairs in the bi-level setting, with a red accent wall and mismatched farm tables adding a warm, rustic note.

Bedford Post, The Farmhouse Ⓜ American
25 | 26 | 23 | $78

Bedford | Bedford Post | 954 Old Post Rd./Rte. 121 (bet. Indian Hill Rd. & Rte. 137) | 914-234-7800 | www.bedfordpostinn.com

"Elegance and class" define the more formal of Richard Gere's Bedford Post eateries, a "charming" "getaway" that "romances its guests" with a "relaxed pace", "lovely ambiance" and "unfailingly excellent" New American cuisine focused on "local meat and produce"; a relatively new chef is in the kitchen, and there's still some murmuring about "small portions", occasionally "mediocre" service and tabs "not for the faint of wallet", but overall it's a "treat."

Big W's Roadside Bar-B-Que Ⓜ BBQ
26 | 7 | 21 | $19

Wingdale | 1475 Rte. 22 (Rock Hill Dr.) | 845-832-6200 |
www.bigwsbbq.com

"Ace pitmaster" and "gregarious" host Warren Norstein (aka Big W) gets "kudos" for his Wingdale "winner" of a BBQ joint that's "worth a drive" for "melt-in-your-mouth, marvelous" pulled pork and brisket, "tender, meaty ribs" and chicken "smoked to perfection", all at "low prices"; those who find the "sterile, fluorescent-lit" setting a turnoff get the grub "boxed to take home", or picnic roadside under the willow when it's warm.

Blue Hill at Stone Barns ⓜ *American*

28 | 28 | 28 | $108

Pocantico Hills | Stone Barns Ctr. | 630 Bedford Rd. (Lake Rd.) | 914-366-9600 | www.bluehillfarm.com

"The wow factor" is high at this "epitome of farm-to-table dining" in Pocantico Hills, where Dan Barber offers "exquisite", "obsessively seasonal" New American tasting menus with ingredients "based on the day's harvest" and grown on the "gorgeous", "manicured" grounds; an "earnest", "knowledgeable" staff (rated tops in our Survey) "pampers you" in the "wonderfully understated" refurbished barn setting, so even if "outrageous prices" for "petite portions" can be irksome, "if you can get a reservation", it's worth "saving your pennies" for; P.S. "go early, stroll the property" or try the cafe for an alfresco lunch.

Buffet de la Gare ⓜ *French*

28 | 23 | 26 | $67

Hastings-on-Hudson | 155 Southside Ave. (Spring St.) | 914-478-1671 | www.buffetdelagareny.com

"If you want classic", this taste of "Paris-on-Hudson" in Hastings delivers "*magnifique*" "old-line" meals in an "enchanting", "intimate" setting just off the river; add in "lovely owners" and "polished" service "with a personal touch", and it's no wonder it's long been "a favorite" for a "memorable" evening, with equally memorable bills; P.S. "reservations a must."

Caterina de Medici ⓩ *Italian*

27 | 27 | 25 | $53

Hyde Park | Culinary Institute of America | 1946 Campus Dr. (Rte. 9) | 845-471-6608 | www.ciarestaurants.com

"You'll think you've died and gone to Tuscan heaven" at this "high-end", student-staffed eatery at the Hyde Park CIA, where "eager-to-please" budding chefs "strut their stuff" cooking and serving "top-of-the-line Italian" cuisine in a "beautiful" setting with "crystal chandeliers"; "earnestness" compensates for any "lack of polish", so overall, it's "five-star dining at two-star prices" – and the menu in the less-formal Al Forno room "is a steal"; P.S. closed weekends.

The Cookery ⓜ *Italian*

26 | 17 | 22 | $46

Dobbs Ferry | 39 Chestnut St. (Main St.) | 914-305-2336 | www.thecookeryrestaurant.com

A true "foodies' spot", this "ambitious" Dobbs Ferry Italian from "talented" chef-owner Dave DiBari is a find for "fabulous", "but not overly fussy" cooking including "amazing" homemade pastas that'll make you "lick your plate clean"; all comes served by a "knowledgeable" crew in a "tiny", "buzzing" room "with a Brooklyn vibe", so the only downsides are its limited reservations policy and acoustics "so noisy you can't hear yourself chew."

Crabtree's Kittle House *American*

25 | 25 | 25 | $63

Chappaqua | Crabtree's Kittle House Inn | 11 Kittle Rd. (Rte. 117) | 914-666-8044 | www.kittlehouse.com

A Westchester "classic", this "genteel", "well-appointed" Chappaqua "country inn" provides "a grand experience" via "outstanding" New American cuisine, a "legendary" wine list "as thick as the telephone book" and service that leaves patrons feeling "coddled" amid a "beautiful setting" that makes each visit a "special occasion"; those who find it a "bit stuffy" may enjoy the "more casual" taproom or "magnif-icent" "bordering on decadent" Sunday brunch.

Crimson Sparrow *American*

| - | - | - | E |

Hudson | 746 Warren St. (8th St.) | 518-671-6565 |
www.thecrimsonsparrow.com

Hudson gastronomes are chirpy over this ambitious New American launched by alumni of NYC's WD-50 and serving sophisticated, cre-ative large and small plates, like venison tartare with breakfast radish and lamb sweetbreads, matched by equally out-of-the-ordinary drinks (there are more traditional offerings at brunch); a million-dollar make-over of the 1850 building blends industrial chic with tin ceilings and brick walls in several inviting spaces, while the sleek courtyard fea-tures a large window looking into the kitchen; cheap it's not, but rates are not outrageous.

Cucina *Italian*

| 25 | 23 | 23 | $48 |

Woodstock | 109 Mill Hill Rd./Rte. 212 (Rte. 375) | 845-679-9800 |
www.cucinawoodstock.com

"Noteworthy pastas and risottos", "creative" thin-crust pizzas and other "genuine", "A-one Italian food" get taken "to new heights" by "inventive" chef Giovanni Scappin in this "chic", "renovated farm-house" restaurant at the "gateway to Woodstock"; an "attentive" staff serves in the "streamlined" setting with its long communal table and cozy booths, while the porch "has its charms" come summer, and al-though it's "on the pricey side", it's a "good value."

Equus *American/French*

| 25 | 28 | 25 | $80 |

Tarrytown | Castle on the Hudson | 400 Benedict Ave. (Martling Ave.) |
914-631-3646 | www.castleonthehudson.com

"Old-world elegance" is alive and well at this "hilltop oasis" in Tarrytown, a "real castle" whose "fairy-tale" setting includes "gorgeous views" of the Hudson and a "baronial" dining room with "flowers everywhere"; service is "spectacular" and the "exorbitantly" priced French–New American cuisine suitably "fit for a king", so even if it's a tad "stodgy" for some, you can't beat it for a "special occasion"; P.S. brunch is a "less formal" affair.

Escoffier Restaurant 🅢🅜 *French*

| 27 | 25 | 26 | $63 |

Hyde Park | Culinary Institute of America | 1946 Campus Dr. (Rte. 9) |
845-471-6608 | www.ciarestaurants.com

The "crème de la crème" at the Hyde Park CIA, this "dressy" "foodie's delight" presents "first-rate", "fine French cuisine" prepared by "fu-ture Iron Chefs", with the "cavalry" (aka "chef-professors") "to back 'em up"; the decor recently underwent an "elegant" "buffing", so add "delightful", "retro service" from "earnest" students, and although it's "expensive", it's "perfect" for a "celebration."

42 🅢 *American*

| 22 | 27 | 22 | $72 |

White Plains | Ritz-Carlton Westchester | 1 Renaissance Sq., 42nd fl.
(Main St.) | 914-761-4242 | www.42therestaurant.com

"So very ritzy" with its "stunning views" and "sophisticated vibe", this "elegant" 42nd-floor dining room at the Ritz-Carlton in White Plains makes you want to "dress up" to celebrate "special occasions" and sa-vor "talented" chef Anthony Goncalves' "inventive riffs" on New

FOOD DECOR SERVICE COST

American cuisine; however, service "varies from visit to visit" (sometimes "personable", other times "snooty"), which can be irksome given the "sky-high prices."

Freelance Cafe & Wine Bar Ⓜ *American*   28 | 21 | 26 | $56

Piermont | 506 Piermont Ave. (Ash St.) | 845-365-3250 | www.xaviars.com
"Everyone raves about" Peter Kelly's "marvelous" Piermont New American, a "relaxed" "baby sister" to Xaviars next door, offering "predictably" "superior food" that's "every bit as good" and a "deal" by comparison; a "charming host" lights up the "small, plain dining room" and oversees a "top-flight" staff, so even though the no-rez policy can mean "frustrating" waits on line, it's a "magic spot" – just "pick odd times to go."

Glenmere Ⓜ *American*   24 | 29 | 25 | $71

Chester | Glenmere Mansion | 634 Pine Hill Rd. (Glenmere Ave.) | 845-469-1900 | www.glenmeremansion.com
"You feel like you're rich" at this "stunning" Chester New American dining room set in an Italianate mansion "miraculously restored" into a "Gatsby"-esque, "luxury" setting that's ranked No. 1 for Decor in Westchester/Hudson Valley; the "well-executed" prix fixe dinners are served Thursdays–Sundays in the "exquisite" Supper Room with its painted mirrored panels, while a simpler, less "crazy-expensive" menu is offered daily in the equally "classy" Frog's End tavern; "exceptional service" and the "nice perk" of dining in the "delightful courtyard" add to the "mesmerizing" experience.

Harvest on Hudson *Italian/Mediterranean*   22 | 27 | 22 | $55

Hastings-on-Hudson | 1 River St. (Main St., off Southside Ave.) | 914-478-2800 | www.harvest2000.com
This "romantic" Hastings respite is set in a "fairy-tale" "farmhouse" "on the Hudson River" amid "lush gardens" that "bring back memories of Tuscany"; service is "professional" and the Italian-Med fare "well prepared", and if some feel it "doesn't live up to" the "idyllic" setting or the "expensive" prices, overall it's a "magical" package.

Il Barilotto Ⓢ *Italian*   27 | 23 | 25 | $48

Fishkill | 1113 Main St. (North St.) | 845-897-4300 |
www.ilbarilottorestaurant.com
They're "at the top of their game" at this "fantastic" Fishkill cousin to Aroma Osteria, where a "polished staff" serves "sublime" Italian dishes and "scrumptious specials" matched by a "terrific wine list"; "lovely, exposed brick" lends the restored 1800s carriage house a "casual but smart" feel, and although "you can rack up a bill" and it's often "noisy", those who "go again and again" say it's a "stellar experience."

Il Cenàcolo *Italian*   28 | 24 | 26 | $62

Newburgh | 228 S. Plank Rd./Rte. 52 (bet. I-87 & Rte. 300) | 845-564-4494 | www.ilcenacolorestaurant.com
"Consistently *molto buono*", this "first-class" Newburgh Northern Italian may look "unimposing outside" but "sets the bar very high", greeting diners in "nicely decorated" digs with a "groaning board" of "second-to-none" antipasti and an "impressive staff" that recites a "long list" of "mouthwatering" specials; it's "expensive, yes, but cheaper than a trip to Tuscany, and no pat-down."

	FOOD	DECOR	SERVICE	COST

Iron Horse Grill ⑧Ⓜ *American* | 27 | 21 | 26 | $60 |

Pleasantville | 20 Wheeler Ave. (bet. Bedford & Manville Rds.) |
914-741-0717 | www.ironhorsegrill.com

"Always a pleasure" purr fans of this "inviting" New American set within
a restored railroad station in Pleasantville, where "genial" chef-owner
Philip McGrath oversees "a near-perfect dining experience" from the
"fabulous", "inventive" fare to the "approachable wine list" and "warm",
"pro" service; seating is either "intimate" or too "snug", depending on
your point of view, but it's "romantic" nonetheless; just "bring saddle-
bags of money" or try one of the "good-value" prix fixe specials.

La Crémaillère Ⓜ *French* | 27 | 26 | 26 | $81 |

Bedford | 46 Bedford-Banksville Rd. (Round House Rd.) | 914-234-9647 |
www.cremaillere.com

"Memorable evenings" transpire at this "gold standard" of "fine dining"
in Bedford, where "superb" French cuisine is elevated by an "extensive
wine cellar" and "outstanding" service in a "beautiful" farmhouse that
"oozes charm"; "such excellence comes at a price", but for a "special
treat" "you can't ask for much more"; P.S. jackets suggested.

La Panetière *French* | 27 | 27 | 27 | $78 |

Rye | 530 Milton Rd. (Oakland Beach Ave.) | 914-967-8140 |
www.lapanetiere.com

"Decidedly elegant", this "stately" Rye manor is "worth spiffing up
for" thanks to its "divine" "haute" New French cuisine that's "exquisitely presented" and served with "wonderful wines" by a "flawless"
staff; factor in a "fairy-book" setting that "transports you to Provence",
and it's a perfect place to "drop a bundle", although the lunchtime prix
fixe is an absolute "bargain"; P.S. jackets suggested.

Mercato Ⓜ *Italian* | 25 | 16 | 21 | $47 |

Red Hook | 61 E. Market St./Rte. 199 (Cherry St.) | 845-758-5879 |
www.mercatoredhook.com

A "scion" of the famed "pasta family", "inspired" chef Francesco
Buitoni mans the stove at his "trendy" Italian "gem" in "lucky Red
Hook", dispensing "deeply satisfying" dishes matched by a "terrific
list" of vino, all at "reasonable" rates; a "lovely" team attends in the
"plain" rooms of the "little porched house", where it's "ear-splitting"
at times, but always "convivial."

Nina *Eclectic* | 25 | 23 | 24 | $45 |

Middletown | 27 W. Main St. (bet. Canal & North Sts.) | 845-344-6800 |
www.nina-restaurant.com

"Haute cuisine in Middletown – who knew?" ask those discovering chef
Franz Brendle's Eclectic "standout", which adds a "fashionable" note
to the neighborhood with "phenomenal" fare ferried by a staff that
"genuinely tries to please"; the "pretty", brick-walled space has a "sophisticated" air, especially when it's full of weekenders, so although a
tad costly, it "thrives"; "these people are doing something right."

No. 9 Ⓜ *American* | 27 | 23 | 25 | $49 |

Millerton | Simmons' Way Village Inn | 53 Main St. (bet. Dutchess &
N. Maple Aves.) | 518-592-1299 | www.number9millerton.com

Ensconced in the dining room of Millerton's "luxury" Simmons'
Way Inn, chef Tim Cocheo's "fantastic" entry offers a "daring"

FOOD DECOR SERVICE COST

French- and Austrian-accented New American menu and "pulls it off superbly", with "sublime", "mouthwatering" cooking that draws "fans from a 10-town radius"; the "congenial", "sophisticated country setting", "personal service" and "midweek prix fixe offering even greater value" have devotees declaring "its name is off by one – it should be a 10!"

Ocean House ⓜ *Seafood*   27 | 16 | 24 | $46

Croton-on-Hudson | 49 N. Riverside Ave. (Farrington Rd.) | 914-271-0702

It may "not look like much from the outside", but this "New England"-style seafooder in Croton specializes in "incredibly fresh fish" so "delectable" "you'd think you were in Nantucket"; service is "pleasant" and its BYO policy makes for "affordable" bills, but it's so "tiny" you'll need to dine with "your elbows tucked in", and the no-reservations policy means "come early or plan to wait."

Peter Pratt's Inn ⓜ *American*   25 | 22 | 24 | $58

Yorktown | 673 Croton Heights Rd. (Rte. 118) | 914-962-4090 | www.prattsinn.com

Brimming with "character", from its "nestled-in-the-woods" location to its "lovely" fireplace-blessed interior, this Yorktown New American is a "perennial favorite" for "fabulous" "locally sourced" fare elevated by an "impressive wine list" and "gracious" service; it's expensive, and you'll need to "test the GPS" to find it, but smitten customers "can't wait to go back."

Plates ⓜ *American*   25 | 21 | 22 | $56

Larchmont | 121 Myrtle Blvd. (Murray Ave.) | 914-834-1244 | www.platesonthepark.com

"A true gem", this "pleasantly grown-up" Larchmont American "just keeps getting better" with "inventive, beautifully presented" seasonal cuisine (and "outstanding" desserts) courtesy of chef-owner Matthew Karp; it's set in a "lovely" "historic" home overlooking a "charming" park, so in spite of some service hiccups and "pricey" bills, most find it "well worth the cost", and the once-a-week BYO special is a steal.

Restaurant North ⓈⓂ *American*   26 | 22 | 25 | $60

Armonk | 386 Main St. (bet. Bedford Rd. & Elm St.) | 914-273-8686 | www.restaurantnorth.com

A "terrific addition" to the Northern Westchester scene, this "chic" "hot spot" from Union Square Cafe alums brings "destination dining" to Armonk with "sublime" "farm-to-table" New American fare, a "fantastic" wine list and a "sharp, solicitous" staff; it's "pricey" and the din can be "deafening" (upstairs is more "serene"), but the biggest hurdle may be scoring a reservation.

Restaurant X & Bully Boy Bar ⓜ *American*   27 | 24 | 26 | $63

Congers | 117 Rte. 303 N. (Hilltop Rd.) | 845-268-6555 | www.xaviars.com

"X is for extraordinary" exclaim those "floored" by Peter Kelly's "magical" Congers New American that's like "Xaviars on a budget" but turning out equally "transcendent" food; "inviting" rooms in the "lovely" "country" house are tended by a "savvy" staff willing to "bend over backward", and although it's "high-priced", the $25 prix fixe lunch and Sunday's "food orgy" of a brunch are truly a "great deal."

Serevan *Mediterranean*   27 | 23 | 25 | $54

Amenia | 6 Autumn Ln. (Rte. 44, west of Rte. 22) | 845-373-9800 | www.serevan.com

"A beacon amid the hayfields", this "outstanding" Amenia Med is a "gourmet paradise" where "gifted", "passionate" chef-owner Serge Madikians uses "top-quality ingredients" and "aromatic spices" to create "superb" "Middle Eastern–tinged" dishes so "scrumptious" you could "point at random" to the menu and have an "inspired" meal; slightly "pricey" tabs are trumped by the "quiet, welcoming farmhouse" setting, "polished" service and overall "convivial" experience.

Sonora *Nuevo Latino*   24 | 22 | 22 | $49

Port Chester | 179 Rectory St. (Willett Ave.) | 914-933-0200 | www.sonorarestaurant.net

"Like a vacation in South America", this "festive" Port Chester "favorite" from Rafael Palomino charms guests with an "innovative" mix of "refined", "artistic" Nuevo Latino plates elevated by "fabulous" cocktails "that will knock you off your barstool"; a "knowledgeable" staff shows "attention to detail", now if only they could do something about the "incredibly noisy" acoustics.

Sushi Nanase *Japanese*   29 | 15 | 23 | $72

White Plains | 522 Mamaroneck Ave. (Shapham Pl.) | 914-285-5351

He may be "a man of few words", but chef Yoshimichi Takeda is a "true master" at this "tiny" 18-seat White Plains Japanese "secret" where he fashions "pristine" fish into "truly spectacular", "delectable" creations, voted No. 1 for Food in Westchester/Hudson Valley; the setting's spare and it's certainly not cheap, but if you "put yourself in their hands" you're in for an "unforgettable" experience; P.S. "reservations are a must."

Swoon Kitchenbar *American*   24 | 21 | 18 | $51

Hudson | 340 Warren St. (bet. 3rd & 4th Sts.) | 518-822-8938 | www.swoonkitchenbar.com

"Talented chef" Jeffrey Gimmel is a "master" at "flavorful", "seasonal sustenance" declare those "swooning" over the "original", "locavore" cuisine at this Hudson New American, where his wife, Nina, makes the "best desserts"; "lovely surroundings top it all" ("even the flowers are fanciful"), although many surveyors find prices "a little high-end for this neck of the woods", especially given sometimes "lackluster" service.

Tarry Lodge *Italian*   24 | 23 | 22 | $53

Port Chester | 18 Mill St. (Abendroth Ave.) | 914-939-3111 | www.tarrylodge.com

"An absolute winner" cheer champions of this "foodie delight" in Port Chester from Mario Batali and Joe Bastianich, where chef Andy Nusser turns out "amazing", "chichi" pizzas and "sophisticated", "wonderfully prepared" pastas in a "casually elegant" marble-clad space that feels "unique for the 'burbs"; of course, it's "crazy crowded", "high decibel" and a "tough reservation", but the "pricey" tab is a "bargain if you choose wisely."

Wasabi *Japanese*   26 | 21 | 22 | $49

Nyack | 110 Main St. (bet. Cedar & Park Sts.) | 845-358-7977
Wasabi Grill *Japanese*
New City | Town Plaza | 195 S. Main St. (3rd St.) | 845-638-2202
www.wasabichi.com

Rockland County residents are "hooked" on this "happening" two-some that "redefines Japanese cuisine" with "exceptional food" and "exciting sushi", plus hibachi at the "smaller", more affordable New City sibling; the "SoHo"-esque spaces are "packed wall-to-wall on weekends", with "good-looking" servers adding to the "chic" "scene", so although all this "swank" "isn't cheap", it's "worth every penny."

Xaviars at Piermont Ⓜ *American*   28 | 25 | 27 | $82

Piermont | 506 Piermont Ave. (Ash St.) | 845-359-7007 | www.xaviars.com
"Foodies" "feel pampered" at Peter Kelly's "jewel box of a restaurant" in Piermont, thanks to "memorable", "marvelous" New American fare, "well-chosen wines", "on-point", practically "flawless service" and a "quietly elegant", "intimate" room with "beautiful flower arrangements" and "lovely" china; you need "deep pockets", whether you choose an "exemplary tasting menu" or go à la carte, but "treat yourself" – it's "heaven sent" for a "celebratory meal."

X2O Xaviars on the Hudson Ⓜ *American*   27 | 28 | 26 | $68

Yonkers | Historic Yonkers Pier | 71 Water Grant St. (Main St.) | 914-965-1111 | www.xaviars.com
"Nothing short of spectacular" swoon fans of Peter Kelly's "splurge-worthy" New American "showcase" – once again voted Westchester/Hudson Valley's Most Popular – set in a "strikingly beautiful" "glass cube" on the Yonkers pier with "majestic views of the Hudson, even from the restrooms"; "superb" food "that inspires 'oohs' from neighboring tables" and a "deep wine list" plus "exceptional, but not at all stuffy" service (including tableside visits from the chef himself) add up to an experience that's "worth every penny"; P.S. the prix fixe lunch and "free-flowing champagne brunch" are "easier on the wallet", or try nibbles at the bar.

Zephs' Ⓜ *American/Eclectic*   25 | 19 | 25 | $54

Peekskill | 638 Central Ave. (bet. Briarcliff-Peekskill Pkwy. & Washington St.) | 914-736-2159 | www.zephsrestaurant.com
"Always on the mark", this "sophisticated" Peekskill "favorite" from chef Victoria Zeph "excels" with an "imaginative" New American-Eclectic menu that "changes with the seasons" and is served with "gracious aplomb"; never mind that some say the "simple", white-tablecloth setting's overly "conservative" and it's a bit of a "schlep", because "there's real value" in the pricing, and overall it's a "treat."

ALPHABETICAL
PAGE INDEX

ALPHA INDEX